THE
OXFORD BOOK OF
MILITARY
ANECDOTES

THE
OXFORD BOOK OF
MILITARY
ANECDOTES

EDITED BY
MAX HASTINGS

GUILD PUBLISHING
LONDON

This edition published 1985 by
Book Club Associates
By arrangement with Oxford University Press

Oxford is a trade mark of Oxford University Press

Introduction and compilation © Max Hastings 1985

Set by Promenade Graphics Ltd.
Printed in Great Britain by
Richard Clay (The Chaucer Press) Ltd.
Bungay, Suffolk

CONTENTS

INTRODUCTION

AN anthology which seeks to reach out across the vast expanse of military history will discomfit each of its readers by omitting the stories he himself holds most dear. A few months after accepting the commission to compile this selection, I began to understand the enormity of the task, and the difficulty of defining its limits. When does the narrative of a battle become an anecdote? Given a choice of descriptions of a given event, to what extent should the integrity of a source be allowed to override the quality of prose? How far is it realistically possible to scan the wilder shores of say, Persian or Japanese military experience when the purpose is to create a single volume for an English-speaking readership?

This selection is principally British and American, with occasional forays among foreign armies. Although it begins in earliest times, it emphasizes the post-eighteenth-century period when anecdotage achieved the form we most readily recognize today. Many pages of the Old Testament, of course, are filled with bloodcurdling military history. Classical literature is rich in evocative battlefield experience. Yet searching the narratives of Xenophon, Thucydides, Caesar and others, I found surprisingly few passages that possess the quality of whimsy, and stand well enough alone to be characterized as anecdotes. Here, as throughout the book, I have compromised, by including such memorable descriptions as that of Hannibal's crossing of the Alps and Caesar's first landing in Britain, while generally seeking a quality of drollness, even at the expense of passing by many great military moments. A collection of this kind is not designed to rival Creasey's or Fuller's studies of decisive battles of the world, but to divert and entertain by exploring the margins of experience. In the military narratives of the early Middle Ages there are many arresting phrases and sentences, but relatively little of a length and coherence to justify inclusion here. Marlborough's wars, sadly, yield far less anecdotage than those of Wellington. I have tried to discriminate principally upon literary merit, rather than with the intention of preserving a balance between wars and centuries. The book includes such classics as the loss of Uxbridge's leg at Waterloo and some celebrated glimpses of Wellington and Napoleon's Marshals, but it also seeks to explore less predictable ground, such as my personal favourite about a classical don in the guise of a lieutenant-colonel of the British army in the North African Desert.

I have sought stories that illuminate the condition of the soldier through the ages in barracks and on the battlefield. Voltaire wrote that 'anecdotes are the gleanings left over from the vast harvest-field of history; they are details that have been long hidden, and hence their name of *anecdotes*; the public is interested in them when they concern illustrious personages'. Yet some of the best military anecdotes concern rankers rather than generals. I have omitted many bloody tales, especially from the classical and medieval periods, that seem illustrative of the contemporary nature of kingship or statecraft rather than of war. It is striking—for those conducting them if not for the hapless civilians over whose country they were waged—that some conflicts have seemed a great deal more entertaining than others. Many familiar quotations are attributed to Cromwell, for instance, and a host of remarkable military achievements; but there are scarcely any good battlefield anecdotes concerning him. Britain's nineteenth-century wars, on the other hand, offer an embarrassment of riches, many of them most wittily recorded by Byron Farwell in his delightful book *Queen Victoria's Little Wars*. Mrs Woodham-Smith's superb works on the Crimea are so filled with anecdote that editing her narratives is an exercise in self-denial. Throughout this book I have allowed the best stories to run at their natural length, to avoid depriving the reader of gems.

There need be no excuses for filling so many pages from the Peninsula, because no campaign in European history has yielded such a plethora of joyful memoirs. On the French side, for instance, while few officers found anything amusing to say about the 1812 Russian campaign, almost all have marvellous stories of Spain and Portugal. The admirers of Conan Doyle's Brigadier Gerard will find all their hero's originals, enchantingly alike both in style and substance, among the pages of Marbot and Thiébault. The exhilarating marriage of military professionalism with the spirit of a great family in arms achieved by Wellington's Peninsula army, and reflected in the memoirs of Smith, Kincaid, Brotherton, Costello, Wheeler, Larpent, and so many others, was not matched for more than a century, until the apotheosis of the Eighth Army in the North African desert in 1941–3. And this later experience, sadly, yielded less memorable prose.

The coming of the twentieth-century nation in arms created a new kind of war literature, the tales of men to whom a soldier's life was not their natural condition, but a strange venture into the unknown. The anecdotage of the First World War is overwhelmingly founded upon irony or the blackest of black farce, rather than on the innocent professional laughter of Victoria's columns on the North-West Frontier. 'White corpses are . . . far more repulsive than black', wrote Colonel Rawlinson, the veteran of Omdurman, as he gazed upon the dead during the siege of Ladysmith. And as the wars of the twentieth century began, so they continued.

The history of wars is, in the last analysis, the story of men's efforts to kill each other, and thus a collection that aspires to embrace the soldier's experience must include tales of horror and tragedy. Where there is comedy, I have tried to choose stories that rise above mere barrack-room humour, of which many anthologies exist already. Thus there are few of the old soldiers' tales, many of them delightful in their way, that adorn regimental magazines. I have confined myself to published sources. All the stories lay claim to a real historical basis, or at least to plausibility, but no attempt has been made to confirm their scholarly credentials. It is painful to omit Homer and Virgil, Thackeray's Waterloo Ball, and Stendhal's view of the battlefield, but the collection had to end somewhere. The only compromise with this principle is the enchanting portrait of Alan Brooke from one of Anthony Powell's novels, which was of course drawn from life.

The book is arranged chronologically. When faced with a choice between narrative quality and purity of source, I have almost invariably favoured the former, for instance by including Elizabeth Longford's masterly account of the Duchess of Richmond's ball, which brings together a wealth of material otherwise fragmented among several memoirs. For the reader disappointed by the paucity of German stories from the two World Wars, I can only say that I have laboured through all the translated memoirs of the period with which I am familiar, and found almost nothing to compare with the quality of the English and American material. Anecdotes snatched from the midst of the battlefield, as at Marston Moor or Waterloo, may irritate some readers who hanker to see them placed within a coherent narrative framework of the battle. I could see no way of resolving this difficulty without straying far beyond the boundaries of an anthology. The difficulty of making a collection of this kind more than fleetingly representative of the huge field from which it is drawn was emphasized when it proved necessary to cut my original manuscript by half, to produce a book of publishable length.

I inherited the pleasure of compiling this selection in 1981, from the incomparably worthier hands of Lord Ballantrae, on his death. He left behind an unedited collection of papers for the book, from which several anecdotes have found their way into these pages. He was able to draw upon the assistance of some splendidly literate and imaginative friends, notable among them Brigadier Peter Young. I must acknowledge a debt to readers of the *Spectator*, who offered some delightful references when the nature of my quest was publicized. The librarians of the London Library and the Royal United Services Institution are always helpful, but for this book they contributed especially patiently and generously. Mrs Penny O'Rorke carried out weeks of invaluable research, often based upon the most tenuous guidance and vaguest memories of mine. Joan Bailey checked many of my references. Will Sulkin of Oxford University Press grappled tolerantly with the sea of scrawls and photocopies with which at last I presented him, and contributed decisively to the final selection. Any pleasure that readers find in these pages owes as much to all these hands as to mine, and is matched by my delight in having been granted an excuse and an opportunity to burrow in the communication trenches of military history, so to speak, where I was able to discover at leisure how little I knew.

Guilsborough Lodge   MAX HASTINGS
Northamptonshire
1985

NOW Jericho was straitly shut up because of the children of Israel; none went out, and none came in.

And the LORD said unto Joshua, See, I have given into thine hand Jericho, and the king therof, *and* the mighty men of valour.

And ye shall compass the city, all *ye* men of war, *and* go round about the city once. Thus shalt thou do six days.

And seven priests shall bear before the ark seven trumpets of rams' horns: and the seventh day ye shall compass the city seven times, and the priests shall blow with the trumpets.

And it shall come to pass, that when they make a long *blast* with the ram's horn, *and* when ye hear the sound of the trumpet, all the people shall shout with a great shout; and the wall of the city shall fall down flat, and the people shall ascend up every man straight before him.

And Joshua the son of Nun called the priests, and said unto them, Take up the ark of the covenant, and let seven priests bear seven trumpets of rams' horns before the ark of the LORD.

And he said unto the people, Pass on, and compass the city, and let him that is armed pass on before the ark of the LORD.

And it came to pass, when Joshua had spoken unto the people, that the seven priests bearing the seven trumpets of rams' horns passed on before the LORD, and blew with the trumpets: and the ark of the covenant of the LORD followed them.

And the armed men went before the priests that blew with the trumpets, and the rereward came after the ark, *the priests* going on, and blowing with the trumpets.

And Joshua had commanded the people, saying, Ye shall not shout, nor make any noise with your voice, neither shall *any* word proceed out of your mouth, until the day I bid you shout; then shall ye shout.

So the ark of the LORD compassed the city, going about *it* once: and they came into the camp, and lodged in the camp.

And Joshua rose early in the morning, and the priests took up the ark of the LORD.

And seven priests bearing seven trumpets of rams' horns before the ark of the LORD went on continually, and blew with the trumpets: and the armed men went before them; but the rereward came after the ark of the LORD, *the priests* going on, and blowing with the trumpets.

And the second day they compassed the city once, and returned into the camp: so they did six days.

And it came to pass on the seventh day, that they rose early about the dawning of the day, and compassed the city after the same manner seven times: only on that day they compassed the city seven times.

And it came to pass at the seventh time, when the priests blew with the trumpets. Joshua said unto the people, Shout; for the LORD hath given you the city.

And the city shall be accursed, *even* it, and all that *are* therein, to the LORD: only Rahab the harlot shall live, she and all that *are* with her in the house, because she hid the messengers that we sent.

And ye, in any wise keep *yourselves* from the accursed thing, lest ye make *yourselves* accursed, when ye take of the accursed thing, and make the camp of Israel a curse, and trouble it.

But all the silver, and gold, and vessels of brass and iron, *are* consecrated unto the LORD: they shall come into the treasury of the LORD.

So the people shouted when *the priests* blew with the trumpets: and it came to pass, when the people heard the sound of the trumpet, and the people shouted with a great shout, that the wall fell down flat, so that the people went up into the city, every man straight before him, and they took the city.

And they utterly destroyed all that *was* in the city, both man and woman, young and old, and ox, and sheep, and ass, with the edge of the sword.

But Joshua had said unto the two men that had spied out the country, Go into the harlot's house, and bring out thence the woman, and all that she hath, as ye sware unto her.

And the young men that were spies went in, and brought out Rahab, and her father, and her mother, and her brethren, and all that she had; and they brought out all her kindred and left them without the camp of Israel.

And they burnt the city with fire, and all that *was* therein: only the silver, and the gold, and the vessels of brass and of iron, they put into the treasury of the house of the LORD.

And Joshua saved Rahab the harlot alive, and her father's household, and all that she had; and she dwelleth in Israel *even* unto this day; because she hid the messengers, which Joshua sent to spy out Jericho.

And Joshua adjured *them* at that time, saying, Cursed *be* the man before the LORD, that riseth up and buildeth this city Jericho: he shall lay the foundation thereof in his firstborn, and in his youngest *son* shall be set up the gates of it.

So the LORD was with Joshua; and his fame was *noised* throughout all the country.

Joshua 6

2.

The Israeli army has always regarded Gideon, who fought his battles around 1100 BC, as the forefather of their modern commando forces.

THEN Jerubbaal, who *is* Gideon, and all the people that *were* with him, rose up early, and pitched beside the well of Harod: so that the host of the Midianites were on the north side of them, by the hill of Moreh, in the valley.

And the LORD said unto Gideon, The people that *are* with thee *are* too many for me to give the Midianites into their hands, lest Israel vaunt themselves against me, saying, Mine own hand hath saved me.

Now therefore go to, proclaim in the ears of the people, saying, Whosoever *is* fearful and afraid, let him return and depart early from mount Gilead. And there returned of the people twenty and two thousand; and there remained ten thousand.

And the LORD said unto Gideon, The people *are* yet *too* many; bring them down unto the water, and I will try them for thee there: and it shall be, *that* of whom I say unto thee, This shall go with thee, the same shall go with thee; and of whomsoever I say unto thee, This shall not go with thee, the same shall not go.

So he brought down the people unto the water: and the LORD said unto Gideon, Every one that lappeth of the water with his tongue, as a dog lappeth, him shalt thou set by himself; likewise every one that boweth down upon his knees to drink.

And the number of them that lapped, *putting* their hand to their mouth, were three hundred men: but all the rest of the people bowed down upon their knees to drink water.

And the LORD said unto Gideon, By the three hundred men that lapped will I save you, and deliver the Midianites into thine hand: and let all the *other* people go every man unto his place.

So the people took victuals in their hand, and their trumpets: and he sent all *the rest of* Israel every man unto his tent, and retained those three hundred men: and the host of Midian was beneath him in the valley.

And it came to pass the same night, that the LORD said unto him, Arise, get thee down unto the host; for I have delivered it into thine hand.

But if thou fear to go down, go thou with Phurah thy servant down to the host:

And thou shalt hear what they say; and afterward shall thine hands be strengthened to go down unto the host. Then went he down with Phurah his servant unto the outside of the armed men that *were* in the host.

And the Midianites and the Amalekites and all the children of the east lay along in the valley like grasshoppers for multitude; and their camels *were* without number, as the sand by the sea side for multitude.

And when Gideon was come, behold, *there was* a man that told a dream unto his fellow, and said, Behold, I dreamed a dream, and, lo, a cake of barley bread tumbled into the host of Midian, and came unto a tent, and smote it that it fell, and overturned it, that the tent lay along.

And his fellow answered and said, This *is* nothing else save the sword of Gideon the son of Joash, a man of Israel: *for* into his hand hath God delivered Midian, and all the host.

And it was *so*, when Gideon heard the telling of the dream, and the interpretation thereof, that he worshipped, and returned into the host of Israel, and said, Arise; for the LORD hath delivered into your hand the host of Midian.

And he divided the three hundred men *into* three companies, and he put a trumpet in every man's hand, with empty pitchers, and lamps within the pitchers.

And he said unto them, Look on me, and do likewise: and, behold, when I come to the outside of the camp, it shall be *that*, as I do, so shall ye do.

When I blow with a trumpet, I and all that *are* with me, then blow ye the trumpets also on every side of all the camp, and say, *The sword* of the LORD, and of Gideon.

So Gideon, and the hundred men that *were* with him, came unto the outside of the camp in the beginning of the middle watch; and they had but newly set the watch: and they blew the trumpets, and brake the pitchers that *were* in their hands.

And the three companies blew the trumpets and brake the pitchers, and held the lamps in their left hands, and the trumpets in their right hands to blow *withal*: and they cried, The sword of the LORD, and of Gideon.

And they stood every man in his place round about the camp: and all the host ran, and cried, and fled.

And the three hundred blew the trumpets, and the LORD set every man's sword against his fellow, even throughout all the host: and the host fled to Beth-shittah in Zererath, *and* to the border of Abel-meholah, unto Tabbath.

And the men of Israel gathered themselves together out of Naphtali, and out of Asher, and out of all Manasseh, and pursued after the Midianites.

And Gideon sent messengers throughout all mount Ephraim, saying, Come down against the Midianites, and take before them the waters unto Beth-barah and Jordan. Then all the men of Ephraim gathered themselves together, and took the waters unto Beth-barah and Jordan.

And they took two princes of the Midianites, Oreb and Zeeb; and they slew Oreb upon the rock Oreb, and Zeeb they slew at the wine-press of Zeeb, and pursued Midian, and brought the heads of Oreb and Zeeb to Gideon on the other side Jordan.

Judges 7

3.

AND the men of Ephraim gathered themselves together [*c.*1100 BC], and went northward, and said unto Jephthah, Wherefore passedst thou over to fight against the children of Ammon, and didst not call us to go with thee? we will burn thine house upon thee with fire.

And Jephthah said unto them, I and my people were at great strife with the children of Ammon; and when I called you, ye delivered me not out of their hands.

And when I saw that ye delivered *me* not, I put my life in my hands, and passed over against the children of Ammon, and the LORD delivered them into my hand: wherefore then are ye come up unto me this day, to fight against me?

Then Jephthah gathered together all the men of Gilead, and fought with Ephraim: and the men of Gilead smote Ephraim, because they said, Ye Gileadites *are* fugitives of Ephraim among the Ephraimites, *and* among the Manassites.

And the Gileadites took the passages of Jordan before the Ephraimites: and it was *so*, that when those Ephraimites which were escaped said, Let me go over; that the men of Gilead said unto him, *Art* thou an Ephraimite? If he said, Nay;

Then said they unto him, Say now Shibboleth: and he said Sibboleth: for he could not frame to pronounce *it* right. Then they took him, and slew him at the passages of Jordan: and there fell at that time of the Ephraimites forty and two thousand.

Judges 12

4.

AND [*c*.1000 BC] there went out a champion out of the camp out of the Philistines, named Goliath of Gath, whose height was six cubits and a span. And he had a helmet of brass upon his head, and he was armed with a coat of mail—and the weight of the coat was five thousand shekels of brass. And he had greaves of brass upon his legs, and a target of brass between his shoulders. And the staff of his spear was like a weaver's beam; and his spear's head weighed six hundred shekels of iron, and one bearing a shield went before him.

And he stood and cried unto the armies of Israel, and said unto them, Why are ye come to set your battle in array? am not I a Philistine, and ye servants to Saul? choose you a man for you—and let him come down to me. If he be able to fight with me, and to kill me, then will we be your servants—but if I prevail against him, and kill him, then shall ye be our servants, and serve us. And the Philistine said,—I defy the armies of Israel this day; give me a man, that we may fight together.

When Saul and all Israel heard those words of the Philistine, they were dismayed and greatly afraid. Now David was the son of that Ephraimite of Bethlehem-judah, whose name was Jesse. And David was the youngest; and the three eldest followed Saul. But David went and returned from Saul to feed his father's sheep at Bethlehem. And the Philistine drew near morning and evening, and presented himself forty days. And Jesse said unto David his son, Take now for thy brethren an ephah of this parched corn, and these ten loaves, and run to the camp to thy brethren; and carry these ten cheeses unto the captain of their thousand, and look how thy brethren fare. And David rose up early in the morning, and left the sheep with a keeper, and took, and went, as Jesse had commanded him—and he came to the trench as the host was going forth to the fight, and shouted for the battle. And David left his carriage in the hand of the keeper of the carriage, and ran into the army, and came and saluted his brethren. And as he talked with them, behold, there came up the champion, the Philistine of Gath, Goliath by name, out of the armies of the Philistines, and spake according to the same words—and David heard them. And all the men of Israel, when they saw the men, fled from him, and were sore afraid.

And David spake to the men that stood by him, saying, What shall be done to the man that killeth this Philistine, and taketh away the reproach from Israel? For who is this uncircumcised Philistine, that he should defy the armies of the living God?

And Eliab his eldest brother heard when he spake unto the men; and Eliab's anger was kindled against David, and he said, Why camest thou down hither? and with whom hast thou left those few sheep in the wilderness? I know thy pride, and the naughtiness of thine heart; for thou art come down that thou mightest see the battle.

And David said, What have I now done? Is there not a cause? And David said to Saul, Let no man's heart fail because of him—thy servant will go and fight the Philistine. And Saul said to David, Thou art not able to go against this Philistine to fight with him; for thou art but a youth, and he a man of war from his youth. And David said unto Saul, Thy servant kept his father's sheep, and there came a lion, and a bear, and took a lamb out of the flock—And I went out after him, and smote him, and delivered it out of his mouth; and when he arose against me, I caught him by his beard, and smote him, and slew him. David said moreover, The LORD that delivered me out of the paw of the lion, and out of the paw of the bear, he will deliver me out of the hand of this Philistine. And Saul said to David, Go, and the LORD be with thee.

And Saul armed David with his armour, and he put an helmet of brass upon his head; also he armed him with a coat of mail. And David girded his sword upon his armour and he assayed to go—for he had not proved it. And David said unto Saul, I cannot go with these—for I have not proved them. And David put them off him. And he took his staff in his hand, and chose him five smooth stones out of the brook, and put them in a shepherd's bag which he had, even in a scrip,—and his sling was in his hand, and he drew near to the Philistine. And the Philistine came on and drew near unto David—and the man that bare the shield went before him. And when the Philistine looked about, and saw David, he disdained him; for he was but a youth, and ruddy, and of a fair countenance. And the Philistine said unto David, Am I a dog, that thou comest to me with staves? And the Philistine cursed David by his gods. And the Philistine said unto David, Come to me, and I will give thy flesh unto the fowls of the air, and to the beasts of the field. Then said David to the Philistine, Thou comest to me with a sword, and with a spear, and with a shield—but I come to thee in the name of the LORD of hosts, the God of the armies of Israel, whom thou hast defied. This day will the LORD deliver thee into mine hand; and I will smite thee, and take thine head from thee; and I will give the carcases of the host of the Philistines this day unto the fowls of the air, and to the wild beasts of the earth; that all the earth may know that there is a God in Israel.

And it came to pass, when the Philistine arose, and came and drew nigh to meet David, that David hasted, and ran toward the army to meet the Philistine. And David put his hand in his bag, and took thence a stone, and slang it, and smote the Philistine in his forehead, that the stone sunk into his forehead, and he fell upon his face to the earth. Therefore David ran, and stood upon the Philistine, and took his sword, and drew it out of the sheath thereof, and slew him, and cut off his head therewith. And when the Philistines saw their champion was dead, they fled. And the men of Israel and of Judah arose, and shouted, and pursued the Philistines, until thou come to the valley and to the gates of Ekron.

1 Samuel 17

5.

On the eve of battle with the Syrians (850 BC), King Ahab seeks to circumvent Micaiah's prophecy of his death in the action.

AND the king of Israel said unto Jehoshaphat, I will disguise myself, and enter into the battle; but put thou on thy robes. And the king of Israel disguised himself and went into the battle. But the king of Syria commanded his thirty and two captains that had rule over his chariots, saying, Fight neither with small or great, save only with the king of Israel. And it came to pass, when the captains of the chariots saw Jehoshaphat, that they said, Surely it is the king of Israel. And they turned aside to fight against him; and Jehoshaphat cried out. And it came to pass, when the captains of the chariots perceived that it was not the king of Israel, that they turned back from pursuing him. And a certain man drew a bow at a venture, and smote the king of Israel between the joints of the harness—wherefore he said unto the driver of his chariot, Turn thine hand, and carry me out of the host; for I am wounded. And the battle increased that day—and the king was stayed up in his chariot against the Syrians, and died at even—and the blood ran out of the wound into the midst of the chariot. And there went a proclamation throughout the host about the going down of the sun, saying, Every man to his city, and every man to his own country. So the king died and was brought to Samaria; and they buried the king in Samaria. And one washed the chariot in the pool of Samaria; and the dogs licked up his blood; and they washed his armour; according unto the word of the LORD which he spake.

1 Kings 22

6.

The claims of this passage of Herodotus to historical verisimilitude are sketchy, to say the least. But it is such a delightful piece of nonsense that it seemed churlish to exclude it.

IN the war between the Greeks and the Amazons, the Greeks, after their victory at the river Thermodon, sailed off in three ships with as many Amazons on board as they had succeeded in taking alive. Once at sea, the women murdered their captors, but, as they had no knowledge of boats and were unable to handle either rudder or sail or oar, they soon found themselves, when the men were done for, at the mercy of wind and wave, and were blown to Cremni—the Cliffs—on Lake Maeotis, a place within the territory of the free Scythians. Here they got ashore and made their way inland to an inhabited part of the country. The first thing they fell in with was a herd of horses grazing; these they seized, and, mounting on their backs, rode off in search of loot. The Scythians could not understand what was happening and were at a loss to know where the marauders had come from, as their dress, speech, and nationality were strange to them. Thinking, however, that they were young men, they fought in defence of their property, and discovered from the bodies which came into their possession after the battle that they were women. The discovery gave a new direction to their plans; they decided to make no further attempt to kill the invaders, but to send out a detachment of their youngest men, about equal in number to the Amazons, with orders to camp near them and take their cue from whatever it was that the Amazons then did: if they pursued them, they were not to fight, but to give ground; then, when the pursuit was abandoned, they were once again to encamp within easy range. The motive behind this policy was the Scythians' desire to get children by the Amazons. The detachment of young men obeyed their orders, and the Amazons, realizing that they meant no harm, did not attempt to molest them, with the result that every day the two camps drew a little closer together. Neither party had anything but their weapons and their horses, and both lived the same sort of life, hunting and plundering.

Towards midday the Amazons used to scatter and go off to some little distance in ones and twos to ease themselves, and the Scythians, when they noticed this, followed suit; until one of them, coming upon an Amazon girl all by herself, began to make advances to her. She, nothing loth, gave him what he wanted, and then told him by signs (being unable to express her meaning in words, as neither understood the other's language) to return on the following day with a friend, making it clear that there must be two men, and that she herself would bring another girl. The young man then left her and told the others what had happened, and on the next day took a friend to the same spot, where he found his Amazon waiting for him and another one with her. Having learnt of their success, the rest of the young Scythians soon succeeded in getting the Amazons to submit to their wishes. The two camps were then united, and Amazons and Scythians lived together, every man keeping as his wife the woman whose favours he had first enjoyed. The men could not learn the women's language, but the women succeeded in picking up the men's; so when they could understand one another, the Scythians made the following proposal: 'We', they said, 'have parents and property. Let us give up our present way of life and return to live with our people. We will keep you as our wives and not take any others.' The Amazons replied: 'We and the women of your nation could never live together; our ways are too much at variance. We are riders; our business is with the bow and the spear, and we know nothing of women's work; but in your country no woman has anything to do with such things—your women stay at home in their waggons occupied with feminine tasks, and never go out to hunt or for any other purpose. We could not possibly agree. If, however, you wish to keep us for your wives and to behave as honourable men, go and get from your parents the share of property which is due to you, and then let us go off and live by ourselves.' The young men agreed to this, and when they came back, each with his portion of the family possessions, the Amazons said: 'We dread the prospect of settling down here, for we have done much damage to the country by our raids, and we have robbed you of your parents. Look now—if you think fit to keep us for your wives, let us get out of the country altogether and settle somewhere on the other side of the Tanais.' Once again the Scythians agreed, so they crossed the Tanais and travelled east for three days, and then north, for another three, from Lake Maeotis, until they reached the country where they are today, and settled down there. Ever since then the women of the Sauromatae have kept to their old ways, riding to the hunt on horseback sometimes with, sometimes without, their menfolk, taking part in war and wearing the same sort of clothes as men. The language of these people is the Scythian, but it has always been a corrupt form of it because the Amazons were never able to learn to speak it properly. They have a marriage law which forbids a girl to marry until she has killed an enemy in battle; some of their women, unable to fulfil this condition, grow old and die in spinsterhood.

Herodotus

7.

A legend of the sixth century BC, whose claims to historical reality remain doubtful, but which it would be unforgivable to omit.

BY this time the Tarquins had fled to Lars Porsena, king of Clusium. There, with advice and entreaties, they besought him not to suffer them, who were descended from the Etrurians and of the same blood and name, to live in exile and poverty; and advised him not to let this practice of expelling kings to pass unpunished. Liberty, they declared, had charms enough in itself, and unless kings defended their crowns with as much vigour as the people pursued their liberty, the highest must be reduced to a level with the lowest; there would be nothing exalted, nothing distinguished above the rest; hence there must be an end of regal government, the most beautiful institution both among gods and men. Porsena, thinking it would be an honour to the Tuscans that there should be a king at Rome, especially one of the Etrurian nation, marched towards Rome with an army. Never before had such terror seized the Senate, so powerful was the state of Clusium at the time, and so great the renown of Porsena. Nor did they only dread their enemies, but even their own citizens, lest the common people, through excess of fear should, by receiving the Tarquins into the city, accept peace even though purchased with slavery. Many concessions were therefore granted to the people by the Senate during that period. Their attention, in the first place, was directed to the markets, and persons were sent, some to the Volscians, others to Cumae, to buy up corn. The privilege of selling salt, because it was farmed at a high rate, was also taken into the hands of the government, and withdrawn from private individuals; and the people were freed from port-duties and taxes, in order that the rich, who could bear the burden, should contribute; the poor paid tax enough if they educated their children. This indulgent care of the fathers accordingly kept the whole state in such concord amid the subsequent severities of the siege and famine, that the highest as well as the lowest abhorred the name of the king; nor was any individual afterwards so popular by intriguing practices as the whole Senate was by their excellent government.

Some parts of the city seemed secured by the walls, others by the River Tiber. The Sublician Bridge well-nigh afforded a passage to the enemy, had there not been one man, Horatius Cocles (fortunately Rome had on that day such a defender) who, happening to be posted on guard at the bridge, when he saw the Janiculum taken by a sudden assault and the enemy pouring down thence at full speed, and that his own party, in terror and confusion, were abandoning their arms and ranks, laying hold of them one by one, standing in their way and appealing to the faith of gods and men, he declared that their flight would avail them nothing if they deserted their post; if they passed the bridge, there would soon be more of the enemy in the Palatium and Capitol than in the Janiculum. For that reason he charged them to demolish the bridge, by sword, by fire, or by any means whatever; declaring that he would stand the shock of the enemy as far as could be done by one man. He then advanced to the first entrance of the bridge, and being easily distinguished among those who showed their backs in retreating, faced about to engage the foe hand to hand, and by his surprising bravery he terrified the enemy. Two indeed remained with him from a sense of shame: Sp. Lartius and T. Herminius, men eminent for their birth, and renowned for their gallant exploits. With them he for a short time stood the first storm of the danger, and the severest brunt of the battle. But as they who demolished the bridge called upon them to retire, he obliged them also to withdraw to a place of safety on a small portion of the bridge that was still left. Then casting his stern eyes toward the officers of the Etrurians in a threatening manner, he now challenged them singly, and then reproached them, slaves of haughty tyrants who, regardless of their own freedom, came to oppress the liberty of others. They hesitated for a time, looking round one at the other, to begin the fight; shame then put the army in motion, and a shout being raised, they hurled weapons from all sides at their single adversary; and when they all stuck in his upraised shield, and he with no less obstinacy kept possession of the bridge, they endeavoured to thrust him down from it by one push, when the crash of the falling bridge was heard, and at the same time a shout of the Romans raised for joy at having completed their purpose, checked their ardour with sudden panic. Then said Cocles: 'Holy Father Tiber, I pray thee, receive these arms, and this thy soldier, in thy propitious stream.' Armed as he was, he leaped into the Tiber, and amid showers of darts, swam across safe to his party, having dared an act which is likely to obtain with posterity more fame than credit. The state was grateful for such valour; a statue was erected to him in the comitium, and as much land given to him as he could plough in one day. The zeal of private individuals was also conspicuous among his public honours. For amid the great scarcity, each contributed something, according to his supply, depriving himself of his own support.

Livy

8.

AFTER the Persian fleet had sailed for Samos, Babylon revolted [c.516 BC]. The revolt had been long and carefully planned; indeed, preparations for withstanding a siege had been going quietly on all through the reign of the Magus and the disturbances which followed the rising of the seven against him, and for some reason or another the secret never leaked out. When the moment finally came to declare their purpose, the Babylonians, in order to reduce the consumption of food, herded together and strangled all the women in the city—each man exempting only his mother, and one other woman whom he chose out of his household to bake his bread for him. When the news reached Darius, he marched against them with all the forces at his disposal, and laid siege to the city. The Babylonians, however, were unimpressed; they climbed gaily on to their battlements and hurled insulting jibes at Darius and his army, calling out: 'What are you sitting there for, men of Persia? Why don't you go away? Oh yes, you will capture our city—when mules have foals.'

Now whoever it was who made this last remark, naturally supposed that no mule would ever have a foal.

A year and seven months went by, and Darius and his army began to chafe at their inability to make any progress towards taking the city. Every trick of strategy, every possible device, had been tried; but to no purpose. The town could not be taken, not even when Darius, after all else had failed, attempted to repeat the method which Cyrus had previously used with success. The Babylonians were always on the watch with extraordinary vigilance, and gave the enemy no chance.

At last, in the twentieth month of the siege, a marvellous thing happened to Zopyrus, son of the Megabyzus who was one of the seven conspirators who killed the Magus: one of his sumpter-mules foaled. When Zopyrus was told of this, he refused to believe it till he had seen the foal with his own eyes; then, forbidding the others who had seen it to say a word to anyone of what had occurred, he began to think hard, and came to the conclusion that the time had come when Babylon could be taken—for had not that Babylonian, at the beginning of the siege, said that the city would fall when mules foaled? That the man should have used the phrase, and that the miracle should actually have happened—surely that meant that the hand of God was in it.

Convinced, therefore, that Babylon was now doomed to destruction, he went to Darius and asked him if the capture of the city was really of supreme importance to him, and, on being told that it was, set himself to devise a way of bringing it about by his own sole act and initiative; for in Persia any special service to the king is very highly valued. Accordingly he passed in review every scheme he could think of, and finally decided that there was one way only in which he could bring the place under, namely by maiming himself and then going over to the enemy as a deserter. Taking this dreadful expedient as a mere matter of course, he at once put it into practice, and there were no half-measures in the way he set about it: he cut off his nose and ears, shaved his hair like a criminal's, raised weals on his body with a whip, and in this condition presented himself to Darius. Darius was shocked at the sight of a man of Zopyrus' eminence so fearfully mutilated, and springing from his chair with an exclamation of horror, asked who it was that had inflicted this punishment upon him, and what Zopyrus had done to deserve it. 'My lord,' Zopyrus answered, 'there is no one but yourself who has power enough to reduce me to this condition.

The hands that disfigured me were none other than my own, for I could not bear to hear the Assyrians of Babylon laugh the Persians to scorn.'

'You speak like a madman;' said Darius; 'to say you did this horrible thing because of our enemies in the beleaguered city, is merely to cloak a shameful act in fine words. Are you fool enough to think that the mutilation of your body can hasten our victory? When you did that to yourself, you must have taken leave of your senses.'

'Had I told you of my intention,' Zopyrus answered, 'you would not have allowed me to proceed. So I acted upon my own initiative. And now—if you too will play your part—we will capture Babylon. I will go as I am to the city walls, pretending to be a deserter, and I will tell them that it was you who caused my misery. They will believe me readily enough—and they will put their troops under my command. Now for your part: wait till the tenth day after I enter the town, and then station by the gates of Semiramis a detachment of a thousand men, whose loss will not worry you. Then, seven days later, send 2,000 more to the Nineveh gates and, twenty days after that, another 4,000 to the Chaldaean gates. None of these three detachments must be armed with anything but their daggers—let them carry daggers only. And then, after a further interval of twenty days, order a general assault upon the city walls from every direction, taking care that our own Persian troops have the sectors opposite the Belian and Cissian gates. It is my belief that the Babylonians, when they see that I have done them good service, will increase my responsibility—even to trusting me with the keys of the gates. And after that—I and our Persians will see what must be done.'

Having given these directions to the king, Zopyrus fled towards the gates of Babylon, glancing over his shoulder as he ran, like a deserter in fear of pursuit. When the soldiers on watch saw him, they hurried down from the battlements, and opening one of the gates just a crack, asked him his name and business. Saying he was Zopyrus and had deserted from the Persian army, he was let in, and conducted by the sentries to the magistrates. Here he poured out his tale of woe, pretending that the injuries he had done to himself had been inflicted upon him by Darius, and all because he had advised him to abandon the siege, as there appeared to be no means of ever bringing it to a successful conclusion. 'And now,' he added, 'here I am, men of Babylon; and my coming will be gain to you, but loss—and that the severest—to Darius and his army. He little knows me if he thinks he can get away with the foul things he has done me—moreover, I know all the ins and outs of his plans.'

The Babylonians, seeing a Persian of high rank and distinction in such a state—his nose and ears cut off and his body a mess of blood from the lash of whips—were quick to believe that he spoke the truth and had really come to offer them his services, and in this belief were prepared to give him whatever he asked. At once he asked for the command of some troops, and, when the request was granted, proceeded to put into practice the plan he had arranged with Darius. The tenth day after his arrival he marched his force out of the city, and surrounded and killed the first detachment of a thousand men which he had instructed Darius to send. This was enough to show the Babylonians that his deeds were as good as his words; they were in high glee, and ready to put themselves under his orders in anything he might propose. After waiting, therefore, the agreed number of days, he picked another party from the troops in the city, marched out, and made mincemeat of the two thousand Persians which Darius had posted by the Nineveh gates. As a result of this second service, the reputation of Zopyrus went up with a jump and his name was on everybody's lips. The same thing happened with the four thousand—once more, after the agreed interval, he marched his men out through the Chaldaean gates, surrounded the Persians there, and cut them down to a man. This was his crowning success; Zopyrus was now the one and only soldier in Babylon, the city's hero, and was created General in Chief and Guardian of the Wall.

And now Darius did not fail to do his part: as had been agreed, he ordered a general assault upon the walls from every direction—which was the signal for Zopyrus to reveal the full extent of his cunning. Waiting till the Babylonian forces had mounted the battlements to repel Darius' onslaught, he opened the Cissian and Belian gates and let the Persians in. Those of the Babylonians who were near enough to see what had happened, fled to the temple of Bel; the rest remained at their posts until they, too, realized that they had been betrayed.

Thus Babylon was captured for the second time, and Darius after his victory—unlike Cyrus, its previous conqueror— destroyed its defences, pulled down all the city gates, and impaled the leading citizens to the number of about three thousand. The rest he allowed to remain in their homes. I mentioned at the beginning of my account how the Babylonians strangled their women to save food, and it was in consequence of this that Darius, in order to prevent the race from dying out, compelled the neighbouring peoples each to send a certain stated number of women to Babylon. In all, as many as fifty thousand were collected there. It is from them that the present inhabitants are descended.

Herodotus

9.

Marching upon Greece in 480 BC, the army of Xerxes beholds an eclipse at the crossing of the Hellespont. The King himself is satisfied by the assurances of the soothsayers that this augurs evil to the cities of the Greeks, not to himself. But others are less convinced.

THE army . . . had not gone far when Pythius the Lydian, in alarm at the sign from heaven, was emboldened by the presents he had received to come to Xerxes with a request. 'Master,' he said, 'there is a favour I should like you to grant me—a small thing, indeed, for you to perform, but to me of great importance, should you consent to do so.' Xerxes, who thought the request would be almost anything but what it actually turned out to be, agreed to grant it and told Pythius to say what it was he wanted. This generous answer raised Pythius' hopes, and he said, 'My lord, I have five sons, and it happens that every one of them is serving in your army in the campaign against Greece. I am an old man, Sire, and I beg you in pity to release from service one of my sons—the eldest—to take care of me and my property. Take the other four—and may you return with your purpose accomplished.'

Xerxes was furiously angry. 'You miserable fellow,' he cried, 'have you the face to mention your son, when I, in person, am marching to the war against Greece with my sons and brothers and kinsmen and friends—*you*, my slave, whose duty it was to come with me with every member of your house, including your wife? Mark my words: it is through the ears you can touch a man to pleasure or rage—let the spirit which dwells there hear good things, and it will fill the body with delight; let it hear bad, and it will swell with fury. When you did me good service, and offered more, you cannot boast that you were more generous than I; and now your punishment will be less than your impudence deserves. Yourself and four of your sons are saved by the entertainment you gave me; but you shall pay with the life of the fifth, whom you cling to most.'

Having answered Pythius in these words Xerxes at once gave orders that the men to whom such duties fell should find Pythius' eldest son and cut him in half and put the two halves one on each side of the road, for the army to march out between them. The order was performed.

And now between the halves of the young man's body the advance of the army began . . .

Herodotus

10.

In the spring of 480 BC, as Xerxes' 100,000 marched south into Greece, the main body of the Greek army retired beyond the Isthmus of Corinth, leaving a rearguard of 300 at the Pass of Thermopylae, commanded by Leonidas of Sparta.

THE Greeks at Thermopylae had their first warning of the death that was coming with the dawn from the seer Megistias, who read their doom in the victims of sacrifice; deserters, too, had begun to come in during the night with news of the Persian movement to take them in the rear, and, just as day was breaking, the look-out men had come running from the hills. At once a conference was held, and opinions were divided, some urging that they must on no account abandon their post, others taking the opposite view. The result was that the army split: some dispersed, the men returning to their various homes, and others made ready to stand by Leonidas.

There is another account which says that Leonidas himself dismissed a part of his force, to spare their lives, but thought it unbecoming for the Spartans under his command to desert the post which they had originally come to guard. I myself am inclined to think that he dismissed them when he realized that they had no heart for the fight and were unwilling to take their share of the danger; at the same time honour forbade that he himself should go. And indeed by remaining at his post he left a great name behind him, and Sparta did not lose her prosperity, as might otherwise have happened; for right at the outset of the war the Spartans had been told by the oracle, when they asked for advice, that either their city must be laid waste by the foreigner or one of their kings be killed. The prophecy was in hexameter verse and ran as follows:

Hear your fate, O dwellers in Sparta of the wide spaces;
Either your famed, great town must be sacked by Perseus' sons,
Or, if that be not, the whole land of Lacedaemon
Shall mourn the death of a king of the house of Heracles,
For not the strength of lions or of bulls shall hold him,

Strength against strength; for he has the power of Zeus,
And will not be checked till one of these two he has consumed.

I believe it was the thought of this oracle, combined with his wish to
lay up for the Spartans a treasure of fame in which no other city should
share, that made Leonidas dismiss those troops; I do not think that
they deserted, or went off without orders, because of a difference of
opinion. Moreover, I am strongly supported in this view by the case of
Megistias, the seer from Acarnania who foretold the coming doom by
his inspection of the sacrificial victims: this man—he was said to be
descended from Melampus—was with the army, and quite plainly
received orders from Leonidas to quit Thermopylae, to save him from
sharing the army's fate. But he refused to go, sending away instead an
only son of his, who was serving with the forces.

Thus it was that the confederate troops, by Leonidas' orders, abandoned their posts and left the pass, all except the Thespians and the
Thebans who remained with the Spartans. The Thebans were
detained by Leonidas as hostages very much against their will—unlike
the loyal Thespians who refused to desert Leonidas and his men, but
stayed, and died with them. They were under the command of Demo-
philus the son of Diadromes.

In the morning Xerxes poured a libation to the rising sun, and then
waited till about the time of the filling of the market-place, when he
began to move forward. This was according to Ephialtes' instructions,
for the way down from the ridge is much shorter and more direct than
the long and circuitous ascent. As the Persian army advanced to the
assault, the Greeks under Leonidas, knowing that the fight would be
their last, pressed forward into the wider part of the pass much further
than they had done before; in the previous days' fighting they had been
holding the wall and making sorties from behind it into the narrow
neck, but now they left the confined space and battle was joined on
more open ground. Many of the invaders fell; behind them the company commanders plied their whips, driving the men remorselessly on.
Many fell into the sea and were drowned, and still more were trampled
to death by their friends. No one could count the number of the dead.
The Greeks, who knew that the enemy were on their way round by the
mountain track and that death was inevitable, fought with reckless desperation, exerting every ounce of strength that was in them against the
invader. By this time most of their spears were broken, and they were
killing Persians with their swords.

In the course of that fight Leonidas fell, having fought like a man indeed. Many distinguished Spartans were killed at his side—their names, like the names of all the three hundred, I have made myself acquainted with, because they deserve to be remembered. Amongst the Persian dead, too, were many men of high distinction—for instance, two brothers of Xerxes, Habrocomes and Hyperanthes, both of them sons of Darius by Artanes' daughter Phratagune.

There was a bitter struggle over the body of Leonidas; four times the Greeks drove the enemy off, and at last by their valour succeeded in dragging it away. So it went on, until the fresh troops with Ephialtes were close at hand; and then, when the Greeks knew that they had come, the character of the fighting changed. They withdrew again into the narrow neck of the pass, behind the walls, and took up a position in a single compact body—all except the Thebans on the little hill at the entrance to the pass, where the stone lion in memory of Leonidas stands today. Here they resisted to the last, with their swords, if they had them, and, if not, with their hands and teeth, until the Persians, coming on from the front over the ruins of the wall and closing in from behind, finally overwhelmed them.

Of all the Spartans and Thespians who fought so valiantly on that day, the most signal proof of courage was given by the Spartan Dieneces. It is said that before the battle he was told by a native of Trachis that, when the Persians shot their arrows, there were so many of them that they hid the sun. Dieneces, however, quite unmoved by the thought of the terrible strength of the Persian army, merely remarked: 'This is pleasant news that the stranger from Trachis brings us: for if the Persians hide the sun, we shall have our battle in the shade.' He is said to have left on record other sayings, too, of a similar kind, by which he will be remembered. After Dieneces the greatest distinction was won by the two Spartan brothers, Alpheus and Maron, the sons of Orsiphantus; and of the Thespians the man to gain the highest glory was a certain Dithyrambous, the son of Harmatides.

The dead were buried where they fell, and with them the men who had been killed before those dismissed by Leonidas left the pass.

Over them is this inscription, in honour of the whole force:

> Four thousand here from Pelops' land
> Against three million once did stand.

The Spartans have a special epitaph; it runs:

> Go tell the Spartans, you who read:
> We took their orders, and are dead.

For the seer Megistias there is the following:

I was Megistias once, who died
When the Mede passed Spercheius' tide.
I knew death near, yet would not save
Myself, but share the Spartans' grave.

The columns with the epitaphs inscribed on them were erected in
honour of the dead by the Amphictyons—though the epitaph upon the
seer Megistias was the work of Simonides, the son of Leoprepes, who
put it there for friendship's sake.

Two of the three hundred Spartans, Eurytus and Aristodemus,
are said to have been suffering from acute inflammation of the eyes,
on account of which they were dismissed by Leonidas before the
battle and went to Alpeni to recuperate. These two men might have
agreed together to return in safety to Sparta; or, if they did not wish
to do so, they might have shared the fate of their friends. But,
unable to agree which course to take, they quarrelled, and Eurytus
had no sooner heard that the Persians had made their way round by
the mountain track than he called for his armour, put it on, and
ordered his servant to lead him to the scene of the battle. The servant obeyed, and then took to his heels, and Eurytus, plunging into
the thick of things, was killed. Aristodemus, on the other hand, finding that his heart failed him, stayed behind at Alpeni. Now if only
Aristodemus had been involved—if he alone had returned sick to
Sparta—or if they had both gone back together, I do not think that
the Spartans would have been angry; but as one was killed and the
other took advantage of the excuse, which was open to both of them,
to save his skin, they could hardly help being very angry indeed with
Aristodemus.

There is another explanation of how Aristodemus got back alive to
Sparta: according to this, he was sent from camp with a message, and
though he might have returned in time to take part in the fighting, he
deliberately loitered on the way and so saved himself, while the man
who accompanied him on the errand joined in the battle and was
killed. In any case, he was met upon his return with reproach and disgrace; no Spartan would give him a light to kindle his fire, or speak to
him, and he was nicknamed the Trembler. However, he afterwards
made amends for everything at the battle of Plataea.

There is also a story that one more of the three hundred—Pantites
—survived. He had been sent with a message into Thessaly, and on

return to Sparta found himself in such disgrace that he hanged himself.

Herodotus

II.

*In 401 BC, Greek mercenaries in the service of Cyrus of Persia, fighting to seize the
crown from his elder brother Artaxerxes II, were victorious at the battle of Cunaxa, but
found themselves leaderless when Cyrus himself was killed and their own officers
treacherously put to the sword. The Greeks chose new officers, among them Xenophon,
who subsequently described their historic fighting march north to the Armenian mountains, and thence onwards to reach the Euxine at Trapezus.*

THE Greeks next arrived at the river Harpasus, the breadth of which
was four plethra. Hence they proceeded through the territory of the
Scythini, four days' journey, making twenty parasangs, over a level
tract, until they came to some villages, in which they halted three days,
and collected provisions. From this place they advanced four days'
journey, twenty parasangs, to a large, rich, and populous city, called
Gymnias, from which the governor of the country sent the Greeks a
guide, to conduct them through a region at war with his own people.
The guide, when he came, said that he would take them in five days to
a place whence they should see the sea; if not, he would consent to be
put to death. When, as he proceeded, he entered the country of their
enemies, he exhorted them to burn and lay waste the lands; whence it
was evident that he had come for this very purpose, and not from any
good will to the Greeks. On the fifth day they came to the mountain;
and the name of it was Theches. When the men who were in the front
had mounted the height, and looked down upon the sea, a great shout
proceeded from them; and Xenophon and the rear-guard, on hearing
it, thought that some new enemies were assailing the front, for in the
rear, too, the people from the country that they had burnt were following them, and the rear-guard, by placing an ambuscade, had killed
some, and taken others prisoners, and had captured about twenty
shields made of raw ox-hides with the hair on. But as the noise still
increased, and drew nearer, and as those who came up from time to
time kept running at full speed to join those who were continually
shouting, the cries becoming louder as the men became more numerous, it appeared to Xenophon that it must be something of very great
moment. Mounting his horse, therefore, and taking with him Lycius

and the cavalry, he hastened forward to give aid, when presently they heard the soldiers shouting, 'The sea, the sea!' and cheering on one another. They then all began to run, the rear-guard as well as the rest, and the baggage-cattle and horses were put to their speed; and when they had all arrived at the top, the men embraced one another, and their generals and captains, with tears in their eyes. Suddenly, whoever it was that suggested it, the soldiers brought stones, and raised a large mound, on which they laid a number of raw ox-hides, staves, and shields taken from the enemy. The shields the guide himself hacked in pieces, and exhorted the rest to do the same. Soon after, the Greeks sent away the guide, giving him presents from the common stock, a horse, a silver cup, a Persian robe, and ten darics; but he showed most desire for the rings on their fingers, and obtained many of them from the soldiers. Having then pointed out to them a village where they might take up their quarters, and the road by which they were to proceed to the Macrones, when the evening came on he departed, pursuing his way during the night.

Xenophon

12.

In 394 BC, the great Roman dictator Camillus was besieging Falerii, one of the twelve Etruscan cities. One of its inhabitants, the teacher charged with the care of the city's boys, was in the habit of taking his pupils for a daily walk outside the walls, between the garrison and the Roman outposts.

THIS teacher, then, wishing to betray Falerii by means of its boys, led them out every day beyond the city walls, at first only a little way, and then brought them back inside when they had taken their exercise. Presently he led them, little by little, further and further out, accustomed them to feel confident that there was no danger at all, and finally pushed in among the Roman outposts with his whole company, handed them over to the enemy, and demanded to be led to Camillus. So led, and in that presence, he said he was a boys' schoolteacher, but chose rather to win the general's favour than to fulfil the duties of his office, and so had come bringing to him the city in the persons of its boys. It seemed to Camillus, on hearing him, that the man had done a monstrous deed, and turning to the bystanders he said: 'War is indeed a grievous thing, and is waged with much injustice and violence; but even war has certain laws which good and brave men will respect, and we must not so hotly pursue victory as not to flee the favours of base and impious doers. The great general will wage war relying on his own native valour, not on the baseness of other men.' Then he ordered his attendants to tear the man's clothing from him, tie his arms behind his back, and put rods and scourges in the hands of the boys, that they might chastise the teacher and drive him back to the city.[1]

Plutarch

13.

In 390 BC, the Gauls seized Rome, and the inhabitants were besieged on the Capitoline Hill where one night they found themselves in mortal danger.

. . . the Gauls had noticed the tracks of a man, where the messenger from Veii had got through, or perhaps had observed for themselves that the cliff near the shrine of Carmentis afforded an easy ascent. So on a starlit night they first sent forward an unarmed man to try the way; then handing up their weapons when there was a steep place, and supporting themselves by their fellows or affording support in their turn, they pulled one another up, as the ground required, and reached the summit, in such silence that not only the sentries but even the dogs—creatures easily troubled by noises in the night—were not aroused. But they could not elude the vigilance of the geese, which, being sacred to Juno, had, notwithstanding the dearth of provisions, not been killed. This was the salvation of them all; for the geese with their gabbling and clapping of their wings woke Marcus Manlius—consul of three years before and a distinguished soldier—who, catching up his weapons and at the same time calling the rest to arms, strode past his bewildered comrades to a Gaul who had already got a foothold on the crest and dislodged him with a blow from the boss of his shield.

As he slipped and fell, he overturned those who were next to him, and the others in alarm let go their weapons and grasping the rocks to which they had been clinging, were slain by Manlius.

And by now the rest had come together and were assailing the invaders with javelins and stones, and presently the whole company lost their footing and were flung down headlong to destruction.

Livy

---

[1] Falerii fell anyway.

14.

During the war against the Latins in 340 BC, the consul Manlius insisted that the most ruthless discipline should be preserved within the Roman ranks, and also decreed that to avoid misunderstandings in battle against a people whose appearance, armour, and organization so closely resembled their own, no Roman should engage the enemy without specific orders.

IT happened that among the other prefects of the troops, who had been sent out in all directions to reconnoitre, Titus Manlius, the consul's son, came with his troop to the back of the enemy's camp, so near that he was scarcely distant a dart's throw from the next post. In that place were some Tusculan cavalry; they were commanded by Geminus Metius, a man distinguished among his countrymen both by birth and exploits. When he recognized the Roman cavalry, and conspicuous among them the consul's son marching at their head (for they were all known to each other, especially the men of note), he asked: 'Romans, are ye going to wage war with the Latins and allies with a single troop? What in the interim will the consuls, what will the two consular armies be doing?' 'They will be here in good time,' says Manlius, 'and with them will be Jupiter himself, as a witness of the treaties violated by you, who is stronger and more powerful. If we fought at the lake Regillus until you had quite enough, here also we shall so act, that a line of battle and an encounter with us may afford you no very great gratification.' In reply to this, Geminus, advancing some distance from his own party, says, 'Do you choose then, until that day arrives on which you are to put your armies in motion with such mighty labour, to enter the lists with me, that from the result of a contest between us both, it may be seen how much a Latin excels a Roman horseman?' Either resentment, or shame at declining the contest, or the invincible power of fate, arouses the determined spirit of the youth. Forgetful therefore of his father's command, and the consul's edict, he is driven headlong to that contest, in which it made not much difference whether he conquered or was conquered. The other horsemen being removed to a distance as if to witness the sight, in the space of clear ground which lay between them they spurred on their horses against each other; and when they were together in fierce encounter, the spear of Manlius passed over the helmet of his antagonist, and that of Maecius passed over the neck of the other's horse. Then, as they pulled their horses round, Manlius, who was the first to gather himself up for a second thrust, pricked his enemy's charger between the ears. The smart of this wound made the horse rear and toss his head so violently that he threw off his rider, who, raising himself with spear and shield, was struggling to his feet after the heavy fall, when Manlius plunged his lance into his throat so that it came out between the ribs and pinned him to the ground. He then gathered up the spoils and rode back to his troopers, who attended him with shouts of triumph to the camp, where he sought at once the headquarters of his father, knowing not what doom the future held for him, or whether praise or punishment were his appointed guerdon.

'Father,' he said, 'that all men might truly report me to be your son, I bring these equestrian spoils, stripped from the body of an enemy who challenged me.' On hearing this, the consul straightway turned from his son and commanded a trumpet to sound the assembly. When the men had gathered in full numbers, the consul said, 'Inasmuch, Titus Manlius, as you have held in reverence neither consular authority nor a father's dignity, and despite our edict have quitted your place to fight the enemy, and so far as in you lay, have broken military discipline, whereby the Roman state has stood until this day unshaken, thus compelling me to forget either the republic or myself, we will sooner endure the punishment of our wrong-doing than suffer the republic to expiate our sins at a cost so heavy to herself; we will set a stern example, but a salutary one, for the young men of the future. For my own part, I am moved, not only by a man's instinctive love of his children, but by this instance you have given of your bravery, perverted though it was by an idle show of honour. But since the authority of the consuls must either be established by your death, or by your impunity be forever abrogated, and since I think that you yourself, if you have a drop of my blood in you, would not refuse to raise up by your punishment the military discipline which through your misdemeanour has slippped and fallen,—go, lictor, bind him to the stake.'

All were astounded at so shocking a command; every man looked upon the axe as lifted against himself, and they were hushed with fear more than with reverence. And so, after standing, as if lost in wonder, rooted to the spot, suddenly, when the blood gushed forth from the severed neck, their voices burst out in such unrestrained upbraiding that they spared neither laments nor curses; and covering the young man's body with his spoils, they built a pyre outside the rampart, where they burned it with all the honours that can possibly attend a soldier's funeral; and the 'orders of Manlius' not only caused men to shudder at the time, but became a type of severity with succeeding ages.

Nevertheless the brutality of the punishment made the soldiers more obedient to their general; and not only were guard-duties, watches, and the ordering of outposts, everywhere more carefully observed, but in the final struggle, as well, when the troops had gone down into battle, that stern act did much good.

Livy

15.

Origins of Alexander the Great's legendary war horse.

ONCE upon a time Philoneicus the Thessalian brought Bucephalas, offering to sell him to Philip [of Macedon, Alexander's father] for thirteen talents, and they went down into the plain to try the horse, who appeared to be savage and altogether intractable, neither allowing any one to mount him, nor heeding the voice of any of Philip's attendants, but rearing up against all of them. Then Philip was vexed and ordered the horse to be led away, believing him to be altogether wild and unbroken; but Alexander, who was near by, said: 'What a horse they are losing, because, for lack of skill and courage, they cannot manage him!' At first, then, Philip held his peace; but as Alexander many times let fall such words and showed great distress, he said: 'Dost thou find fault with thine elders in the belief that thou knowest more than they do or art better able to manage a horse?' 'This horse, at any rate,' said Alexander, 'I could manage better than others have.' 'And if thou shouldst not, what penalty wilt thou undergo for thy rashness?' 'Indeed,' said Alexander, 'I will forfeit the price of the horse.' There was laughter at this, and then an agreement between father and son as to the forfeiture, and at once Alexander ran to the horse, took hold of his bridle-rein, and turned him towards the sun; for he had noticed, as it would seem, that the horse was greatly disturbed by the sight of his own shadow falling in from of him and dancing about. And after he had calmed the horse a little in this way, and had stroked him with his hand, when he saw that he was full of spirit and courage, he quietly cast aside his mantle and with a light spring safely bestrode him. Then, with a little pressure of the reins on the bit, and without striking him or tearing his mouth, he held him in hand; but when he saw that the horse was rid of the fear that had beset him, and was impatient for the course, he gave him his head, and at last urged him on with sterner tone and thrust of foot. Philip and his company were speechless with anxiety at first; but when Alexander made the turn in proper fashion and came back towards them proud and exultant, all the rest broke into loud cries, but his father, as we are told, actually shed tears of joy, and when Alexander had dismounted, kissed him, saying: 'My son, seek thee out a kingdom equal to thyself; Macedonia has not room for thee.'

Plutarch

16.

THE Macedonians used to celebrate a festival in honour of Dionysus, and it was Alexander's custom to offer sacrifice each year on the sacred day. The story is that on this particular occasion [328 BC] Alexander, for some reason best known to himself, sacrificed not to Dionysus but to Castor and Polydeuces, the Dioscuri. There had been some pretty heavy drinking (another innovation—in drink, too, he now tended to barbaric excess), and in the course of talk the subject of the Dioscuri came up, together with the common attribution of their parentage to Zeus instead of to Tyndareus. Some of the company—the sort of people whose sycophantic tongues always have been and always will be the bane of kings—declared with gross flattery that, in their opinion, Polydeuces and Castor were not to be compared with Alexander and his achievements; others, being thoroughly drunk, extended the invidious comparison to Heracles himself: for it was only envy, they maintained, which deprived the living of due honour from their friends.

Now Cleitus for some time past had quite obviously deprecated the change in Alexander: he liked neither his move towards the manners of the East, nor the sycophantic expressions of his courtiers. When, therefore, he heard what was said on this occasion (he, too, had been drinking heavily), he angrily intervened; it was intolerable, he declared, to offer such an insult to divine beings, and he would allow no one to pay Alexander a compliment at the expense of the mighty ones of long ago—such a compliment was not for his honour but for his shame. In any case, he continued, they grossly exaggerated the marvellous nature of Alexander's achievements, none of which were mere personal triumphs of his own; on the contrary, most of them were the work of the Macedonians as a whole.

Alexander was deeply hurt—and I, for my part, feel that Cleitus' words were ill-judged; in view of the fact that most of the party were drunk, he could, in my opinion, have quite well avoided the grossness of joining in the general flattery simply by keeping his thoughts to himself. But there was more to come: for others of the company, hoping, in their turn, to curry favour with Alexander, brought up the subject of Philip, and suggested, absurdly enough, that what he had done was, after all, quite ordinary and commonplace. At this Cleitus could control himself no longer; he began to magnify Philip's achievements and belittle Alexander's; his words came pouring out—he was, by now, very drunk indeed—and, among much else, he taunted Alexander with the reminder that he had saved his life, when they fought the Persian cavalry on the Granicus.

'This is the hand', he cried, holding it out with a flourish, 'that saved you, Alexander, on that day.'

Alexander could stand no more drunken abuse from his friend. Angrily he leapt from his seat as if to strike him, but the others held him back. Cleitus continued to pour out his insulting remarks, and Alexander called for the Guard. No one answered.

'What?' he cried, 'have I nothing left of royalty but the name? Am I to be like Darius, dragged in chains by Bessus and his cronies?'

Now nobody could hold him; springing to his feet, he snatched a spear from one of the attendants and struck Cleitus dead.

Accounts of this incident differ. Some authorities say it was not a spear but a pike; Aristobulus does not mention the occasion of the drinking bout: according to him, Cleitus need not have been killed but for his own action; for when Alexander sprang up in rage to kill him, Ptolemy, son of Lagus, a member of the King's personal guard, hurried him out of the door and over the wall and ditch of the fortress. But, unable to control himself, he went back to the banquet room and met Alexander just at the moment when he was calling his name.

'Here I am, Alexander!' he cried, and, as he spoke, the blow fell.

Personally, I strongly deprecate Cleitus' unseemly behaviour to his sovereign; and for Alexander I feel pity, in that he showed himself on this occasion the slave of anger and drunkenness, two vices to neither of which a self-respecting man should ever yield. But when the deed was done, Alexander immediately felt its horror; and for that I admire him. Some have said that he fixed the butt of the pike against the wall, meaning to fall upon it himself, because a man who murdered his friend when his wits were fuddled with wine was not fit to live. Most writers, however, say nothing of this; they tell us that Alexander lay on his bed in tears, calling the name of Cleitus and of his sister Lanice, who had been his nurse. 'Ah,' he cried, 'a good return I have made you for your care, now I am a man! You have lived to see your sons die fighting for me, and now with my own hand I have killed your brother.' Again and again he called himself the murderer of his friends, and for three days lay without food or drink, careless of all personal comfort.

Arrian

17.

In 323 BC, Alexander was at Babylon preparing for a great new expedition into Ambia when he was taken with a fever after a boating expedition on the Euphrates.

NEXT day he was carried out on his bed to perform his daily religious duties as usual, and after the ceremony lay in the men's quarters till dark. He continued to issue orders to his officers, instructing them who were to march by land to be ready to start in three days and those who were going with himself by sea to sail one day later. From there he was carried on his bed to the river, and crossed in a boat to the park on the further side, where he took another bath and rested. Next day he bathed again and offered sacrifice as usual, after which he went to lie down in his room, where he chatted to Medius and gave orders for his officers to report to him early next morning. Then he took a little food, returned to his room, and lay all night in a fever. The following morning he bathed and offered sacrifice, and then issued to Nearchus and the other officers detailed instructions about the voyage, now due to start in two days' time. Next day he bathed again, went through his regular religious duties, and was afterwards in constant fever. None the less he sent for his staff as usual and gave them further instructions on their preparations for sailing. In the evening, after another bath, his condition was grave, and the following morning he was moved to the building near the swimming-pool. He offered sacrifice, and in spite of his increasing weakness, sent for his senior officers and repeated his orders for the expedition. The day after that he just managed to have himself carried to his place of prayer, and after the ceremony still continued, in spite of his weakness, to issue instructions to his staff. Another day passed. Now very seriously ill, he still refused to neglect his religious duties; he gave orders, however, that his senior officers should wait in the court, and the battalion and company commanders outside his door. Then, his condition already desperate, he was moved from the park back to the palace. He recognized his officers when they entered his room but could no longer speak to them. From that moment until the end he uttered no word. That night and the following day and for the next twenty-four hours, he remained in a high fever.

These details are all to be found in the Diaries. It is further recorded in these documents that the soldiers were passionately eager to see him; some hoped for a sight of him while he was still alive; others wished to see his body, for a report had gone round that he was already dead, and they suspected, I fancy, that his death was being concealed by his guards. But nothing could keep them from a sight of him, and the motive in almost every heart was grief and a sort of helpless bewilderment at the thought of losing their king. Lying speechless as the men filed by, he yet struggled to raise his head, and in his eyes there was a look of recognition for each individual as he passed. The Diaries say that Peitho, Attalus, Demophon and Peucestas, together with Cleomenes, Menidas, and Seleucus, spent the night in the temple of Serapis and asked the God if it would be better for Alexander to be carried into the temple himself, in order to pray there and perhaps recover; but the God forbade it, and declared it would be better for him if he stayed where he was. The God's command was made public, and soon afterwards Alexander died—this, after all, being the 'better' thing.

Arrian

18.

A delightfully preposterous device attributed to Alexander's former secretary and sub-ordinate commander Eumenes of Cardia, when after his old master's death he was being besieged by Antigonus in a town named Nora in Phrygia (319 BC).

. . . fearing that by remaining in one place he might ruin the horses of his army, because there was no room for exercising them, Eumenes hit upon a clever device by which an animal standing in one place might be warmed and exercised, so that it would have a better appetite and not lose its bodily activity. He drew up its head with a thong so high that it could not quite touch the ground with its forefeet, and then forced it by blows of a whip to bound and kick out behind, an exercise which produced no less sweat than running on a racecourse. The result was that, to the surprise of all, the animals were led out of the

fortress after a siege of several months in as good condition as if he had
kept them in pasture.

Cornelius Nepos

19.

*Pyrrhus, King of Epirus (b.319 BC) aspired to emulate Alexander the Great, but was
never able to translate his considerable military talents into secure political power. In
280 BC, he fought alongside the Tarentines against Rome, and defeated the consul
Laevinus at Heraclea. According to Plutarch, 15,000 men died in the battle, which
also contributed the most lasting memorial of Pyrrhus to history.*

THE two armies separated; and we are told that Pyrrhus said to one
who was congratulating him on his victory, 'If we are victorious in one
more battle with the Romans, we shall be utterly ruined.'

Plutarch

20.

The end of Pyrrhus, 274 BC.

THE same ambitious, quarrelsome prince fell upon Argos, at a time
when it was divided by the factions of Aristias and Aristippus. The
Argives at first sent to Pyrrhus to beg him to evacuate their territories.
He promised to do so, but that very same night entered their gates,
aided by the treachery of Aristias. A great part of his troops had already
spread themselves throughout the city, when an act of imprudence
deprived him of his victory and his life. Whoever reads the life of
Pyrrhus will observe the importance he always attached to his
elephants—engines of war, if we may so call them, introduced for a
time into Europe by the conquests of Alexander. He had tried to terrify
the Romans with these monstrous animals but without success. So
partial was he to these bulky assistants, that he insisted upon their
being brought into Lacedaemon, though the gates were not large
enough, or the streets sufficiently wide, to make them at all available.
Alarmed by the noise created by the confusion the elephants produced, the Argives flew to arms, and their houses became so many
citadels, from which they poured all sorts of missiles down upon the
troops of the king of Epirus. The elephants so completely blocked up

the way, as to prevent the entrance of fresh troops, and were of more injury to their masters than to the Spartans. Abandoned by his people, Pyrrhus maintained his character for personal valour by the brave manner in which he fought his way through the enemy. An Argive attacked him, and hurled his javelin at him; but the point was blunted by the thickness of his cuirass. The furious prince was about to strike him dead, when the mother of the Argive, who beheld the fight from the roof of her house, threw a tile at Pyrrhus, which, striking him on the head, stretched him senseless on the ground. One of the soldiers of Antigonus coming up, was rejoiced to find their great enemy in such a state, and immediately cut off his head. His soldiers, deprived of their leader, were soon put to the rout. Thus perished, by the hand of an old woman, a captain famous for his exploits against both Rome and Carthage, and whose victorious arms had made Greece tremble more than once.

William Robson

21.

Hannibal crosses the Alps, 218 BC.

FROM that time the mountaineers fell upon them in smaller parties, more like an attack of robbers than war, sometimes on the van, sometimes on the rear, according as the ground afforded them advantage, or stragglers advancing or loitering gave them an opportunity. Though the elephants were driven through steep and narrow roads with great loss of time, yet wherever they went they rendered the army safe from the enemy, because men unacquainted with such animals were afraid of approaching too nearly. On the ninth day they came to a summit of the Alps, chiefly through places trackless; and after many mistakes of their way, which were caused either by the treachery of the guides, or, when they were not trusted, by entering valleys at random, on their own conjectures of the route. For two days they remained encamped on the summit; and rest was given to the soldiers, exhausted with toil and fighting: and several beasts of burden, which had fallen down among the rocks, by following the track of the army arrived at the camp. A fall of snow, it being now the season of the setting of the constellation of the Pleiades, caused great fear to the soldiers, already worn out with weariness of so many hardships. On the standards being moved forward at day-break, when the army proceeded slowly over all places entirely blocked up with snow, and languor and despair strongly appeared in the countenances of all, Hannibal, having advanced before the standards, and ordered the soldiers to halt on a certain eminence, whence there was a prospect far and wide, points out to them Italy and the plains of the Po, extending themselves beneath the Alpine mountains; and said 'that they were now surmounting not only the ramparts of Italy, but also of the city of Rome; that the rest of the journey would be smooth and down-hill; that after one, or, at most, a second battle, they would have the citadel and capital of Italy in their power and possession'. The army then began to advance, the enemy now making no attempts beyond petty thefts, as opportunity offered. But the journey proved much more difficult that it had been in the ascent, as the declivity of the Alps being generally shorter on the side of Italy is consequently steeper; for nearly all the road was precipitous, narrow, and slippery, so that neither those who made the least stumble could prevent themselves from falling, nor, when fallen, remain in the same place, but rolled, both men and beasts of burden, one upon another.

They then came to a rock much more narrow, and formed of such perpendicular ledges, that a light-armed soldier, carefully making the attempt, and clinging with his hands to the bushes and roots around, could with difficulty lower himself down. The ground, even before very steep by nature, had been broken by a recent falling away of the earth into a precipice of nearly a thousand feet in depth. Here when the cavalry had halted, as if at the end of their journey, it is announced to Hannibal, wondering what obstructed the march, that the rock was impassable. Having then gone himself to view the place, it seemed clear to him that he must lead his army round it, by however great a circuit, through the pathless and untrodden regions around. But this route also proved impracticable; for while the new snow of a moderate depth remained on the old, which had not been removed, their footsteps were planted with ease as they walked upon the new snow, which was soft and not too deep; but when it was dissolved by the trampling of so many men and beasts of burden, they then walked on the bare ice below, and through the dirty fluid formed by the melting snow. Here there was a wretched struggle, both on account of the slippery ice not affording any hold to the step, and giving way beneath the foot more readily by reason of the slope; and whether they assisted themselves in rising by their hands or their knees, their supports themselves giving way, they would tumble again; nor were there any stumps or roots near, by pressing against which, one might with hand or foot support himself; so that they only floundered on the smooth ice and amid the melted snow. The beasts of burden sometimes also cut into this lower ice by merely treading upon it, at others they broke it completely through, by the violence with which they struck in their hoofs in their struggling, so that most of them, as if taken in a trap, stuck in the hardened and deeply frozen ice.

At length, after the men and beasts of burden had been fatigued to no purpose, the camp was pitched on the summit, the ground being cleared for that purpose with great difficulty, so much snow was there to be dug out and carried away. The soldiers being then set to make a way down the cliff, by which alone a passage could be effected, and it being necessary that they should cut through the rocks, having felled and lopped a number of large trees which grew around, they make a huge pile of timber; and as soon as a strong wind fit for exciting the flames arose, they set fire to it, and, pouring vinegar on the heated stones, they render them soft and crumbling. They then open a way with iron instruments through the rock thus heated by the fire, and soften its declivities by gentle windings, so that not only the beasts of burden, but also the elephants could be led down it. Four day were spent about this rock, the beasts nearly perishing through hunger: for the summits of the mountains are for the most part bare, and if there is any pasture the snows bury it. The lower parts contain valleys, and some sunny hills, and rivulets flowing beside woods, and scenes more worthy of the abode of man. There the beasts of burden were sent out to pasture, and rest given for three days to the men, fatigued with forming the passage: they then descended into the plains, the country and the dispositions of the inhabitants being now less rugged.

In this manner chiefly they came to Italy in the fifth month (as some authors relate) after leaving New Carthage, having crossed the Alps in fifteen days.

Livy

22.

Fabius Cunctator enhances his reputation for probity.

. . . in Italy the prudent delay of Fabius had procured the Romans some intermission from disasters; which conduct, as it kept Hannibal disturbed with no ordinary degree of anxiety, for it proved to him that

the Romans had at length selected a general who would carry on the
war with prudence, and not in dependence on fortune; so was it treated
with contempt by his countrymen, both in the camp and in the city;
particularly after that a battle had been fought during his absence from
the temerity of the master of the horse, in its issue, as I may justly
designate it, rather joyful than successful. Two causes were added to
augment the unpopularity of the dictator: one arising out of a stratagem and artful procedure of Hannibal; for the farm of the dictator
having been pointed out to him by deserters, he ordered that the fire
and sword and every outrage of enemies should be restrained from it
alone, while all around were levelled with the ground; in order that it
might appear to have been the term of some secret compact: the other
from an act of his own, at first perhaps suspicious, because in it he had
not waited for the authority of the senate, but in the result turning
unequivocally to his highest credit, with relation to the change of prisoners: for, as was the case in the first Punic war, an agreement had
been made between the Roman and Carthaginian generals, that
whichever received more prisoners than he restored, should give two
pounds and a half of silver for every man. And when the Roman had
received two hundred and forty-seven more than the Carthaginian,
and the silver which was due for them, after the matter had been frequently agitated in the senate, was not promptly supplied, because he
had not consulted the fathers, he sent his son Quintus to Rome and
sold his farm, uninjured by the enemy, and thus redeemed the public
credit at his own private expense.

                                                                    Livy

23.

*Under the Roman system, by which each of the two consuls commanded the army on
alternate days, the plebeian Terentius Varro took the ill-judged decision to attack at
Cannae (3 August 216 BC), against the advice of his colleague Lucius Aemilius, with
disastrous results: close to 50,000 of the Romans and their allies are said to have been
killed. Varro escaped; and Lucius Aemilius was wounded.*

CN. LENTULUS, a military tribune, saw, as he rode by, the consul
covered with blood sitting on a boulder. 'Lucius Aemilius,' he said,
'the one man whom the gods must hold guiltless of this day's disaster,
take this horse while you have still some strength left, and I can lift you

into the saddle and keep by your side to protect you. Do not make this day of battle still more fatal by a consul's death, there are enough tears and mourning without that.' The consul replied: 'Long may you live to do brave deeds, Cornelius, but do not waste in useless pity the few moments left in which to escape from the hands of the enemy. Go, announce publicly to the senate that they must fortify Rome and make its defence strong before the victorious enemy approaches, and tell Q. Fabius privately that I have ever remembered his precepts in life and in death. Suffer me to breathe my last among my slaughtered soldiers, let me not have to defend myself again when I am no longer consul, or appear as the accuser of my colleague and protect my innocence by throwing the guilt on another.' During this conversation a crowd of fugitives came suddenly upon them, followed by the enemy, who, not knowing who the consul was, overwhelmed him in a shower of missiles. Lentulus escaped on horseback in the rush.

Livy

24.

After Cannae.

HANNIBAL'S officers crowded round him with congratulations on his victory. The others all advised him, now that he had brought so great a war to a conclusion, to repose himself and to allow his weary soldiers to repose for the remainder of that day and the following night. But Maharbal, the commander of the cavalry, held that no time should be lost. 'Nay,' he cried, 'that you may realize what has been accomplished by this battle, in five days you shall banquet in the Capitol! Follow after; I will precede you with the cavalry, that the Romans may know that you are there before they know that you are coming!' To Hannibal the idea was too joyous and too vast for his mind at once to grasp it. And so, while praising Maharbal's goodwill, he declared that he must have time to deliberate regarding his advice. Then said Maharbal, 'In very truth the gods bestow not on the same man all their gifts; you know how to gain a victory, Hannibal: you know not how to use one.' That day's delay is generally believed to have saved the City and the empire.

Livy

25.

Archimedes, the Greek inventor and mathematician, was among the population of Syracuse when the city was besieged by Claudius Marcellus in 213 BC. He put his genius at the disposal of the garrison to design artillery for them, and was the most distinguished victim when the Romans at last took Syracuse in 211.

WHEN, therefore, the Romans assaulted them by sea and land, the Syracusans were stricken dumb with terror; they thought that nothing could withstand so furious an onset by such forces. But Archimedes began to ply his engines, and shot against the land forces of the assailants all sorts of missiles and immense masses of stones, which came down with incredible din and speed; nothing whatever could ward off their weight, but they knocked down in heaps those who stood in their way, and threw their ranks into confusion. At the same time huge beams were suddenly projected over the ships from the walls, which sank some of them with great weights plunging down from on high; others were seized at the prow by iron claws, or beaks like the beaks of cranes, drawn straight up into the air, and then plunged stern foremost into the depths, or were turned round and round by means of enginery within the city, and dashed upon the steep cliffs that jutted out beneath the wall of the city, with great destruction of the fighting men on board, who perished in the wrecks. Frequently, too, a ship would be lifted out of the water into mid-air, whirled hither and thither as it hung there, a dreadful spectacle, until its crew had been thrown out and hurled in all directions, when it would fall empty upon the walls, or slip away from the clutch that had held it.

. . . But what most of all afflicted Marcellus [on the fall of the city] was the death of Archimedes. For it chanced that he was by himself, working out some problem with the aid of a diagram, and having fixed his thoughts and his eyes as well upon the matter of his study, he was not aware of the incursion of the Romans or of the capture of the city. Suddenly a soldier came upon him and ordered him to go with him to Marcellus. This Archimedes refused to do until he had worked out his problem and established his demonstration, whereupon the soldier flew into a passion, drew his sword, and dispatched him. Others, however, say that the Roman came upon him with drawn sword threatening to kill him at once, and that Archimedes, when he saw him, earnestly besought him to wait a little while, that he might not leave the result that he was seeking incomplete and

without demonstration; but the soldier paid no heed to him and
made an end of him. There is also a third story, that as Archimedes
was carrying to Marcellus some of his mathematical instruments,
such as sun-dials and spheres and quadrants, by means of which he
made the magnitude of the sun appreciable to the eye, some soldiers
fell in with him, and thinking that he was carrying gold in the box,
slew him. However, it is generally agreed that Marcellus was
afflicted at his death, and turned away from his slayer as from a polluted person, and sought out the kindred of Archimedes and paid
them honour.

Plutarch

26.

*After his defeat at Zama in 202 BC, Hannibal remained at Carthage until he was
driven into exile with Antiochus III of Syria in 193 BC. It was at Ephesus during this
period, claim Greek writers quoted by Livy, that Hannibal's conqueror Scipio
Africanus met the Carthaginian while on an ambassadorial mission to Syria.*

. . . when Africanus asked who, in Hannibal's opinion, was the greatest general, Hannibal named Alexander, the king of the Macedonians,
because with a small force he had routed armies innumerable and
because he had traversed the most distant regions, even to see which
transcended human hopes. To the next request, as to whom he would
rank second, Hannibal selected Pyrrhus; saying that he had been the
first to teach the art of castrametation; besides, no one had chosen his
ground or placed his troops more discriminatingly; he possessed also
the art of winning men over to him, so that the Italian peoples preferred the lordship of a foreign king to that of the Roman people, so
long the master in that land. When he continued, asking whom Hannibal considered third, he named himself without hesitation. Then
Scipio broke into a laugh and said 'What would you say if you had
defeated me?' 'Then, beyond doubt,' he replied, 'I should place myself
both before Alexander and before Pyrrhus and before all other
generals.'

Livy

27.

Spartacus was a Thracian shepherd who served for a time in the Roman army before deserting and becoming a brigand. On his capture, he was sold to a trainer of gladiators, and in 73 BC was in the barracks of one Lentulus, at Capua, when he persuaded some seventy of his comrades to join him in a break for freedom. Some estimates place the eventual number of his followers at 90,000. By the end of his first year of liberty, he controlled most of southern Italy after defeating two Roman forces. In 72 BC, he defeated both consuls, and reached the foot of the Alps. But here his movement collapsed, and in 71 he was defeated and killed by Crassus on the river Silarus, his surviving followers being crucified. This is a somewhat partisan Roman account of the slaves' revolt.

ONE can tolerate, indeed, even the disgrace of a war against slaves; for although, by force of circumstances, they are liable to any kind of treatment, yet they form as it were a class (though an inferior class) of human beings and can be admitted to the blessings of liberty which we enjoy. But I know not what name to give to the war which was stirred up at the instigation of Spartacus; for the common soldiers being slaves and their leaders being gladiators—the former men of the humblest, the latter men of the worse, class—added insult to the injury which they inflicted upon Rome.

Spartacus, Crixus and Oenomaus, breaking out of the gladiatorial school of Lentulus with thirty or rather more men of the same occupation, escaped from Capua. When, by summoning the slaves to their standard, they had quickly collected more than 10,000 adherents, these men, who had been originally content merely to have escaped, soon began to wish to take their revenge also. The first position which attracted them (a suitable one for such ravening monsters) was Mt Vesuvius. Being besieged here by Clodius Glabrus, they slid by means of ropes made of vine-twigs through a passage in the hollow of the mountain down into its very depths, and issuing forth by a hidden exit, seized the camp of the general by a sudden attack which he never expected. They then attacked other camps, that of Varenius and afterwards that of Thoranus; and they ranged over the whole of Campania. Not content with the plundering of country houses and villages, they laid waste Nola, Nuceria, Thurii and Metapontum with terrible destruction. Becoming a regular army by the daily arrival of fresh forces, they made themselves rude shields of wicker-work and the skins of animals, and swords and other weapons by melting down the iron in the slave-prisons. That nothing might be lacking which was proper to a regular army, cavalry was procured by breaking in herds of horses which they encountered, and his men brought to their leader the insignia and fasces captured from the praetors, nor were they refused by the man who, from being a Thracian mercenary, had become a soldier, and from a soldier a deserter, then a highwayman, and finally, thanks to his strength, a gladiator. He also celebrated the obsequies of his officers who had fallen in battle with funerals like those of Roman generals, and ordered his captives to fight at their pyres, just as though he wished to wipe out all his past dishonour by having become, instead of a gladiator, a giver of gladiatorial shows. Next, actually attacking generals of consular rank, he inflicted defeat on the army of Lentulus in the Apennines and destroyed the camp of Publius Cassius at Mutina. Elated by these victories he entertained the project—in itself a sufficient disgrace to us—of attacking the city of Rome. At last a combined effort was made, supported by all the resources of the empire, against this gladiator, and Licinius Crassus vindicated the honour of Rome. Routed and put to flight by him, our enemies—I am ashamed to give them this title—took refuge in the furthest extremities of Italy. Here, being cut off in the angle of Bruttium and preparing to escape to Sicily, but being unable to obtain ships, they tried to launch rafts of beams and casks bound together with withies on the swift waters of the straits. Failing in this attempt, they finally made a sally and met a death worthy of men, fighting to the death as became those who were commanded by a gladiator. Spartacus himself fell, as became a general, fighting most bravely in the front rank.

Florus

28.

Julius Caesar (101–44 BC) describes his first landing in Britain in 55 BC.

SUMMER was now drawing to a close, and winter sets in rather early in these parts, as Gaul lies wholly in northern latitudes. Nevertheless I hurried on preparations for an expedition to Britain, knowing that Britain had rendered assistance to the enemy in nearly all my Gallic campaigns. Although it was too late in the year for military operations I thought it would be a great advantage merely to have visited the island, to have seen what kind of people the inhabitants were, and to have learned something about the country with its harbours and landing-places. Of all this the Gauls knew virtually nothing; for no one except traders makes the journey with any regularity, and even their knowledge is limited to the sea coast immediately facing Gaul. Interviews with numerous merchants elicited nothing as to the size of the island, the names and strength of the native tribes, their military and civil organization, or the harbours which might accommodate a large fleet. Nevertheless it seemed essential to obtain this information before risking an expedition, and Caius Volusenus appeared to me the best man for the job. He travelled in a warship with orders to make a general reconnaissance and report back as early as possible. Meanwhile the whole army moved into Artois, where the mainland is nearest to the coast of Britain; and ships were ordered to assemble there from all neighbouring districts, including the fleet which had been built last year for the Venetian campaign. Meanwhile, however, some traders revealed our plans to the Britons, and a number of tribes sent envoys promising hostages and offering their submission. They were received in audience, promised generous terms, and urged to abide by their undertaking. They were accompanied on their return journey by Commius, whom I had appointed ruler of the Atrebates after the subjugation of that people, and of whose honour, discretion, and loyalty I had received abundant proof. Commius was greatly respected in Britain, and his orders were to visit all the states he could, impressing on them the advantages of Roman protection, and to announce my impending arrival.

Volusenus completed his survey as far as he was able without disembarking and risking a hostile reception from the natives. Five days later he returned and made his report. . . . A fleet of about eighty ships, which seemed adequate for the conveyance of two legions, was eventually commissioned and assembled, together with a number of warships commanded by the chief of staff, officers of general rank, and auxiliary commanders. At another port, some eight miles higher up the coast, were eighteen transports which had been prevented by adverse winds from joining the main fleet at Boulogne: these were allotted to the cavalry. The remainder of the army under Sabinus and Cotta was sent on a punitive expedition against the Menapii and those cantons of the Morini which had not been represented in the recent delegation. Another general officer, Publius Sulpicius Rufus, was ordered to guard the harbour with a force that seemed large enough for that purpose.

Arrangements were now complete, the weather was favourable, and we cast off just before midnight. The cavalry had been ordered to make for the northern port, embark there, and follow on; but they were rather slow about carrying out these instructions, and started, as we shall see, too late. I reached Britain with the leading vessels at about 9 a.m., and saw the enemy forces standing under arms all along the heights. At this point of the coast precipitous cliffs tower over the water, making it possible to fire from above directly on to the beaches. It was clearly no place to attempt a landing, so we rode at anchor until about 3.30 p.m. awaiting the rest of the fleet. During this interval I summoned my staff and company commanders, passed on to them the information obtained by Volusenus, and explained my plans. They were warned that, as tactical demands, particularly at sea, are always uncertain and subject to rapid change, they must be ready to act at a moment's notice on the briefest order from myself. The meeting then broke up: both wind and tide were favourable, the signal was given to weigh anchor, and after moving about eight miles up channel the ships were grounded on an open and evenly shelving beach.

The natives, however, realized our intention: their cavalry and war chariots (a favourite arm of theirs) were sent ahead, while the main body followed close behind and stood ready to prevent our landing. In the circumstances, disembarkation was an extraordinarily difficult business. On account of their large draught the ships could not be beached except in deep water; and the troops, besides being ignorant of the locality, had their hands full: weighted with a mass of heavy armour, they had to jump from the ships, stand firm in the surf, and fight at the same time. But the enemy knew their ground: being quite unencumbered, they could hurl their weapons boldly from dry land or shallow water, and gallop their horses which were trained to this kind of work. Our men were terrified: they were inexperienced in this kind of fighting, and lacked that dash and drive which always characterized their land battles.

The warships, however, were of a shape unfamiliar to the natives; they were swift, too, and easier to handle than the transports. Therefore, as soon as I grasped the situation I ordered them to go slightly astern, clear of the transports, then full speed ahead, bringing up on the Britons' right flank. From that position they were to open fire and force the enemy back with slings, arrows, and artillery. The manœuvre was of considerable help to the troops. The Britons were scared by the strange forms of the warships, by the motion of the oars, and by the artillery which they had never seen before: they halted, then fell back a little; but our men still hesitated, mainly because of the deep water.

At this critical moment the standard-bearer of the Tenth Legion, after calling on the gods to bless the legion through his act, shouted:

'Come on, men! Jump, unless you want to betray your standard to the
enemy! I, at any rate, shall do my duty to my country and my commander.' He threw himself into the sea and started forward with the
eagle. The rest were not going to disgrace themselves; cheering wildly
they leaped down, and when the men in the next ships saw them they
too quickly followed their example.

The action was bitterly contested on both sides. But our fellows
were unable to keep their ranks and stand firm; nor could they follow
their appointed standards, because men from different ships were falling in under the first one they reached, and a good deal of confusion
resulted. The Britons, of course, knew all the shallows: standing on
dry land, they watched the men disembark in small parties, galloped
down, attacked them as they struggled through the surf, and surrounded them with superior numbers while others opened fire on the
exposed flank of isolated units. I therefore had the warships' boats and
scouting vessels filled with troops, so that help could be sent to any
point where the men seemed to be in difficulties. When every one was
ashore and formed up, the legions charged: the enemy was hurled
back, but pursuit for any distance was impossible as the cavalry transports had been unable to hold their course and make the island. That
was the only thing that deprived us of a decisive victory.

The natives eventually recovered from their panic and sent a delegation to ask for peace, promising to surrender hostages and carry out my
instructions. These envoys brought with them Commius, who, it will
be remembered, had preceded us to Britain. When he had landed and
was actually delivering my message in the character of an ambassador
he had been arrested and thrown into prison. Now, after their defeat,
the natives sent him back: in asking for peace they laid the blame for
this outrage upon the common people and asked me to overlook the
incident on the grounds of their ignorance. I protested against this
unprovoked attack which they had launched after sending a mission to
the Continent to negotiate a friendly settlement, but agreed to pardon
their ignorance and demanded hostages. Some of these were handed
over at once, others, they said, would have to be fetched from a distance and would be delivered in a few days. Meanwhile they were
ordered to return to their occupations on the land, and chieftains
began to arrive from the surrounding districts, commending themselves and their tribes to my protection. Peace was thus concluded.

Late on the fourth day after our landing in Britain the eighteen
transports with cavalry on board had sailed from the northern port with

a gentle breeze; but as they neared the British coast and were within sight of the camp a violent storm had blown up, and none of them could hold their course. Some had been driven back to the point of embarkation; others, in great peril, had been swept down channel, westwards, towards the southernmost part of the island. Notwithstanding the danger, they had dropped anchor, but now shipped so much water that they were obliged to stand out to sea as darkness fell and return to the Continent.

It happened to be full moon that night; and at such times the Atlantic tides are particularly high, a fact of which we were ignorant. The result was that the warships, which had been beached, became waterlogged: as for the transports riding at anchor, they were dashed one against another, and it was impossible to manœuvre them or do anything whatever to assist. Several ships broke up, and the remainder lost their cables, anchors, and rigging. Consternation naturally seized the troops, for there were no spare ships in which they could return and no means of refitting. It had been generally understood, too, that we should winter in Gaul, and consequently no arrangements had been made for winter food supplies in Britain.

The British chieftains at my headquarters sized up the situation and put their heads together. They knew we had no cavalry and were short of grain and shipping; they judged the weakness of our forces from the inconsiderable area of the camp, which was all the smaller because we had brought no heavy equipment; and they decided to renew the offensive. Their aim was to cut us off from food supplies and other material and to prolong the campaign until winter. They were confident that if the present expeditionary force were wiped out or prevented from returning, an invasion of Britain would never again be attempted. Accordingly they renewed their vows of mutual loyalty, slipped away one by one from our camp, and secretly reassembled their forces from the countryside.

I had not yet been informed of their intention; but, in view of the disaster to our shipping and the fact that they had ceased to deliver hostages, I had a suspicion of what might happen, and was prepared for any emergency. Corn was brought in every day from the fields; timber and bronze from the badly damaged vessels were used to repair others; the necessary equipment was ordered from the Continent; and, thanks to the energy and efficiency of the troops, all but twelve ships were made tolerably seaworthy.

One day while these repairs were in progress the Seventh Legion was doing its turn in the harvest field: nothing had occurred as yet to arouse suspicion of an impending attack, for many of the natives were still at work on the land and others were frequent visitors to our camp. Suddenly, however, the sentries on the gates reported an unusually large dust cloud in the direction in which the legion had gone. My suspicions were confirmed—the natives had hatched some new plot.

The battalions on guard duty were detailed to go with me to the scene of action, two others were ordered to relieve them, and the rest to arm and follow on immediately. We had not been marching long before I noticed the Seventh was in difficulties: they were only just managing to hold their ground with their units closely packed and under heavy fire. The fact was, the enemy had guessed their destination, as the fields were already stripped elsewhere: they had hidden themselves in the woods by night, and attacked while the men were unarmed and busy reaping. We lost a few killed. The rest were in confusion before they could form up, and found themselves hemmed in by cavalry and war chariots.

The following will give some idea of British charioteers in action. They begin by driving all over the field, hurling javelins; and the terror inspired by the horses and the noise of the wheels is usually enough to throw the enemy ranks into disorder. Then they work their way between their own cavalry units, where the warriors jump down and fight on foot. Meanwhile the drivers retire a short distance from the fighting and station the cars in such a way that their masters, if outnumbered, have an easy means of retreat to their own lines. In action, therefore, they combine the mobility of cavalry with the staying power of foot soldiers. Their skill, which is derived from ceaseless training and practice, may be judged by the fact that they can control their horses at full gallop on the steepest incline, check and turn them in a moment, run along the pole, stand on the yoke, and get back again into the chariot as quick as lightning.

Our troops were unnerved by these tactics, and help reached them in the nick of time: for as we approached the enemy halted, and the legion recovered its morale. The moment, however, was clearly inopportune to precipitate a general engagement; so I advanced no further, and shortly afterwards led the troops back to camp. This episode kept us all fully occupied, and such natives as were still at work in the fields made off.

There followed several days of bad weather, which confined us to camp besides preventing an enemy attack. But during this interval the

Britons sent runners all over the countryside to inform the population that our force was very weak, and that if it could be driven from its base they had every chance of obtaining valuable loot and of securing their freedon once and for all. A strong British force of both arms was assembled and marched on our camp. It was fairly evident that what had happened before would happen again—even if we routed them, their speed would enable them to get clear of further danger. Nevertheless, there were now available some thirty horses brought over by Commius. So the legions were drawn up in battle formation in front of the camp, and after a brief action the enemy was overwhelmed and fled. We followed as far as our speed and endurance allowed, killed a large number of them, then burned all their dwellings over a wide area, and returned to base.

That same day envoys came to sue for peace: they were met with a demand for twice as many hostages as before, and were ordered to bring them over to the Continent, because the equinox was close at hand and the ill condition of our ships made it inadvisable to postpone the voyage until winter. Taking advantage of fair weather we set sail a little after midnight, and the whole fleet reached the mainland in safety.

Julius Caesar

29.

Caesar halted his forces at Ravenna while he waited to hear whether the Senate would accept the tribunes' veto on the disbandment of his army, 49 BC.

. . . when news reached him that the tribunes' veto had been disallowed, and that they had fled the city, he at once sent a few cohorts ahead with all secrecy, and disarmed suspicion by himself attending a theatrical performance, inspecting the plans of a school for gladiators which he proposed to build, and dining as usual among a crowd of guests. But at dusk he borrowed a pair of mules from a bakery near Headquarters, harnessed them to a gig, and set off quietly with a few of his staff. His lights went out, he lost his way, and the party wandered about aimlessly for some hours; but at dawn found a guide who led them on foot along narrow lanes, until they came to the right road. Caesar overtook his advanced guard at the river Rubicon, which formed the frontier between Gaul and Italy. Well aware how critical a decision confronted him, he turned to his staff, remarking: 'We may still draw back: but, once across that little bridge, we shall have to fight it out.'

As he stood, in two minds, an apparition of superhuman size and beauty was seen sitting on the river bank playing a reed pipe. A party of shepherds gathered around to listen and, when some of Caesar's men, including some of the trumpeters, broke ranks to do the same, the apparition snatched a trumpet from one of them, ran down to the river, blew a thunderous blast, and crossed over. Caesar exclaimed: 'Let us accept this as a sign from the Gods, and follow where they beckon, in vengeance on our double-dealing enemies. The die is cast.'

He led his army to the farther bank, where he welcomed the tribunes of the people who had fled to him from Rome. Then he tearfully addressed the troops and, ripping open his tunic to expose his breast, begged them to stand faithfully by him. The belief that he then promised to promote every man present to the Equestrian Order is based on a misunderstanding. He had accompanied his pleas with the gesture of pointing to his left hand, as he declared that he would gladly reward those who championed his honour with the very seal ring from his thumb; but some soldiers on the fringe of the assembly, who saw him better than they could hear his words, read too much into the gesture. They put it about that Caesar had promised them all the right to wear a knight's gold ring, and the 4,000 gold pieces required to support a knighthood.

Suetonius

30.

AFTER defeating Scipio [at Thapsus, April 46 BC], Caesar celebrated four triumphs in one month with a few days' interval between them; and, after defeating the sons of Pompey, a fifth. These triumphs were the Gallic—the first and most magnificent—the Alexandrian, the Pontic, the African, and lastly the Spanish. Each differed completely from the others in its presentation.

As Caesar rode through the Velabrum on the day of his Gallic triumph, the axle of his triumphal chariot broke, and he nearly took a toss; but afterwards ascended to the Capitol between two lines of elephants, forty in all, which acted as his torch-bearers. In the Pontic triumph one of the decorated wagons, instead of a stage-set representing scenes from the war, like the rest, carried a simple three-word inscription:

I CAME, I SAW, I CONQUERED!

This referred not to the events of the war, like the other inscriptions, but to the speed with which it had been won.

Suetonius

31.

Mark Antony, mounting his ill-fated invasion of Parthia in 36 BC, receives a brisk demonstration of the tactics for which his opponents were celebrated.

THE Parthians, who were crafty as well as confident in their arms, pretended to be panic-stricken and to fly across the plains. Antonius immediately followed them, thinking that he had already won the day, when suddenly a not very large force of the enemy unexpectedly burst forth, like a storm of rain, upon his troops in the evening when they were weary of marching, and overwhelmed two legions with showers of arrows from all sides. No disaster had ever occurred comparable with that which threatened the Romans on the following day, if the gods in pity had not intervened. A survivor from the disaster of Crassus dressed in Parthian costume rode up to the camp, and having uttered a salutation in Latin and thus inspired trust by speaking their language, informed them of the danger that was threatening them. The king, he said, would soon be upon them all with his forces; they ought, therefore, to retreat and make for the mountains, though, even so, they would probably have no lack of enemies to face. The result was that a smaller body of the enemy than was anticipated came up with them. However, it did come up with them, and the rest of their forces would have been destroyed, had not some of the soldiers, as though they had been drilled to it, by chance kneeled down, when the missiles fell like hail upon them, and raising their shields above their heads presented the appearance of dead men; whereupon the Parthians refrained from further use of their bows. Then, when the Romans rose up again, it seemed so like a miracle that one of the barbarians cried out 'Depart, Romans, and farewell; rumour deservedly calls you victorious over the nations, since you have escaped the weapons of the Parthians.'

Florus

32.

Gaius Caesar—the Emperor Caligula, thus nicknamed 'Bootikins' from his days in camp as a child—campaigning in Germany, AD 39.

AFTER reaching his headquarters, Gaius showed how keen and severe a commander-in-chief he intended to be by ignominiously dismissing any general who was late in bringing along from various places the auxiliaries he required. Then, when he reviewed the legions, he discharged many veteran leading-centurions on grounds of age and incapacity, though some had only a few more days of their service to run; and, calling the remainder a pack of greedy fellows, scaled down their retirement bonus to sixty gold pieces each.

All that he accomplished in this expedition was to receive the surrender of Adminius, son of the British King Cunobelinus, who had been banished by his father and come over to the Romans with a few followers. Gaius, nevertheless, wrote an extravagant dispatch to Rome as if the whole island had surrendered to him, and ordered the couriers not to dismount from their post-chaise on reaching the outskirts of the city but make straight for the Forum and the Senate House, and take his letter to the Temple of Mars the Avenger for personal delivery to the Consuls, in the presence of the entire Senate.

Since the chance of military action appeared very remote, he presently sent a few of his German bodyguard across the Rhine, with orders to hide themselves. After lunch scouts hurried in to tell him excitedly that the enemy were upon him. He at once galloped out, at the head of his friends and part of the Guards cavalry, to halt in the nearest thicket, where they chopped branches from the trees and dressed them like trophies; then, riding back by torchlight, he taunted as timorous cowards all who had failed to follow him, and awarded his fellow-heroes a novel fashion in crowns—he called it 'The Ranger's Crown'—ornamented with sun, moon, and stars. On another day he took some hostages from an elementary school and secretly ordered them on ahead of him. Later, he left his dinner in a hurry and took his cavalry in pursuit of them, as though they had been fugitives. He was no less melodramatic about this foray: when he returned to the hall after catching the hostages and bringing them back in irons, and his officers reported that the army was marshalled, he made them recline at table, still in their corselets, and quoted Virgil's famous advice: 'Be steadfast, comrades, and preserve yourselves for happier occasions!' He also severely reprimanded the absent Senate and People for enjoying banquets and festivities, and for hanging about the theatres or their luxurious country-houses while the Emperor was exposed to all the hazards of war.

In the end, he drew up his army in battle array facing the Channel and moved the arrow-casting machines and other artillery into position as though he intended to bring the campaign to a close. No one had the least notion what was in his mind when, suddenly, he gave the order: 'Gather sea-shells!' He referred to the shells as 'plunder from the ocean, due to the Capitol and the Palace', and made the troops fill their helmets and tunic-laps with them; commemorating this victory by the erection of a tall lighthouse, not unlike the one at Pharos, in which fires were to be kept going all night as a guide to ships. Then he promised every soldier a bounty of four gold pieces, and told them: 'Go happy, go rich!' as though he had been excessively generous.

He now concentrated his attention on his forthcoming triumph. To supplement the few prisoners and the deserters who had come over from the barbarians, he picked the tallest Gauls of the province— 'those worthy of a triumph'—and some of their chiefs as well. These had not only to grow their hair and dye it red, but also to learn German and adopt German names. The triremes used in the Channel were carted to Rome overland most of the way; and he sent a letter ahead instructing his agents to prepare a triumph more lavish than any hitherto known, but at the least possible expense; and added that everyone's property was at their disposal.

Before leaving Gaul he planned, in an excess of unspeakable cruelty, to massacre the legionaries who long ago, at the news of Augustus's death, had mutinously besieged the headquarters of his father Germanicus, who was their commander; he had been there himself as a little child. His friends barely restrained him from carrying this plan out, and he could not be dissuaded from ordering the execution of every tenth man; for which purpose they had to parade without arms, not even wearing their swords, and surrounded by armed horsemen. But when he noticed that a number of legionaries, scenting trouble, were slipping away to fetch their weapons, he hurriedly fled from the gathering and headed straight for Rome.

Suetonius

33.

On the fall of the town of Jotapata to its Roman besiegers (AD 67), the Jewish garrison commander Josephus sought refuge in a nearby cave. Here the Romans sent word of their willingness to offer him mercy, which he was eager to accept. But to his dismay, his forty companions preferred the prospect of collective suicide.

JOSEPHUS argued at great length in his desire to avert mass suicide. But desperation made his hearers deaf; they had long ago devoted themselves to death, and now they were furious with him. Running at him from all directions sword in hand, they reviled him for cowardice, everyone appearing about to strike him. But he called one by name, glared like a general at another, shook hands with a third, pleaded with a fourth till he was ashamed, and distracted by conflicting emotions in his critical situation, he kept all their swords away from his throat, turning like an animal at bay to face each assailant in turn.

In this predicament his resourcefulness did not fail him. Putting his trust in divine protection he staked his life on one last throw. 'You have chosen to die,' he exclaimed; 'well then, let's draw lots and kill each other in turn. Whoever draws the first lot shall be dispatched by number two, and so on down the whole line as luck decides. In this way no one will die by his own hand—it would be unfair when the rest were gone if one man changed his mind and saved his life.' The audience swallowed this bait, and getting his way Josephus drew lots with the rest. Without hesitation each man in turn offered his throat for the next man to cut, in the belief that a moment later his commander would die too. Life was sweet, but not so sweet as death if Josephus died with them! But Josephus—shall we put it down to divine providence or just to luck?—was left with one other man. He did not relish the thought either of being condemned by the lot or, if he was left till last, of staining his hand with the blood of a fellow Jew. So he used persuasion, they made a pact, and both remained alive.

Josephus

34.

[THE Emperor Vespasian (AD 69–79)] missed no opportunity of tightening discipline: when a young man, reeking of perfume, came to thank him for a commission he had asked for and obtained, Vespasian turned his head away in disgust and cancelled the order, saying crushingly: 'I should not have minded so much if it had been garlic.'

Suetonius

35.

Having attempted to check the licence of the Praetorian Guard, the Emperor Pertinax was murdered by them on 28 March AD 193.

THE Praetorians had violated the sanctity of the throne, by the atrocious murder of Pertinax; they dishonoured the majesty of it, by their subsequent conduct. The camp was without a leader, for even the Praefect Laetus, who had excited the tempest, prudently declined the public indignation. Amidst the wild disorder Sulpicianus, the emperor's father-in-law, and governor of the city, who had been sent to the camp on the first alarm of mutiny, was endeavouring to calm the fury of the multitude, when he was silenced by the clamorous return of the murderers, bearing on a lance the head of Pertinax. Though history has accustomed us to observe every principle and every passion yielding to the imperious dictates of ambition, it is scarcely credible that, in these moments of horror, Sulpicianus should have aspired to ascend a throne polluted with the recent blood of so near a relation, and so excellent a prince. He had already begun to use the only effectual argument, and to treat for the Imperial dignity; but the more prudent of the Praetorians, apprehensive that, in this private contract, they should not obtain a just price for so valuable a commodity, ran out upon the ramparts; and, with a loud voice, proclaimed that the Roman world was to be disposed of to the best bidder by public auction.

This infamous offer, the most insolent excess of military licence, diffused an universal grief, shame, and indignation throughout the city. It reached at length the ears of Didius Julianus, a wealthy senator, who, regardless of the public calamities, was indulging himself in the luxury of the table. His wife and his daughter, his freedmen and his parasites, easily convinced him that he deserved the throne, and earnestly conjured him to embrace so fortunate an opportunity. The vain old man (AD 193, 28 March) hastened to the Praetorian camp where Sulpicianus was still in treaty with the guards; and began to bid against him from the foot of the rampart. The unworthy negotiation was transacted by faithful emissaries, who passed alternately from one candidate to the other, and acquainted each of them with the offers of his rival. Sulpicianus had already promised a donative of five thousand drachms (above one hundred and sixty pounds) to each soldier, when Julian, eager for the prize, rose at once to the sum of six thousand two hundred and fifty drachms, or upwards of two hundred pounds sterling. The gates of the camp were instantly thrown open to the purchaser; he was declared emperor, and received an oath of allegiance from the soldiers, who retained humanity enough to stipulate that he should pardon and forget the competition of Sulpicianus.

It was now incumbent on the Praetorians to fulfil the conditions of the sale. They placed their new sovereign, whom they served and despised, in the centre of their ranks, surrounded him on every side with their shields, and conducted him in close order of battle through the deserted streets of the city. The senate was commanded to assemble; and those who had been the distinguished friends of Pertinax, or the personal enemies of Julian, found it necessary to affect a more than common share of satisfaction at this happy revolution. After Julian had filled the senate-house with armed soldiers, he expatiated on the freedom of his election, his own eminent virtues, and his full assurance of the affections of the senate. The obsequious assembly congratulated their own and the public felicity; engaged their allegiance, and conferred on him all the several branches of the Imperial power. From the senate Julian was conducted, by the same military procession, to take possession of the palace. The first objects that struck his eyes were the abandoned trunk of Pertinax and the frugal entertainment prepared for his supper. The one he viewed with indifference; the other with contempt. A magnificent feast was prepared by his order, and he amused himself till a very late hour with dice, and the performances of Pylades, a celebrated dancer. Yet it was observed, that after the crowd of flatterers dispersed, and left him to darkness, solitude, and terrible reflection, he passed a sleepless night; revolving most probably in his mind his own rash folly, the fate of his virtuous predecessor, and the doubtful and dangerous tenure of an empire, which had not been acquired by merit, but purchased by money.

Edward Gibbon

36.

The Chinese general Wu Ch'i, on the eve of action against the Ch'in State.

BEFORE the battle had begun, one of his soldiers, a man of matchless daring, sallied forth by himself, captured two heads from the enemy, and returned to camp. Wu Ch'i had the man instantly executed, whereupon an officer ventured to remonstrate, saying: 'This man was a good soldier, and ought not have been beheaded.' Wu Ch'i replied: 'I fully believe he was a good soldier, but I had him beheaded because he acted without orders.'

Tu Mu

37.

An incident in the wars of China, AD 241, when Sun Pin and T'ien Chi led the armies of the Ch'i State against those of Wei, whose armies were commanded by P'ang Chuan.

SUN PIN said: 'The Ch'i State has a reputation for cowardice, and therefore our adversary despises us. Let us turn this circumstance to account.' Accordingly, when the army had crossed the border into Wei territory, he gave orders to show 100,000 fires on the first night, 50,000 on the next, and the night after only 20,000. P'ang Chuan pursued them hotly, saying to himself 'I knew these men of Ch'i were cowards; their numbers have already fallen away by more than half.' In his retreat, Sun Pin came to a narrow defile, which he calculated that his pursuers would reach after dark. Here he had a tree stripped of its bark, and inscribed upon it the words: 'Under this tree shall P'ang Chuan die.' Then, as night began to fall, he placed a strong body of archers in ambush near by with orders to shoot directly they saw a light. Later on, P'ang Chuan arrived at the spot, and noticing the tree, struck a light in order to read what was written on it. His body was immediately riddled by a volley of arrows, and his whole army thrown into confusion.

Tu Mu

38.

SUN TZU whose personal name was Wu was a native of the Ch'i State. His *Art Of War* brought him to the notice of Ho Lu, King of Wu. Ho Lu said to him, 'I have carefully perused your thirteen chapters. May I submit your theory of managing soldiers to a slight test?'

Sun Tzu replied, 'You may.'

The King asked, 'May the test be applied to women?'

The answer was again in the affirmative, so arrangements were made to bring 180 ladies out of the palace. Sun Tzu divided them into two companies and placed one of the King's favourite concubines at the head of each. He then made them all take spears in their hands and addressed them thus: 'I presume you know the difference between front and back, right hand and left hand?'

The girls replied, 'Yes.'

Sun Tzu went on. 'When I say eyes front, you must look straight ahead. When I say "left turn", you must face towards your left hand. When I say "right turn", you must face towards your right hand. When I say "about turn", you must face right around towards the back.'

Again the girls assented. The words of command having been thus explained, he set up the halberds and battle axes in order to begin the drill. Then to the sound of drums he gave the order 'right turn', but the girls only burst out laughing.

Sun Tzu said patiently, 'If words of commands are not clear and distinct, if orders are not thoroughly understood, then the general is to blame.' He started drilling them again and this time gave the order 'left turn', whereupon the girls once more burst into fits of laughter.

Then he said, 'If words of command are not clear and distinct, if orders are not thoroughly understood, the general is to blame. But, if his orders are clear and the soldiers nevertheless disobey, then it is the fault of their officers.' So saying, he ordered the leaders of the two companies to be beheaded.

Now the King of Wu was watching from the top of a raised pavilion, and when he saw his favourite concubines about to be executed, he was greatly alarmed and hurriedly sent down the following message: 'We are now quite satisfied as to our general's ability to handle troops. If we are bereft of our two concubines, our meat and drink will lose their savour. It is our wish that they shall not be beheaded.'

Sun Tzu replied even more patiently, 'Having once received His Majesty's commission to be general of his forces, there are certain commands of His Majesty which, acting in that capacity, I am unable to accept.'

Accordingly and immediately, he had the two leaders beheaded and straight away installed the pair next in order as leaders in their place. When this had been done the drum was sounded for the drill once more. The girls went through all the evolutions, turning to the right or to the left, marching ahead or wheeling about, kneeling or standing, with perfect accuracy and precision, not venturing to utter a sound.

Then Sun Tzu sent a messenger to the King saying: 'Your soldiers,

Sire, are now properly drilled and disciplined and ready for Your Majesty's inspection. They can be put to any use that their sovereign may desire. Bid them go through fire and water and they will not now disobey.'

But the King replied: 'Let our general cease drilling and return to camp. As for us, we have no desire to come down and inspect the troops.'

Thereupon Sun Tzu said calmly: 'The King is only fond of words and cannot translate them into deeds.'

After that the King of Wu saw that Sun Tzu was one who knew how to handle an army, and appointed him general. In the West Sun Tzu defeated the Ch'u State and forced his way into Ying, the capital; and to the North he put fear into the States of Ch'i and Ch'in, and spread his fame abroad amongst the feudal princes. And Sun Tzu shared in the might of the Kingdom.

Su-Ma Ch'ien

39.

Gibbon at his most superbly sardonic describes the sack of Rome in AD 410.

A ROMAN lady, of singular beauty and orthodox faith, had excited the impatient desires of a young Goth, who, according to the sagacious remark of Sozomen, was attached to the Arian heresy. Exasperated by her obstinate resistance, he drew his sword, and, with the anger of a lover, slightly wounded her neck. The bleeding heroine still continued to brave his resentment and to repel his love, till the ravisher desisted from his unavailing efforts, respectfully conducted her to the sanctuary of the Vatican, and gave six pieces of gold to the guards of the church on condition that they should restore her inviolate to the arms of her husband. Such instances of courage and generosity were not extremely common. The brutal soldiers satisfied their sensual appetites without consulting either the inclination or the duties of their female captives; and a nice question of casuistry was seriously agitated, Whether those tender victims, who had inflexibly refused their consent to the violation which they sustained, had lost, by their misfortune, the glorious crown of virginity. There were other losses indeed of a more substantial kind and more general concern. It cannot be presumed that all the barbarians were at all times capable of perpetrating such amorous outrages; and the want of youth, or beauty, or chastity, protected the greatest part of the Roman women from the danger of a rape. But avarice is an insatiate and universal passion; since the enjoyment of almost every object that can afford pleasure to the different tastes and tempers of mankind may be procured by the possession of wealth. In the pillage of Rome a just preference was given to gold and jewels, which contain the greatest value in the smallest compass and weight; but, after these portable riches had been removed by the more diligent robbers, the palaces of Rome were rudely stripped of their splendid and costly furniture. The sideboards of massy plate, and the variegated wardrobes of silk and purple, were irregularly piled in the waggons that always followed the march of a Gothic army. The most exquisite works of art were roughly handled or wantonly destroyed: many a statue was melted for the sake of the precious materials; and many a vase, in the division of the spoil, was shivered into fragments by the stroke of a battle-axe. The acquisition of riches served only to stimulate the avarice of the rapacious barbarians, who proceeded by threats, by blows, and by tortures, to force from their prisoners the confession of hidden treasure. Visible splendour and expense were alleged as the proof of a plentiful fortune; the appearance of poverty was imputed to a parsimonious disposition; and the obstinacy of some misers, who endured the most cruel torments before they would discover the secret object of their affection, was fatal to many unhappy wretches, who expired under the lash for refusing to reveal their imaginary treasures. The edifices of Rome, though the damage has been much exaggerated, received some injury from the violence of the Goths. At their entrance through the Salarian gate they fired the adjacent houses to guide their march and to distract the attention of the citizens; the flames, which encountered no obstacle in the disorder of the night, consumed many private and public buildings, and the ruins of the palace of Sallust remained in the age of Justinian a stately monument of the Gothic conflagration. Yet a contemporary historian has observed that fire could scarcely consume the enormous beams of solid brass, and that the strength of man was insufficient to subvert the foundations of ancient structures. Some truth may possibly be concealed in his devout assertion, that the wrath of Heaven supplied the imperfections of hostile rage, and that the proud Forum of Rome, decorated with the statues of so many gods and heroes, was levelled in the dust by the stroke of lightning.

Edward Gibbon

40.

Attila the Hun on the eve of the Battle of Chalons, AD 451.

HIS own warriors believed him to be the inspired favourite of their deities, and followed him with fanatic zeal: his enemies looked on him as the preappointed minister of Heaven's wrath against themselves; and, though they believed not in his creed, their own made them tremble before him.

In one of his early campaigns, he appeared before his troops with an ancient iron sword in his grasp, which he told them was the god of war whom their ancestors had worshipped. It is certain that the nomadic tribes of Northern Asia, whom Herodotus described under the name of Scythians, from the earliest times worshipped as their god a bare sword. That sword-god was supposed, in Attila's time, to have disappeared from earth; but the Hunnish king now claimed to have received it by special revelation. It was said that a herdsman, who was tracking in the desert a wounded heifer by the drops of blood, found the mysterious sword standing fixed in the ground, as if it had been darted down from Heaven. The herdsman bore it to Attila, who thenceforth was believed by the Huns to wield the Spirit of Death in battle; and the seers prophesied that that sword was to destroy the world. A Roman, who was on an embassy to the Hunnish camp, recorded in his memoirs Attila's acquisition of this supernatural weapon, and the immense influence over the minds of the barbaric tribes which its possession gave him. In the title which he assumed, we shall see the skill with which he availed himself of the legends and creeds of other nations as well as of his own. He designated himself 'Attila, Descendant of the Great Nimrod. Nurtured in Engaddi. By the Grace of God, King of the Huns, the Goths, the Danes, and the Medes. The Dread of the World.'

. . . It was during the retreat from Orleans that a Christian hermit is reported to have approached the Hunnish king, and said to him, 'Thou art the Scourge of God for the chastisement of Christians.' Attila instantly assumed this new title of terror, which thenceforth became the appellation by which he was most widely and most fearfully known.

Sir Edward Creasey

41.

A Persian foray against a Roman town in Mesopotamia.

CABADES, in besieging Amida [January AD 503], brought against every part of the defences the engines known as rams; but the townspeople constantly broke off the heads of the rams by means of timbers thrown across them. However, Cabades did not slacken his efforts until he realized that the wall could not be successfully assailed in this way. For, though he battered the wall many times, he was quite unable to break down any portion of the defence, or even to shake it; so secure had been the work of the builders who had constructed it long before. Failing in this, Cabades raised an artificial hill to threaten the city, considerably overtopping the wall; but the besieged, starting from the inside of their defences, made a tunnel extending under the hill, and from there stealthily carried out the earth, until they hollowed out a great part of the inside of the hill. However, the outside kept the form which it had at first assumed, and afforded no opportunity to anyone of discovering what was being done. Accordingly many Persians mounted it, thinking it safe, and stationed themselves on the summit with the purpose of shooting down upon the heads of those inside the fortifications. But with the great mass of men crowding upon it with a rush, the hill suddenly fell in and killed almost all of them. Cabades, then, finding no remedy for the situation, decided to raise the siege, and he issued orders to the army to retreat on the morrow. Then indeed the besieged, as though they had no thought of their danger, began laughingly from the fortifications to jeer at the barbarians. Besides this some courtesans shamelessly drew up their clothing and displayed to Cabades, who was standing close by, those parts of a woman's body which it is not proper that men should see uncovered. This was plainly seen by the Magi, and they thereupon came before the king and tried to prevent the retreat, declaring as their interpretation of what had happened that the citizens of Amida would shortly disclose to Cabades all their secret and hidden things. So the Persian army remained there.

Not many days later one of the Persians saw close by one of the towers the mouth of an old underground passage, which was insecurely concealed with some few small stones. In the night he came there alone, and, making trial of the entrance, got inside the circuit-wall; then at daybreak he reported the whole matter to Cabades. The king himself on the following night came to the spot with a few men, bringing ladders which he had made ready. And he was favoured by a piece of good fortune; for the defence of the very tower which happened to be nearest to the passage had fallen by lot to those of the Christians who are most careful in their observances, whom they call monks. These men, as chance would have it, were keeping some annual religious festival to God on that day. When night came on they all felt great weariness on account of the festival, and, having sated themselves with food and drink beyond their wont, they fell into a sweet and gentle sleep, and were consequently quite unaware of what was going on.[1] So the Persians made their way through the passage inside the fortifications a few at a time, and, mounting the tower, they found the monks still sleeping and slew them to a man. When Cabades learned this, he brought his ladders up to the wall close by this tower. It was already day. And those of the townsmen who were keeping guard on the adjoining tower became aware of the disaster, and ran thither with all speed to give assistance. Then for a long time both sides struggled to crowd back the other, and already the townsmen were gaining the advantage, killing many of those who had mounted the wall, and throwing back the men on the ladders, and they came very near to averting the danger. But Cabades drew his sword and, terrifying the Persians constantly with it, rushed in person to the ladders and would not let them draw back, and death was the punishment for those who dared turn to leave. As a result of this the Persians by their numbers gained the upper hand and overcame their antagonists in the fight. So the city was captured by storm on the eightieth day after the beginning of the siege. There followed a great massacre of the townspeople, until one of the citizens—an old man and a priest—approached Cabades as he was riding into the city, and said that it was not a kingly act to slaughter captives. Then Cabades, still moved with passion, replied: 'But why did you decide to fight against me?' And the old man answered quickly: 'Because God willed to give Amida into thy hand not so much because of our decision as of thy valour.' Cabades was pleased by this speech, and permitted no further slaughter, but he bade the Persians plunder the property and make

---

[1] An unknown hand has scrawled upon the page of my copy: 'Moral: Don't go to church on active service.'

slaves of the survivors, and he directed them to choose out for himself
all the notables among them.

                                                              Procopius

42.

*Geoffrey of Monmouth (1100?–1154) was one of the principal begetters of the legend
of King Arthur and his Round Table. Here he describes the Battle of Saussy, a misty
encounter at some undefined moment in the Dark Ages; two of the boldest Arthurian
knights, Hoel and Gawain, have just seen a party of their followers cut their way
through to the Roman commander, Lucius, only to be surrounded and killed.*

No better knights than Hoel and Gawain have ever been born down
the ages. When they learned of the death of their followers, they
pressed on even more fiercely. They spurred on this way and that, first
in one direction, then in another, in their relentless attack on the
Emperor's bodyguard. Gawain, fearless in his courage, did his utmost
to come up with Lucius himself in the fight. He made every effort to
push forward, for he was the bravest of all the knights. He decimated
the enemy by his onslaught and as he killed them he moved ever forward. Hoel was in no way less brave. He was raging like a thunderbolt
in another sector, encouraging his own men and bringing death to his
enemies. He parried their attacks with the utmost courage, giving and
receiving blows, but not drawing back for a second. It would be difficult to say which of these two was the braver.

As Gawain and Lucius fought bitterly in this way, the Romans suddenly recovered. They attacked the Bretons and so brought help to
their general. They repulsed Hoel, Gawain and their troops, and
began to cut their way into them. It was at this juncture that the
Romans suddenly came face to face with Arthur and his division. He
had heard a moment before of this slaughter which was being inflicted
on his men. He moved up with his own division, drew his wonderful
sword Caliburn and encouraged his fellow-soldiers by shouting loudly
at them. 'What the Devil are you doing, men?' he demanded. 'Are you
letting these effeminate creatures slip away unhurt? Not one must
escape alive! Think of your own right hands, which have played their
part in so many battles and subjected thirty kingdoms to my sover-
eignty! Remember your ancestors, whom the Romans, then at the
height of their power, made tributaries. Remember your liberty, which
these halflings, who haven't anything like your strength, plan to take

away from you! Not one must escape alive! Not one must escape, I say!'

As he shouted these insults, and many others, too, Arthur dashed straight at the enemy. He flung them to the ground and cut them to pieces. Whoever came his way was either killed himself or had his horse killed under him at a single blow. They ran away from him as sheep run from a fierce lion whom raging hunger compels to devour all that chance throws in his way. Their armour offered them no protection capable of preventing Caliburn, when wielded in the right hand of this mighty King, from forcing them to vomit forth their souls with their life-blood. Ill luck brought two Kings, Sertorius of Libya and Politetes of Bithynia, in Arthur's way. He hacked off their heads and bundled them off to hell.

Geoffrey of Monmouth

43.

THE noble Charlemagne [King of the Franks 768–814, Holy Roman Emperor 800–16] was often angry because he was obliged to go out and fight against barbarous peoples when one of his leaders seemed well suited to the task. This I can prove from the action of a man who came from my own neighbourhood. He was a man called Eishere, from the Thurgau, who, as his name implies, formed 'a large part of a terrifying army'. He was so tall that you would have thought that he was descended from the race of Anak, if these last had not lived so far away and so long ago. Whenever he came to the River Thur, swollen and foaming with mountain torrents, and was unable to force his great horse into the stream, which was more like solid ice than flowing water, he would seize the reins and force his horse to swim behind him, saying 'By Saint Gall, you must follow me, whether you want to or not!' This man marched with the Emperor in his troop of soldiers, and mowed down the Bohemians and Wiltzes and Avars as a man mows a meadow. He spitted them on his spear as if they were tiny birds. When he came back victorious, the stay-at-homes asked him how he liked it in the land of the Winides. Contemptuous of some and angry with others, he used to answer: 'What were these tadpoles to me? I used to spit seven, or eight, or sometimes nine of them on my spear, and carry them about all over the place, squealing their incomprehensible lingo.

The King my master and I ought never to have worn ourselves out fighting such worms.'

Notker the Stammerer

44.

Successes and failure of Danegeld.

1002

In this year the king and his councillors determined that tribute should be paid to the fleet and peace made with them on condition that they should cease their evil-doing. Then the king sent Ealdorman Leofsige to the fleet, and he then, by the command of the king and his councillors, arranged a truce with them and that they should receive provisions and tribute. And they then accepted that, and 24,000 pounds were paid to them. Then meanwhile Ealdorman Leofsige killed the king's high-reeve, Æfic, and the king then banished him from the country. And then in the spring the queen, Richard's daughter, came to this land. And in the same summer Archbishop Ealdwulf died.

And in that year the king ordered to be slain all the Danish men who were in England—this was done on St Brice's day—because the king had been informed that they would treacherously deprive him, and then all his councillors, of life, and possess this kingdom afterwards.

1003

In this year Exeter was stormed on account of the French *ceorl* Hugh, whom the queen had appointed as her reeve, and the Danish army then destroyed the borough completely and seized much booty there. And in that same year the army went inland into Wiltshire. Then a great English army was gathered from Wiltshire and from Hampshire, and they were going very resolutely towards the enemy. Then Ealdorman Ælfric was to lead the army, but he was up to his old tricks. As soon as they were so close that each army looked on the other, he feigned him sick, and began retching to vomit, and said that he was taken ill, and thus betrayed the people whom he should have led. As the saying goes: 'When the leader gives way, the whole army will be much hindered.' When Swein saw that they were irresolute, and that they all dispersed, he led his army into Wilton, and they ravaged and burnt the borough, and he betook him then to Salisbury, and from there went back to the sea to where he knew his wave-coursers were.

1004

In this year Swein came with his fleet to Norwich and completely ravaged and burnt the borough. Then Ulfcetel with the councillors in East Anglia determined that it would be better to buy peace from the army before they did too much damage in the country, for they had come unexpectedly and he had not time to collect his army. Then, under cover of the truce which was supposed to be between them, the Danish army stole inland from the ships, and directed their course to Thetford. When Ulfcetel perceived that, he sent orders that the ships were to be hewn to bits, but those whom he intended for this failed him; he then collected his army secretly, as quickly as he could. And the Danish army then came to Thetford within three weeks after their ravaging of Norwich, and remained inside there one night, and ravaged and burnt the borough. Then in the morning, when they wished to go to their ships, Ulfcetel arrived with his troops to offer battle there. And they resolutely joined battle, and many fell slain on both sides.There the flower of the East Anglian people was killed. But if their full strength had been there, the Danes would never have got back to their ships; as they themselves said that they never met worse fighting in England than Ulfcetel dealt to them.

The Anglo-Saxon Chronicle

45·

Rodrigo Díaz de Vivar (b. 1043), El Campeador—'*The Fighter*', *or El* Cid—'*The Lord*', *from the Arabic* Sayyidi, *passed into Christian legend for his struggle against the Moorish infidels in Spain. In reality, at one time or another he fought almost anybody who stood in the way of his considerable ambitions, and was not in the least averse to tactical alliances with the Moors when these were convenient. He was a ruthless outlaw for most of his life. Here, in 1090 by his defeat and capture of the Count of Barcelona, he puts his unfortunate ruler off his food.*

. . . widespread rumours that the Cid Ruy Díaz was harrying the whole countryside reached the ears of the Count of Barcelona, who was highly incensed and considered this action as a personal injury.

The Count was a hasty and foolish man and spoke without due reflection: 'The Cid, Rodrigo of Vivar, has done me great wrongs. In my own palace he gave me great offence by striking my nephew and never giving satisfaction for it. Now he is ravaging the lands under my protection. I never challenged him nor showed enmity towards him in return, but since he seeks me out, I shall demand redress.' Great numbers of Moors and Christians flocked in haste to join his forces, and they went in search of the Cid, the mighty Ruy Díaz of Vivar. They journeyed three days and two nights and came up with the Cid in the pine wood of Tévar, so confident in their strength that the Count was certain of laying hands on him. The Cid, Don Rodrigo, carrying large quantities of booty, descended from the mountains to a valley. There he received the message of Count Ramón. When the Cid heard it he sent word, saying: 'Tell the Count not to take offence. I am carrying off nothing of his, so let him leave me to go in peace.' The Count replied: 'Not so! He shall pay for past and present injuries here and now. The exile from Castile will learn what sort of a man he has wronged.' The messenger returned with all speed, and the Cid realized that there was nothing for it but to fight.

'Knights' (he said), 'put aside the booty, and make ready quickly to take up arms. Count Ramón is about to engage us in a great battle. He has brought with him a vast host of Moors and Christians and is determined to fight. As they are advancing towards us, let us engage them here. Tighten your saddle-girths and put on your armour. The enemy are coming downhill, all wearing hose (without boots). They have racing saddles and loose girths, but we shall ride with Galician saddles and wear boots over our hose. Though we number only one hundred knights we have got to defeat this large army. Before they reach the plain we shall attack with our lances. For each man you strike, three saddles will go empty. Ramón Berenguer will see the kind of man he has come to find today in the pine woods of Tévar to deprive me of my booty.'

All were ready by the time the Cid had finished speaking, with their armour on and mounted on their horses. They watched the forces of the Franks ride down the hill, and when these reached the bottom, close now to the plain, the Cid, fortunate in battle, ordered the attack. His men were delighted to obey and they used their pennoned lances to good effect, striking some and overturning others. The Cid won the battle and took Count Ramón prisoner.

There he won for himself Colada, a sword worth more than a thousand silver marks. This was a victorious battle which brought honour to the Cid. He brought the Count as a prisoner to his tent and commanded his faithful vassals to stand guard over him. He then left his tent, in great good humour at the amount of the booty, while his men crowded in from all sides. A great feast was prepared for Don Rodrigo, but Count Ramón showed no relish for it. They brought the dishes and placed them in front of him, but he refused to eat and scorned all they offered. 'I shall not eat a mouthful,' he said, 'for all the wealth of Spain. I had rather die outright since such badly shod fellows have defeated me in battle.'

To that the Cid replied in these words: 'Eat this bread, Count, and drink this wine. If you do as I say you will go free, but if not, you will never see Christendom again for the rest of your life.'

Count Ramón said: 'You eat, Don Rodrigo, and take your ease, for I would rather starve to death than eat anything.' For three days they tried in vain to persuade him. While they were dividing up the great booty they could not get him to eat even a morsel of bread.

The Poem of the Cid

46.

OUTSIDE the walls of Acre during the Third Crusade, a Welsh and a Turkish archer agreed to a trial of skills. Each promised to stand still while his adversary took a shot at him. The Turk fired and missed, then suggested they allow themselves two shots each. The Welsh archer—says the Norman poet Ambroise—agreed, but while the Turk was getting his second arrow ready, the Welshman took careful aim and shot him through the heart:

> 'You kept the pact not,' so he spoke,
> 'So, by Saint Denis, mine I broke.'

Ronald Finucane

47.

In the last hours of the defence of Acre before its fall to the Saracens in May 1291, William de Beaujeu, Grand Master of the Temple, was hit.

. . . Even as he got his death wound, he was accused of cowardice. An arrow had penetrated to a hand's depth into his arm pit, unnoticed by those around him. He rode on as best he could in the press of battle, erratically as his powers failed. This was at last remarked, and a troup of Crusaders intercepted him, exhorting him not to flee and leave them. He replied, 'Seigneurs, je ne peu plus, car je suys mort: vées le coup', and sank into the arms of his attendants, dead.

Edith Simon

48.

At the beginning of the thirteenth century the Tartar leader Temuchin, better known to the world as Genghis Khan, created by conquest an empire in Asia such as the world had never seen.

IT was a progression that made the savagery and destruction brought upon the world by Attila the Hun look like reasoned acts of statesmanship. Temuchin drowned in blood all the nations that dared to resist him and obliterated towns, villages and *ordus* in his path, leaving no one but the steppe wolves and carrion crows to bury the butchered millions.

'Unchecked by human valour, they were able to overcome the terrors of vast deserts, the barriers of mountains and seas, the severities of climate, and the ravages of famine and pestilence. No dangers could appall them, no stronghold could resist them, no prayer for mercy could move them,' is the assessment of the *Cambridge Medieval History* of Genghis Khan and his horsemen.

Within a quarter of a century he subdued all the steppe nations and the *kuriltai*, the council of the Mongol chiefs, proclaimed him Genghis Khan, the Khan of Khans in 1206. It was a fitting name, although the names Mighty Killer of Man and the Perfect Warrior used by the subjects and neighbours of his empire were nearer the truth.

'The merit of an action', he cautioned his sons, 'lies in finishing it to the end.' The empire-building could not be considered completed until three powerful states bordering his realm were destroyed.

But these were not simple steppe kingdoms with armies unable to match the organization, discipline and massed attacks of Mongol cavalry. The Chin empire, with its well-fortified capital city of Peking, then called Yenking, had all the advantages of an ancient civilization over the Mongol nomads, and furthermore the Chinese army was well versed in the use of sophisticated war machines and gun powder.

The Tangut kingdom of Hsia Hsi, on the upper reaches of the Hoang Ho (Yellow River) was also a state of town-dwellers, while Kara Khitai was a powerful Muslim kingdom.

Genghis chose Hsia Hsi, the weakest of the three, as his first target.

In 1207 he invaded part of the Tangut kingdom, but fortifications of the city of Volohai appeared too much for his steppe horsemen. But what he could not get with brute force he won with fox-like cunning. He offered to withdraw if he was given by way of tribute one thousand cats and one thousand swallows. The startled Tangut complied. But instead of withdrawing Genghis set them alight and released them in one great rush of living fire. The hapless cats and birds set the city on fire in hundreds of places and, while the garrison fought the flames, the Mongols breached the walls.

By the end of 1211 the Tangut empire was subdued and the golden bit of slavery was forced into its emperor's mouth. The following year Genghis invaded the Chin empire and, after battles of gigantic scale and atrocities of terrifying proportions, the Mongol horsemen overran North China to the Yellow Sea. After a prolonged siege, Genghis took Peking in 1215, but by then his reputation was such that, according to a Persian chronicler, some 60,000 Chinese virgins hurled themselves from the city walls to their deaths rather than fall alive into the hands of his soldiery.

Gabriel Ronay

49.

LOUIS VI of France [1108–37] in one of his engagements was in considerable danger; a soldier of the enemy took hold of the bridle of his horse, crying out, 'the king is taken.' 'No, sir,' replied Louis, raising his battle axe, with which he hewed down the soldier, 'no, sir, a king is never taken, not even at chess.'

The Percy Anecdotes

50.

IN order to deter Godfrey of Bouillon from his siege of Arsuf, the Moslems tied up one of his friends, Gerard, and slung him over the wall. Gerard shouted down to Godfrey begging him to spare him, but Godfrey claimed that he would attack even if his own brother were

hanging there. After being punctured by twelve arrows, Gerard was
reeled in by the Moslems and, amazingly enough, was able to recover,
thanks to Moslem medical care. The next year, Godfrey rewarded him
with the fief of Hebron as compensation for those terrifying moments
spent as a wriggling target.

Ronald Finucane

51.

*Some six miles from the town of Tiberias lie the Horns of Hattin, the high ground on
which the Saracens entrapped the Crusader army under King Guy on 4 July 1187,
inflicting a crushing defeat upon the Christians from which their cause in the Holy
Land never recovered.*

THE Moslem attack began soon after daybreak. The Christian infantry had only one thought, water. In a surging mass they tried to break
through down the slope towards the lake gleaming far below. They
were driven up a hillock, hemmed in by the flames and by the enemy.
Many of them were slaughtered at once, many others were taken prisoner; and the sight of them as they lay wounded and swollen-mouthed
was so painful that five of Raymond's knights went to the Moslem
leaders to beg that they might be slain, to end their misery. The horsemen on the hills fought with superb courage. Charge after charge of
the Moslem cavalry was driven back with losses, but their own
numbers were dwindling. Enfeebled by thirst, their strength began to
fail them. Before it was too late, at the King's request, Raymond led
his knights . . . to burst through the Moslem lines (which) closed up
again behind them. They could not make their way back again to their
comrades, so, miserably, they rode . . . away to Tripoli. A little later
Balian of Ibelin and [the lord] of Sidon broke their way out. They were
the last to escape.

There was no hope left for the Christians; but they still fought on,
retiring up the hill to the Horns. The King's red tent was moved to the
summit, and his knights gathered round him. Saladin's young son
al-Afdal was at his father's side witnessing his first battle. 'When the
Frankish King had withdrawn to the hilltop [he relates], his knights
made a gallant charge and drove the Moslems back upon my father. I
watched his dismay. He changed colour and pulled at his beard, then

rushed forward crying: "Let us give the devil the lie!" When I saw the Franks flying I cried out with glee: "We have routed them!" But they charged again and drove our men back again to where my father stood. Again he urged our men forward and again they drove the enemy up the hill. Again I cried out: "We have routed them!" But my father turned to me and said: "Be quiet. We have not beaten them so long as that tent stands there.' At that moment the tent was overturned. Then my father dismounted and bowed to the ground, giving thanks to God, with tears of joy.'

. . . The Holy Cross . . . was in the hands of the Infidel. Few of the horses had survived. When the victors reached the hilltop, the knights themselves, the King among them, were lying on the ground . . . with hardly the strength to hand their swords over and surrender. Their leaders were taken off to the tent that was erected on the battlefield for the Sultan.

The only magnate to have been killed outright in the battle was the Bishop of Acre, who contrary to usage had concealed a mail shirt under his vestments. God had justly made an example of him for his lack of faith.

. . . Saladin received King Guy and his brother the Constable Amalric, Reynald de Châtillon and his stepson Humphrey of Toron, the Grand Master of the Temple Gerard de Ridefort, the aged Marquis of Montferrat, the lords of Jebail and Botrun, and many of the lesser barons of the realm. [Saladin] seated the King next to him and, seeing his thirst, handed him a goblet of rose water, iced with the snows of Hermon. Guy drank from it and handed it on to Reynald who was at his side. By the laws of Arab hospitality to give food and drink to a captive meant that his life was safe; so Saladin said quickly to the interpreter, 'Tell the King that he gave that man to drink, not I.'

Saladin turned to Reynald and berated him for his crimes. Reynald answered back and Saladin there and then struck off his head; after which he gave orders that none of the other lay knights was to be harmed or offered any indignity. But with the exception of the Grand Master of the Temple, all captives belonging to the Military Orders were sent to execution. The gallant Countess of Tripoli was allowed to leave Tiberias with honour and to rejoin her husband.

The prisoners were sent to Damascus, where the barons were lodged in comfort and the poorer folk sold in the slave market. So many were there that the price of a single prisoner fell to three dinars, and you could buy a whole healthy family, a man, his wife, his three sons and two daughters, for eighty dinars the lot. One Moslem even thought it a good bargain to exchange a prisoner for a pair of sandals.

Steven Runciman

52.

RICHARD COEUR DE LION, in besieging the castle of Chalus [1199], was shot in the shoulder with an arrow; and an awkward surgeon, in endeavouring to extract the weapon, mangled the wound in such a manner that a gangrene ensued. The castle being taken, and the king perceiving he should not live; ordered Bertram de Gourdon, who had shot the arrow, to be brought into his presence. 'What harm did I ever do thee,' asked the king, 'that thou shouldst kill me?' Bertram replied with great magnanimity and courage, 'You killed with your own hand my father and two of my brothers; and you likewise designed to have killed me. You may satiate your revenge. I should cheerfully suffer all the torments that can be inflicted, were I sure of having delivered the world of a tyrant who filled it with blood and carnage.' This bold and spirited answer struck Richard with remorse. He ordered the prisoner to be presented with one hundred marks, and set at liberty; but one of the courtiers, like a true ruffian, ordered him to be flayed alive, according to the barbarous practices of the times.

Naval and Military Anecdotes

53.

A tale of the Mongols.

. . . in the year of the Cock (AD 1201) the Khadagin and ten other clans met at the Alkhui Spring and consulted together, intending to make Jamukha their lord. When they had sacrificed a horse and sworn oaths they went down along the Ergune river and when they reached the river-island at the Ken river they set up Jamukha as their Khan. They meant to attack Chingis [i.e. Genghis] and the Ong Khan. But news of their intention was brought to Chingis at Gurelgu by Khoridai of the Khorilas. Chingis informed the Ong Khan and the Ong Khan collected his forces and joined Chingis. When the Ong Khan and Chingis had met they went down the Kerulen river to face Jamukha.

Chingis sent out Altan and two others as scouts; the Ong Khan sent his son Sengum and two others as scouts. From among these scouts some were sent on to Enegen-guiletu, Chekcher and Chikhurkhu to prospect. When Altan and the others got to Utkiya, the man who had been scouting at Chikhurkhu came and announced that the enemy was about to arrive. Altan and the others then went towards them to get news. On the way they met Jamukha's scout A'uchu the Valiant and three others and spoke to them. But they saw that night was coming on and went back to spend the night in the camp of their main forces.

Next day the armies of Chingis and Jamukha got into contact at Koyiten and drew up in battle-order, facing one another. While they were marshalling their forces two members of Jamukha's army, called Buyirukh-khan and Khudukha, who possessed the art of raising storms, wanted to attack Chingis's army down the storm. But unfortunately for them the storm ricochetted, utter darkness filled Heaven and Earth, and Jamukha's army was unable to advance. They all fell into gulleys, and Jamukha and the others said to one another, 'This can only mean that Heaven is not supporting us!' His army broke up in complete confusion.

After Jamukha's army broke up, the Naiman and the other ten peoples who had supported him all returned to their own settlements. Jamukha seized the people who had raised him to be their Khan and took them back with him down the Ergune river. Upon this, the Ong Khan set out in pursuit of Jamukha, while Chingis pursued the Taichi'ut leader A'uchu. When A'uchu got back to his own settlement he moved his people across the Onan river, marshalled his armies and waited for Chingis to come and do battle with him. When Chingis arrived they fought several bouts, and then when night came the two armies bivouacked facing one another where they had fought.

When Chingis was fighting with the Taichi'ut he got a wound in the neck which bled to a frightening extent. It fell to his retainer Jelme to suck out the obstructed blood. At midnight Chingis came to himself and said, 'My blood has dried up of itself. I am very thirsty.' Jelme took off all his clothes, went straight into the enemy's camp and looked in the lockers of their carts for fresh mare's milk, but could find none. There was only a pail of sour milk, so he brought this back. No one had seen him come or go. Then he went to get water to mix with the sour milk and gave the mixture to Chingis to drink. The more he drank the thirstier he became. He had drunk three times before he stopped. Then he said, 'Now I can see clearly with my eyes and understand with my mind.' He sat up and while he was sitting there, dawn came. He then saw that round where he was sitting the ground was flowing with a regular slush of blood. He said, 'Why did you deal with it like that? Surely it would have been better to dispose of it a bit further off?' Jelme said, 'I was far too busy to go to a distance. Moreover I was frightened of leaving you. I swallowed as much of the blood as I could and only spat out the rest. Still, I did manage to swallow quite a lot!' Chingis again said, 'With me wounded like this, how came you to go naked into the enemy's camp? If they had caught you, I suppose you would have had to tell them I was wounded.' Jelme said, 'If I had been captured I would have said to them, "I was intending to desert your side, but having found out I meant to desert they took away my clothes and were about to kill me when I managed to break away." They would certainly have believed that all this was true and would have given me clothes and taken me into their service. And just as certainly—I would have jumped on to one of their horses and escaped.' Chingis said, 'Once before, when the Merkits were harrying me at Mount Burkhan, you saved my life; and now you sucked out the blood from my neck. When I was thirsty, you risked your life to get me sour milk to drink and so brought me back to my senses. These three good deeds that you have done to me will remain for ever in my heart.'

Arthur Waley

54.

26 August 1346, the field of Crécy.

THE English, who were drawn up in three divisions, and seated on the ground, on seeing their enemies advance, rose undauntedly up, and fell into their ranks. That of the prince was the first to do so, whose archers were formed in the manner of a portcullis, or harrow, and the men at arms in the rear. The earls of Northampton and Arundel, who commanded the second division, had posted themselves in good order on his wing, to assist and succour the prince, if necessary.

You must know, that these kings, earls, barons and lords of France, did not advance in any regular order, but one after the other, or any way most pleasing to themselves. As soon as the king of France came in sight of the English, his blood began to boil, and he cried out to his marshals, 'Order the Genoese forward, and begin the battle, in the name of God and St Denis.' There were about fifteen thousand

Genoese cross-bowmen; but they were quite fatigued, having marched on foot that day six leagues, completely armed, and with their cross-bows. They told the constable, they were not in a fit condition to do any great things that day in battle. The earl of Alençon, hearing this, said, 'This is what one gets by employing such scoundrels, who fall off when there is any need for them.' During this time a heavy rain fell, accompanied by thunder and a very terrible eclipse of the sun; and before this rain a great flight of crows hovered in the air over all those battalions, making a loud noise. Shortly afterwards it cleared up, and the sun shone very bright; but the Frenchmen had it in their faces, and the English in their backs. When the Genoese were somewhat in order, and approached the English, they set up a loud shout, in order to frighten them; but they remained quite still, and did not seem to attend to it. They then set up a second shout, and advanced a little forward; but the English never moved. They hooted a third time, advancing with their cross-bows presented, and began to shoot. The English archers then advanced one step forward, and shot their arrows with such force and quickness, that it seemed as if it snowed. When the Genoese felt these arrows, which pierced their arms, heads, and through their armour, some of them cut the strings of their cross-bows, others flung them on the ground, and all turned about and retreated quite discomfited. The French had a large body of men at arms on horseback, richly dressed, to support the Genoese. The king of France, seeing them thus fall back, cried out, 'Kill me those scoun-drels; for they stop up our road, without any reason.' You would then have seen the above-mentioned men at arms lay about them, killing all they could of these runaways.

The English continued shooting as vigorously and quickly as before; some of their arrows fell among the horsemen, who were sumptuously equipped, and, killing and wounding many, made them caper and fall among the Genoese, so that they were in such confusion they could never rally again. In the English army there were some Cornish and Welshmen on foot, who had armed themselves with large knives: these, advancing through the ranks of the men at arms and archers, who made way for them, came upon the French when they were in this danger, and, falling upon earls, barons, knights, and squires, slew many, at which the king of England was afterwards much exasperated. The valiant king of Bohemia was slain there. He was called Charles of Luxembourg; for he was the son of the gallant king and emperor, Henry of Luxembourg: having heard the order of the battle, he enquired where his son, the lord Charles, was: his attendants answered, that they did not know, but believed he was fighting. The king said to them; 'Gentlemen, you are all my people, my friends and brethren at arms this day: therefore, as I am blind, I request of you to lead me so far into the engagement that I may strike one stroke with my sword.' The knights replied, they would directly lead him forward; and in order that they might not lose him in the crowd, they fastened all the reins of their horses together, and put the king at their head, that he might gratify his wish, and advanced towards the enemy. The lord Charles of Bohemia, who already signed his name as king of Germany, and bore the arms, had come in good order to the engagement; but when he perceived that it was likely to turn out against the French, he departed, and I do not well know what road he took. The king, his father, had rode in among the enemy, and made good use of his sword; for he and his companions had fought most gallantly. They had advanced so far that they were all slain; and on the morrow they were found on the ground, with their horses all tied together.

The earl of Alençon advanced in regular order upon the English, to fight with them; as did the earl of Flanders, in another part. These two lords, with their detachments, coasting, as it were, the archers, came to the prince's battalion, where they fought valiantly for a length of time. The king of France was eager to march to the place where he saw their banners displayed, but there was a hedge of archers before him. He had that day made a present of a handsome black horse to sir John of Hainault, who had mounted on it a knight of his, called sir John de Fusselles, that bore his banner: which horse ran off with him, and forced his way through the English army, and, when about to return, stumbled and fell into a ditch and severely wounded him: he would have been dead, if his page had not followed him round the battalions, and found him unable to rise: he had not, however, any other hindrance than from his horse; for the English did not quit the ranks that day to make prisoners. The page alighted, and raised him up; but he did not return the way he came, as he would have found it difficult from the crowd. This battle, which was fought on one Saturday between la Broyes and Crécy, was very murderous and cruel; and many gallant deeds of arms were performed that were never known. Towards evening, many knights and squires of the French had lost their masters: they wandered up and down the plain, attacking the English in small parties: they were soon destroyed; for the English had determined that day to give no quarter, or hear of ransom from any one.

Early in the day, some French, Germans, and Savoyards, had broken through the archers of the prince's battalion, and had engaged with the men at arms; upon which the second battalion came to his aid, and it was time, for otherwise he would have been hard pressed. The first division, seeing the danger they were in, sent a knight in great haste to the King of England, who was posted upon an eminence, near a windmill. On the knight's arrival, he said, 'Sir, the earl of Warwick, the lord Stafford, the lord Reginald Cobham, and the others who are about your son, are vigorously attacked by the French; and they entreat that you would come to their assistance with your battalion, for, if their numbers should increase, they fear he will have too much to do.' The king replied, 'Is my son dead, unhorsed, or so badly wounded that he cannot support himself?' 'Nothing of the sort, thank God,' rejoined the knight; 'but he is in so hot an engagement that he has great need of your help.' The king answered, 'Now, sir Thomas, return back to those that sent you, and tell them from me, not to send again for me this day, or expect that I shall come, let what will happen, as long as my son has life; and say, that I command them to let the boy win his spurs; for I am determined, if it please God, that all the glory and honour of this day shall be given to him, and to those into whose care I have intrusted him.' The knight returned to his lords, and related the king's answer, which mightily encouraged them, and made them repent they had ever sent such a message.

It is a certain fact, that sir Godfrey de Harcourt, who was in the prince's battalion, having been told by some of the English, that they had seen the banner of his brother engaged in the battle against him, was exceedingly anxious to save him; but he was too late, for he was left dead on the field, and so was the earl of Aumarle his nephew. On the other hand, the earls of Alençon and of Flanders were fighting lustily under their banners, and with their own people; but they could not resist the force of the English, and were there slain, as well as many other knights and squires that were attending on or accompanying them. The earl of Blois, nephew to the king of France, and the duke of Lorraine, his brother-in-law, with their troops, made a gallant defence; but they were surrounded by a troop of English and Welsh, and slain in spite of their prowess. The earl of St Pol and the earl of Auxerre were also killed, as well as many others. Late after vespers, the king of France had not more about him than sixty men, every one included. Sir John of Hainault, who was of the number, had once remounted the king; for his horse had been killed under him by an arrow: he said to the king, 'Sir, retreat whilst you have an opportunity, and do not expose yourself so simply: if you have lost this battle, another time you will be the conqueror.' After he had said this, he took the bridle of the king's horse, and led him off by force; for he had before entreated of him to retire. The king rode on until he came to the castle of la Broyes, where he found the gates shut, for it was very dark. The king ordered the governor of it to be summoned: he came upon the battlements, and asked who it was that called at such an hour? The king answered, 'Open, open, governor; it is the fortune of France.' The governor, hearing the king's voice, immediately descended, opened the gate and let down the bridge. The king and his company entered the castle; but he had only with him five barons, sir John of Hainault, the lord Charles of Montmorency, the lord of Beaujeu, the lord of Aubigny, and the lord of Montfort. The king would not bury himself in such a place as that, but, having taken some refreshments, set out again with his attendants about midnight, and rode on, under the direction of guides who were well acquainted with the country, until, about day-break, he came to Amiens, where he halted. This Saturday the English never quitted their ranks in pursuit of any one, but remained on the field, guarding their position, and defending themselves against all who attacked them. The battle was ended at the hour of vespers.

When, on this Saturday night, the English heard no more hooting or shouting, nor any more crying out to particular lords or their banners, they looked upon the field as their own, and their enemies as beaten. They made great fires, and lighted torches because of the obscurity of the night. King Edward then came down from his post, who all that day had not put on his helmet, and, with his whole battalion, advanced to the prince of Wales, whom he embraced in his arms and kissed, and said, 'Sweet son, God give you good perseverance: you are my son, for most loyally have you acquitted yourself this day: you are worthy to be a sovereign.' The prince bowed down very low, and humbled himself, giving all honour to the king his father.

Sir John Froissart

55.

CHIVALRY'S finest military expression in contemporary eyes was the famous Combat of the Thirty in 1351. An action of the perennial conflict in Brittany, it began with a challenge to single combat issued by Robert de Beaumanoir, a noble Breton on the French side, to his opponent Bramborough of the Anglo-Breton party. When their partisans clamored to join, a combat of thirty on each side was agreed upon. Terms were arranged, the site was chosen, and after participants heard mass and exchanged courtesies, the fight commenced. With swords, bear-spears, daggers, and axes, they fought savagely until four on the French side and two on the English were slain and a recess was called. Bleeding and exhausted, Beaumanoir called for a drink, eliciting the era's most memorable reply: 'Drink thy blood, Beaumanoir, and thy thirst will pass!' Resuming, the combatants fought until the French side prevailed and every one of the survivors on either side was wounded. Bramborough and eight of his party were killed, the rest taken prisoner and held for ransom.

In the wide discussion the affair aroused, 'some held it as a very poor thing and others as a very swaggering business,' with the admirers dominating. The combat was celebrated in verse, painting, tapestry, and in a memorial stone erected on the site. More than twenty years later Froissart noticed a scarred survivor at the table of Charles V, where he was honored above all others. He told the ever-inquiring chronicler that he owed his great favor with the King to his having been one of the Thirty. The renown and honor the fight earned reflected the knight's nostalgic vision of what battle should be. While he practised the warfare of havoc and pillage, he clung to the image of himself as Sir Lancelot.

Barbara Tuchman

56.

The anarchy which prevailed across large tracts of France even during periods of truce in the Anglo-French conflict greatly profited freebooters ruthless and skilful enough to take advantage of them.

POOR rogues took advantage of such times, and robbed both towns and castles; so that some of them, becoming rich, constituted themselves captains of bands of thieves: there were among them those worth forty thousand crowns. Their method was, to mark out particular towns or castles, a day or two's journey from each other: they then collected twenty or thirty robbers, and, travelling through by-roads in the night-time, entered the town or castle they had fixed on about day-break, and set one of the houses on fire. When the inhabitants perceived it, they thought it had been a body of forces sent to destroy them, and took to their heels as fast as they could. The town of Donzere was treated in this manner; and many other towns and castles were taken, and afterwards ransomed. Among other robbers in Languedoc, one had marked out the strong castle of Cobourne in Limosin, which is situated in a very strong country. He set off in the night-time with thirty companions, took and destroyed it. He seized also the lord of Cobourne, whom he imprisoned in his own castle, and put all his household to death. He kept him in prison until he ransomed himself for twenty-four thousand crowns paid down. The robber kept possession of the castle and its dependencies, which he furnished with provisions, and thence made war upon all the country round about. The king of France, shortly afterwards, was desirous of having him near his person: he purchased the castle of him for twenty thousand crowns, appointed him his usher at arms, and heaped on him many other honours. The name of this robber was Bacon, and he was always mounted on handsome horses of a deep roan colour, or on large palfreys, apparelled like an earl, and very richly armed; and this state he maintained as long as he lived.

There were similar disorders in Brittany; and robbers carried on the like methods of seizing and pillaging different towns and castles, and then selling them back again to the country at a dear rate: by which means many of their leaders became very rich. Among others, there was one of the name of Croquart, who was originally but a poor boy, and had been page to the lord d'Ercle in Holland. When this Croquart arrived at manhood, he had his discharge, and went to the wars in Brittany, where he attached himself to a man at arms, and behaved very well. It happened, that in some skirmish his master was taken and slain; when, in recompense for his prowess, his companions elected him their leader in the place of his late master: he then made such profit by ransoms, and the taking of towns and castles, that he was said to be worth full forty thousand crowns, not including his horses, of which he had twenty or thirty, very handsome and strong, and of a deep roan colour. He had the reputation of being the most expert man at arms of the country, was chosen to be one of the thirty that engaged against a similar number, and was the most active combatant on the side of the English. King John of France made him the offer of knighting him, and marrying him very richly, if he would quit the English party, and promised to give him two thousand livres a year; but Croquart would never listen to it. It chanced one day, as he was riding a young horse, which he had just purchased for three hundred crowns, and was putting him to his full speed, that the horse ran away with him, and in leaping a ditch, stumbled into it, and broke his master's neck. Such was the end of Croquart.

Sir John Froissart

57.

For much of their history, Scots soldiers fought alongside the French against the English, and several of their lords were among the stricken French host at Poitiers in 1356. The wounded Lord Douglas might have received short shrift from his captors but for the remarkable presence of mind of his sympathetic kinsman Sir William Ramsay, who had fought with the Black Prince.

ARCHIBALD DOUGLAS, having been made prisoner along with the rest, appeared in more sumptuous armour than the other Scottish prisoners; and, therefore, he was supposed by the English to be some great lord. Late in the evening after the battle, when the English were about to strip off his armour, sir William Ramsay of Colluthy, happening to be present, fixed his eyes on Archibald Douglas, and, affecting to be in a violent passion, cried out, 'You cursed, damnable murderer, how comes it, in the name of mischief, that you are thus proudly decked out in your master's armour? Come hither, and pull off my boots.' Douglas approached trembling, kneeled down, and pulled off one of the boots. Ramsay, taking up the boot, beat Douglas with it. The English bystanders, imagining him out of his senses, interposed, and rescued Douglas. They said, that the person whom he had beaten was certainly of great rank, and a lord. 'What, he a lord?', cried Ramsay 'he is a scullion, and a base knave, and, as I suppose, has killed his master. Go, you villain, to the field, search for the body of my cousin, your master; and when you have found it, come back, that at least I may give him a decent burial.' Then he ransomed the feigned servingman for forty shillings; and, having buffeted him smartly, he cried, 'Get you gone; fly.' Douglas bore all this patiently, carried on the deceit, and was soon beyond the reach of his enemies.

Lord Hailes

58.

TIMOUR, whom I [Voltaire] shall call Tamerlane, in conformity with the general custom, was, according to the best historians, descended from Genghis Khan by the female side. He was born in the year 1357, in the city of Cash, in the territories of the ancient Sogdiana, whither the Greeks formerly penetrated under Alexander the Great, and settled some colonies. It is at present inhabited by the Usbeg Tartars. It begins at the borders of the Gihon, or Oxus; which river has its source in Lesser Thibet, about seven hundred leagues from the source of the Tigris and Euphrates. This is the river Gihon, which we find mentioned in the Book of Genesis.

At the mention of the city of Cash, we are ready to figure to ourselves a desert country. It lies, however, in the same latitude with Naples and Provence, and, in a word, is a delightful country.

At the name of Tamerlane, we are again apt to form an idea of a barbarian, little removed from a brute: but let it be remembered, as we have before observed, that there never was a great conqueror among princes, nor in private life any person remarkably fortunate, without that kind of merit which always meets with success for its reward. Now, Tamerlane must undoubtedly have had the greater share of the merit peculiar to ambition, who, born without any dominions of his own, subdued more countries than Alexander, and almost as many as Genghis Khan. His first conquest was the city of Balk, the capital of Khorasan, on the borders of Persia. After that he subdued the province of Kandahar, and reduced all ancient Persia; then returning, he conquered the people of Transoxana, and made himself master of Bagdad. He went to India, which he also subdued, and took possession of Delhi, which is its capital. We find that all those who have made themselves masters of Persia have in like manner conquered or ravaged India. Thus Darius Ochus reduced it after many others; and after him Alexander, Genghis Khan, and Tamerlane found it an easy conquest. Shah Nadir in our time only showed himself there, gave it laws, and brought off immense treasures.

Tamerlane, after having conquered India, returned and fell upon Syria, whose capital city, Damascus, he took. He then hastened back to Bagdad, which he had lately conquered, and which now attempted to throw off his yoke: he reduced it, and gave it up to plunder and the sword. It is said that on this occasion more than eight hundred thous-

and inhabitants were put to death. The city was razed to the foundations. In these countries cities were easily destroyed, and as easily
rebuilt, the houses being, as we have elsewhere remarked, built only of
bricks dried in the sun. It was in the midst of this series of victories that
the Greek emperor, after having in vain solicited aid from the Christians, addressed himself at length to the Tartar. Five Mahometan
princes, whom Bajazet had driven out of their kingdoms on the borders of the Pontus Euxinus, came at the same time to implore his
assistance. Thus invited by Mussulmans and Christians, he marched
into Asia Minor.

There is one circumstance which may give us an advantageous idea
of Tamerlane's character, which is, that we find him, through the
whole course of this war, strictly observant of the laws of nations.
Before he began hostilities, he sent ambassadors to Bajazet, requiring
him to raise the siege of Constantinople, and do justice to the Mussul-
man princes, whom he had deprived of their kingdoms. Bajazet
received these proposals with the utmost rage and contempt; upon
which Tamerlane declared war against him, and continued his march.
Bajazet immediately raised the siege of Constantinople; and between
Caesarea and Ancira, in 1401, was fought that great battle, in which
all the forces of the world seemed met together. Tamerlane's troops
must doubtless have been extremely well disciplined; for, after a most
obstinate resistance, they conquered those which had defeated the
Greeks, the Hungarians, the Germans, the French, and many other
warlike nations. We may be almost certain that, on this occasion,
Tamerlane, who till then had always fought with the bow and scimitar,
made use of cannon against the Ottomans; and that it was he who sent
those pieces of ordnance into the Mogul country which are to be seen
there to this day, and on which are engraved certain unintelligible
characters. The Turks, on their side, not only made use of cannon,
but also of the ancient wild-fire. This double advantage would have
infallibly given them the victory over Tamerlane, had he not made use ·
of artillery.

Bajazet, in this battle, saw his son Mustapha slain, fighting by his
side; and he himself fell captive into the hands of the conqueror, with
another of his sons, named Musa, or Moses.

It may not be displeasing to know the consequences of this memorable battle, between two nations which seemed to dispute for the
mastery of Europe and Asia, and two mighty conquerors, whose names
are still celebrated by posterity; a battle likewise, which, for a time,

preserved the Greek Empire from ruin, and might have contributed to the overthrow of the Turkish power.

The Turkish annals tell us that Tamerlane shut Bajazet up in an iron cage; but we meet with nothing like this in any of the Persian or Arabian authors who have written the life of Tamerlane.

. . . We find him soon after ravaging all Syria which belonged to the Egyptian Mamelukes. He then repassed the Euphrates, and returned to the city of Samarcand, which he considered as the capital of his vast empire. He had conquered almost as great an extent of territory as Genghis Khan, for although this latter made himself master of a part of China and Korea, Tamerlane was for some time in possession of Syria and a part of Asia Minor, whither Genghis had never been able to penetrate. He was also master of almost all Hindostan; whereas Genghis had subdued only the northern provinces of that vast empire. While he remained at Samarcand, he meditated the conquest of China, although far from being firmly established in the immense dominions he already possessed, and at an age when his death could not be far distant.

It was in this city that he, like Genghis Khan, received the homage of several princes of Asia, and ambassadors from many sovereigns, particularly from the Greek emperor, Manuel, and even from Henry III, king of Castile. On this occasion he gave one of those feasts which resembled the magnificent entertainments given of old by the first kings of Persia. All the different orders of the state, and the several artificers, passed in review before him, each carrying the badge of their profession. He married all his grandsons and granddaughters in the same day: at length he died in an extreme old age, in 1406, after a reign of thirty-six years, happier with respect to his length of days, and having lived to see his grandchildren happy, than Alexander, to whom the Orientals are so fond of comparing him; but otherwise far inferior to the Macedonian, being born in a barbarous nation, and having, like Genghis Khan, destroyed a multitude of cities without having built one; whereas Alexander, during the course of a very short life, and in the midst of his rapid conquests, built Alexandria and Scanderoon, and rebuilt this very city of Samarcand, which afterward became the seat of Tamerlane's empire, as likewise a number of other cities in India: he also established several colonies of Greeks beyond the Oxus, sent the astronomical observations of the Babylonians into Greece, and entirely changed the commerce of Asia, Europe, and Africa, making Alexandria the magazine of the universe; so far then, in my opinion, Alexander

surpasses Tamerlane, Genghis, and all the conquerors who have been
put up in competition with him.

                                                              Voltaire

59.

OF [Bertrand] Du Guesclin [created Constable of France in 1370],
whom St-Palaye calls the flower of chivalry, two stories are told that
throw a different but curious light on the manners of those times. Having on one occasion defeated the English and taken many of them prisoners, Du Guesclin tried to observe the rules of distributive justice in
the partition of the captives, but failing of success and unable to discover to whom the prisoners really belonged, he and Clisson (who
were brothers in arms) in order to terminate the differences which the
victorious French had with one another on the subject, conceived that
the only fair solution was to have them all massacred, and accordingly
more than 500 Englishmen were put to death in cold blood outside the
gates of Bressière. So, on a second occasion, such a quantity of English
were taken that 'there was not, down to the commonest soldier, anyone
who had not some prisoner of whom he counted to win a good ransom;
but as there was a dispute between the French to know to whom each
prisoner belonged, Du Guesclin, to put them all on a level, ordered
them to put all to the sword, and only the English chiefs were spared'.
This ferocious warrior, the product and pride of his time, and the
favourite hero of French chivalry, was hideous in face and figure; and
if we think of him, with his round brown face, his flat nose, his green
eyes, his crisp hair, his short neck, his broad shoulders, his long arms,
short body, and badly made legs, we have evidently one of the worst
specimens of that type which was for so long the curse of humanity, the
warrior of medieval Europe.

                                                            James Farrar

60.

*A perfectly characteristic little tale of chivalry, of a kind of which Froissart recounts
scores of examples between Poitiers and Agincourt.*

THE earl of Buckingham and his whole army were quartered at Toury
in Beauce, and in the environs, where they found plenty of provisions.

During the skirmish at Toury, a squire from Beauce, a gentleman of tried courage, who had advanced himself by his own merit, without any assistance from others, came to the barriers, and cried out to the English, 'Is there among you any gentleman who for love of his lady is willing to try with me some feat of arms? If there should be any such, here I am, quite ready to sally forth completely armed and mounted, to tilt three courses with the lance, to give three blows with the battle-axe, and three strokes with the dagger. Now look, you English, if there be none among you in love.'

This squire's name was Gauvain Micaille. His proposal and request was soon spread among the English, when a squire, an expert man at tournaments, called Joachim Cator, stepped forth and said, 'I will deliver him from his vow: let him make haste and come out of the castle.' Upon this, the lord Fitzwalter, marshal of the army, went up to the barriers, and said to sir Guy le Baveux, 'Let your squire come forth: he has found one who will cheerfully deliver him; and we will afford him every security.'

Gauvain Micaille was much rejoiced on hearing these words. He immediately armed himself, in which the lords assisted, in the putting on the different pieces, and mounted him on a horse, which they gave to him. Attended by two others, he came out of the castle; and his varlets carried three lances, three battle-axes, and three daggers. He was much looked at by the English, for they did not think any Frenchman would have engaged body to body. There were besides to be three strokes with a sword, and with all other sorts of arms. Gauvain had had three brought with him for fear any should break.

The earl of Buckingham, hearing of this combat, said he would see it, and mounted his horse, attended by the earls of Stafford and Devonshire. On this account, the assault on Toury ceased. The Englishman that was to tilt was brought forward, completely armed and mounted on a good horse. When they had taken their stations, they gave to each of them a spear, and the tilt began; but neither of them struck the other, from the mettlesomeness of their horses. They hit the second onset, but it was by darting their spears; on which the earl of Buckingham cried out, 'Hola hola! it is now late.' He then said to the constable, 'Put an end to it, for they have done enough this day: we will make them finish it when we have more leisure than we have at this moment, and take great care that as much attention is paid to the French squire as to our own: and order some one to tell those in the castle not to be uneasy about him, for we shall carry him with us to

complete his enterprise, but not as a prisoner; and that when he shall
have been delivered, if he escape with his life, we will send him back in
all safety.'

These orders of the earl were obeyed by the marshal, who said to
the French squire, 'You shall accompany us without any danger, and
when it shall be agreeable to my lord you will be delivered.' Gauvain
replied, 'God help me!' A herald was sent to the castle, to repeat to the
governor the words you have heard.

The following day, they marched towards Geneville in Beauce,
always in expectation of having an engagement with the enemy; for
they well knew they were followed and watched by the French, in
greater numbers than themselves. True it is, that the French dukes,
counts, barons, knights, and squires, eagerly wished for a battle, and
said among themselves, that it was very blameable and foolish not to
permit them to engage, and suffer the enemy thus to slip through their
hands. But, when it was mentioned to the king, he replied, 'Let them
alone: they will destroy themselves.' The English continued their
march, with the intent to enter Brittany.

You before heard, that there were three hundred spears in Geneville, so the whole army passed by it. There was indeed at the barriers
some little skirmishing, which lasted not long, as it was time thrown
away. Without Geneville a handsome mill was destroyed. The earl
came to Yterville, and dismounted at the house of the Templars. The
van-guard went forwards to Puiset, where they heard that sixty companions had posted themselves in a large tower: they marched to the
attack, for it was situated in the open plain without any bulwarks. The
assault was sharp, but did not last long, for the archers shot so briskly
that scarcely any one dared to appear on the battlements: the tower was
taken, and those within slain or made prisoners. The English then set
fire to it, and marched on, for they were in the utmost distress for
water. From thence they went to Ermoyon, where they quartered
themselves, and then to the forest of Marchenoir. In this forest there is
a monastery of monks, of the Cistertian order, which is called the Cistertian Abbey, and has several handsome and noble edifices, where
formerly a most renowned and noble knight, the count de Blois,
received great edification, and bequeathed to it large revenues; but the
wars had greatly diminished them. The earl of Buckingham lodged in
this abbey, and heard mass there on the feast of our Lady in
September. It was there ordered, that Gauvain Micaille and Joachim
Cator should on the morrow complete their enterprise. That day the

English came to Marchenoir: the governor was a knight of that country, called sir William de St Martin, a prudent and valiant man at arms. The English, after having reconnoitred the castle, retired to their quarters. In another part, the lord Fitzwalter came before the castle of Verbi, not to attack it, but to speak with the governor at the barriers, with whom he was well acquainted, having been together formerly in Prussia. The lord Fitzwalter made himself known to the lord de Verbi, and entreated him, out of courtesy, to send him some wine, and in return he would prevent his estate from being burnt or spoiled. The lord de Verbi sent him a large quantity, and thirty great loaves with it; for which the lord Fitzwalter was very thankful, and kept his promise.

On the day of the feast of our Lady, Gauvain Micaille and Joachim Cator were armed, and mounted to finish their engagement. They met each other roughly with spears, and the French squire tilted much to the satisfaction of the earl: but the Englishman kept his spear too low, and at last struck it into the thigh of the Frenchman. The earl of Buckingham as well as the other lords were much enraged at this, and said it was tilting dishonourably; but he excused himself, by declaring it was solely owing to the restiveness of his horse. Then were given the three thrusts with the sword; and the earl declared they had done enough, and would not have it longer continued, for he perceived the French squire bled exceedingly: the other lords were of the same opinion. Gauvain Micaille was therefore disarmed and his wound dressed. The earl sent him one hundred francs by a herald, with leave to return to his own garrison in safety, adding that he had acquitted himself much to his satisfaction. Gauvain Micaille went back to the lords of France: and the English departed from Marchenoir, taking the road to Vendôme.

Sir John Froissart

61.

Many of the interminable Italian wars of the late fourteenth century were fought by condottieri, *mercenaries of whom a considerable number were English veterans of the campaigns in France. The most celebrated, or notorious, was the White Company led by an archer named John Hawkwood.*

AT the Battle of Brentelle in 1386 the Paduans captured, *inter alia*, two hundred and eleven courtesans in what might excusably be termed the enemy baggage-train. These girls they crowned with flowers and provided with bouquets—it was fittingly midsummer, and a delightful sequel to an unexpectedly easy battle, the Venetian condottieri having been bribed to retreat. The courtesans were led in procession into Padua and entertained to breakfast by Francesco Carrara in his palace. Life evidently was not all rape and ruin.

. . . The White Company was organized very much as the Great Company had been. Like Montreal, Hawkwood had a staff to assist him. His principal lieutenants were the German, Sterz, whom he had supplanted, and an aristocratic Englishman, Andrew de Belmonte, whom the Italians called 'Dubramonte', and credited with royal blood, because his gentle manners contrasted with those of his more barbaric followers. It was perhaps for this reason that Andrew had a romantic affair with a certain Monna Tancia, wife of one Guido, Lord of the Forest, but the identities and fates of these characters are no longer traceable.

The company treasurer was a highly important figure. This was William Turton, to whom, as 'Guglielmo Toreton', the chamberlain of the Pisan republic paid over the contracted sums. The names of many a humble soldier, 'Marco' and 'Marcuccio', the trumpeters, and others, are preserved in the Pisan accounts, though their original form and nationality are often obscured by the spelling of the native clerks. There was a surprising amount of paperwork and the treasurer needed the help of a considerable staff. There were negotiations with employing governments, reports, requests, instructions, and complaints. There were applications for permission to march through the territory of friendly or neutral states—a recurring necessity in a land that was a jigsaw puzzle of interlocking principalities. Within the company there were the accounts, the pay due to each member according to his grade, and a record of any monies advanced. The troops were apt to gamble and otherwise fritter away their earnings. If they got into debt, they might pawn or sell their arms and equipment, thereby becoming useless to their employers. Florence, at this same date, was meeting the difficulty with her own mercenaries. She opened a credit fund in February 1362, making interest-free loans of public money to embarrassed warriors. If a knight borrowed from the fund, two constables, or high-ranking officers, had to stand surety for him. The constable himself was good for six times as large a loan, if he needed it.

Altogether, Hawkwood and his administrative staff had to combine the functions of lawyers, diplomats, accountants, and paymasters. It could not have been done without taking on Italians. Sterz, with his knowledge of Italy, must have been indispensable in those early days. But Hawkwood himself became, in time, fluent in the language of the country in which he was to spend the rest of his life.

Geoffrey Trease

62.

Although he was dead at 25, Thomas Holland, Duke of Surrey and Earl of Kent, in his brief life proved an accomplished villain, profiting greatly from his sponsorship of the execution of his uncle Arundel and from performing lesser acts useful to himself and Richard II. On Richard's fall and the elevation of Henry of Lancaster to the throne, the Earl of Kent (as he became again on being stripped of his dukedom) made a bold final bid to restore his own fortunes, and those of Richard, which displayed the courage that Froissart, among others, conceded him in full measure.

AND, in [1399] being in Ireland, with King Richard, when that dreadful News came to him, of Henry Duke of Lancaster's arrival in England; he return'd back with him; whose Resignation and Deposal soon after ensued. And thereupon a Parliament, viz. on the Feast-day of St Faith the Virgin, wherein this Duke was doom'd to lose that his great Title, in regard he had been one of the prosecutors of Thomas of Wodstoke, Duke of Glocester.

But to this grand alteration, neither he, nor some others, who had born the greatest sway, during King Richard's Reign, could be content to submit: And, therefore, plotted to come into Windsore-Castle, where King Henry then kept his Christmass, under the disguise of Mummers; so to Murther him (with his sons) and to restore King Richard. But King Henry, having notice thereof, got privily to London; so that this Duke, and the rest (who thought to have accomplish'd their work, as they had design'd) coming thither, on the Sunday evening, next after New-years-day, in the twilight, with about four hundred Men in Armes, found that they were disappointed of their purpose. Whereupon they went away much displeased. But dissembling his discontent, he rode to Sunning (near Reading) where King Richard's Queen then was; and, in the presence of divers of her servants, signing himself, with his right hand, on the fore-head; said 'Bless me! What is the reason that Henry of Lancaster, who hath so much boasted of his valor, doth thus shun me?' Adding, 'My Lords and Friends, be it known to you all, that Henry of Lancaster who pursued me, is now fled to the Tower of London, with his sons and friends: and, that it is my purpose to go to King Richard, my rightfull King; who, being escaped out of prison, lieth at Pontfract, with an Hundred thousand Men.'

And, that the more credit might be given to what he said, he pull'd King Henries Badges from some of his servants necks, with disdain; saying, That hereafter none such should be used; and tore off the Crescents from the Armes of such Gentlemen as wore them: And so, having cheered up the Queen (though all in vain) rode to Walingford, and so to Abendon, exhorting the people to put themselves in Armes for King Richard. And, at length, came to Cirencester, in the dark of the night, with the like report. But, the Townsmen, suspecting all this to be but counterfeit, blockt up the Avenues the place whereunto they came: and, about midnight, when they attempted to get privily away, with Bowes and Arrowes, hindred their passage.

Discerning therefore the danger; he and the rest Arm'd themselves, supposing they might easily conquer those Rusticks: which, after three houres fight, seeing they could not do, they submitted; intreating that their lives might be spared, till they could speak with the King. But, so it fell out; that, during this bustle, a Priest of their Company, presuming, that if he could set some Houses on fire, the Inhabitants would be so busied in quenching them, that they might then have an opportunity to escape: thereupon, presently did so, though to no purpose. For the people, by reason thereof, grew the more enraged; and, letting the houses burn, took this Earl, with the Earl of Salisbury, out of the Abby, and beheaded them. This hapned on Wednesday, after the Feast of the Epiphany [17 January 1400].

The Baronage of England

63.

In the ranks of the English army on the eve of Agincourt, 24 October 1415.

AND when at last we were at the last rays of light, and darkness fell between us and them, we still stood in the field and heard our foes, everyone calling as the manner is, for his comrade, servant and friend, dispersed by chance in so great a multitude. Our men began to do the same, but the king ordered silence throughout the whole army, under penalty of the loss of horse and harness in the case of a gentleman, . . . and of the right ear in the case of a yeoman or below, with no hope of pardon, for anyone who might presume to break the king's order. And he at once went in silence to a hamlet nearby, in a place where we had only a few houses; most of us had to rest in gardens and orchards, through a night of pouring rain. And when our enemies considered the quietness of our men and our silence, they thought that we were struck with fright at our small numbers and contemplated flight during the night; so they established fires and strong watches throughout the fields and routes. And as it was said they thought they were so sure of us that they cast dice that night for our king and nobles.

Henrici Quinti Angliae Regis Gesta

64.

Agincourt, 25 October 1415.

As the morning wore on, Henry's confidence, real or assumed, began to waver. He had hoped that the French would have attacked him soon after dawn and would have exhausted themselves in doing so; but now, three hours after daybreak, they still remained motionless. And he must fight his battle that day, for his men would be incapable of fighting it tomorrow. 'The army', as one of his chaplains put it, 'was very much wearied with hunger, diseases, and marching, and was not likely to obtain any food in this country. The longer they remained there, so much the more would they be subjected to the effects of debility and exhaustion.'

Henry sought the advice of the more experienced soldiers among his knights and asked them whether or not they thought he should attack as the enemy showed no signs of attacking him. They all agreed that he should, and he appeared to be ready to accept their guidance when three horsemen were seen to move out of the ranks of the French army and ride across towards him.

One of these horsemen, the Sire de Heilly (who had been taken prisoner by the English in a previous campaign and had escaped) went up to Henry and, without the polite preamble that custom and etiquette demanded, told him that he had heard it said that his captors accused him of having escaped 'in a way unbecoming a knight', and that if anyone dared to repeat the accusation he would challenge him to single combat and prove him a liar.

The King replied that there could be no question of personal quarrels being settled at such a time and advised Heilly to return to his companions and tell them to begin their attack.

'I trust in God', Henry added coldly, 'that if you did disgrace the honour of knighthood in the manner of your escape you will today either be killed or recaptured.'

Heilly refused to deliver the King's message. His companions, he said, were not his servants but subjects of the King of France and they would begin the battle at their own pleasure, not at the will of their enemy.

'Depart, then, to your host', Henry said dismissively, turning his horse's head. 'And however fast you ride, you may find that we shall be there before you.' . . .

A body of eighteen knights, it is believed, led by Brunelet de Masinguehen and Ganiot de Bournonville, swore that they would get near enough to [King Henry] to strike the crown from his head, or die in the attempt. Whether or not they did so, it is certain that someone struck a fleuron from his crown during the fight and that a battle-axe dented his helmet which can still be seen, to attest the fact, above his tomb in Westminster Abbey.

Christopher Hibbert

65.

This decently cynical view of the Maid of Orleans seems much preferable to the reverent portraits of more respectful historians.

A GENTLEMAN upon the frontiers of Lorraine, whose name was Baudricourt, happened to meet with a young servant wench at an inn in the town of Vaucouleurs, whom he thought a fit person to act the character of a female warrior and a prophetess. Joan of Arc—which was the name of this heroine—whom the vulgar look upon as a shepherdess, was in fact only a tavern girl; 'of a robust make,' as Monstrelet says, 'and who could ride without a saddle, and perform other manly exercises which young maidens are unaccustomed to'. She was made to pass for a young shepherdess of eighteen; and yet it is evident from her confession that she was at that time twenty-seven. She had courage and wit sufficient to engage in this delicate enterprise, which afterward became a heroic one, and suffered herself to be carried before the king at Bourges, where she was examined by matrons, who took care to find her a virgin, and by certain doctors of the university, and some members of the parliament, who all without hesitation declared her inspired. Whether they were really imposed upon, or were crafty enough to adopt the project, the vulgar swallowed the bait, and that was sufficient.

The English were at that time, in 1428, besieging Orleans, Charles's last resource, and were upon the point of making themselves masters of the town, when this amazon in man's dress, directed by able officers, undertook to throw reinforcements into the town. Previous to her attempt she harangued the soldiers, as one sent from God, and inspired them with that enthusiastic courage peculiar to all who imagine they behold the Deity Himself fighting their cause. After this she put herself at their head, delivered Orleans, beat the English, foretold to Charles that she would see him consecrated at Rheims, fulfilled her promise, sword in hand, and assisted at the coronation, holding the standard with which she had so bravely fought.

These rapid victories obtained by a girl, with all the appearances of a miracle, and the king's coronation, which conciliated the public respect to his person, had almost restored the lawful prince, and expelled the foreign pretender, when the instrument of all these wonders, Joan of Arc, was wounded and taken prisoner in 1430, while defending Compiègne. Such a person as the Black Prince would have honored and respected her courage; but the regent, Bedford, thought it necessary to detract from it, in order to revive the drooping spirits of the English. She had pretended to perform a miracle, and Bedford pretended to believe her a witch.

My principal end is always to observe the spirit of the times, since it is that which directs the great events of the world.

The university of Paris presented a complaint against Joan, accusing her of heresy and witchcraft. Therefore this university either believed what the regent would have it believe; or if it did not believe it, it was guilty of most infamous baseness. This heroine, who was worthy of that miracle which she had feigned, was tried at Rouen by Cauchon, bishop of Beauvais, by five other French bishops, and one English bishop, assisted by a Dominican monk, vicar to the Inquisition, and by the doctors to the university; who declared her 'a superstitious prophetess of the devil, a blasphemer against God and His saints, and one who had been guilty of numberless errors against the faith of Christ'. As such she was condemned to perpetual imprisonment, and to fast on bread and water. She made a reply to her judges, which, in my opinion, is worthy of eternal memory. She was asked why she dared to assist at the consecration of Charles, as his standard-bearer.

'Because', answered she, 'it is but just that the person who shared in the toil should partake likewise of the honor.'

Some time after this, being accused of having again put on men's clothes, which had been left in her way purposely to tempt her, her judges, who certainly had no right to try her, as she was a prisoner of war, declared her a relapsed heretic, in 1431; and without further ceremony condemned to the flames a person who, for the services she had rendered her king, would have had altars erected to her in those heroic times when mankind were wont to decree such honors to their deliverers. Charles VII afterward restored her memory with honor, which indeed had been sufficiently honored by her punishment.

Voltaire

66.

The petition of Thomas Hostelle, 1429.

To the king, our sovereign lord,

Beseecheth meekly your povere [poor] liegeman and humble horatour [petitioner], Thomas Hostelle, that, in consideration of his service done to your noble progenitors of full blessed memory, king Henry the iiijth and King Henry the fifth (whose souls God assoile!), being at the siege of Harfleur there smitten with a springolt through the head, losing his one eye and his cheek bone broken; also at the battle of Agincourt, and afore at the taking of the carracks on the sea, there with a gadde of yrene [iron] his plates smitten in to his body and his hand smitten in sunder, and sore hurt, maimed and wounded, by mean whereof he being sore feebled and debrused, now falle to great age and poverty, greatly endetted, and may not help him self, having not wherewith to be sustained ne relieved, but of men's gracious almesse [alms], and being for his said service never yet recompensed ne rewarded, it please your high and excellent grace, the premises tenderly considered, of your benign pity and grace to relieve and refresh your said povere oratour as it shall please you with your most gracious almesse, at the reverence of God and in work of charity, and he shall devoutly pray for the souls of your said noble progenitors and for your most noble and high estate.

Thomas Hostelle

67.

The King of Hungary launches an ill-fated invasion of the Turkish empire, 1444.

LADISLAUS, seduced by false hopes, and a manner of thinking which success alone can justify, invaded the sultan's territories. The janissaries upon this went in a body to beseech Amurath to quit his retirement, and put himself at their head, to which he consented; and the two armies met near the Pontus Euxinus, in that country now known by the name of Bulgaria, but which was then called Moesia. The battle was fought near the city of Varna, in 1444 [10 November]. Amurath wore in his bosom the treaty of peace which he had concluded with the Christians, and which they had so lately infringed; and holding it up in the midst of the crowd, at a time that he found his troops began to give way, he called aloud to God, beseeching Him to punish the perjured Christians, and revenge the insult offered to the laws of nations. This is what has given rise to the fabulous report, that the peace was sworn on the eucharist, and the host deposited in the hands of Amurath, and that it was to this host that he addressed himself in the day of battle. Perjury for this time met with the punishment it deserved. The Christians were defeated after an obstinate resistance. King Ladislaus, after receiving a number of wounds, had his head struck off by a janissary, who carried it in triumph through the ranks of the Turkish army; at this fatal sight the rout of the Christians became general.

Amurath, after his victory, caused the body of Ladislaus to be buried in the field of battle, with all military honors. It is even said that he caused a pillar to be erected on his gravethis fatal sight the rout of the Christians became general.

Amurath, after his victory, caused the body of Ladislaus to be buried in the field of battle, with all military honors. It is even said that he caused a pillar to be erected on his grave; with an inscription, which was so far from insulting his memory, that it extolled his courage, and lamented his misfortunes.

Some writers say that Cardinal Julian, who was present at this battle, endeavoring to cross a river in his flight, was drowned by the weight of gold which he carried about him. Others again say that he was slain by the Hungarians. It is certain that he perished on that day.

But what is most remarkable is, that Amurath, after having gained this signal victory, betook himself again to solitude; and a second time abdicated the crown, which he was afterward obliged to resume, to go forth again to battle, and to conquer.   Voltaire

68.

The fall of Constantinople, 1453.

IN the confusion of darkness an assailant may sometimes succeed; but in this great and general attack, the military judgment and astrological knowledge of Mahomet advised him to expect the morning, the memorable twenty-ninth of May, in the fourteen hundred and fifty-third year of the Christian era. The preceding night had been strenuously employed: the troops, the cannon, and the fascines were advanced to the edge of the ditch, which in many parts presented a smooth and level passage to the breach; and his fourscore galleys almost touched, with the prows and their scaling ladders, the less defensible walls of the harbour. Under pain of death, silence was enjoined; but the physical laws of motion and sound are not obedient to discipline or fear: each individual might suppress his voice and measure his footsteps; but the march and labour of thousands must inevitably produce a strange confusion of dissonant clamours, which reached the ears of the watchmen of the towers. At daybreak, without the customary signal of the morning gun, the Turks assaulted the city by sea and land; and the similitude of a twined or twisted thread has been applied to the closeness and continuity of their line of attack. The foremost ranks consisted of the refuse of the host, a voluntary crowd who fought without order or command; of the feebleness of age or childhood, of peasants and vagrants, and of all who had joined the camp in the blind hope of plunder and martyrdom. The common impulse drove them onwards to the wall; the most audacious to climb were instantly precipitated; and not a dart, not a bullet, of the Christians, was idly wasted on the accumulated throng. But their strength and ammunition were exhausted in this laborious defence: the ditch was filled with the bodies of the slain; they supported the footsteps of their companions; and of this devoted vanguard the death was more serviceable than the life. Under their respective bashaws and sanjaks, the troops of Anatolia and Romania were successively led to the charge: their progress was various and doubtful; but, after a conflict of two hours, the Greeks still maintained and improved their advantage; and the voice of the emperor was heard, encouraging his soldiers to achieve, by a last effort, the deliverance of their country. In that fatal moment the Janizaries arose, fresh, vigorous, and invincible. The sultan himself on horseback, with an iron mace in his hand, was the spectator and judge of their valour; he was surrounded by ten thousand of his domestic troops, whom he reserved for the decisive occasion; and the tide of battle was directed and impelled by his voice and eye. His numerous ministers of justice were posted behind the line, to urge, to restrain, and to punish; and if danger was in the front, shame and inevitable death were in the rear, of the fugitives. The cries of fear and of pain were drowned in the martial music of drums, trumpets, and attaballs; and experience has proved that the mechanical operation of sounds, by quickening the circulation of the blood and spirits, will act on the human machine more forcibly than the eloquence of reason and honour. From the lines, the galleys, and the bridge, the Ottoman artillery thundered on all sides; and the camp and city, the Greeks and the Turks, were involved in a cloud of smoke, which could only be dispelled by the final deliverance or destruction of the Roman empire. The single combats of the heroes of history or fable amuse our fancy and engage our affections: the skilful evolutions of war may inform the mind, and improve a necessary, though pernicious, science. But in the uniform and odious pictures of a general assault, all is blood, and horror, and confusion; nor shall I strive, at the distance of three centuries and a thousand miles, to delineate a scene of which there could be no spectators, and of which the actors themselves were incapable of forming any just or adequate idea.

The immediate loss of Constantinople may be ascribed to the bullet or arrow, which pierced the gauntlet of John Justiniani. The sight of his blood, and the exquisite pain, appalled the courage of the chief, whose arms and counsels were the firmest rampart of the city. As he withdrew from his station in quest of a surgeon, his flight was perceived and stopped by the indefatigable emperor. 'Your wound', exclaimed Palaeologus, 'is slight; the danger is pressing: your presence is necessary; and whither will you retire?'—'I will retire', said the trembling Genoese, 'by the same road which God has opened to the Turks'; and at these words he hastily passed through one of the breaches of the inner wall. By this pusillanimous act he stained the honours of a military life and the few days which he survived in Galata, or the isle of Chios, were embittered by his own and the public reproach. His example was imitated by the greatest part of the Latin auxiliaries, and the defence began to slacken when the attack was pressed with redoubled vigour. The number of the Ottomans was fifty, perhaps a hundred, times superior to that of the Christians; the double walls were reduced by the cannon to a heap of ruins: in a circuit of several miles some places must be found more easy of access, or more feebly guarded; and if the besiegers could penetrate in a single point, the whole city was irrecoverably lost. The first who deserved the sultan's reward was Hassan the Janizary, of gigantic stature and strength. With his scimitar in one hand and his buckler in the other, he ascended the outward fortification: of the thirty Janizaries who were emulous of his valour, eighteen perished in the bold adventure. Hassan and his twelve companions had reached the summit: the giant was precipitated from the rampart: he rose on one knee, and was again oppressed by a shower of darts and stones. But his success had proved that the achievement was possible: the walls and towers were instantly covered with a swarm of Turks; and the Greeks, now driven from the vantage ground, were overwhelmed by increasing multitudes. Amidst these multitudes, the emperor, who accomplished all the duties of a general and a soldier, was long seen and finally lost. The nobles, who fought round his person, sustained, till their last breath, the honourable names of Palaeologus and Cantacuzene: his mournful exclamation was heard, 'Cannot there be found a Christian to cut off my head?' and his last fear was that of falling alive into the hands of the infidels. The prudent despair of Constantine cast away the purple: amidst the tumult he fell by an unknown hand, and his body was buried under a mountain of the slain. After his death resistance and order were no more: the Greeks fled towards the city; and many were pressed and stifled in the narrow pass of the gate of St Romanus. The victorious Turks rushed through the breaches of the inner wall; and as they advanced into the streets, they were soon joined by their brethren, who had forced the gate Phenar on the side of the harbour. In the first heat of the pursuit about two thousand Christians were put to the sword; but avarice soon prevailed over cruelty; and the victors acknowledged that they should immediately have given quarter, if the valour of the emperor and his chosen bands had not prepared them for a similar opposition in every part of the capital. It was thus, after a siege of fifty-three days, that Constantinople, which had defied the power of Chosroes, the Chagan, and the caliphs, was irretrievably subdued by the arms of Mahomet the Second. Her empire only had been subverted by the Latins: her religion was trampled in the dust by the Moslem conquerors.

The tidings of misfortune fly with a rapid wing; yet such was the extent of Constantinople, that the more distant quarters might prolong,

some moments, the happy ignorance of their ruin. But in the general
consternation, in the feelings of selfish or social anxiety, in the tumult
and thunder of the assault, a *sleepless* night and morning must have
elapsed; nor can I believe that many Grecian ladies were awakened by
the Janizaries from a sound and tranquil slumber. On the assurance of
the public calamity, the houses and convents were instantly deserted;
and the trembling inhabitants flocked together in the streets, like a
herd of timid animals, as if accumulated weakness could be productive
of strength, or in the vain hope that amid the crowd each individual
might be safe and invisible. From every part of the capital they flowed
into the church of St Sophia: in the space of an hour, the sanctuary,
the choir, the nave, the upper and lower galleries, were filled with the
multitudes of fathers and husbands, of women and children, of priests,
monks, and religious virgins: the doors were barred on the inside, and
they sought protection from the sacred dome which they had so lately
abhorred as a profane and polluted edifice. Their confidence was
founded on the prophecy of an enthusiast or impostor, that one day the
Turks would enter Constantinople, and pursue the Romans as far as
the column of Constantine in the square before St Sophia: but that this
would be the term of their calamities; that an angel would descend
from heaven with a sword in his hand, and would deliver the empire,
with that celestial weapon, to a poor man seated at the foot of the column. 'Take this sword,' would he say, 'and avenge the people of the
Lord.' At these animating words the Turks would instantly fly, and the
victorious Romans would drive them from the West, and from all Anatolia, as far as the frontiers of Persia. It is on this occasion that Ducas,
with some fancy and much truth, upbraids the discord and obstinacy of
the Greeks. 'Had that angel appeared,' exclaims the historian, 'had he
offered to exterminate your foes if you would consent to the union of
the church, even then, in that fatal moment, you would have rejected
your safety, or have deceived your God.'

    While they expected the descent of the tardy angel, the doors were
broken with axes; and as the Turks encountered no resistance, their
bloodless hands were employed in selecting and securing the multitude of their prisoners. Youth, beauty, and the appearance of wealth,
attracted their choice; and the right of property was decided among
themselves by a prior seizure, by personal strength, and by the authority of command. In the space of an hour the male captives were
bound with cords, the females with their veils and girdles. The sena-

tors were linked with their slaves; the prelates with the porters of the church; and young men of a plebeian class with noble maids whose faces had been invisible to the sun and their nearest kindred. In this common captivity the ranks of society were confounded; the ties of nature were cut asunder; and the inexorable soldier was careless of the father's groans, the tears of the mother, and the lamentations of the children. The loudest in their wailings were the nuns, who were torn from the altar with naked bosoms, outstretched hands, and dishevelled hair; and we should piously believe that few could be tempted to prefer the vigils of the harem to those of the monastery. Of these unfortunate Greeks, of these domestic animals, whole strings were rudely driven through the streets; and as the conquerors were eager to return for more prey, their trembling pace was quickened with menaces and blows. At the same hour a similar rapine was exercised in all the churches and monasteries, in all the palaces and habitations, of the capital; nor could any place, however sacred or sequestered, protect the persons or the property of the Greeks. Above sixty thousand of this devoted people were transported from the city to the camp and fleet; exchanged or sold according to the caprice or interest of their masters, and dispersed in remote servitude through the provinces of the Otto- man empire. Among these we may notice some remarkable characters. The historian Phranza, first chamberlain and principal secretary, was involved with his family in the common lot. After suffering four months the hardships of slavery, he recovered his freedom: in the ensuing winter he ventured to Adrianople, and ransomed his wife from the *mir bashi*, or master of the horse; but his two children, in the flower of youth and beauty, had been seized for the use of Mahomet himself. The daughter of Phranza died in the seraglio, perhaps a virgin: his son, in the fifteenth year of his age, preferred death to infamy, and was stabbed by the hand of the royal lover. A deed thus inhuman cannot surely be expiated by the taste and liberality with which he released a Grecian matron and her two daughters, on receiving a Latin ode from Philelphus, who had chosen a wife in that noble family. The pride or cruelty of Mahomet would have been most sensibly gratified by the capture of a Roman legate; but the dexterity of Cardinal Isidore eluded the search, and he escaped from Galata in a plebeian habit. The chain and entrance of the outward harbour was still ocupied by the Italian ships of merchandise and war. They had signalized their valour in the siege: they embraced the moment of retreat, while the Turkish mariners were dissipated in the pillage of the city. When they hoisted sail, the beach was covered with a suppliant and lamentable crowd; but the means of transportation were scanty; the Venetians and Genoese selected their countrymen; and, notwithstanding the fairest promises of the sultan, the inhabitants of Galata evacuated their houses, and embarked with their most precious effects.

In the fall and the sack of great cities an historian is condemned to repeat the tale of uniform calamity: the same effects must be produced by the same passions; and when those passions may be indulged without control, small, alas! is the difference between civilized and savage man. Amidst the vague exclamations of bigotry and hatred, the Turks are not accused of a wanton or immoderate effusion of Christian blood: but according to their maxims (the maxims of antiquity), the lives of the vanquished were forfeited; and the legitimate reward of the conqueror was derived from the service, the sale, or the ransom of his captives of both sexes. The wealth of Constantinople had been granted by the sultan to his victorious troops; and the rapine of an hour is more productive than the industry of years. But as no regular division was attempted of the spoil, the respective shares were not determined by merit; and the rewards of valour were stolen away from the followers of the camp, who had declined the toil and danger of the battle. The narrative of their depredations could not afford either amusement or instruction: the total amount, in the last poverty of the empire, has been valued at four millions of ducats; and of this sum a small part was the property of the Venetians, the Genoese, the Florentines, and the merchants of Ancona. Of these foreigners the stock was improved in quick and perpetual circulation: but the riches of the Greeks were displayed in the idle ostentation of palaces and wardrobes, or deeply buried in treasures of ingots and gold coin, lest it should be demanded at their hands for the defence of their country.

Edward Gibbon

69.

A vivid demonstration of the confusions of civil war at the Battle of Barnet, 14 April 1471, where Edward IV at last prevailed and Warwick the Kingmaker was killed.

KING HARRY was then in London, and the Archbishop of York, in the palace of the Bishop of London. And on the Wednesday next before Easter Day King Harry and the Archbishop of York with him rode about London, and desired the people to be true to him; and every man said they would. Nevertheless, Christopher Urswick, Recorder of London, and divers alderman, who had the government of the city, commanded all the people who were in arms, protecting the city and King Harry, to go home to dinner; and during the dinner time King Edward was let in, and so went to the palace of the Bishop of London and there took King Harry and the Archbishop of York and put them in ward, the Thursday next before Easter Day. And the Archbishop of Canterbury, the Earl of Essex, Lord Berners, and such others as bore towards King Edward good will, as well in London as in other places, produced as many men as they could to strengthen the said King Edward; so then he had 7,000 men and there they refreshed themselves well all that day and Good Friday [12 April 1471].

And upon Easter Eve he and all his host went towards Barnet and took King Harry with him; for he understood that the Earl of Warwick and the Duke of Exeter, the Marquis Montagu, the Earl of Oxford, and many other knights, squires, and commons, to the number of 20,000 men, were gathered together to fight against King Edward. But it happened that he with his host entered the town of Barnet before the Earl of Warwick and his host. And so the Earl of Warwick and his host lay outside the town all night, and each of them fired guns at the other all night. And on Easter Day in the morning, the 14th April, right early, each of them came upon the other; and there was such a thick mist that neither of them might see the other perfectly. There they fought, from 4 o'clock in the morning unto 10 o'clock of the forenoon. And at various times the Earl of Warwick's party had the victory, and supposed that they had won the field. But it happened so that the Earl of Oxford's men had upon them their lord's livery, both in front and behind, which was a star with streams, which was much like King Edward's livery, a sun with streams. And the mist was so thick that a man might not properly judge one thing from another; so the Earl of Warwick's men shot and fought against the Earl of Oxford's men, thinking and supposing that they had been King Edward's men. And at once the Earl of Oxford and his men cried 'Treason! Treason!' and fled away from the field with 800 men. The lord Marquis Montagu had an agreement and understanding with King Edward and put upon him King Edward's livery; and a man of the Earl of Warwick saw that and fell upon him and killed him.

Warkworth's Chronicle

70.

How to sack a divisional commander: Tewkesbury, 4 May 1471.

LORD WENLOCK not having advanced to the support of the first line, but remaining stationary, contrary to the expectations of Somerset, the latter, in a rage, rode up to him, reviled him, and beat his brains out with an axe.

Richard Brooke

71.

The morning of Bosworth, 22 August 1485.

THE first persons who attended the king, were Lovell, the Lord Chamberlain; Catesby, the Attorney-General; and Sir Richard Ratcliffe, all privy councellors, to whom he uttered the ill-bodings of his heart. Issuing from his tent, by twilight, he observed a centinel asleep, and is said to have stabbed him, with this remark, 'I found him asleep, and have left him as I found him.' Perhaps this was the only person Richard ever put to death, who deserved it.

William Hutton

72.

PIERRE DU TERRAIL, chevalier de Bayard, who was a real knight-errant and deemed the flower of chivalry, descended from an ancient and honorable family in Dauphiny. His great-grandfather's father fell at the feet of King John in the battle of Poitiers; his great-grandfather was slain at the battle of Agincourt; his grandfather lost his life in the battle of Montlhéry; and his father was desperately wounded in the battle of Guinegate, commonly called the battle of the Spurs. The chevalier himself had signalized himself from his youth by incredible acts of personal valor; first of all at the battle of Fornovo [6 July 1495]: in the reign of Louis XII he, with his single arm, defended the bridge at Naples against two hundred knights: in the reign of Francis I he fought so valiantly at the battle of Marignano [15 September 1515], under the eye of his sovereign, that, after the action, Francis insisted upon being knighted by his hand, after the manner of chivalry. Having given his king the slap on the shoulder, and dubbed him knight, he addressed himself to his sword in these terms: 'How happy art thou, in having this day conferred the order of knighthood on such a virtuous and powerful monarch. Certes, my good sword, thou shalt henceforth be kept as a relic, and honored above all others, and never will I wear thee except against the infidels.' So saying, he cut a caper twice, and then sheathed his sword. He behaved with such extraordinary courage and conduct on a great number of delicate occasions, that he was promoted to the rank of lieutenant-general, and held in universal esteem. It was at the retreat of Rebec that his back was broken with a musket shot. Perceiving himself mortally wounded, he exclaimed: 'Jesus, my God, I am a dead man.' Then he kissed the cross of his sword, repeated some prayers aloud, caused himself to be laid under a tree, with a stone supporting his head, and his face toward the enemy, observing that he would not, in the last scene of his life, begin to turn his back on the enemy. He sent a dutiful message to the king by the lord of Alegre; and having made a military will by word of mouth, was visited and caressed by the constable of Bourbon and Marquis de Pescara. He died on the spot, in the forty-eighth year of his age.

Voltaire

73.

FERNANDO CORTES set sail from the island of Cuba in 1519, on a new expedition to the continent. This man, who was no more than a private lieutenant to the governor of a newly-discovered island, and had with him only six hundred men, eighteen horses, and a few field-pieces, set out to conquer the most powerful state of America. At first he was fortunate to meet with a Spaniard who, having been nine years a prisoner at Yucatan, on the road to Mexico, served him as an interpreter. An American lady, whom he called Doña Marina, became at once his mistress and chief counsellor, having learned Spanish enough to be an interpreter for him also. To complete his good fortune, he met with a volcano full of sulphur and saltpetre; which served him to replace the powder he spent in his engagements. He coasted all along the Gulf of Mexico, sometimes caressing the natives, and at others making war upon them. On his way he met with several well-governed towns, where the arts were held in estimation. The powerful republic of Tlaxcala, which flourished under an aristocratic government, opposed his further passage; but the sight of the horses, and the report of the cannon, soon put this ill-armed multitude to flight, and he made

peace with them on his own terms. Six thousand of these new allies
accompanied him from Tlaxcala on his journey to Mexico, which
empire he entered without resistance, though forbidden by the sovereign; who, nevertheless, had thirty vassal kings under his command,
each of whom could appear in the field at the head of a hundred thous-
and men, armed with those sharp stones which they used instead of
steel . . .

[By 1521] Cortes had . . . made himself absolute master of the city
of Mexico, and the whole empire was reduced to the Spanish domi-
nion, as were also Golden Castile, Darien, and all the neighboring
territories.

What now was the reward Cortes met with for such unheard-of services? The same as Columbus; he was persecuted, and by that very
bishop, Fonseca, who, after having been instrumental in sending home
the discoverer of America, loaded with chains, wanted now to treat its
conqueror in the same manner. In short, notwithstanding the titles
which his country bestowed upon him, at his return he was held but in
slight estimation. It was with difficulty that he could even obtain an
audience with Charles V. One day, he pushed through the crowd that
surrounded the emperor's coach, and got on the step of the door, when
Charles asked who that man was. 'It is he', answered Cortes, 'who has
given you more dominions than your ancestors left you towns.'

Voltaire

74.

The supreme weapon of the Spanish conquistadores *against the Indians of Mexico*
was the horse, which the Indians had never seen before, and at first believed to be
invested with supernatural powers in battle. This illusion was shattered, however,
when after a series of striking Spanish victories a Tlascalan force on the battlefield suc-
cessfully broke through to Cortes' horsemen.

A BODY of the Tlascalans, . . . acting in concert, assaulted a soldier
named Moran, one of the best riders in the troop. They succeeded in
dragging him from his horse, which they despatched with a thousand
blows. The Spaniards, on foot, made a desperate effort to rescue their
comrade from the hands of the enemy—and from the horrible doom of
the captive. A fierce struggle now began over the body of the prostrate
horse. Ten of the Spaniards were wounded, when they succeeded in
retrieving the unfortunate cavalier from his assailants, but in so disas-

trous a plight that he died on the following day. The horse was borne off in triumph by the Indians, and his mangled remains were sent, a strange trophy, to the different towns of Tlascala. The circumstance troubled the Spanish commander, as it divested the animal of the supernatural terrors with which the superstition of the natives had usually surrounded it. To prevent such a consequence, he had caused the two horses, killed on the preceding day, to be secretly buried on the spot.

William H. Prescott

75.

A tale from the military memoirs of Blaise de Monlue, of 'a young virgin of Siena' at the siege of 1555.

I HAD made a decree at the time when I was dictator, that no one upon pain of severe punishment should fail to go to The Guard in his turn. This young maid seeing a brother of hers who was concerned to be upon duty not able to go, she took his morian and put it upon her head, his breeches and a collar of buff and put them on, and with his halberd upon her shoulder in this equipage marched the guard, passing when the list was read by her brother's name, and stood sentinel in turn without being discovered till the morning that it was fair light day, when she was conducted home with great honour. In the afternoon Signor Cornelio showed her to me.

Blaise de Lasseran-Massencenere, Seigneur de Monlue

76.

An incident during the campaign in the Low Countries, 22 September 1586.

WHEN that unfortunate stand was to be made before Zutphen, to stop the issuing out of the Spanish Army from a streict; with what alacrity soever he [Sir Philip Sidney] went to actions of honor, yet remembring that upon just grounds the ancient Sages describe the worthiest persons to be ever best armed, he had compleatly put on his; but meeting the Marshall of the Camp lightly armed (whose honor in that art would not suffer this unenvious Themistocles to sleep) the unspotted emulation of his heart, to venture without any inequalitie, made him cast off his Cuisses; and so, by the secret influence of destinie, to disarm that part, where God (it seems) had resolved to strike him. Thus they go on, every man in the head of his own Troop; and the weather being misty, fell unawares upon the enemie, who had made a strong stand to receive them, near to the very walls of Zutphen; by reason of which accident their Troops fell, not only unexpectedly to be engaged within the levell of the great shot, that played from the Rampiers, but more fatally within shot of their Muskets, which were layd in ambush within their own trenches.

Now whether this were a desperate cure in our Leaders, for a desperate disease; or whether misprision, neglect, audacity, or what else induced it, it is no part of my office to determine, but onely to make the narration clear, and deliver rumor, as it passed then, without any stain, or enammel.

Howsoever, by this stand, an unfortunate hand out of those forespoken Trenches, brake the bone of Sir Philip's thigh with a Musketshot. The horse he rode upon, was rather furiously cholleric, than bravely proud, and so forced him to forsake the field, but not his back, as the noblest, and fittest biere to carry a Martiall Commander to his grave. In which sad progress, passing along by the rest of the Army, where his Uncle the Generall was, and being thirstie with excess of bleeding, he called for drink, which was presently brought him; but as he was putting the bottle to his mouth, he saw a poor Souldier carryed along, who had eaten his last at the same Feast, gastly casting up his eyes at the bottle. Which Sir Philip perceiving, took it from his head, before he drank, and delivered it to the poor man, with these words, 'Thy necessity is yet greater than mine.' And when he had pledged this poor souldier, he was presently carried to Arnheim.

Sir Fulke Greville

77.

In March 1590 Colonel Theodoric Schomberg was commanding a regiment of German mercenaries in the service of King Henry IV of France against the Spaniards.

THIS officer, for whose valour and abilities he [the King] had a great respect, came to him (pressed by the mutinous spirit of his men) the day before the battle of Ivry, to urge the payment of part of their arrears. Henry, irritated in the midst of his anxieties and arrangements, previous to a battle where the enemy's numbers were fully double the army he commanded, hastily asked him, 'Was that a time to come for pay, when he ought to be asking for his orders to prepare for battle?' Schomberg withdrew overwhelmed with vexation and distress at this unmerited treatment, for his only object had been, to secure the obedience of his unmanageable troops, until the battle should have taken place. Next day he appeared at the head of his Germans with a countenance of deep depression, which Henry observed, and immediately recollecting what had passed the previous evening, rode up to him with kindness and friendship in his looks, and said loud enough to be heard by all around, 'Monsieur Schomberg, I have offended you. This day may, perhaps, be the last of my life: God forbid that I should fall, under the impression that I had insulted the honour of a gentleman, without any offer for the reparation of such an injury! I am convinced both of your valour and your merit. I entreat you to pardon me.'—'It is true', answered the Colonel, 'that your Majesty wounded me lately, but today you kill me; for your conduct at this instant will force me to sacrifice my life in your service.' Before the end of the combat this brave man was slain, fighting by the side of the King.

Lord de Ros

78.

GUSTAVUS ADOLPHUS, King of Sweden, happening at a public review to have some dispute with Colonel Seaton, an officer in his service, gave him a blow, which the latter resented so highly, that when the field-day was over, he repaired to the King's apartment, and demanded his discharge, which his majesty signed, and the colonel withdrew, not a word being said on the subject by either party. Gustavus, however, having coolly considered the matter, and being informed that Seaton intended to set out the next morning for Denmark, he followed him, attended by an officer and two or three grooms. When his majesty came to the Danish frontier, he left all his attendants, except one, and overtaking Seaton on a large plain, he rode up to him, saying, 'Dismount, Sir; that you have been injured I acknowledge; I am, therefore, now come to give you the satisfaction of a gentleman, for being now out of my own dominions, Gustavus and you are equal. We have both, I see, pistols and swords; alight, sir, immediately, and the affair shall be decided.' Seaton recovering from his surprise, dismounted, as the king had already done, and falling on his knee, said,

'Sire, you have more than given me satisfaction, in condescending to
make me your equal. God forbid that my sword should do any mischief
to so brave and gracious a prince! Permit me to return to Stockholm;
and allow me the honour to live and die in your service.' The king
raised him from the ground, embraced him, and they returned in the
most amicable manner to Stockholm, to the astonishment of the whole
court.

Naval and Military Anecdotes

79.

THE deputies of a great metropolis in Germany, once offered the
great Turenne, one hundred thousand crowns not to pass with his
army through their city. 'Gentlemen,' said he, 'I can't in conscience
accept your money, as I had no intention to pass that way.'

The Percy Anecdotes

80.

*Albrecht von Wallenstein (1583–1634), the son of a petty Bohemian aristocrat,
became one of the most powerful princes in Europe during the Thirty Years War, serving the Emperor who was at last moved to have his over-mighty subject assassinated.
Wallenstein's craft and ruthlessness made him a legend in his own lifetime. A slight
sample is given here by Sydnam Poyntz, the English soldier of fortune who served for
some years in his army.*

BUT his [Wallenstein's] onely maister-piece was how to get in Don
Baltazar ye Spaniard, which hee tryed to doe very politickly, as you
shall heare. Taking occasion to discourse with Don Baltazar of
Honours the now Emp^r had bestowed on seuerall persons in this tyme
of warres, naming many that were not worthy of that honour they had:
at length said there was one who better deserved Honour then the best
of all and quoth hee whether it bee out of modestie, or humility or
pride never seeks after any. Baltazar wondering who that should bee,
Walleston said it was hymself. Baltazar said hee was contented. It was
enough for hym to doe well for it was his duty to his maister the Emp^r.
Quoth Walleston, I love you so well, as I will whilest I am in Office,
that you make vse of it, and you shall finde it: and all that I can doe for
you is that the Emp^r bestow some honour on you, and that I thinke hee

will doe at my request, and if it please you, quoth hee, to take my Letter with you and make a iourny to the Court, your labour will bee well payed. Don Baltazar modestly refused it, but must needs accept of his kind offer, the next day hee was to have Walleston his Letter and came for it, and because you shall know, quoth hee, what you carry, made his owne Secretary to read it: the effect of it was to desire his Ma^{ty} in lieu of Don Baltazars many services to make hym a Duke with wonderfull praises of his valour and Vertue &c. hee set his hand to it in his presence & sealed before them but it was so finely handled that Walleston popt an other Letter into Don Baltazar his hand of an other content: which was that Don Baltazar had bene earnest with hym to write in his behalf to his Ma^{ty} to bestow on hym the Honour of a Duke, for his faithfull service: that was all hee requested. Hee did confesse to his Ma^{ty} that hee did deserve it well but at this tyme hee besought his Ma^{ty} to hold his hands till these troublesome Warres were over, for quoth Walleston, I find by experience that after one hath gotten such honour on theyr backes, they grow troublesome to the Generall and will not bee ruled but ready to rise in rebellion against hym and hee could not keep them in aw as before, and that hee would bee pleased to pvt hym of to some other tyme with some good answeare or other. So Walleston delivered the Letter to the Don, with a Kisse in reverence of the Emp^r & the other receaved it with the like. Walleston desirous to heare of his successe at his leasurable returne, away went the Don with his Encomiendum verily expecting hee should bee a present Duke. And the Emp^r was willing enough to doe hym that honour & more for hee loved hym very well, & knew Don Baltazar loved hym as well; and that hee was a good souldier & had donne hym brave & faithfull service and a good and Vertuous man besides notwithstanding hee was and must bee ruled by his Generall especially thinges standing as they did. But welcomed Don Baltazar very kindly, and promised hym faithfully that if hee would but stay his leasure a little while, hee would finde out both honour & that which should support that honour besides and so the Emp^r meaned indeed. Don Baltazar with these kinde words from the Emp^r hymself went away very well satisfied and after comming to Walleston the first thing Walleston said to hym, I doe not doubt but I may give you the ioy of your new Honour hee had from the Emp^r; who answeared hym no: that the Emp^r was very busie, but that hee woud doe it an other tyme, wherein hee would load hym with honour & Revenews, with that Walleston gave a great stamp on the ground tearing his heire and swearing a great Othe Who would serve such a simple

Emperour that knew not to whome to bestow his honour, nor will not believe his Generall who is a continuall ey-witnesse in the field of souldiers merits or demerits, and you especially that have donne hym such honourable and faithfull service and not to gratifie you with so small a request, the dishonour hee hath donne to you in it is the more, because the whole Camp taketh notice of it, and will the more when they see & heare you returne without your desert and will despise you as a man of little merit hereafter, your owne souldiers will hardly obey you; and for my owne part I my self am deeply disgraced in it, for what will not others under mee [be] ready to contemne mee when they see mee of so little credit with the Emp^r, that I can not get honour to be bestowed on them that so well deserve it.

                                                            Sydnam Poyntz

81.

Poyntz's memoirs vividly reveal the chaos amid which the soldiers of Europe fought the Thirty Years War, with dramatic upturns and collapses of personal fortune, overnight transfers of loyalty from one army to another, and in Poyntz's case, even a period as a slave in the hands of the Turks. As he also shows, his prosperity rose and fell sharply according to the strength of the troop under his command, so that heavy losses in action were a personal disaster for a commander, as well as a military one.

. . . when I began first as many others did to follow after Mansfield like mad folkes wee knew not whither I came into Germany with other troopes of souldiers wee passed thorough many brave Princes Countries in all which wee had supply of Men and Money and where wee found such plenty of all things for backe and belly that heart could desire and had got pretty store of Crownes: but at the length wee had a Crosse of fortune, for Tilly met with us & stript us naked of all Canon, Amunition and whatsoever wee had, yea with the death of most but those that saved their lives by running away: yet at length our Army was encreased againe by those Protestant Princes thorough whose plentifull Countries wee had marched; that at that tyme when we met wth Bethlem Gabor wee were got to 30 thousand which also as I told you before came to nothing, and worse then nothing by the death of Mansfield and Weymar, and most of many brave souldiers fell into miserable captivity where wee were stript of all that wee lightly got in that long journy, but lost in an hower, and made slavish Slaves & nightly chayned by the feet to a great log after our sharpe dayes Labour, which

was so terrible to fellowes of brave spirits that they did strive to dy &
could not, and that which grieved mee as much as for my self was for a
brave young gentleman of a Duke of Barlamonts house in Italy, and
wee called hym Count Barlamont, who was beaten to death before our
faces, because his Spirit was so great as would not yield to bee a
drudge. But now to my self I saw there was no striving tooke upon mee
an humble spirit and fell to my drudgery hoping once for a light night
as they say and went merrily to my Worke and strove to get the
language and now & then some money by hooke or by crooke & hid it
in od corners: so after 2 or 3 yeares patience, opportunity fell that I got
away and some 40 myles but was brought backe with a vengeance and
had 300 blowes on my feet which cooled my running for one yeare. But
God at length did prosper my intentions, for I got a brave horse which
at length brought mee to the skirts of Christendome, but fortune threw
mee againe on my backe, met with theeves got all my little Mony and
horse and all: O how that went to my heart to part with my horse,
which had brought mee out of the Devills Mouth, and so neare Christendome, I meane Austria, where hee would have given mee a hundred
pound if some other had had hym, but no remedy. After all these
Crosses the Sunne began to shyne clearly upon mee as I have formerly
showed you how luckily I light upon a poore franciscan an Englishman by name A. More, and somewhat allyed by marriage to our name
in Sussex. Then I rise by fortunes from a Lieutenant to a Captn of a
troop of Horse in Saxons Armie, but beeing taken Prisoner by the
Imperialists I lost againe all that I had under the Saxon Duke. Thus
fortune tossed mee up and downe, but I sped better than I expected;
for I was taken Prisoner by Count Butler with whome after I got in
favour hee raysed mee extreamely: for by his favour hee got mee my
first Wife, a rich Merchants Daughter, who though wee lived not two
yeares together, shee dying in child-bed to my great grief, yet shee left
mee rich, and she was of an humble condition and very houswifly, wee
should have lived very happily togeather; and if shee had lived but halfe
a yeare longer I had come to greater Wealth: for within that tyme after
her death, her father & Mother, who lived in Aegre where I got my
wife, dyed, and left a World of Wealth which came to strangers, having
no child nor childs child; and not content with this the good Count
Butler got me an other Wife, rich in Land and mony, but of a higher
birth & spirit, and therefore would live at a higher rate than our
meanes would well afford, for no Lady in this Land wore better close
than she did, besides her Coach and 6 Coach-horses wch with

Attendants answearable to it would bee very expensive and had great
Kindred that lay vpon vs. But I beeing come to this height got to bee by
Count Butlers favour Sergeant Maior of a Troop of 200 horse but I
was to raise them at my owne charge, which was no small matter for
mee to doe, beeing so well underlayd and so well aforehand, for I had
then £3000 which I carried into the field with mee besides that I left at
home with my Wife, and besides that I had layd out about some land I
bought which lay nere my Wives Lande. And I made good use of my
place for I could and did send home often tymes Mony to my Wife,
who it seemes spent at home what I got abroad, but fortune turned
against mee againe for in that cruell bloody Battaille where in the King
of Sweveland was killed, my horses were all ether killed or ranne away.

    . . . presently that night the Army was comaunded to march away
without sound of Drum or Trumpet, and so wee marched 8 Miles that
night before wee refreshed ourselves againe: but the march was so
suddaine, that every one that had baggage, horse and Wagons were
glad to leave his baggage behinde hym, for our horses were all strayd
and run away beeing played upon continually by the Swevish Canon
though they stood a Mile of. For Walleston to make his Army seeme
bigger, had together all the Women, struggers and boys of the Camp
with horses and wagon-Jades to stand togeather to make as it were a
great Troop with sheets for their flags, who when they saw the Canon
shoot so fast upon them, run all away; though souldiers were sent to
keep them togeather, where I lost most of my wealth, and could bring
no more away then I and my 3 weary Officers could carry; and Walleston was in the same predicament hymself for hee was faine to leave all
his canon and baggage behinde.

    At the beginning great store of prisoners were taken on both sides, I
my self was taken prisoner three tymes but twice I was rescued by my
fellowes; the third tyme beeing taken hold of by my belt, having my
sword in my hand, I threw the belt over my Eares and rescued myself. I
lost three horses that day beeing shot under mee, and I hurt under my
right side and in my thigh, but I had horses without maisters enough to
choose and horse my self; all had pistols at their saddle bowe but shot
of and all that I could doe, was with my sword without a scabard, and a
daring Pistol but no powder nor shot: my last horse that was shot had
almost killed mee for beeing shot in the guts, as I thinke, hee mounted
on a suddaine such a height, yea I thinke on my conscience two yards,
and suddaine fell to the ground upon his bum, and with his suddaine
fall thrust my bum a foot into the ground and fell upon mee and there

lay groveling upon mee, that hee put mee out of my senses. I knew not how I was, but at length coming to myself, with much a doe got up, and found 2 or 3 brave horses stand fighting togeather. I tooke the best, but when I came to mount hym I was so bruised & with the weight of my heavy Armour that I could not get my leg into the saddle that my horse run away with mee in that posture half in my saddle and half out, and so run with mee till he met with Picolominie comming running with a Troop of horse und my horse run among them that I scaped very narrowly of beeing throwne cleane of but at length got into my saddle full of paine and could hardly sit, and followed the Troop having nothing but a daring Pistol and a naked Sword.

No more Prisoners taken that day, every one strove to save hymself. Here fortune left mee almost bare againe, and well she left mee at so bloody a battaile with life. But this losse I did prittily well recover that Winter beeing billeted in Austria among rich Boores, by hooke or by crooke, I got mee strong in horse and men as I thought any had; but it fell out so that with continuall marching this spring from one side of Germany to the other, to help the miserly Duke of Saxon against the Sweve: and from thence backe againe to Loraine from whence wee went at first to Gallas who lay there entrenched with the Army, and the famine wee endured so long there, my Troop grew so short & poore & the Country growne so poore that nothing was to bee got amongst the Boores upon whome alwais lay the Comaunders hopes whilest they were in good plight, for wee might bee our own carvers, for we had no other pay: these failing, my thoughts were in despaire of ever raising my companie againe: And I had almost £2000 in my purse with mee at that tyme, yet I considered it would goe hard to part with my ready Money, and nothing to bee got, and I knew not how things stood at home, and to goe empty handed home would not doe so well, considering also I had left a costly Wife at home: and having bene almost a whole yeare in Warres, I set up my rest of going home, and mee thought a private life after these wandring wearisome marches did relish sweetly in my thoughts and so after a long march I came nere home, where I heare the true tryall of fortunes mutability, which was that my Wife was killed & my child, my house burned and my goods all pillaged: My Tenants and Neighbours all served in the same sauce, the whole Village beeing burned; nether horse, Cowe, sheep nor Corne left to feed a Mouse. This when I came home I found too true some poore people got into the ruines living with roots: this went nere mee. This was donne by a party of french that came out of Italy going

homewards: here was little comfort for mee to stay here: then I presently determined to go see my deare friend Count Buttler Governour
of that Country, . . . but my hopes were turned upside downe, for it
was my good hap to see hym, but he was dying, which strucke more
nere to mee, or as much as my owne losse, but there was no remedy,
but yet it somewhat revived hym and what show of love a dying man
can expresse, hee did grasping my hand with all his strength and calling for his Will gave mee a thousand pound therein and not long after
having receaved his Viaticum with a great sylver Crucifix in his hand
and in my Armes yielded up the Ghost. I had thought my heart would
have burst with grief, but could get out no teares out of my stony heart:
but to my owne heart I cryed Spes et Fortuna Valete, my hopes and
fortune now farewell, who if hee had lived, I had had fortune almost at
my becke; but hee beeing dead about the £1000 hee gave mee his Wife
beeing the Executrix and not so friendly to mee as she might have
bene, and her husbands love to me required, kept mee so of with
delayes, and at last I was forced to goe to Ratisbone where the Emp^r
was expected about it, but never the nearer, and there also I was as
nere but the charge in expecting was so great as the debt it self would
not countervaile it and finding there an English Embassadour made as
much use of his favour as I could in my passe hither, away I went for
England loosing my frend and his guift.

Sydnam Poyntz

82.

A Parliamentary soldier writes from Essex's army.

Aylesbury, August 1642

ON Monday August 8th we marched to Acton; but being the sixth
company, we were belated, and many of our soldiers were constrained
to lodge in beds whose feathers were above a yard long. Tuesday, early
in the morning, several of our soldiers inhabiting the out parts of the
town sallied out unto the house of one Penruddock, a papist, and being
basely affronted by him and his dog, entered his house and pillaged
him to the purpose. This day, also the soldiers got into the church,
defaced the ancient and sacred glazed pictures, and burned the holy
rails.

Wednesday: Mr Love gave us a famous sermon this day—also the soldiers brought the holy rails from Chiswick, and burned them in our town. At Chiswick they also intended to pillage the Lord Portland's house also also Dr Duck's, but by our commanders they were prevented. This day our soldiers generally manifested their dislike of our Lieutenant-Colonel, who is a Goddam blade, and will doubtless hatch in hell, and we all desire that either the Parliament would depose him, or the devil fetch him away quick. This day, towards even, our regiment marched to Uxbridge, but I was left behind, to bring up thirty men with ammunition the next morning.

Thursday: I marched towards Uxbridge; and at Hillingdon, one mile from Uxbridge, the rails being gone, we got the surplices, to make us handkerchieves, and one of our soldiers wore it to Uxbridge. This day the rails of Uxbridge, formerly removed was, with the service book, burned. This evening Mr Harding gave us a worthy sermon.

Saturday morning . . . We came to Wendover, where we refreshed ourselves, burnt the rails and accidentally, one of the Captain Francis's men, forgetting he was charged with a bullet, shot a maid through the head, and she immediately died.

Sabbath day, August 15th. In this town, a pulpit was built in the market place, where we heard two worthy sermons. This evening our ungodly Lieutenant-Colonel, upon an ungrounded whimsy, commanded two of our captains, with their companies, to march out the town, but they went not. I humbly entreat you, as you desire the success of our just and honourable cause, that you would endeavour to root out our Lieutenant-Colonel for if we march further under his command, we fear, upon sufficient grounds, we are all but dead men.

Sergeant Nehemiah Wharton

83.

On the field of Edgehill, Buckinghamshire, 23 October 1642: as the Royalists marched south from Nottingham, they fought the first significant battle of the English Civil War against the Parliamentary army sent from London to meet them.

THE Royalists were in the stronger position but for the last two days they had come through hostile country where food and shelter were hard to find. The troops were hungry and the tempers of the leaders were at breaking point. Lindsey, who had advised marching through the enclosed land in the valleys among the villages, in the interests of the infantry, had been overruled by Rupert, and the advance had been made through the open country on the higher ground where the cavalry could move—and see—best. In the swift seizure of Edgehill and the drawing up of the battle Rupert's advice had again prevailed. Lindsey refused to allow him to direct the ordering of the infantry on the field. Rupert, with more military judgment than social tact, protested that the battle could not be planned piecemeal and further insisted that pikemen and musketeers be interspersed with each other in the modern Swedish fashion. Lindsey's sulks flared into rage. In front of the troops, he flung his baton to the ground and declared that if he 'was not fit to be a general he would die a colonel at the head of his regiment'. In the embarrassing circumstances, his place as commander of the foot was taken by Sir Jacob Astley, a mature and competent soldier who had once been Prince Rupert's tutor and understood how to get on with him.

The quarrels concluded, they completed the ordering of the field. Rupert with four cavalry regiments and the King's lifeguards, was on the right wing, Wilmot with five regiments of horse on the left, the infantry in the centre. The King's standard, borne by Sir Edmund Verney, floated at the head of his red-coated foot guard. His lifeguard of cavalry, under his cousin and Richmond's brother, Lord Bernard Stuart, had asked and been given permission to serve with Prince Rupert.

The King, in a black velvet coat lined with ermine, now rode along the lines with words of encouragement. He had already briefly addressed the principal officers in his tent: 'Your King is both your cause, your quarrel and your captain,' he said, 'come life or death, your King will bear you company, and ever keep this field, this place, and this day's service in his grateful remembrance.'

Rupert also addressed his troops, not on politics, but on tactics. He knew that his cavalry, short of firearms and scantily trained, must achieve the utmost by the impact of their first charge, and consequently instructed them to ride in the closest possible formation, and to hold their fire until they had closed with the enemy.

It was afternoon before both armies were in position and Essex, hoping to gain the initiative and cause some preliminary disorder in the King's lines, opened fire with his cannon. At this the King with his own hand ignited the charge and the Royalist guns gave answer. Sir Jacob Astley uttered a brief prayer: 'O Lord, thou knowest how busy I must be this day. If I forget thee, do not thou forget me.' Rupert waited no longer, and suddenly Essex saw the Royalist horse on his left sweep down the slope and hurl themselves upon his wavering lines. Rupert's men came in at an oblique angle, riding down not only the Parliamentary cavalry on that wing, but some of the infantry nearest them. The opposing forces made no stand but fled 'with the enemy's horse at their heels and amongst them, pell mell'. In their flight they battered their way through their own reserve drawn up in the rear, and although Denzil Holles gallantly 'planted himself just in the way' and tried to rally the fugitives he brought very few of them to a stand. The rest shamefully scattered with Rupert's men hallooing after them. Some stragglers made a wide cross country circuit and carried the news of Parliament's defeat down the London road as far as Uxbridge. Most fled to Kineton and were beaten through it by the Royalists. A mile beyond the town John Hampden and his regiment, marching up with the rest of the delayed artillery, met the dismayed rout, and by expeditiously planting a battery across the road checked or at least deflected the pursuers.

All this time on the slope of Edgehill the King's forces were faring badly. Contrary to instructions the very small reserve of cavalry on the right wing, which should have stayed to give cover to the infantry, had followed Prince Rupert's charge and joined in the pursuit, leaving the centre, with the infantry, the guns, and the King's standard, bare of defence on one side. Before the Prince and his few experienced officers could extricate their men from the enjoyable chase and bring them back to the field, the infantry had been very roughly handled.

The resolution of Essex and the skill of the old Scottish veteran, Sir William Balfour, had prevented the total defeat of Parliament. Wilmot, on the Royalist left, had charged when Rupert did, and had driven the greater part of the opposing cavalry from the field, but the wily Balfour, with a party of Parliamentary horse, drew out of the range of Wilmot's onslaught, and while the Royalists pursued the fliers, he made his way up the hill under cover of the hedges until, with a sudden charge, he fell upon the King's guns and the infantry in the centre. At the silencing of the Royalist guns, the Parliamentary infantry took heart and closed with the now defenceless and disordered Royalist centre, who manfully stood their ground. Lindsey, badly wounded, was taken prisoner; the King's standard bearer Sir Edmund Verney was killed and the standard taken. The Prince of Wales, to his joy, found himself almost at grips with the rebels. 'I fear them not,' he shouted, and cocked his pistol, but his startled attendants hustled him to the rear.

Some of Rupert's cavalry were now returning, by scattered parties.

Captain John Smith rounded up a couple of hundred men and fell in on the Parliamentary flank, diverting them from their prey. Sometime in this hot action he retrieved the King's standard in a hand-to-hand struggle with several of the enemy. Exhaustion, and the harassing onslaught of the returning Royalists, forced the Parliamentary infantry to give ground and fall back as the early darkness fell.

Both armies camped in the field, neither being willing to allow the other to claim sole possession. Through a night of bitter frost they strove, vainly, to keep warm, and on the next day Essex, while formally announcing his victory, drew off towards Warwick. His cavalry was in total disorder; he had lost about fifty colours and much baggage and equipment. On the retreat to Warwick, Rupert's cavalry harassed him all the way, forced him to abandon some of his cannon and blew up four of his ammunition waggons. The Royalists were now between him and London with an almost clear road, and he wrote urgently to Westminster to call out all available troops to defend the capital. But his claim of a 'victory' had this much truth: he had, with Balfour's invaluable help and by his own calm and tenacity, retrieved his army from what might easily have been irremediable disaster.

*

The Royalist prisoners in the Parliamentary camp were among the few who at first truly believed in the Parliamentary claim of victory. Lord Lindsey, angry and in pain, declared that he would never fight in a field with boys again; he never did, for he died that day. Those who had watched Prince Rupert's charge from the other side cursed this boy of twenty-three for a different reason. He was a soldier to be reckoned with, and his men had a spirit which needed only a little more discipline to make them irresistible. Oliver Cromwell in later years recorded a conversation that he had with his cousin Hampden about this time: 'Your troopers said I, are most of them old decaying servingmen and tapsters, and such kind of fellows. Their troopers are gentlemen's sons, younger sons and persons of quality . . . You must get men of a spirit that is likely to go on as far as gentlemen will go, or else I am sure you will be beaten still.' Cromwell was not altogether fair to the quality of the Parliamentary cavalry or the sources whence it came, but he saw that the Cavaliers, at Powicke and again at Edgehill, had established a superiority that it would be very hard to challenge.

C. V. Wedgwood

84.

One of the most moving communications in the history of warfare: in June 1643 Sir
Ralph Hopton, commanding for the King in the West, wrote a letter to his old friend
Sir William Waller, commanding for Parliament, to suggest a meeting at which the
Royalist plainly hoped to gain a change of heart in the rebel. This was Waller's reply.

To my Noble friend Sr Ralphe Hopton at Wells.
Sr

The experience I have had of your Worth, and the happinesse I have
enjoyed in your friendship are woundinge considerations when I look
upon this present distance betweene us. Certainly my affections to you
are so unchangeable, that hostility itselfe cannot violate my friendship
to your person, but I must be true to the cause wherein I serve: The
ould limitation *usque ad aras* holds still, and where my conscience is
interested, all other obligations are swallowed up. I should most gladly
waite on you according to your desire, but that I looke upon you as you
are ingaged in that partie, beyond a possibility of retraite and conse-
quentlie uncapable of being wrought upon by any persuasion. And I
know the conference could never be so close betweene us, but that it
would take wind and receive a construction to my dishonour; That
great God, which is the searcher of my heart, knows with what a sad
sence I goe upon this service, and with what a perfect hatred I detest
this warr without an Enemie, but I looke upon it as *Opus Domini*, which
is enough to silence all passion in mee. The God of peace in his good
time send us peace, and in the meane time fitt us to receive it: Wee are
both upon the stage and must act those parts assigned us in this Tragedy: Lett us do it in a way of honour, and without personall animosit-
ies, whatever the issue be, I shall never willingly relinquish the dear
title of

Your most affectionate friend
and faithful servant,
Wm. Waller.

Bath, 16 June 1643

85.

Sir Arthur Hazelrigg's Parliamentary horse became known as 'Hazelrigg's Lobsters' for the formidable headpieces in which they encased themselves in battle. The Royalists won the battle of Roundaway Down on 13 July 1643, but the best efforts of the cavalier officer Richard Atkyns failed to defeat Hazelrigg.

'Twas my fortune in a direct line to charge their general of horse; he discharged his carbine first, and afterwards one of his pistols, before I came up to him; and missed with both; I then immediately struck into him and touched him before I discharged mine, and I am sure I hit him for he staggered and presently wheeled off from his party. Follow him I did and discharged the other pistol at him and I'm sure I hit his head for I touched it before I gave fire and it amazed him at that present but he was too well armed all over for a pistol bullet to do him any hurt, having a coat of mail over his arms and a headpiece musket proof.

I came up to him again and having a very swift horse stuck by him for a good while and tried him from the head to the saddle and could not penetrate him or do him any hurt; but in this attempt he cut my horse's nose that you might put your finger in the wound and gave me such a blow on the inside of my arms amongst the veins that I could hardly hold my sword: he went on as before and I slackened my pace again, and found my horse drop blood, but not so bold as before.'

Atkyns stuck to his task and now tried to pull Hazelrigg off his horse. Hazelrigg slashed at Atkyns's horse, cutting its cheek and half the headstall from the bridle. Reluctantly Atkyns decided that his only course was to kill Hazelrigg's horse. He stabbed at it with his sword. As Hazelrigg's horse began to stumble Atkyns aimed a further blow at his opponent and managed to prick him behind his helmet. Atkyns was then joined by two other cavaliers and thereupon demanded Hazelrigg's surrender. Hazelrigg had no option but was reluctant to give up his sword. Just as he had done so, a troop of Roundhead cavalry saw what was happening and charged up. Hazelrigg was rescued and in the process Atkyns was wounded in the shoulder by a pistol shot.[1]

Philip Warner

---

[1] [This was] 'an exploit which later caused the King to say, with one of his rare jests, that had Sir Arthur "been victualled as well as fortified he might have endured a siege".'
C. V. Wedgwood, *The King's War*

86.

Lord Falkland, who died at Newbury on 20 September 1643, was widely believed to have deliberately sacrificed himself in the face of an unhappy love life and the misery of civil war. John Aubrey took a somewhat more cynical view.

IN the civil wars, he adhered to King Charles I, who after Edgehill fight made him Principal Secretary of State (with Sir Edward Nicholas) which he discharged with a great deal of wit and prudence, only his advice was very unlucky to his majesty, in persuading him (after the victory at Roundway Down and the taking of Bristol) to sit down before Gloucester, which was so bravely defended by that incomparably vigilant governor Colonel Massey, and the diligent and careful soldiers and citizens (men and women) that it so broke and weakened the king's army that 'twas the primary cause of his ruin: *vide* Mr Hobbes. After this, all the king's matters went worse and worse. Anno domini 1643 at the fight at Newbury, my Lord Falkland being there, and having nothing to do decided to charge; as the two armies were engaging, rode in like a madman (as he was) between them, and was (as he needs must be) shot. Some that were your superfine discoursing politicians and fine gentlemen, would needs have the reason of this mad action of throwing away his life so, to be his discontent for the unfortunate advice given to his master as aforesaid; but, I have been well informed, by those that best knew him, and knew the intrigues behind the curtain (as they say) that it was the grief of the death of Mrs Moray, a handsome lady at Court, who was his mistress, and whom he loved above all creatures, was the true cause of his being so madly guilty of his own death, as aforementioned: *there is no great wit without an admixture of madness.*

The next day, when they went to bury the dead, they could not find his lordship's body, it was stripped, trod upon and mangled; so there was one that had waited on him in his chamber would undertake to know it from all other bodies, by a certain mole his lordship had on his neck, and by that mark did find it. He lies interred at Great Tew aforesaid, but, I think, yet without any monument.

John Aubrey

87.

From the order book of the Staffordshire County Committee of the Parliamentary Army.

December 27th 1643:

That whosoever shall committ Fornication, or frequent companie of light women, whether officer or souldier, shall be forthwith casheered and the woman carted.

March 18th, 1644:

Ordered, that the Gunner which did committ fornication, shall bee set upon the greate gun, with a marke uppon his backe through the Garrison and then disgracefully expulsed.

Mark Bence-Jones

88.

Prince Rupert of the Rhine, ablest of the King's commanders, ranked foremost in the demonology of his enemies.

HIS very name struck terror in Puritan hearts. All kinds of legends grew up about him, and were broadcast by the Roundhead pamphleteers. He was said to have observed the strength of Essex's army by disguising himself as an apple vendor and peddling his fruit among the soldiers. Two Roundhead merchants who were brought before him at Henley and found him, for some reason, in bed with his clothes on, were quick to report that he had vowed never 'to undress or shift himself until he had reseated King Charles at Whitehall'. He was invested with diabolical powers, and his white dog, Boy, was seen as his familiar spirit. The tales told about Boy surpassed those told about his master. He could prophesy, he could make himself invisible, he was endowed with the gift of languages. 'He is weapon-proof himself, and probably hath made his master so too . . . they lie perpetually in one bed, sometimes the Prince upon the Dog, and sometimes the Dog upon the Prince; and what this may in time produce, none but the close committee can tell.' . . .

[Then, at Marston Moor on 2 July 1644] in an hour's fighting on that damp July evening he . . . lost both his army and his reputation. And as though that were not enough, he also lost his beloved dog, Boy, who had been with him when he was eating supper and had followed him as he galloped into the fray. His carcase was found next morning among the dead. The Roundheads rejoiced, convinced that without his familiar spirit the Bloody Prince could no longer harm them. And indeed, after Marston Moor, Rupert's luck did not return.

Mark Bence-Jones

89.

Of all the sieges of history, that of the Marquis of Winchester's Basing House, from the early spring of 1644 until October 1645, stands among the most heroic and romantic.

BASING 'was the largest of any subject's house in England, yea, larger than most (eagles have not the biggest nests of all birds) of the King's palaces. The motto "Love Loyaltie" was often written in every window thereof, and was well practised in it, when, for resistance on that account, it was lately levelled to the ground' [wrote Dr Thomas Fuller, once its chaplain]. Their enemies styled the Basing garrison 'foxes and wolves', but they showed in many a daring foray that they could bite as well as bark.

A plot was . . . formed by some disheartened malcontents within the walls to surrender the house to Sir William Waller, with whom a correspondence was carried on by 'the Lord Edward Pawlet, brother to the Marquis of Winchester, and then with him as unsuspected as a brother ought to be'. The plot was discovered through the unexpected desertion to the King of Sir Richard Granville, who was ever after called by his old comrades 'Skellum' or 'Rogue'; and the conspirators were all executed, with the exception of Lord Edward, who was forced to act as hangman at all future garrison executions.

On June 11th, 1644, the siege of Basing House began in earnest. Colonel Norton, aided by Colonel Onslow and a Surrey contingent, showed himself a daring and resolute foe, and was reinforced by Colonel Herbert Morley with five hundred foot from Farnham. He blockaded the house with his cavalry, occupied Basing village, and cut off supplies. On June 14th there was a smart skirmish near The Vine, and on the same day it was reported in London that the garrison was already suffering severely, Sir William Waller having burnt both their mills. Salt and other necessaries were also lacking. On June 18th—a day to be hereafter memorable for fighting—a jet of flame at midnight made the old church tower stand out in bold relief. Half Basing was in a blaze, and it seemed as if a fierce sortie made from the house would raise the siege. But it was not to be. For eighteen weeks the struggle went on. Sorties, assaults, mines, desertions, famines, and feasting came in quick succession. The story of this period alone would fill a volume. Basing House began to be styled 'Basting House' by rejoicing Cavaliers. The besiegers laboured, like Nehemiah's workmen, with a sword in one hand and a tool in the other, and on June 24th 'three of ours runne to them'. The gallows was always ready for would-be deserters. A heavy fire of shells, some eighty pounds in weight, which the garrison styled 'baubles', and of cannon shot was kept up, and 'they did shoot the Marquisse himselfe through his clothes'. Owing to a lack of salt, on July 24th, 'stinking beef was thrown over Basing walls'. In vain did Colonel Morley summon the Marquis to surrender, in spite of disease making havoc in the ranks of the defenders. Several dashing sorties were made, and once or twice the besiegers were driven off as far as Basingstoke.

In the second week in September, Colonel Sir Henry Gage, a gallant Roman Catholic soldier, led a relieving force from Oxford, and, after a fiercely-contested action on Chinham Down, against desperate odds, with sorely wearied troops, and shrouded in blinding fog, relieved the garrison in masterly fashion. The wounded Roundheads 'were next day sent forth unto the care of their own chirurgeons, and two that ran from us had execution'. 'That lovers met that day, and blushed and kissed; and old grey-bearded friends embraced each other, and, aye marry, pledged each other, too; that good Catholic comrades exchanged prayers at Basing altar; that brave fathers kissed the wives and children they had left shut up in brave old "Loyalty", needs no telling. But not alone in kissing and quaffing did Gage and his troops spend those two merry days.'

On September 14th the Cavaliers were celebrating their relief, 'drinking in the town, and in no good order'. Colonel Norton made an unexpected attack, and 'one hour's very sharp fight followed'. Basing Church was taken and retaken, as, indeed, it was several times during the siege, though, strangely enough, the Virgin and Child on the west front still remained unharmed.

The assailants were at length repulsed with heavy loss, but in the struggle the wise and learned Lieutenant-Colonel Johnson, doctor and botanist, was mortally wounded. Ten days later there was another fierce fight. The stern besiegers again closed tenaciously around Basing, and things went on much as before, the gallant little garrison being in vain summoned to surrender. In October, 1644, the King himself was in the neighbourhood, returning from his western campaign to Oxford, as were also Cromwell and the Earl of Manchester, who were then not on the best of terms. Manchester intended the engagement which was afterwards the second Battle of Newbury to have been fought at Basing, and even marked out the positions which his regiments were to occupy.

Famine was now pressing the garrison hard, and surrender seemed imminent. On November 28th it was said in London that 'Basing garrison had neither shoes nor stockings, drank water, and looked all as if they had been rather the prisoners of the grave than the keepers of a castle.' The diary of the siege closes with these noble words:

Let no man, therefore, think himself an instrument, only in giving thanks that God had made him so, for here was evidently seen 'He chose the weak to confound the strong.' *Non nobis Domine.* 'Not unto us, not unto us, O Lord, but to Thine own Name be all glory for ever. Amen!'

For some months Basing was left in peace, and many a successful foray and capture of road waggons took place, bold riders scouring the country as far as Hindhead. But unfortunately religious dissensions, which have ruined many noble causes, broke out. On May Day, 1645, there was a sorry sight. All the defenders who were not Roman Catholics marched out of Loyalty House some five hundred strong. They were refused admission to Donnington Castle by stout-hearted Sir John Boys, who expected to be besieged, but was unable to feed so large a contingent. After a running fight with Colonel Butler's Horse, they succeeded in joining the army of the dissolute Lord Goring, at Lambourne in Berkshire.

At the end of August, the Parliament sent Colonel Dalbier, a Dutchman, from whom it is said that Cromwell learned the mechanical part of soldiering, to reduce Basing at all costs. 'Mercurius Britannicus' said that the Marquis of Winchester spent his time in bed at the bottom of a cellar, 'out of reach of gunshot, for, you know, generals and governors should not be too venturous'. Dalbier occupied Basing village, and tried in vain to take the house by means of mines. Shells, known as 'granado shells', proved more effective. One mortar, which was sent direct from London—the bridges being strengthened so that it might cross them—fired shells of sixty-three pounds weight and eighteen inches in diameter. Ammunition was sent from Windsor Castle, then a Parliamentarian arsenal. 'A compounded stifling smoke', emitted by damp straw, brimstone, arsenic, and other ingredients, made the lives of the besiegers a misery. On Sunday, September 21st, 1645, the Rev. William Beech, a Wykehamist, gave the besiegers a remarkable sermon, which occupies, in small type, thirty-two small quarto pages. It was entitled 'More Sulphur for Basing', and is a marvellous specimen of the sermon militant. On the following day, Dalbier's guns brought down 'the great tower in the old house'. Deserters and a released prisoner said that 'in the top of this tower was hid a bushel of Scots twopences, which flew about their ears'. Shot and shell now poured in thick and fast, and when on October 8th Lieutenant-General Cromwell, at the head of a brigade detached from General Fairfax's new model army, arrived from recently-captured Winchester, the fate of the fortress was sealed. The besiegers were seven thousand in number, whilst the walls, which needed from eight hundred to a thousand men to hold them, sheltered but three hundred, many of whom were but eighteen and some scarcely twelve years of age, including also the priests and the wounded. Only its natural strength saved the fortress so long. There was no chance of relief.

On October 13th the besieged made their last sortie, and, during a fog, captured Colonel Robert Hammond and Colonel King, the former of whom was afterwards the King's gaoler at Carisbrook Castle. They received fair treatment, and it was alleged that they were taken by previous arrangement, so that Colonel Hammond might save the life of the Marquis during the final assault. At five o'clock in the morning of October 14th the attack began, and the invincible Ironsides formed up in column. The garrison was utterly worn out, but it is said that some of them were surprised as they were playing cards. 'Clubs are trumps, as when Basing House was taken', is a well-known Hampshire phrase. Rush of pike and pistol shot put a speedy end alike to game and players. Four cannon shots boomed out, and, by a breach which is still plainly visible, the storming party entered the New House, and then made their way inch by inch over the huge mounds faced with brickwork into the Old House. In spite of the black flags of defiance which they hung out, and of the heroism of those who 'fought it out at sword's point', superior numbers prevailed. When opposition ceased, plundering began. But in the midst of the pillage, the dread cry of 'Fire' was raised, for a fireball had been left to smoulder unheeded. Ere long, Basing House was but a pile of smoking ruins. Many of the garrison were suffocated or burned to death in the cellars and vaults in which they had taken refuge, and which have been recently opened out by Lord Bolton. Hugh Peters, 'the ecclesiastical newsmonger', heard them crying in vain for help. 'There were four more Roman Catholic priests beside, who were plundered of their vestments, and themselves reserved for the gallows.' The prisoners were two hundred in number, including the stout old Marquis, who, after being confined with Sir Robert Peake for a day or two at the Bell Inn at Basingstoke, was sent up to London, and committed to the Tower. He was afterwards allowed to retire to France. William Faithorne and Wenceslaus Hollar were also taken. Inigo Jones, the celebrated architect, who is said to have designed the west door of Basing Church, 'was carried away in a blanket, having lost his clothes', doubtless borrowed by some trooper. Seventy-four men were killed, but only one woman, the daughter of Dr Griffith, of St Mary Magdalen, Old Fish Street, 'a gallant gentlewoman, whom the enemy shamefully left naked'. We are told by 'Mercurius Veridicus' of 'the ladies' wardrobe, which furnished many of the soldiers' wives with gowns and petticoats'. The ladies themselves were 'entertained somewhat coarsely, yet they left them with some clothes upon them'. A hundred gentlewomen's rich gowns and petticoats were among the spoil, which was reckoned to be worth £200,000, and was styled by Cromwell 'a good encouragement'. The victors chaffered with the dealers, who had hired all the available horses between Basing and London, lowering their prices as the hour for marching drew nigh. At dawn on October 15th, 1645, Cromwell's trumpets sounded 'to horse', and the long column of the Ironsides marched away from smoke-blackened, ruined Basing, to reduce Longford House, near Salisbury, and the House of Commons ordered that all and sundry might take brick or stone at will from the ruins. Basing House soon became the picturesque ruin which it has ever since remained.

G. N. Godwin

90.

AFTER the battle of Marston Moor [2 July 1644], Cromwell, returning from the pursuit of a party of the royalists, purposed to stop at Ripley, the seat of Sir William Ingleby; and having an officer in his troop, a relation of Sir William's, he sent him to announce his arrival. Having sent in his name, and obtained an audience, he was answered by the lady that no such person should be admitted there; adding, that she had force sufficient to defend herself and that house against all rebels. The officer, on his part, represented the extreme folly of making any resistance; and that the safest way would be to admit the general peaceably. After much persuasion, the lady took the advice of her kinsman, and received Cromwell at the gate of the lodge, with a pair of pistols stuck in her apron-strings; and having told him she expected that neither he nor his soldiers would behave improperly, led the way to the hall, where, sitting on a sofa, jealous of his intentions, she passed the whole night. At his departure in the morning, the lady observed, It was well he had behaved in so peaceable manner; for that, had it been otherwise, he should not have left that house alive.

Naval and Military Anecdotes

91.

The most romantic campaign of the Civil War was that of James Graham, Marquis of Montrose, who rode north with only two followers after the Royalist defeat at Marston Moor, to raise Scotland for the King. In the autumn of 1644, with a wild little Highland army, he won a series of extraordinary victories until, with the coming of winter, his enemies assumed that campaigning was ended until the snows melted. Instead, Montrose led his men across the mountains from Blair Atholl to Inverary in an epic march which inflicted a devastating surprise upon the Marquis of Argyll and his Campbells. Then Montrose turned north, and was deep in the mountains when he learned that a much superior force under Argyll was in close pursuit. On 1 February 1645, the Covenanters pitched camp at Inverlochy, just north of the modern town of Fort William.

IT is said that it was Ian Lom Macdonald, the bard of Keppoch himself, who walked to tell Montrose at Kilcummin the news of the Campbell army at his back. Montrose at first simply did not believe him. He had heard nothing to suggest that any Campbell force was anywhere within days of him. His own army had dwindled to barely 1500 men. All the others, the Atholl men and most of the Clanranald amongst them, had retired home with their plunder. He knew that there were at least 5000 levies under Seaforth at Inverness. He had few doubts of his ability to defeat them. His concern was that whether he did so or not, after fighting one major battle he would be in no condition instantly to turn and grapple the Campbells in another. . . .

Montrose questioned Ian Lom Macdonald with deadly patience, for the fortunes of the King's cause in Scotland hung upon his answers. He asked him about the paths over the hills and the state of the drifts on the higher ground, about the strength of the Campbells and the slightest clues as to their intentions. If Macdonald lied, said the Lord Marquis coldly, he would hang for it. Stubbornly the poet insisted that he told the truth. The critical moment had come. Montrose ordered his officers to rouse the army and prepare to march against the Campbells.

'I was willing to let the world see that Argyll was not the man his Highlanders believed him to be,' he wrote cheerfully to the King in his later dispatch, 'and that it was possible to beat him in his own Highlands.'

Montrose reckoned that, left to his own devices, Argyll would dog his footsteps until he was entangled with Seaforth, and then fall upon him from the rear. Such a strategy suited perfectly the Campbell's temperament. It was essential that Montrose destroy his southern, most dangerous enemy, before moving on at his leisure to deal with the vacillating Seaforth. His first move was to plant strong pickets along the main track southwards through the Great Glen, to prevent Campbell scouts moving forward or informers going back to report that the royalist army was gone from Kilcummin. Then he led his men from their billets to begin one of the greatest flank marches in the annals of warfare.

The weather was worse than on the hardest stages of the descent on Inverary. The army must move fast to have any hope of achieving vital surprise. Montrose had chosen once again to attempt the impossible in order to confound his opponent. Instead of approaching Argyll down the passes of the Great Glen like any lesser mortal, he planned to take to the mountains and march parallel with the main road southwestwards, hidden by the intervening range of hills. The going, naturally, would be a thousand times more difficult. The snow-drifts lay virgin upon the hillsides. The very deer floundered clumsily in their midst. The steep faces were untrodden even by cowherds and deer hunters since winter began. The cold was appalling. Even if somehow Montrose could lead his army to confront Argyll without benefit of maps or compasses through the wilderness, his exhausted men must then do battle against odds of two to one. . . .

Up the valley of the Tarff they laboured, high into the hills towards the fierce summit of Carn Dearg. That first day of the march, Friday, January 31st, they had well over two thousand feet to climb before they were over the shoulder of Carn Dearg and could begin the descent into Glen Roy. Once over the watershed, somewhere high in the pass they may have rested for a few hours on the first night. But they had little enough time to spare, and to many of them it must have seemed worse to lie endlessly shivering in their plaids than to stagger on through the snow. Clumsily improvised deerskin sandals and ragged clothes worn to shreds by weeks of exposure under intolerable conditions offered little protection against the freezing January night. For those who were thirsty there was only the shocking chill of the burn water. If some of the men managed to bring down a deer, they ate their chunks of bloody flesh unsalted. They had no bread and only a little oatmeal. . . .

Somewhere on these last stages of the march, Montrose's vanguard suddenly found themselves face to face with a small party of Campbells. There was a startled, brutal little struggle in which most of the Campbells were cut down. But a few escaped. Away they fled, down the hill to report to Argyll's leaguer at Inverlochy that an enemy was afoot, close at hand. Around the friendly Campbell camp fires on the loch shore, it was unthinkable that Montrose and his army were anywhere nearby. They were known to be thirty miles further north at Kilcummin. It was obvious that this must be some clan raiding party on the loose, perhaps skirmishers sent by Montrose to harass the advancing Campbells. Auchinbreck was a cautious man, so he strengthened his pickets and pushed out patrols to probe the hills, but he left the bulk of his army to its food and sleep.

Montrose's clansmen reached their objective on the hillside above Inverlochy just as night was falling on that Saturday, February 1st. As the order was given to halt, men slipped into the shelter of the burn beds and the folds of the hill to rest their aching limbs. Montrose's officers fell in around him to report: the army was utterly exhausted, and the tail of stragglers stretched dangerously for miles behind them. It would be hours before they were all assembled. They were hungry, although there was little enough to be done about that. They could mark Argyll's camp fires below them well enough, but they had no clues as to his dispositions. It was unthinkable to attack immediately. 'So be it then,' said the Lord Marquis calmly. 'We will take them at dawn.'

For the royalists crouching shivering on the hillside, it must have seemed that that night could never end. There was no fuel for fires, and it would anyway have been dangerous to light them. It was all but impossible to sleep when there was the cold, the constant movement of men and confused coming of stragglers, the murmur of orders and arguments. A huge moon hung over the mountains, bathing royalists and Campbells in the eerie grey light that seems to promise dragons and fairies whenever it lights Lochaber in winter. Many men must have lain silent, watching the flicker of Campbell fires far below, computing grimly how many claymores lay around each one.

. . . At dawn on the morning of February 2nd, Sir Duncan Campbell of Auchinbreck was rousing his army to fight, still uncertain whom he faced. All night his pickets had skirmished indecisively against the mysterious enemy on the hills, exchanging occasional shots and cries in the darkness, marking the dark shadows flitting across the hill in the moonlight. The Marquis of Argyll announced that he was taking to his galley. It lay off-shore, ready to hand as usual. Argyll was rowed out with his companions, amongst them the tiresome Covenanting minister Mr Mungo Law, and Montrose's own brother-in-law Sir James Rollo. With his arm still disabled from his fall, Argyll would be of no practical value on shore, as he could point out with his usual unanswerable logic. His capture would be a disaster for the Covenant. The MacCailein Mhor felt no romantic compulsion to stand beside his clan army in battle to offer his moral support in their struggle to the death. As the grey light brightened reluctantly, the Campbells on the shore and their chief on his galley stood silent, gazing curiously upwards at the hillside to discover what this day would bring.

As the first shaft of sunlight appeared in the sky, the sound of the fanfare saluting the raising of the Royal Standard echoed down upon the Campbells with the majesty of the last trump. The presence of the Standard signified the presence of the King's Lieutenant, of Montrose himself at the head of his army. A shock of dismay and astonishment ran down the ranks. Then as the trumpet fanfare died away, the pipes took up the tale. They were playing the terrible Cameron pibroch, 'Sons of dogs come and I will give you flesh.'

On the hillside as the royalists deployed in their clan regiments, Montrose, Airlie and the rest of his staff crouched in the snow eating a mess of oatmeal and water off the point of their dirks. This was all the breakfast the army could look for that morning. Their supper still lay in Campbell pouches. They prepared themselves to go and fetch it. Impatiently the Irish took up their positions, half under Alasdair's command on the right, the rest under Magnus O'Cahan on the left. The order of battle for the centre of the army reads like a rollcall of the great names of Highland history: the men of Glengarry, of Maclean, Keppoch, Glencoe, Atholl, Appin, Lochaber; each contingent headed by its chieftain and eager to outdo its rivals. Behind them stood a reserve of Irish musketeers. Thomas Ogilvy's handful of horse gathered around the Royal Standard. Their poor beasts were already on the verge of collapse, hopelessly lame and constantly underfed. But this day they would be driven to their utmost, if they collapsed under their riders at the end of it.

The priests walked before the ranks blessing the men, and the Catholics knelt to pray, their arms at their feet. Alasdair was dismayed to see Ian Lom Macdonald, the bard of Keppoch who had guided them through such hazards to reach this battlefield, now walking alone away from the army. 'Ian Lom, wilt thou leave us?' he cried. 'If I go with thee today and fall in battle, who will sing thy praises and thy prowess tomorrow?' called back the poet calmly. He turned again and walked away up the hillside until he reached a knoll from which he could see Loch Eil and Inverlochy fairly below him. There that lonely figure stood unmoving through the morning, watching the ebb and surge of the battle beneath.

Magnus O'Cahan began the struggle with a headlong charge upon Gillespie's vanguard. Gillespie's men leapt forward to meet them. Axe and sword and pike crashed headlong in the snow. Gillespie's men reeled back, appalled by the wave of slashing steel and point-blank musketry from O'Cahan's downhill attack. As they fell back on the main Campbell position, Alasdair's men threw themselves on Auchinbreck's left. Then the whole royalist army poured down the hillside and drove madly at the Campbell battle line. The Lowland musketeers were trained to fight like-minded regiments of their opponents. For a few minutes they rhythmically loaded and fired by ranks as they were accustomed. Then the Gaelic fury broke upon them, and all their experience and discipline lapsed into chaos. Their ranks disintegrated. A company which attempted to withdraw at night, amidst the host of prisoners who surrendered on quarter, included some of the greatest of the Campbell name. With a full heart, Montrose wrote his dispatch to his King.

' . . . As to the state of affairs in this kingdom, the bearer will fully inform your Majesty in every particular. And give me leave, with all humility, to assure your Majesty that, through God's blessing, I am in the fairest hopes of reducing this Kingdom to your Majesty's obedience. And, if the measures I have concerted with your Majesty's other loyal subjects fail me not, which they hardly can, I doubt not before the end of this summer I shall be able to come to your Majesty's assistance with a brave army which, backed with the justice of your Majesty's cause, will make the Rebels in England, as well as in Scotland, feel the just rewards of Rebellion. Only give me leave, after I have reduced this country to your Majesty's obedience, and conquered from Dan to Beersheba, to say to your Majesty then, as David's General did to his master, 'come thou thyself lest this country be called by my name'. For in all my actions I aim only at your Majesty's honour and interest, as becomes one that is to his last breath, may it please your Sacred Majesty—

Your Majesty's most humble, most faithful, and most obedient Subject and Servant,

MONTROSE.

Inverlochy in Lochaber,
February 3rd, 1645.'

When the battle was over, Ian Lom Macdonald came down from his post on the hillside above Inverlochy. He was true to his promise. To honour this Candlemas of 1645, he wrote one of the greatest of all Gaelic odes. . . .

Montrose's army marched north from Inverlochy leaving the shore strewn with the naked bodies of their enemies. None came to the battlefield to bury the dead. The Camerons had fulfilled the ghastly promise of their pibroch. The dogs came down to feast upon Campbell flesh.

Max Hastings

92.

One of the last significant skirmishes of the First Civil War took place at Stow-on-the-Wold, Gloucestershire, on 21 March 1646, where Sir Jacob Astley conducted a gallant, vain last stand for the King with a body of Welsh levies, who rapidly surrendered.

ASTLEY himself, unhorsed and surrounded, gave up his sword to one of Colonel Birch's men. 'You have done your work, boys,' said the old cavalier, 'you may go play, unless you fall out among yourselves.'

C. V. Wedgwood

93·

The decisive moment of the Battle of Dunbar, 3 September 1650, when Cromwell's Foot had launched their devastating attack upon the Scottish position.

JUST then the sun rose out of the sea beyond St Abb's, and Oliver, in a voice which rang above the din, cried, 'Let God arise, let His enemies be scattered!' And again, 'They run, they run—I profess they run.'

By six o'clock the battle was over. Leslie's horse was driven back on his foot, and the foot, penned in between the enemy and the upper ravine of the burn, was a helpless mob: much of it had never come into action. Some fled towards Cockburnspath, but more across the hills towards Haddington. Oliver, before the pursuit began, halted his men and sang the 117th Psalm, and the ministers who, says Sir Edward Walker, were the first to flee, heard behind them words which they had often used to other purposes:

> O give you praise unto the Lord,
>   All nations that be;
> Likewise you people all accord
>   His name to magnify.

John Buchan

94·

Oliver Cromwell's dispatch from Dublin, 17 September 1649, describing the capture of Drogheda on 12 September, in which an estimated 4,000 defenders were put to the sword.

DIVERS of the enemy retreated into the Millmount, a place very strong and of difficult access; being exceedingly high, having a good graft [ditch], and strongly palisadoed. The Governor, Sir Arthur Aston, and divers considerable officers, being there, our men, getting up to them, were ordered by me to put them all to the sword. And, indeed, being in the heat of action, I forbade them to spare any that were in arms in the town; and, I think, that night they put to the sword about two thousand men—divers of the officers and soldiers being fled over the bridge into the other part of the town, where about one hundred of them possessed St Peter's church steeple, some the west gate, and others a strong round tower next the gate called St Sunday's. These, being summoned to yield to mercy, refused. Whereupon I ordered the steeple of St Peter's church to be fired, when one of them was heard to say, in the midst of the flames, 'G—d d—n me! G—d confound me! I burn, I burn!'

The next day, the other two towers were summoned; in one of which was about six or seven score; but they refused to yield themselves: and we, knowing that hunger must compel them, set only good guards to secure them from running away until their stomachs were come down. From one of the said towers, notwithstanding their condition, they killed and wounded some of our men. When they submitted, their officers were knocked on the head, and every tenth man of the soldiers killed; and the rest shipped for the Barbadoes. The soldiers in the other tower were all spared, as to their lives only, and shipped likewise for the Barbadoes. I am persuaded that this is a righteous judgment of God upon these barbarous wretches, who have imbrued their hands in so much innocent blood; and that it will tend to prevent the effusion of blood for the future. Which are the satisfactory grounds to such actions, which otherwise cannot but work remorse and regret.

Oliver Cromwell

95.

WHILE Louis XIV was besieging Lisle in 1667, the Count de Brouai, governor of the town, had occasion to send a flag of truce into the besiegers' camp. When the officer who bore it was returning, the Duke de Charrost, captain of the king's guard, called out, 'Tell Brouai not to follow the example of the governor of Douay, who yielded like a coward.' The King turned round laughing, and said, 'Charrost, are you mad?'—'How, sir?' answered he; 'Brouai is my cousin.'

Lord de Ros

96.

The childhood of the future Tsar Peter the Great in the 1680s.

HIS favorite game, as it had been from earliest childhood, was war. During Fedor's reign, a small parade ground had been laid out for Peter in the Kremlin where he could drill the boys who were his playmates. Now, with the open world of Preobrazhenskoe around him, there was infinite space for these fascinating games. And, unlike most boys who play at war, Peter could draw on a government arsenal to supply his equipment. The arsenal records shows that his requests were frequent. In January 1683, he ordered uniforms, banners and two wooden cannon, their barrels lined with iron, mounted on wheels to allow them to be pulled by horses—all to be furnished immediately. On his eleventh birthday, in June 1683, Peter abandoned wooden cannon for real cannon with which, under the supervision of artillerymen, he was allowed to fire salutes. He enjoyed this so much that messengers came almost daily to the arsenal for more gunpowder. In May 1685, Peter, nearing thirteen, ordered sixteen pairs of pistols, sixteen carbines with slings and brass mountings and, shortly afterward, twenty-three more carbines and sixteen muskets.

By the time Peter was fourteen and he and his mother had settled permanently at Preobrazhenskoe, his martial games had transformed the summer estate into an adolescent military encampment. Peter's first 'soldiers' were the small group of playmates who had been appointed to his service when he reached the age of five. They had been selected from the families of boyars to provide the Prince with a personal retinue of young noblemen who acted the roles of equerry, valet and butler; in fact they were his friends. Peter also filled his ranks by drawing from the enormous, now largely useless group of attendants of his father, Alexis, and his brother Fedor. Swarms of retainers, especially those involved in the falconry establishment of Tsar Alexis, remained in the royal service with nothing to do. Fedor's health had prevented him from hunting, Ivan was even less able to enjoy the sport and Peter disliked it. Nevertheless, all these people continued to receive salaries from the state and be fed at the Tsar's expense, and Peter decided to employ some of them in *his* sport.

The ranks were further swelled by other young noblemen presenting themselves for enrollment, either on their own impulse or on the urging of fathers anxious to gain the young Tsar's favor. Boys from other classes were allowed to enroll, and the sons of clerks, equerries, stable grooms and even serfs in the service of noblemen were set beside the sons of boyars. Among these young volunteers of obscure origin was a boy one year younger than the Tsar named Alexander Danilovich Menshikov. Eventually, 300 of these boys and young men had mustered on the Preobrazhenskoe estate. They lived in barracks, trained like soldiers, used soldiers' talk and received soldiers' pay. Peter held them as his special comrades, and from this collection of young noblemen and stableboys he eventually created the proud Preobrazhensky Regiment. Until the fall of the Russian monarchy in

1917, this was the first regiment of the Russian Imperial Guard, whose colonel was always the Tsar himself and whose proudest claim was that it had been founded by Peter the Great.

Soon, all the quarters available in the little village of Preobrazhenskoe were filled, but Peter's boy army kept expanding. New barracks were built in the nearby village of Semyonovskoe; in time, this company developed into the Semyonovsky Regiment, and it became the second regiment of the Russian Imperial Guard. Each of these embryo regiments numbered 300 and was organized into infantry, cavalry and artillery—just like the regular army. Barracks, staff offices and stables were built, more harnesses and caissons were drawn from the equipment of the regular horse artillery, five fifers and ten drummers were detached from regular regiments to pipe and beat the tempo of Peter's games. Western-style uniforms were designed and issued: black boots, a black three-cornered hat, breeches and a flaring, broad-cuffed coat which came to the knees, dark bottle green for the Preobrazhensky company and a rich blue for the Semyonovsky. Levels of command were organized, with field officers, subalterns, sergeants, supply and administrative staffs and even a pay department, all drawn from the ranks of boys. Like regular soldiers, they lived under strict military discipline and underwent rigorous military training. Around their barracks they mounted guard and stood watches. As their training advanced, they set off on long marches through the countryside, making camp at night, digging entrenchments and setting out patrols.

Peter plunged enthusiastically into this activity, wanting to participate fully at every level. Rather than taking for himself the rank of colonel, he enlisted in the Preobrazhensky Regiment at the lowest grade, as a drummer boy, where he could play with gusto the instrument he loved. Eventually, he promoted himself to artilleryman or bombardier, so that he could fire the weapon which made the most noise and did the most damage. In barracks or field, he allowed no distinction between himself and others. He performed the same duties, stood his turn at watch day and night, slept in the same tent and ate the same food. When earthworks were built, Peter dug with a shovel. When the regiment went on parade, Peter stood in the ranks, taller than the others but otherwise undistinguished.

Peter's boyhood refusal to accept senior rank in any Russian military or naval organization became a lifelong characteristic. Later, when he marched with his new Russian army or sailed with his new fleet, it was always as a subordinate commander. He was willing to be promoted from drummer boy to bombardier, from bombardier to sergeant and eventually up to general or, in the fleet, up to rear admiral and eventually vice admiral, but only when he felt that his competence and service merited promotion. In part, at the beginning, he did this because in peacetime exercises drummer boys and artillerymen had more fun and made more noise than majors and colonels. But there was also his continuing belief that he should learn the business of soldiering from the bottom up. And if he, the Tsar, did this, no nobleman would be able to claim command on the basis of title.

Robert K. Massie

97.

The defence of Derry against the Catholic Jacobites ranks among the foremost legends of Protestant Ulster. As the Redshanks—James II's bare-legged Highlanders— marched towards the city's gates, the citizens within remained in doubt whether to allow them passage.

THE moment of crisis was at hand, for the watchers on the walls could see that the Redshanks had reached the Waterside and were beginning to come across the river in boats. Two of their officers, who swaggered haughtily up to the gates, were admitted and presented their warrant, demanding quarters for their men and forage for their horses. A technical defect in the warrant enabled the sheriffs to procrastinate and, meanwhile, a number of young men— 'the younger sort who are seldom so dilatory in their actions'—decided to act. 'While we were in this confused hesitation,' wrote Captain Ash in his journal, 'on the 7th December, 1688, a few resolute APPRENTICE BOYS determined for us.' There were thirteen of them, those apprentice boys whose names, English and Scottish names, have never been forgotten in Ulster. The sun was high in the midday sky when these thirteen young men drew their swords, ran to the mainguard and seized the keys, then rushed down to the Ferryquay gate to raise the drawbridge and close the gate in the astonished faces of Antrim's troops, only sixty yards away.

The Redshanks stared in disbelief at the great gate closing ponderously in front of them and stood around for a while as if under the impression that it must soon be re-opened. A citizen called James Morrison shouted at them from the walls to be off, and when they still lingered hopefully he called loudly to an invisible and perhaps imaginary colleague to 'bring about the great gun here'. At this threat the

Redshanks hastily retreated to their boats and returned to the Water-side to work off their annoyance in petty assaults upon the inhabitants of that suburb.

At the last possible moment, by an apparently spontaneous interven-tion by thirteen young men, Derry had been saved for the Protestant cause.

Patrick Macrory

98.

Many of the stories surrounding the massacre of the Macdonalds of Glencoe on 13 February, 1692, properly belong as legends rather than historical anecdotes, but this is one of the most vivid.

A WOMAN of Inverrigan, it was said, took shelter with her child and a dog beneath the bridge that crossed the burn of Allt-na-Muidhe. The crying of the child was heard, and a soldier was sent to kill it. He came to the bridge, and saw the woman holding her plaid over the child's mouth to stifle its cries. He bayoneted the dog and went back, holding up the wet steel. 'That's not human blood,' said the officer, though the story does not explain how he knew. 'Kill the child, or I'll kill you.' So the soldier went back to the bridge. He drew his hanger and he cut the little finger from the child's hand, smearing its blood on his sword. . . . The story has a sequel, of course. Many years later the soldier was tra-velling homeward through Appin, and he stopped at a cottage for the night. About the fire he talked of his soldiering, and when he was asked to name the most terrible thing he had seen he said it was the Massacre of Glencoe. As he slept, his host said, 'I'll make an end to him in the morning.' At breakfast the soldier was again asked to tell of Glencoe, and he told the story of the child, at which his host held up a hand from which the little finger was missing. They parted as friends.

John Prebble

99.

A legendary figure of her period, Mother Ross, enlists in 1693 in search of her lost husband.

IN the morning I thought of going in search of my dear Richard, and this gave some ease to my tortured mind. I began to flatter myself that I should meet no great difficulty in finding him out, and resolved in one of his suits, for we were both of a size, to conceal my sex, and go directly for Flanders, in search of him whom I preferred to everything else the world could afford me, which, indeed, had nothing alluring, in comparison with my dear Richard, and whom the hopes of seeing had lessened every danger to which I was going to expose myself. The pleasure I found in the thoughts of once more regaining him, recalled my strength, and I was grown much gayer than I had been at any time in my supposed widowhood. I was not long deliberating, after this thought had possessed me, but immediately set about preparing what was necessary for my ramble; and disposing of my children, my eldest with my mother, and that which was born after my husband's departure, with a nurse (my second son was dead), I told my friends, that I would go to England in search of my husband, and return with all possible expedition after I had found him. My goods I left in the hands of such friends as had spare house room, and my house I let to a cooper. Having thus ordered my affairs, I cut off my hair, and dressed me in a suit of my husband's having had the precaution to quilt the waistcoat, to preserve my breasts from hurt, which were not large enough to betray my sex, and putting on the wig and hat I had prepared, I went out and bought me a silver-hilted sword, and some Holland shirts: but was at a loss how I should carry my money with me, as it was contrary to law to export above £5 out of the kingdom; I thought at last of quilting it in the waistband of my breeches, and by this method I carried with me fifty guineas without suspicion.

I had nothing upon my hands to prevent my setting out; wherefore, that I might get as soon as possible to Holland, I went to the sign of the Golden Last, where Ensign Herbert Laurence, who was beating up for recruits, kept his rendezvous. He was in the house at the time I got there, and I offered him my service to go against the French, being desirous to show my zeal for his majesty King William, and my country. The hopes of soon meeting with my husband, added a sprightliness to my looks, which made the officer say, I was a clever brisk young fellow; and having recommended my zeal, he gave me a guinea enlisting money, and a crown to drink the king's health, and ordered me to be enrolled, having told him my name was Christopher Walsh, in Captain Tichbourn's company of foot, in the regiment commanded by the Marquis de Pisare. The lieutenant of our company was Mr Gardiner, our ensign, Mr Welsh.

We stayed but a short time in Dublin after this, but, with the rest of the recruits, were shipped for Holland, weighed anchor, and soon arrived at Williamstadt, where we landed and marched to Gorcum. Here our regimentals and first mountings were given us. The next day we set out for Gertrudenburg, and proceeded forward to Landen, where we were incorporated in our respective regiments, and then joined the grand army, which was in expectation of a general battle, the enemy being very near within cannon-shot. Having been accustomed to soldiers, when a girl, and delighted with seeing them exercise, I very soon was perfect, and applauded by my officers for my dexterity in going through it.

Daniel Defoe

100.

Richard Steele became a cadet in the Life Guards on leaving Oxford in 1694, and represents the story below as one that he heard from a Corporal of his regiment who had served in the civil wars, which would have made the man a very great age indeed.

THIS gentleman was taken by the enemy; and the two parties were upon such terms at that time, that we did not treat each other as prisoners of war, but as traitors and rebels. The poor corporal, being condemned to die, wrote a letter to his wife when under sentence of execution. He writ on the Thursday, and was to be executed on the Friday: but, considering that the letter would not come to his wife's hands until Saturday, the day after execution, and being at that time more scrupulous than ordinary in speaking exact truth, he formed his letter rather according to the posture of his affairs when she should read it, than as they stood when he sent it: though, it must be confessed, there is a certain perplexity in the style of it, which the reader will easily pardon, considering his circumstances.

'Dear Wife,

Hoping you are in good health, as I am at this present writing; this is to let you know, that yesterday, between the hours of eleven and twelve, I was hanged, drawn, and quartered. I died very penitently, and every body thought my case very hard. Remember me kindly to my poor fatherless children.

Yours until death,
W.B.'

It so happened, that this honest fellow was relieved by a party of his friends, and had the satisfaction to see all the rebels hanged who had been his enemies. I must not omit a circumstance which exposed him to raillery his whole life after. Before the arrival of the next post, that would have set all things clear, his wife was married to a second husband, who lived in the peaceable possession of her; and the corporal, who was a man of plain understanding, did not care to stir in the matter, as knowing that she had the news of his death under his own hand, which she might have produced upon occasion.

Richard Steele

101.

WHEN Peter the Great took by storm the city of Narva, in 1704, which was defended by General Horn and a Swedish garrison, the soldiers, in defiance of the express orders of the Czar, carried fire and destruction into every quarter of the town, slaughtering the inhabitants without mercy. Peter the Great threw himself, sword in hand, into the midst of the massacre; and rescued many of the defenceless women and children from his merciless and savage troops. He killed, with his own hand, one of his ferocious soldiers, whom the heat of the carnage rendered deaf to his voice; and at last succeeded in curbing the fury of this unlicensed scene. Covered with dust, sweat, and blood, he then hastened to the townhouse, where the principal inhabitants of the place had taken refuge. His terrible and threatening air greatly alarmed these unhappy people. As soon as he had entered the hall, he laid his sword on a table; and then addressing himself to the affrighted multitude, who waited their doom in anxious silence, 'It is not', said he, 'with the blood of your fellow-citizens that this sword is stained; but with that of my own soldiers, whom I have been sacrificing for your preservation.'

Lord de Ros

102.

Marlborough met his great friend and comrade-in-arms Prince Eugene of Savoy for the first time on 10 June 1704, at Gross Heppach. Next morning, Eugene inspected Marlborough's cavalry escort.

'MY Lord,' said Eugene, 'I never saw better horses, better clothes, finer belts and accoutrements; but money, which you don't want in

England, will buy clothes and fine horses, but it can't buy that lively air I see in every one of these troopers' faces.' 'Sir,' said Marlborough, 'that must be attributed to their heartiness for the public cause and the particular pleasure and satisfaction they have in seeing your Highness.'

Dr Hare

103.

It is not infrequently the case that when an officer falls on the battlefield, enquiries are made as to which side shot him.

A COMMANDER who served under Marlborough, Brigadier-General Richard Kane, warned in his memoirs that officers who ill-treated their men could expect to 'meet with their fate in the day of battle from their own men'. He was by no means the only military writer to sound this caution. There is a story of a major of the 15th Foot who, on the field of Blenheim, turned to address his regiment before the assault, and apologized for his past ill behaviour. He requested that, if he must fall, it should be by the bullets of the enemy. If spared, he would undertake to mend his ways. To this abject performance, a grenadier said: 'March on, sir; the enemy is before you, and we have something else to do than think of you now.' After several attacks, the regiment carried its position and the major, gratified, no doubt, to be still alive, turned to his troops and removed his hat to call for a cheer. No sooner had he said 'Gentlemen, the day is ours' than he was struck in the forehead by a bullet and killed. There was a decided suspicion that the bullet was no accident.

E. S. Turner

104.

After his great victory at Blenheim, Marlborough honoured his defeated opponent, Marshal Tallard, by inviting him to accompany him as he inspected the Allied army. Their dialogue is said to have gone something like this:

MARLBOROUGH: 'I am very sorry that such a cruel misfortune should have fallen upon a soldier for whom I have had the highest regard.'

TALLARD: 'And I congratulate you on defeating the best soldiers in the world.'

MARLBOROUGH: 'Your Lordship, I presume, excepts those who had the honour to beat them.'

Lives of the Two Illustrious Generals

105.

To those familiar with the conditions of modern campaigning and the privations of modern defeat, those endured by the Comte de Merode-Westerloo with the French army in the wake of Blenheim may not sound too severe. But they obviously exercised the Count severely, and may help to explain his change of sides later in the war.

THE moment we left Ulm all the heavy baggage and carts were set on fire in the interests of mobility. Three great waggon-parks were formed in the countryside, and we had the sorrow of watching them burn as we marched away. I, like all the others, lost in addition to my carts all my field furniture, chairs, tables, beds, utensils, field ovens— the lot. I was fortunate to keep my two dozen mules which carried my most vital possessions. I lost still more horses through the ravages of the so-called 'German sickness' which put all our cavalrymen on their feet. The disease started in my stable the day of the battle. From the time I lost my first horse, besides the thirteen that were killed or injured on the battlefield, one or two fell sick every day, dying forty-eight hours later. Thus between Blenheim and Brussels I lost ninety-seven horses and all their harness had to be left behind too. The mules alone were not subject to this plague, but one slight consolation was that the enemy also caught it after camping on some of our vacated sites.

Robert Parker and the Comte de Merode-Westerloo

106.

The end of the story of 'Mother Ross'.

ALMOST the last shot fired by the French at the battle of Ramillies, in 1706, wounded a trooper in Lord Hay's Regiment of Dragoons (now the Royal Scots Dragoon Guards). With a fractured skull, the soldier underwent the operation of trepanning, when it was discovered that the supposed man was really a woman. It turned out that she had followed her husband to the war, and after discovering him had continued to serve, making her partner promise not to disclose her sex. She had enlisted under the name of Christopher Walsh in 1693, and, until her discovery thirteen years later, had served in different regiments through several campaigns. Naturally, the news of the exploit of Mrs Richard Walsh, which was her married name, spread rapidly through the army, and the plucky woman received many kindnesses from officer and men. The great Duke of Marlborough himself took an interest in her, and persuaded her to be remarried to her husband. The ceremony was attended by a large number of officers, who all kissed the bride before leaving.

'Mother Ross', as she afterwards was called, was appointed cook in her husband's regiment; but at the siege of Ath she could not resist the sound of battle, so, seizing a musket, she killed one of the enemy. Unfortunately, at the same moment, a ball from the enemy struck her in the mouth, splitting her underlip and knocking one of her teeth into her mouth.

Mrs Walsh's husband was killed at the battle of Malplaquet (1709), but at the end of eleven weeks she married Hugh Jones, a grenadier in the same regiment. Her second husband being killed, she married a soldier of the Welsh Fusiliers, named Davies, who survived her. Eventually 'Mother Ross' retired on a pension of a shilling a day, given by Queen Anne, and on her death in 1739 was buried with military honours in the cemetery belonging to Chelsea Hospital.

James Settle

107.

Private Bishop admits to having written just three letters of this sort to his wife in six years' campaigning. He was astonished and aggrieved, on his eventual discharge at Dover, to discover that she had married another man in his absence.

I WILL now make bold to trouble the Reader with a line or two that I sent to my Wife before I went to Camp [in 1707], then I will proceed forward to the rest of my Actions.

'My Dear, be so candid as to excuse my annual Letters, as my Thoughts hitherto have been taken up with Business of great Importance that required great Attention, and rendered me unfit to think of my private Affairs. But as we have accomplished all we undertook the last Campaign, I am in Hopes we shall not meet with any Obstruction the next ensuing; and I don't doubt in the least but that our Desires will be fulfilled, if we trust to the Providence of God: For he is our Rock, our Shield, and strong Tower: For my part, I trust in him to aid and assist me, knowing that he is our only Support. So I conclude with Fervency of Heart to what is abovementioned; liikewise give me Leave to subscribe myself yours for ever, not forgetting my Mother.'

Matthew Bishop

108

Fraternization in Flanders, 1708.

A SERGEANT, that belonged to my Lord Hartford's Regiment, had a Sister in the French Service; he was very desirous of going to make an Enquiry after her; therefore he took Courage, and asked the Major Leave, who readily gave his Consent. With that the Sergeant went off, in order to make a strict Inquisition after her, and she readily came to him. The Joy they expressed at Meeting were inconceivable, and created a great deal of Mirth, both amongst our Officers, and private Men in general. I remember she brought a Bottle of Brandy in order to treat her Brother, and they were in great Raptures during the Time they continued together. In the Interim our Officers were prodigious jocular and pleasant, and desired the Woman to sit down in Company with them. They were a jovial Crew, and drank round the Table like Sons of Bacchus. The Woman, being in excessive high Spirits, was as quick with her Repartees as possible. In the first Place our Officers boasted of our Provisions being far better than the French Army's, that we had good Beef, Bacon, and extremely fine Geneva; good Bread, and, above all, the English Pay was double that of the French. One would have imagined these were Arguments sufficient to work upon a Woman's Heart; but all they said had no Effect on her. She told them, She thought the French Provisions were preferable to ours; that all the World would allow their Bread to be better than that of any other Nation; they had fine juicy Beef, none better to her Palate; and Brandy enough, which revived her Soul; what could a Woman desire more? Such like Conversation passed between our Officers and the Woman as they sat all round the Table. But her stay created a Jealousy in the French, so that they sent a Drum over their Breast-works to our Guard. Then we sent another to their's. Upon this, one of the French Officers came over, and advanced forward; and one of our's went and met him half way. They saluted each other with a great deal of

Ceremony, and a great many Compliments passed between them. Then they both returned to their respective Posts, and soon after we sent the Woman and a Drum in order to conduct her safe; upon which they sent back our's. But the poor Sergeant's Joy was turned to Mourning; for he took on greatly, when he saw himself disappointed of getting his Sister into our Army.

Matthew Bishop

109.

THERE was [a] . . . Man that was remarkable for a great Eater, his Name was John Jones, who belonged to Captain Cutler's Company: He said he was prodigious hungry. With that the Men asked him how many Cannon Balls he had eaten for his Breakfast. Then I said to him, Thou deservest Preferment, if thou canst digest Cannon Balls. Then Sergeant Smith came up to me, and told me, He had eaten four or six twenty-four Pounders, and as many six or twelve Pounders in a Morning for his Breakfast. Now this Sergeant was not addicted to tell fabulous Stories, though it seemed incredible to any one's Thinking. But he explained it in this Manner, that the Man often frequented the Fields in Search of those Cannon Balls; that he had used to dig them out of the Banks, and had brought a great Number in a Morning to the Artillery, in order to dispose of them for Money; and the Money he bought his Provision with. Had there been no Cannon Balls flying, he certainly could not have subsisted; for he both eat and drank more than ten moderate Men: So that his daily Study was to provide for his Belly.

Matthew Bishop

110.

THE sole legitimate offspring of Maurice de Saxe lived for only a few days [of January 1715]. On the day of the baby's death the father was not at his wife's side, but was rollicking with a sledging party on the frozen Elbe. In the middle of a wild race the ice gave way, and plunged horses, sledges and riders into the freezing water. Maurice and his companions almost drowned.

The death of his boy freed him from family ties, and soon he was heading once more for the fighting that was still devastating his father's dominions. One evening the young count, with his suite of five officers and a dozen servants, arrived at a remote Polish inn while on their way to join the main Saxon army at Sandomierz on the Vistula. While they were at supper, a band of enemy cavalry attacked the village in which the inn stood. In later years Maurice used to say that there were eight hundred of them; but as he grew older he was increasingly given to Falstaffian embroidery. At any rate, there were at least eighty or ninety, and Maurice and his score of companions hastily barricaded themselves inside the inn. In the fight that followed three of the defenders were killed, and Maurice himself received a wound in the thigh. By nightfall it seemed that their chances of surviving until dawn were slim. Maurice decided to risk a break-out. He and his men ran for the stables, saddled up, and made a dash for the forest. A few sabre-slashes and they were through.

Next day they joined the Saxon detachment that was marching to besiege Usedom, a small fortress on an island off the Pomeranian coast. After many weeks of hard fighting, it fell to Frederick Augustus' troops. Usedom had been the town where Gustavus Adolphus, the Lion of the North, had landed from Sweden seventy-five years before. Its loss in 1715 was an indication of the rapid collapse of the Swedish empire, the downward spiral towards disintegration.

Maurice and his regiment were next transferred to Stralsund, where events had taken a suddenly dramatic turn. After five years in captivity, Charles XII had escaped from his captors and, accompanied by only a single companion had traversed the eleven hundred miles between Thrace and Pomerania. After seven weeks in the saddle and a series of extraordinary adventures, the mud-encrusted pair presented themselves to the astounded garrison of Stralsund at midnight on November 11th, 1714. Charles stood once more on what was technically Swedish soil.

Inspired by the return of their king, the Swedish defenders beat off the storming parties of five nations: Saxony, Denmark, Hanover, Russia, and Prussia. But as the months went by, the walls and installations of the port were reduced to heaps of useless rubble. Stralsund became indefensible. In December 1715, the Swedes were forced to take their last desperate measures. Charles evacuated the survivors of his forces at dead of night and pushed out to sea in a rowing boat with his senior officers. The departure from reeking Stralsund was symbolic of his whole career. It was the ruin of his ambitions; it was the end of the Great Northern War; it wrote finis to the imperial greatness of

Sweden. Within three years Charles was dead, killed by a dubious hand before the petty fortress of Frederikshald in Norway. 'Voilà la pièce finie', observed a cynical French military engineer who witnessed the event: 'Allons souper.'

John Manchip White

III.

A stratagem suggested by Marshal Saxe.

THE affair of Denin [1712] puts me in mind of an accident, which it is not unseasonable *en passant* to give an account of. The French cavalry being dismounted after the action was over, the Marshal, who was always in high spirits, says to the soldiers of a regiment upon his right, as he was passing along the line, 'Well, my lads, we have beat 'em!' upon which some begun to cry out, 'Long live the King!' others to throw their hats into the air, and to fire their pieces: the cavalry joining in the acclamation, alarmed the horses to such a degree, that they broke loose from the men, and galloped quite away, insomuch that if there had been four men in the front of them, they might very easily have led them all off to the enemy; it moreover occasioned some considerable damage, as well as disorder, great numbers of the men being wounded, and a quantity of arms lost. I was unwilling to omit here the relation of this circumstance, for the sake of introducing a description of the method of decoying horses, as there are but few partisans, who are acquainted with it.

Maurice de Saxe

112.

From the diary of a soldier in the garrison of Gibraltar under siege, 1727.

March 9th. Came a deserter who reports that while our guns were firing at them an officer pulled off his hat, huzzaed and called God to damn us all, when one of our balls with unerring justice took off the miserable man's head and left him a wretched example of the Divine justice.

April 12th. A recruit who refused to work, carry arms, eat or drink was whipped for the fifth time, after which being asked by the officer he said he was now ready to do his duty.

May 7th. This morning Ensign Stubbs of Colonel Egerton's regiment retired a little out of the camp and shot himself.

June 17th. Today two corporals of the Guards boxed over a rail until both expired, but nobody can tell for what reason.

October 11th. One of Pearce's regiment went into the belfry of a very high steeple, threw himself into the street, and broke his skull to pieces.

October 16th. Will Garen, who broke his back, was hanged.

December 9th. Last night a deserter clambered up within a little of Willis's battery and was assisted by a ladder of ropes by our men. When the officers came to examine his face, they found him to have deserted out of the Royal Irish two months ago. Asking the reason of his return, he said he chose rather to be hanged than continue in the Spanish service, so is to have his choice.

January 2nd 1728. Here is nothing to do nor any news, all things being dormant and in suspense, with the harmless diversions of drinking, dancing, revelling, whoring, gaming and other innocent debaucheries to pass the time—and really, to speak my own opinion I think and believe that Sodom and Gomorrah were not half so wicked and profane as this worthy city and garrison of Gibraltar.

An unknown British soldier who signed himself 'S.H.'

113.

RICHELIEU . . . at the siege of Philippsburg [1734], found himself in the same army group as his wife's cousins, the Prince de Lixin and the Prince de Pons. The Prince de Conti, who was commanding a regiment, gave a party to celebrate his own seventeenth birthday. Richelieu was an old friend of the Prince's father; he felt he could go to the party straight from a day in the trenches, without changing his clothes. When the Prince de Lixin saw him he remarked in a loud voice that M. de Richelieu, in spite of his marriage, still seemed to have a good deal of dirt clinging to him. The Duke called him out; they decided to fight at once, because fighting among officers was forbidden and they were afraid of being stopped. So they proceeded, with their friends, to a deserted place behind the trenches and told the servants to light flares. These attracted the enemy's fire, and the duel took place amid falling shells; the Germans soon found the range and one of the servants was killed. The opponents were evenly matched; Lixin almost immediately wounded Richelieu in the thigh. The Duke's seconds, who were liking the situation less and less, urged him to give up. He refused and the fight went on a good long time. In the end Richelieu ran Lixin through the heart. The officers present, thankful to be alive themselves, carried the two principals off the field, one to his grave and the other to the hospital.

Nancy Mitford

114.

IN 1739, the Russian and Turks, who had been at war, met to conclude terms of peace. The commissioners were Marshal Keith for the Russians and the Grand Vizier for the Turks. These two personages met, and carried on their negotiations by means of interpreters. When all was concluded they rose to separate, but just before leaving the Grand Vizier suddenly went to Marshal Keith, and, taking him cordially by the hand, declared in the broadest Scotch dialect that it made him 'unco' happy to meet a countryman in his exalted station'. As might be expected, Keith, who himself was a Scotsman in the service of Russia, stared with astonishment, and was eager for an explanation of the mystery. 'Dinna be surprised', the Grand Vizier exclaimed; 'I'm o' the same country wi' yoursell, mon! I mind weel seein' you and your brother, when boys, passin' by to the school at Kirkaldy; my father, sir, was bellman o' Kirkaldy.'

James Settle

115.

[COLONEL] Guise going over one campaign to Flanders, observed a young raw officer, who was in the same vessel with him, and with his usual humanity told him that he would take care of him, and conduct him to Antwerp, where they were both going; which he accordingly did, and then took leave of him. The young fellow was soon told by some arch rogues, whom he happened to fall in with, that he must signalize himself by fighting some man of known courage, or else he would soon be despised in the regiment. The young man said he knew no one but Colonel Guise, and he had received great obligations from him. It was all one for that, they said, in these cases; the colonel was the fittest man in the world, as every body knew his bravery. Soon afterwards, up comes the young officer to Colonel Guise, as he was walking up and down the coffee-room, and began in a hesitating manner to tell him how much obliged he had been to him, and how sensible he was of his obligations. 'Sir (replied Colonel Guise), I have done my duty by you, and no more.' 'But, colonel (added the young officer, faltering), I am told that I must fight some gentleman of known courage, and who has killed several persons, and that nobody—'. 'Oh, Sir (interrupted the colonel), your friends do me too much honour; but there is a gentleman (pointing to a fierce-looking black fellow, that was sitting at one of the tables), who has killed half the regiment.' So up goes the officer to him, and tells him, he is well-informed of his bravery, and that for that reason he must fight him. 'Who, I, Sir? (said the gentleman) why, I am the *apothecary*.'

Naval and Military Anecdotes

116.

The caption to a portrait of Hannah Snell.

BORN at Worcester 1723—Inlisted herself by the name of James Gray in Colonel Guise's regiment then at Carlisle 1745, where she received 500 lashes. Deserted from thence and went to Portsmouth, where she Inlisted in Colonel Fraser's Regiment of Marines, went in Admiral Boscawen's Squadron to the East Indies, at the siege of Pondicherry where she received 12 shot, one in her Groin, Eleven in her legs; 1750 came to England without the least discovery of her Sex, and on her petitioning His Royal Highness the Duke of Cumberland he was pleased to order her a Pension of £30 a year.

Anon.

117.

An incident at Fontenoy, 11 May 1745, as the opposing armies closed in silence to within fifty paces of each other, recounted by a French pen.

A REGIMENT of the English guards, that of Campbell, and the Royal Scots, formed the front rank: M. de Campbell was their lieutenant-general; the Count of Albremarle their major-general; and M. de

Churchill, natural grandson of the great Duke of Marlborough, their brigadier. The English officers saluted the French by raising their hats. The Count de Chabannes, the Duke de Biron, who had advanced along with all the officers of the French guards, returned the salute. Lord Charles Hay, captain of the English guards, cried: 'Gentlemen of the French guards, open fire.'

The Count d'Auteroche, then a lieutenant although later a captain of grenadiers, called back in a loud voice: 'Gentlemen, we shall not be the first to fire; fire yourselves!' The English then loosed a rolling volley.[1]

Voltaire

118.

Sir John (later Earl) Ligonier (1680–1770), the French Huguenot émigré who escaped from France at the age of 17 and joined the British service, was taken prisoner by the French at the Battle of Laffeldt on 2 July 1747: he was leading a cavalry charge which covered the retreat of the British and Austrian army under the Duke of Cumberland. Ligonier wrote to Prince William of Hesse, describing his reception by Louis XV, who was in the field with Marshal Saxe.

I HASTEN to tell you of the good treatment I received from the King. The official reports as well as the papers will tell you what happened in general terms. As for me, I was far from expecting such a thing. The soldier who captured me, would have had his head broken if I had still had a loaded pistol. He knocked off my hat and taking his off to salute me, said 'General, you are my prisoner and I bid you welcome.' He had six others wih him and I gave him my purse. Without dismounting they led me off towards the King, who was quite close, being in the thick of the fight. On the way some of the Household Provost guards, whom I recognized by their uniform, pressed in on me and I thought, seeing my situation, they were going to kill me. But when I came to the King, he greatly reassured me, saying, with a charming smile, 'Well, General, we will have the pleasure of your company at supper tonight.' Whereupon a musketeer was commanded to accompany me to my quarters, and a moment later came an officer, who said 'Sir, the King bids me bring you good news. Your carriage and equipment which were captured, are here and it is the King's orders that you have them

---

[1] It seems churlish to record the verdict of later historians, that at Fontenoy the French fired first.

back.' I thought I was dreaming, for the idea of being executed returned again and again to my mind. However, the King was very gracious to me that evening and paid me every attention at table, which set an example to the others. At the end, when I took leave of his Majesty, mustering all the French vocabulary I could still remember, the King said to me, 'M. Ligonier, your captivity will not be harsh, for you know that I am a kind hearted man.' At that my heart swelled and I could only answer by putting a knee to the ground, and the King stretched out to me his beautiful gloveless hand, on which I planted, I swear you, a very warm kiss mingled with some tears. The King of France is a great and good King believe me, who have the good luck to serve such an admirable Prince.

Earl Ligonier

119.

ACCORDING to French writers it was Saxe himself who introduced Ligonier to Louis with the words, 'Sire, I here present to your Majesty a man who has defeated all my plans by a single glorious action.' It was at this interview that the king observed to Ligonier that not only did the English pay all but they fought all and let it be known he was tired of war. 'Would it not be better to think seriously of making peace, rather than killing so many brave men?' he is reported to have said to Ligonier by Voltaire, who in his history hints that the proper thing would have been to have had Ligonier executed.

Scotsmen in the French service thought poorly of the king's kindness to Ligonier, where an English king would have shown little mercy to them in such circumstances. The king naturally inquired of Ligonier if he was not a Frenchman and if so how and why he had left France. The General searching for a quick answer that would incriminate no one and assure his own future, replied, 'Sire, when I left France, before the age of ten, I was only a child, not knowing what I did.' He had been sent to the protection of an uncle, he said, and was not responsible for his own actions. Satisfied with this tactful explanation, the king asked the prisoner whether he would like to witness the feu-de-joie and personally conducted him to watch the ritual celebration of victory. Valfons then escorted Ligonier round the French lines, discussing the day's fighting as they went. During the tour of inspection an arrogant young French officer pointed out the Regiment of Navarre saying, 'Sir, there is the finest Regiment in Europe', to which Ligonier with true Gascon spirit replied, 'Yes, I know: I saw them taken prisoner at Hochstadt', meaning Blenheim, forty-three years before. During further exchanges, perhaps at supper, Ligonier told the king the full story of his capture, commending the honesty and loyalty of the two carabiniers who had refused his bribe of a purse and jewelled watch. The king at once ordered the men to be given a present of 50 louis each as well as a pension and a commission.

Rex Whitworth

120.

AFTER the peace of Aix La Chapelle [1748] a number of officers of regiments were reduced. One of these gentlemen accidentally introducing himself into a subscription billard room, at a coffee house near St James's, found the Duke of Cumberland, his late Majesty's uncle, at play with a colonel of the Guards; it was a match for a considerable sum, and the termination of it was looked for with apparent eagerness by the numerous spectators. His Royal Highness lost the game and immediately putting his hand into his pocket, discovered that he had lost a gold snuff box on the top of which was a fine portrait of Frederick of Prussia, set round with brilliants.

A general confusion ensued, the door was immediately locked, and a search called for, which was readily assented to by all present except the stranger, who declared that he would lose his life before he would submit to the proposal; little doubt was then entertained but he was the pickpocket; and resistance appeared useless. The indignant soldier then requested that His Royal Highness would honour him with a private interview; to this the Duke instantly assented, and the company remained in the greater suspense. On entering the room, the officer thus addressed the Duke: 'May it please your Royal Highness, I am a soldier; but my sword is no longer of service to me or my country, and the only means I have to support the character of a gentleman (which no distress shall induce me to forfeit) is the half pay which I receive from the bounty of my sovereign.

'My name is C—, my rank a lieutenant in the Old Buffs. I dined this day at a chop house, where I paid for a rump steak; but eating only half of it I have the remainder wrapped up in paper in my pocket, for another scanty meal at my humble lodgings'; and immediately producing it, added, 'I am now, Sir, ready to undergo the strictest search.' 'I'll be d—d if you shall', replied the Duke, and on their returning to the billiard room the flap of His Highness's coat struck against the entrance; when it was discovered that the seam of his pocket was unsewed and the lost valuable was safe in the silk lining. A few days after, the gallant officer received a Captain's Commission, with a flattering letter from the Royal Duke of future promotion.

The Soldier's Companion

121.

THERE is little doubt that a mean jealousy of Prince Ferdinand was the real cause of Lord George Sackville's reluctance to advance with the cavalry, and complete the rout of the army of Marechal de Contades at Minden, in 1757. At the celebrated court-martial, by the sentence of which Lord George was dismissed the service, every effort was made on his part to prove that he was embarrassed and hampered by the contradictory orders received from the Prince. On the other hand, his enemies (and he was very unpopular in the service) tried to show that he was influenced by personal fear. But this is very improbable; the enemy were in full retreat, and the advance of the cavalry was only required to complete their confusion and harass their flight, and that is not a moment at which even a coward would betray his alarm.

The whole question of the contradictory orders seems to have been this. One of the Prince's Staff-officers sent with the order to Lord George desired him to advance *with* 'the cavalry'. Another who arrived on the heels of the first, said, 'with the British cavalry.' Lord George took advantage of this discrepancy, to send them both back with the inquiry whether he was to move forward *all* the cavalry (there were several foreign regiments), or only the British. Meantime the opportunity for charging and routing the retreating French infantry was lost, and, though the victory was gained, yet its consequences were not near what they ought to have been. Prince Ferdinand, as soon as the action was over, issued a severe order reflecting upon Lord George; and the Court-martial appear to have only done their duty by dismissing him. Strange it now appears, that a man cashiered under such circumstances, should afterwards, when he became Lord George Germaine (a name he took for a large inheritance) have held the office of Secretary of State. To such height parties ran at the period, that his great interest, and, it must be added, his remarkable talents, enabled him to rise from so fatal a disgrace as dismissal from the army for misconduct before the enemy.

Lord de Ros

122.

FREDERICK THE GREAT of Prussia [1688–1740], asked Sir Robert Sutton, at a review of his tall grenadiers, if he thought an equal number of Englishmen could beat them? 'Sir,' replied Sir Robert, 'I do not venture to assert that; but I know that half the number would try.'

Naval and Military Anecdotes

123.

IN the first war of Silesia, the king [Frederick] being desirous of making, in the night time, some alterations in his camp, ordered that under pain of death, neither fire nor candle should be burning in the tents after a certain hour. He went round the camp himself, to see that his orders were obeyed; and, as he passed by Captain Zietern's camp, he perceived a light. He entered, and found the captain sealing a letter, which he had just written to his wife, whom he tenderly loved. 'What are you doing there?' said the king: 'Do you not know the orders?' Zietern threw himself at his feet, and begged mercy, but he neither could nor attempted to deny his fault. 'Sit down,' said the king to him, 'and add a few words I shall dictate.' The officer obeyed, and the king dictated: 'Tomorrow I shall perish on the scaffold.' Zietern wrote it, and he was executed the next day.

The Percy Anecdotes

124.

When Frederick invaded Saxony on 28 August 1756, the Saxon Minister of State Count Brühl was, in name at least, foremost among the enemy commanders.

. . . his personal interests were far removed from the rough and tumble of the battlefield. Though he had been appointed General of

Infantry at his own request this was solely a political move designed to impose his authority on his King's military advisers. Brühl's private ambitions lay in the sartorial field. He possessed 200 pairs of shoes, 802 embroidered nightshirts, 500 suits, 102 watches, 843 snuffboxes, 87 rings, 67 smelling-bottles, 1,500 wigs, and 29 carriages. The choice of dress which faced this unfortunate man each morning was thus a formidable one; to ease his task, he had an album prepared containing coloured reproductions of his entire wardrobe. After the basic ensemble had been selected, it was at least possible for him to get up. Then the accessories—rings, snuffboxes, etcetera—could be chosen at leisure. Nor was his collecting mania confined to inanimate objects. At bedtime he had again to act with promptitude and decision, declaring his preference among an *embarras de maîtresses*. He lacked nothing, in fact, except intelligence. For the last ten years he had been supplying the Courts of Europe with cautionary tales of the King of Prussia's misdeeds, some true, some imaginary, but all in due course reaching the King's ears through his paid informers in the Dresden Chancellory.

As his army marched unopposed through Saxony, Frederick's opinion of Brühl proved accurate: 'Fifteen hundred wigs, but no head!' Taken completely by surprise, Brühl's only action was to withdraw hurriedly with his Sovereign to inaccessible country near Dresden, where, at a place called Pirna, the Saxon army was then slowly assembled. Nightshirts, smelling-salts, even the incriminating State archives were left behind in the capital, where the last were soon seized by a resolute Prussian general despite the Queen's efforts to hide some of the documents in her bed.

Ludwig Reiners

125.

. . . he [Frederick the Great, at the outset of his campaign of 1757] wrote a secret letter of instructions to the Minister for Home Affairs, his boyhood friend Count Finckenstein:

In the critical state of our affairs, I ought to give you my orders so that you may have authority to take the necessary decisions in case of necessity. If I should be killed, affairs must be carried on without the slightest change and without it becoming apparent that they are in other hands. Should I be taken prisoner by the enemy, I forbid the smallest consideration for my person or the least notice to be taken of anything I may write from captivity. If such a misfor-

tune occurs I wish to sacrifice myself for the State and allegiance must be paid
to my brother, who, together with all my ministers and generals, shall answer
to me with his head that neither province nor ransom shall be offered for me
and that the war shall be prosecuted and advantages exploited exactly as
though I had never existed in the world.

At the same time he wrote to [his sister] Wilhelmina:

It is shameful at my age to be knocking about with four furious females
[Maria Theresa, the Empress Elizabeth, Madame de Pompadour, and Frederick's sister Queen Ulrike of Sweden]. But I have got to defend my skin and
persuade these ladies to lay down the sword and return to their spinning-
wheels. As for me, dear sister, fear nothing from this war. Only the worthy get
killed; my type always survives.

Ludwig Reiners

126.

On the evening of 24 August 1758, Frederick lay in a mill on the river Mutzel, pre-
paring to fight a desperate battle at Zorndorf the next morning against the invading
Russian army. On this occasion as on so many in his wars, Frederick preferred the
company of his young Swiss lecteur, *de Catt, to that of his generals.*

ATTRACTED by his tact, modesty and good sense, Frederick used
him during these war years as a kind of sounding-board for his
opinions, an audience for his recitations and a critic and editor of his
verses. Whenever he had the time, in the afternoons or evenings, he
would summon him for a chat and de Catt kept a record of their conversations. 'When you look at it in later years,' the King told him, 'you
will say: this is what that garrulous old warrior told me who was always
bemoaning his lot, always in a fever-heat, wondering anxiously how
matters would end and shouting at me, his life was no better than a
dog's . . . '

That evening, on 24th August, de Catt was summoned to the King:

. . . I found him writing busily in a very small room in the mill. I thought he
was making his plans for the battle. Not at all. He was writing verses. 'Verses,
Sire? And tomorrow Your Majesty intends to fight a battle!' 'What's so unusual
about that? My thoughts have been on the main business all day, my plan is
ready, I have made my decisions. So now I think I might be allowed to scribble
verses like any other man.' . . .

The King then remarked that Racine's odes were not nearly so good
as his tragedies. The record continues:

'I think, Sire, it would be very difficult to write verse in the style of Racine, starting, for instance, with: "Celui qui des flots assouvit la fureur . . ." 'You are right, that would be difficult. But, mon cher, suppose I try?' He had seized his pen when the generals were announced. 'Wait a moment in my room. I want to give them their instructions. Everyone must know exactly what he has to do . . . ' The King went out and returned after talking to his generals for half an hour. 'Well, all's said. Now, what can I say about "Celui qui des flots . . ."?'

In a quarter of an hour he had finished the verses, which he allowed me to keep. 'Now, my friend,' said the King, 'let us eat these grapes, for who knows who may eat them tomorrow. We move at dawn.'

Next morning, Frederick's servant told de Catt that the King had slept so soundly he had had difficulty in waking him.

Ludwig Reiners

127.

The story of Frederick that every schoolboy knows.

IT was customary with Frederick the Great of Prussia, whenever a new soldier appeared in his guards, to ask him three questions, viz., 'How old are you? How long have you been in my service? Are you satisfied with your pay and treatment?' It happened that a young soldier, a native of France, who had served in his own country, desired to enlist into the Prussian service, and his figure was such as to cause him to be immediately accepted. He was, however, totally ignorant of the German language, but his captain gave him notice that the King would ask him certain questions in that language the first time he saw him, and therefore instructed him to learn by heart the three answers which he was to make the King. The soldier learned them by the next day; and as soon as he appeared in the ranks, Frederick came up to interrogate him. His Majesty, however, happened to begin with the second question first; and asked him 'How long have you been in my service?' 'Twenty-one years, answered the soldier.' The King, struck with his youth, which contradicted his answer, said to him much astonished, 'How old are you?' 'One year, an't please your Majesty.' Frederick, still more astonished, cried, 'You or I must certainly be bereft of our senses.' The soldier, who took this for the third question about 'pay and treatment', replied firmly, 'Both an't please your Majesty.' 'This is the first time I ever was treated as a madman at the head of my army,' rejoined Frederick. The soldier, who had exhausted his stock of German, stood silent; and when the King again addressed him, in order to penetrate the mystery, the soldier told him in French, that he did not understand a word of German. The King laughed heartily, and, after exhorting him to perform his duty, left him.

Naval and Military Anecdotes

128.

Mr Edward Gibbon recalls his military experience.

IN the act of offering our names and receiving our commissions, as major and captain in the Hampshire regiment (June 12, 1759), we had not supposed that we should be dragged away, my father from his farm, myself from my books, and condemned, during two years and a half (May 10, 1760–December 23, 1762), to a wandering life of military servitude. But a weekly or monthly exercise of thirty thousand provincials would have left them useless and ridiculous; and after the pretence of an invasion had vanished, the popularity of Mr Pitt gave a sanction to the illegal step of keeping them till the end of the war under arms, in constant pay and duty, and at a distance from their respective homes. When the King's order for our embodying came down, it was too late to retreat, and too soon to repent. The south battalion of the Hampshire militia was a small independent corps of four hundred and seventy-six, officers and men, commanded by Lieutenant-Colonel Sir Thomas Worsley, who, after a prolix and passionate contest, delivered us from the tyranny of the Lord Lieutenant, the Duke of Bolton. My proper station, as first captain, was at the head of my own, and afterwards of the grenadier company; but in the absence, or even in the presence, of the two field officers, I was entrusted by my friend and my father with the effective labour of dictating the orders, and exercising the battalion. With the help of an original journal, I could write the history of my bloodless and inglorious campaigns; but as these events have lost much of their importance in my own eyes, they shall be dispatched in a few words. From Winchester, the first place of assembly (June 4, 1760), we were removed, at our own request, for the benefit of a foreign education. By the arbitrary, and often capricious orders of the

War Office, the battalion successively marched to the pleasant and hospitable Blandford (June 17); to Hilsea barracks, a seat of disease and discord (September 1); to Cranbrook in the Weald of Kent (December 11); to the seacoast of Dover (December 27); to Winchester camp (June 25, 1761); to the populous and disorderly town of Devizes (October 23); to Salisbury (February 28, 1762); to our beloved Blandford a second time (March 9): and finally, to the fashionable resort of Southampton (June 2); where the colours were fixed till our final dissolution (December 23). On the beach at Dover we had exercised in sight of the Gallic shores. But the most splendid and useful scene of our life was a four months' encampment on Winchester Down, under the command of the Earl of Effingham. Our army consisted of the thirty-fourth regiment of foot and six militia corps. The consciousness of defects was stimulated by friendly emulation. We improved our time and opportunities in morning and evening field-days; and in the general reviews the South Hampshire were rather a credit than a disgrace to the line. In our subsequent quarters of the Devizes and Blandford, we advanced with a quick step in our military studies; the ballot of the ensuing summer renewed our vigour and youth; and had the militia subsisted another year, we might have contested the prize with the most perfect of our brethren.

The loss of so many busy and idle hours was not compensated by any elegant pleasure; and my temper was insensibly soured by the society of our rustic officers. In every state there exists, however, a balance of good and evil. The habits of a sedentary life were usefully broken by the duties of an active profession: in the healthful exercise of the field I hunted with a battalion, instead of a pack; and at that time I was ready, at any hour of the day or night, to fly from quarters to London, from London to quarters, on the slightest call of private or regimental business. But my principal obligation to the militia was the making me an Englishman, and a soldier. After my foreign education, with my reserved temper, I should long have continued a stranger to my native country, had I not been shaken in this various scene of new faces and new friends: had not experience forced me to feel the characters of our leading men, the state of parties, the forms of office, and the operation of our civil and military system. In this peaceful service I imbibed the rudiments of the language, and science of tactics, which opened a new field of study and observation. I diligently read, and meditated, the *Mémoires Militaires* of Quintus Icilius (Mr Guichardt), the only writer who has united the merits of a professor and a veteran. The discipline and evolutions of a modern battalion gave me a clearer notion of the phalanx and the legion; and the captain of the Hampshire grenadiers (the reader may smile) has not been useless to the historian of the Roman empire.

Edward Gibbon

129.

One of General James Wolfe's biographers recounts the tale told by Lord Temple of an incident following Wolfe's appointment to command in Canada in 1759.

'AFTER Wolfe's appointment', we are told, 'and on the day preceding his embarkation for America, Pitt, desirous of giving his last verbal instructions, invited him to dinner, Lord Temple being the only other guest. As the evening advanced, Wolfe, heated perhaps by his own aspiring thoughts and the unwonted society of statesmen, broke forth into a strain of gasconade and bravado. He drew his sword, he rapped the table with it, he flourished it round the room, he talked of the mighty things which that sword was to achieve. The two Ministers sat aghast at an exhibition so unusual from any man of real sense and real spirit. And when at last Wolfe had taken his leave, and his carriage was heard to roll from the door, Pitt seemed for the moment shaken in his high opinion which his deliberate judgment had formed of Wolfe; he lifted up his eyes and arms, and exclaimed to Lord Temple, "Good God! that I should have entrusted the fate of the country and of the Administration to such hands!" '

Now Temple was hardly the man to understand Wolfe, who was probably very different from the officers of his acquaintance, who were not supposed to exhibit zeal at the dinner-table, nor any particular enthusiasms unconnected with women, horse-racing and cards. He himself was sedateness and apathy personified. As Pitt bitterly (but anonymously) wrote years afterwards, when he quarrelled with his brother-in-law, Temple 'might have crept out of life with as little notice as he crept in, and gone off with no other degree of credit than that of adding a single unit to the bills of mortality', had he not derived lustre from his association with himself.

B. Willson

130.

AGED only thirty-two, Wolfe was chosen by Pitt to command the expedition to take Quebec, which would mean the conquest of Canada. With the splendid seamanship and co-operation of Admiral Saunders his troops were taken from Louisburg and arrived before Quebec. The heights opposite the town were seized; the first assault, somewhat ill-conceived, was costly and unsuccessful, and finally Wolfe decided to take a force downstream secretly; the cliffs were scaled by a narrow path which led to the summit. Montcalm, though commanding superior numbers, was led to attack before his whole force was ready. Wolfe died in the moment of victory, and his noble opponent Montcalm also died soon after. Four days later Quebec surrendered. This was the year when, guided by Pitt, England gained great victories: Horace Walpole said in one of his letters, 'One is forced to ask every morning what victory there is, for fear of missing one.'

The night before the battle [12 September 1759] Wolfe told John Jervis, an old school-fellow and later Earl St Vincent, that he did not expect to survive the action. Taking from his neck a miniature of Miss Lowther, he asked Jervis to deliver it to her in person. She was the sister of the first Earl of Lonsdale, and Wolfe had become engaged to her.

For full two hours the procession of boats, borne on the current, steered silently down the St Lawrence. The stars were visible, but the night was moonless and sufficiently dark. The General was in one of the foremost boats, and near him was a young midshipman, John Robison, afterwards professor of natural philosophy in the University of Edinburgh. He used to tell in his later life how Wolfe, with a low voice, repeated Gray's *Elegy in a Country Churchyard* to the officers about him. Probably it was to relieve the intense strain of his thoughts. Among the rest was the verse which his own fate was soon to illustrate—

> The paths of glory lead but to the grave.

'Gentlemen,' he said, as his recital ended, 'I would rather have written those lines than take Quebec.'

As they neared their destination, the tide bore them in towards the shore, and the mighty wall of rock and forest towered in darkness on their left. The dead stillness was suddenly broken by the sharp Qui vive! of a French sentry, invisible in the thick gloom. 'France!' answered a Highland officer of Fraser's regiment from one of the boats of the light infantry. He had served in Holland, and spoke French fluently.

'A quel régiment?'

'De la Reine', replied the Highlander. He knew that a part of that corps was with Bougainville. The sentry, expecting the convoy of provisions, was satisfied, and did not ask for the password.

Soon after, the foremost boats were passing the heights of Samos, when another sentry challenged them, and they could see him through the darkness running down to the edge of the water, within range of a pistol-shot. In answer to his questions, the same officer replied, in French: 'Provision-boats. Don't make a noise; the English will hear us.' In fact, the sloop-of-war *Hunter* was anchored in the stream not far off. This time, again, the sentry let them pass. In a few moments they rounded the headland above the Anse du Foulon. There was no sentry there. The strong current swept the boats of the light infantry a little below the intended landing-place. They disembarked on a narrow strand at the foot of heights as steep as a hill covered with trees can be. The twenty-four volunteers led the way, climbing with what silence they might, closely followed by a much larger body. When they reached the top they saw in the dim light a cluster of tents at a short distance, and immediately made a dash at them. Vergor leaped from bed and tried to run off, but was shot in the heel and captured. His men, taken by surprise, made little resistance. One or two were caught, and the rest fled.

The main body of troops waited in their boats by the edge of the strand. The heights near by were cleft by a great ravine choked with forest trees; and in its depths ran a little brook called Ruisseau St-Denis, which, swollen by the late rains, fell plashing in the stillness over a rock. Other than this no sound could reach the strained ear of Wolfe but the gurgle of the tide and the cautious climbing of his advance-parties as they mounted the steeps at some little distance from where he sat listening. At length from the top came a sound of musket-shots, followed by loud huzzas, and he knew that his men were masters of the position. The word was given; the troops leaped from the boats and scaled the heights, some here, some there, clutching at trees and bushes, their muskets slung at their backs. Tradition still points out the place, near the mouth of the ravine, where the foremost reached the top. Wolfe said to an officer near him: 'You can try it, but I don't think you'll get up.' He himself, however, found strength to drag himself up with the rest. The narrow slanting path on the face of the heights had been made impassable by trenches and abattis; but all obstructions were soon cleared away, and then the descent was easy. In the gray of the morning the long file of red-coated soldiers moved quickly upward, and formed in order on the plateau above.

Francis Parkman

131.

The battle on the Heights of Abraham began about 9 a.m. on 13 September 1759 with a charge by the French which was repulsed by volley fire from the British ranks, Wolfe being wounded in the wrist. He was hit twice more, this time mortally, as he advanced with his men against the reeling French regiments, but he ordered an officer to support him as his van swept past, lest they should see that he was wounded.

AFTER our late worthy General, of renowned memory, was carried off wounded to the rear of the front line, he desired those who were about him to lay him down; being asked if he would have a Surgeon he replied, 'it is needless; it is all over with me'. One of them cried out, 'They run, see how they run.' 'Who runs?' demanded our hero with great earnestness, like a person aroused from sleep. The Officer answered, 'The Enemy, Sir; Egad, they give way everywhere.' Thereupon the General rejoined, 'Go one of you, my lads, to Colonel Burton; tell him to march Webb's regiment with all speed down to Charles's river, to cut off the retreat of the fugitives from the bridge.' Then, turning on his side, he added, 'Now, God be praised, I will die in peace'; and thus expired.

Captain John Knox

132.

A notable example of government ingratitude for military sacrifice as characteristic of the twentieth century as of the eighteenth.

MRS WOLFE was a woman cast in the antique mould. Although she could not bring herself to reply to letters of condolence, she was not blind either to the dignity or the duties of her position as mother and chief surviving representative of her celebrated son. On November 6 she addressed a letter to Chatham, observing,

As you did my dear son the honour to entrust him with so great and important an office as the taking of Quebec, which you, Sir, planned, and he executed, I hope to his Majesty's, your and his country's satisfaction, though to my irreparable loss, it occurs to me that there may be some papers or orders of yours relating to the Government service which will come to me. If you will honour me with your commands, I shall send them by a faithful and trusty gentleman, who carries this, Lieutenant Scott; and no eye shall see them but your own.

But it was over a fortnight before the papers reached her at the hands of Captain Bell, who no doubt thought he was doing his duty by examining and sorting them beforehand, not realizing either the capacity or the imperiousness of the old lady at Blackheath. She was as angry as if a slight had been intentionally put upon her.

Her patience had much to endure. It will be recalled that Wolfe had made a will disposing of some seven or eight thousand pounds which he supposed he had inherited on the death of his father. It appeared, however, that the old General, seeing his son well and profitably employed in the service, had given his wife a life interest in his small fortune, which, as her health was but poor, seemed to offer but little injustice to his son. When the nature of James's will was revealed, Mrs Wolfe once again addressed Chatham.

MRS WOLFE *to* CHATHAM

Blackheath, November 30th, 1759

Sir. The great honour your letter of the 28th of Nov. does me, has given me resolution which no other consideration could do to make an application which I hope you will not disprove. My dear son, not knowing the disposition his father had made of his fortune—which was wholly settled on me for life and magnified by fame greatly beyond what it really is—has left to his friends more than a third part of it; and though I should have the greatest pleasure imaginable in discharging these legacies in my lifetime, I cannot do it without distressing myself to the highest degree. My request to you, good and great Sir, is that you will honour me with your instructions how I may in the properest manner address His Majesty for a pension to enable me to fulfil the generous and kind intentions of my most dear lost son to his friends, and to live like the relict of General Wolfe and General Wolfe's mother. I hope, Sir, you will pardon this liberty. I have the honour to be, etc., etc.

CHATHAM *to* MRS WOLFE

St James's Square, January 17, 1760

Madam. I think myself much favoured by your letter wherein you are pleased to desire my advice in a matter that concerns your ease. Had I more than information in my power to offer on a subject so interesting, I beg you will be assured, Madam, that your trouble would be rendered very short, as well my own satisfaction become very sensible. But the thing you are pleased to mention being totally in the Duke of Newcastle's department, I can only desire leave to apprise you that it is to his Grace that all applications of such a nature are to be addressed. If you shall judge proper to take that step (with regard to which I cannot venture to advise), you will command, in that, as well as every other occasion, all good offices and sincerest endeavours for your service from him who has the honour ever to remain, with the truest respect, Madam,

Your most obedient and most humble servant,

WM. PITT.

It only remains to add that the hero's mother was not only unsuccessful in this application to the Government, but also in another transaction which redounds little to the credit of the Government or the nation. It was supposed that Wolfe, being a Commander-in-Chief of an expedition, would be entitled to a Commander-in-Chief's pay. Not until February 1761 were the warrants made out for the payment of the staff of the Quebec expedition. As Mrs Wolfe's agent, Fisher based his demand at the rate of £10 a day from the date of his last commission until his death—a matter of nearly £2500. Promptly was the claim rejected by the War Office, then presided over by Charles Townshend, a brother of Wolfe's brigadier. Acting according to the counsel of friends, amongst whom were the Lord Shelburne and Sir Robert Rich, Mrs Wolfe addressed a memorial to the young king, George III. But the representations of Barrington were successful, and after a melancholy correspondence lasting three years, Townshend's successor, Wellbore Ellis, wrote finally to say that the application was refused.

It is to be feared the old lady got a reputation for eccentricity by the tenacity with which she clung to her claims and to the memory of her son and husband.

B. Willson

133.

The field of Landeshut, 23 June 1760.

FIELD-MARSHAL LOUDON attacked the Prussian general, Heinrich Fouqué, 'one of those tigerish lieutenant-generals whom the Prussian service bred in such profusion'. Fouqué was badly cut up by the Austrian cavalry whilst making a last stand with his few remaining men. Colonel Voit of the Austrian Lowenstein Dragoons brought up his parade horse and courteously begged Fouqué to mount. The Prussian declined, saying 'the blood would spoil your fine saddlery'. Voit replied 'it will become far more precious, when it is stained with the blood of a hero'. There was one officer who was vulgar enough to taunt the captured commander for his misfortune to his very face. But all the officers who were present condemned his bad manners. Fouqué interrupted, and merely said, 'let him speak, gentlemen! You know how it goes in war; it's my turn today, and tomorrow it's yours.'

Christopher Duffy

134.

OFFICERS of [the American] militia were, up to the end of 1776, appointed by popular vote or ballot. A New Jersey man or a Maryland man looked upon the whole proceedings as being of the nature of a vestry meeting. Wherever he went he carried his voting ticket in his pocket, and whether the post to be filled was that of a mayor, sheriff, magistrate, collector, or captain, the principle for him remained the same. The militiamen enrolled themselves according to a form of contract drawn on democratic lines; as thus:

We the subscribers do hereby severally enlist ourselves into the service of the United American Colonies until the first day of January next . . . and we severally consent to be formed by such person or persons as the general court shall appoint into a company of ninety men, including one captain, two lieutenants, one ensign, four sergeants, four corporals, one drum, and one fife *to be elected by the company*.

The practice of election extended even to field officers. A Maryland regiment having been called together to poll for a field officer, the colonel fixed a day for the poll and appointed himself returning officer for the declaration of the poll. The men of the regiment disregarded the date fixed by the colonel, refused his services as returning officer, and threatened him with personal violence should he dare to interfere, so fiercely was the democratic principle asserted even in a state of the aristocratic origin which Maryland was proud to claim.

Henry Belcher

135.

IN the course of the late action [September 1777], Lieutenant Harvey of the 62nd, a youth of sixteen and a nephew of the Adjutant General of the same name, received several wounds and was repeatedly ordered off the field by Colonel Anstruther. But his heroic ardor would not allow him to quit the battle, while he could stand and see his brave lads fighting beside him. A ball striking one of his legs, his removal became absolutely necessary, and while they were conveying him away, another wounded him mortally. In this situation the Surgeon recommended him to take a powerful dose of opium, to avoid seven or eight hours of most exquisite torture. This he immediately consented to, and when the Colonel entered the tent with Major Harnage, who were both wounded, they asked whether he had any affairs they could settle for him? His reply was, 'That being a minor, everything was already adjusted.' But he had one request, which he had just life enough to utter, 'Tell my uncle I died like a soldier!'

Lieutenant Aubusey

136.

The American army straggled into winter quarters at Valley Forge, Pennsylvania, on 21 December 1777, to begin an experience that passed into national legend as an epic of endurance, and ended only with the coming of spring.

IN all, Washington's army numbered 11,000 officers and men, of whom 8200 were fit for duty. They made a camp in a fine strategic site, but there was much about it that added to their misery—and they were miserable when they arrived. They lacked almost everything an army needs for survival. They had been hungry for several weeks, and their new quarters were in a part of Pennsylvania barren of provisions. They had lived for weeks in the open and required barracks or housing that would give them protection from the winter. Valley Forge had virtually no buildings; the troops would have to put up their own.

The recent campaign had worn out shoes and clothing as well as men. The hills offered no more in the way of clothing than of food. Almost everything else was in short supply as well. A few days after their arrival Washington remarked that there was no soap in the army but, he concluded, there was not much use for it since few men had more than one shirt, and some none at all. And he might have noted that, though Valley Creek and the Schuylkill bordered the camp, water for all uses had to be carried for considerable distances, in some places a mile or more.

The woods afforded the materials for housing, and the soldiers fell to building huts almost immediately. Washington ordered that the camp be carefully laid out. Huts, fourteen by sixteen feet, were to be constructed of logs, roofed with 'split slabs'. Clay sealed the sides and was used to make fireplaces. Nails were not to be had of course, and the logs had to be notched. Each hut housed a squad of twelve men. Washington promised to share his soldiers' hardships until the first huts were completed and lived in a tent before finally moving into one of the few houses near by. By January 13 the last of the huts were completed.

Comfort did not abound inside the huts' walls. Many had only the ground for floors, and straw for beds was not readily available. Worst of all, the troops frequently had nothing to eat. At the time of their arrival the commissary seems to have contained only twenty-five barrels of flour—nothing else, neither meat nor fish. During the days that followed the soldiers chopped down trees and put up huts with empty stomachs. At night, according to Albigence Waldo, a surgeon of the Connecticut line, there was a general cry that echoed through the hills—'No meat! No meat!' The troops added to this 'melancholy sound' their versions of the cawing of crows and the hooting of owls.

Imitating bird calls suggests that the troops' sense of humor saw them through the worst of their sufferings. They had their hatreds, too, and these also may have helped sustain them. One was firecake, a thin bread made of flour and water and baked over the campfire. Another was the commissaries who were supposed to provide food for the army. Waldo reconstructed a number of conversations along the following lines: 'What have you for your dinners, boys?' 'Nothing but firecake and water, Sir.' At night: 'Gentlemen, the supper is ready. What is your supper, lads?' 'Firecake and water, Sir.' In the morning: 'What have you got for breakfast, lads?' 'Firecake and water, Sir.' And from Waldo, the snarl: 'The Lord send that our Commissary of Purchases may live [on] firecake and water till their glutted gutts are turned to pasteboard.'

Robert Middlekauff

137.

A volunteer in the South Carolina infantry describes an incident at Eutaw Springs, 8 September 1781.

ONE of his [Colonel William Washington's] dragoons, Billy Lunsford, requested of his captain leave to steal upon and shoot a British senti- nel. The captain told him it could not do the cause any good, and, as the sentinel was doing his duty, it was a pity to shoot him. Billy swore his time was out, and, as he was going home to Virginia, he would have it to tell that he had killed 'one damned British son of a bitch'. Accordingly, Billy commenced passing backwards and forwards with a pistol, creeping on his all fours and grunting like a hog. The sentinel was heard to slap his cartouche box and fired, and Billy changed his grunting to groaning, being shot through the body, entering his right and coming out his left side. It was as pretty a shot as could have been made in daylight. The British sentinel, being reinforced, carried Billy a prisoner into their camp, where, by the kind attention of a British sur- geon who nursed him and had him nursed all night to prevent his bleeding inwardly and to make him bleed outwardly, he recovered.

John Chaney

138.

One of the Franco-American force besieging the British garrison of Savannah in 1779 was Samuel Warren, formerly an officer in the British service.

AN English aunt sent him word that if the report was true she hoped he would have an arm or a leg shot off in his first battle. She had her wish, as he lost one on 9th October. After the war, he placed the leg bone in an elegant mahogany case to which he affixed a plate bearing the date of its loss. This Warren sent to his aunt with a note to the effect that, while her wish had been fulfilled, he would rather be a rebel with one leg than a royalist with two. William B. Stevens

139.

Later in the siege of Savannah, Colonel Arthur Dillon offered his men of the LXXX Infanterie a hundred guineas for the first to brave the hail of British fire and plant a fascine in the ditch below their works.

NOT a soldier moved. Much mortified, Colonel Dillon began to upbraid them for cowardice. A sergeant-major stepped forward. 'Had you not, sir,' he protested, 'held out a sum of money as a temptation, your grenadiers would, one and all, have presented themselves.' With this, the soldiers to a man advanced. Of one hundred and ninety-four, only ninety were to return, it is said.

Alexander Lawrence

140.

Count Matthieu Dumas describes the moment on 19 October 1781, when he rode out from the American lines to meet Lord Cornwallis's emissary, Brigadier-General Charles O'Hara, and commence the formal surrender of Yorktown.

I PLACED myself at General O'Hara's left hand . . . He asked me where General Rochambeau was. 'On our left,' I said, 'at the head of the French line.' The English general urged his horse forward to present his sword to the French general. Guessing his intention, I galloped on to place myself between him and M. de Rochambeau, who at that moment made me a sign, pointing to General Washington who was opposite to him . . .

'You are mistaken,' said I to General O'Hara. 'The commander-in-chief of our army is on the right.'

I accompanied him, and the moment that he presented his sword, General Washington, anticipating him said, 'Never from such a good hand.'

[*An American officer wrote that:*] The British officers in general behaved like boys who had been whipped at school. Some bit their lips, some pouted, others cried. Their round, broad-brimmed hats were well adapted to the occasion, hiding those faces they were ashamed to show. The foreign regiments made a more military appearance, and the conduct of their officers was far more becoming men of fortitude.

[*Captain Graham of the 76th Foot described the scene in the British lines:*] Drums were beat, but the colors remained in their cases—an idle retaliation for a very idle sight which had been put by our people on the American garrison of Charleston, and the regiments having formed in columns at quarter distance the men laid down their arms.

It is a sorry reminiscence, this. Yet the scene made a deep impression at the moment, for the mortification and unfeigned sorrow of the soldiers will never fade from my memory. Some went so far as to shed tears, while one man, a corporal, who stood near me, embraced his firelock and then threw it on the ground exclaiming, 'May you never get so good a master again!'

Nevertheless, to do them justice, the Americans behaved with great delicacy and forbearance, while the French, by what motive actuated I will not pretend to say, were profuse in their protestations of sympathy . . . When I visited their lines . . . immediately after our parade had been dismissed, I was overwhelmed with the civility of my late enemies.

[*Lord Cornwallis wrote the next day to General Clinton, on passage to relieve him, too late:*] I have the mortification to inform your Excellency that I have been forced to give up the posts of York and Gloucester, and to surrender the troops under my command, by capitulation on the 19th inst. as prisoners of war to the combined forces of America and France.

[*And on 22 October, Lafayette wrote to a friend:*] The play, sir, is over. Washington has given a dinner for British General O'Hara.

Esmond Wright

141.

At the port of Leith late one April evening in 1779, Highland soldiers of the 42nd and 71st regiments, abruptly drafted to serve with a detested Glasgow Lowland regiment, refused the order and fought a brief, bloody little battle with men of the South Fencibles sent to compel them. Fourteen of the combatants died and many more were wounded. Three of the captured Highlanders were sentenced to death by a court martial.

[AT Holyrood] . . . early on Friday, May 28, they were brought up to the chamber of the Great Hall and out into the sunlight of Palace Yard, their heads bare and their hands tied behind them. Preceded by muffled drums and escorted by a platoon of the Argyll Fencibles, now the garrison regiment and soon to be in revolt itself, they were slow-marched from the citadel under the narrow arch of Foog's Gate, northward past the foot of the Lang Stairs to the Portcullis and Inner Barrier until they crossed the drawbridge to the mound of Castle Hill. Here five companies of the Argyll Fencibles were drawn up in hollow square facing the fortress, and three ranks of red dragoons held back the press of the crowd from the Royal Mile. The sun was strong, but a brisk wind moved across the high ground, pulling at the belted plaids of the Argylls and of the other Highland prisoners who had been brought out to watch the death of their friends. By the wall of the dry ditch and below the Half Moon Battery were three open coffins to which the condemned men were led. Each man knelt beside the plain box allotted to him, MacGregor with them, but as the minister began to pray he was stopped by Major Hugh Montgomerie of the Argylls. Before the condemned men could submit their souls to God they must listen to the General Orders issued two days before by Robert Skene.

Although these orders were brief the reading took some minutes, for the Major frequently paused, awaiting MacGregor's whispered translation. The court having found the accused guilty of mutiny and a breach of the second, third, fourth and fifth Articles of War, and having duly considered the evil tendency to mutiny and sedition, especially when carried to such enormous lengths in the present case, did adjudge Charles Williamson, Archibald MacIver and Robert Budge to be shot to death. Which sentence had been transmitted to the King, and His Majesty had been pleased to signify his pleasure. Having regard to the former commendable behaviour of the 42nd Regiment, and that Robert Budge, only now recovering from the wounds he had received in the affray, did not appear to have any forward part in the mutiny, His Majesty was most graciously pleased to grant the condemned a free pardon 'in full consideration that they will endeavour upon every future occasion, by a prompt obedience and orderly demeanour, to atone for this unpremeditated but atrocious offence'.

Quickly stripped of their muffling crêpe, the Argyll drums now beat a spirited march, the companies turning and wheeling toward the Royal Mile in a river of green tartan. The bewildered prisoners rose from their knees. Their hands were untied and they stumbled from the coffins to the waiting, weeping embrace of their comrades.

John Prebble

142.

After three days and nights of continuous gunfire in the streets of Gibraltar, on 15 April 1781 Sergeant Ancell encountered a well-known private of his regiment.

I MET Jack Careless in the street, singing with uncommon glee (notwithstanding that the enemy were firing with prodigious warmth) part of the old song:

A soldier's life's a merry life,
From care and trouble free.

He ran to his comrade with eagerness and, presenting his bottle, cried: 'Damn me if I don't like fighting! I'd like to be ever tanning the Dons. Plenty of good liquor for carrying away—never was the price so cheap—fine stuff—enough to make a miser quit his gold.'

'Why, Jack,' said he, 'what have you been about?'

With an arch grin he replied: 'That would puzzle a heathen philosopher, or yearly almanack-maker to unriddle—I scarce know myself, I have been constantly on foot and watch, half-starved and without money, facing a parcel of pitiful Spaniards. I have been fighting, wheeling, marching and counter-marching—sometimes with a firelock, then with a handpike, and now my bottle,' brandishing it in the air, 'I am so pleased with the melody of great guns that I consider myself a Roman general, gloriously fighting for my country's honour and liberty.'

A shell that instant burst, a piece of which knocked the bottle out of his hand. With the greatest composure he replied (having first graced it with an oath): 'This is not any loss. I have found a whole cask by good luck.' And he brought his comrade to view his treasure.

'But Jack,' says he, 'are you not thankful to God for your preservation?'

'How do you mean?', answered Jack, 'Fine talking of God with a soldier, whose trade and occupation is cutting throats. Divinity and slaughter sound very well together. They jingle like a cracked bell in the hand of a noisy crier. Our King is answerable to God for us! I fight for him. My religion consists in a firelock, open touch-hole, good flint, well-rammed charge and seventy rounds of powder and ball. This is the military creed. Come, comrade, drink success to the British arms!'

On his asking him for a glass, he seemed surprised.

'Why,' says he, 'you may well know there is not one to be had. But there is something that will do as well', and he took up a piece of shell. 'Here is a cup fit for a monarch. This was not purchased with gold or friendship, but with the streams of our countrymen's blood.'

Having filled the piece of shell, he gave it to his comrade to drink. 'Come, Jack', said he. 'Here is to King George and victory!'

'And he that would not drink the same', replied Jack, 'I'd give him an ounce of lead to pay Charon to ferry him over the river Styx!'

Sergeant Ancell

143.

William Cobbett goes for a soldier.

IN one of these walks I happened to cast my eye on an advertisement, inviting all loyal young men, who had a mind to gain riches and glory, to repair to a certain rendezvous, where they might enter into His Majesty's Marine Service, and have the peculiar happiness and honour of being enrolled in the Chatham division. I was not ignorant enough to be the dupe of this morsel of military bombast; but a change was what I wanted; besides, I knew that marines went to sea, and my desire to be on that element had rather increased than diminished by my being penned up in London. In short, I resolved to join this glorious corps; and, to avoid all possibility of being discovered by my friends, I went down to Chatham, and enlisted into the marines as I thought, but the next morning I found myself before a Captain of a marching regiment. There was no retreating; I had taken a shilling to drink His Majesty's health, and his further bounty was ready for my reception.

When I told the Captain that I thought myself engaged in the marines, 'By Jasus, my lad,' said he, 'and you have had a narrow escape.' He told me, that the regiment into which I had been so happy as to enlist was one of the oldest and boldest in the whole army, and that it was at that time serving in that fine, flourishing and plentiful country, Nova Scotia. He dwelt long on the beauties and riches of this terrestrial paradise, and dismissed me, perfectly enchanted with the prospect of a voyage thither.

I enlisted in 1784, and, as peace had then taken place, no great haste was made to send recruits off to their regiments. I remember well what sixpence a day was, recollecting the pangs of hunger felt by me, during the thirteen months that I was a private soldier at Chatham, previous to my embarkation for Nova Scotia. Of my sixpence, nothing like five-pence was left to purchase food for the day. Indeed, not fourpence. For there was washing, mending, soap, flour for hair-powder, shoes, stockings, shirts, stocks and gaiters , pipe-clay and several other things to come out of the miserable sixpence! Judge then of the quantity of food to sustain life in a lad of sixteen, and to enable him to exercise with a musket (weighing fourteen pounds) six to eight hours every day. The best battalion I ever saw in my life was composed of men, the far greater part of whom were enlisted before they were sixteen, and who, when they were first brought up to the regiment, were clothed in coats made much too long and too large, in order to leave room for growing.

We had several recruits from Norfolk (our regiment was the West Norfolk); and many of them deserted from sheer hunger. They were lads from the plough-tail. All of them tall, for no short men were then taken. I remember two that went into a decline and died during the year, though when they joined us, they were fine hearty young men.

I have seen them lay in their berths, many and many a time, actually crying on account of hunger. The whole week's food was not a bit too much for one day.

My leisure time was spent, not in the dissipations common to such a way of life, but in reading and study. In the course of this year I learnt more than I had ever done before. I subscribed to a circulating library at Brompton, the greatest part of the books in which I read more than once over. The library was not very considerable, it is true, nor in my reading was I directed by any degree of taste or choice. Novels, plays, history, poetry, all were read, and nearly with equal avidity.

Such a course of reading could be attended with but little profit: it was skimming over the surface of everything. One branch of learning, however, I went to the bottom with, and that the most essential too: the grammar of my mother tongue. I had experienced the want of knowledge of grammar during my stay with Mr Holland; but it is very probable that I never should have thought of encountering the study of it, had not accident placed me under a man whose friendship extended beyond his interest. Writing a fair hand procured me the honour of being copyist to Colonel Debieg, the commandant of the garrison. I transcribed the famous correspondence between him and the Duke of Richmond. The Colonel saw my deficiency, and strongly recommended study. He enforced his advice with a sort of injunction, and with a promise of reward in case of success. I procured me a Lowth's grammar, and applied myself to the study of it with unceasing assiduity.

The edge of my berth, or that of the guard-bed, was my seat to study in; my knapsack was my bookcase; a bit of board lying on my lap was my writing desk; and the task did not demand anything like a year of my life. I had no money to purchase candle or oil; in winter time it was rarely that I could get any evening light but that of the fire, and only my turn even of that. To buy a pen or a sheet of paper I was compelled to forgo some portion of food, though in a state of half-starvation; I had no moment of time that I could call my own; and I had to read and to write amidst the talking, laughing, singing, whistling and brawling of at least half a score of the most thoughtless of men, and that, too, in the hours of their freedom from all control. Think not lightly of the farthing that I had to give, now and then, for ink, pen, or paper. That farthing was, alas! a great sum to me! I was as tall as I am now, I had great health and great exercise. I remember, and well I may! that, upon one occasion, I, after all absolutely necessary expenses, had, on a Friday, made shift to have a halfpenny in reserve, which I had destined for the purchase of a red herring in the morning; but, when I pulled off my clothes at night, so hungry then as to be hardly able to endure life, I found that I had lost my halfpenny! I buried my head under the miserable sheet and rag, and cried like a child.

Though it was a considerable time before I fully comprehended all that I read, still I read and studied with such unremitted attention, that, at last, I could write without falling into any very gross errors. The pains I took cannot be described: I wrote the whole grammar out two or three times; I got it by heart. I repeated it every morning and every evening, and, when on guard, I imposed on myself the task of saying it all over once every time I was posted sentinel. To this exercise of my memory I ascribe the retentiveness of which I have since found it capable, and to the success with which it was attended, I ascribe the perseverance that has led to the acquirement of the little learning of which I am master.

I was soon raised to the rank of Corporal, a rank, which, however contemptible it may appear in some people's eyes, brought me in a clear twopence per diem, and put a very clever worsted knot upon my shoulder, too. As promotion began to dawn, I grew impatient to get to my regiment, where I expected soon to bask under the rays of royal favour. The happy days of departure at last came: we set sail from Gravesend, and, after a short and pleasant passage, arrived at Halifax in Nova Scotia.

William Cobbett

144.

Henry James Pye, created Poet Laureate in 1790, like many others who have occupied the post found himself a figure of ridicule.

MR PYE, the present poet laureate, with the best intentions at this momentous period [1795], if not with the very best poetry, translated the verses of Tyrtaeus the Spartan. They were designed to produce animation throughout the kingdom, and among the militia in particular. Some of the *Reviewing* Generals (I do not mean the Monthly or Critical) were much impressed with their *weight* and importance, and at a board of General Officers, an experiment was agreed upon, which fortunately failed. They were read aloud at Warley Common, and at Barham Downs, by the adjutants, at the head of five different regiments, at each camp, and much was expected. But before they were half finished, all the front ranks, and as many of the others as were within hearing or verse-shot, dropped their arms suddenly, and were *all found fast asleep*! Marquis Townsend, who never approved of the scheme, said, with his usual pleasantry, that the first of all poets observed, 'that sleep is the brother of death'.

                                                            Thomas James Mathias

145.

The brief and disastrous military experience of the poet Samuel Taylor Coleridge, 1794, at the depths of his own impecuniosity.

TOWARDS morning he came upon a recruiting poster for the 15th (Elliott's) Light Dragoons. It seemed suddenly that the pacifist and the pantisocrat must face his antithesis; the country lad who wore so uneasily the brilliant trappings of a man of the world must immerse his misery in the thing he feared most, to experience the physical discomfort, to face the fact of being a soldier.

He went at once to the recruiting office. An old and benevolent sergeant listened to his agitated request to be recruited into the army, and asked him if he had been in bed.

The answer was apparent before the pale young man with the black dishevelled hair had time to shake his head. The sergeant gave him breakfast and persuaded him to rest for a few hours. In the evening he offered a guinea, and told him to go to the play and cheer himself up. He did so, but came back afterwards. To withdraw now would seem to be weakness. The sergeant shook his head sadly, almost burst into tears. 'Then it must be so', he said.

Next morning he mustered his recruits. The General made an inspection. He stopped before the drooping and somewhat ungainly figure. 'Your name, sir?'

'Cumberbatch, sir,' he extemporized quickly.

'What do you come here for, sir?'

'To be a soldier, sir.'

'Do you think you can run a Frenchman through the body?'

'I don't know, sir, as I never tried. But I'll let a Frenchman run *me* through the body before I'll run away.'

'Good enough', said the General, and passed on.

So he became a cavalry man. 'Never make a proper soldier out of he', said the drill sergeant. His horse was liable to bite. He couldn't even rub her down himself. With charm and volubility he bribed a lad to do it for him, paying him by writing letters and love stanzas.

As soon as he mounted his horse on one side, he was off on the other. 'Silas is off again!' they cried. They thought him a 'talking natural'.

He won them over with his stories. He sat at the foot of his bed with a group of dragoons round him. He told them of the Peloponnesian war, which lasted 27 years.

'There must have been some fine fine promotion there', said one soldier. 'Aye', said another. 'How many rose from the ranks, I wonder.'

He related the feats of Archimedes, but they couldn't swallow them. 'Silas, that's a lie', they shouted. 'Do you think so?' he said mildly, and went on. 'That Silas—his fancy's always on the stretch.' He switched to Alexander the Great and recaptured their interest. 'Ah, he were a great general. Who were his father? Was he a Cornishman? I did know an Alexander in Truro.' They protested when he told them of the retreat of the ten thousand. 'Don't like to hear about retreat. I'm for marching on.'

'What rations did they have on that campaign?'

'Sure every time the sun rose they had two pounds of good ox beef and plenty of whisky', said an Irishman, and that clinched the matter.

That was probably later, after he had proved hopeless as a trooper, and had been removed to the medical department, where his stories were better than physic.

He had told the story of his army experiences so many times, such a maze of fantasy and legend had grown from it, that even he could not remember the true story of his release. He had told Cottle he was acting as sentry at the door of the officers' ballroom. Two officers passed, talking of the Greek drama, quoting what they thought was Euripides.

'Excuse me, sir,' he interrupted. 'The lines are not quite accurately quoted. Besides, they're not from Euripides; they're from the second antistrophe of the Oedipus of Sophocles.'

'Who the devil are you?' said the officers in astonishment, 'Old Faustus grown young again?'

'I am your honour's humble sentinel.'

'Damme, sir,' said the second officer. 'The fellow must be a gentleman.'

'An odd fish.'

'Not an odd fish, but a stray bird from the Oxford or Cambridge aviary.'

Or was the truth that Captain Ogle found pencilled on the door of his stable: 'Eheu! quam infortunii miserrimum est fuisse felicem'?

A confidential letter to one of his Cambridge friends must have been passed on to his brother George. He was at Henley Workhouse, nursing a comrade through smallpox. He carried a memory of a solitary summer house in a garden, and the face of a beautiful girl. The imagination that had been touched by Mary Evans could only too easily find a new symbol. . . .

The family had got to work to procure his release. Investigations were made, and about this time George Cornish, a school friend, arrived and lent him a guinea. Colonel James, the soldier of the family, proved his interest at the War Office. On April 10th 1794 S. T. Cumberbatch was discharged as insane.

Maurice Carpenter

146.

Captain George Brummell of the 10th Light Dragoons was one of the Prince Regent's less plausible military appointments of 1794. The Beau (for it was he) was fortunate never to find himself under the command of any more exacting leader than his Prince.

. . . since he spent more time in front of a cheval glass than on horseback, and in attendance on the Prince than with his troop, it was not surprising that he was still unfamiliar with most of his men. Fortunately one of his dragoons had a nose which remained bright blue even in the warmest weather; Brummell ordered that this man should be stationed in the front rank and he was thus always able to identify his own troop. And then one day, as he sat immaculate and motionless on his glossily groomed charger, his squadron commander rode up and sharply demanded what he was doing there.

Brummell gazed at him in polite astonishment. 'You are with the wrong troop!' shouted the colonel. Brummell, casting a quick glance over his shoulder, caught a reassuring glimpse of the blue nose. 'No, no, Sir!' he said. 'I know better than that—a pretty thing indeed if I did not know my own troop!' Alas, because of his estrangement from regimental affairs he did not know that he had recently received some recruits and lost blue nose. . . .

[In 1797] Captain Brummell was involved in a brief burst of serious military activity. One afternoon when the 10th Light Dragoons were quartered at Dorchester and the Prince of Wales was fox-hunting with some of his officers at Crichel House, the estate he had rented five miles north of Wimborne Minster, word came of a French fleet making for the Dorset coast. It was known that the French had constructed barges and shallow craft for an invasion. The warships were no doubt escorting them. The Prince, throwing himself into the saddle anew, and galloping as wildly as his seventeen-and-a-half stone would permit, led his officers through Blandford, where he alerted a squadron of the Bays, and then on another seventeen miles to Dorchester, arriving well after nightfall. To the blare of trumpets and clatter of startled hooves the Prince of Wales's Own readied themselves for battle while their Colonel went off to confer with the General commanding the district. The General, unaware of the impending invasion of his shore, only half-a-dozen miles distant, had gone early to bed. The Prince routed him out, informed him of the perilous situation, and had him despatch scouts in all directions. They returned with confirmation that a fleet was sailing along the coast. Only in one respect was the Prince's information defective—the ships were English, not French.

Hubert Cole

147.

One evening early in 1798, to his horror Brummell found himself ordered north with his regiment to take part in the suppression of the industrial disturbances there.

. . . The following morning Brummell called upon the Prince who, astonished to see his young friend up and about at so early an hour, asked what urgent business had brought him.

'Why, the fact is, Your Highness,' said Brummell, 'I have heard that we are ordered to Manchester. Now you must be aware how disagreeable that would be to *me*.'

The Prince waited.

'Think, Your Royal Highness,' Brummell continued, 'Manchester!'

While the Prince considered the horrors of provincial garrison life, Brummell clinched his argument: 'Besides—*you* would not be there.' After the briefest of pauses for the gross flattery to sink in: 'I have therefore, with Your Royal Highness's permission, determined to sell out.'

'Oh, by all means, Brummell,' said the Prince. 'Do as you please, do as you please!'

Hubert Cole

148.

The Russian army in the last years of the eighteenth century found the Tsar Paul a somewhat difficult master: mad, dangerous and subject to extraordinary military obsessions.

HE had a passion for parades and for useless ceremonials. Soldiers must be made beautiful, he declared, regardless of military efficiency. New uniforms were designed which were so tight that the wearers were scarcely able to breathe, let alone fight. Soldiers staggered under the weight of wigs which had thick, stinking grease plastered over them, and which had iron rods inserted into the queues to make them fall straight. Men were obliged to wear a type of strait-jacket in order to train them to stand erect, and steel plates were strapped round their knees to prevent legs bending when marching on parades. Hours had to be spent polishing weapons, buttons and buckles, pipe-claying belts and powdering the greasy wigs. Musket-butts were hollowed out and filled with loose shot to make them rattle nicely as the men went through the various exercises. Discipline was intensified so that the troops would behave in puppet fashion. 'The guard-parade became for him the most important institution and focal point of government,' wrote Frederic Masson, tutor to Alexander. 'Every day, no matter how cold it might be, he dedicated the same time to it, spending each morning in plain deep green uniform, great boots and a large hat exercising his guards. . . . Surrounded by his sons and aides-de-camp he would stamp his heels on the stones to keep himself warm, his bald head bare, his nose in the air, one hand behind his back, the other raising, and falling, a baton as he beat time, crying out 'One, two—one, two.'

Roger Parkinson

149.

AN anecdote is told of Sir Ralph Abercromby, which strikingly shows that characteristic consideration for others which was the ruling spirit of his life. When, after the Battle of Alexandria in 1801, he was being carried off mortally wounded, a soldier's blanket was placed under his head to ease it. He felt the relief, and asked what it was. 'Only a soldier's blanket,' was the reply. 'Whose blanket is it?' 'Only one of the men's.' 'I wish to know the name of the man to whom the blanket belongs,' persisted Sir Ralph. A short pause ensued, until the information had been obtained. When the reply was given: 'Duncan Roy's, of the 42nd, Sir Ralph.' 'Then', declared the wounded general, 'see that Duncan Roy gets his blanket this night.'

James Settle

150.

ONE day in 1805 fourteen-year-old Joseph Anderson was in a serious scrape at Banff Academy. He had been shooting sparrows with a gun which he had no right to possess, and when taxed with the offence he denied it.

His form master, a Mr Simpson, exclaimed:

'You have told a lie, sir, and I must punish you; so down with your breeches.'

Indignantly the culprit refused, saying:

'I am an officer and won't submit.'

Mr Simpson was no doubt aware that his pupil had recently been commissioned an ensign in the 78th Foot—all the more reason, he may have thought, why prevarication should not be overlooked. But young Anderson kicked, thumped and created such a din that the rector of the Academy came hurrying up. After hearing explanations from both sides, he said to the pupil:

'I will not disgrace you, sir. You are an officer.'

Joseph Anderson went on to soldier with honour in the Peninsula and to rule a convict island off the coast of Australia, ending his service as a lieutenant-colonel, a Commander of the Bath and a Knight of Hanover.

E. S. Turner

151.

For those who imagine that Conan Doyle parodied history to create his enchanting Brigadier Gerard, the memoirs of such Napoleonic generals as Thiébault, Marbot and Caulincourt suggest that reality outdid Gerard. This is one of Thiébault's stories of the Army of Italy.

THE review took place at the gates of Verona. Complete full-dress had been ordered, and the care taken to execute the order caused all the more surprise at the appearance of La Salle, who, usually the most brilliant as he was the handsomest officer in the army, turned up in an old pelisse, pantaloons, and dirty boots, and riding an Austrian hussar's horse, on which he had been careful to leave its saddle, its bridle, and even its rope-halter.

The surprise caused by this get-up was universal, and the commander-in-chief's first question was: 'What horse have you got there?' The answer was ready: 'A horse I have just taken from the enemy!' 'Where?' 'At Vicenza, general.' 'Are you mad?' 'I have just come thence; indeed I bring news from thence, which you will, perhaps, deem not unimportant.'

Bonaparte at once took him aside, talked with him for a quarter of an hour, and came back to the group formed by Generals Berthier, Masséna and Augereau, and by the staff-officers present, announcing that he had just promoted La Salle major. Here is the rest of the story.

La Salle, who was a man of many accomplishments and a highly susceptible temperament, found, amid all his enthusiasm for his military duties, some time at his disposal for love-affairs. He was carrying on one of these with a Marchesa di Sale, one of the cleverest and most charming women of Upper Italy, who afterwards poisoned herself in despair at the loss of him. She lived at Vicenza, and the withdrawal of our army across the Adige had interrupted the *liaison*. The lovers had found means to correspond across the Austrian army, but correspondence was not enough for La Salle, and he resolved on one of those enterprises which success alone will justify. Selecting twenty-five men from the 1st Regiment of Cavalry—one of the best that we then had— he assembled them after nightfall and set out at once, without orders, without letting anyone know, without even a show of authority. He passed the enemy's vedettes unperceived, escaped his pickets, got through the hills to the rear of the Austrian army, and, marching without cockades and with cloaks unfolded, by mountain roads which he knew, reached Vicenza, where he knew there was no garrison, toward midnight, concealed his little troop, and hastened to the Marchesa.

About half-past two in the morning, as he was preparing to be off some pistol-shots were heard. He mounted at once and rejoined his escort, learning then that he had been discovered and surrounded. The most direct roads were strongly guarded, but he recollected one point which was likely still to be open, and hastened thither. Thirty-six hussars were occupying it; he charged them without knowing their numbers, overturned them, captured and brought away nine horses; then he returned by a different road which involved a long way round, avoided cantonments, spoke German, and passed himself off for an Austrian to the men of a picket through which he had to pass. Lastly, marching as fast as possible, he fell upon the rear of the last Austrian advanced post, sabred all that he could get at, and returned by daylight to San Martino d'Albaro, whence he had started, without having lost a single man.

But the fleeting moments which La Salle had passed at Vicenza were not devoted solely to making love. The Marchesa, prepared for the interview, had procured some valuable information, which she had passed on to him. Moreover, he had chosen for his prank the night preceding the commander-in-chief's review. On his return he had avoided showing himself, so as not to have to report to anyone, and then had waited for the moment when, by appearing before Bonaparte in the get-up and on the horse which I have mentioned, he might make the most he could of an attempt which would have either to be punished or rewarded.

General Thiébault

152.

Another memory of the Army of Italy.

IN some of these fights I had occasion to see Brigadier-General Macard, a soldier of fortune, who had been carried by the whirlwind of the Revolution, almost without intermediate steps, from the rank of trumpet-major to that of general officer. He was an excellent specimen of the officers who were called into existence by chance and their own courage, and who, while they displayed a very genuine valour before the enemy, were none the less unfitted by their want of education for filling exalted positions. He was chiefly remarkable for a very quaint peculiarity. Of colossal size and extraordinary bravery, this singular person, when he was about to charge at the head of his troops, invariably cried, 'Look here! I'm going to dress like a beast.' Therewith he would take off his coat, his vest, his shirt, and keep on nothing except his plumed hat, his leather breeches, and his boots. Stripped thus to the waist, General Macard offered to view a chest almost as shaggy as a bear's, which gave him a very strange appearance. When he had once got on what he very truly called his beast's clothing, General Macard would dash forward recklessly, sabre in hand, and swearing like a pagan, on the enemy's cavalry. But he very seldom got at them, for at the sight of this giant, half-naked, hairy all over, and in such a strange outfit, who was hurling himself at them and uttering the most fearful yells, his opponents would bolt on all sides, scarcely knowing if they had a man to deal with or some strange wild animal.

General Macard was, as might be expected, completely ignorant, which sometimes caused great amusement to the better-educated officers under his command. One day one of these came to ask leave to go into the neighbouring town to order himself a pair of boots. 'By Jove!' said the general, 'that will suit well; as you are going to a shoemaker, just come here and take my measure and order me a pair too.' The officer, much surprised, replied that he could not take his measure, as, never having been a shoemaker, he had not the least idea how to set about it. 'What!' cried the general, 'I sometimes see you pass whole days looking at the mountains, pencilling and drawing lines, and when I ask you what you are doing, you answer that you are measuring the mountains; well, if you can measure objects more than a league away from you, what do you mean by telling me that you cannot take my measure for a pair of boots when you have got me under your hand? Come, take my measure without any more ado.' The officer assured him that it was impossible; the general insisted, got angry, began to swear; and it was only with great difficulty that other officers, attracted by the noise, succeeded in bringing this ridiculous scene to an end. The general never would understand how an officer who measured the mountains could be unable to measure a man for a pair of boots.

Baron de Marbot

153.

1 December 1805, the eve of Austerlitz.

TOWARDS evening an order of the day announced the forthcoming battle to the army. One phrase especially roused the troops; that, namely, in which the Emperor proclaimed that, if they justified his expectations, he should confine himself to directing the movements; but, in the contrary event, he should expose himself where danger was greatest. No sooner had the order been read to all the corps than the Emperor passed *incognito* and without escort along the front of several regiments. He was at once recognized, and was the object of the greatest enthusiasm. Just as he was in front of the 28th a soldier cried, 'We promise you that you will only have to fight with your eyes tomorrow!' Halting in front of Ferny's brigade, composed of the 46th and 57th, he asked the men if their supply of cartridges were complete. 'No,' answered one; 'but the Russians taught us in the Grisons that only bayonets were needed for them. We will show you tomorrow!'

Between one army excited to this point and another composed of fanatics, the battle of the next day was bound to be decisive and merciless. But the next day was December 2, the anniversary of the coronation. This coincidence, joined with the conviction of success, put the troops into such a state of enthusiasm that they wished to give some sign of general rejoicing as an announcement to the Emperor of the celebration they were preparing for him; in which they also wanted to let the enemy share, as he had just allowed us to witness those last manœuvres executed under our very noses, as if to terrify us. Hardly had night fallen when, by a spontaneous impulse hardly credible, nearly 80,000 men, distributed among a dozen bivouacs, suddenly armed themselves with long poles bearing bundles of lighted straw. They kept renewing them for half an hour, carrying them about and waving them, as they danced a *farandole* and shouted 'Long live the Emperor!' Out of the 80,000, 25,000 to 30,000 were to transform this festival field into a field of slaughter; but it is the way of our soldiers to mingle the gayest with the most terrible images. At the first shouts, and still more at the way in which they were redoubled on all sides, our surprise made us turn out; and, as the Imperial Guard was shouting louder than the rest, Morand and I leapt on our horses and galloped to the Emperor's bivouac. What were my astonishment and delight to find there General Junot, whom I believed to be still ambassador at Lisbon. He had galloped from Lisbon to Bayonne, there had jumped into a carriage, and had continued his race without losing a minute all the way to Austerlitz. Excited by his successful journey, he related every sort of crazy performance—laughing like a madman, for example, when he told us how a Spanish postilion, who was galloping with him through a regular hurricane wet to the skin, said, at sight of the white pelisse with all its embroideries and orders, which he wore as Colonel of Hussars, as wet as his own clothes, 'Sir, this is not ambassador's weather.'

General Thiébault

154.

Keeping up appearances in Napoleon's cavalry.

ONE of our captains, named B—, a fine young fellow, would have been one of the handsomest men in the army if his calves had been in keeping with the rest of his person; but he had legs like stilts, which had a very bad effect with the tight—so-called Hungarian—pantaloons worn at that time by the chasseurs. In order to meet this inconvenience, Captain B— had had some good-sized pads made in the shape of calves, which made his handsome figure complete. You shall see how these false calves cost me an arrest, though they were not the sole cause of it. It was prescribed by the regulations that the officers should have their horses' tails long, like those of the troopers. Our colonel, M. Moreau, was always admirably mounted, but all his horses had their tails docked, and, as he feared that General Bourcier, who was very strict in maintaining the regulations, would reprimand him for setting a bad example to his officers, he had caused, for the purpose of the inspection, false tails to be attached to all his horses. There were so marvellously well fitted that unless you knew you would have thought them natural. We went to the inspection, to which General Bourcier had invited General Suchet, inspector of infantry, as well as General Gudin, commanding the territorial division. They were accompanied by a numerous and brilliant staff; the business took a long time, the movements were nearly all carried out at a gallop, and ended with several charges at full speed. I was commanding a section in the centre, forming part of the squadron under M. B—, near whom the colonel placed himself. They were, therefore, two paces in front of me, when the generals came forward to congratulate M. Moreau on the admirable style in which the manœuvres were carried out. But what did I see? The extreme rapidity of the movements which we had just made had deranged the symmetry of the additions which the captain and the colonel had made to their get-up. The false tail of the colonel's horse had become partly detached; the stump, composed of a plug of tow, was dragging almost on the ground, like a skein, while the false hair was up in the air, several feet higher, and spread out fan-shaped over the horse's croup, so that he seemed to have an enormous peacock's tail. As for M. B——'s sham calves, under the pressure of the saddle flaps they had slipped forward without his perceiving it, and presented a round lump on his shin bones, which produced a most comical effect; the captain all the while sitting proudly upright on his horse, as who should say, 'Look at me! What a handsome man I am!' At twenty years old one has not much gravity; mine was overcome by the grotesque spectacle which I had under my eyes, and, in spite of the imposing presence of three generals, I could not restrain myself from shouting wildly with laughter. I writhed on my saddle, I gnawed the sleeve of my jacket: it was no use; I laughed and laughed until my sides ached. Thereupon the inspector-general, not knowing the cause of my merriment, ordered me to fall out of the ranks and put myself under arrest. I obeyed, but, as I was obliged to pass between the horses of the colonel and of the captain, my eyes fell again, in spite of myself, on that infernal tail and also on the new-fashioned calves, and there I was again seized with an inextinguishable laugh which nothing could check. The generals must have thought that I was gone mad; but as soon as they had departed, the officers of the regiment, coming up to the colonel and Captain B——, soon knew what was the matter, and laughed like me—but at least with less danger to themselves.

Baron de Marbot

155.

Major John Blakiston enjoyed his service in India in the first decade of the nineteenth century.

ONE thing, however, struck me as disagreeable, that was the parade and nonsense kept up in the army, and which, without adding to discipline, only served to create disgust to the service. However hot the weather might be, an officer could scarcely stir out of his tent without being buckled up in sword and sash, for fear of meeting some jack-in-office of a staff-officer, who, if he found him straying out of his lines not altogether *en militaire*, would send him back to his tent with a flea in his ear. In truth, the airs which these favourites of fortune gave themselves, towards those who continued to trudge on in the beaten path of their profession, were insufferable. I recollect about this time a brother officer of mine asking one of these upstarts, with whom he had formerly been on most intimate terms, whether we should halt the next day? 'I really do not know the intentions of the general', was the reply. Returning to his tent somewhat disgusted with the airs of his former companion, and soliloquizing on the nature of man, and the fantastic tricks which he plays, when 'dressed in a little brief authority', he was met by his maty-boy with the information that the army was to halt the next day. 'Where did you learn that?' said my friend. 'Major M—'s washerman tell.'

. . . This circumstance reminds me also of a story which was told me of Captain Grose of the Madras army, who was killed at the siege of Seringapatam. He was son of Grose, the antiquary, whose talents he inherited. He was remarkable for his wit and humour, and his memory is still cherished by all the lovers of fun who knew him. Having had occasion to make some communication to head-quarters, he was received much in the usual manner by one of the under-strappers, who told him that no verbal communication could be received, but that what he had to say must be sent through the medium of an official letter. He happened, some days afterwards, to have a party dining with him, and among others were a few members of the staff. In the midst of dinner a jack-ass came running among the tent-ropes, exerting his vocal organs in a manner by no means pleasing to the company. Grose immediately rose, and thus addressed the intruder:

'I presume, sir, you come from head-quarters. I receive no verbal communications whatever, sir. If you have anything to say to me, sir, I beg you will commit it to paper.' The will which Captain Grose made the night before the storming of Seringapatam, under a presentiment of his fate, was quite in character. It began with the apostrophe of 'O my nose!' and among other bequests contained the present of a wooden sword to an officer of rank to whom he bore no good will, and who was supposed not to be endowed with any superfluous quantity of personal valour.

John Blakiston

156.

GENERAL MEDOWS, equally renowned for his wit and bravery, being on a reconnoitring party in the Mysore country, a twenty-four pound shot struck the ground at some distance from the general, and was passing in such a direction as would have exposed him to danger had he continued his road. Quick as lightning he stopped his horse, and pulling off his hat very gracefully, as the shot rolled on, good humouredly said, 'I beg you to proceed, sir; I never dispute precedence with any gentleman of your family.'

The Percy Anecdotes

157.

Colonel Harvey Aston, a notorious duellist, fell at last in an encounter with a brother officer.

HE had seen a good deal of the world before he came out to India, had been a great fox-hunter, a patron of the fancy, and a leading member in the sporting circles. He had many good points about him; was generous and brave; but he had a most inveterate disposition to quizzing, which involved him in many personal encounters, whereby he obtained the reputation of a professed duellist. He used to tell a story of one of his affairs, which, though not at all creditable to himself, was the best satire on the practice of duelling that can well be imagined. 'I was in the theatre one night,' said he, 'and, seeing a fellow eating apples in the box where there were some ladies, I took the liberty of poking one into his throat with my finger. The man struck me. I knocked him down, and gave him a sound drubbing' (for the Colonel was a famous bruiser). 'He called me out. I shot him through the arm; and the fool called that *satisfaction*.' One of the few instances in which he was known to have been right, was on the occasion which proved fatal to him. On receiving his antagonist's shot, which took effect in his body, he staggered a few paces; then, recovering himself, he presented his pistol deliberately at his opponent, and said, 'I could kill him' (for he was a capital shot); 'but the last act of my life shall not be an act of revenge!'

John Blakiston

158.

Eylau, 8 February 1807.

To enable you to understand my story, I must go back to the autumn of 1805, when the officers of the Grand Army, among their preparations for the battle of Austerlitz, were completing their outfits. I had two good horses, the third, for whom I was looking, my charger, was to be better still. It was a difficult thing to find, for though horses were far less dear than now, their price was pretty high, and I had not much money; but chance served me admirably. I met a learned German, Herr von Aister, whom I had known when he was a professor at Sorèze. He had become tutor to the children of a rich Swiss banker, M. Scherer, established at Paris in partnership with M. Finguerlin. He informed me that M. Finguerlin, a wealthy man, living in fine style, had a large stud, in the first rank of which figured a lovely mare, called Lisette, easy in her paces, as light as a deer, and so well broken that a child could lead her. But this mare, when she was ridden, had a terrible fault, and fortunately a rare one: she bit like a bulldog, and furiously attacked people whom she disliked, which decided M. Finguerlin to sell her. She was bought for Mme de Lauriston, whose husband, one of the Emperor's aides-de-camp, had written to her to get his campaigning outfit ready. When selling the mare, M. Finguerlin had forgotten to mention her fault, and that very evening a groom was found disembowelled at her feet. Mme de Lauriston, reasonably alarmed, brought an action to cancel the bargain; not only did she get her verdict, but, in order to prevent further disasters, the police ordered that a written statement should be placed in Lisette's stall to inform purchasers of her ferocity, and that any bargain with regard to her should be void unless the purchaser declared in writing that his attention had been called to the notice. You may suppose that with such a character as this the mare was not easy to dispose of, and thus Herr von Aister informed me that her owner had decided to let her go for what anyone would give. I offered 1,000 francs, and M. Finguerlin delivered Lisette to me, though she had cost him 5,000. This animal gave me a good deal of trouble for some months. It took four or five men to saddle her, and you could only bridle her by covering her eyes and fastening all four legs; but once you were on her back, you found her a really incomparable mount.

However, since while in my possession she had already bitten several people, and had not spared me, I was thinking of parting with her. But I had meanwhile engaged in my service Francis Woirland, a man who was afraid of nothing, and he, before going near Lisette, whose bad character had been mentioned to him, armed himself with a good hot roast leg of mutton. When the animal flew at him to bite him, he held out the mutton; she seized it in her teeth, and burning her gums, palate, and tongue, gave a scream, let the mutton drop, and from that moment was perfectly submissive to Woirland, and did not venture to attack him again. I employed the same method with a like result. Lisette became as docile as a dog, and allowed me and my servant to approach her freely. She even became a little more tractable towards the stablemen of the staff, whom she saw every day, but woe to the strangers who passed near her! . . .

Such was the mare which I was riding at Eylau at the moment when the fragments of Augereau's army corps, shattered by a hail of musketry and cannon-balls, were trying to rally near the great cemetery. You will remember how the 14th of the line had remained alone on a hillock, which it could not quit except by the Emperor's order.

*

I found the 14th formed in square on the top of the hillock, but as the slope was very slight the enemy's cavalry had been able to deliver several charges. These had been vigorously repulsed, and the French regiment was surrounded by a circle of dead horses and dragoons, which formed a kind of rampart, making the position by this time almost inaccessible to cavalry; as I found, for in spite of the aid of our men, I had much difficulty in passing over this horrible entrenchment. At last I was in the square. Since Colonel Savary's death at the passage of the Wkra, the 14th had been commanded by a major. While I imparted to this officer, under a hail of balls, the order to quit his position and try to rejoin his corps, he pointed out to me that the enemy's artillery had been firing on the 14th for an hour, and had caused it such loss that the handful of soldiers which remained would inevitably be exterminated if they went down into the plain, and that, moreover, there would not be time to prepare to execute such a movement, since a Russian column was marching on him, and was not more than a hundred paces away. 'I see no means of saving the regiment,' said the major; 'return to the Emperor, bid him farewell from the 14th of the line, which has faithfully executed his orders, and bear to him the eagle which he gave us, and which we can defend no longer: it would add too much to the pain of death to see it fall into the hands of the enemy.'

Then the major handed me his eagle. Saluted for the last time by the glorious fragment of the intrepid regiment with cries of 'Vive l'Empereur!' they were going to die for him. It was the *Cæsar morituri te salutant* of Tacitus,[1] but in this case the cry was uttered by heroes. The infantry eagles were very heavy, and their weight was increased by a stout oak pole on the top of which they were fixed. The length of the pole embarrassed me much, and as the stick without the eagle could not constitute a trophy for the enemy, I resolved with the major's consent to break it and only carry off the eagle. But at the moment when I was leaning forward from my saddle in order to get a better purchase to separate the eagle from the pole, one of the numerous cannon-balls which the Russians were sending at us went through the hinder peak of my hat, less than an inch from my head. The shock was all the more terrible since my hat, being fastened on by a strong leather strap under the chin, offered more resistance to the blow. I seemed to be blotted out of existence, but I did not fall from my horse; blood flowed from my nose, my ears, and even my eyes; nevertheless I still could hear and see, and I preserved all my intellectual faculties, although my limbs were paralysed to such an extent that I could not move a single finger.

Meanwhile the column of Russian infantry which we had just perceived was mounting the hill; they were grenadiers wearing mitre-shaped caps with metal ornaments. Soaked with spirits, and in vastly superior numbers, these men hurled themselves furiously on the feeble remains of the unfortunate 14th, whose soldiers had for several days been living only on potatoes and melted snow; that day they had not had time to prepare even this wretched meal. Still our brave Frenchmen made a valiant defence with their bayonets, and when the square had been broken, they held together in groups and sustained the unequal fight for a long time.

During this terrible struggle several of our men, in order not to be struck from behind, set their backs against my mare's flanks, she, contrary to her practice, remaining perfectly quiet. If I had been able to move I should have urged her forward to get away from this field of slaughter. But it was absolutely impossible for me to press my legs so as to make the animal I rode understand my wish. My position was the more frightful since, as I have said, I retained the power of sight and thought. Not only were they fighting all round me, which exposed me to bayonet-thrusts, but a Russian officer with a hideous countenance

---

[1] It was Suetonius.

kept making efforts to run me through. As the crowd of combatants prevented him from reaching me, he pointed me out to the soldiers around him, and they, taking me for the commander of the French, as I was the only mounted man, kept firing at me over their comrades' heads, so that bullets were constantly whistling past my ear. One of them would certainly have taken away the small amount of life that was still in me had not a terrible incident led to my escape from the mêlée.

Among the Frenchmen who had got their flanks against my mare's near flank was a quartermaster-sergeant, whom I knew from having frequently seen him at the marshal's, making copies for him of the 'morning states'. This man, having been attacked and wounded by several of the enemy, fell under Lisette's belly, and was seizing my leg to pull himself up, when a Russian grenadier, too drunk to stand steady, wishing to finish him by a thrust in the breast, lost his balance, and the point of his bayonet went astray into my cloak, which at that moment was puffed out by the wind. Seeing that I did not fall, the Russian left the sergeant and aimed a great number of blows at me. These were at first fruitless, but one at last reached me, piercing my left arm, and I felt with a kind of horrible pleasure my blood flowing hot. The Russian grenadier with redoubled fury made another thrust at me, but, stumbling with the force which he put into it, drove his bayonet into my mare's thigh. Her ferocious instincts being restored by the pain, she sprang at the Russian, and at one mouthful tore off his nose, lips, eyebrows, and all the skin of his face, making of him a living death's-head, dripping with blood. Then hurling herself with fury among the combatants, kicking and biting, Lisette upset everything that she met on her road. The officer who had made so many attempts to strike me tried to hold her by the bridle; she seized him by his belly, and carrying him off with ease, she bore him out of the crush to the foot of the hillock, where, having torn out his entrails and mashed his body under her feet, she left him dying on the snow. Then, taking the road by which she had come, she made her way at full gallop towards the cemetery of Eylau.

Baron de Marbot

159.

Marshal Lefèbvre was made Duke of Danzig for his success in seizing the city for Napoleon.

ON March 11th, 1807, the town was invested. The first shot was fired by the French batteries on April 24th—Lefèbvre was no hustler—and by the end of May the town had fallen, and not so long afterwards Madame la Maréchale-Duchesse de Danzig, the buxom, kindhearted, jolly old washerwoman, was visiting the Tuileries to thank the Empress on behalf of herself and her husband the Duke. They were simple souls, the new Duke and Duchess. She used to begin half her sentences with the words 'When I used to do the washing', and he was naïvely proud of his new grandeur. But at the same time he was very conscious of the years of hard work that had raised him so high. On an occasion when an old friend of his youth was admiring enviously the splendours of his house in Paris: 'So you're jealous of me,' exclaimed the veteran, 'very well; come out into the courtyard and I'll have twenty shots at you at thirty paces. If I don't hit you, the whole house and everything in it is yours.' The friend hastily declined to take the chance, whereupon Lefèbvre remarked drily, 'I had a thousand bullets fired at me from much closer range before I got all this.'

A. G. Macdonell

160.

BERTHIER, the great organizer of the marches of the Army-Corps, tried his hand at organizing a shoot in order to please Napoleon. Every detail for the day's sport was worked out with the same meticulous accuracy with which the *Grande Armée* had been swept from Boulogne to Austerlitz. The carriages arrived on the stroke at the Tuileries, the beaters were ready, the keepers in their best clothes, a beautiful lunch waiting to be eaten, and a thousand rabbits, brought the night before and dumped in the park, waiting to be shot. But poor, ugly little Berthier made one trivial mistake. Instead of buying wild rabbits, he bought tame ones and did not know that they were accustomed to be fed twice a day. When the Emperor took his gun in hand and advanced into the park, the rabbits, all thousand of them, mistook him for the man who provided their daily lettuce, and leapt to their feet and charged towards him. Berthier and his staff beat them off with horse-whips, but the rabbits, who were more expert in the Napoleonic warfare than some of the Marshals, wheeled round on both flanks and actually reached the Emperor's carriage before the Emperor could mount and drive off back to Paris.

Another curious incident of the shooting-parties of these splendid days was when Napoleon, who was a better hand with a field-gun than he was with a fowling-piece, accidentally shot Masséna in the eye. With characteristic readiness, the Emperor put the blame of the accident on Berthier, who with characteristic subservience accepted the blame, while Masséna, who lost his eye, with characteristic tact accepted the transference of blame.

A. G. Macdonell

161.

. . . Henry Francis Mellish [a captain of the 10th Hussars] was ADC to Sir Ronald Ferguson, one of Wellington's generals. It was reported one day that Mellish had been taken prisoner but when Wellington heard of it he said, 'They'll not keep him long.' Sure enough, the next day he was seen riding into the British camp on a donkey. Everyone laughed at his mount and said it was not worth £5. He retorted, 'I'll soon make it £35.' He then rode towards the enemy lines, had it shot from under him, and returned to claim £35 from the government for the loss of his mount in battle.

Philip Warner

162.

The 28th Foot, in which the author was a subaltern, on the retreat to Corunna, 1 January 1809.

OUR stay at Cambarros was but short, for scarcely had the men laid down to repose, which was much wanted in consequence of the manner in which they had passed the previous night, when some of our cavalry came galloping in, reporting that the enemy were advancing in force. We were immediately ordered to get under arms, and hurried to form outside the town on that part facing Bembibre. While we were forming a dragoon rode up, and an officer who being ill was in one of the light carts which attended the reserve, cried out, 'Dragoon, what news?' 'News, sir? The only news I have for you is that unless you step

out like soldiers, and don't wait to pick your steps like bucks in Bond
Street of a Sunday with shoes and silk stockings, damn it! you'll be all
taken prisoners.' 'Pray, who the devil are you?' came from the cart. 'I
am Lord Paget,' said the dragoon; 'and pray, sir, may I ask who you
are?' 'I am Captain D——n, of the 28th Regiment, my lord.' 'Come
out of that cart directly,' said his lordship; 'march with your men, sir,
and keep up their spirits by showing them a good example.' The captain scrambled out of the cart rear, face foremost, and from slipping
along the side of the cart and off the wheels, and from the sudden jerks
which he made to regain his equilibrium, displayed all the ridiculous
motions of a galvanized frog. Although he had previously suffered a
good deal from both fatigue and illness, yet the circumstance
altogether caused the effect desired by his lordship, for the whole regiment were highly diverted by the scene until we arrived at Bembibre,
and it caused many a hearty laugh during the remainder of the retreat.

Robert Blakeney

163.

*At Corunna on 16 January 1809, Sir John Moore was fighting a rearguard action
against a superior French force under Marshal Soult, to cover the evacuation of the
14,000 British troops under his command.*

THE French having brought up reserves, the battle raged fiercely: fire
flashing amidst the smoke, and shot flying from the adverse guns;
when Hardinge rode up and reported that the Guards were coming
quickly. As he spoke, Sir John Moore was struck to the ground by a
cannon-ball, which lacerated his left shoulder and chest.

He had half-raised himself, when Hardinge having dismounted,
caught his hand: and the General grasped his strongly, and gazed with
anxiety at the Highlanders, who were fighting courageously: and when
Hardinge said, 'They are advancing', his countenance lightened.

Colonel Graham now came up, and imagined, from the composure
of the General's features, that he had only fallen accidentally, until he
saw blood welling from his wound. Shocked at the sight, he rode off
for surgeons. Hardinge tried in vain to stop the effusion of blood with
his sash: then, by the help of some Highlanders and Guardsmen, he
placed the General upon a blanket. In lifting him, his sword became

entangled, and Hardinge endeavoured to unbuckle the belt to take it off; when he said with soldierly feelings, 'It is as well as it is; I had rather it should go out of the field with me.'

His serenity was so striking, that Hardinge began to hope the wound was not mortal; he expressed his opinion, and said, that he trusted the surgeons would confirm it, and that he would still be spared to them.

Sir John turned his head, and cast his eyes steadily on the wounded part, and then replied, 'No, Hardinge, I feel that to be impossible.— You need not go with me; report to General Hope, that I am wounded and carried to the rear.' He was then raised from the ground by a Highland serjeant and three soldiers, and slowly conveyed towards Corunna. . . .

The soldiers had not carried Sir John Moore far, when two surgeons came running to his aid. They had been employed in dressing the shattered arm of Sir David Baird; who, hearing of the disaster which had occurred to the commander, generously ordered them to desist, and hasten to give him help. But Moore, who was bleeding fast, said to them, 'You can be of no service to me: go to the wounded soldiers, to whom you may be useful'; and he ordered the bearers to move on. But as they proceeded, he repeatedly made them turn round to view the battle, and to listen to the firing; the sound of which, becoming gradually fainter, indicated that the French were retreating.

Before he reached Corunna, it was almost dark, and Colonel Anderson met him; who, seeing his general borne from the field of battle for the third and last time, and steeped in blood, became speechless with anguish. Moore pressed his hand, and said in a low tone: 'Anderson, don't leave me.' As he was carried into the house, his faithful servant François came out, and stood aghast with horror: but his master, to console him, said smiling, 'My friend, this is nothing.'

He was then placed on a mattress on the floor, and supported by Anderson, who had saved his life at St Lucia; and some of the gentlemen of his staff came into the room by turns. He asked each, as they entered, if the French were beaten, and was answered affirmatively. They stood around; the pain of his wound became excessive, and deadly paleness overspread his fine features; yet, with unsubdued fortitude, he said, at intervals, 'Anderson, you know that I have always wished to die this way. I hope the people of England will be satisfied! I hope my country will do me justice!'

'Anderson, you will see my friends as soon as you can. Tell them— every thing.—Say to my mother—.' Here his voice faltered, he became excessively agitated, and not being able to proceed, changed the subject.

'Hope!—Hope! I have much to say to him—but cannot get it out. Are Colonel Graham, and all my aides-de-camp, safe?' (At this question, Anderson, who knew the warm regard of the General towards the officers of his staff, made a private sign not to mention that Captain Burrard was mortally wounded.) He then continued, 'I have made my will, and have remembered my servants. Colborne has my will, and all my papers.' As he spoke these words, Major Colborne, his military secretary, entered the room. He addressed him with his wonted kindness; then, turning to Anderson, said, 'Remember you go to Willoughby Gordon, and tell him it is my request, and that I expect he will give a Lieutenant-Colonelcy to Major Colborne;—he has been long with me—and I know him to be most worthy of it.'

He then asked the Major, who had come last from the field, 'Have the French been beaten?' He assured him they had on every point. 'It's a great satisfaction', he said, 'for me to know that we have beat the French. Is Paget in the room?' On being told he was not, he resumed, 'Remember me to him; he is a fine fellow.'

Though visibly sinking, he then said, 'I feel myself so strong—I fear I shall be long dying.—It's great uneasiness—it's great pain!'—

'Everything François says is right.—I have great confidence in him.' He thanked the surgeons for their attendance. Then seeing Captains Percy and Stanhope, two of his aides-de-camp, enter, he spoke to them kindly, and repeated to them the question 'if all his aides-de-camp were safe'; and was pleased on being told they were.

After a pause, Stanhope caught his eye and he said to him, 'Stanhope! remember me to your sister.' He then became silent.

James Carrick Moore

164.

GENERAL SIR WILLIAM PAYNE, Bt, at that time [July–August 1809] commanding the cavalry, was noted for his eccentricity. During the retreat from Talavera he addressed the cavalry commissaries as follows: 'Owing to the exertions it would entail, a commissary who did his duty in this country could not possibly remain alive. He would be forced to die. Of all my commissaries, not one has yet sacrificed his life; consequently they are not doing their duty.' Schaumann (a

German) commented: 'Most Englishmen of high position, particularly when they are serving in a hot climate, are a little mad.'

H. B. C. Rogers

165.

WELLINGTON could put up with rows between firebrands, especially when they were first-class officers, but there were more serious staff problems to be faced as well.

Few of the new officers sent out to him by the Horse Guards [in 1810] possessed the solid ability and agreeable temperament of an Edward Pakenham or a Lowry Cole.

There was General Sir William Erskine, drunken, 'blind as a beetle', according to a fellow officer, and probably mad, whom he had sent home 'indisposed' the year before. Back he came in 1810, along with other known disasters such as Generals Lumley and Lightburne and Colonel Landers. Landers had also been sent home once already, by Sir John Moore from Sicily. Wellington would at least keep Landers off the battlefield by appointing him 'perpetual President of General Courts-Martial', with Lightburne, if Wellington had his way, as the perpetual President's first customer—Lightburne's conduct having been 'scandalous'. Wellington gave Colonel Torrens, Military Secretary at the Horse Guards, the full blast of his indignation:

Really when I reflect upon the characters and attainments of some of the General officers of this army . . . on whom I am to rely . . . against the French Generals . . . I tremble: and, as Lord Chesterfield said of the Generals of his day, 'I only hope that when the enemy reads the list of their names he trembles as I do.' Sir William Erskine and General Lumley will be a very nice addition to this list! However I pray God and the Horse Guards to deliver me from General Lightburne and Colonel Landers.

Wellington always liked to give his favourite quotations a good run. The Chesterfield epigram would have often sparkled at his dinner table, enhanced with characteristic 'By Gods!' and divested of references to authorship, until in due course his enchanted aides-de-camp handed it down to posterity as the great man's own work.

He was eventually delivered from Erskine when the unfortunate general committed suicide at Lisbon in 1813.

Elizabeth Longford

166.

This story from a French officer later gave birth to a host of literary legends.

A FRENCH sergeant, wearied of the misery in which the army was living, resolved to decamp and live in comfort. To this end he persuaded
about a hundred of the worst characters in the army, and going with
them to the rear, took up his quarters in a vast convent deserted by the
monks, but still full of furniture and provisions. He increased his store
largely by carrying off everything in the neighbourhood that suited
him; well-furnished spits and stewpans were always at the fire, and
each man helped himself as he would; and the leader received the
expressive if contemptuous name of 'Marshal Stockpot'. The scoun-
drel had also carried off numbers of women; and being joined before
long by the scum of the three armies attracted by the prospect of
unrestrained debauchery, he formed a band of some three hundred
English, French, and Portuguese deserters, who lived as a happy
family in one unbroken orgy. This brigandage had been going on for
some months, when one day, a foraging detachment having gone off in
pursuit of a flock as far as the convent which sheltered the so-called
'Marshal Stockpot', our soldiers were much surprised to see him coming to meet them at the head of his bandits, with orders to respect his
grounds and restore the flock which they had just taken there. On the
refusal of our officers to comply with this demand, he ordered his men
to fire on the detachment. The greater part of the French deserters did
not venture to fire on their compatriots and former comrades, but the
English and Portuguese obeyed, and our people had several men killed
or wounded. Not being in sufficient numbers to resist, they were compelled to retreat, accompanied by all the French deserters, who came
back with them to offer their submission. Masséna pardoned them on
condition that they should march at the head of the three battalions
who were told off to attack the convent. That den having been carried
after a brief resistance, Masséna had 'Marshal Stockpot' shot, as well
as the few French who had remained with him. A good many English
and Portuguese shared their fate, the rest were sent off to Wellington,
who did prompt justice on them.

                                                              Baron de Marbot

167.

A matching tale from the English camp.

WHILE at Campo Mayor [in 1809] the convalescents of my [Harry Smith's] Light Brigade were ordered to our old fortress, called Onguala, on the immediate frontier of Portugal, and opposite to Abuchucha, the frontier of Spain. They consisted of forty or fifty weakly men. I was first for Brigade duty, and I was sent in command, with a Lieut. Rentall of the 52nd Regiment and my brother Tom, who was sick. I knew this country well, for we had had some grand battues there, and shot red deer and wild boars. So soon, therefore, as I was installed in my command, lots of comrades used to come from Campo Mayor to breakfast with me and shoot all day. On one occasion Jack Molloy, Considine, and several fellows came, and while out we fell into the bivouac of a set of banditti and smugglers. We hallooed and bellowed as if an army were near us. The bandits jumped on their horses and left lots of corn-sacks, etc., in our hands; but on discovering our numbers, and that we fired no balls (for we had only some Rifle buttons pulled off my jacket), being well armed, they soon made us retreat. This, after my friends returned to Campo Mayor, so disconcerted me that I made inquiry about these same rascals, and ascertained there were a body of about twenty under a Catalan, the terror of the country. I immediately sent for my sergeant (a soldier in every sense of the word) to see how many of our convalescents he could pick out who could *march at all*. He soon returned. He himself and ten men, myself, Rentall, and my sick brother Tom (who *would* go) composed my army. I got a guide, and ascertained that there were several haunts of these bandits; so off I started. We moved on a small chapel (many of which lone spots there are in all Roman Catholic countries), at which there was a large stable. On approaching we heard a shot fired, then a great and lawless shouting, which intimated to us our friends of the morning were near at hand. So Pat Nann and I crept on to peep about. We discovered the fellows were all inside a long stable, with a railed gate shut, and a regular sentry with his arms in his hand. They were all about and had lights, and one very dandy-looking fellow with a smart dagger was cutting tobacco to make a cigar. Pat and I returned to our party and made a disposition of attack, previously ascertaining if the stable had a back door, which it had not. I then fell in our men very silently, Mr Rentall being much opposed to our attack, at which my brother Tom blew him up in no bad style of whispering abuse, and our men went for the gate. The sentry soon discovered us and let fly, but hit no one. The gate was fast and resisted two attempts to force it, but so amazed were the bandits, they [never] attempted to get away their horses, although their arms were regularly piled against the supports of the roof of the stable, and we took twelve banditti with their captain, a fine handsome fellow, horses, etc. His dagger I sent to my dear father. I sent my prisoners on the next day to Campo Mayor, galloping ahead myself, in an awful funk lest General Craufurd should blow me up. However, I got great credit for my achievement in thus ridding the neighbourhood of a nest of robbers; and the captain and five of his men (being Spaniards) were sent to Badajos and sentenced to the galleys for life, being recognized as old offenders. The remainder received a lesser punishment. My men got forty Spanish dollars each prize money, the amount I sold the horses for. I bought for forty dollars the captain's capital horse. The men wanted me to keep him as my share, but I would not. Dr Robb, our surgeon, gave sixty Spanish dollars for a black mare.

Sir Harry Smith

168.

A Rifle Brigade officer in the campaign of 1811.

IN a few days, as we had got well up to the French rear-guard and were about to attack, a General Order was received, to my astonishment, appointing me Brigade Major to the 2nd Light Brigade, not dear old Sydney's. *He* expected it, since he and Colonel Pakenham (dear Sir Edward!) were trying to do something for me on account of my lame leg. Beckwith says, 'Now give your Company over to Layton, and set off immediately to Colonel Drummond,' who commanded the Brigade. Hardly had I reached it, when such a cannonade commenced, knocking the 52nd about in a way I never saw before and hardly since. We were soon all engaged, and drove the French, with very hard fighting, into and over the river, with a severe loss in killed, prisoners, and drowned. A very heavy fight it was, ending just before dark. I said to my Brigadier, 'Have you any orders for the picquets, sir?' He was an old Guardsman, the kindest though oddest fellow possible. 'Pray, Mr Smith, are you my Brigade Major?' 'I believe so, sir.' 'Then let me tell

you, it is your duty to post the picquets, and mine to have a d—d good
dinner for you every day.' We soon understood each other. He cooked
the dinner often himself, and I *commanded* the Brigade.

Sir Harry Smith

169.

A day with Lord Wellington's hounds.

ONE day, when Wellington was not present, hounds found a strong
fox, and away went the field at a great pace with a breast-high scent.
The fox was headed by a working party of infantry returning from the
trenches, and forthwith made for the outpost line, No Man's Land,
and enemy country. 'Hold hard, gentlemen', sung out the Master. The
Whips were about to call off hounds, when Tom Crane shouted 'Leave
'em!', and turning to the astonished Master said, 'where my fox goes,
so do I', and galloped off with hounds in full cry before him. He killed,
and as his excitement cooled, he found himself in an awkward situation. A patrol of French light cavalry cut him off and took him prisoner. The French were thoroughly puzzled. At first they thought he
was a milord, but later decided that he was not. He was returned,
hounds and all, under a flag of truce, with many mutual courtesies
between the officers.

Douglas Bell

170.

A French officer describes a truly Gerardian brush with an English challenger.

I WAS no great distance from the enemy's skirmishers, posted in the
woods surrounding the clearing. Although I knew that Marshal Ney
had a strong escort, I was uneasy on his account, fearing that the English might have cut him off, until I saw him on the other side of the
brook. Pelet was with him, and both were going in the direction of Masséna. So, being sure that the orders had been conveyed, I was about to
return, when a young English light infantry officer trotted up on his
pony, crying, 'Stop, Mr Frenchman; I should like to have a little fight
with you!' I saw no need to reply to this bluster, and was making my way
towards our outposts, 500 yards in arrear, while the Englishman

followed me, heaping insults on me. At first I took no notice, but presently he called out, 'I can see by your uniform that you are on the staff of a marshal, and I will put in the London papers that the sight of me was enough to frighten away one of Masséna's or Ney's cowardly aides-de-camp!' I admit that it was a serious error on my part, but I could no longer endure this impudent challenge coolly; so, drawing my sword, I dashed furiously at my adversary. But just as I was about to meet him, I heard a rustling in the wood, and out came two English hussars, galloping to cut off my retreat. I was caught in a trap, and understood that only a most energetic defence could save me from the disgrace of being taken prisoner, through my own fault, in sight of the whole French army, which was witness to this unequal combat. So I flew upon the English officer; we met; he gave me a slash across the face, I ran my sword into his throat. His blood spurted over me, and the wretch fell from his horse to the ground, which he bit in his rage. Meanwhile, the two hussars were hitting me all over, chiefly on the head. In a few seconds my shako, my wallet, and my pelisse were in strips, though I was not myself wounded by any of their blows. At length, however, the elder of the two hussars, a grizzled old soldier, let me have more than an inch of his point in my right side. I replied with a vigorous backhander; my blade struck his teeth and passed between his jaws, as he was in the act of shouting, slitting his mouth to the ears. He made off promptly, to my lively satisfaction, for he was by far the braver and more energetic of the two. When the younger man found himself left alone with me, he hesitated for a moment, because as our horses' heads were touching, he saw that to turn his back to me was to expose himself to be hit. However, on seeing several soldiers coming to my aid, he made up his mind, but he did not escape the dreaded wound, for in my anger I pursued him for some paces and gave him a thrust in the shoulder, which quickened his speed. During this fight, which lasted less time than it has taken to tell it, our scouts had come up quickly to set me free, and on the other side the English soldiers had marched towards the place where their officer had fallen. The two groups were firing at each other, and I was very near getting in the way of the bullets from both sides. But my brother and Ligniville, who had seen me engaged with the English officer and his two men, had hastened up to me, and I was badly in want of their help, for I was losing so much blood from the wound in my side that I was growing faint, and I could not have stayed on my horse if they had not held me up. As soon as I rejoined the staff, Masséna said, taking my hand, 'Well done;

rather too well done! A field officer has no business to expose himself in fighting at the outposts.' He was quite right, but when I told him the motives which had led me on, he blamed me less, and the more fiery Ney, remembering his own hussar days, cried, 'Upon my word, in Marbot's place I should have done the same!' All the generals and my comrades came to express their concern, while Dr Brisset was attending to me. The wound in my cheek was not important; in a month's time it had healed over, and you can scarcely see the mark of it along my left whisker. But the thrust in my right side was dangerous, especially in the middle of a long retreat, in which I was compelled to travel on horseback, without being able to get the rest which a wounded man needs. Such, my children, was the result of my fight, or, if you like, my prank at Miranda de Corvo. You have still got the shako which I wore, and the numerous notches with which the English sabres have adorned it prove that the two hussars did not let me off. I brought away my wallet also, the sling of which was cut in three places, but it has been mislaid.

Baron de Marbot

171.

The mirror image: a similar affray described by an English pen, outside Salamanca in 1812.

I HAD an encounter in single combat this day with a very young French officer between the two lines of skirmishers, French and English, who stood still, by mutual consent, to witness it. The French officer showed great cunning and skill, seeing the superiority of my horse, for he remained stationary to receive me, and allowed me to ride round and round him while he remained on the defensive. He made several cuts at the head of my horse and succeeded in cutting one of my reins and the forefinger of my bridle hand which was, however, saved by the thick glove I wore, though the finger was cut very deeply to the joint. As my antagonist was making the last cut at me I had the opportunity of making a thrust at his body which staggered him, and he made off. I thought I had but slightly wounded him, but I found on enquiry the next day, when sent on a flag of truce, that the thrust had proved mortal, having entered the pit of his stomach. I felt deeply on this occasion and was much annoyed, as I had admired the chivalrous and noble bearing of this young officer. He was a mere youth, who, I suppose, thought it necessary to make this display as a first essay, as French officers usually do on their first appearance on the field and, indeed I believe, it is expected of them by their comrades. I shall never forget his good-humoured, fine countenance during the whole time we were engaged in this single combat, talking cheerfully and politely to me as if we were exchanging civilities instead of sabre cuts. The cut I received on the forefinger of my bridle hand proved a great grievance for some time, as it prevented me from playing the violin for weeks—a great deprivation, as I always played in the bivouac at night.

Captain T. W. Brotherton

172.

WE had in my old corps, amongst other 'characters', one that, at the period I am writing about, was well known in the army to be as jovial a fellow as ever put his foot under a mess-table. His name was Fairfield; and though there were few who could sing as good a song, there was not in the whole British army a worse duty officer. Indeed, it was next to impossible to catch hold of him for any duty whatever; and so well known was his dislike to all military etiquette, that the officer next to him on the roster, the moment Fairfield's name appeared for guard-mounting or court-martial, considered himself as the person meant, and he was right nine times out of ten. The frequent absence of Fairfield from drill, at a time too when the regiment was in expectation of being inspected by the general of division, obliged the officer commanding to send the surgeon to ascertain the nature of his malady, which from its long continuance (on occasions of duty!) strongly savoured of a chronic complaint. The doctor found the invalid traversing his chamber rather lightly clad for an indisposed person; he was singing one of Moore's melodies, and accompanying himself with his violin, which instrument he touched with great taste. The doctor told him the nature of his visit, and offered to feel his pulse, but Fairfield turned from him, repeating the lines of Shakespeare, 'Canst thou minister,' etc. etc. 'Well,' replied the surgeon, 'I am sorry for it, but I cannot avoid reporting you fit for duty.'—'I'm sorry you cannot,' rejoined Fairfield; 'but my complaint is best known to myself! and I feel that were I to rise as early as is necessary, I should be lost to the service in a month.' 'Why,' said the doctor, 'Major Thompson says you have been lost to it ever since he first knew you, and that is now something about six years,' and he took his leave for the purpose of making his report.

The Major's orderly was soon at Fairfield's quarters with a message to say that his presence was required by his commanding officer. Fairfield was immediately in attendance. 'Mr Fairfield,' said the Major, 'your constant habit of being absent from early drill has obliged me to send the surgeon to ascertain the state of your health, and he reports that you are perfectly well, and I must say that your appearance is anything but that of an invalid—how is this?' 'Don't mind him, sir,' replied Fairfield; 'I am, thank God! very well *now*, but when the bugle sounded this morning at four o'clock a cold shivering came over me—I think it was a touch of ague!—and besides, Dr Gregg is too short a time in the Connaught Rangers to know my *habit*.'—'Is he?' rejoined the old Major, 'he must be d—d stupid then. But that is a charge you surely can't make against me. I have been now about nineteen years in the regiment, during six of which I have had the pleasure of knowing you, and you will allow me to tell you, that I am not only well acquainted with 'your habit', but to request you will, from this moment, *change it*'—and with this gentle rebuke he good-humouredly dismissed him. He was an excellent duty officer ever after.

William Grattan

173.

A French officer describes an episode in the Peninsular campaign of 1811.

ONE evening, just as I was finishing my game of chess with the duchess, a servant announced M. de Canouville. An instant of silence testified to our astonishment and our curiosity; after which a piteous voice besought food and admission for a poor worn-out and famished traveller. Then as a face worthy of the voice came through the doorway, that face, which indeed was that of Jules de Canouville, was greeted with a general shout of laughter. With an instinctive movement everyone rose and went towards him, with exclamations appropriate to the doleful get-up of this dandy of the court, this most fashionable of the young men of the day, to the mud with which he was covered, to the disorder of his dress, to his beard, which nowadays would be too short, but at that time was regarded as untidy. After the first outburst and many repetitions of his name, after disconnected words uttered at random, everybody having ejaculated in his own way and in different keys, 'Canouville!—you!—he! Is it possible?—how?—why?'—it became possible to frame a sentence, and a dialogue on the whole as comic as the entrance was succeeded by something resembling a conversation. After having told us that he was the bearer of dispatches for the Prince of Essling, with orders to discover an army which in Paris was supposed to be lost, he came to the real motive for his journey, and repeated to all of us twenty times what he declared he could not tell anybody once, what everybody knew, what he was all on fire to tell us. Being aide-de-camp to the Prince of Neuchâtel, he had recently become the lover of Pauline Bonaparte, Princess Borghese. In order to put a stop to the intrigue the Emperor had had this duty entrusted to him with orders to start at once, and the crazy fellow, in order to get back quickly, had galloped without rest or respite. While he related the details of his adventure he mingled them with alas's and sighs fit, as the duchess said, to blow the candles out.

Nothing equally melancholy could have been more comical or more lively. His supper was another comedy, for complaining all the while that he was being left to starve, he did not hear or did not notice when his meal was announced, and at the table, where he took his position like a man ready to eat up everything, he went on talking and forgot to eat. At midnight I wanted to retire, but he begged me not to go without him, and it was striking one when I succeeded in getting him to adjourn the meeting. At the duchess's door such of the party as had remained till then separated; I thought that he also would take his leave and make his way to wherever he was staying, but he stopped, and resuming his lamentable voice there in the middle of the road, said to me, 'General, would you have the heart to desert an unhappy young man?' 'Surely not,' I replied; 'and if you do not breakfast or dine with the duchess, I am sure I hope that you will look upon my table as your own.' 'But for to-night?' 'For to-night? Why, you're going back to bed and to sleep.' 'What bed?' 'Why, hang it, the bed at your lodging.' 'I haven't got any lodging.' 'What, didn't you get a lodging when you arrived?' 'No, general, and if you desert me I don't know what will become of me'; and, roaring with laughter, I took him along to my house.

There we had another display. When I ordered my servant to get a bed made for him in my sitting-room, he went on, 'General, you are so kind.' 'Well?' 'Well, I am too unhappy to sleep alone.' 'Oh indeed; you don't want to sleep with me?' 'No, general, but pray have a bed made for me in your room,' and I did so. Instead of going to bed, I had to hear the whole story of his happiness and his misfortunes, a panegyric of the excellent qualities and the charms of the princess, and the confession of his passion for her. The poor lad had lost everything, his heart and his head alike; with the exception of a few minutes my night was equally lost, but one does not often have a more amusing one. However, I did get to bed, and finally to sleep. As for him, when I woke up he had gone out; by eight in the morning he had presented himself at the duchess's, and had her woke up to get a letter from her to the duke. She sent answer that he was mad; indeed, I had given him the day before all the reasons to show that as communication with the Army of Portugal was interrupted it would be no use for him to continue his journey, and that he must wait for a more propitious moment to discharge his errand. After he had left the duchess I saw him again; he wanted to push on at least as far as Ciudad Rodrigo or Almeida, but I made him see that even if he got there, which appeared impossible without an escort—and with that I had no excuse for furnishing him— he would be none the less cut off from the Army of Portugal; while if, contrary to all probability, a column of that army succeeded sooner or later in cutting its way through to one of those towns, it would not go away without communicating with me and receiving my orders and dispatches, so that there would be nothing gained for his errand by leaving Salamanca. 'But in that case,' he returned, 'what would be the good of my staying here? My dispatches will go just as well with yours as by themselves. And what impropriety would there be in my handing them to you?' 'I should not receive them.' 'And if I left them on your desk?' 'Well, I should have to have them taken up. But you would not get any receipt for them; you would remain responsible for them, and I should report the matter.'

No one can imagine what these simpletons after Berthier's sort were, charming young people, all in good style and possessed of some fortune, in some cases of sufficient distinction and position to attain to anything, and of whom none ever played any part unless in ladies' boudoirs. Canouville was one of the most agreeable of them. He got more and more excited till he persuaded himself that he would be bearing an important piece of news if he went to Paris and said that it was impossible to communicate, although I represented to him that twenty dispatches of mine had informed, and were still informing, the Prince of Neuchâtel of the fact. Although I repeated to him that it was ridiculous to ride 600 or 700 leagues in order to get a blowing up and perhaps something worse, he declared that for him an hour passed at

Paris was worth a whole lifetime. Finding this a sublime reply and reason, he departed on the strength of them, crossed all the north of Spain without taking a single man to escort him, reached Paris at night, was run down at once, and forced to decamp at daybreak. Three weeks had not passed when he came back very melancholy, and begged me to give him back his dispatches.

General Thiébault

174.

BOTH Wellington and Napoleon were eminently practical men. They knew there was a time for dressing-up and a time for undressing too. I am reminded of the anecdote told by Wellington to his confidante, Mrs Arbuthnot, on the methods Napoleon wished to employ in order to distract the Parisian public's attention from the appalling losses in the Russian campaign then in progress. He ordered that the ballet dancers at the opera were to appear *sans culotte*. The order was given, but the dancers flatly refused to comply. 'Wellington added', says Mrs Arbuthnot in her journal, 'that if the women had consented he did not doubt but that it would have obliterated all recollection of the Russian losses. Wellington was categoric. "This anecdote," he said, "he knew for a fact." '

The Iron Duke had a sound understanding of human nature: and he was being realistic, rather than cynical, when, during the Peninsular campaigns he set a limit of forty-eight hours for his officers' leaves in Lisbon, or behind the lines. This, he said, was as long as any reasonable man could wish to spend in bed with any woman.

Lesley Blanch

175.

A British officer, wounded at Badajoz, is at last brought to his tent on the morning of 7 April 1812.

THE two faithful soldiers, Bray and Macgowan, that conducted me there, on entering, found my truss of straw, or bed, if the reader will so allow me to designate it, occupied by Mrs Nelly Carsons, the wife of my batman, who, I suppose, by the way of banishing care, had taken to drinking divers potations of rum to such an excess that she lay down in my bed, thinking, perhaps, that I was not likely again to be its occupant; or, more probably, not giving it a thought at all. Macgowan attempted to wake her, but in vain—a battery of a dozen guns might have been fired close to her ear without danger of disturbing her repose! 'Why then, sir,' said he, 'sure the bed's big enough for yees both, and she'll keep you nate and warm, for, be the powers, you're kilt with the cold and the loss ov blood.' I was in no mood to stand on ceremony, or, indeed, to stand at all. I allowed myself to be placed beside my partner, without any further persuasion; and the two soldiers left us to ourselves and returned to the town. Weakness from loss of blood soon caused me to fall asleep, but it was a sleep of short duration. I awoke, unable to move, and, in fact, lay like an infant. The fire of small arms, the screams of the soldiers' wives, and the universal buzz throughout the camp, acted powerfully upon my nervous and worn-out frame; but Somnus conquered Mars, for I soon fell into another doze, in which I might have remained very comfortable had not my companion awoke sooner than I wished; discharging a huge grunt, and putting her hand upon my leg, she exclaimed, 'Arrah! Dan, jewel, what makes you so stiff this morning?'

William Grattan

176.

The most celebrated and romantic tale of the Peninsula is that of Juanita, who became the wife of Harry Smith of the Rifle Brigade, and followed him through campaigns for the next forty years, giving her name to the town of Ladysmith in South Africa before she died. Here a fellow Rifleman describes her first appearance in the British ranks, during the murderous sack of Badajoz in April 1812.

I WAS conversing with a friend the day after, at the door of his tent, when we observed two ladies coming from the city, who made directly towards us; they seemed both young, and when they came near, the elder of the two threw back her *mantilla* to address us, showing a remarkably handsome figure, with fine features; but her sallow, sunburnt, and careworn, though still youthful, countenance showed that in her 'the time for tender thoughts and soft endearments had fled away and gone'.

She at once addressed us in that confident, heroic manner so characteristic of the high-bred Spanish maiden, told us who they were—the last of an ancient and honourable house—and referred to an officer high in rank in our army, who had been quartered there in the days of her prosperity, for the truth of her tale.

Her husband, she said, was a Spanish officer in a distant part of the kingdom; he might, or he might not, still be living. But yesterday she and this her young sister were able to live in affluence and in a handsome house; to-day they knew not where to lay their heads, where to get a change of raiment or a morsel of bread. Her house, she said, was a wreck; and, to show the indignities to which they had been subjected, she pointed to where the blood was still trickling down their necks, caused by the wrenching of their ear-rings through the flesh by the hands of worse than savages, who would not take the trouble to unclasp them!

For herself, she said, she cared not; but for the agitated and almost unconscious maiden by her side, whom she had but lately received over from the hands of her conventual instructresses, she was in despair, and knew not what to do; and that, in the rapine and ruin which was at that moment desolating the city, she saw no security for her but the seemingly indelicate one she had adopted—of coming to the camp and throwing themselves upon the protection of any British officer who would afford it; and so great, she said, was her faith in our national character, that she knew the appeal would not be made in vain, nor the confidence abused. Nor was it made in vain! Nor could it be abused, for she stood by the side of an angel! A being more transcendingly lovely I had never before seen—one more amiable I have never yet known!

Fourteen summers had not yet passed over her youthful countenance, which was of a delicate freshness—more English than Spanish; her face, though not perhaps rigidly beautiful, was nevertheless so remarkably handsome, and so irresistibly attractive, surmounting a figure cast in nature's fairest mould, that to look at her was to love her; and I did love her, but I never told my love, and in the mean time another and a more impudent fellow stepped in and won her! But yet I was happy, for in him she found such a one as her loveliness and her misfortunes claimed—a man of honour, and a husband in every way worthy of her!

That a being so young, so lovely, and so interesting, just emancipated from the gloom of a convent, unknowing of the world and to the world unknown, should thus have been wrecked on a sea of troubles, and thrown on the mercy of strangers under circumstances so dreadful, so uncontrollable, and not have sunk to rise no more, must be the wonder of every one. Yet from the moment she was thrown on her own resources, her star was in the ascendant.

Guided by a just sense of rectitude, an innate purity of mind, a singleness of purpose which defied malice, and a soul that soared above circumstances, she became alike the adored of the camp and of the drawing-room, and eventually the admired associate of princes. She yet lives, in the affections of her gallant husband, in an elevated situation in life, a pattern to her sex, and everybody's *beau ideal* of what a wife should be.

Sir John Kincaid

177.

Salamanca, 22 July 1812.

MARMONT came down upon us the first night with a thundering cannonade, and placed his army *en masse* on the plain before us, almost within gunshot. I was told that, while Lord Wellington was riding along the line, under a fire of artillery, and accompanied by a numerous staff, a brace of greyhounds in pursuit of a hare passed close to him. He was at the moment in earnest conversation with General Castanos; but the instant he observed them he gave the view hallo and went after them at full speed, to the utter astonishment of his foreign accompaniments. Nor did he stop until he saw the hare killed; when he returned and resumed the commander-in-chief as if nothing had occurred.

Sir John Kincaid

178.

AMONG the soldiers, robbery of beehives was a favourite crime, the 4th Division being known for their prowess as 'honeysuckers'. Wellington told the story of a beehive-robber he himself caught redhanded.

'Hillo, sir! where did you get that beehive?' The soldier, misunderstanding his intention, replied obligingly that the beehives were just over the hill but he'd better hurry or they'd all be gone.

Elizabeth Longford

179.

Wellington's Judge-Advocate dispensing justice with what might reasonably be termed gay abandon.

WE arrived at Guinaldo in two hours, finished a case and tried a man for shooting a Portuguese, acquitted him of murder, but found him guilty of very disorderly conduct, and sentenced him to receive eight hundred lashes. I then walked round the town, looked into the church, and came back; wrote the whole out fair on six sides of folio paper; dined with the president at six, had a hospitable reception; and in the evening went to a sort of frolicsome masked ball, given extra on account of the Courts-martial.

F. S. Larpent

180.

As the Grand Army approached Moscow, the Russian rearguard marched out of it.

THE final Russian regiments moved through Moscow unmolested by the French. A military band began to beat out a defiant tune in an attempt to lift the spirits of the soldiers, but [General Mikhail] Milora-dovich rode in a fury to the commander, thrusting forward his promi-nent jaw and shouting: 'What idiot told your band to play?' The band officer replied that a garrison must play suitable music when leaving a fortress, under a regulation laid down by Peter the Great. 'Where do the regulations of Peter the Great provide for the surrender of Moscow?' bellowed back Miloradovich. 'Order that damned music to be stopped!'

Roger Parkinson

181.

On the banks of the Niemen on 14 December 1812, the ruins of the Grand Army fought their last action of the Russian campaign.

AWAKENED by the sound of cannon-fire, the Marshal [Ney] ran to the Vilna gate [of Kovno]. He found his own cannon had been spiked, and that the artillerymen had fled! Enraged, he darted forward, and elevating his sword, would have killed the officer who commanded them had it not been for his *aide-de-camp* (Fézensac), who warded off the blow and allowed the miserable fellow to escape.

Ney then summoned his infantry, but only one of the two feeble battalions of which it was composed had taken up arms; these were the three hundred Germans. He drew them up, encouraged them, and as the enemy was approaching, was just about to give them the order to fire when a Russian cannon ball, grazing the palisade, came in and broke the thigh of their commanding officer. He fell, and without the least hesitation, finding that his wound was mortal, he coolly drew his pistols and blew out his brains before his troops. Terrified at this act of despair, his soldiers were completely scared. All of them at once threw down their arms and fled in disorder.

Ney, abandoned by all, neither deserted himself nor his post. After vain efforts to detain these fugitives, he collected their muskets, which were still loaded, became once more a common soldier, and with only a few others kept facing thousands of the Russians. His very audacity stopped them; it made some of his artillerymen ashamed, who then returned to join their Marshal; and it gave time to another *aide-de-camp*, Heymès, and to General Marchand to assemble thirty soldiers and bring forward two or three light pieces. Meanwhile Marchand went to collect the only battalion which remained intact.

At about 2.00 p.m. the second Russian attack began from the other side of the Niemen, although still directed against the bridge. Obviously the last desperate action of the 1812 campaign was now approaching its climax. Ney sent Marchand and his four hundred men forward to secure the bridge.

As to himself, without giving way, or disquieting himself further as to what was happening at the rear, he kept on fighting at the head of his thirty men and maintained himself until night at the Vilna gate. He then traversed the town and crossed the Niemen, constantly fighting, retreating but never flying, marching after all the others, supporting to the last moment the honour of Napoleon's arms, and for the hundredth time during the last forty days and forty nights, putting his life and liberty in jeopardy just to save a few more Frenchmen.

At Gumbinnen in East Prussia on 15 December General Matthieu Dumas was just sitting down to his first decent breakfast in months when someone kicked the door open. 'There stood before him a man in a ragged brown coat, with a long beard, dishevelled and with his face darkened as if it had been burned, his eyes red-rimmed and glaring. Underneath his coat he wore the rags and shreds of a discoloured and filthy uniform.'

'Here I am then,' the newcomer exclaimed.

'But who are you?' the general cried, alarmed.

'What! Don't you recognize me? I am Marshal Ney: the rearguard of the *Grande Armée*! I have fired the last shot on the bridge at Kovno. I have thrown the last of our muskets into the Niemen. I have made my way here across a hundred fields of snow. Also I'm damnably hungry. Get someone to bring me a plate of soup . . . '

Once fed, bathed and with his uniform stitched up he hurried off to Königsberg and a traumatic conference with the King of Naples . . .

Raymond Horricks

182.

A soldier of the 51st Foot writes home from Spain.

Moimento, 28 April 1813

Since I wrote last . . . I am sorry to say we have had a Serjeant, Corporal and private punished by sentence of a division court martial for what the Earl of Dalhousie considers a great crime, and I must myself confess that in a Military point of view the private could scarcely be guilty of a greater. I shall relate the story to you, then you will be able to form your own opinion on it.

It being fine weather the General had some tents pitched in a field belonging to the house he was staying in. A mail had just arrived from England and the General and his staff were looking over the newspapers. One of our men, sentry at the tent, having got some rum had drank so much that he was quite intoxicated. Seeing the papers he began to be anxious to know how things were going on in England, so without any ceremony he walks up to the tent door, but unfortunately the tent peg or cords caught his toe and in he bolted head foremost and lay prostrate at the Earl's feet, and not having the benefit of a polite education without making an apology for his abrupt intrusion with much sang froid asked the General 'What news from England'. It is easy to guess what followed, the man with the Serjeant and Corporal of the Guard were confined, a Division Court Martial followed. The Serjeant was tried for passing the man, the Corporal for planting him on sentry, and the man for being drunk on duty. As a matter of course they were all found guilty. The Serjeant and Corporal to be reduced to the ranks and receive 300 lashes and the private 500. These sentences were carried into execution in presence of as many troops of the Division as could be conveniently assembled.

. . . You have often hinted in your letters that I ought to endeavour to get promoted. I have no desire . . . I have always declined every offer made to me, before this. I am young and I have so far kept out of trouble. I always endeavour to perform my duty in the best way I am able. I have therefore nothing to fear. But should I be entrusted with a guard perhaps I might get into a scrape through their neglect. There is time enough after the razor has passed round my chin some hundred times more before I think about accepting of any responsible situation.

Private William Wheeler

183.

After Lutzen, 2 May 1813.

. . . Napoleon expressed great alarm at the sight of Ney. 'My dear Cousin! But you are covered in blood!' The Marshal looked down at his gory uniform. 'It isn't mine, Sire,' he replied calmly; ' . . . except where that damned bullet passed through my leg!'

Raymond Horricks

184.

Wellington's army in the campaign of 1813.

[LORD] Bathurst was told on 29 June that 'our vagabond soldiers' had been 'totally knocked up' by their night of plunder, and until discipline could be enforced we should 'do no good' even by our greatest victories. Three days later (2 July) the thunders pealed more loudly still.

It is quite impossible for me or any other man to command a British army under the existing system. We have in the service the scum of the earth as common soldiers—

and what with proposals in Parliament for reforms and soft-hearted officers in the field, it was impossible to keep 'such men as some of our soldiers are' in order.

The fatal phrase, *scum of the earth*, had long been and was to remain a favourite with Wellington. He was to rub in his point to Stanhope in 1831 during one of his many arguments about flogging.

'Do they beat them in the French Army?' asked Stanhope.

'Oh, they bang them about very much with ramrods and that sort of thing, and then they shoot them.'

But the reason why the British Army needed the terror of the triangle as an ultimate deterrent, whereas the French did not, was because the French was an army of conscripts and the British of volunteers:

The conscription calls out a share of every class— no matter whether your son or my son—all must march; but our friends—I may say it in this room— are the very scum of the earth.

Wellington then went on to analyse the volunteer material:

People talk of their enlisting from their fine military feeling—all stuff—no such thing. Some of our men enlist from having got bastard children—some for minor offences—many more for drink; but you can hardly conceive such a set brought together, and it really is wonderful that we should have made them the fine fellows they are.

Elizabeth Longford

185.

Harry Smith finds himself billeted upon a Spaniard of somewhat alarming personal habits in the campaign of 1813.

AFTER I had dressed myself, he came to me and said, 'When you dine, I have some capital wine, as much as you and your servants like; but,' he says, 'come down and look at my cellar.' The fellow had been so civil, I did not like to refuse him. We descended by a stone staircase, he carrying a light. He had upon his countenance a most sinister expression. I saw something exceedingly excited him: his look became fiend-like. He and I were alone, but such confidence had we Englishmen in a Spaniard, and with the best reason, that I apprehended no personal evil. Still his appearance was very singular. When we got to the cellar-door, he opened it, and held the light so as to show the cellar; when, in a voice of thunder, and with an expression of demoniacal hatred and antipathy, pointing to the floor, he exclaimed, 'There lie four of the devils who thought to subjugate Spain! I am a Navarrese. I was born free from all foreign invasion, and this right hand shall plunge this stiletto in my own heart as it did into theirs, ere I and my countrymen are subjugated!' brandishing his weapon like a demon. I see the excited patriot as I write. Horror-struck as I was, the instinct of self-preservation induced me to admire the deed exceedingly, while my very frame quivered and my blood was frozen, to see the noble science of war and the honour and chivalry of arms reduced to the practices of midnight assassins. Upon the expression of my admiration, he cooled, and while he was deliberately drawing wine for my dinner, which, however strange it may be, I drank with the gusto its flavour merited, I examined the four bodies. They were Dragoons—four athletic, healthy-looking fellows. As we ascended, he had perfectly recovered the equilibrium of his vivacity and naturally good humour. I asked him how he, single-handed, had perpetrated this deed on four armed men (for their swords were by their sides). 'Oh, easily enough. I pretended to love a Frenchman' (or, in his words, 'I was an Afrancesado'), 'and I proposed, after giving them a good dinner, we should drink to the extermination of the English.' He then looked at me and ground his teeth. 'The French rascals, they little guessed what I contemplated. Well, we got into the cellar, and drank away until I made them so drunk, they fell, and my purpose was easily, and as joyfully, effected.' He again brandished his dagger, and said, 'Thus die all enemies to Spain.' Their horses were in his stable.

Sir Harry Smith

186.

I KNEW an officer of the 18th Hussars, W.R., young, rich, and a fine-looking fellow, who joined the army not far from St Sebastian. His stud of horses was remarkable for their blood; his grooms were English, and three in number. He brought with him a light cart to carry forage, and a fourgon for his own baggage. All went on well till he came to go on outpost duty; but not finding there any of the comforts to which he had been accustomed, he quietly mounted his charger, told his astonished sergeant that campaigning was not intended for a gentleman, and instantly galloped off to his quarters, ordering his servants to pack up everything immediately, as he had hired a transport to take him off to England. He left us before any one had time to stop him; and though despatches were sent off to the Commander-in-Chief, requesting that a court-martial might sit to try the young deserter, he arrived home long enough before the despatches to enable him to sell out of his regiment. He deserved to have been shot.

Captain Gronow

187.

Aftermath of a skirmish, November 1813.

I WAS resting myself on a wall or rather a bank, thinking to what trouble and misery many lovely young women of respectable connections had brought themselves into by marrying soldiers who but a few years since I had seen in old England in the full enjoyment of health etc. when I was roused from my reverie by a well known voice saying 'Then you have caught it at last, Corporal.' I looked up and there stood Marshall who I had once saved from a watery grave, his arm was in a sling. I was about to spake to him when I was interupted by a female voice in a trembling accent, 'Oh W— have you seen my husband or can you give me any account of him.' I shook my head. 'Oh it is too true, your silence confirms what I have just been told, he is dead.' She then ran away towards the hill where the severe conflict had taken place. 'Ah Marshall' said I 'her fears are but too true, he is dead indeed, he fell not many yards from where I lay.' 'Who the D— is she' said M— 'I did not see her to notice her.' 'Not know her' said I. 'It was Mrs Foster.' 'Oh Damn it' said he, 'was it, I am sorry for her, but you know there is so many of these damned women running and blubbering about, enquiring after their husbands. Why the D—l dont they stop at home where they ought to be. This is no place for them. Come let us go in and get something to drink, not stop here to be pestered to death by a parcel of women. Come make haste, here comes Cousins' wife, snivelling as if she was a big girl going to school without her breakfast.' 'She has reason to snivel as you calls it' said I 'she is the most unfortunate creature in the army.' 'Unfortunate indeed' said M—'why I think she is devilish lucky in getting husbands, she has had a dozen this campaign.' M— was drunk and had rather stretched the number. This unfortunate woman was now a widow for the third time since the battle of Victoria.

Private William Wheeler

188.

DURING the action of the 10th of December 1813, commonly known as that of the Mayor's House, in the neighbourhood of Bayonne, the Grenadier Guards, under the command of Colonel Tynling, occupied an unfinished redoubt on the right of the high-road. The Duke of Wellington happened to pass with Freemantle and Lord A. Hill, on his return to head-quarters, having satisfied himself that the fighting was merely a feint on the part of Soult. His Grace on looking around saw, to his surprise, a great many umbrellas, with which the officers protected themselves from the rain that was then falling. Arthur Hill came galloping up to us saying 'Lord Wellington does not approve of the use of umbrellas during the enemy's firing, and will not allow "the gentlemen's sons" to make themselves ridiculous in the eyes of the army.' Colonel Tynling, a few days afterwards, received a wigging from Lord Wellington for suffering his officers to carry umbrellas in the face of the enemy; his Lordship observing, 'The Guards may in uniform, when on duty at St James's, carry them if they please; but in the field it is not only ridiculous but unmilitary.'

Captain Gronow

189.

AN hour after Wellington's entry into Toulouse [on 12 April 1814], while he was dressing for a dinner he was to give in the Prefecture, Colonel Frederick Ponsonby galloped in from the royalist town of Bordeaux.

'I have extraordinary news for you.'

'Ay, I thought so. I knew we should have peace; I've long expected it.'

'No; Napoleon has abdicated.'

'How abdicated? Ay, 'tis time indeed.'

Suddenly the penny dropped.

'You don't say so, upon my honour! Hurrah!' The Commander-in-Chief, still in his shirt sleeves, spun round on his heel snapping his fingers like a schoolboy.

Elizabeth Longford

190.

. . . while the Duke of Wellington was Ambassador at Paris, after the capture and occupation of that city by the Allied armies, in 1814, an atrocious attempt was made to assassinate him when returning one evening to his hotel in his carriage. The assassin had placed himself in the Rue Royale, just outside the gateway of the court-yard of the hotel, and firing his pistol at the Duke, just as the carriage turned into the gateway, ran up the street, and made his escape, before he could be seized by the sentries who were on duty at the entrance. There were two of them on this post, but the gate being narrow, they both stood back on the inside, to get out of the way of the carriage; for the coachman, on seeing the flash of the pistol, whipped his horses up to a gallop as he turned in. Consequently the fellow was off before they could rush out after him. Great display of zeal for discovery of the criminal was made afterwards by the French Minister of Police, but assisted by the villains who had employed him, the man escaped out of Paris, and got safe away into Belgium.

It is deplorable to think that Buonaparte, after his exile, should have looked upon this cowardly and bloody design as a subject for acknowledgment and gratitude in his Will, but there stands the document, all written in his own hand, recording in the following words this perverted sentiment: 'Je laisse au sous-officier Cantillon prévenu de l'assassinat du Duc de Wellington la somme de 10,000 francs. Il avoit autant de droit de tuer cet oligarch, que l'autre avoit de m'envoyer périr sur les rochers de Ste Hélène.'

Lord de Ros

191.

Harry Smith was one of many Peninsular veterans who took part in the doomed and bloody British assault on New Orleans in December 1814.

LATE in the afternoon I was sent to the enemy with a flag of truce, and a letter to General Jackson, with a request to be allowed to bury the dead and bring in the wounded lying between our respective positions. The Americans were not accustomed to the civility of war, like our old *associates* the French, and I was a long time before I could induce them to receive me. They fired on me with cannon and musketry, which excited my choler somewhat, for a round shot tore away the ground under my right foot, which it would have been a bore indeed to have lost under such circumstances. However, they did receive me at last, and the reply from General Jackson was a very courteous one.

After the delivery of the reply to General Lambert, I was again sent out with a fatigue party—a pretty large one too—with entrenching tools to bury the dead, and some surgeons to examine and bring off the wounded. I was received by a rough fellow—a Colonel Butler, Jackson's Adjutant-General. He had a drawn sword, and no scabbard. I soon saw the man I had to deal with. I outrode the surgeon, and I apologized for keeping him waiting; so he said, 'Why now, I calculate as your doctors are tired; they have plenty to do today.' There was an awful spectacle of dead, dying, and wounded around us. '*Do?*' says I, 'why this is nothing to us Wellington fellows! The next brush we have with you, you shall see how a Brigade of the Peninsular army (arrived yesterday) will serve you fellows out with the bayonet. They will lie piled on one another like round shot, if they will only stand.' 'Well, I calculate you must get at 'em first.' 'But,' says I, 'what do you carry a drawn sword for?' 'Because I reckon a scabbard of no use so long as one of you Britishers is on our soil. We don't wish to shoot you, but we must, if you molest our property; we have thrown away the scabbard.'

Sir Harry Smith

192.

On his escape from Elba in 1815, Napoleon faced the decisive crisis whose outcome determined his ability to regain command of France.

AT the Laffrey Defile, not far from Grenoble, the narrow way was found blocked on 7 March by the 5th Regiment of the Line, drawn up in battle order. It was a tense moment, but as each side looked to their muskets' priming, Napoleon strode forward and in a superb if theatrical gesture threw open the breast of his grey overcoat and invited the Bourbon troops ' . . . to fire upon your Emperor'. Heedless of their officers, the rank and file flung down their muskets and flocked forward with repeated cheers to mingle with Napoleon's supporters. Next day, the 7th Regiment behaved in the same way, and for Napoleon the great crisis was over. 'Before Grenoble I was only an adventurer,' Napoleon later mused upon St Helena, 'after Grenoble, I was a Prince.'

David Chandler

193.

Grammont, 29th May, 1815

THE 13th of April [according to Wylly, the 51st marched from Brussels on the 9th] we marched from Brussels to Grammont. Before we left we were delighted by a General Order issued by H.R.H. the Prince of Orange, in which order he 'Surrenders the Command of the Army into the more able hands of His Grace the Duke of Wellington'. I never remember anything that caused such joy, our men were almost frantic, every soldier you met told the joyful news. I happened to be out in the city when the order was delivered. I met some dozen soldiers as I was returning to the Convent. I was accosted by every one, thus 'Sergt. W— have you seen the order?' My answer was invariably 'No.' The reply would be 'Glorious news, Nosey has got the command, wont we give them a drubbing now?' When I arrived at the Convent I had a bottle of gin thrust up to my mouth, and twenty voices shouting 'drink hearty to the health of our old Commander, we dont care a d—n for all France, supposing everyone was a Napoleon etc.' Let it suffice to say that it caused a general fuddle, the evening was spent by reminding each other of the glorious deeds done in the Peninsular, mingled with song and dance, good hollands and tobacco.

Private William Wheeler

194.

When Wellington received news of Napoleon's advance towards Quatre Bras on 15 June 1815, he declined to hasten precipitately from Brussels to the battlefield. 'The numerous friends of Napoleon who are here', he declared, 'will be on tip toe; the well-intentioned must be pacified; let us therefore go all the same to the Duchess of Richmond's ball, and start for Quatre Bras at 5 a.m.'

THE most famous ball in history was the climax of Wellington's psychological warfare which always involved 'pleasure as usual'. The question of holding it or not had first come up in May.

'Duke,' said the Duchess of Richmond one day, 'I do not wish to pry into your secrets . . . I wish to give a ball, and all I ask is, may I give my ball? If you say, "Duchess, don't give your ball", it is quite sufficient, I ask no reason.'

'Duchess, you may give your ball with the greatest safety, without fear of interruption.' At that date, indeed, the Duke had intended to give a ball himself on 21 June, the second anniversary of the battle of Vitoria. Operations were not expected to begin before 1 July.

Since those dignified ducal exchanges circumstances had altered with a vengeance, more radically than Wellington even now supposed. That very afternoon there had been a close run thing, though a small one, at Quatre Bras. Prince Bernhard of Saxe-Weimar with 4,000 infantry and eight guns had occupied on his own initiative the empty crossroads at Quatre Bras and had easily driven off 1,700 French skirmishers unsupported by artillery; next moment, however, Marshal Ney himself rode forward to reconnoitre and but for shoulder-high rye which concealed the true weakness of the Prince's position, Ney might have ridden straight through into Brussels. It was a splendid initial triumph for Prince Bernhard and his Dutch–Belgian troops, many of whom were afterwards to behave with the unsteadiness of raw boys called from the plough. Neither Ney nor Wellington knew anything of the crisis which had come and gone. Ney, only just recalled by Napoleon to his post from having been rusticated in the country, was still getting his bearings. All Wellington knew was that the Prince of Orange, who was now dancing at the ball, had reported all quiet on the Nivelles–Namur *chaussée* earlier in the day.

It has often been asked why Wellington did not cancel the ball at 3 p.m. instead of going to hear the fiddlers while Rome burned, or at any rate did not ride out to Quatre Bras at midnight to see for himself what was on the other side of the hill. Apart from Wellington's extreme sensitivity to the chances of a Belgian stab in the back, his place was in Brussels. Having at last redirected his whole army towards Quatre Bras, nothing more remained for him to do there that night. He was personally to lead out the reserve in the morning. Orders had still to be distributed among officers in Brussels and personal interviews held. Why not under the convenient camouflage and at the ready-made rendezvous of a ball? This was to be Wellington's explanation to his friends during later post-mortems of Waterloo, and it is confirmed by Lord Fitzroy Somerset's own brief statement: 'As it [the ball] was the place where every British officer of rank was likely to be found, perhaps for that reason the Duke dressed & went there.'

Morale-building, duty, convenience—they all played their part in getting Wellington to the ball. Why not admit also that the Irish devil in him wanted to go? He would go; and see 'those fellows' damned.

Wellington's decision gave Byron his chance to include Brussels in Childe Harold's Pilgrimage and Thackeray to make Becky Sharp roll her green eyes and flaunt her pink ball dress in a perfect setting.

> There was a sound of revelry by night,
> And Belgium's Capital had gather'd then
> Her Beauty and her Chivalry—and bright
> The lamps shone o'er fair women and brave men. . . .

The ball-room, situated on the ground floor of the Richmonds' rented house in the rue de la Blanchisserie, had been transformed into a glittering palace with rose-trellised wallpaper, rich tent-like draperies and hangings in the royal colours of crimson, gold and black, and pillars wreathed in ribbons, leaves and flowers. Byron's 'lamps' were the most magnificent chandeliers and the list of chivalry, if not beauty, was headed by H.R.H. the Prince of Orange, G.C.B. All the ambassadors, generals and aristocrats were present as well as dashing young officers like Arthur Shakespear of the Light Dragoons, and Captain Pakenham of the Royal Artillery—Sir Charles Stuart, General Alava, the Mountnorrises and Wedderburn-Websters, the Capels, Grevilles and Mrs Pole. Creevey's step-daughters, the Misses Ord, got their tickets, for the amusing Radical moved in the best circles, treasuring the probably correct conviction that he was the illegitimate son of a former Lord Sefton. The rear was brought up by the diplomat Mr Chad, Wellington's surgeon Dr John Hume and his chaplain the Reverend Samuel Briscall whose name as usual was spelt wrong.

Wellington arrived 'rather late' at the entrance, where streams of light poured through the open windows into the warm streets and over the thronged carriages. In the ball-room those officers whose regiments were at any distance were already beginning to slip quietly away. The seventeen-year-old Lady Georgiana Lennox, whose sisters used to enjoy riding across the Phœnix Park with 'the great Sir Arthur' in 1807, was dancing. She immediately broke off and went up to Wellington to ask whether the rumours were true (Arthur Shakespear wrote in his diary, 'about twelve o' clock it was rumoured that we were to march in the morn!') Wellington replied, as she thought, very gravely,

'Yes, they are true, we are off tomorrow.' As this terrible news (Georgiana's words) rapidly circulated, the ball-room was like a hive that someone had kicked: an excited buzz arose from all the tables and elegantly draped embrasures. The Duke of Brunswick felt a premonition of death and gave such a shudder that he dropped the little Prince de Ligne off his lap. Some officers flew to and fro saying their goodbyes and departed, others clung so desperately to the loved one's hand or to the champagne bottle that when the hour struck there was no time to change and, like the heroine of *The Red Shoes*, they had to march in their dancing pumps. The Duke meanwhile appeared to the two youthful Miss Ords to be as composed as ever, while the even younger William Lennox, covered with plaster after a riding accident at Enghien, particularly noticed the serenity that 'beamed' all over his face.

'On with the dance! Let joy be unconfined.'

A rather more perspicacious guest, however, Lady Hamilton-Dalrymple, who sat for some time beside Wellington on a sofa, was struck by his preoccupied and anxious expression beneath the assumed gaiety: 'Frequently in the middle of a sentence he stopped abruptly and called to some officer, giving him directions, in particular to the Duke of Brunswick and Prince of Orange, who both left the ball before supper.' But even the lady on the sofa did not suspect the degree of drama with which the Prince of Orange's departure was attended.

Shortly before supper, as Wellington stood with Lady Charlotte Greville on his arm, a despatch was brought in by Lieutenant Henry Webster from Quatre Bras for the Prince of Orange. Slender Billy, merry as a marriage bell, handed it unopened to Wellington who quietly slipped it into his pocket for the moment. The message, dated about 10 p.m. that night, announced the repulse of Prussian forces from Fleurus on the road north-east of Charleroi and less than eight miles as the crow flies from Quatre Bras. As soon as Wellington had read this enlightening but grim piece of news he recommended the Prince to miss supper and return straight to his headquarters in the field.

'Webster!' he called to the Prince's aide-de-camp, 'four horses instantly to the Prince of Orange's carriage . . . ' After other instructions now made necessary had been delivered in whispers or scribbles, Wellington proceeded to the supper-room.

Hardly had he sat down before the Prince of Orange reappeared and whispered something to him for several minutes. Wellington looked incredulous but said nothing except to repeat that the Prince should go back to his quarters at Braine-le-Comte and to bed. Wellington kept up an animated and smiling conversation for twenty minutes more, when a lesser man would had fled the moment he heard Slender Billy's news. A notable Belgian arisocrat, indeed, the Marquise d'Assche, who sat next to the Duke of Richmond and opposite the Duke of Wellington at supper, did not relish the English nonchalance. Painfully conscious that her brother was somewhere out there where the cannon had been booming at dusk she looked across at the Duke with a jaundiced eye. His own *placement* was agreeable: Georgy Lennox on one side, who received from him a miniature of himself painted by a Belgian artist, and Frances Webster on the other. 'I would willingly have throttled him,' recalled the Marquise d'Assche, 'from the impatience which his phlegm caused me, and the ease of his conversation with Lady Withesburne [*sic*] to whom he paid ardent court.'

At last the necessary interval was up and Wellington turned casually to the Duke of Richmond.

'I think it is time for me to go to bed likewise. . . . ' The party rose and moved into the hall. As Wellington was saying good-night to his host he whispered something in Richmond's ear—the last recorded and most celebrated whisper of an evening remarkable for its undertones.

'Have you a good map in the house?' He needed to discover the exact implications of the almost incredible message verbally passed on to him at the supper table by the Prince of Orange. The written message which the Prince had received from his headquarters at Braine-le-Comte was dated 15 June 1815 '10$\frac{1}{2}$ p.m.' and signed by Baron Jean de Constant Rebecque, the Prince's chief-of-staff.

The enemy, de Constant Rebecque reported, were said to have pushed up the *chaussée* towards Brussels as far as Quatre Bras. . . .

The Duke of Richmond took him into his study next to the ballroom and spread out a map. Wellington looked at it wryly:

'Napoleon has *humbugged* me, by God! he has gained twenty-four hours' march on me.'

'What do you intend doing?'

'I have ordered the army to concentrate at Quatre Bras; but we shall not stop him there, and if so, I must fight him *here*.' Wellington passed his thumb-nail over the map just south of the Waterloo position. Then he left the scene of his acute discomfort, avoiding for once the hall-door.

Elizabeth Longford

195.

THAT night [17 June] Uxbridge slept at Waterloo, but before he went to bed he consulted Vivian upon a subject that was weighing heavily on his mind. According to Sir William Fraser, he said to Sir Hussey [Vivian],

I find myself in a very difficult position. A great battle will take place tomorrow.

The Duke, as you know, will not economize his safety. If any accident happens to him, I shall suddenly find myself Commander in Chief. Now, I have not the slightest idea what are the projects of the Duke. I would give anything in the world to know the dispositions which, I have no doubt, have been profoundly calculated. It will be impossible for me to frame them in a critical moment. I dare not ask the Duke what I ought to do.

Vivian advised him to consult Count Alava, the Spanish general, whose friendship with Wellington led to his being attached to his staff during the campaign. Uxbridge at once went to him and found that Alava agreed that the question was a serious one, but suggested that it was for Uxbridge himself to tackle it. Alava therefore went to the Duke and told him that Uxbridge wished to see him. Uxbridge then explained to the Duke 'the motive of his visit with all the delicacy imaginable'. The Duke listened to him to the end, without saying a single word, and then asked: 'Who will attack the first tomorrow, I or Bonaparte?' 'Bonaparte,' was the reply. 'Well,' continued the Duke, 'Bonaparte has not given me any idea of his projects: and as my plans will depend upon his, how can you expect me to tell you what mine are?' The Duke then rose, and putting his hand on Uxbridge's shoulder, added, 'There is one thing certain, Uxbridge, that is, that whatever happens, you and I will do our duty.' The two men then shook hands, and Uxbridge retired to sleep.

Lord Anglesey

196.

The repulse of the French assault upon the Château d'Hougoumont was one of the decisive actions of the day.

A GIGANTIC subaltern named Legros and reinforced with the nick-name of *l'Enfonceur*, the Smasher, stove in a panel of the great north door and followed by a handful of wildly cheering men, dashed into the courtyard. Pandemonium broke out. The defenders slashed and hewed at the invaders in desperate hand-to-hand duels. But the real thing was to prevent any more of the enemy from entering the yard. Five powerful Coldstreamers—Macdonnell, three other officers and a sergeant—threw themselves bodily against the huge door and slowly, slowly, by main force pushed it back against the pressure outside. This done they turned their attention to the invaders. . . .

'The success of the battle of Waterloo depended on the closing of the gates of Hougoumont.' So said Wellington afterwards.

Among the heroic five was Henry Wyndham, who had opened the door of King Joseph's coach at Vitoria. Now he shut a door to more purpose. It was said afterwards by his niece when she found herself sitting in a draught, that no Wyndham had ever closed a door since Hougoumont.

Elizabeth Longford

197.

TRIP'S Dutch–Belgian cavalry was now at hand. [Lord] Uxbridge, pleased with their fine appearance, and desirous of exciting in them a courageous enthusiasm, placed himself conspicuously in their front, and ordering the 'charge', led them towards the enemy. He had proceeded but a very short distance, when his aide-de-camp, Captain Horace Seymour, galloped close up to him, and made him aware that not a single man of them was following him. Turning round his horse, he instantly rode up to Trip, and addressed himself to this officer with great warmth. Then, appealing to the brigade in terms the most exhorting and encouraging, and inciting them by gestures the most animated and significant, he repeated the order to charge, and again led the way in person. But this attempt was equally abortive; and Uxbridge, exasperated and indignant, rode away from the brigade, leaving it to adopt any course which its commander might think proper.

William Siborne

198.

THE Duke was running short of aides-de-camp. It was said that once or twice he was reduced to using stray civilians, with whom the battlefield was still supplied, to carry his messages—a young Swiss, perhaps a traveller in buttons from Birmingham, as well as a small Londoner on a pony who turned out to be a commercial traveller for a City firm.

'Please, Sir, any orders for Todd and Morrison?'

'No; but will you do me a service? Go to that officer and tell him to refuse a flank.'

Elizabeth Longford

199.

AT one point of the battle when the Duke was surrounded by several of his staff, it was very evident that the group had become the object of the fire of a French battery. The shot fell fast about them, generally striking and turning up the ground on which they stood. Their horses became restive, and 'Copenhagen' himself so fidgety that the Duke, getting impatient, and having reasons for remaining on the spot, said to those about him, 'Gentlemen, we are rather too close together—better to divide a little.' Subsequently, at another point of the line, an officer of the artillery came up to the Duke, and stated that he had a distinct view of Napoleon, attended by his staff; that he had the guns of his battery well pointed in that direction, and was prepared to fire. His Grace instantly and emphatically exclaimed, 'No! no! I'll not allow it. It is not the business of commanders to be firing upon each other.'

William Siborne

200.

ALL along the battered ridge Wellington pursued his charmed course, reining in Copenhagen wherever the tension was greatest to speak a word of caution or encouragement.

'Are we to be massacred here? Let us go at them, let us give them *Brummegum*!' the men shouted at him, brandishing their bayonets.

'Wait a little longer, my lads, you shall have at them presently.' To their officers he said,

'Hard pounding, this, gentlemen; try who can pound the longest.' Once there was an echo of *Henry V*:

'Standfast . . . we must not be beat—what will they say in England?'

Elizabeth Longford

201.

. . . the Duke was told that Napoleon having asked Soult whether he
had sent for Grouchy, Soult answered that he had despatched an officer at a particular hour. 'Un officier!', exclaimed Napoleon, turning
round to his suite; 'un officier! Ah, mon pauvre Berthier! S'il avait été
ici il en aurait envoyé vingt.'

Lord Stanhope

202.

'JUST as Sir H. Vivian's Brigade were going down to the charge,'
wrote Wildman the day after the battle, 'Lord Uxbridge was struck by a
grape shot on the right knee which shattered the joint all to pieces. I
did not see him fall & went on to the charge, but soon missed him and
perceived Seymour taking him to the rear.' The Duke told his brother
William (also on the day after the battle) that Uxbridge was wounded
when talking to him 'during the last attack, almost by the last shot'. To
Stanhope Wellington explained that he was on the side from which the
shot proceeded, and that it passed over the neck of his horse till it
reached Uxbridge. The Duke supported him and prevented his falling
from the saddle. Writing as a very old man, and thirty-seven years after
the event, Uxbridge himself remembered that he was hit 'in the low
ground beyond La Haye Sainte, and perhaps $\frac{1}{4}$ of an hour before Dusk,
at the moment when I was quitting the Duke to join Vivian's Brigade of
Hussars which I had sent for, being the only fresh Corps I had'. In the
popular version, Uxbridge exclaims 'By God, sir, I've lost my leg!'
Wellington momentarily removes the telescope from his eye, considers
the mangled limb, says 'By God, sir, so you have!' and resumes his
scrutiny of the victorious field.

Men of a Hanoverian infantry battalion, advancing rapidly behind
the cavalry, helped to remove the wounded hero from his horse, and
six of them, with the faithful aide-de-camp Seymour walking at their
head, bore him from the field. A number of old soldiers claimed in
years to come that they had assisted in this 'melancholy duty', among
them one with the name of Esau Senior of the Inniskilling Dragoons.

Back at his headquarters in Waterloo, the surgeons who examined
the wound all agreed that it would be at the imminent danger of his life
to attempt to save the limb. His comment was typical: 'Well, gentlemen,' he said, 'I thought so myself. I have put myself in your hands

and, if it is to be taken off, the sooner it is done the better.' He at once wrote a letter to Char [his wife], saying that had he been a young single man he might have run the risk of keeping his leg, but that as it was he would, if possible, preserve his life for her and his children. Then, while the surgeons prepared for their task, he put the coming agony quite out of his mind, and conversed at length with his staff about the action, forgetting his wound 'in the exultation for the Victory'. Wildman, who was present at the amputation, tells how

he never moved or complained: no one even held his hand. He said once perfectly calmly that he thought the instrument was not very sharp. When it was over, his nerves did not appear the least shaken and the surgeons said his pulse was not altered. He said, smiling, 'I have had a pretty long run, I have been a beau these forty-seven years and it would not be fair to cut the young men out any longer' and then asked us if we did not admire his vanity. I have seen many operations, [continues Wildman] but neither Lord Greenock nor myself could bear this, we were obliged to go to the other end of the room.

Thank God he is doing as well as possible. He had no fever and the surgeons say nothing could be more favourable.

Later that night Vivian looked in, fresh from the pursuit. He was greeted with: 'Vivian, take a look at that leg, and tell me what you think of it. Some time hence, perhaps, I may be inclined to imagine it might have been saved, and I should like your opinion upon it.' Confronted with the gruesome object, Vivian readily confirmed that it was best off, and left his chief to compose himself for sleep.

The owner of the house where the operation was performed, a M. Paris, placed the leg in a wooden coffin and asked its owner's permission 'de placer le membre du noble et intéressant Milord dans notre petit jardin'. Permission was granted, and in due course a weeping willow was planted over the site. M. Paris erected a commemorative plaque, which may still be seen today; upon it these words appear:

> Ci est enterré la Jambe
> de l'illustre et vaillant Comte Uxbridge,
> Lieutenant-Général de S.M. Britannique,
> Commandant en chef la cavalerie anglaise,
> belge et hollandaise, blessé le 18 juin,
> 1815, à la mémorable bataille de Waterloo;
> qui, par son héroisme, a concouru au
> triomphe de la cause du genre humain;
> glorieusement décidée par l'éclatante
> victoire du dit jour.

Some wag is said to have scribbled beneath the inscription:

> Here lies the Marquis of Anglesey's limb;
> The Devil will have the remainder of him.

The wife of the Bishop of Norwich, visiting the house on the first anniversary of the battle, was shown 'as a relic almost as precious as a Catholic bit of bone or blood, the blood upon a chair in the room where the leg was cut off, which M. Paris had promised my lord "de ne jamais effacer" '. When in later years Uxbridge visited the place, it was said that he found the very table on which he had lain for the amputation of the limb, and that by his direction dinner was spread upon it for himself and two of his sons who were with him.

Lord Anglesey

203.

Having played a decisive role in repelling the French cavalry charges throughout the day, Mercer's battery of horse artillery, in the last minutes of the battle, found themselves under devastating fire from the guns of the arriving Prussians.

ONE shell I saw explode under the two finest wheel-horses in the troop—down they dropped. In some instances the horses of a gun or ammunition waggon remained, and all their drivers were killed. The whole livelong day had cost us nothing like this. Our gunners too—the few left fit for duty of them—were so exhausted that they were unable to run the guns up after firing, consequently at every round they retreated nearer to the limbers; and as we had pointed our two left guns towards the people who were annoying us so terribly, they soon came altogether in a confused heap, the trails crossing each other, and the whole dangerously near the limbers and ammunition waggons, some of which were totally unhorsed, and others in sad confusion from the loss of their drivers and horses, many of them lying dead in their harness attached to their carriages. I sighed for my poor troop—it was already but a wreck.

I had dismounted, and was assisting at one of the guns to encourage my poor exhausted men, when through the smoke a black speck caught my eye, and I instantly knew what it was. The conviction that one never sees a shot coming towards you unless directly in its line flashed across my mind, together with the certainty that my doom was sealed. I had barely time to exclaim 'Here it is then!'—much in that gasping sort of way one does when going into very cold water takes away the breath— 'whush' it went past my face, striking the point of my pelisse collar, which was lying open, and smash into a horse close behind me. I breathed freely again.

Under such a fire, one may be said to have had a thousand narrow escapes; and, in good truth, I frequently experienced that displacement of air against my face caused by the passing of shot close to me; but the two above recorded, and a third which I shall mention, were remarkable ones, and made me feel in full force the goodness of Him who protected me among so many dangers. Whilst in position on the right of the second line, I had reproved some of my men for lying down when shells fell near them until they burst. Now my turn came. A shell, with a long fuse, came slop into the mud at my feet, and there lay fizzing and flaring, to my infinite discomfiture. After what I had said on the subject, I felt that I must act up to my own words, and, accordingly, there I stood, endeavouring to look quite composed until the cursed thing burst—and, strange to say, without injuring me, though so near. The effect on my men was good. We had scarcely fired many rounds at the enfilading battery when a tall man in the black Brunswick uniform came galloping up to me from the rear, exclaiming, 'Ah! mine Gott!— mine Gott! vat is it you doos, sare? Dat is your friends de Proosiens; an you kills dem! Ah mine Gott!—mine Gott! vill you no stop, sare?—vill you no stop? Ah! mine Gott!—mine Gott! vat for is dis? De Inglish kills dere friends de Proosiens! Vere is de Dook von Vellington?—vere is de Dook von Vellington? Oh, mine Gott!—mine Gott!' etc. etc., and so he went on raving like one demented. I observed that if these were our friends the Prussians they were treating us very uncivilly; and that it was not without sufficient provocation we had turned our guns on them, pointing out to him at the same time the bloody proofs of my assertion. Apparently not noticing what I said, he continued his lamentations, and, 'Vill you no stop, sare, I say?' Wherefore, thinking he might be right, to pacify him I ordered the whole to cease firing, desiring him to remark the consequences. *Psieu, psieu, psieu,* came our *friends'* shot, one after another; and our friend himself had a narrow escape from one of them. 'Now, sir,' I said, 'you will be convinced; and we will continue our firing, whilst you can ride round the way you came, and tell them they kill their friends the English; the moment their fire ceases, so shall mine.' Still he lingered, exclaiming, 'Oh, dis

is terreebly to see de Proosien and de Inglish kill vonanoder!' At last
darting off I saw no more of him.

Cavalier Mercer

204.

IT was 9 p.m. on 18 June 1815 and nearly dark when Blücher and
Wellington rode forward to greet one another on the Brussels road
between *La Belle-Alliance* and Rossomme.

'Mein lieber Kamerad!' cried the old hero, leaning forward from his
horse to kiss Wellington; 'Quelle affaire!' That was about all the
French he knew, said the Duke long afterwards.

Elizabeth Longford

205.

IN his [Wellington's] quarters at Waterloo, the table had been laid for
the whole of the staff. He sat down at it alone, and people noticed that
whenever the door was opened he glanced at it eagerly, as if he hoped
to see some of his friends who had eaten breakfast there and now were
missing. When he had eaten, he lay down to sleep on a pallet on the
floor, because an officer was dying in his bed.

David Howarth

206.

LOOTING the enemy's dead was a soldier's right, and fortunes were
lying on the field for anyone cold-blooded enough to take them. Dead
officers, in particular, had purses, watches, pistols, swords, lockets and
sentimental charms. Their epaulettes and gold braid were worth
money. When all those were gone, there were clothes and equipment,
and when even the clothes were gone there were teeth. False teeth
were either carved out of ivory or made up of human teeth, and den-
tists would pay well for the raw materials. Such a haul was made from
the field of Waterloo that dentures for years afterwards were often
called Waterloo teeth.

But the looting after Waterloo was out of hand. Wounded who resisted the looters were quietly stabbed, and successful looters killed and robbed each other. All the armies blamed the Belgian peasants for these excesses, but in the night after the battle few if any peasants had ventured back, and the prowlers were British or Prussian. The peasants' turn came later, when the armies had moved away.

David Howarth

207.

The morning after the battle: on the field of Waterloo, Cavalier Mercer and his surviving comrades ate for the first time in twenty-four hours.

H OW we enjoyed the savoury smell! and, having made ourselves seats of cuirasses, piled upon each other, we soon had that most agreeable of animal gratifications—the filling of empty stomachs. Never was a meal more perfectly military, nor more perfectly enjoyed.

We had not yet finished our meal, when a carriage drove on the ground from Brussels, the inmates of which, alighting, proceeded to examine the field. As they passed near us, it was amusing to see the horror with which they eyed our frightful figures; they all, however, pulled off their hats and made us low bows. One, a smartly dressed middle-aged man, in a high cocked-hat, came to our circle, and entered into conversation with me on the events of yesterday. He approached holding a delicately white perfumed handkerchief to his nose; stepping carefully to avoid the bodies (at which he cast fearful glances *en passant*), to avoid polluting the glossy silken hose that clothed his nether limbs. May I be pardoned for the comparison: Hotspur's description of a fop came forcibly to my mind as we conversed; clean and spruce, as if from a bandbox, redolent of perfume, he stood ever and anon applying the 'kerchief to his nose. I was not leaning on my sword, but I arose to receive him from my seat of armour, my hands and face begrimed and blackened with blood and smoke—clothes too. 'I do remember when the fight was done,' etc. etc. It came, as I said, forcibly to my mind as I eyed my friend's costume and sniffed the sweet-scented atmosphere that hovered round him. The perfumed handkerchief, in this instance, held the place of Shakespeare's 'pouncet-box'—the scene was pleasant to remember! With a world of bows my man took leave, and proceeded, picking his steps with the same care as he followed the route of his companions in the direction of Hougoumont.

Cavalier Mercer

208.

Mercer hears a Frenchman upbraid a wounded comrade for screaming in his agony with 'unsoldierlike want of fortitude'.

THE speaker was sitting on the ground, with his lance stuck upright beside him—an old veteran, with a thick bushy, grizzly beard, countenance like a lion—a lancer of the Old Guard, and no doubt had fought in many a field. One hand was flourished in the air as he spoke, the other, severed at the wrist, lay on the earth beside him; one ball (case-shot, probably) had entered his body, another had broken his leg. His suffering, after a night of exposure so mangled, must have been great; yet he betrayed it not. His bearing was that of a Roman, or perhaps of an Indian warrior, and I could fancy him concluding appropriately his speech in the words of the Mexican king, 'And I too; am I on a bed of roses?' I could not but feel the highest veneration for this brave man, and told him so, at the same time offering him the only consolation in my power—a drink of cold water, and assurances that the waggons would soon be sent round to collect the wounded. He thanked me with a grace peculiar to Frenchmen, and eagerly inquired the fate of their army. On this head I could tell him nothing consolatory, so merely answered that it had retired last night, and turned the conversation to the events of yesterday. This truly brave man spoke in most flattering terms of our troops, but said they had no idea in the French army we should have fought so obstinately, since it was generally understood that the English Government had, for some inexplicable reason, connived at Napoleon's escape from Elba, and therefore had ordered their army only to make a show of resistance. After a very interesting conversation, I begged his lance as a keepsake, observing that it never could be of further use to him. The old man's eyes kindled as I spoke, and he emphatically assured me that it would delight him to see it in the hands of a brave soldier, instead of being torn from him, as he had feared, by those vile peasants. So I took my leave, and walked away with the lance in my hand.

Cavalier Mercer

209.

[JOHN WILSON] Croker gave me an interesting account of his receiving the news of the battle of Waterloo—I believe from the naval officers in the Channel—and his communication to the Duchess of Angoulême [niece by marriage of King Louis XVIII]. It was in the middle of the night, and Her Royal Highness was residing at a house near Fulham. With some difficulty he obtained admittance, had her awakened, and saw her come down to him in her nightcap and *robe de chambre*. With a profound bow he began to announce the gain of a great battle in Flanders where—'Stop,' she cried, 'stop!' and to his great astonishment immediately left the room. But in a few moments she returned, bringing a map. 'Now,' she said, 'show me where was the allied army before the battle?' 'Here, madam.' 'And where after the battle?'—'Here.' Then on hearing the account—she sunk on her knees and remained a few minutes in silent prayer. On rising, she turned to Croker, and thanked him for the trouble he had taken, expressing also her joy at the event, but added that from her experience of military news, she never trusted the account of any success unless she found that the army said to have gained it was in a more forward position after than before the engagement.

Lord Stanhope

210.

AFTER the battle of Waterloo, all the wounded horses of the Household Brigade of cavalry were sold by auction. Sir Astley [Cooper] attended the sale, and bought twelve, which he considered so severely hurt as to require the greatest care and attention in order to effect a cure. Having had them conveyed, under the care of six grooms, to his park in the country, the great surgeon followed, and with the assistance of his servants, commenced extracting bullets and grape-shot from the bodies and limbs of the suffering animals. In a very short time after the operations had been performed, Sir Astley let them loose in the park; and one morning, to his great delight, he saw the noble animals form in line, charge and then retreat, and afterwards gallop about, appearing greatly contented with the lot that had befallen them. These manœuvres were repeated generally every morning, to his great satisfaction and amusement.

Captain Gronow

211.

The 51st Foot on the road from Waterloo to Paris, June 1815.

ON the morning of the 24th inst. we marched on Cambray, about a league from the town we fell in with some cavalry piquets. After passing them we soon came in sight of the town, saw the tricolour flag flying on the citadel. This place had been strongly fortified, but the guns were withdrawn from the works, except the citadel. A great many stragglers were collected here, and these with the national guard belonging to the place seemed to threaten us with some resistance.

Our brigade marched to the opposite side of the town, the remainder of the Division halted on the side nearest to Cato. We had collected what ladders and ropes we could find in the farmhouses, then we began splicing to enable us to scale the walls if necessary. A flag of truce was sent to the Town but they were fired at, which caused them to return, and a ball had passed through the Trumpeter's cap. We were now ready for storming and were only waiting the order to advance. In a short time our field pieces opened when a shell, I believe the first thrown from the Howitzer, set a large building on fire. We now pushed on to the works, near the gate, got into the trenches, fixed our ladders and was soon in possession of the top of the wall. The opposition was trifling, the regular soldiers fled to the citadel, and the shopkeepers to their shops. We soon got possession of the gate and let in the remainder of the brigade, formed and advanced to the great square. We were as was usual, received by the people with vivas, many of whom had forgot to wash the powder off their lips caused by biting off the cartridges when they were firing at us from the wall. The remainder of the division entered the town at the same time on the opposite side.

Piquets were established at the citadel, and about dusk the remainder of the division were marched out of the town and encamped. We had picked up some money in the town, or more properly speaking we had made the people hand it over to us to save us the trouble of taking it from them, so we were enabled to provide ourselves with what made us comfortable. About an hour after we had left the town we heard an explosion and soon learned that a Serjt. Corporal and four men fell in with a barrel of gunpowder. They being drunk took it for brandy, and Corporal C— fired into it as he said to make a bung hole, while the others were waiting with tin canteens to catch the supposed liquor, but it blew up and all the brandy merchants were dreadfully mutilated.

The loss of the regiment was 2 rank and file killed, and ten wounded, exclusive of the brandy merchants, who are so dreadfully scorched it is feared that four cannot recover, and other two will not be fit for service again.

The 25th we halted and His pottle belly Majesty, Louis 18th, marched into the loyal town of Cambray. His Majesty was met by a deputation of his beloved subjects who received their father and their king with tears of joy. Louis blubbered over them like a big girl for her bread and butter, called them his children, told them a long rigmarole of nonsense about France, and his family, about his heart, and about their hearts, and I don't know what. The presence of their good old fat King had a wonderful effect on their tender consciences, the air rent with their acclamations. The Loyal and faithful soldiers of the Great Napoleon followed their example and surrendered the citadel to their beloved master Old Bungy Louis.

No doubt the papers will inform you how Louis 18th entered the loyal city of Cambray, how his loyal subjects welcomed their beloved king, how the best of monarchs wept over the sufferings of his beloved people, how the Citadel surrendered with acclamations of the joy to the best of kinds, and how his most Christian Majesty effected all this without being accompanied by a single soldier. But the papers will not inform you that 4th Division and a brigade of Hanoverian Huzzars (red) were in readiness within half a mile of this faithful city, and if the loyal citizens had insulted their kind, how it was very probable we should have bayoneted every Frenchman in the place. The people well knew this, and this will account for the sudden change in their loyalty or allegiance from their Idol Napoleon (properly named) the Great, to an old bloated poltroon, the Sir John Falstaff of France.

Private William Wheeler

212.

Cavalier Mercer, in France with the victorious Allied army, observes a timeless example of the wanton destruction which accompanies every army in every war.

In front of the church was a small open space, whence a handsome lodge and *grille* gave a view of a long avenue terminated by a chateau. In this place about twenty or thirty hussar horses were standing linked together under charge of one hussar. I believe these people were Prussians, but I can't say. From this man we learned that his comrades were at the chateau, and thither we went, curious to ascertain what they did there. We were certainly not quite so much shocked at the scene of ruin and havoc which presented itself as we went down the avenue as we should have been a week ago; they are becoming familiar now. The fragments of sofas, chairs, tables, etc., lying about the grass, bespoke a richly furnished house, and the nearer we drew to the house the thicker became these signs of vengeance. Large pieces of painted paper torn from the walls, remnants of superb silk window-curtains, with their deep rich fringe, hung amongst the bushes; broken mirrors and costly lustres covered the ground in such a manner as to render it difficult to avoid hurting our horses' feet—the brilliant drops of these last, scattered amongst the grass, might, with a little stretch of imagination, have induced us to believe ourselves traversing Sinbad's valley of diamonds; slabs of the rarest marble, torn from the chimney-pieces, lay shattered to atoms; even the beds had been ripped open, and the contents given to the winds, and conveyed by them to all parts of the park, covering in some places the ground like newly fallen snow. The trees of the avenue were cut and hacked, and large patches of bark torn off—many were blackened and scorched by fires made at the foot of them, with the mahogany furniture for fuel; the shrubs cut down or torn up by the roots; the very turf itself turned up or trampled into mud by the feet of men and horses. Hitchins and I dismounted at the grand entrance into the house; and, by way of securing our horses, shut them up in a little room to which a door was still left, and proceeded to inspect the interior of this once splendid mansion. Shouts and laughter resounded through the building. The hussars were busy completing the work of destruction; and as we passed the magnificent stairs leading up from the hall, we narrowly escaped being crushed under a large mirror which these gentlemen at that very moment launched over the banisters above with loud cheers. The ground-floor on the side fronting the park consisted of a suite of magnificent rooms, lofty, finely proportioned, and lighted by a profusion (as we should deem it) of windows down to the floor. These had been most luxuriously and richly furnished; now they were empty, the papering hanging in rags from the walls, and even the cornices destroyed more or less. Every kind of abuse of France and the French was written on the walls. In one room was the remnant of a grand piano. The sad reflections awakened by this sight may be more easily conceived than described, and I turned from it with a sickening and overwhelming sensation of disgust, in which I am sure Hitchins fully participated. The next room seemed to have been chosen as the place of execution of all the porcelain in the house, which had there been collected for a grand smash. The hand-somest Sèvres and Dresden vases, tea and dinner services, formed heaps of fragments all over the floor, and a large porcelain stove had shared the same fate. Another room had been lined with mirrors from the ceiling to the floor; it appeared these had been made targets of, for many were the marks of pistol-balls on the walls they had covered; little remained of these except some parts of their rich gilt frames. The last room of the suite had the end farthest from the windows semi-circular, and this end had been fitted up with benches, *en amphithéâtre*. The whole of this room was painted to represent the interior of a for-est, and on one side was a pool of water, in which several naked nymphs were amusing themselves. The plaster was torn down in large patches, and the nymphs stabbed all over with bayonets. The upper floor consisted of bedrooms, dressing-rooms, and baths, and exhibited the same melancholy destruction as those below; even the leaden lining of the baths, the leaden water-pipes, etc., were cut to pieces. On inquiring of one hussar why they so particularly wreaked their vengeance on this house, he said because it belonged to Jerome Buonaparte, whom every German detested.

Cavalier Mercer

213.

Marshal Blücher showed a notably less forgiving disposition towards his late enemies than his British allies.

A MEMORABLE instance occurred subsequently to the convention of Paris, at a large dinner party given by the Duke of Wellington, when, rising from his seat between the latter and the British minister, Viscount Castlereagh, he gave the following toast: 'May the diploma-tists not again spoil with their pens, that which the armies have at so much cost won with their swords!' Not long after this, when the terms of the peace were under discussion, Blücher, conceiving that these would again be made too favourable to France, evinced the greatest mistrust, amounting almost to hatred, of the diplomatists. Happening to meet the Prussian minister, Prince Hardenberg, he thus boldly addressed him—'I only wish I had you, gentlemen of the pen, exposed for once to a pretty smart skirmishing fire, that you might learn what it is when the soldier is obliged to repair with his life's blood the errors which you so thoughtlessly commit on paper.' The following fact shows that no personal considerations restrained him from indulging in his splenetic humour against the great diplomatists of the day. It is well known that immediately after the convention of Paris, he was extremely desirous of destroying the bridge of Jena, and that he would undoubtedly have carried his intentions into effect had it not been for the urgent representations of the Duke of Wellington. On that occasion, Count von der Golz, formerly his aide-de-camp, and then Prussian ambassador in Paris, made a written application to him, in behalf, and in the name, of Prince Talleyrand; beseeching the preservation of the bridge. Blücher replied in his own hand-writing—'I have resolved upon blowing up the bridge; and I cannot conceal from your excellency how much pleasure it would afford me if M. Talleyrand would previously station himself upon it; and I beg you will make my wish known to him.'

William Siborne

214.

A dinner at Hythe, Kent, in honour of the Peninsular veteran General Sir George Murray, in the early 1820s.

THERE were present Officers of the 95th Rifles, the Tipperary Militia and the South Devon Militia, making some fifty persons in all. In many regiments it was normal to allow a bottle of port a head and sometimes two or three would be drunk. No one was allowed to escape a bumper toast without a certificate from a doctor. In order to avoid the inevitable drunkenness our Militia Captain, with a softer head than his companions, used to quietly draw his bumper glass off the table and pour his wine into his jackboots, which were then worn high up to the knee with knee-breeches before Wellington boots and trousers were introduced.

The dinner to Sir George Murray commenced at six o'clock in the evening and did not terminate until seven o'clock the following morning. Drunkenness prevailed, many dropped off their seats, while others fell when trying to get out of the room without assistance. The Tipperary boys were noisy and full of obscene and indecent toasts, while the General himself thrice appeared to fall asleep. Whilst the General was in one of these slumbers the President of the day gave the toast 'To the Immortal Memory of the lamented Sir John Moore, to be drunk in silence.' Whether the word silence or a jog of the General's elbow roused him is not clear, but he attempted to rise from his chair and said 'Mr President, I rise' but, instead of rising, fell to his knees and then continued, 'Mr President, this is a toast I always drink kneeling.' Tremendous applause followed from everyone present sober enough to witness this drama.

I left as the clock struck seven, followed separately by the Colonel and then the Captain. A few remnants of this extraordinary banquet remained until breakfast time when the General washed himself, had his boots cleaned and apparently sober appeared on parade at ten o'clock, when as a joke he put an officer under arrest for being drunk.

Dr John Butter

215.

The Duke of Wellington reminisces about Blücher's last years.

POOR Blücher went mad for some time. He had shown off before some of our ladies, and got a fall from his horse and a blow on his head. This gave him all sorts of strange fancies. When I went to take leave of him, he positively told me that he was pregnant! And what do you think he said he was pregnant of?—An elephant! And who do you think he said had produced it?—A French soldier! . . .

It was the last time I ever saw him. I went to him; he could hardly speak French, but he said (striking his side) 'Je sens un éléphant là!' . . . I could only say, 'Je vous assure que vous vous méprenez!' and that he would soon get better. But he continued to express his surprise at there being a Frenchman in the case. 'Imaginez que moi—moi! un soldat français!' I suppose he had dreamt it the night before.

He was a very fine fellow, and whenever there was any question of fighting, always ready and eager—if anything too eager.

Lord Stanhope

216.

A demonstration of the hazards of writing military history.

Sir,

London, October 1832

I have just received a letter from my brother-in-law, dated Missouree, the 17th April last, in which he informs me that it was only on the day before he had read a paragraph in your third volume of the 'Peninsular War' reflecting upon his conduct at the battle of Barrosa. He desires me to inform you without delay, that immediately on the termination of his military duties in India (which will take place in the latter part of the next year) he will return to this country and require from you that satisfaction which is due from one officer to another for this most unfounded calumny.

I have the honour to be, &c. &c.

****

To Colonel W. Napier, C.B.

H. A. Bruce

217.

The novelist Dostoevsky spent an impecunious and undistinguished period of his life as a cadet at an army engineer academy in 1838-9.

DOSTOEVSKY may have held most of his fellow students in contempt, but he obviously could not endure the idea of being considered by them both personally odd *and* socially inferior; and the struggle to maintain his social status and self-esteem is quite naïvely evident in his letters. He writes his father in June 1838 that all of his money had been spent, explaining that, for the May parade of the Academy before the royal family, he had bought himself a new shako. 'Absolutely all my new comrades acquired their own shakos; and my government issue might have caught the eye of the Tsar.' Since, a bit earlier, he notes proudly that 140,000 troops had participated in the spectacle, this eventuality hardly seems a likelihood.

Joseph Frank

218.

Cecil Woodham-Smith's incomparable portrait of Lord Cardigan, one of the most pernicious boobies in the history of the British Army, commanding the 11th Light Dragoons in 1840.

HE was now in his glory. When he went to London it was his practice to give a number of his smartest men a day's leave and five shillings, and each posted himself at some point which he intended to pass. People ran to stare as Lord Cardigan sauntered down St James's Street, saluted at every few yards by his Hussars, brilliant as parrakeets.

But if only he could have got rid of the 'Indian' officers—it was incredible to him, he used to remark to his friends, that any of them could be so thick-skinned as to stay. No 'Indian' officer ever received an invitation to his own house, and when cards of invitation for dinners and balls were sent to the mess by gentlemen living in the neighbourhood, he had made it a rule that they were not to be given to those officers whom, he said, he had 'found sticking to the regiment in the East Indies'. Yet 'Indian' officers obstinately remained, a perpetual hindrance to his work of bringing the regiment to perfection.

Take their drinking habits. In India it had been the custom for officers to drink porter—it was healthier and cheaper. To this the Lieutenant-Colonel furiously objected. Porter was the drink of factory hands and labourers, and he wished to make the 11th famous for its splendid hospitality, for he loved the pomp and ceremony of 'great' dinners. He forbade bottled porter to appear on the mess table.

On May 18th, 1840, Major-General Sleigh, the Inspector-General of Cavalry, and his staff were to dine in the mess of the 11th after an inspection. Arrangements were made on a magnificent scale, and the Lieutenant-Colonel gave orders that nothing but champagne was to be served at dinner. The result of the inspection was most gratifying: Lord Cardigan was highly complimented on the brilliant appearance, the magnificent mounts and the fine performance of the 11th, and as he entered the mess with General Sleigh he was seen to be in high good humour.

At dinner one of General Sleigh's aides was sitting next to a certain Captain John Reynolds, an 'Indian' officer and the son of a distinguished 'Indian' officer. General Sleigh's aide asked if he might have Moselle instead of champagne, and John Reynolds gave the order to a mess waiter, who, anxious to supply the wine at once, did not stop

to decant it, but placed it on the table in its bottle. At this moment
Lord Cardigan looked down the table, and there, among the silver,
the glass, the piles of hot-house fruit, he saw a black bottle—it must
be porter! He was transported with rage. John Reynolds, an 'Indian'
officer, was drinking porter under his very nose, desecrating the
splendour of his dinner-table. When it was explained to him that the
black bottle contained Moselle, he refused to be appeased; gentlemen, he said, decanted their wine. Next day he sent a message to
John Reynolds through the president of the Mess Committee, a
Captain Jones, who was one of his favourites. Captain Jones found
him with two other officers, one of whom did not belong to the regiment. 'The Colonel has desired me to tell you', said Captain Jones,
'that you were wrong in having a black bottle placed on the table at a
great dinner like last night. The mess should be conducted like a
gentleman's table and not like a pot-house.' John Reynolds was
'utterly astonished', especially as the message was delivered before
an audience, but, controlling himself, he told the other 'in a quiet
manner, that he had no right to bring him an offensive message, and
as a brother captain it would have been better taste if he had
declined to deliver it'. Almost at once he was summoned to the
orderly-room, where, before Captain Jones and the Adjutant, Lord
Cardigan attacked him in furious rage. 'If you cannot behave quietly,
sir, why don't you leave the regiment? That is just the way with you
Indian officers; you think you know everything, but I tell you, sir,
you neither know your duty nor discipline. . . . Oh yes! I believe you
do know your duty, but you have no idea whatever of discipline. I
put you under arrest.'

John Reynolds remained silent. Captain Jones then offered his
hand, but Reynolds refused to shake it, 'I have no quarrel with you',
he said 'and nothing has passed that makes shaking hands necessary.'

Lord Cardigan burst out in a loud voice. 'You have insulted Captain
Jones.' John Reynolds quietly repeated, 'I have not, my lord.' Lord
Cardigan shouted, 'I say you have. You are under arrest, and I shall
report the matter to the Horse Guards.' John Reynolds replied, 'I am
sorry for it', and retired.

He was then placed under close arrest, but brought up from time to
time, to be examined by Lord Cardigan, who railed at him, taunted
him with being an 'Indian' officer, and ordered him to explain himself.
These interviews lasted as long as two hours, and John Reynolds

stated, 'I never can describe the mental torture I underwent during the probing and cross-examination of my feelings, lest I should say something that might afterwards be used against me, especially as Lieutenant-Colonel the Earl of Cardigan condescended to assure me that he waived the consideration of being my commanding officer, and afterwards resumed it, so that I had great difficulty in knowing when I was addressing his Lordship as a private gentleman and when in his capacity as Lieutenant-Colonel.'

After three days he received a memorandum from Lord Hill, the Commander-in-Chief, recommending him to admit the impropriety of his conduct towards his commanding officer and to resume friendly relations with Captain Jones. He obeyed the first instruction, but refused to drink wine with Captain Jones or to shake hands with him, and remained under arrest. On June 9th Major-General Sleigh came once more to Canterbury, summoned the officers of the 11th to appear before him, and without holding an investigation, read aloud a letter from headquarters, condemning John Reynolds in the strongest poss-ible language and approving and supporting Lord Cardigan. Rey-nolds's behaviour was described as 'pernicious and vindictive', and an enquiry was 'absolutely refused' on the ground that 'many things would come to light which are not for the good of the service'. John Reynolds then asked that he might be court-martialled for the offences he was alleged to have committed, and at this General Sleigh flew into a rage. There was to be no court-martial, no enquiry, no further dis-cussion of the affair; the Commander-in-Chief had made up his mind once and for all that the matter was to be considered as settled. And, turning angrily on John Reynolds, General Sleigh told him that he had 'forfeited the sympathy of every officer of rank in the service'.

General Sleigh and Lord Cardigan then left the room together, and Captain John Reynolds resumed his regimental duties with the 11th. The following week the regiment left Canterbury for duty at Brighton Pavilion.

The Army authorities had found themselves in a dilemma; since Lord Cardigan had been reinstated [after an earlier absurdity], for better or worse he must be supported. It was too late to draw back, and the best policy seemed to be firmness: the officers of the 11th must be shown that it was useless to oppose Lord Cardigan.

Unfortunately the 'Black Bottle' affair became a nine days' wonder, the phrase caught the public fancy, and 'black bottle' became a catch-word. Jokes about the 11th appeared in newspapers and mock reports were circulated of 'The Battle of the Moselle, in which His Royal Highness Prince Albert's Regiment has severely suffered, being so completely broken in pieces as to require "*reforming*".' A private of the 11th was arrested for assaulting a guardsman in the street; when reprimanded by Lieutenant-Colonel Lord Cardigan, the man stammered out, 'But, my Lord, he called me a black bottle.' Meanwhile Captain John Reynolds's guardian (his father had died in India) pestered Lord Hill for an explanation of General Sleigh's reprimand, for production of the correspondence, and for a court-martial. When he got no satisfaction he sent an account of the affair and copies of his letters to Lord Hill to every leading newspaper in London, and in almost every instance they were printed in full.

To Lord Cardigan, however, 'Black Bottle' brought unmixed satisfaction. Once more he had been supported, once more he had been proved right.

Cecil Woodham-Smith

219.

NAPIER is said to have sent back a one-word announcement of his conquest of Sind: 'Peccavi.' Of course he did not—no more than did General Pershing cry 'Lafayette we are here!' But if generals have the wit to win battles there will always be wits to put words in their mouths later.

Byron Farwell

220.

At the Battle of Chilianwala on 13 January 1849 in the Second Sikh War, confused orders by Brigadier Pope, commanding the cavalry, caused them to turn in headlong flight.

ON they galloped, crowding too close together, they overturned four of their own guns, upset wagons and horses. The flight of the cavalrymen was halted by a chaplain, the Rev. W. Whiting. He was attending the sick and wounded at a field hospital when he saw some frightened dragoons fleeing the battlefield. The chaplain stopped them, and demanded to know what had happened. 'The day is lost!' cried a dragoon. 'All our army is cut up, and the Sikhs have taken our guns and everything.'

'No, sir!' the chaplain said. 'The Almighty God would never will it that a Christian army should be cut up by a pagan host. Halt, sir! or as I am a minister of the word of God, I'll shoot you!' Whiting's knowledge of history may have been faulty, but he stopped the rout . . . Gough, with a soldier's view of the hierarchy of the Church of England, proposed that the chaplain be made a brevet-bishop.

Byron Farwell

221.

One of West Point Military Academy's more notable failures was the attempt to make a soldier of James Whistler, later the well-known artist but in 1853 a mere gentleman cadet.

GENERAL WEBB says that it was not unusual at cavalry drill for Whistler, a sorry horseman, to go sliding over his horse's head. On such occasions Major Sacket . . . would call:

'Mr Whistler, aren't you a little ahead of the squad?'

Adjutant-General George D. Ruggles . . . also refers to Whistler's habit of parting company with his horse during drills.

In the first mounted drill in the riding academy in which Whistler took part, he had a hard horse. The instructor . . . gave the command: 'Trot out!'

At this command Whistler, who had journeyed from the withers to his croup and back again several times, tumbled in a bundle into the tanbark. He lay for a moment without movement. The dragoon soldiers, who imagined him seriously injured, ran to him and picked him up, to carry him to the hospital; but he told them to let him down. Major Porter . . . called to him from his horse: 'Mr Whistler, are you hurt?'

Whistler, leisurely drawing off his gauntlet and brushing the tanbark away from his hips, replied, 'No, Major! but I do not understand how any man can keep a horse for his own amusement!'

There was in the squad a horse named Quaker. This horse . . . had thrown the most expert riders in the cavalry detachment. . . . One day . . . this horse fell to Whistler, who coming up blinking with his myopia, said: 'Dragoon, what horse is this?' The soldier answered: 'Quaker, sir,' and Whistler replied: 'My God! He's no friend.'

*

The most famous moment in Whistler's West Point career occurred during his chemistry examination. Asked to discuss silicon, he supposedly asserted, 'Silicon is a gas,' causing his interrogator to end the questioning by saying, 'That will do; Mr Whistler.' The episode was concluded years later when Whistler declared, 'If silicon had been a gas, I might have become a general.'

Gordon Fleming

222.

John Nicholson (1821-57) was one of a handful of British officers ruling India before the Mutiny who achieved epic stature, not least for the ruthlessness with which he dispensed justice, in this case against a local thief.

HE [Nicholson] rode off alone to the village of the robber, who by a curious coincidence was the first person he met. Upon being ordered to surrender the man rushed at Nicholson, who ran him through, rode back and had the body brought to him. Cutting the head off, he placed it beside him in the office and contemptuously asked every village headman who entered whether he recognized to whom it belonged.

*

One night the officers of the Movable Column were waiting for their dinner, which was overdue. A messenger was sent to the cooking tent bringing back word that dinner would soon be ready. About half an hour after the appointed time Nicholson stalked in, saying abruptly: 'I am sorry, gentlemen, to have kept you waiting for your dinner, but I have been hanging your cooks.' Later they learnt what had happened. Nicholson had heard from one of his spies that the soup had been poisoned with aconite, so just before dinner he sent for the soup and arrested the cooks, who denied the accusation; but as they refused to taste it on the ground of caste, he gave some to a monkey, which died. A few minutes later, reported an officer who was present, 'our regimental cooks were ornamenting a neighbouring tree'.

Hesketh Pearson

223.

The Battle of Balaclava on 25 October 1854 gave birth to two British legends, one entirely honourable, the second chiefly grotesque. This was the first.

THE Russians had now advanced far enough to bring Sir Colin Campbell's force within range of their guns, and they opened fire with considerable effect. Sir Colin had drawn up his force on a hillock at the entrance to the gorge leading to Balaclava, and he ordered his men to lie on their faces in a line two deep on the far slope. Lying helpless under artillery fire is notoriously a strain, and at this moment the four squadrons came into view, bearing rapidly down from the Causeway Heights, while behind them, just becoming visible, was the main body of the Russian cavalry. The sight was once more too much for the Turks; they leapt to their feet and officers and men fled for the port, again crying 'Ship! ship! ship!' As they passed the camp of the Argylls a soldier's wife rushed out and fell upon them, belabouring them with a stick, kicking them, cursing them for cowards, pulling their hair and boxing their ears, and so pursued them down to the harbour.

Five hundred and fifty men of the Argylls and 100 invalids were now left to stand between the Russian army and Balaclava, and Sir Colin rode down the line telling them, 'Men, remember there is no retreat from here. You must die where you stand.'

To the Russian cavalry as they came on, the hillock appeared unoccupied, when suddenly, as if out of the earth, there sprang up a line two deep of Highlanders in red coats—the line immortalized in British history as 'the thin red line'. Every man in that line expected to be killed and, determined to sell his life as dearly as possible, faced the enemy with stern steadiness.

The Russians were taken aback. Their intelligence service was quite as inadequate as the British; they had no idea of the strength and disposition of the British troops and they suspected once more that they had fallen into an ambush. Indeed, the gorge ahead would have been perfect for that purpose had the idea of an ambush ever occurred to the British command.

The Russian cavalry checked, halted, and from the thin red line came a volley of the deadly musket-fire, every bullet aimed, which formation in line made possible. The Russians wavered, steadied, advanced, and a second volley was fired. Once more the Russians wavered, and such was the eagerness of the Argylls that there was a movement forward: the men wanted to dash out and engage the cavalry hand to hand, and Sir Colin Campbell was heard shouting sternly, 'Ninety-third! Ninety-third! Damn all that eagerness.' The British line steadied, a third volley was fired, and the Russians wheeled and withdrew in the direction of the main body of their cavalry. The Highlanders burst into hurrahs. Balaclava, for the moment, was saved.

Cecil Woodham-Smith

224.

This account of the Charge of the Light Brigade by a young officer who took part has the merit of being much less familiar than William Howard Russell's epic of war correspondence.

Heights of Sebastopol
December 1st (1854)

My dear Father,

Since I wrote last nothing decisive has been done towards finishing our now truly wretched campaign, my last letter would prove from its date that I was not present at the last engagement on the Inkerman Heights, the only affair that I have not had a share in. I was in the Black Sea on board of ship at the time lying outside the bay of Varna. The account of the battle which will reach you before this you may fully believe, I don't think the papers will exaggerate, it was without exception the most sanguinary on record for the numbers engaged. I have of course heard all the accounts about it and been over the ground, where there still remain ample proofs of a desperate slaughter. It is well known here that the Russians confess to 20,000 hors de combat—they attacked us 40,000 strong led on by the two Grand Dukes at daybreak, having been allowed to bring up a great number of heavy guns during the night, a fool of an ensign hearing them all the time without reporting it, they were there, and taking the English, it was on our side, by surprise, we turned out just as we were in our great coats, the Russians came on most furiously mistaking us in the great coats for Turks, our Guards and 4 other regiments were the only troops at hand, they held their ground bravely as long as they could, but of course were obliged to fall back on the next support. The French came up about this time and enabled us to attack the serfs, on which they turned in every direction and then commenced the most horrific slaughter. Our fellows charged them with the bay right down to the bottom of the heights. The deserters say that they got such a lesson that day, that they have tried several times since to get them on without success; and I really think there is no chance of their attacking again. Now for the other massacres as of the 25th October. I have abstained from making a report about this affair, except just that I had a most wonderful escape and got slightly wounded with a spent shot as I should have unnecessarily alarmed you because it is impossible to describe it otherwise than as the most downright useless, ridiculous, except to those in it, sacrifice seen now by *The Times* of the 13th that they have described the thing truly, so I may as well confirm it. *The Times* account is so good that I shall only say what happened to myself.

Our order to charge was brought by a half madman Capt. Nolan, the order was very difficult to understand rightly. On Lord Lucan asking what he was to charge, the only information was, there is the enemy and there is your order. There the enemy consisted of 15,000 infantry, 4,000 cavalry protected by 10 guns, to reach them we had to go down a ravine between two hills with 10 guns on each besides a host of riflemen. Down we went very steadily, the fire was terrific, it seemed impossible to escape, we were well in range of grape shot on each side besides the barkers in front. I got through safe up to the guns, cut down all that came within reach and then at the cavalry behind, but to our horror the heavy brigade had not followed in support and there was an alarm that we were cut off in rear, which was true. There was nothing left for it, but to cut our way back the same way we came, the Lancers who cut us off made a very mild resistance, they seemed to be astonished at our audacity at charging them in the wretched confusion we were in, we got through them with very little loss. Just after getting through these beggars, I thought I heard a rattle behind and, by Jove, I was only just in time, we were pursued and on looking behind a Muscovite had his sword up just in my range and in the act of cutting me down, I showed him the point of my sword instantly close to his throat, he pulled his horse almost backwards and gave me an opportunity of getting more forward. I now had nothing to fear being on a good horse except going through those infernal guns again—about a quarter of a mile from the batteries I felt a tremendous blow on the calf of the leg, and instantly my poor old horse was hit on the offside and was going to fall. I jumped off in a second with the pistol in one hand and sword in the other, and had the satisfaction of seeing my old friends only ten yards behind in full pursuit. Things looked very bad indeed, but in spite of my game leg, I ran faster than ever I did before in my life and kept pace with my friends behind till their own fire got so thick that they thought fit to drop it. I was now between these two batteries and could only raise a walk. I must have been a quarter of an hour under fire on foot, and much to the astonishment of my real friends, the few who escaped, I turned up about half an hour after the rest of the stragglers. I have finished my romance, for really my escape was almost romantic, but dont on that account put it in print as some of my brave companions like.

Enough of war, in spite of living in a tent at this time of the year with 3 inches of mud inside and 12 out, I am not down in the mouth. My fortnight at sea put my leg to rights, and those two fools who command us Lucan and C. have been kind enough to place us such a distance from our supplies, the roads being very deep, that they can't feed the wretched little wreck of a brigade, the consequence is that they are dying 8 and 10 a day, now it requires no mathematician to see that this cant last, besides the horses are so weak that I don't think any one of them could trot a mile. They cant bring us into action again. Tomorrow we move down to Balaclava to be near our supplies and if we have luck get some sort of a roof for man and beast.

The Russians are worse, if possible, off than ourselves, they are beginning to starve inside and outside of Sebastopol, still they fire away as briskly as ever, we can't assault it without large reinforcements, the army outside would instantly attack us, I fancy it will not fall for some time yet, and I have also I think a chance of going home to command the depot in about two months time. So things are looking up. The newspapers arrive very irregularly, please to speak about it and have via Marseilles put upon them. I want also the Illustrated News. Don't put any more money at the bank, but on account, and put it into the 15 per cents.

    With best love,
  Your affectionate son,
        E. A. Cook

225.

Conditions for the British Army in the Crimea became slightly more tolerable in the spring of 1855.

FOOD had been miraculously improved by Alexis Soyer, the famous chef of the Reform Club, who arrived in March 1855 with full authority from Lord Panmure. Soyer came out at his own expense attended by a 'gentleman of colour' as his secretary. In manner and appearance he was a comic opera Frenchman, but Miss Nightingale recognized his genius and became his friend. 'Others', she wrote, 'have studied cookery for the purpose of gormandizing, some for show. But none but he for the purpose of cooking large quantities of food in the most nutritive and economical manner for great quantities of people.' Though the authorities received him 'very coolly', Soyer was armed with authority and he proceeded to attack the kitchens of the Barrack Hospital which Miss Nightingale never entered. He composed recipes for using the army rations to make excellent soup and stews. He put an end to the frightful system of boiling. He insisted on having permanently allocated to the kitchens soldiers who could be trained as cooks. He invented ovens to bake bread and biscuits and a Scutari teapot which made and kept tea hot for fifty men. As he walked the wards with his tureens of soup the men cheered him with three times three. Finally, he gave a luncheon attended by Lord and Lady Stratford and their suite, at which he served delicious dishes made from army rations.

In one thing Soyer failed. Like Miss Nightingale, he strongly objected to the way the meat was divided; since weight was the only criterion one man might get all bone; why should not the meat be boned, and each man receive a boneless portion, with the bones being used for broth? The answer from Dr Cumming was that it would need a new Regulation of the Service to bone the meat.

Cecil Woodham-Smith

226.

At the outbreak of the Indian Mutiny the 1st Bengal Irregular Cavalry, Skinner's Horse, were stationed at Multan under the command of Captain Neville Chamberlain.

APART from Skinner's Horse, there were two regiments of Bengal Native Infantry and a battery of native horse-gunners; no European troops except fifty artillerymen. The senior officer in the station had thirty-four years' service and was quite unfit for duty but he was ready to let Chamberlain take the initiative and virtually command the station. It was a dangerous responsibility to assume. There was reason to suppose that the infantry and artillery would prove no more reliable here than they had elsewhere and Chamberlain decided that he must get help from another station and disarm them. He sent for help; there was no hope of British troops but the 1st Punjab Cavalry and the 2nd Punjab Infantry were ordered to march. Until they arrived, he must rely implicitly on his own men, Skinner's Horse; he told them he trusted them and he showed it by the tasks he gave them to do. Skinner's had always recruited near Delhi; their men were counted Hindustanis by the Punjabis. They were Hindustani Muslims, Rajputs and Jats and the people known to the army as Ranghars, that is, Muslims who claim Rajput origin. They did not come from Oudh but were of just the same class as the Bengal Regular Cavalry such as the 3rd with whom the trouble had started at Meerut. They differed mainly in having only three picked British officers to a regiment. Their native officers were therefore much more used to taking responsibility; they had to command their squadrons and troops.

At this anxious juncture, the native officer commanding the squadron of Ranghars came to Chamberlain and asked for a private interview. He was unhappy because something had given the Ranghars the impression that the captain did not trust them as completely as he trusted the other squadrons. Chamberlain heard him out, then sent his orderly to the bank, with a note requesting the banker to send him a sword he had deposited for safe custody. It was a jewelled sword, valuable to anyone, but doubly so to Chamberlain because, as everyone in the regiment knew, it had been given him by a close friend who had captured it in battle in Sind. He handed this sword to Shaidad Khan, the ressaldar of the Ranghar squadron. 'Give me this back', he said, 'when this war is over.' The ressaldar's eyes filled with tears; he knelt and touched the captain's knees. Nothing but death could sever the bond between them.

Skinner's were loyal throughout the Mutiny and became the senior regiment of Indian cavalry.

Philip Mason

227.

By 10 November 1857, Sir Colin Campbell's relief force was poised to move upon Lucknow, but the garrison possessed no means of communicating with him about the best line of advance. At last, a 36-year-old minor civil servant named Thomas Kavanagh, married with fourteen children, volunteered to carry a message from Lucknow's commander, Sir James Outram. Without a word to his wife, he slipped out of the Residency disguised as an Indian and made his way safely through the enemy lines. For his deed he became the first civilian to be awarded the Victoria Cross. Campbell followed the suggested route to the triumphant relief of Lucknow. Lacking ciphers, Outram was compelled to improvise a classically Victorian method of disguising his dispatch. Kavanagh carried the following message.

Sir,

I σενδ un σκετch du γρουνδ ιντερυενινγ βετωην αλυμ βαγ et cette ποσιτιον et βεγ à συγεστ θη φολοωινγ μοδε d'οπερατιονς as that whereby vous may εφεκτ une jυνκτιον avec nous avec le λεαστ διφικυλτη. φρομ αλυμ βαγ πασινγ ρουνδ le σουθερν φασε de l'ενκλοσυρε et βετωην les υιλαγες de ὑσητνυγρ et πορωα et προςηδινγ αλμοστ δυε εαστ pour αβουτ trois μιλες ουερ un λευελ κουντρη de γρας λανδ et κλτιυατιον avec un σηαλοω jηηλ à κρος σηορτλη après ληυινγ αλυμ βαγ (προβαβλη pas plus θαν ανκλε δηπ νοω et νο οβστακλε aux γυνς) vous will αριυε οποσιτε à la υιλαγε de jαμαιτα sur votre λεφτ—σλαντινγ παστ wʰ pour αβουτ une μιλε à νορθ εαστ vous αριυε à la διλκυσηαρ παλασε—rien mais le παρκ ωαλ ιντερυενινγ αβουτ εiτ φητ ί, wʰ est βροκεν δοων dans μανη πλασες et κουλδ βη νοκεδ δοων ανηωηερε par a κουπλε δες πιονηρς. Le παλασε ἁωυινγ λαργε ωινδοως en ευροπεαν στιλε n'est pas λικλη être δεφενδεδ, mais ιφ σο, a φευ κανον σηοτ wᵈ σοον εμτη ιτ et ινδηδ j'αντισιπατε λιτλε ορ νο οποσιτιον à votre οκυπατιον de διλκυσηαρ παλασε et παρκ ορ des νειγηβουρινγ μαρτινιὲρσ or βιβιαπορε maisons shᵈ vous θινκ νεσεσαρη, l'ενεμη'ς τρωπς βεινγ chηφλη sur θις σιδε du καναλ. L'υνιον jακ ὁιστεδ au τοπ de la παλασε et un ρογαλ σαλυτε φρομ υος γυνς à δραω notre ατεντιον το ιτ, shᵈ vous ἁυε ἁδ νο πρευιους φιρινγ wᵈ ινφορμ nous de votre αριυαλ et notre υνιον wʰ nous wᵈ θεν ὁιστ sur la chυτρ μανζιλ παλασε (δισταντ deux à trois μιλες) will show vous que nous sommes ινφορμεδ. A la διλκυσηαρ vous avez un οπεν μαιδαν pour ενκαμπμεντ οφ νηρλη une μιλε βετωην le παλασε & un δηπ καναλ βετωην vous et la ville, les βριδγες sur wʰ sont βροκεν δοων. Par ενκαμπινγ avec votre φροντ to θη καναλ avec vos γυνς en votre φροντ ετ φλανκς vous wᵈ κηπ δοων ανη φιρε wʰ l'ενεμη cᵈ βρινγ αγαινστ vous φϱομ λε ville σιδε pour ils ont ονλη sept οϱ huit γυνς en διφεϱεντ ποσιτιονς sur cette σιδε de la γοομτη γυαϱδινγ les διφεϱεντ ἠγϱεσσες τοωαϱδς la διλκυσηαϱ φϱομ νοτϱε ποσιτιον w^h sont οφ διφεϱεντ καλιβϱε et σο βαδλη φουνδ εν καϱιαγες ils w^d have σομε διφικυλτη ιν τακινγ θεμ αωαι à τυϱν αγαινστ vous et ιφ ιλς διδ ϱεμουε θεμ πουϱ θατ πυϱποσε it w^d φασιλιτατε notre δαση ουτ à μητ vous quand vous δο αδυανσε à θις σιδε du καναλ where however ils ne sont pas λικελη à στανδ εξποσεδ as ils θεν w^d be à ατακ φϱομ φϱοντ et ϱεαϱ. Under κουεϱ de vos γυνς vous n'aurez pas de διφικυλτη εν σλοπινγ πασαγες pour votre αϱτιλεϱη δοων votre σιδε ιντο le καναλ et υπ νοτϱε σιδε δυϱινγ θη φιϱστ νιτε ϱεαδη à κϱοςς εϱλη νεξτ μοϱνινγ. φυϱθεϱ δελαι, je pense, w^d be ιμπολιτικ, as it w^d give l'ενεμη τιμε à βϱινγ γυνς φϱομ δισταντ πλασες. λεστ μεσενγεϱς sh^d μισκαϱη votre σιγναλ pour ιντενδινγ à κϱοςς le καναλ ιν θη μοϱνινγ might be τϱοις γυνς φολοωεδ par trois ϱοκετς la nuit βεφοϱε, après une ϱεκοναισανσε ἁδ σατισφιεδ vous de la φησιβιλιτη de πϱεπαϱινγ les σλοπες δυϱινγ λα νυιτ. Les βανκς du καναλ sont φϱομ vingt à vingt cinq φητ ἰ, πεϱαπς λεςς τοωαϱδς votre droit avec λιτλε οϱ νο eau et σουνδ βοτομ. Vous w^d οφ κουϱσε ἁυε παϱτης en οκυπατιον de la διλκυσηαϱ παλασε, et après πασινγ le καναλ en σομε des πϱινσιπαλ βυιλδινγς κομ^v votre λινε de κομ$^{v.}$ mais nous sh^d μητ vous ἁλφ ωαι avec un πϱετη στϱονγ κολυμν d'ευϱοπεανς et γυνς et w^d θεν αϱανγε τογεθεϱ le μοδε de μαινταινινγ la κομ$^{v.}$ βετωην votre καμπ sur le καναλ et notre εντϱενχμεντ. Vous w^d πεϱαπς ἁλτ deux trois jours à αλυμ βαγ et may κοντϱιυε à donner nous νοτισε du jour de votre αδυανσε. Of course tous les τϱωπς à αλυμ βαγ seront υνδεϱ vos κομανδ et un petit γυαϱδ ινκλυδινγ λες κονυαλεσεντς will συφισε à μαινταιν θατ πλασε, θυς πλασινγ σομε cinq ou σιξ cents ευϱοπεανς à votre δισποσαλ—βεσιδες γυνς.

True Copy.   J. Outram.

George Couper,
Secy. Chief Comr.

228.

The Times correspondent *William Howard Russell vividly described the palace plunder that fell to Campbell's force that finally stormed Lucknow.*

IN the next court, which was sheltered from fire by the walls around it, our men had made a great seizure of rich plunder. They had burst into some of the state apartments, and they were engaged in dividing the spoil of shawls and lace and embroidery of gold and silver and pearls. . . . Two men of the 90th were in before us, and, assisted later by some of the 38th, we saw them appropriate money's worth enough to make them independent for life. . . . In one box they found diamond bracelets, emeralds, rubies, pearls and opals, all so large and bright and badly set that we believed at the time they were glass.

William Howard Russell

229.

His biographer records his distress at being unable to take much personal advantage of the sack.

RUSSELL had no moral objection to looting, which was universally accepted as one of the perquisites of being with the vanguard. His only regret was that he was not able to take full advantage of his chances. In one of the palaces, the Kaiserbagh, a soldier found a boxful of diamonds, emeralds and pearls and offered them all to Russell for a hundred rupees. But he had no money on him: 'I might have made my fortune if I had had a little ready money with me. As it was I loaded myself with jade and got a diamond drop etc. I might have secured a small sackful. I could not believe these things were real which I saw.'

Alan Hankinson

230.

Russell's editor, Delane, added his commiserations about missed opportunities.

YOU have done so admirably well that everyone admits that your story of Lucknow equals the very best of your Crimea achievements. It has been fully appreciated and you have not, as you had in the Crimea, a large party interested in running you down and contradicting you. . . . Pray draw £10 on my account and carry it all in gold about you when you next accompany a storming party. It makes one blasphemous to think that you got nothing out of the Kaiserbagh for the want of a few rupees.

John Thadeus Delane

231.

A private soldier of the 9th Foot took a less sympathetic view of Russell's activities.

MR HENRY [*sic*] RUSSELL has been pleased to write declamatory letters from the inactivity of the troops at Nawabgunge. He hinted that the Brigadier was unfit to command the brigade, but the Commander-in-Chief gave the lie to this by appointing him Brigadier of the 2nd class at Byram Ghat in December. It so happens that there are men in India who are well acquainted with this newspaper writer and I myself prove to the falseness of his letters on more than one occasion. Russell is a man who is easily brought [*sic*] over, but such men as Brigadier Purnell care not for his declamatory letters. Neither does he wish to purchase his favour at the expense of dinners to this detested correspondent, for detested he is by every honest English soldier. If a colonel or a general wishes to figure in prominence in the home papers, let him make friends with Russell by entertaining him at dinners where there is plenty of wine and spirituous liquors and furnish him with camp equipage and carriage for the same when in the march, and he may soon expect to see his name in the Gazette with a C.B. attached.

Still what he calls inactivity I call harassing duty. Suppose that Russell had been a common soldier instead of a correspondent. I fancy that I see him fully accoutred, falling in on parade with sixty rounds of ammunition, his rifle and bayonet weighing 11 pounds and a half, his haversack with two days' provisions in it and lastly a water bottle slung by his side. Having imagined him to have fallen in on parade with his regt, he now marches off with it. The regt halts after having gone over 11 mile of ground knee-deep in dust and almost dying for a drop of water. He is next put on piquet, where he remains till the next morning, when he is permitted to take his belts off, while he washes his hands and face. And before he has been able to get a drop of coffee, the regt is again on the move. Fresh ground is taken up either to the right or left or maybe we go a mile farther, where there is a bridge and we are there to intercept them. Three or four days at a time are passed in this way. Yet all this marching out and in in all weather and at all hours of the night or day was, in Mr Russell's opinion, three months' ease—we were lying inactive at Nawabgunge. Would he not have sung a different song if he was there to have gone through the above? I think he would.

Charles Wickins

232.

A reminiscence of Lord Roberts, at a time when he was an ambitious young quartermaster-general in India, in 1860.

FOR some time I had been indulging a hope that I might be sent to China with my old General, Hope Grant, who had been nominated to the command of the expedition which, in co-operation with the French, was being prepared to wipe out the disgrace of the repulse experienced early in the year, by the combined French and English naval squadrons in their attack on the Taku forts. My hope, however, was doomed to disappointment. Lord Clyde [the C-in-C] decided to send Lumsden and Allgood as A.Q.M.G.'s with the force, and I was feeling very low in consequence. A day or two afterwards we dined with the Cannings, and Lord Clyde took my wife in to dinner. His first remark to her was: 'I think I have earned your gratitude, if I have not managed to satisfy everyone by these China appointments.' On my wife asking for what she was expected to be grateful, he said: 'Why, for not sending your husband with the expedition, of course. I suppose you would rather not be left in a foreign country alone a few months after your marriage? If Roberts had not been a newly-married man, I would have sent him.' This was too much for my wife, who sympathized greatly with my disappointment, and she could not help retorting: 'I am afraid I cannot be very grateful to you for making my husband feel I am ruining his career by standing in the way of his being sent on service. You have done your best to make him regret his marriage.' The poor old Chief was greatly astonished, and burst out in his not too refined way: 'Well, I'll be hanged if I can understand you women! I have done the very thing I thought you would like, and have only succeeded in making you angry. I will never try to help a woman again.'

Lord Roberts

233.

Sir Harry Smith's Arab charger Aliwal had been with him through all the battles of the Sutlej campaign, followed him home to England in 1847 and thence to South Africa and back again in 1852. In 1859 the old general concluded that his day was done. His aide-de-camp's daughter describes the parting.

MY sister and I have a vivid recollection of the lovely horse, and how, when we used to meet Sir Harry when we were out walking and he was

riding, he would call out, 'Stand still, children', and then come galloping up at full speed, and Aliwal would stop at our very feet; and my
mother used to tell us that on the anniversary of the Battle of Aliwal,
when there was always a full-dress dinner at the General's house,
some one would propose Aliwal's health, and Sir Harry would order
him to be sent for. The groom would lead the beautiful creature all
round the dinner-table, glittering with plate, lights, uniforms, and brilliant dresses, and he would be quite quiet, only giving a snort now and
then, though, when his health had been drunk and the groom had led
him out, you could hear him on the gravel outside, prancing and caper-
ing. The horse was now old, and Sir Harry, in his new house in
London, would not be able to keep him; and though Sir Robert Gerard (now Lord Gerard) kindly offered him a home, Sir Harry feared
that his old age would perhaps be an unhappy one, and he resolved to
shoot him. My father and the faithful groom were with Sir Harry when
he did so, and I believe they all shed tears.

Miss Payne

234.

Sir Harry Smith's epitaph for himself, composed in 1844. He died in 1860.

I HAVE now served my country nearly forty years, I have fought in
every quarter of the globe, I have driven four-in-hand in every quarter,
I have never had a sick certificate, and only once received leave of
absence, which I did for eight months to study mathematics. I have
filled *every* staff situation of a Regiment and of the General Staff. I
have commanded a Regiment in peace, and have had often a great
voice in war. I entered the army perfectly unknown to the world, in ten
years by force of circumstances I was Lieutenant-Colonel, and I have
been present in as many battles and sieges as any officer of my standing
in the army. I never fought a duel, and only once made a man an apology, although I am as hot a fellow as the world produces; and I may
without vanity say, the friendship I have experienced equals the love I
bear my comrade, officer or soldier.

My wife has accompanied me throughout the world; she has ever
met with kind friends and never has had controversy or dispute with
man or woman.

Sir Harry Smith

235.

The Third China War of 1860 was one of a long series of nineteenth-century clashes in which the European powers—in this case, Britain and France—sought to assert their will against the Chinese on highly doubtful pretexts. Having stormed the Taku forts at the mouth of the Pai Ho river, the army proceeded to Peking where the French comprehensively looted the Summer Palace, a Chinese Versailles. The British, not to be outdone, then burned down what was left 'to teach the Chinese a lesson'. A modern newspaper correspondent reviewing the contemporary justification that was offered for this act of vandalism may be forgiven for mourning the passing of an age in which such stirring deeds were done to secure the goodwill of the media.

As regards the burning of the palace, we have never at any time hesitated to assume the responsibility of the deed, but not from the motives attributed by General de Montauban, who now justifies an act in which at the time he refused to participate. The General states: 'We hoped, therefore, that this vigorous demonstration would have a good result. Unfortunately, our hopes were not realized soon enough to save some unfortunate European envoys from frightful tortures; still more, the correspondent of the "Times" was put to death; and it was when the bloody fragments of his body were found that the English resolved to burn the palace in revenge for the murder of their countryman. I perfectly remember that I then made some observations to Lord Elgin, [the British Envoy] who replied in a form of discreet confidence, "What would the 'Times' say of me if I did not avenge its correspondent?" '

An unnamed British medical officer

236.

In the summer of 1861 Ulysses S. Grant was appointed Colonel of the 21st Illinois Volunteers, and soon afterwards ordered to march against a Confederate force at the little town of Florida, commanded by Colonel Thomas Harris.

In the twenty-five miles we had to march we did not see a person, old or young, male or female, except two horsemen who were on a road that crossed ours. As soon as they saw us they decamped as fast as their horses could carry them. I kept my men in the ranks and forbade their entering any of the deserted houses or taking anything from them. We halted at night on the road and proceeded the next morning at an early hour. Harris had been encamped in a creek bottom for the sake of being near water. The hills on either side of the creek extend to a considerable height, possibly more than a hundred feet. As we approached

the brow of the hill from which it was expected we could see Harris'
camp, and possibly find his men ready formed to meet us, my heart
kept getting higher and higher until it felt to me it was in my throat. I
would have given anything then to have been back in Illinois, but I had
not the moral courage to halt and consider what to do; I kept right on.
When we reached a point from which the valley below was in full view I
halted. The place where Harris had been encamped a few days before
was still there and the marks of a recent encampment were plainly
visible, but the troops were gone. My heart resumed its place. It
occurred to me at once that Harris had been as much afraid of me as I
had been of him. This was a view of the question I had never taken
before, but it was one I never forgot afterwards. From that event to the
close of the war, I never experienced trepidation upon confronting an
enemy, though I always felt more or less anxiety. I never forgot that he
had as much reason to fear my forces as I had his. The lesson was
valuable. . .

                                                              U. S. Grant

237.

[LOU] Wallace as a boy had longed to go to West Point, and when that
dream failed he tried earnestly to become a novelist. That failed too—
the train of thought that would eventually become 'Ben Hur' had not
yet taken shape in his mind—and so he turned to the law and politics,
and when the war began he was made Colonel of the 11th Indiana. He
was sent to Paducah soon after the place was occupied by Union
troops, and—his political connections being first-rate—it was not long
before he learned that he was being made a brigadier general. This
unsettled him a bit, and he went to General [Charles F.] Smith to ask
advice.

    Smith had taken over a big residence for headquarters, and Wallace
found him sitting by the fire after dinner, taking his ease, his long legs
stretched out, a decanter on the table. Smith was, said Wallace, 'by all
odds the handsomest, stateliest, most commanding figure I had ever
seen'. Somewhat hesitantly Wallace showed him his notice of promotion and asked if he should accept.

    Smith had worked thirty-five years to get his own commission as a
brigadier, and the idea that any officer might hesitate to accept such a

thing stumped him. Why on earth, he asked, should Wallace not take it?

'Because', confessed Wallace 'I don't know anything about the duties of a brigadier.' Smith blinked at him.

'This', he said at last, 'is extraordinary. Here I have been spending a long life to get an appointment like this one about which you are hesitating. And yet,—that isn't it. That you should confess your ignorance—good God!'

Then Smith reached for the decanter, poured Wallace a drink, and told him to accept the promotion and stop worrying. He dug into a table drawer, got out a copy of the United States Army Regulations, and declared that a general should know these rules 'as the preacher knows his Bible'. Then he went on to sum up his own soldierly philosophy in words which Wallace remembered:

Battle is the ultimate to which the whole life's labour of an officer should be directed. He may live to the age of retirement without seeing a battle; still, he must always be getting ready for it as if he knew the hour of the day it is to break upon him. And then, whether it come late or early, he must be willing to fight—he *must* fight.

Bruce Catton

238.
General Thomas J. Jackson at Bull Run, 21 July 1861.

JACKSON, like Bee and Bartow, had been ordered to the Stone Bridge. Hearing the heavy fire to his left increasing in intensity, he had turned the head of his column towards the most pressing danger, and had sent a messenger to Bee to announce his coming. As he pushed rapidly forward, part of the troops he intended to support swept by in disorder to the rear. Imboden's battery came dashing back, and this officer, meeting Jackson, expressed with a profanity which was evidently displeasing to the general his disgust at being left without support. 'I'll support your battery', was the brief reply; 'unlimber right here.' At this moment appeared General Bee, approaching at full gallop, and he and Jackson met face to face. The latter was cool and composed; Bee covered with dust and sweat, his sword in his hand, and his horse foaming. 'General,' he said, 'they are beating us back!' 'Then, sir, we will give them the bayonet'; the thin lips closed like a vice, and the First Brigade, pressing up the slope, formed into line on the eastern edge of the Henry Hill.

Jackson's determined bearing inspired Bee with renewed confidence. He turned bridle and galloped back to the ravine where his officers were attempting to reform their broken companies. Riding into the midst of the throng, he pointed with his sword to the Virginia regiments, deployed in well-ordered array on the height above. 'Look!', he shouted, 'there is Jackson standing like a stone wall! Rally behind the Virginians!' The men took up the cry; and the happy augury of the expression, applied at a time when defeat seemed imminent and hearts were failing, was remembered when the danger had passed away.

G. F. R. Henderson

239.

Jackson's subordinates were frequently exasperated by his passion for secrecy—security, as we should call it in the twentieth century—concerning his future intentions.

WHEN Jackson was informed of the irritation of his generals he merely smiled, and said, 'If I can deceive my own friends I can make certain of deceiving the enemy.' Nothing shook his faith in Frederick the Great's maxim, which he was fond of quoting: 'If I thought my coat knew my plans, I would take it off and burn it.' An anecdote told by one of his brigadiers illustrates his reluctance to say more than necessary. Previous to the march to Richmond this officer met Jackson riding through Staunton. 'Colonel,' said the general 'have you received the order?' 'No, sir.' 'Want you to march.' 'When, sir?' 'Now.' 'Which way?' 'Get in the cars. Go with Lawton.' 'How must I send my train and battery?' 'By the road.' 'Well, general, I hate to ask questions, but it is impossible to send my wagons off without knowing which road to send them.' 'Oh!' —laughing—'send them by the road the others go.'

G. F. R. Henderson

240.

Gettysburg, 1 July 1863, from the Confederate ranks.

LATE in the afternoon of this first day's battle, when the firing had greatly decreased along most of the lines, General Ewell and I were riding through the streets of Gettysburg. In a previous battle he had lost one of his legs, but prided himself on the efficiency of the wooden one which he used in its place. As we rode together, a body of Union soldiers, posted behind some buildings and fences on the outskirts of the town, suddenly opened a brisk fire. A number of Confederates were killed or wounded, and I heard the ominous thud of a Minié ball as it struck General Ewell at my side. I quickly asked: 'Are you hurt, sir?' 'No, no,' he replied; 'I'm not hurt. But suppose that ball had struck you: we would have had the trouble of carrying you off the field, sir. You see how much better fixed for a fight I am than you are. It don't hurt a bit to be shot in a wooden leg.'

General John B. Gordon

241.

Death of General John Sedgwick, CG VI Corps, Spottsylvania Court House, Virginia 9 May 1864.

DURING the morning, after a conference with Grant, Sedgwick rode forward to an elevation near the center of his position, found that his men were a little nervous because of the fire of Confederate sharp-shooters, assured them that there was nothing to worry about because 'they couldn't hit an elephant at this distance . . . ', and then himself fell dead with a sharpshooter's bullet in his brain.

Bruce Catton

242.

After the Spottsylvania battles of 10–12 May 1864.

I BREAKFASTED about 3 p.m., and then, feeling frisky, volunteered to go to a spring a quarter of a mile to the rear, the first portion of the path to which was commanded by Confederate rifles. The crew of the gun I belonged to loaded me down with their empty canteens, and I ran, to avoid the sharpshooters' fire, to the protection of the forest behind us. There I saw many soldiers. Hollow-eyed, tired-looking men they were too, but not 'coffee-boilers', lying on the ground, sleeping soundly. They had sought the comparative safety of the forest to sleep. Near the spring, which rose in a dense thicket through which a spring run flowed, the shade was thick and the forest gloomy. The water in the spring had been roiled, so I searched for another higher up the run. While searching for it I saw a colonel of infantry put on his war paint. It was a howling farce in one act—one brief act of not more than twenty seconds' duration, but the fun of the world was crowded into it. This blonde, bewhiskered brave sat safely behind a large oak tree. He looked around quickly; his face hardened with resolution. He took a cartridge out of his vest pocket, tore the paper with his strong white teeth, spilled the powder into his right palm, spat on it, and then, first casting a quick glance around to see if he was observed, he rubbed the moistened powder on his face and hands, and then dust-coated the war paint. Instantly he was transformed from a trembling coward who lurked behind a tree into an exhausted brave taking a little well-earned repose. I laughed silently at the spectacle, and filled my canteens at a spring I found, and then rejoined my comrades, and together we laughed at and then drank to the health of the blonde warrior. That night I slept and dreamed of comic plays and extravagant burlesques; but in the wildest of dream vagaries there was no picture that at all compared with the actual one I had seen in the forest. That colonel is yet alive. I saw him two years ago.

Frank Wilkeson

243.

Treatment of a war correspondent in the Union lines that many another general on many another battlefield would have relished the opportunity to carry out.

ON one of these six Cold Harbour days, when my battery was in action, I saw a party of horsemen riding towards us from the left. I smiled as the absurdity of men riding along a battle-line for pleasure filled my sense of the ridiculous; but as I looked I saw that the party consisted of a civilian under escort. The party passed close behind our guns, and in passing the civilian exposed a large placard, which was fastened to his back, and which bore the words, 'Libeller of the Press'. We all agreed that he had been guilty of some dreadful deed, and were pleased to see him ride the battle-line. He was howled at, and the wish to tear him limb from limb and strew him over the ground was fiercely expressed. This man escaped death from the shot and shells and bullets that filled the air. I afterwards met him in Washington, and he told me that he was a newspaper war correspondent, and that his offence was in writing, as he thought, truthfully, to his journal, that General Meade advised General Grant to retreat to the north of the Rapidan after the battle of the Wilderness.[1]

Frank Wilkeson

244.

Leonidas Polk, who was killed at Pine Mountain in June 1864 during Sherman's advance on Atlanta, was distinguished by being both a Confederate general and a bishop.

LIKE his opponent, General Sherman, Johnston had been aware of the unwieldy length of his position. He could shorten and strengthen it by withdrawing from Pine Mountain, and anchoring his line on Kennesaw. On the morning of June 14 he rode with Hardee and Polk to the crest of Pine Mountain to look the situation over. Three quarters of a mile below, a Union battery, looking like toy cannon tended by toy soldiers, lobbed two shells in their direction.

Johnston and Hardee took cover, as did other officers who had joined the group from curiosity. Polk remained unruffled, viewing through his glass the scene below. A third shell whistled from the Union guns. It struck the bishop-general squarely in the chest, tearing his lungs out. For a second or two he remained erect—even in death he would not be hurried—then slipped to the ground without a sound. Ignoring the Federal cannon, Johnston ran to his side, raising the head of the fallen general on his arm. Weeping unrestrainedly he whispered, 'I would rather anything than this.'

An ambulance was summoned by the signal station. While waiting, his fellow officers discovered in Polk's bloodied tunic a copy of Dr Quintard's poems, 'Balm for the Weary and Wounded', with the corner of a page turned down to mark the stanza:

> There is an unseen battlefield
> In every human breast
> Where two opposing forces meet
> And where they seldom rest. . . .

Later a sad and silent cavalcade wound down the mountain, with

---

[1] The correspondent was Edward Crapsey of the *Philadelphia Inquirer*. General Meade later claimed that his punishment delighted the army 'for the race of newspaper correspondents is universally despised by the soldiers'.

Johnston riding bareheaded beside the body of his general. Polk's remains were carried to the Marietta depot to be taken to Atlanta, and Johnston returned to the front to break the news to his assembled army. 'In this most distinguished leader', he told the troops, 'we have lost the most courteous of gentlemen, the most gallant of soldiers. The Christian patriot has neither lived nor died in vain. His example is before you; his mantle rests with you.'

Polk's loss was not a major military tragedy to the defending army. His fellow officers agreed that he was 'more theoretical than practical', and even the troops considered him a little ineffectual. Yet they loved him withal, as even hardened troops can love a man for his humanity rather than his skill in combat. Perhaps the most eloquent tribute was found by Federal troops who occupied Pine Mountain two days later. Greeting them was a crudely lettered sign: YOU YANKEE SONS OF BITCHES HAVE KILLED OUR OLD GEN. POLK.

Samuel Carter III

245.

After being expelled from Atlanta by Sherman in September 1864, Hood's Confederate army swung in a wide arc towards Tennessee along the route by which Sherman had advanced, hoping to induce him to follow them. Along their line of march, they summoned Union positions that they encountered to surrender, provoking such exchanges of civilities as those that follow.

Around Allatoona, October 5, 1864

Commanding Officer, United States Forces, Allatoona.

I have placed the forces under my command in such positions that you are surrounded, and to avoid a needless effusion of blood I call on you to surrender your forces at once, and unconditionally.

Five minutes will be allowed you to decide. Should you accede to this, you will be treated in the most honourable manner as prisoners of war,

I have the honour to be, very respectfully yours,

S. G. FRENCH

Major-General commanding forces Confederate States.

General Corse replied immediately:

Allatoona, Georgia, 8.30 a.m. October 5 1864

Major-General S. G. French, Confederate States etc.

Your communication demanding surrender of my command I

acknowledge receipt of, and respectfully reply that we are prepared for the 'needless effusion of blood' whenever it is agreeable to you.

I am, very respectfully, your obedient servant,

JOHN M. CORSE

Brigadier-General commanding forces United States.

In the Field, October 12, 1864

To the Officer commanding the United States forces at Resaca, Georgia.

Sir, I demand the immediate and unconditional surrender of the post and garrison under your command, and, should this be acceded to, all white officers and soldiers will be parolled in a few days. If the place is carried by assault, no prisoners will be taken. Most respectfully, your obedient servant,

J. B. HOOD, General

Resaca, Georgia, October 12, 1864

To General J. B. Hood

Your communication of this date just received. In reply, I have to state that I am somewhat surprised at the concluding paragraph to the effect that, if the place is carried by assault, no prisoners will be taken. In my opinion I can hold this post. If you want it, come and take it.

I am, general, very respectfully, your most obedient servant,

CLARK R. WEAVER, Commanding Officer.

W. T. Sherman

246.

Sherman tells a somewhat sanctimonious tale of the manner in which the memory of his friendship saved a Carolinan lady from being despoiled by his men.

TOWARD evening of February 17th [1865], the mayor, Dr Goodwin, came to my quarters at Duncan's house, and remarked that there was a lady in Columbia who professed to be a special friend of mine. On his giving her name, I could not recall it, but inquired as to her maiden or family name. He answered Poyas. It so happened that, when I was a lieutenant at Fort Moultrie, in 1842–'46, I used very often to visit a family of that name on the east branch of Cooper River, about forty miles from Fort Moultrie, and to hunt with the son, Mr James Poyas, an elegant young fellow and a fine sportsman. His father, mother, and several sisters, composed the family, and were extremely hospitable.

One of the ladies was very fond of painting in water-colors, which was one of my weaknesses, and on one occasion I had presented her with a volume treating of water-colors. Of course, I was glad to renew the acquaintance, and proposed to Dr Goodwin that we should walk to her house and visit this lady, which we did. The house stood beyond the Charlotte depot, in a large lot, was of frame, with a high porch, which was reached by a set of steps outside. Entering this yard, I noticed ducks and chickens, and a general air of peace and comfort that was really pleasant to behold at that time of universal desolation; the lady in question met us at the head of the steps and invited us into a parlor which was perfectly neat and well furnished. After inquiring about her father, mother, sisters, and especially her brother James, my special friend, I could not help saying that I was pleased to notice that our men had not handled her house and premises as roughly as was their wont. 'I owe it to you, general,' she answered. 'Not at all. I did not know you were here till a few minutes ago.' She reiterated that she was indebted to me for the perfect safety of her house and property, and added. 'You remember, when you were at our house on Cooper River in 1845, you gave me a book'; and she handed me the book in question, on the fly-leaf of which was written: 'To Miss — Poyas, with the compliments of W. T. Sherman, First-lieutenant Third Artillery.' She then explained that, as our army approached Columbia, there was a doubt in her mind whether the terrible Sherman who was devastating the land were W. T. Sherman or T. W. Sherman, both known to be generals in the Northern army; but, on the supposition that he was her old acquaintance, when Wade Hampton's cavalry drew out of the city, calling out that the Yankees were coming, she armed herself with this book, and awaited the crisis. Soon the shouts about the market-house announced that the Yankees had come; very soon men were seen running up and down the streets; a parcel of them poured over the fence, began to chase the chickens and ducks, and to enter her house. She observed one large man, with full beard, who exercised some authority, and to him she appealed in the name of 'his general'. 'What do you know of Uncle Billy?' 'Why,' she said, 'when he was a young man he used to be our friend in Charleston, and here is a book he gave me.' The officer or soldier took the book, looked at the inscription, and, turning to his fellows, said: 'Boys, that's so; that's Uncle Billy's writing, for I have seen it often before.' He at once commanded the party to stop pillaging, and left a man in charge of the house, to protect her until the regular provost-guard should be established. I then asked her if the

regular guard or sentinel had been as good to her. She assured me that
he was a very nice young man; that he had been telling her all about his
family in Iowa; and that at that very instant of time he was in another
room minding her baby. Now, this lady had good sense and tact, and
had thus turned aside a party who, in five minutes more, would have
rifled her premises of all that was good to eat or wear.

                                                        W. T. Sherman

247.

*The French Foreign Legion's annual parade of the wooden hand of Captain Jean
Danjou is one of history's odder military traditions. The hand was the only relic of the
officer recovered after the action in which he died, and which remains today the
Legion's proudest memory.*

CAMERONE . . . is the most evocative name in Legion history, even
though it will not be found on any but the largest-scale maps. Yet it is
important to know what happened on 30th April 1863 at the farmhouse whose ruins, visible until a few years ago, inspired this inscription on a marble plaque placed among the other trophies of war in Les
Invalides in Paris:

> QUOS HIC NON PLUS LX
> ADVERSI TOTIUS AGMINIS
> MOLES CONSTRAVIT
> VITA PRIUS QUAM VIRTUS
> MILITES DESERVIT GALLICOS
> DIE XXX MENSI APR. ANNI MDCCCLXIII

(Those who lie here, though less than sixty in number, fought an entire army
before being overwhelmed by sheer weight. Life abandoned these French soldiers before honour did on the 30 of April, 1863.)

These few words epitomize the story of Captain Jean Danjou, thirty-
five years old, veteran of the Crimea, Italy, and North Africa, and his
company of sixty-four men—men with names like Bartolotto, Katau,
Wenzel, Kunassek, Gorski. Captain Danjou's orders were to keep
open the highway connecting Vera Cruz and Mexico City so that the
French could send through a convoy of 60 carts and 150 mules carrying arms, ammunition, and three million francs in gold to headquarters
in the capital.

For this purpose he volunteered to lead a depleted company of sixty-
two men together with two officers from another unit on a reconnaissance

mission along the Vera Cruz–Puebla road. He had volunteered for this assignment because the commanding officer and fifty men of the Third Company were all ill with malaria or dysentery. So with his under-strength company, Danjou left camp at one o'clock in the morning and, marching all night, reached high ground at seven in the morning when it was decided to brew up coffee. The Legion troop had, in the meantime, been observed by the Mexicans whose leader, Colonel Milan, now decided to wipe them out before attacking the convoy coming from Vera Cruz.

As soon as he was harassed by the Mexican cavalry, Captain Danjou withdrew his men to a farmhouse in the village of Camerone, no doubt hoping to be able to hold off sporadic attacks by small groups of horse-men until the main body of the Legion came to his relief. But he was mistaken; within a matter of hours, his company was besieged by a small army of at least 2,000 men—300 regular cavalry, 350 guerillas, and three battalions of infantry. Of his own company of sixty-four, six-teen were already dead, wounded, or missing, leaving only three offi-cers and forty-six legionnaires to defend the farmhouse. They could not hope to survive against such odds, which may explain why Captain Danjou, before he died, demanded that each of them take an oath to fight to the end. The end came in the evening after a day of non-stop fighting during which the defenders had had nothing to eat and, worse, nothing to drink. By six o'clock the original company of three officers and sixty-two men was reduced to one officer, Second-lieutenant Maudet, and eleven legionnaires. The others were either dead or badly wounded, among them Captain Danjou, shot in the head, and his second-in-command, Lieutenant Vilain, mortally wounded. Soon after six the Mexicans decided on an all-out attack on the barn urged on by Colonel Milan who realized that to lose this battle would be a lasting disgrace to the Mexican army and the cause of liberation. This time the assault was overwhelming. But as the Mexicans swarmed in through the now undefended windows and doors of the farmhouse, Lieutenant Maudet ordered a bayonet charge. At the head of his four remaining legionnaires, he rushed out into the courtyard to meet the cross-fire of the besiegers and fell, hit in the face and body. One of his men was shot dead in this last charge; the other three were taken pris-oner. The battle in the farmhouse at Camerone had lasted nine hours, and when it was over, two officers and twenty legionnaires were dead; one officer and twenty-two legionnaires were wounded; and twenty legionnaires had been taken prisoner. The Mexican casualties were around three hundred. The Third Company of the Second Battalion of the Legion had been wiped out, but the convoy of arms and money passed through without incident and reached Mexico City safely.

Camerone was symbolic—'a glorious defeat' on the one hand, a 'glorious victory' on the other. The defeat was the loss of a company of sixty-five professional fighting-men; the victory was the saving of the convoy. But there were very few opportunities in Mexico for the 'bravura' of Camerone; on the contrary, the casualties among the Legion were mostly the result of disease and the inevitable desertions. The final toll was thirty-one officers and 1,917 men dead or missing out of 4,000 sent to Mexico during the four years of Maximilian's reign.

James Wellard

248.

An episode during America's Indian wars.

LATE in December [1867] the survivors of Black Kettle's band began arriving at Fort Cobb. They had to come on foot, because Custer had killed all of their ponies. Little Robe was now the nominal leader of the tribe, and when he was taken to see [General Phil.] Sheridan he told the bearlike soldier chief that his people were starving. Custer had burned their winter meat supply; they could find no buffalo along the Washita; they had eaten all their dogs.

Sheridan replied that the Cheyennes would be fed if they all came into Fort Cobb and surrendered unconditionally. 'You cannot make peace now and commence killing whites again in the spring,' Sheridan added. 'If you are not willing to make a complete peace, you can go back and we will fight this thing out.'

Little Robe knew there was but one answer he could give. 'It is for you to say what we have to do', he said.

Yellow Bear of the Arapahos also agreed to bring his people to Fort Cobb. A few days later, Tosawi brought in the first band of Comanches to surrender. When he was presented to Sheridan, Tosawi's eyes brightened. He spoke his own name and added two words of broken English. 'Tosawi, good Indian', he said.

It was then that General Sheridan uttered the immortal words: 'The only good Indians I ever saw were dead.' Lieutenant Charles Nordstrom, who was present, remembered the words and passed them on, until in time they were honed into an American aphorism: *The only good Indian is a dead Indian.*

Dee Brown

249.

QUEEN VICTORIA, listening to a military band at Windsor, was captivated by a certain tune and sent a messenger to ascertain the title of it. He returned in some embarrassment and said it was called 'Come Where the Booze is Cheaper'.

Christopher Pulling

250.

Sedan, on 1 September 1870, was not merely the decisive battle of the Franco-Prussian War, but the last battlefield of its kind that Europe would ever see.

IT was now a superb day, and Moltke's staff had found for the King [of Prussia] a vantage-point from which a view of the battle could be obtained such as no commander of an army in Western Europe was ever to see again. In a clearing on the wooded hills above Frénois, south of the Meuse, there gathered a glittering concourse of uniformed notabilities more suitable to an opera-house or a race-course than to a climactic battle which was to decide the destinies of Europe and perhaps of the world. There was the King himself; there was Moltke, Roon and their staff officers watching the crown to their labours, while Bismarck, Hatzfeldt and the Foreign Office officials watched the beginnings of theirs. There was Colonel Walker from the British army and General Kutusow from the Russian; there was General Sheridan from the United States, Mr W. H. Russell of *The Times*, and a whole crowd of German princelings; Leopold of Bavaria and William of Württemberg, Duke Frederick of Schleswig-Holstein and the Duke of Saxe-Coburg, the Grand Duke of Saxe-Weimar and the Grand Duke of Mecklenburg-Strelitz and half a dozen others, watching the remains of their independence dwindling hour by hour as the Prussian, Saxon, and Bavarian guns decimated the French army round Sedan.

*

As at Morsbach, as at Vionville, it was shown that when faced with resolute men armed with breech-loading rifles all the anachronistic splendour and courage of French chivalry was impotent. The German skirmishing-lines were overrun, but the supporting formations stood immovable and poured their volleys into the advancing mass. At no point was the German line broken. The cavalry torrent divided and swept by it to either side, northwards towards Illy to return to their own ranks, southward to crash into the quarries of Gaulier or to be rounded up in the valley towards Glaire, leaving the carcasses of horses and the bodies of their riders lying thick in front of the German lines.

As the survivors of the charge rallied, Ducrot sought out their commander, General de Gallifet, and asked him whether they could try again. 'As often as you like, mon général,' replied Gallifet cheerfully, 'so long as there's one of us left.' So the scattered squadrons were rallied and once more the watchers above Frénois saw them plunging down the hill to certain destruction. King William was stirred to exclaim at their courage in words still carved on their memorial above Floing: 'Ah! Les braves gens!' but it was not for him to lament that it was courage tragically wasted. Even now the cavalry were not exhausted. At 3 p.m. Ducrot, his front everywhere crumbling, threw them in yet again, while he and his staff rode along the ranks of the infantry trying in vain to rouse them to advance in the wake of the horse. This last attack, its cohesion gone, was repulsed as decisively as the rest, and with the greatest bloodshed of all. A pleasing legend speaks of Gallifet and his last followers passing exhausted within a few feet of the German infantry regiment. The Germans ceased fire; their officers saluted; and the Frenchmen were allowed to ride slowly away, honoured and unharmed.

With the business of the day safely over, Bismarck considered it safe to send for the King of Prussia. The interview between the sovereigns was brief and embarrassed. There was little for Napoleon to say, except to compliment William on his army—above all on his artillery—and lament the inadequacy of his own. He asked only one favour—that he might go into captivity, not by the same road as his army, but through Belgium, which would avoid an embarrassing passage through the French countryside. Bismarck approved. Napoleon might still be useful 'and it would not even do any harm if he took another direction . . . if he failed to keep his word it would not injure us'. Peace would eventually have to be made, and it could hardly be negotiated with a captured sovereign. Napoleon free in London—or even on

French soil—would be no less inclined to end the disastrous war. His word would carry more weight with his countrymen, and a weak empire would be as good a régime for France in Bismarckian Europe as any other. And if Napoleon was no longer the legal sovereign of France, who was?

So on 3rd September Napoleon with his suite, his powdered postilions, and the train of waggons which had so encumbered the movements of his army, drove into captivity, bound for the palace of Wilhelmshöhe above Cassel. His troops, marching through pouring rain to the makeshift internment camp which the Germans had improvised for them in the loop of the Meuse round Iges—le camp de la misère as they called it after a week of starvation under pelting rain— watched his departure with indifference punctuated by abuse. Both Moltke and Bismarck watched the carriage drive away. Moltke wondered, a little tortuously, whether Napoleon might not have devised the whole operation to secure his untroubled retreat from his responsibilities. Bismarck merely remarked reflectively, 'There is a dynasty on its way out.' Then both returned to the gigantic problems which their victory had set them to solve.

Michael Howard

251.

It is noteworthy how often in military history a deluge of decorations have been conferred on survivors to ease the pain of catastrophe. On 22 January 1879, King Cetewayo's Zulu impis inflicted a bitter humiliation upon elements of Lord Chelmsford's column encamped at Isandhlwana. Of 1,800 men, only some 350 escaped alive. The 24th Foot, later the South Wales Borderers, were almost totally destroyed. Yet on the same day, eleven Victoria Crosses were won at Rorke's Drift, a mission station a few miles distant where the Zulus also swept down, confident of annihilating the ragtag of a British garrison.

RORKE'S DRIFT had been churned into a muddy quagmire by the passing army and the continued movement of oxen and supply wagons. A mission station-farm was located about a quarter of a mile from the drift on the Natal side of the river and this had been turned into a field hospital and supply centre. On the morning of 22 January there were thirty-six men in the hospital, together with a surgeon, a chaplain, and one orderly; eighty-four men of B Company of the 2nd Battalion of the 24th Regiment and a company of Natal Kaffirs were there to guard the crossing; there was also an engineer officer who helped wagons to cross the river, and a few casuals.

Neither of the two regular officers entitled to hold a command (the surgeon-major did not count) was regarded as outstanding. At least neither of them had ever done anything remarkable in their careers up to this point. The senior of the two was black-bearded Lieutenant John Rouse Merriot Chard, the Royal Engineer officer. Commissioned at the age of twenty-one he had served for more than eleven years without ever seeing action or receiving a promotion.

Lieutenant Gonville Bromhead was in charge of B company of the 24th at Rorke's Drift. His brother, Major Charles Bromhead, was in the same regiment, as was natural, for members of the Bromhead family had served in the 24th Regiment for more than 120 years. Charles was regarded as a brilliant officer; he had been in the Ashanti War with Wolseley and was now on staff duty in London. But Gonville, thirty-three years old with nearly twelve years of service, had been a lieutenant for eight years; he was not so bright and was almost totally deaf. He ought not to have been in the army at all. That he was left behind and assigned to the dull job of watching the river crossing was probably due to the natural reluctance of Pulleine to allow him to command a company in battle.

It was about the middle of the afternoon before Chard and Bromhead learned from two volunteer officers of the Natal Kaffirs of the disaster at Isandhlwana and of their own danger. There were no defences at all at Rorke's Drift, but Chard decided that it would be impossible to bring away all the sick and injured men in hospital so they must do what they could to make the mission defensible. Using wagons, biscuit boxes, bags of mealies and existing walls, they managed to enclose the house, barn and kraal. Fortunately, the buildings were of stone, as was the wall around the kraal, but the house, now being used as a hospital, had a thatched roof, making it vulnerable. All the sick and injured who were well enough to shoot were given rifles and ammunition and Chard counted on having about 300 men to defend his little improvised fort.

A few refugees from Isandhlwana reached Rorke's Drift, but most continued their flight. The mounted natives who had been stationed at the drift and the native contingent with Chard all fled, together with their colonial officers and non-commissioned officers. Chard was left with only 140 men, including the patients from the hospital, to man his 300 yard perimeter. Late in the afternoon a man came racing down the hill in back of the station shouting 'Here they come, black as hell and thick as grass!' And a Zulu impi of 4,000 warriors now descended on Rorke's Drift.

The soldiers were still carrying biscuit boxes and mealie bags to the walls when the Zulus, with their black and white cowhide shields and with assegais flashing in the sun, came running into view. Boxes and bags were dropped, rifles and cartridge pouches were seized and the soldiers ran to man the barricades. Rifles crashed as the defenders fired into the black masses of Zulu warriors that swept down on them. The Zulus had a deadly open space to cross and took terrible casualties—but they came on in waves. The soldiers could not shoot fast enough and as the Zulus swept around the walls of the hospital there were hand to hand fights along the makeshift barricades, bayonets against assegais, the Zulus mounting the bodies of their own dead and wounded to grab at the rifle barrels and jab at the soldiers.

The men of the 24th had already been enraged before the Zulus arrived by the sight of their native allies and colonial volunteers deserting them. One soldier had even put a bullet into the retreating back of a European non-commissioned officer of the Native Contingent. They were in a fighting mood, and now with the Zulus upon them they fought with a frenzy.

Some of the Zulus who were armed with rifles crouched behind boulders on the rocky slopes behind the mission and fired at the backs of the defenders on the far wall. Fortunately their shooting was erratic, and they did little damage. The steady marksmanship of the soldiers was better; one private downed eight Zulus with eight cartridges during the first charge. The soldiers had found plenty of ammunition among the stores in the barn and the chaplain circulated among them distributing handfuls of fresh cartridges.

There was wild, vicious room to room fighting when the Zulus broke into the hospital; the sick and wounded, together with a few men from B Company, held them off with desperate courage until they set fire to the thatched roof. Meanwhile, Chard was trying to withdraw his men into a narrower perimeter encompassing only the barn, kraal and the yard in front of the barn. Into this area the men who had escaped from the hospital, the freshly wounded and Chard's remaining effectives retreated and continued the fight. It was dark now, but the Zulus still came on and by the light of the burning hospital the fight went on.

In rush after rush the Zulus pressed back the soldiers. The kraal, which had been defended by bayonets and clubbed rifles when there was no time to reload, had at last to be abandoned. Rifles had now been fired so often and so fast that the barrels burned the fingers and the fouled guns bruised and battered the shoulders and frequently jammed. The wounded cried for water and the canteens were empty, but Chard led a sally over the wall to retrieve the two-wheeled water cart that stood in the yard by the hospital. It was about four o'clock in the morning before the Zulu attacks subsided, but even then flung assegais continued to whistle over the walls.

It seems nearly incredible that even brave, disciplined British soldiers could have sustained such determined attacks by men equally brave and in such numbers. But they did. By morning, Chard and Bromhead had about eighty men still standing. Fifteen had been killed, two were dying and most were wounded. When dawn broke over the hills, the soldiers looked over the walls and braced their tired, wounded bodies for another charge. Their faces were blackened and their eyes were red; their bodies ached and their nerves were stretched taut from the strain. But the Zulus were gone. Around them were hundreds of black corpses; a few wounded Zulus could be seen retreating painfully over a hill; the ground was littered with the debris of battle: Zulu shields and assegais; British helmets, belts and other accoutrements; broken wagons, biscuit boxes and mealie bags, and the cartridge cases of the 20,000 rounds of ammunition the defenders had fired. Chard sent out some cautious patrols, but there were no signs of the enemy in the immediate vicinity. The soldiers cleared away some dead Zulus from the cook house and began to make tea.

About seven-thirty the Zulus suddenly appeared again. Chard called his men and they manned the walls, but the Zulus simply sat down on a hill out of rifle range. They, too, were exhausted, and they had not eaten for more than two days. They had no desire to renew the fight. Besides, the leader of the impi had disobeyed the order of Cetewayo by crossing the Buffalo River into Natal and he was doubtless considering how he would explain to his chief the costly night of savage fighting outside the boundaries of Zululand. While Chard and his men grimly watched, the Zulus rose and wearily moved off over the hills.

Later in the morning, some mounted infantry rode up and soon after Chelmsford appeared with what was left of his main force. He had hoped that some portion of his troops had been able to retreat from Isandhlwana to Rorke's Drift, but he found only the survivors of those who had been left there. With the remnants of his column and the handful of men from Rorke's Drift, he sadly retreated into Natal.

Eleven Victoria Crosses were awarded the defenders of Rorke's Drift: the most ever given for a single engagement. There might have been even more, but posthumous awards were not then made. Both Chard and Bromhead received the medal. There were many Welshmen in the 24th (which later became the South Wales Borderers), and among the eighty-four men of B Company there were five men named Jones and five named Williams; two of the Joneses and one Williams won the Victoria Cross. Private Williams's real name, however, was John Williams Fielding; he had run away from home to enlist and had changed his name so that his father, a policeman, would not find him.

Private Frederick Hitch, twenty-four, also won a Victoria Cross and survived his years of service to enjoy the wearing of it as a commissionaire. The bad luck of his regiment seemed to pursue Hitch and his medal, even to the grave. One day while Hitch was in his commissionaire's uniform and wearing his medals a thief snatched the Victoria Cross from his chest. It was never seen again. King Edward VII eventually gave him another to replace it, but when Hitch died in 1913 this one, too, had disappeared. Fifteen years later it turned up in an auction room; his family bought it and it is now in the museum of his old regiment. Mounted on his tomb in Chiswick cemetery was a bronze replica of the Victoria Cross. In 1968 thieves stole that.

Lieutenant Chard finally received his first promotion—to brevet major, becoming the first officer in the Royal Engineers ever to skip the rank of captain. He was also invited to Balmoral where Queen Victoria gave him a gold signet ring. He served for another eighteen years in Cyprus, India and Singapore, but he received only one more promotion. In 1897 cancer of the tongue caused him to retire and he died three months later.

Bromhead was also promoted to captain and brevet major, though he never rose any higher. He, too, was invited to Balmoral by the Queen, but being on a fishing trip when the invitation arrived he missed the occasion. He died in 1891 at the age of forty-six in Allahabad, still in the 24th Regiment.

Bromhead and Chard were fortunate in a sense when their moment for glory arrived: fighting with their backs to the wall, they had only to show the kind of stubborn bravery and simple leadership for which the British officer was conditioned and which he was best equipped to display. No great decision or military genius was required of them. But this is not to detract from their feat of courage and the British army was rightly proud of them.

Byron Farwell

252.

On 1 June 1879 the Empress Eugenie's only son the Prince Imperial, attached to Lord Chelmsford's column in Zululand, was accompanying a reconnaissance patrol ambushed by the Zulus. The horsemen dashed for safety. But the Prince, together with three British troopers, was brought down and killed. Four survivors, together with an officer named Lieutenant Jahleel Carey who had impulsively asked to join the party, returned to camp.

WHEN Lieutenant Carey entered the officers' mess he was greeted for the last time by a cheerful remark from a fellow officer: Major Grenfell called out, 'Why, Carey, you're late for dinner. We thought you'd been shot.'

'I'm all right', Carey said glumly, 'but the Prince has been killed.'

The word soon spread through the camp. Chelmsford was shaken. All those responsible knew the importance of the tragedy, not only to the world at large but to their own careers and reputations. The wretched Lieutenant Carey sat down that night and wrote the whole story to his wife: 'I am a ruined man, I fear . . . But it might have been my fate. The bullets tore round us and with only my revolver what could I do? . . . I feel so miserable and dejected!' He had reason to feel sorry for himself. It was probably true that there was little he could have done to save the Prince and that he probably would have been killed himself had he tried. But he did not try. And for this he was condemned by every officer in Zululand; indeed, by every officer in the British Army. He tried to find excuses for himself. Apparently he came to believe in his own blamelessness and to resent the scorn of his fellow officers. He demanded a court of inquiry to clear his name. The court met and recommended that he be court-martialled. At his trial Carey maintained that he had not been in command of the party but had only accompanied the Prince to correct his sketches. He did everything possible to shift the blame for the disaster onto the victim. He did not succeed. The court found him guilty of misbehaviour in the face of the enemy.

Carey was sent back to England where he found considerable sympathy among civilians who did not understand the soldiers' code and who thought that Chelmsford and the Duke of Cambridge were more to be blamed than he. Carey, in his talks with the many reporters who interviewed him, put more and more of the blame on the Prince. In spite of everything, Eugenie pleaded with Queen Victoria not to allow him to be punished and the Queen reluctantly wrote to the review board to ask them to drop the charge, which they did. Carey was ordered to report to his regiment, but he was still not content. He felt that he would be completely vindicated only if Eugenie received him. He wrote time and time again requesting this, but unknown to him the text of the letter he had written his wife immediately after the fight admitting his cowardice, had been sent to Eugenie. He wrote and talked so much that at last the Empress released the letter to the press. Carey was ruined.

When he rejoined his regiment Carey found himself a pariah. No one spoke to him. Officers turned their backs when he approached them. He had disgraced his regiment and the army, and he was never forgiven. Oddly enough, he did not resign but endured this social hell for six years until he died in Bombay.

Soldiers and civilians obviously had different views of the affair. For the most part the soldiers kept their mouths shut, but Wolseley, writing to his wife, expressed the view of many soldiers when he said [of the Prince Imperial] 'He was a plucky young man, and he died a soldier's death. What on earth could he have better? Many other brave men have also fallen during this war, and with the Prince's fate England has no concern. Perhaps I have insufficient sympathy with foreign nations; I reserve all my deep feeling for Her Majesty's subjects.'

Byron Farwell

253.

By the late nineteenth century the armies of the world were thickly populated with European commanders who had left their homelands either in search of adventure, or under a cloud. Valentine Baker (1827–89) was a classic example of the latter breed. All his life he dreamt of rehabilitation in the British army. Instead he is remembered for leading an Egyptian army to disaster against the dervishes at El Teb on 6 February 1884.

HE was born in Enfield, England, the son of a rich merchant who had large estates in Jamaica and Mauritius. At the age of twenty-one he went with his elder brothers, John and Samuel (later Sir Samuel

Baker, the great African explorer) to establish an English settlement in Ceylon at a place in the hills 115 miles from Colombo. Valentine soon decided that he did not want to be a pioneer farmer and joined the Ceylon Rifles as an ensign. Four years later he transferred to the 13th Lancers and distinguished himself fighting in the Kaffir War of 1855–57. During the Crimean War he saw more action at the battle of Tchernaya and during the siege of Sevastopol.

In 1859 he obtained his majority and exchanged into the 10th Hussars. The following year, at the age of thirty-three, he was given command of the regiment. Valentine Baker was a keen, serious student of military science. He wrote pamphlets and books on national defence and the organization of British cavalry, and he brought his own regiment to a high state of efficiency. Not content to remain unoccupied in England, he went as a spectator to see the Austro-Prussian War and the Franco-Prussian War, and he travelled and explored in the remoter parts of Persia and Russia. In 1874 he was appointed assistant quartermaster-general at Aldershot.

In 1875 Valentine Baker, now forty-eight years old and married to a squire's daughter, appeared to be a happy man leading an interesting life and in the middle of a successful career. As *The Times* later said in his obituary, 'his career might have been among the most brilliant in our military service'. Might have been. On 2 August 1875 he was convicted of 'indecently assaulting a young lady in a railway carriage' and sentenced to a year in prison and a fine of £500. His career and his reputation were in ruins. He was, of course, dismissed from the army, 'Her Majesty having no further occasion for your services'.

Good officers who assaulted young ladies in railway carriages were not banned from the Turkish army, and Valentine Baker, after his release from prison, went to Turkey and was at once made a major-general.

Byron Farwell

254.

One of the most splendidly colourful adventurers accompanying Wolseley's 1884 expedition up the Nile to rescue General Gordon was Colonel Frederick Gustavus Burnaby (1842–85).

In appearance he was most un-British: he had a swarthy complexion and stood six feet four inches high. He had a high thin voice and a forty-six-inch chest. In his youth he was thought to have been the strongest man in Europe and he is said to have once carried a small pony under his arm. He had joined the army as a cornet in the household cavalry when he was sixteen, but he had such a passion for gymnastics and muscle-building that he ruined his health. To regain it he took to travelling. He travelled in Central and South America, and Central Asia, hardly places one would normally choose to go for one's health, particularly in the last century, but that was his excuse and that is what he did. He was *The Times* correspondent in Spain during the Carlist War and he visited Gordon in the Sudan in 1875. A linguist, he spoke French, German, Spanish, Russian, Italian and some Turkish. His experiences in Central Asia were written up in a successful book, *A Ride to Khiva*. A trip through Asia Minor resulted in another popular book. As a 'visitor' to the Russo-Turkish War he commanded the 5th Brigade of the Turkish army at the battle of Tashkesan. In Turkey he had known Valentine Baker and the two of them were once poisoned in the home of a Greek archbishop. He had at one time stood for parliament, but had been defeated. Burnaby was passionately interested in ballooning and had made nineteen ascents, on one of which, in 1882, he crossed the English Channel.

Without leave he went to Egypt and was with his friend Valentine Baker in the Eastern Sudan. As a volunteer with Gerald Graham's expedition, he cleared out a stone building at El Teb with a double-barrelled shotgun. Saying that he was going to Bechuanaland, Burnaby, now forty-two years old, went to Korti and joined Wolseley, who was delighted to see him. It was illegal, but Wolseley put him on his staff.

Byron Farwell

255.

The British column advancing across the desert from Jakdul Wells to the Nile at last met the dervishes in strength on 17 January 1885, at Abu Klea, where they prevailed only after desperate fighting in which Burnaby was mortally wounded.

LORD BINNING, a Lieutenant in the Blues, reached him where he lay, thirty yards outside the square, before he died.

I was not the first to find him. A young private in the Bays, a mere lad, was already beside him, endeavouring to support his head on his knee; the lad's genuine grief was touching, as were his simple words: 'Oh! sir, here is the bravest man in England, dying, and no one to help him.'

Binning took his hand, but Burnaby was indeed beyond help. In a few moments he was dead, upon his face 'the composed and placid smile of one who had been suddenly called away in the midst of a congenial and favourite occupation'. The death of a man who, by his courage and gigantic size, had seemed almost immortal, deeply affected his comrades, particularly the men in the Blues, some of whom sat down and cried.

Julian Symons

256.

A pen portrait of the commanding officer of the Fourth Hussars in 1893.

COLONEL BRABAZON was an impoverished Irish landlord whose life had been spent in the British Army. He personified the heroes of Ouida. From his entry into the Grenadier Guards in the early 60s he had been in the van of fashion. He was one of the brightest military stars in London society. A close lifelong friendship had subsisted between him and the Prince of Wales. At Court, in the Clubs, on the racecourse, in the hunting field, he was accepted as a most distinguished figure. Though he had always remained a bachelor, he was by no means a misogynist. As a young man he must have been exceptionally good-looking. He was exactly the right height for a man to be. He was not actually six feet, but he looked it. Now, in his prime, his appearance was magnificent. His clean-cut symmetrical features, his bright grey eyes and strong jaw, were shown to the best advantage by a moustache which the Kaiser might well have taken as his unattainable ideal. To all this he added the airs and manners of the dandies of the generation before his own, and an inability real or affected to pronounce the letter 'R'. Apt and experienced in conversation, his remarkable personality was never at a loss in any company, polite or otherwise.

His military career had been long and varied. He had had to leave the Grenadier Guards after six years through straitened finances, and passed through a period of serious difficulty. He served as a gentleman volunteer—a great privilege—in the Ashanti Campaign of 1874. Here he so distinguished himself that there was a strong movement in high circles to restore to him his commission. This almost unprecedented favour was in fact accorded him. The Prince of Wales was most anxious that he should be appointed to his own regiment—the 10th Hussars—in those days probably the most exclusive regiment in the Army. However, as no vacancy was immediately available he was in the interval posted to an infantry regiment of the Line. To the question, 'What do you belong to now, Brab?' he replied, 'I never can wemember, but they have gween facings and you get at 'em from Waterloo.'

Of the stationmaster at Aldershot he enquired on one occasion in later years: 'Where is the London twain?' 'It has gone, Colonel.' 'Gone! Bwing another.'

Translated at length into the 10th Hussars he served with increasing reputation through the Afghan War in 1878 and 1879 and through the fierce fighting round Suakim in 1884. As he had gained two successive brevets upon active service he was in army rank actually senior to the Colonel of his own regiment. This produced at least one embarrassing situation conceivable only in the British Army of those days. The Colonel of the 10th had occasion to find fault with Brabazon's squadron and went so far in his displeasure as to order it home to barracks. Brabazon was deeply mortified. However, a few weeks later the 10th Hussars were brigaded for some manœuvres with another cavalry regiment. Regimental seniority no longer ruled, and Brabazon's army rank gave him automatically the command of the brigade. Face to face with his own commanding officer, now for the moment his subordinate, Brabazon had repeated the same remarks and cutting sentences so recently addressed to him, and finished by the harsh order, 'Take your wegiment home, Sir!' The fashionable part of the army had been agog with this episode. That Brabazon had the law on his side could not be gainsaid. In those days men were accustomed to assert their rights in a rigid manner which would now be thought unsuitable. There were, however, two opinions upon the matter.

As it was clear that his regimental seniority would never enable him to command the 10th, the War Office had offered him in 1893 the command of the 4th Hussars. This was in itself an inevitable reflection upon the senior officers of that regiment. No regiment relishes the arrival of a stranger with the idea of 'smartening them up'; and there must have been a great deal of tension when this terrific Colonel, blazing with medals and clasps, and clad in all his social and military prestige, first assumed command of a regiment which had even longer traditions than the 10th Hussars. Brabazon made little attempt to conciliate. On the contrary he displayed a masterful confidence which won not only unquestioning obedience from all, but intense admiration, at any rate from the Captains and subalterns. Some of the seniors, however, were made to feel their position. 'And what chemist do you get this champagne fwom?' he enquired one evening of an irascible Mess president.

To me, apart from service matters in which he was a strict disciplinarian, he was always charming. But I soon discovered that behind all his talk of war and sport, which together with questions of religion or irreligion and one or two other topics formed the staple of Mess conversation, there lay in the Colonel's mind a very wide reading. When, for instance, on one occasion I quoted, 'God tempers the wind to the shorn lamb', and Brabazon asked 'Where do you get that fwom?' I had replied with some complacency that, though it was attributed often to the Bible, it really occurred in Sterne's *Sentimental Journey*. 'Have you ever wead it?' he asked, in the most innocent manner. Luckily I was not only naturally truthful, but also on my guard. I admitted that I had not. It was, it seemed, one of the Colonel's special favourites.

The Colonel, however, had his own rebuffs. Shortly before I joined the regiment he came into sharp collision with no less a personage than Sir Evelyn Wood who then commanded at Aldershot. Brabazon had not only introduced a number of minor irregularities, mostly extremely sensible, into the working uniform of the regiment—as for instance chrome yellow stripes for drill instead of gold lace—but he had worn for more than thirty years a small 'imperial' beard under his lower lip. This was of course contrary to the Queen's Regulations, Section VII: 'The chin and underlip are to be shaved (except by pioneers, who will wear beards).' But in thirty years of war and peace no superior authority had ever challenged Brabazon's imperial. He had established it as a recognized privilege and institution of which no doubt he was enormously proud. No sooner had he brought his regiment into the Aldershot command than Sir Evelyn Wood was eager to show himself no respecter of persons. Away went the chrome yellow stripes on the pantaloons, away went the comfortable serge jumpers in which the regiment was accustomed to drill; back came the gold lace stripes and the tight-fitting cloth stable-jackets of the old regime. Forced to obey, the Colonel carried his complaints unofficially to the War Office. There was no doubt he had reason on his side. In fact within a year these sensible and economical innovations were imposed compulsorily upon the whole army. But no one at the War Office or in London dared override

Sir Evelyn Wood, armed as he was with the text of the Queen's Regulations. As soon as Sir Evelyn Wood learned that Brabazon had criticized his decisions, he resolved upon a bold stroke. He sent the Colonel a written order to appear upon his next parade 'shaved in accordance with the regulations'. This was of course a mortal insult. Brabazon had no choice but to obey. That very night he made the sacrifice, and the next morning appeared disfigured before his men, who were aghast at the spectacle, and shocked at the tale they heard. The Colonel felt this situation so deeply that he never referred to it on any occasion. Except when obliged by military duty, he never spoke to Sir Evelyn Wood again.

Winston S. Churchill

257.

Marcel Proust (1871–1922) was asked in a Confession Album: 'What event in military history do you admire most?' He replied unhesitatingly 'My own enlistment as a volunteer.' Proust the novelist profited greatly from the experience of Proust the soldier, as Anthony Powell illustrates.

CAPTAIN DE BORODINO, Saint-Loup's Squadron Commander, is one of the characters in the novel drawn from life. His prototype was Captain Walewski, a Company Commander in the 76th, grandson of Bonaparte by a Polish lady, an affair well known to history. As it happened the Captain's mother, in addition to his grandmother's imperial connections, had been mistress to Napoleon III. That such a figure, with origins, appearance and behaviour all crying out for chronicling, should turn up in Proust's regiment illustrates one of those peculiar pieces of literary luck which sometimes attend novelists.

General de Froberville's prototype in real life was General de Gallifet, a well-known personality in the world with which Proust deals. Gallifet, who had led the cavalry charge at Sedan, suppressed the Commune with an almost Communist savagery, and (though not Dreyfusard) insisted on a revisionist approach to the Dreyfus case, was also a wit and a womanizer. Mr Painter mentions several stories about him: the silver plate covering the wound in his abdomen (received in the Mexican campaign) alleged to lend physical subtlety to his many love affairs; the distinguished lady archaeologist, rather masculine in dress, who insisted on joining the men after dinner, at which the

General took her by the arm with the words 'Come along, my dear fellow, let's go and have a pee.'

. . . In *Jean Santeuil* he [Proust] does, however, devote a good deal of space to Colonel Picquart, another good instance of Proust's approach to army matters, and also his technique of absorbing 'real people' into his writing.

Picquart's story should be briefly recalled. An Alsatian, sixteen years old when Alsace was annexed by Germany, he was regarded as an ambitious and very promising officer, he had served on Gallifet's staff, been present at Dreyfus's court-martial, and, in due course, put in charge of the Secret Service Section—an outstandingly ramshackle one—at the French War Office. On taking over, Picquart re-examined the Dreyfus file held by his Section, coming to the conclusion that something had gone badly wrong in the Court's examination of evidence. He drew this fact to the attention of his superiors, with the consequence that he was himself posted to North Africa (stationed where there was a good chance of death in action) then, when he persisted in making further representations about Dreyfus, put under arrest, imprisoned, and placed in the running for condemnation to five years in a fortress.

All this is striking enough; but when it is added that Picquart, if not a rabid anti-semite, was decidedly unfriendly towards Jews, he will at once be seen to be building up the sort of character upon which a writer likes to get to work. When Dreyfus was cleared, Picquart refused to meet him; and when, in due course, Picquart rose in rank and was in a position to be of some assistance in Dreyfus's professional rehabilitation in the army, he would take no step to make things easier. Clemenceau, in a slapstick mood, appointed him his Minister of War, a post Picquart filled without great distinction, behaving rather badly to officers who had merely been carrying out orders issued by former anti-Dreyfusard superiors. Picquart remained unmarried all his life; dying, in consequence of being thrown from his horse, when in command of an Army Corps, about six months before the outbreak of war in 1914.

Proust's own health was naturally far too precarious for there to be any question of serving again in the army. That did not prevent the routine requirements of medical boards, which he accepted—one recalls the great to-do D. H. Lawrence made in similar circumstances—as inevitable consequences of a world war. All the same, there was one aspect of them that was exceedingly troublesome to

Proust—the time the boards took place. He dreaded these orders to present himself, merely because they threatened the hour or two's sleep he could achieve only during daytime. By one of those clerical errors endemic to military administration, certainly a classical one, he was ordered on one occasion to report to the Invalides for medical examination at 3.30 a.m., instead of the same hour in the afternoon. To many people such an instruction would have been disturbing. Proust was charmed. This nocturnal summons seemed just another example of how accommodating the military authorities could sometimes show themselves.

Anthony Powell

258.

Few military reputations have been won as briskly as that of Theodore Roosevelt, the future President of the United States. The American war against the Spanish in Cuba was proclaimed on 20 April 1898. Roosevelt and his 'Rough Riders' landed with the American expeditionary force on 15 June. They were back in New York two months later. Yet in the interval Roosevelt, merely a celebrity before the war, made himself a national hero.

ON Saturday [23 April] the President issued a call for 125,000 volunteers to swell the ranks of the 28,000-man Regular Army. Included in this general summons was an extraordinary provision for three regiments 'to be composed exclusively of frontiersmen possessing special qualifications as horsemen and marksmen'. Secretary Alger would not have to look far for someone to be colonel of the first regiment, since the nation's most prominent frontiersman, horseman, and marksman was already pounding on his desk at the War Department. That same day, he offered the command to Theodore Roosevelt.

As long ago as 1886 Roosevelt had talked of leading a troop of 'harum-scarum roughriders' into battle, without much conviction that such a dream would ever come true. Now, miraculously, it had; fate seemed to be adapting itself to his own peculiar abilities. Here at last was supreme opportunity for personal and military glory. Yet with supreme self-control Roosevelt turned the offer down. He told the Secretary that while he had been a captain in the New York National Guard, he lacked experience in hard military organization. He was sure he could 'learn to command the regiment in a month', but that very month might make the difference between fighting at the front or languishing behind and missing the war. He would be happy to serve as lieutenant colonel if the colonelcy went to Leonard Wood.

After some deliberation, Alger accepted this arrangement. . . .

Although neither man had yet received his commission, the announcement of their appointment was made on April 25, and by April 27 sacks of applications were thumping in from all parts of the country. The majority of these applications (which eventually numbered twenty-three thousand, enough for an entire division) were addressed to Roosevelt. He, Secretary Alger, the President, and Congress might imagine Wood to be the true commander of the regiment, but the American public was not fooled. Already Western newspapers were hailing the formation of 'Teddy's Terrors', and every day brought a fresh crop of suggested names, all with the same alliterative connotation: 'Teddy's Texas Tarantulas', 'Teddy's Gilded Gang', 'Teddy's Cowboy Contingent', 'Teddy's Riotous Rounders' (and then, gradually, as the Lieutenant Colonel let it be known he did not like the nickname), 'Roosevelt's Rough 'Uns', and 'Roosevelt's Rough Riders'. The last name stuck, and was soon common usage. 'Colonel Wood', commented the *New York Press*, 'is lost sight of entirely in the effulgence of Teethadore. . . .'

It did not take the men long to size Roosevelt up, to compare him with 'Old Poker Face', and find Wood wanting. Although some cowpunchers were put off by the New Yorker's overbearing courtesy ('he was polite almost to the extent of making one uneasy'), they could not help being impressed by his drive. 'It was evident to all who met him that he was tremendously ambitious.' They noticed that Wood often asked advice, but seldom information; Roosevelt asked information, but never advice. For all the punctilious deference of the older man to the younger, for all Wood's mastery of military bureaucracy (the Rough Riders were easily the best-armed and best-equipped regiment in the Army) there was no doubt, within a week of Roosevelt's arrival, as to whom they considered to be colonel *malgré lui*. Wood knew it, and knew that his superiors in Washington knew it. 'I realized that if this campaign lasted for any considerable length of time I would be kicked upstairs to make room for Roosevelt.'

Yet the Colonel did not hesitate to exercise authority over his subordinate when he deemed it necessary. Roosevelt was still inexperienced in matters of military discipline, and when Wood heard that he had treated an entire squadron to unlimited beer—apparently as a reward for their improvement in drill—he made a pointed remark over supper 'that, of course, an officer who would go out with a large batch of men and drink with them was quite unfit to hold a commission'. There was a dead silence. Later Roosevelt visited Wood privately in his tent and confessed to the crime. 'I wish to say, sir, that I agree with what you said. I consider myself the damndest ass within ten miles of this camp. Good night.'

. . . Not until the evening of [25 June] were battle orders broadcast among the thirty-one transport ships. When the news reached Roosevelt, he entertained the Rough Riders to his patented war-dance evolved from years of prancing around the carcasses of large game animals. Hand on hip, hat waving in the air, he sang:

> Shout hurrah for Erin-go-Bragh,
> And all the Yankee nation!

Aboard the *Yucatán* a macabre toast was drunk: 'To the Officers, may they get killed, wounded or promoted!' Only Roosevelt, presumably, could relish such sentiments to the full. . . .

At the battle of San Juan, 1 July 1898.

It was now well past noon, and the insect-like figures of General Kent's infantry could be seen beginning a slow, toiling ascent of San Juan Hill. Roosevelt sent messenger after messenger to General Sumner, imploring permission to attack his own hill, and was just about to do so unilaterally when the welcome message arrived: 'Move forward and support the regulars in the assault on the hills in front.' It was not the total advancement he had been hoping for, but it was enough. 'The instant I received the order I sprang on my horse, and then my "crowded hour" began.'

Soldiers are apt to recollect their wartime actions, as poets do emotions, in tranquillity, imposing order and reason upon a dreamlike tumult. Roosevelt was honest enough to admit, even when minutely describing his charge up the hill, that at the time he was aware of very little that was going on outside the orbit of his ears and sweat-fogged spectacles. It was as if some primeval force drove him. 'All men who feel any power of joy in battle', he wrote, 'know what it is like when the wolf rises in the heart.'

Yet enough original images, visual and auditory, survive in Roosevelt's written account of the battle to give a sense of the rush, the roar, the pounce of that vulpine movement. To begin with, there was the sound of his own voice rasping and swearing as he cajoled terrified soldiers to follow him. 'Are you afraid to stand up when I am on horseback?' Then the sight of a Rough Rider at his feet being drilled lengthwise with a bullet intended for himself. Next, line after line of cavalry parting before his advance, like waves under a Viking's prow. The puzzled face of a captain refusing to go farther without permission from some senior colonel, who could not be found.

Roosevelt: 'Then I am the ranking officer here and I give the order to charge.' Another refusal. Roosevelt: 'Then let my men through, sir!' Grinning white faces behind him; black men throwing down a barbed-wire fence before him. A wave of his hat and flapping blue neckerchief. The sound of shouting and cheering. The sound of bullets 'like the ripping of a silk dress'. Little Texas splashing bravely across a stream, galloping on, and on, up, up, up. Another wire fence, forty yards from the top, stopping her in her tracks. A bullet grazing his elbow. Jumping off, wriggling through, and running. Spaniards fleeing from the *hacienda* above. Only one man with him now: his orderly, Bardshar, shooting and killing two of the enemy. And then suddenly a revolver salvaged from the *Maine* leaping into his own hand and firing: a Spaniard not ten yards away doubling over 'neatly as a jackrabbit'. At last the summit of the hill—his and Bardshar's alone for one breathless moment before the other Rough Riders and cavalrymen swarmed up to join them. One final incongruous image: 'a huge iron kettle, or something of the kind, probably used for sugar-refining'.

As his head cleared and his lungs stopped heaving, Roosevelt found that Kettle Hill commanded an excellent view of Kent's attack on San Juan Hill, still in progress across the valley about seven hundred yards away. The toiling figures seemed pitifully few. 'Obviously the proper thing to do was help them.' For the next ten minutes he supervised a continuous volley-fire at the heads of Spaniards in the San Juan blockhouse, until powerful Gatlings took over from somewhere down below, and the infantry on the left began their final rush. At this the wolf rose again in Roosevelt's heart. Leaping over rolls of wire, he started down the hill to join them, but forgot to give the order to follow, and found that he had only five companions. Two were shot down while he ran back and roared imprecations at his regiment. 'What, are you cowards?' 'We're waiting for the command.' 'Forward MARCH!' The Rough Riders willingly obeyed, as well as members of the 1st and 10th Cavalry. Again Roosevelt pounded over lower ground under heavy fire; again he surged up grassy slopes, and again he saw Spaniards deserting their high fortifications. To left and right, all along the crested line of San Juan Heights, other regiments were doing the same. 'When we reached these crests we found ourselves overlooking Santiago.' . . . 'Look at all these damned Spanish dead!' he exulted to Trooper Bob Ferguson, an old family friend.

Official tallies revealed a fair score of American casualties—680 according to one count, 1071 according to another. The Rough Riders contributed 89, but this only increased Roosevelt's sense of pride: he noted that it was 'the heaviest loss suffered by any regiment in the cavalry division'.

'No hunting trip so far has ever equalled it in Theodore's eyes,' Bob Ferguson wrote to Edith. 'It makes up for the omissions of many past years . . . T. was just revelling in victory and gore.'

Roosevelt's exhilaration at finding himself a hero (already there was talk of a Medal of Honor) and, by virtue of his two charges, sent as officer in command of the highest crest and the extreme front of the American line, was so great that he could not sit, let alone lie down even in the midst of a surprise bombardment at 3.00 a.m. A shell landed right next to him, besmirching his skin with powder, and killing several nearby soldiers; but he continued to strut up and down, 'snuffing the fragrant air of combat', silhouetted against the flares like a black lion rampant.

'I really believe firmly now they can't kill him', wrote Ferguson.

Edmund Morris

259.

Churchill's description of the charge of the 21st Lancers at Omdurman on 2 September 1898 is a classic of battlefield narrative just as the episode itself was a classic of military futility. The curse of British cavalry throughout its history has been its inability to know when to stop charging.

EVERYONE expected that we were going to make a charge. That was the one idea that had been in all minds since we had started from Cairo. Of course there would be a charge. In those days, before the Boer War, British cavalry had been taught little else. Here was clearly the occasion for a charge. But against what body of enemy, over what ground, in which direction or with what purpose, were matters hidden from the rank and file. We continued to pace forward over the hard sand, peering into the mirage-twisted plain in a high state of suppressed excitement. Presently I noticed, 300 yards away on our flank

and parallel to the line on which we were advancing, a long row of
blue-black objects, two or three yards apart. I thought there were
about a hundred and fifty. Then I became sure that these were men—
enemy men—squatting on the ground. Almost at the same moment the
trumpet sounded 'Trot', and the whole long column of cavalry began
to jingle and clatter across the front of these crouching figures. We
were in the lull of the battle and there was perfect silence. Forthwith
from every blue-black blob came a white puff of smoke, and a loud
volley of musketry broke the odd stillness. Such a target at such a distance could scarcely be missed, and all along the column here and
there horses bounded and a few men fell.

The intentions of our Colonel had no doubt been to move round the
flank of the body of Dervishes he had now located, and who, concealed
in a fold of the ground behind their riflemen, were invisible to us, and
then to attack them from a more advantageous quarter; but once the
fire was opened and losses began to grow, he must have judged it inex-
pedient to prolong his procession across the open plain. The trumpet
sounded 'Right wheel into line', and all the sixteen troops swung round
towards the blue-black riflemen. Almost immediately the regiment
broke into a gallop, and the 21st Lancers were committed to their first
charge in war!

I propose to describe exactly what happened to me: what I saw and
what I felt. I recalled it to my mind so frequently after the event that
the impression is as clear and vivid as it was a quarter of a century ago.
The troop I commanded was, when we wheeled into line, the second
from the right of the regiment. I was riding a handy, sure-footed, grey
Arab polo pony. Before we wheeled and began to gallop, the officers
had been marching with drawn swords. On account of my shoulder I
had always decided that if I were involved in hand-to-hand fighting, I
must use a pistol and not a sword. I had purchased in London a
Mauser automatic pistol, then the newest and the latest design. I had
practised carefully with this during our march and journey up the river.
This then was the weapon with which I determined to fight. I had first
of all to return my sword into its scabbard, which is not the easiest
thing to do at a gallop. I had then to draw my pistol from its wooden
holster and bring it to full cock. This dual operation took an appreciable time, and until it was finished, apart from a few glances to my
left to see what effect the fire was producing, I did not look up at the
general scene.

Then I saw immediately before me, and now only half the length of a polo ground away, the row of crouching blue figures firing frantically, wreathed in white smoke. On my right and left my neighbouring troop leaders made a good line. Immediately behind was a long dancing row of lances couched for the charge. We were going at a fast but steady gallop. There was too much trampling and rifle fire to hear any bullets. After this glance to the right and left and at my troop, I looked again towards the enemy. The scene appeared to be suddenly transformed. The blue-black men were still firing, but behind them there now came into view a depression like a shallow sunken road. This was crowded and crammed with men rising up from the ground where they had hidden. Bright flags appeared as if by magic, and I saw arriving from nowhere Emirs on horseback among and around the mass of the enemy. The Dervishes appeared to be ten or twelve deep at the thickest, a great grey mass gleaming with steel, filling the dry watercourse. In the same twinkling of an eye I saw also that our right overlapped their left, that my troop would just strike the edge of their array, and that the troop on my right would charge into air. My subaltern comrade on the right, Wormald of the 7th Hussars, could see the situation too; and we both increased our speed to the very fastest gallop and curved inwards like the horns of the moon. One really had not time to be frightened or to think of anything else but these particular necessary actions which I have described. They completely occupied mind and senses.

The collision was now very near. I saw immediately before me, not ten yards away, the two blue men who lay in my path. They were perhaps a couple of yards apart. I rode at the interval between them. They both fired. I passed through the smoke conscious that I was unhurt. The trooper immediately behind me was killed at this place and at this moment, whether by these shots or not I do not know. I checked my pony as the ground began to fall away beneath his feet. The clever animal dropped like a cat four or five feet down on to the sandy bed of the watercourse, and in this sandy bed I found myself surrounded by what seemed to be dozens of men. They were not thickly-packed enough at this point for me to experience any actual collision with them. Whereas Grenfell's troop next but one on my left was brought to a complete standstill and suffered very heavy losses, we seemed to push our way through as one has sometimes seen mounted policemen break up a crowd. In less time than it takes to relate, my pony had scrambled up the other side of the ditch. I looked round.

Once again I was on the hard, crisp desert, my horse at a trot. I had the impression of scattered Dervishes running to and fro in all directions. Straight before me a man threw himself on the ground. The reader must remember that I had been trained as a cavalry soldier to believe that if ever cavalry broke into a mass of infantry, the latter would be at their mercy. My first idea therefore was that the man was terrified. But simultaneously I saw the gleam of his curved sword as he drew it back for a ham-stringing cut. I had room and time enough to turn my pony out of his reach, and leaning over on the off side I fired two shots into him at about three yards. As I straightened myself in the saddle, I saw before me another figure with uplifted sword. I raised my pistol and fired. So close were we that the pistol itself actually struck him. Man and sword disappeared below and behind me. On my left, ten yards away, was an Arab horseman in a bright-coloured tunic and steel helmet, with chain-mail hangings. I fired at him. He turned aside. I pulled my horse into a walk and looked around again.

In one respect a cavalry charge is very like ordinary life. So long as you are all right, firmly in your saddle, your horse in hand, and well armed, lots of enemies will give you a wide berth. But as soon as you have lost a stirrup, have a rein cut, have dropped your weapon, are wounded, or your horse is wounded, then is the moment when from all quarters enemies rush upon you. Such was the fate of not a few of my comrades in the troops immediately on my left. Brought to an actual standstill in the enemy's mass, clutched at from every side, stabbed at and hacked at by spear and sword, they were dragged from their horses and cut to pieces by the infuriated foe. But this I did not at the time see or understand. My impressions continued to be sanguine. I thought we were masters of the situation, riding the enemy down, scattering them and killing them. I pulled my horse up and looked about me. There was a mass of Dervishes about forty or fifty yards away on my left. They were huddling and clumping themselves together, rallying for mutual protection. They seemed wild with excitement, dancing about on their feet, shaking their spears up and down. The whole scene seemed to flicker. I have an impression, but it is too fleeting to define, of brown-clad Lancers mixed up here and there with this surging mob. The scattered individuals in my immediate neighbourhood made no attempt to molest me. Where was my troop? Where were the other troops of the squadron? Within a hundred yards of me I could not see a single officer or man. I looked back at the Dervish mass. I saw two or three riflemen crouching and aiming their rifles at me from the fringe of it. Then for the first time that morning I experienced a sudden sensation of fear. I felt myself absolutely alone. I thought these rifle-men would hit me and the rest devour me like wolves. What a fool I was to loiter like this in the midst of the enemy! I crouched over the saddle, spurred my horse into a gallop and drew clear of the *mêlée*. Two or three hundred yards away I found my troop all ready faced about and partly formed up.

The other three troops of the squadron were re-forming close by. Suddenly in the midst of the troop up sprung a Dervish. How he got there I do not know. He must have leaped out of some scrub or hole. All the troopers turned upon him thrusting with their lancers: but he darted to and fro causing for the moment a frantic commotion. Wounded several times, he staggered towards me raising his spear. I shot him at less than a yard. He fell on the sand, and lay there dead. How easy to kill a man! But I did not worry about it. I found I had fired the whole magazine of my Mauser pistol, so I put in a new clip of ten cartridges before thinking of anything else.

I was still prepossessed with the idea that we had inflicted great slaughter on the enemy and had scarcely suffered at all ourselves. Three or four men were missing from my troop. Six men and nine or ten horses were bleeding from spear thrusts or sword cuts. We all expected to be ordered immediately to charge back again. The men were ready, though they all looked serious. Several asked to be allowed to throw away their lances and draw their swords. I asked my second sergeant if he had enjoyed himself. His answer was 'Well, I don't exactly say I enjoyed it, Sir; but I think I'll get more used to it next time.'

Winston S. Churchill

260.

No episode in the life of Lord Kitchener took him longer to live down than his treatment of the remains of the Mahdi after Omdurman.

ON 6 September four days after the battle, he issued orders that the Mahdi's tomb should be razed to the ground, and that the bones of Gordon's great enemy should be cast into the Nile.

Gordon's nephew, Major S. W. Gordon, R.E., was entrusted with the execution of that order; and the Madhi's skull, which was unusually large and shapely, was saved from destruction and presented to Kitchener as a trophy. Some members of the 'band of boys' with whom it amused him occasionally to relax, suggested that he should cause the skull to be mounted in silver or gold, and that he should use it as an inkstand or as a drinking-cup.

Kitchener played with that idea and with the skull for a short time; and he acquired somehow the idea that Napoleon's intestines had found their way from St Helena to the museum of the Royal College of Surgeons in London. Accordingly, he announced incautiously to some of his staff that he proposed to send the Mahdi's skull to the College of Surgeons with a request that it should be placed on exhibition alongside the guts of Napoleon.

That story of the Mahdi's skull obtained a wide currency; and it caused, in February 1899, a great howl of rage against Kitchener, which was compounded, in approximately equal parts, of frothy but sincere sentiment and of jealousy. Radical and intellectual circles hated Kitchener at that time; the Army was intensely jealous of him; and he had gone out of his way to insult the Press. For a few weeks, therefore, while unfriendly questions were being asked in Parliament and elsewhere, Kitchener felt extremely uncomfortable.

On 27 February 1899 Salisbury telegraphed to Cromer: 'The Queen is shocked by the treatment the Mahdi's body has received, and thinks the head ought to be buried. Putting it in a museum, she thinks, will do great harm.' On 2 March Cromer replied:

> The dead set against Kitchener was sure to come, sooner or later. Apart from the natural reaction, he has not the faculty of making friends. The soldiers are furiously jealous of him, and many of the newspaper correspondents, whom he took no pains to conciliate, have long been waiting for an opportunity to attack him. He has his faults. No one is more aware of them than myself. But for all that, he is the most able of the English soldiers I have come across in my time.
>
> He was quite right in destroying the Mahdi's tomb, but the details of the destruction were obviously open to objection. . . .
>
> Kitchener is himself responsible for the rather unwise course of sending the skull to the College of Surgeons.

Kitchener's relations with the Press had been bad from the start of the campaign. He made two exceptions among the newspaper correspondents in favour of *The Times* and the *Daily Mail* (Hubert Howard and G. W. Steevens); but that favouritism caused trouble; and he seldom let slip an opportunity of demonstrating the contempt in which he held the profession as a whole. Only a day or two before the Battle of Omdurman he was informed that a group of correspondents had been

waiting outside his tent for some time in the belief that he had a statement to make. He let them wait, until he was ready to emerge, and
then, as he strode angrily through their midst he made a statement,
which consisted only of the words: 'Get out of my way, you drunken
swabs!'

In those circumstances the commotion in the British and American
Press about Kitchener and the Mahdi's skull was prolonged mali-
ciously for several weeks. It was combined with charges that Kitchener
had left all the dervish wounded to die without succour on the battlefield of Omdurman, and that he had personally ordered a massacre of
civilians in Omdurman after the battle. Those attacks worried Kitchener, who wrote (7 March 1899) to the Queen:

Lord Kitchener is much distressed that Your Majesty should think that the
destruction of the Mahdi's tomb, and the disposal of his bones was improperly
carried out. He is very sorry that anything he has done should have caused
Your Majesty a moment's uneasiness.

A few days after the battle, I consulted with some native officers of the
Sudanese troops, and spoke on the matter with some influential natives here;
and they told me that, although no educated person believed in the Mahdi
being anything but an impostor who had attempted to change the Mohamme-
dan religion, . . . some of the soldiers in our ranks still believed in the Mahdi;
and they recommended the destruction of the tomb, and that the bones should
be thrown into the Nile, which would entirely dissipate any such belief.

Nothing in the matter was done in a hurry, but four days after the battle,
before I left for Fashoda, I gave the order for the destruction, thinking it was
the safest and wisest course; and this was carried out in my absence. There
was no coffin, and when the bones were found the soldiers seemed all astonished, and exclaimed—'By God! This was not the Mahdi after all he told us!'
They had previously believed that the Mahdi had been translated bodily to
heaven.

When I returned from Fashoda, the Mahdi's skull, in a box, was brought to
me, and I did not know what to do with it. I had thought of sending it to the
College of Surgeons where, I believe, such things are kept. It has now been
buried in a Moslem cemetery.

                                                              Philip Magnus

261.

Colonel Sir Robert Baden-Powell's relentless high spirits and elephantine sense of fun during the siege of Mafeking (October 1899–May 1900) enchanted his Victorian contemporaries, but tend to persuade a modern reader that enemy action was the least of the miseries that the garrison were compelled to endure.

THE garrison, in the face of increasing losses and decreasing food, lost none of the high spirits which it reflected from its commander. The programme of a single day of jubilee—Heaven only knows what they had to hold jubilee over—shows a cricket match in the morning, sports in the afternoon, a concert in the evening, and a dance, given by the bachelor officers, to wind up. Baden-Powell himself seems to have descended from the eyrie from which, like a captain on the bridge, he rang bells and telephoned orders, to bring the house down with a comic song and a humorous recitation. The ball went admirably, save that there was an interval to repel an attack which disarranged the programme. Sports were zealously cultivated, and the grimy inhabitants of casemates and trenches were pitted against each other at cricket or football.

Sunday cricket so shocked Snyman the [the Boer commander in the later stages of the siege] that he threatened to fire upon it if it were continued.

Arthur Conan Doyle

262.

General Sir Redvers Buller's allegedly sybaritic habits, although disputed by at least one modern historian of the period, were the source of much caustic humour among his contemporaries during his campaign for the relief of Ladysmith, November 1899–February 1900.

FINDING his supply of champagne was getting very low, he telegraphed home to his wine-merchants to send out fifty cases of the usual brand, with strict injunctions that the cases were to be marked 'Castor Oil'. About the time the wine was due, the general wrote to the base and informed the officer in charge that he expected fifty cases of castor oil, which he wished despatched to his headquarters without delay. The reply from the base came in a few days, and was as follows: 'Regret exceedingly no cases as described have yet reached us, but this day we have procured all the castor oil possible (twenty cases), and have despatched it without delay, as you desired. We trust this unavoidable delay has caused no serious inconvenience.'

MacCarthy O'Moore

263.

Frank Richards joined the Royal Welch Fusiliers as a private in 1901 and was soon afterwards posted to India. He was speedily taught by old soldiers the fashion in which the natives were to be kept at bay

WE reached Deolalie at daybreak the following morning and were issued with ground-sheets, blue rugs and Indian kit-bags. On the second morning a few of us strolled around the tents of the time-expired men. The majority of these had gone on a route-march but there were a few of them outside their tents and we got into conversation with one of them who had completed over twelve years' service, eleven of these in India. There was a native sweeping around the tent where we were conversing, and the old soldier ordered him on another job. The native replied in broken English that he would do it after he had finished his sweeping. The old soldier drove his fist into the native's stomach, shouting at the same time: 'You black soor, when I order you to do a thing I expect it to be done at once.' The native dropped to the ground, groaning, and the old soldier now launched out with his tongue in Hindoostani and although I did not understand the language I knew he was cursing the native to some order. The native stopped groaning and rose to his feet, shivering with fright: the tongue of the old soldier was evidently worse than his fist. He made several salaams in front of the old soldier and got on with the job he had been ordered to do.

The old soldier then said: 'My God, it's scandalous the way things are going on in this country. The blasted natives are getting cheekier every day. Not so many years ago I would have half-killed that native, and if he had made a complaint afterwards and had marks to show, any decent Commanding Officer would have laughed at him and told him to clear off. Since old Curzon has been Viceroy things are different, you see. An order has been issued, which every soldier in India believes came from him, that Commanding Officers must severely punish men who are brought in front of them for ill-treating natives. We have to be very careful these days. If we punch them in the face they have marks to show, so we have to punch them in the body. Most of the natives on the Plains have enlarged spleens, and a good punch in the body hurts them more than what it would us. I expect you lads have got six or seven years to do in the country, and if you live to become time-expired you will have the same feeling towards natives as what I have. You will soon find out that the more you are down on them the better they will respect you. Treat them kindly and they will show you no respect at all. What is won by the sword must be kept by the sword, and it's the only law that will ever apply to this country. Old Curzon is no damned good, this country wants a Viceroy who will keep the bleeding natives down. If I had my way I'd give him the sack and recommend him for a job as a Sunday School teacher among the Eskimos around the North Pole.'

It was drawing on towards Canteen-time and he inquired if we were fond of a drop of 'neck-oil', which like 'purge' was a nickname of beer. When we replied that we were, he exclaimed: 'That's good! So long as you are in this country always have your drop of neck-oil and you'll live all the longer for it.' While we were in the Canteen natives came around selling monkey-nuts. They were shouting: 'Monkey-nut wallah, plenty good with the beer.' Monkey-nuts were very cheap and most of the time-expired men were buying them and dipping them in salt to eat with their beer. The old soldier recommended them, saying that they made the neck-oil go down better. Before stop-tap we agreed with him and the ground around us was thick with monkey-nut shells. During our forty-five minutes in the Canteen he gave us some good advice, especially regarding the native prostitutes, and told us to mind that whatever we did we should never go with one of the numerous prostitutes that were always soliciting on the outskirts of camps or in the neighbourhood of barracks.

We left Deolalie on the evening of the following day and the old soldier wished us the best of luck. As the years rolled on I came to agree with him as to how the natives should be treated, and I still agree with him that what is won by the sword must be kept by the sword. During my first two years in the country I found that Lord Curzon was very much disliked by the rank and file of the Army, who all agreed that he was giving the natives too much rope. Another thing that added to his unpopularity was that his wife, Lady Curzon, was supposed to have said that the two ugliest things in India were the water-buffalo and the British private soldier. Every soldier in India at the time believed this story and very much resented it. A water-buffalo is larger than an English cow and a very ugly beast indeed. One of our chaps said that he would like to see the whole of the Battalion parade naked in front of Lady Curzon for inspection, with Lord Curzon also naked in the midst of them: for comparison, like a tadpole among gods.

Frank Richards

264.

General Adrian Carton de Wiart, VC, became a legend in the British Army for bombastic heroism of a kind which subsequently contributed to the creation of Evelyn Waugh's Brigadier Ben Ritchie-Hook. Here he makes an early appearance as a young officer serving as ADC to the C-in-C in South Africa, Sir Henry Hildyard, soon after the end of the Boer War.

LADY HILDYARD was a most charming hostess but an inveterate gambler, and South Africa with its fortunes won and lost overnight was a dangerous centre for the unstable. One day she came to me in great distress. She had gambled and lost an enormous sum, practically all Sir Henry's capital, and what should she do? I advised her to confess at once. All Sir Henry said was: 'Never mind, my dear, I might have done much worse myself.'

I was always a reluctant card player, but bridge was considered as an essential part of an A.D.C.'s equipment. One night Lady Hildyard, who was my partner, had committed what I considered to be several enormities and as she got up to leave the room at the end of our game I shook my fist after her retreating back. Sir Henry entered the room at that unfortunate moment, and I thought I was for home. Instead, he turned to Major Winwood the military secretary and said: 'De Wiart's a very patient man, isn't he?'

Adrian Carton de Wiart

265.

The Royal Military College at Sandhurst was the scene of a number of cadet mutinies in the nineteenth century. Here, in old age, a participant recounts the story of that of 1902, which followed disciplinary action against the entire body of cadets for a series of mysterious fires at the College.

THE cadets had a burning sense of grievance when all leave was stopped on account of something they knew nothing about; so, about half-past nine, after mess, they collected on the Main Entrance steps of the College and they cheered Kruger, Smuts, De Wet and every Boer General they could think of, and there were hoots about 'Bobs' (Field-Marshal Earl Roberts) and the War Office.

While this was going on some of the cadets suggested that we should go to the Fête, which was on in Camberley. In the meantime some of the cadets started to roll the guns and the roller down into the lake. As soon as the Fête was suggested, the body of cadets moved en masse down the drive of the College to the Camberley Gate. Every lamp post we could see was bent double; everything that was breakable was broken; and everything that was movable was thrown into the lake.

The gate-keeper wisely went into his house and left the gate open, and the body of cadets trooped into Camberley singing the well-known songs of the Sandhurst of that day. One small body of cadets went off to the Governor's House, where he was having a dinner party, and serenaded him with similar Sandhurst songs—not of the choicest as you may imagine.

When we got to the Fête ground, the gate-keeper showed great pleasure in seeing us and thought we had been allowed to come and were going to pay to go in. Instead of that, with one wild rush, we made for the gates; over went the money tables, down went the money collectors, and in rushed a number of cadets, how many I don't know, but I was amongst them because I was knocked down in the rush and got through on my hands and knees. Mind you, we were all in red mess kit.

It was a dry night. When we were in the Fair, some of us got on the roundabouts, some on the swings, and the Fair authorities thought it was a bit risky to stop the roundabouts in case we broke them up.

Then the rumour came that they had sent a patrol of officers and senior corporals to round us up; so we asked them to stop the merry-go-round and we all got off and tried to get out of the Fête ground. But we found the gates closed, so we wandered round until we found a barbed-wire fence and crawled over it into the Staff College grounds, from where we got into the RMC. When we got back we found the orderly on duty at the company and he took our names.

The Commandant was perfectly right; the whole disturbance was due to the stoppage of leave, which was strongly resented. It was the most unjust punishment because we knew nothing about who lit the fires . . . whether it was a company officer, a servant or a cadet, or someone from outside. And if the Brass Hats hadn't interfered, all this disturbance would never have happened.

The next morning there were headlines in the Press of mutiny at Sandhurst and of how the cadets had broken out of bounds and gone off to the Fête, and rumours went round the College that we were all going to be rusticated.

However everything quietened down and leave was re-opened. Two days after, however, the fifth fire occurred; and that put the lid on it. A telegram came, I understand from the War Office, to say that all the cadets of 'C' Company were to be rusticated if they could not prove an alibi, and twenty-nine cadets, of whom I was one, were for it.

We were had up by the Adjutant in the lecture hall, all twenty-nine of us together, and told that we were all to be rusticated and had to leave the College next morning. We thought this very unfair but we all went off and packed and were driven, with our luggage, to Camberley station in four-wheeler cabs amidst the cheers of the College. Every window had a cadet cheering. We then proceeded home.

At my home in Eastbourne was a friend of mine, who was in my room in 'C' Company, called Cavendish, and his father had been a Conservative Agent and knew Winston Churchill; so he suggested that his boy and I should go up to London and see Churchill. Churchill was a back bench MP and he was against the Government as far as I remember . . . he was a Liberal or something. In the meanwhile a number of letters had appeared in *The Times* and questions had been asked in the House.

We went up to London and we saw Churchill at his house. Cavendish's father was present at the interview; he brought us in and introduced us. The idea was that Churchill was going to ask a question or move a motion in the House about the whole matter.

I am not sure whether he ever did ask his question or what he did do. But a few days later we got a communication from the War Office to say that the Commander-in-Chief, Bobs, wanted to interview us personally at the War Office . . . all twenty-nine of us. On a certain day . . . we arrived there . . . Cavendish and I . . . and found twenty-six others. In the meantime we had been asked by the War Office to sign an affidavit that we knew nothing about the fires.

We were shown into Bobs' room, each one individually. He shook hands with me, sat me down in an arm chair and checked my name. He then asked if I was any relation of Colonel Hadow's of the 15th Sikhs. I said, 'Yes, I'm his son.'

'Oh indeed,' he said, 'I remember him in Kabul and Kandahar in '79. He was wounded wasn't he, in the Tirah Show?' And I said, 'yes'.

So he said, 'How is he? Remember me to him.'

And I told him, 'Oh, a bit lame, but otherwise all right.'

Well, we chatted for a bit and then at the end of about five minutes he said to me, 'Oh, by the way, do you know anything about these fires . . . who did it . . . or who was likely to have done it? And if you know anything perhaps you would tell me in confidence.'

But I told him that I knew nothing about it and had no more idea than he had who had started them. With that he thanked me and I got up and shook hands with him and went out.

Bobs was very spry and alert and didn't look anything like his age. He had just returned from South Africa. At first, I was naturally rather afraid of him but my father had told me that I should find him a pleasant and affable man—which I did . . . not at all the fierce sort of fellow one might picture as Commander-in-Chief. Shortly after I got a letter from the War Office saying that as the Commander-in-Chief had interviewed me personally and satisfied himself that I knew nothing about the fires and couldn't help in any way, that I was completely exonerated from all blame; I could return to Sandhurst at the beginning of the next term and count my exams of the term before as passed.

Major H. R. Hadow

266.

Private Richards recalls a comrade of the Royal Welch Fusiliers driven to desperate measures to gain a discharge.

He had joined the Army in a fit of despair over the young lady with whom he had been walking out, who had chucked him and taken up with a soldier. It was Archie's idea to be sent to the South African War and win a posthumous V.C., so that she would be sorry for the manner in which she had jilted him. But after he had been in the Army for a time he forgot his broken heart, and the South African War ended, and he wanted to return to civil life.

It was while we were in Jersey that Archie began to 'work his ticket', as it was called. An Adjutant's Parade was the first occasion. His company, which was the leading company on the Square, had already fallen in, the roll had been called and the orderly-sergeant had reported Archie absent, when he came strolling out of his room, trailing his rifle behind him, with a far-away look in his eyes. He fell in on the left of his company, just as the company officer began to inspect it. The Adjutant, who spotted him, rubbed his eyes in amazement and certainly the way Archie was dressed would have made a cat laugh. On his red jacket he had stitched a dozen lids of Day and Martin's Soldier's Friend, together with metal-polish tins, all of them highly polished. Tied to the back of his braces and hanging over his backside was a frying-pan. The Adjutant was too astonished to say a word until Archie was about to be marched to the Guard-room under escort. Then he roared: 'Bring that damned lunatic in front of me.' When questioned as to why he had appeared on parade improperly dressed, Archie assured the Adjutant that he was properly dressed. He said that he was entitled to the decorations and medals he wore on his breast, having won them during the years he had served with the Emperor of Abyssinia's army. He said that the large decoration he wore on his backside was the most coveted honour in Abyssinia; when the Emperor decorated him with it he had also promoted him to full general. He said that the generals and the princes became jealous, and if he hadn't left the country when he did he would have been dead meat in a very short space of time. He said that when he arrived back in England the only proof that he had that he had been full general in the Abyssinian army was his decorations, which he was now wearing and which he was very proud of. The Adjutant ordered the escort to take him to hospital, but after he had been there a week the medical officer came to the conclusion that he was perfectly sane, and Archie was sent back to the Fort under escort. For making a laughing-stock of the King's uniform and pretending he was balmy he was lucky enough to get the light sentence of fourteen days' cells.

He still acted strangely after he came out of the cells. He was determined to leave the Army by some means or other and, like other men who tried to work their tickets, he did not have the necessary twenty-one pounds to buy himself out. He would have deserted but he knew that if he went back to his relatives he would soon be arrested as a deserter, which would mean six months' imprisonment, probably without a discharge at the end to console him for his hardships. He decided to stick to his original plan of action. In India his manner became stranger than ever. He used to have long interesting conversations with himself, mostly about love or Abyssinia, and was twice sent to hospital for observation. He was not punished any more, because the doctors were undecided as to whether he had lost his mental balance or not. A lot of us believed that he was really up the loop from having played at it

so long. On our march back to Meerut we stayed one day at a place
where there was a magnificent temple on the banks of a large deep
lake. That afternoon quite a number of us were enjoying a swim in the
lake and Archie, who could not swim a stroke, sat on the edge of the
lake watching us. Some time later, when most of us had left the water
and were just beginning to dress, I heard a man exclaim: 'By God, that
man must be an expert, otherwise he wouldn't dive in from as high as
that!' I looked around and was surprised to see Archie stripped and
standing on the top of a high pillar of stone on the edge of the lake. I
shouted to him not to be a fool, but at that moment he made a wonderful dive, going in so straight and making so little of a splash that the
men who did not know him very well uttered a cry of amazement and
said: 'That fellow Archie must have been a professional high-diver in
civil life!' But the rest of us, who knew him better, dived in and fished
him out half-drowned. This was a further escapade to be reported to
the doctor who was attached to the Battalion on the march.

Archie's final stunt was a masterpiece. The Divisional Sports were
being held in a few weeks' time and he entered for every running event
from the hundred yards to the mile. He refused to be assisted in his
training, which he did, so he said, about half an hour before twilight
every evening. Late on Sunday evening, on the day before the Sports
were to be held, Archie left the tent, saying that he was going out for a
final spin on his secret training-ground. We who knew him were wondering what new scheme he had evolved for working his ticket. We had
not followed him before when he was going out for his spins, but on
the evening we thought we would. We kept about one hundred yards
behind him. He stuck to the main road after leaving the Camp until he
was about twenty yards from the entrance to the Protestant Church.
There we were surprised to see him cut across country and disappear
among some trees and high tropical plants at the back of the church.

The shadows of twilight were falling as we arrived at the entrance to
the church, where all the best society of Meerut attended evensong.
After a little discussion we decided to enter the grounds, and get
among the trees at the back to see what Archie was up to. But just as
we opened the gate the congregation began to file out and collect in
little groups here and there, as the custom is all over the civilized
world, gossiping together about fashions or the sermon. Suddenly a
man with a pair of running pumps on his feet but otherwise as naked as
the day he was born jumped out from behind the plants and began
running round and round the church with the speed of a hare. It was

Archie. Some of the ladies screamed, others did their best to close
their eyes. I expect that the full-blooded ones who had old and decrepit husbands closed only one eye and gazed with the other in rapturous
admiration at this nude athlete. Archie was physically handsome in
feature and limb and old Mother Nature had been kind to him in many
ways. For a few moments the ladies' esquires were too astonished to do
anything, and it was the same with us. He had completed two laps and
was halfway around the church on a third one before we burst into the
grounds, shouting that the man was a lunatic. We caught him and
rushed him behind the plants out of sight. The three of us now thought
that he was really up the loop. He did not seem to realize that he had
done anything out of the ordinary and said: 'Well, boys, do you think
any man has a ghost of a chance against me tomorrow? You'll see, I'll
cake-walk every event I have entered for.'

An officer of another regiment, who had been in church, ordered us
to conduct him to hospital and in less than a fortnight he was on his
way down to Kalabar under escort to be interned in an asylum there.
Later he was transferred to a military asylum at home. His last words
to the escort were: 'Well, so long, boys. I'll be thinking of you when I'm
back in Blighty. I am supposed to be balmy, and so I was to join the
Army. But, one thing, I'm not half so balmy, and never have been, as
those balmy bastards who still have to do six or seven years in this
God-damned country. You'll be doing me a favour if you convey to
them my deepest, heartfelt sympathies.' Within twelve months we had
news that he had been discharged from the asylum and from the Army,
and that he had an excellent job in his home town and was happily
married to a young lady who, he said, was worth a hundred of the one
for whose sake he had behaved in such a rash manner.

                                                        Frank Richards

267.

IN the murky pre-1914 days, the regiment [4th Prince of Wales' Own
Gurkha Rifles] had an officer whose chief pride was his reputation as a
lady's man. He never failed to attend the regimental ordeal known as
the Tuesday Bunfight. Every Tuesday the ladies of the station, perhaps five or six in number, were invited to the mess for tea, cakes, and
tennis. Every available officer had to be present to entertain them—all
except one, a man who could hardly be induced to speak at all to any

woman, and never spoke to one politely. This man had succeeded, through his known misogyny and addiction to work, in getting permanent permission to absent himself from the Tuesday Bunfights. What few people ever knew—and none at the time—was that every Tuesday, as soon as the ladykiller left for the Bunfight, the misogynist pedalled furiously down the steep road to the former's Indian mistress, and returned late at night with ardour quelled but misogyny unabated.

John Masters

268.

Having failed the Sandhurst entrance exam, to his profound dismay Osbert Sitwell found that family connections had secured him a Yeomanry commission, with an attachment to a Hussar regiment stationed at Aldershot. Here, he spent a miserable spring and summer in 1912.

FROM time to time I still tried to reach London. Though only thirty-six miles away, the capital seemed infinitely distant. There were many things there this spring and summer that I wanted to see; among them, the second Post-Impressionist Exhibition and a small show of drawings and paintings by Augustus John; there were operas to hear, and concerts. I wanted, also, to keep in touch with the few friends I possessed, and from whom my incarceration at Aldershot cut me off no less effectually than a decree of banishment to Siberia. In June, therefore, I asked for the two or three days to which I had become entitled. . . . But when the Commanding Officer enquired where I wished to spend it, and received the reply '*London*', I could see the look of genuine consternation and amazement that passed over his face. 'London!' he plainly said to himself. 'Imagine wishing to leave Aldershot, earthly paradise that it is, for so mean a city!'

'But what can you do there; what can you want to do? There's nothing to do', he reiterated in a tortured voice, and with a soldier's simple vocabulary. When he had recovered sufficiently from the shock, he refused permission. But I think his story of 'the Young Officer who wanted to go to *London*!' went the rounds: for Generals, when they visited us, surveyed me carefully, as if I were a dangerous wild beast, and the senior regimental officers seemed to regard me with increased distaste. 'What can be the state of mind', their eyes clearly goggled the message, 'of a young man who wishes to leave Aldershot to spend a few days in London!' *London*! Why, you could not even kill anything there!

(It was tantalizing, too, to see all those living creatures behind their bars, walking, pacing, climbing, swinging about in the Zoological Gardens, and not be able to get at them, not be able to fire a single shot!) No huntin': no shootin': no polo, even. . . . Of course, there was always Tattersall's, that they admitted, but it need not occupy more than a single afternoon. You could be back in the dear old Mess in time for dinner.

Osbert Sitwell

269.

By the summer of 1913, Osbert Sitwell had relinquished his Yeomanry commission and joined the Grenadier Guards to appease his father's wishes. He still, however, showed few of the instincts of a natural soldier.

. . . one day while I was Ensign on King's Guard at St James's Palace, the Captain of it—an awe-inspiring individual, with a heavy, but regular profile, and moustachios left over from the drawing-rooms of George du Maurier—enquired, after an immense effort that resembled the wheezing of an old clock about to strike, but was none the less born of a kindly intention to try to lessen the tedium of long hours spent in the red-papered guard-room, 'Do you like horses?', and I replied, 'No, but I like giraffes—they have such a beautiful line', he took the answer unexpectedly well, and even attempted to smile. . . . Then, on another occasion this spring, it had been my turn to take the Early Parade at 6 a.m. After breakfast, the Adjutant sent for me to the Orderly Room. I obeyed the intimidating summons. I entered, and saluted the great man. He said, looking up,

'Mr Sitwell, it is reported to me that you were late this morning for Early Parade.'

I expressed dissent.

On this, he enquired, 'Were the men on parade when you arrived?'

I replied, 'I didn't take any notice, sir. I did not look.'

I can see now that my answer, which was quite genuine and unaffected, must have been disconcerting to a mind of such excellent military punctuality and precision.

Osbert Sitwell

270.

On the morning of 1 August 1914, the German ambassador in London, Prince Lich-nowsky, telegraphed Kaiser Wilhelm II to declare his belief that if Germany did not attack France, Britain would agree to remain neutral, and to keep France neutral, in a Russo-German war.

THE Kaiser clutched at Lichnowsky's passport to a one-front war. Minutes counted. Already mobilization was rolling inexorably toward the French frontier. The first hostile act, seizure of a railway junction in Luxembourg, whose neutrality the five Great Powers, including Germany, had guaranteed, was scheduled within an hour. It must be stopped, stopped at once. But how? Where was Moltke? Moltke had left the palace. An aide was sent off, with siren screaming, to intercept him. He was brought back.

The Kaiser was himself again, the All-Highest, the War Lord, blazing with a new idea, planning, proposing, disposing. He read Moltke the telegram and said in triumph: 'Now we can go to war against Russia only. We simply march the whole of our Army to the East!'

Aghast at the thought of his marvellous machinery of mobilization wrenched into reverse, Moltke refused point-blank. For the past ten years, first as assistant to Schlieffen, then as his successor, Moltke's job had been planning for this day, The Day, *Der Tag*, for which all Germany's energies were gathered, on which the march to final mastery of Europe would begin. It weighed upon him with an oppressive, almost unbearable responsibility.

Tall, heavy, bald, and sixty-six years old, Moltke habitually wore an expression of profound distress which led the Kaiser to call him *der traurige Julius* (or what might be rendered 'Gloomy Gus'; in fact, his name was Helmuth). Poor health, for which he took an annual cure at Carlsbad, and the shadow of a great uncle were perhaps cause for gloom. From his window in the red brick General Staff building on the Königplatz where he lived as well as worked, he looked out every day on the equestrian statue of his namesake, the hero of 1870 and, together with Bismarck, the architect of the German Empire. The nephew was a poor horseman with a habit of falling off on staff rides and, worse, a follower of Christian Science with a side interest in anthroposophism and other cults. For this unbecoming weakness in a Prussian officer he was considered 'soft'; what is more, he painted, played the cello, carried Goethe's *Faust* in his pocket, and had begun a translation of Maeterlinck's *Pelléas et Mélisande*.

Introspective and a doubter by nature, he had said to the Kaiser upon his appointment in 1906: 'I do not know how I shall get on in the event of a campaign. I am very critical of myself.' Yet he was neither personally nor politically timid. In 1911, disgusted by Germany's retreat in the Agadir crisis, he wrote to Conrad von Hotzendorff that if things got worse he would resign, propose to disband the army and 'place ourselves under the protection of Japan; then we can make money undisturbed and turn into imbeciles'. He did not hesitate to talk back to the Kaiser, but told him 'quite brutally' in 1900 that his Peking expedition was a 'crazy adventure', and when offered the appointment as Chief of Staff, asked the Kaiser if he expected 'to win the big prize twice in the same lottery'—a thought that had certainly influenced William's choice. He refused to take the post unless the Kaiser stopped his habit of winning all the war games which was making nonsense of manœuvres. Surprisingly, the Kaiser meekly obeyed.

Now, on the climactic night of August 1, Moltke was in no mood for any more of the Kaiser's meddling with serious military matters, or with meddling of any kind with the fixed arrangements. To turn around the deployment of a million men from west to east at the very moment of departure would have taken a more iron nerve than Moltke disposed of. He saw a vision of the deployment crumbling apart in confusion, supplies here, soldiers there, ammunition lost in the middle, companies without officers, divisions without staffs, and those 11,000 trains, each exquisitely scheduled to click over specified tracks at specified intervals of ten minutes, tangled in a grotesque ruin of the most perfectly planned military movement in history.

'Your Majesty,' Moltke said to him now, 'it cannot be done. The deployment of millions cannot be improvised. If Your Majesty insists on leading the whole army to the East it will not be an army ready for battle but a disorganized mob of armed men with no arrangements for supply. Those arrangements took a whole year of intricate labour to complete'—and Moltke closed upon that rigid phrase, the basis for every major German mistake, the phrase that launched the invasion of Belgium and the submarine war against the United States, the inevitable phrase when military plans dictate policy—'and once settled, it cannot be altered'.

In fact it could have been altered. The German General Staff, though committed since 1905 to a plan of attack upon France first, had in their files, revised each year until 1913, an alternative plan against Russia with all the trains running eastward.

'Build no more fortresses, build railways', ordered the elder Moltke who had laid out his strategy on a railway map and bequeathed the dogma that railways are the key to war. In Germany the railway system was under military control with a staff officer assigned to every line; no track could be laid or changed without permission of the General Staff. Annual mobilization war games kept railway officials in constant practice and tested their ability to improvise and divert traffic by telegrams reporting lines cut and bridges destroyed. The best brains produced by the War College, it was said, went into the railway section and ended up in lunatic asylums. . . .

On the night of August 1, Moltke, clinging to the fixed plan, lacked the necessary nerve. 'Your uncle would have given me a different answer', the Kaiser said to him bitterly.

Barbara Tuchman

271.

August 1914.

I ARRIVED in London at six in the morning, and reported to the Reserve Battalion, already in course of formation. In the afternoon I went to say good-bye to many friends, who, as it happened, were never to return to England. Two or three of the most confident I heard instructing their servants to pack their evening-clothes, since they would need them in a week or two in Berlin. . . . Later, I called on my Grandmother Londesborough, now grown a very old lady. She was, as I have explained earlier, a great-niece of Wellington's, and perhaps some lingering anti-Napoleonic tradition inspired her parting remark to me, 'It's not the Germans but the French I'm frightened of.' Still, even then, it was not certain that war was coming. But in the evening, I went to the Mall, and waited. If the Lord Mayor's Coach arrived, it meant war, and presently, after dusk, sure enough it came trundling along through the Admiralty Arch toward the Palace. As it entered the gates I heard the great crowd roar for its own death. It cheered and cried and howled. . . . How many of those voices could have been heard in two years' time?

War hysteria quickly asserted itself. Haldane, the most efficient War Minister of the age, was chivvied out of the War Office, and Lord Kitchener, god of the hour, but a deity who had grown stiff in the joints, sat in his chair, turning a stern face to the world. Recruiting songs vied with genuine patriotic appeals. In the music-halls, Miss

Phyllis Dare was singing, 'Oh, we don't want to lose you, but we think you ought to go.' Soon whole mattresses of white feathers were coming out, and being given away; for in 1914 the reactions were simpler, quicker and more direct than in 1939. Fortune-tellers reaped a rich harvest, and *Old Moore's Almanack* reached a new sales-level. By September, the story of the Russian armies in England had begun, and I find Sacheverell, who wrote to me regularly from Renishaw every day, and who was unusually wise and cautious for his sixteen years, announcing the great news. 'They saw the Russians pass through the station here last night', he wrote, 'and Miss Vasalt telephoned to Mother this afternoon and said trains in great number had passed through Grantham Station all day with the blinds down. So there must, I think, be some truth in it, don't you?'

Osbert Sitwell

272.

One of the first cavalry encounters of the war between a patrol of Russian hussars and a German picket on the eastern front.

SUDDENLY there was a clatter of hooves, and seven horsemen trotted up. Lieutenant Stepanov had started at the same time as Genishta's patrol, but they had had a long distance to cover, and as they had had to reconnoitre the woods, it had taken them much longer. Genishta rode up to Stepanov.

'Stepa, let's have a go at them!' he said.

Now they could clearly see the advancing Germans. Sixteen to eighteen riders were approaching the village in a deployed formation, shooting their carbines as they rode. The distance was about 600 yards; the Russian troopers tensed as they watched their quarry draw near.

Because of the buildings it was impossible to align the men; they clustered in small groups behind houses and sheds. Lieutenant Genishta turned to give a command, but Stepanov anticipated him. Spurring his horse and yelling at the top of his voice, he dashed forward. Pell mell through the narrow alleys the Horse Grenadiers rushed forward shouting 'Hurrah!'

Out in the open a semblance of a line was formed, some of the men galloping with lances couched, others with raised swords. Genishta and Stepanov, both good horsemen and well mounted, had drawn ahead, Stepanov leading.

The German patrol stopped, their leader gave a command, and wheeling about they galloped off in good order. The German lieutenant, however, restrained his horse and stood for a moment or two facing the oncoming Russians. Then he too wheeled and followed his men.

Now the three Russian officers were galloping abreast—Genishta on the right, Stepanov in the middle and Egerstrom on the left. Several lengths behind came their men. Thus they galloped for about a mile. The Germans came to a wide ditch with rather boggy sides. Everyone made it over except the lieutenant. His horse refused suddenly, sinking hock-deep in mud. Lieutenant von Lütken was catapulted over its head and he landed on the other side of the ditch. He jumped quickly to his feet and looked back. His men were galloping away. No one turned back to help him. Undeterred, he drew his revolver and stood alone facing the enemy.

The first to reach the ditch was Lieutenant Stepanov who headed directly at the German standing on the other side. As the horse rose for the jump, von Lütken fired. The bullet hit Stepanov's horse in the head, killing it outright. It crashed into the ditch, sending its rider flying. Stepanov fell at von Lütken's feet, and lost his sword. The German fired and missed.

At this moment Lieutenant Genishta jumped the ditch somewhat to the right. Von Lütken wheeled left and fired, but Genishta galloped right by, too far to reach him with his sword. Stepanov had jumped up and seized the German; they fell struggling to the ground. Von Lütken tried to use his revolver, but Stepanov pinned his arm to the ground. In desperation von Lütken bit Stepanov's finger to the bone.

Several Horse Grenadiers had, in the meanwhile, jumped the ditch. One of the troopers, Semikopenko, hurled himself down from his horse and while still in the air, slashed at the German with his sword. The blow was accurate and deadly: it severed the wrist holding the revolver. Another trooper thrust his lance into the brave von Lütken, killing him. . . .

Knowing the German squadrons to be close at hand, Genishta stopped the pursuit. Scarlet faces dripping with sweat, grey coats torn and spattered with blood, blood dripping too from sword blades and lance heads, the Horse Grenadiers rode in. Someone brought back the dead German lieutenant's dispatch case. Genishta opened it. Inside were two papers. One was the report to his regiment. It read: 'Shumsk occupied by Russian cavalry patrols.' The other was a letter to his parents, written, addressed, but never sent.

That evening Lieutenant Genishta sat down and wrote a letter to the family of the late Lieutenant von Lütken. He told them about their son's brave death and said how sorry he was. He sent the letter c/o the Red Cross.

Several years passed; the war ended—for the Germans in defeat, for the Russians in revolution, chaos, and years of bloody civil war.

The year 1924 found the ex-cavalry officer Genishta an exile in Paris. Living was hard, jobs were scarce and it was difficult to start a new life. The former Guards officer was now eking out an existence driving a taxi cab. One evening, returning tired to his dimly lit garret, he found a letter postmarked Germany. It read:

Dear Lieutenant Genishta:

Please forgive this tardy (10 years) answer, but only now have we learned quite by accident of your whereabouts. My parents, now deceased, and I were deeply touched by your letter describing my brother's death; we always wanted to thank you for your kind words and consideration. Your letter hangs framed below the portrait of my late brother. . . .

Enclosed in the letter was a photograph of a large castle somewhere in Germany, the residence of the von Lütken family.

A long correspondence followed between Genishta and von Lütken's sister. Knowing how difficult life had become for the former cavalry officer, the German lady invited him to come and stay with her family. Poor but proud, the Russian officer thanked her and refused.

Alexis Wrangel

273.

The BEF boards its ships for France, August 1914, described by a staff officer.

I REMEMBER when the Oxfordshire Hussars embarked, they brought with them a vast quantity of kit: tin uniform boxes, suitcases and cabin trunks, as if they were on their way round the world. Someone questioned the loading of this baggage, whereupon a red-faced Major burst into my office in a towering rage: 'This is simply damnable!' he shouted. 'Winston said we could take 'em, and now one of your prize B.F.s says we can't. . . . ' 'All right! All right!' I cut him short. 'What is the trouble about?' And having ascertained what the First Lord of the

Admiralty had sanctioned, I telephoned down to the A.E.S.O. in charge to load the officers' trousseaux—a word which did not seem to please my furious friend. All were loaded, and, I believe, a week later were unpacked by German hands.

No sooner had he left the room than in burst a Hussar Captain. He also was boiling over with anger. He stuttered and had a high-pitched voice: 'Do you expect that *I* am going to get on *that* old barge?' (the *Archimedes*, a cattle-ship, later on torpedoed). 'Why,' he continued, 'there is no notepaper on board.' 'Yes,' I replied, 'that is so; for, since the outbreak of war, Argentine bullocks have been considerate enough to do without it. May I, however, give you a tip—well, they have dispensed with toilet paper also.'

A strange incident was one in which Major Maclean played the part of fairy godmother. It happened on the day upon which the Beaulieu Division marched in. As was often the case, a howling crowd of friends and relatives collected outside the dock gates. An elderly woman was demanding to be let in, and by her side was standing a girl literally dripping tears. Maclean, always good-natured, allowed the two women to enter, and then discovered that the girl was expecting a baby, and that the culprit, a Sergeant, was somewhere in the crowded docks. Pacifying her, Maclean said: 'You leave it to me: it will be all right,' and off he went. Three-quarters of an hour later he came back with the Sergeant: how he found him remains a mystery, for there must have been some twelve to fifteen thousand troops embarking or embarked. Then he took the Sergeant and the girl into the door-keeper's hutch, which stands just inside the gates, and making them sign some document which he hastily concocted, he married them in Scottish fashion. When later on someone chipped him and said: 'Well, that's not a legal marriage', he replied: 'No—but now it is a very good case for breach of promise.' And I am inclined to think that he was right.

J. F. C. Fuller

274.

The 17 August meeting between Sir John French, C.-in-C. of the British Expeditionary Force, and General Lanrezac, commanding the French Fifth Army on his flank, as described by the British liaison officer.

SIR JOHN stepped out of his car looking very spick and span. He was a good deal shorter than General Lanrezac, who came out to greet him. The two men stood for a moment in strong contrast to each other, Lanrezac large, swarthy, revealing his creole origin (he was born in Guadeloupe), Sir John ruddy-faced, his white moustache drooping over the corners of his mouth. His clear penetrating blue eyes, his very upright bearing and quick movements, made him infinitely the more attractive personality, and gave him the appearance of being by far the more soldierly of the two. You had only to look at him to see that he was a brave, determined man.

At that time I did not know him, but later it fell to my lot to see him often, and at times when he was being as highly tried as any individual could be. I learnt to love and to admire the man who never lost his head, and on whom danger had the effect it has on the wild boar: he would become morose, furious for a time, harsh, but he would face up and never shirk. He knew only one way of dealing with a difficulty, and that was to tackle it. When everything seemed to crumble about him he stood his ground undismayed.

I was told a story of him, I think by General Foch, of how during the bad days at Ypres he once arrived at the latter's head-quarters and said: 'I have no more reserves. The only men I have left are the sentries at my gates. I will take them with me to where the line is broken, and the last of the English will be killed fighting.'

If he had once lost confidence in a man, justly or unjustly, that man could do no right in his eyes. He was as bad an enemy as he was a good friend, and that is saying a great deal. He was deeply attached to the French nation, and after the War, being unable to live in his place in Ireland, which had been sacked, he lived in France from choice. But he judged both French and British by the same standards, and when, at the time of Mons, he came to the conclusion that General Lanrezac was not playing the game with him, it was finished. Once he had lost confidence in the Commander of the Fifth Army he ignored him and acted as if he and his Army did not exist.

Today all was still well.

The two men walked into General Lanrezac's sanctum together, the one short, brisk, taking long strides out of proportion to his size, the other big, bulky, heavy, moving with short steps as if his body were too heavy for his legs. . . .

. . . We knew that Lanrezac spoke no English, and Sir John, though he understood a little French, at that time could hardly speak it at all. . . .

. . . Sir John, stepping up to a map in the 3me Bureau, took out his glasses, located a place with his finger, and said to Lanrezac: 'Mon Général, est-ce-que—'. His French then gave out, and turning to one of his staff, he asked: 'How do you say "to cross the river" in French?' He was told, and proceeded: 'Est-ce-que les Allemands vont traverser la Meuse à—à—.' Then he fumbled over the pronunciation of the name. 'Huy' was the place, unfortunately one of the most difficult words imaginable to pronounce, the 'u' having practically to be whistled. It was quite beyond Sir John. 'Hoy', he said at last, triumphantly. 'What does he say? What does he say?' exclaimed Lanrezac. Somebody explained that the Marshal wanted to know whether in his opinion the Germans were going to cross the river at Huy? Lanrezac shrugged his shoulders impatiently. 'Tell the Marshal', he said curtly, 'that in my opinion the Germans have merely gone to the Meuse to fish.' This story gives some idea of Lanrezac's mentality and manners. Evidently his conversation with Sir John had put him out of temper, and he did not hesitate to show it by being deliberately rude. . . .

The staffs of both armies were not slow to realize that the two men had not taken to each other. General Lanrezac did not disguise from his entourage his feelings toward Sir John, and I learnt a few days later at Le Cateau that Sir John had not liked Lanrezac.

The interview had resulted in a complete fiasco.

Sir Edward Spears

275.

A moment in the retreat from Mons recalled by a British medical officer.

27th Aug. As we turned into the Grande Place at St Quentin on that late August afternoon not a single German was to be seen. The whole square was thronged with British infantrymen standing in groups or wandering about in an aimless fashion, most of them without either packs or rifles. Scores had gone to sleep sitting on the pavement, their backs against the fronts of the shops. Many, exhausted, lay at full length on the pavement. Some few, obviously intoxicated, wandered about firing in the air at real or imaginary German aeroplanes. The great majority were not only without their arms but had apparently either lost or thrown away their belts, water-bottles and other equipment.

There must have been several hundred men in the square, and more in the side streets; yet apparently they were without officers—anyway, no officers were to be seen. On the road down to the station we found Major Tom Bridges with part of his squadron and a few Lancers, horse-gunners and other stragglers who had attached themselves to his command. We followed him down to the station. Apparently some hours before our arrival the last train that was to leave St Quentin— Paris-wards—for several years, had steamed out, carrying with it most of the British General Staff. A mob of disorganized soldiery had collected at the station, and I was told some had booed and cheered ironically these senior Staff officers as the Staff train steamed out. Certainly many of these infantrymen appeared to be in a queer, rather truculent, mood. Bridges, who had sized up the situation, harangued this disorganized mob that only a few hours before had represented at least two famous regiments of the 4th Division.

Dismounted and standing far back in the crowd I could not hear what he said, but his words of encouragement and exhortation were received with sullen disapproval and murmurs by the bulk of those around him. One man shouted out: 'Our old man (his Colonel) has surrendered to the Germans, and we'll stick to him. We don't want any bloody cavalry interfering!' and he pointed his rifle at Bridges. I failed at first to understand how all these English soldiers could have surrendered to the Germans whom we had left several miles outside the city. But I was tired and hungry and I didn't much care what happened. Losing interest in what was taking place at the station I rode back up to the Grande Place, hoping I should find some food and a sofa on which I could lie down. As I rode up from the station many of the men in the street stared at me disdainfully, their arms folded; scarcely one saluted—I was for them only 'one of the bloody interfering cavalry officers'.

When I awoke it was dusk, and two or three officers of the 4th Dragoon Guards were in the square with Bridges. Apparently, Bridges was having an interview with some official—I believe, the Mayor of St Quentin—urging him to provide horses and carts to take those of our men who were too sore-footed to be able to march out of town. I walked over to listen. As far as I could understand, the official—Mayor or whoever he was—was very indignant; he kept saying:

'You understand, m'sieur le Majeur, it is now too late. These men have surrendered to the Germans.'

'How? The Germans are not here!'

'Their colonel and officers have signed a paper giving me the numbers of the men of each regiment and the names of the officers who are prepared to surrender, and I have sent a copy of this out under a white flag to the Commander of the approaching German Army!'

'But you have no business, m'sieur, as a loyal Frenchman, to assist allied troops to surrender!'

'What else?' urged the Mayor. 'Consider, m'sieur le Majeur, the alternatives. The German Army is at Gricourt? Very well, I, representing the inhabitants of St Quentin, who do not want our beautiful town unnecessarily destroyed by shell-fire because it happens to be full of English troops, have said to your colonels, and your men: "Will you please go out and fight the German Army *outside* St Quentin", but your men they say: "No! We cannot fight! We have lost nearly all our officers, our Staff have gone away by train, we do not know where to. Also, we have no artillery, most of us have neither rifles nor ammunition, and we are all so very tired!" Then, m'sieur le Majeur, I say to them: "Then please if you will not fight will you please *go right away*, and presently the Germans will enter St Quentin peacefully; so the inhabitants will be glad to be tranquil, and not killed, and all our good shops not burned." But they reply to me: "No, we cannot go away! We are terribly, terribly tired. We have had no proper food nor rest for many days, and yesterday we fought a great battle. We have not got any maps, and we do not even know where to go to. So we will stay in St Quentin and have a little rest!" Then I say to them: "Since you will neither fight nor go away, then please you must surrender." So I send out a list of those who surrender to the German Commander, and now all is properly arranged!'

Arranged! Yet the logic of this argument was irresistible—but for one point, which Bridges had quickly seized upon. The men *could* be got away if every horse and cart in St Quentin was collected for those men too tired to march; his cavalrymen would escort them out of the town. So the shops and streets would be cleared of tired and drunken men, and there would be no more firing off of rifles; but there was to be no more of this wine, only tea or coffee and bread.

So eventually it was arranged; Bridges had saved the situation which though bad was understandable. Disorganized stragglers had arrived by the hundred, many out of sheer fatigue having thrown away their packs and rifles. They had tramped beneath the blazing August sun with empty stomachs, dispirited and utterly weary; many had received quantities of wine from kindly French peasants to revive them in those dusty lanes. Literally, in many cases their bellies were full of wine and their boots half full of blood; that I saw myself. The English soldier's feet like his head, but unlike his heart, are not his strong point. . . .

Bridges asked me to count the men who were collecting in the Square and get them into fours. I counted one hundred and ten fours—that is to say four hundred and forty men. Then he asked me to do something else, I forget what it was. A few men had whistles and Jew's harps, perhaps they had them in their haversacks as soldiers often do, and they formed a sort of band. We persuaded one of the colonels to march in front of his men. My recollection is that he looked very pale, entirely dazed, had no Sam Browne belt, and leant heavily on his stick, apparently so exhausted with fatigue and the heat that he could scarcely have known what he was doing. Some of his men called to him encouraging words, affectionate and familiar, but not meant insolently—such as: 'Buck up, sir! Cheer up, Daddy! Now we shan't be long! We are all going back to "Hang-le-Tear"!'

Actually I saw him saluting one of his own corporals who did not even look surprised. What with fatigue, heat, drink and the demoralization of defeat, many hardly knew what they were doing. I was so tired myself that I went to sleep on my horse almost immediately after I remounted, and nearly fell off, much to the amusement of some of the infantry who supposed I was as drunk with white wine as some of their comrades.

It was nearly half-past twelve before we left St Quentin. The sultry August day had passed to leave a thick summer mist. Our small army was at last collected. Every kind of vehicle had been filled with men with blistered feet. In front of them, on foot, were several hundred infantry, mostly of two regiments, but containing representatives of nearly every unit in the 4th Division, and behind, to form the rear-guard to this extraordinary cavalcade, Tom Bridges' mounted column—the gallant little band of 4th Dragoon Guards with driblets of Lancers, Hussars, Irish Horse, Signallers and the rest of the stragglers. In front of all rode a liaison officer and a guide sent by the Mayor, and I think Tom Bridges. By his side, walking, armed with a walking stick, was one of the two colonels—a thick-set man—who had surrendered. (The other had disappeared.) And immediately behind them the miscellaneous 'band' of Jew's harps and penny whistles. So through the darkness and the thick shrouding fog of that summer night we marched out, literally feeling our way through the countryside, so thick was the mist. At about two in the morning we had reached the villages of Savy and Roupy. Just as we started to leave St Quentin I woke up to the fact that my precious map-case was missing, and I had to return to look for it in the now deserted Grande Place. As for a moment I sat on my horse alone there, taking a last look round, I heard an ominous sound—the metallic rattle on the cobbles, of cavalry in formation entering the town through one of the darkened side-streets that led into the Grande Place.

The Germans must have entered St Quentin but a few minutes after the tail of our queer little column disappeared westward through the fog towards Savy.

Lt.-Col. Arthur Osburn

276.

On 31 August Lt. Lord Castlerosse of the Irish Guards, who was later to achieve a kind of celebrity as a wit and gossip columnist, lifted his arm to knock away a wasp which had just stung his nose, as a German rifleman fired.

AT that precise moment the bullet struck, hitting him in the elbow and breaking bones in both his lower and upper arm. 'It was as if I had been struck by a tidal wave', he said. It was several hours later, when he was lying on the ground in considerable pain, that a German came along, kicking all the corpses as he passed. When he kicked Castlerosse, Castlerosse swore. He was immediately loaded on a cart and transported to a crossroads, where he was laid beside several other wounded prisoners. What happened after that remained vividly in Castlerosse's memory for the rest of his life. He not only never forgot it, but it coloured everything he was ever afterwards to think about war or politics, soldiers or politicians.

His wound was serious, for the elbow was shattered and he had lost much blood, but he rarely lost consciousness during his captivity. At the crossroads he later remembered how a German soldier came and, to amuse his comrades, started pricking him in the leg with his bayonet until Castlerosse raved and swore. Presently an officer came along and ordered the man away and talked to him. Before he left he wrote his name in Castlerosse's notebook and said:

'Remember, if you get back into the war, that we looked after your prisoners and restrained our fanatics.'

His name was von Cramm, and he was the father of a famous tennis champion of the 'twenties and 'thirties.

Leonard Mosley

277.

3rd Sept. The prospect of the retreat [from Mons] being continued was depressing to all of us, and especially exasperating to Commandant Lamotte, the efficient little officer in charge of the distribution of maps for the Army. With the Army moving at such a rate, to supply all units with the vast quantity of maps required was no light task. Lamotte kept dashing off to Paris to exhort the map-printing department, already working day and night, to even greater efforts. Maps of France, always more maps of France, were called for, whilst vast quantities of maps of Germany, carefully prepared for a successful offensive, filled the vaults, never to be disturbed.

At Orbais the special grievance of our little cartographer was that people would insist on fighting battles at the junction of two maps, thereby thoughtlessly and wastefully using two sheets where one should have sufficed.

Sir Edward Spears

278.

The genesis of the Marne: the meeting of Joffre and French on 5 September 1914.

EVERYONE stood: Sir John French, with Murray and Wilson beside him; Joffre put his cap on the table and faced French. At once he began to speak in that low, toneless, albino voice of his, saying he had felt it his duty to come to thank Sir John personally for having taken a decision on which the fate of Europe might well depend. Sir John bowed. Then, without hurry or emphasis, Joffre explained the situation, developing the story of the German advance, and the change of direction of the First German Army . . .

We hung on his every word. We saw as he evoked it the immense battlefield over which the corps, drawn by the magnet of his will, were moving like pieces of intricate machinery, until they clicked into their appointed places . . .

Joffre was now foretelling what would happen on the morrow and on the day after and on the day after that, and as a prophet he was heard with absolute faith. We were listening to the story of the victory of the Marne, and we absolutely believed.

Joffre expounded his plan. He spoke of the British role, asking for the total support of the British Army. Then, turning full on Sir John, with an appeal so intense as to be irresistible, clasping both his own hands so as to hurt them, General Joffre said:

'Monsieur le Maréchal, c'est la France qui vous supplie.'

His hands fell to his sides wearily. The effort he had made had exhausted him.

We all looked at Sir John. He had understood and was under the stress of strong emotion. Tears stood in his eyes, welled over and rolled down his cheeks.

He tried to say something in French. For a moment he struggled with his feelings and with the language, then turning to an English officer . . . who stood beside him, he exclaimed: 'Damn it, I can't explain. Tell him that all that men can do our fellows will do.'

Sir Edward Spears

279.

One of the few eye-witness recollections of the legendary 'taxi-cabs of the Marne', 7 September 1914.

A BLOCK had brought me momentarily to a halt against the boundary wall of a château, when a car with its lights extinguished, ploughing its way through the throng, forced a confused wave of men and beasts against me, the weight of which flattened me against the wall . . .

Another car followed in its wake, then others and still others, in endless, silent, succession.

The moon had risen, and its rays shone reflected on the shiny peaks of taxi-drivers' caps. Inside the cabs, one could make out the bent heads of sleeping soldiers.

Someone asked, 'Wounded?' And a passing voice replied: 'No. Seventh Division. From Paris. Going into the line . . . '

Paul Lintier

280.

GENERAL DE MAUD'HUY had just been roused from sleep [12 September 1914] on the straw of a shed and was standing in the street, when a little group of unmistakable purport came round the corner. Twelve soldiers and an N.C.O., a firing party, a couple of gendarmes, and between them an unarmed soldier. My heart sank and a feeling of horror overcame me. An execution was about to take place. General de Maud'huy gave a look, then held up his hand so that the party halted, and with his characteristic quick step went up to the doomed man. He asked what he had been condemned for. It was for abandoning his post. The General then began to talk to the man. Quite simply he explained discipline to him. Abandoning your post was letting down your pals, more, it was letting down your country that looked to you to defend her. He spoke of the necessity of example, how some could do their duty without prompting but others, less strong, had to know and understand the supreme cost of failure. He told the condemned man that his crime was not venial, not low, and that he must die as an example, so that others should not fail. Surprisingly the wretch agreed, nodded his head. The burden of infamy was lifted from his shoulders. He saw a glimmer of something, redemption in his own eyes, a real hope, though he knew he was to die.

Maud'huy went on, carrying the man with him to comprehension that any sacrifice was worth while if it helped France ever so little. What did anything matter if he knew this?

Finally de Maud'huy held out his hand: 'Yours also is a way of dying for France', he said. The procession started again, but now the victim was a willing one.

The sound of a volley in the distance announced that all was over. General de Maud'huy wiped the beads of perspiration from his brow, and for the first time perhaps his hand trembled as he lit his pipe.

Sir Edward Spears

281.

Although a gunner by training, in the confusion after Mons Lt. James Marshall-Cornwall found himself placed in command of a squadron of the 15th Hussars for the exhilarating advance eastward following the Battle of the Marne.

ON only one occasion did I have a personal encounter with the enemy. As the country seemed deserted, I was riding along some hundreds of yards ahead of my squadron, accompanied only by my trumpeter. On turning the corner of a village street, I ran into a patrol of four Uhlans, not 30 yards away. Drawing my sword, I shouted 'Troop, charge!' and then turned about quickly and fled at a gallop. The enemy patrol also wheeled about and galloped in the opposite direction. It was the only time that I ever drew my sword in the presence of the enemy.

Sir James Marshall-Cornwall

282.

Lt. Bernard Montgomery of the Warwickshire Regiment was compelled to take direct action during an attack on 13 October 1914.

WHEN zero hour arrived I drew my recently sharpened sword and shouted to my platoon to follow me, which it did. We charged forward towards the village; there was considerable fire directed at us and some of my men became casualties, but we continued on our way. As we neared the objective I suddenly saw in front of me a trench full of Germans, one of whom was aiming his rifle at me.

In my training as a young officer I had received much instruction in how to kill my enemy with a bayonet fixed to a rifle. I knew all about the various movements—right parry, left parry, forward lunge. I had been taught how to put the left foot on the corpse and extract the bayonet, giving at the same time a loud grunt. Indeed, I had been considered good on the bayonet-fighting course against sacks filled with straw, and had won prizes in man-to-man contests in the gymnasium. But now I had no rifle and bayonet; I had only a sharp sword, and I was confronted by a large German who was about to shoot me. In all my short career in the Army no one had taught me how to kill a German with a sword. The only sword exercise I knew was saluting drill, learnt under the sergeant-major on the barrack square.

An immediate decision was clearly vital. I hurled myself through the air at the German and kicked him as hard as I could in the lower part of the stomach; the blow was well aimed at a tender spot. I had read much about the value of surprise in war. There is no doubt that the German was surprised and it must have seemed to him a new form of war; he fell to the ground in great pain and I took my first prisoner!

Viscount Montgomery

283.

The Christmas Truce of 1914.

AT 8.30 a.m. I was looking out, and saw four Germans leave their trenches and come towards us; I told two of my men to go and meet them, *unarmed* (as the Germans were unarmed), and to see that they did not pass the half-way line. We were 350–400 yards apart at this point. My fellows were not very keen, not knowing what was up, so I went out alone, and met Barry, one of our ensigns, also coming out from another part of the line. By the time we got to them, they were three quarters of the way over, and much too near our barbed wire, so I moved them back. They were three private soldiers and a stretcher-bearer, and their spokesman started off by saying that he thought it only right to come over and wish us a happy Christmas, and trusted us implicitly to keep the truce. He came from Suffolk, where he had left his best girl and a $3\frac{1}{2}$ h.p. motor-bike! He told me that he could not get a letter to the girl, and wanted to send one through me. I made him write out a post card in front of me, in English, and I sent it off that night. I told him that she probably would not be a bit keen to see him again. We then entered on a long discussion on every sort of thing. I was dressed in an old stocking-cap and a man's overcoat, and they took me for a corporal, a thing which I did not discourage, as I had an eye to going as near their lines as possible. I asked them what orders they had from their officers as to coming over to us, and they said *none*; they had just come over out of goodwill. . . .

I kept it up for half an hour, and then escorted them back as far as their barbed wire, having a jolly good look round all the time, and picking up various little bits of information which I had not had an opportunity of doing under fire! I left instructions with them that if any of them came out later they must not come over the half-way line, and appointed a ditch as the meeting place. We parted after an exchange of Albany cigarettes and German cigars, and I went straight to H.-qrs. to report.

On my return at 10 a.m. I was surprised to hear a hell of a din going on, and not a single man left in my trenches; they were completely denuded (against my orders), and nothing lived! I heard strains of 'Tipperary' floating down the breeze, swiftly followed by a tremendous burst of 'Deutschland über Alles', and as I got to my own Coy. H.-qrs. dug-out, I saw, to my amazement, not only a crowd of about 150 British and Germans at the half-way house which I had appointed opposite my lines, but six or seven such crowds, all the way down our lines, extending towards the 8th Division on our right. I bustled out and asked if there were any German officers in my crowd, and the noise died down (as this time I was myself in my own cap and badges of rank).

I found two, but had to talk to them through an interpreter, as they could neither talk English nor French. . . . I explained to them that strict orders must be maintained as to meeting half-way, and everyone unarmed; and we both agreed not to fire until the other did, thereby creating a complete deadlock and armistice (if strictly observed). . . .

Meanwhile Scots and Huns were fraternizing in the most genuine possible manner. Every sort of souvenir was exchanged, addresses given and received, photos of families shown, etc. One of our fellows offered a German a cigarette; the German said, 'Virginian?' Our fellow said, 'Aye, straight-cut': the German said, 'No thanks, I only smoke Turkish!' (Sort of 10/- a 100 me!) It gave us all a good laugh.

A German N.C.O. with the Iron Cross—gained, he told me, for conspicuous skill in sniping—started his fellows off on some marching tune. When they had done I set the note for 'The Boys of Bonnie Scotland, where the heather and the bluebells grow', and so we went on, singing everything from 'Good King Wenceslaus' down to the ordinary Tommies' song, and ended up with 'Auld Lang Syne', which we all, English, Scots, Irish, Prussians, Wurtembergers, etc., joined in. It was absolutely astounding, and if I had seen it on a cinematograph film I should have sworn that it was faked! . . .

Just after we had finished 'Auld Lang Syne' an old hare started up, and seeing so many of us about in an unwonted spot—did not know which way to go. I gave one loud 'View Holloa', and one and all, British and Germans, rushed about giving chase, slipping up on the frozen plough, falling about, and after a hot two minutes we killed in the open, a German and one of our fellows falling together heavily upon the completely baffled hare. Shortly afterwards we saw four more hares, and killed one again; both were good heavy weight and had evidently been out between the two rows of trenches for the last two months, well-fed on the cabbage patches, etc., many of which are untouched on the 'no-man's land'. The enemy kept one and we kept the other. It was now 11.30 a.m. and at this moment George Paynter arrived on the scene with a hearty 'Well, my lads, a Merry Christmas to you! This is d—d comic, isn't it?' . . . George told them that he thought it was only right that we should show that we could desist from hostilities on a day which was so important in both countries; and he then said, 'Well, my boys, I've brought you over something to celebrate this funny show with', and he produced from his pocket a large bottle of rum (not ration rum, but the proper stuff). One large shout went up, and the nasty little spokesman uncorked it, and in a heavy ceremonious manner, drank our healths, in the name of his 'cameraden'; the bottle was then passed on and polished off before you could say knife . . .

During the afternoon the same extraordinary scene was enacted between the lines, and one of the enemy told me that he was longing to get back to London: I assured him that 'So was I'. He said that he was sick of the war, and I told him that when the truce was ended, any of his friends would be welcome in our trenches, and would be well-received, fed, and given a free passage to the Isle of Man! Another coursing meeting took place, with no result, and at 4.30 p.m. we agreed to keep in our respective trenches, and told them that the truce was ended. . . .

The Border Regiment were occupying this section on Christmas Day, and Giles Loder, our Adjutant, went down there with a party that morning on hearing of the friendly demonstrations in front of my Coy., to see if he could come to an agreement about our dead, who were still lying out between the trenches. The trenches are so close at this point, that of course each side had to be far stricter. Well, he found an extremely pleasant and superior stamp of German officer, who arranged to bring all our dead to the half-way line. We took them over there, and buried 29 exactly half-way between the two lines. Giles collected all personal effects, pay-books and identity discs, but was stopped by the Germans when he told some men to bring in the rifles; all rifles lying on their side of the half-way line they kept carefully! . . .

They apparently treated our prisoners well, and did all they could for our wounded. This officer kept on pointing to our dead and saying, 'Les braves, c'est bien dommage.'

When George heard of it he went down to that section and talked to the nice officer and gave him a scarf. That same evening a German orderly came to the half-way line, and brought a pair of warm, woolly gloves as a present in return for George.

Captain Sir Edward Hulse, Bart.

284.

A staff officer is driven to passionate frustration by attachment to a Home Command in the winter of 1914.

. . . one day the General said to me: 'The War Office is very nervous about an invasion, there are five million [or whatever the number was] sheep in Sussex, Kent and Surrey. When the enemy land, they will at once be moved by route march to Salisbury Plain.' I knew that this was an impossible task, and that Sir John Moore had proclaimed it as such in 1805. But there was no arguing over it, so I spent days and days working out march tables for sheep. One day I said to him: 'Do you realize, sir, that should all these sheep be set in movement, every road will be blocked?' 'Of course,' he answered; 'at once arrange to have a number of signposts ready and marked, "Sheep are not to use this road." 'But', I replied, 'what if the less well-educated sheep are unable to read them?' This brought our conversation to an end, but, unfortunately, not my tribulations; for as none of us was even an amateur farmer, no one of us had thought of the lambing season, and when it came along all our time and space factors had to be readjusted. If ever there was a wicked waste of time, it was this.

Another hare-brained idea was to destroy all intoxicants in the public-houses the moment the enemy landed. Du Cane was against this proposal, yet to consider it he summoned a meeting of the Local Emergency Committee, upon which sat a variety of ancient celebrities, among whom was a General Heath, aged about seventy-five and an ardent teetotaller. To this assembly of notables the General pointed out that, as the enemy were likely to land in Thanet, it would be better to double the liquor than remove what was there, because the drunker they got, the more time we should have in which to collect our scattered forces. Whereupon Heath, white and trembling, rose to exclaim: 'But what of my wife, General, what of my poor wife?' Considering that this good lady must have been over seventy, du Cane quite rightly replied that she ought to be safe enough.

J. F. C. Fuller

285.

It may be difficult to credit the notion that anyone enjoyed the First World War, but Carton de Wiart plainly did. After some early adventures fighting the Mad Mullah in East Africa in 1914, he was invalided home and granted sick leave.

ON my appearing before the Medical Board they seemed rather shocked at my desire to go to France. We argued, and they produced the astonishing solution that if I found I could wear a satisfactory glass eye they would consider me. I imagine they did not wish the Germans to think that we were reduced to sending out one-eyed officers.

At my next board I appeared with a startling, excessively

uncomfortable glass eye. I was passed fit for general service. On emerging I called a taxi, threw my glass eye out of the window, put on my black patch, and have never worn a glass eye since. . .

Having got his wish for a posting to France early in 1915, he was soon wounded again.

My hand was a ghastly sight; two of the fingers were hanging by a bit of skin, all the palm was shot away and most of the wrist. For the first time, and certainly the last, I had been wearing a wrist-watch, and it had been blown into the remains of my wrist. I asked the doctor to take my fingers off; he refused, so I pulled them off myself and felt absolutely no pain in doing it. . .

Once again he qualified for sick leave.

When I had nearly recovered I went along to White's one afternoon and a member known to me by sight, came up and asked me if I would do him a favour. I answered cautiously that I would if it was not a financial transaction, as no good seems to come out of borrowing or lending money. He then told me there was a man paying undue attention to a lady he knew and he wanted to fight him and asked me to second him in a duel! I agreed at once, as I think duelling a most excellent solution in matters of the heart, and saw that my man was a tremendous fire-eater with only one object in view, to kill his opponent. It was a lively change from the sick bed. I went off to see his opponent, whom I knew; true to form, he found the whole idea quite ridiculous. I assured him that my friend was adamant and determined to fight with any suggested weapon, but preferably with pistols at the range of a few feet. It took some time to penetrate into the gentleman's mind that this was serious, and with a great deal of reluctance he appointed the seconds. As a last resort our opponent produced what he considered a telling argument, which was that if this episode was found out we should all get into serious trouble, and still more serious trouble if someone was either hurt or killed. My reply to that was that the war was on, everyone too busy to be interested, and that it would be simple to go to some secluded spot like Ashdown Forest with a can of petrol and cremate the remains of whichever was killed. This suggestion finished him off; the mere thought of his ashes scattered to the four winds, unhonoured and unsung, was too much for him. He promptly sat down and wrote an affidavit not to see the lady again. It was a tame end: it seemed to me that as he did not like the lady enough to fight for her, he needed a thrashing.

Adrian Carton de Wiart

286.

An armistice at Anzac Beach, Gallipoli, 24 May 1915.

WE walked from the sea and passed immediately up the hill, through a field of tall corn filled with poppies, then another cornfield; then the fearful smell of death began as we came upon scattered bodies. We mounted over a plateau and down through gullies filled with thyme, where there lay about 4,000 Turkish dead. It was indescribable. One was grateful for the rain and the grey sky. . . . There were two wounded crying in that multitude of silence. . . . The Turkish Captain with me said: 'At this spectacle even the most gentle must feel savage, and the most savage must weep.' The dead fill acres of ground, mostly killed in the one big attack, but some recently. They fill the myrtle-grown gullies. One saw the result of machine-gun fire very clearly; entire companies annihilated—not wounded, but killed, their heads doubled under them with the impetus of their rush and both hands clasping their bayonets. It was as if God had breathed in their faces. . . .

A good deal of friction at first. The trenches were 10 to 15 yards apart. Each side was on the *qui vive* for treachery. In one gully the dead had got to be left unburied. It was impossible to bury them without one side seeing the position of the other. In the Turkish parapet there were many bodies buried. Fahreddin told Skeen he wanted to bury them, 'but', he said, 'we cannot take them out without putting something in their place.' . . .

I talked to the Turks, one of whom pointed to the graves. 'That's politics', he said. Then he pointed to the dead bodies and said: 'That's diplomacy. God pity all of us poor soldiers.'

. . . Then Skeen came. He told me to get back as quickly as possible to Quinn's Post, as I said I was nervous at being away, and to retire the troops at 4 and the white-flag men at 4.15. . . .

At 4 o'clock the Turks came to me for orders. I do not believe this could have happened anywhere else. I retired their troops and ours, walking along the line. At 4.7 I retired the white-flag men, making them shake hands with our men. Then I came to the upper end. About

a dozen Turks came out. I chaffed them, and said that they would
shoot me next day. They said, in a horrified chorus: 'God forbid!' The
Albanians laughed and cheered, and said: 'We will never shoot you.'
Then the Australians began coming up, and said: 'Good-bye, old
chap; good luck!' And the Turks said: 'Oghur Ola gule gule gedejek-
seniz, gule gule gelejekseniz' (Smiling may you go and smiling come
again). Then I told them all to get into their trenches, and unthinkingly
went up to the Turkish trench and got a deep salaam from it.

Hon. Aubrey Herbert

287.

A skirmish at Gallipoli narrated by a Royal Marine.

THE following is a strictly true account of about the most horrible and
deadly encounter I have so far had the misfortune to be in.

The enemy in enormously strong numbers occupied some strong
positions and simply could not be turned out. They were behind every
small ridge and filled up every crevice of which there was an abundance. We had continually had encounters with them in a casual sort
of way but now it had been determined to shift them at all costs. The
enemy had their bite first however. One night just after we had piped
down and settled ourselves for the night routine of the trenches they
made an attack. We repulsed them with very considerable loss and our
monkey was well up now and as soon as day light appeared we made a
determined counter attack. It was no end of a stiff do. Blood, Blood
everywhere. Even splashes of it on my face and as for my hands, well, I
looked an object indeed. You know too it was Summer time and by
now the sun had risen so that streams of perspiration rolled from us.
We took no prisoners and the slaughter was really terrible. Even as we
killed them off, fresh ones appeared to take our special attention, and
so the slaughter continued. We had at last cleared the place except for
sundry stragglers who would no doubt be seen off later. We had killed
scores, yes hundreds of the loathed enemy.

ON OUR SHIRTS. The next time I enlist and go on Active Service (and
I hope others will take my advice) I shall always carry a plentiful supply
of KEATINGS POWDER for it kills Bugs, fleas, moths, beetles, etc. and
ensures a peaceful night.

Private Horace Bruckshaw

288.

JUST about sunset on a calm evening I was looking in this direction when slowly the brown line of trenches and earth began to change to a dull luminous green. Looking intently I saw great clouds of greenish-yellow vapour creeping across from the German lines, and all clearly issuing from one or two fixed points. We had heard talk of gas, and we had once or twice detected the smell of strange chemical odours, but here was a gas-attack, a mile away, which I could see in action with my own eyes. It was, in fact, one of the last attempts of the Germans at this time to use chlorine and, like its predecessors, which had occurred before we moved up, it failed.

The men had already shown signs of nervousness of gas, a nervousness based only on the wild stories that runners had brought. But here it was for me to see without breathing, to look at impartially so that I could be prepared when I met it. The other signs of battle had filled me with a curious elation. The shells that burst so close, the line ahead of us that we might fill at any moment, gave me a strange pleasure. The gas, with its green paralysis, changed my mood. I was angry rather than frightened, angry as the dog that snaps at the unaccustomed.

Our seniors were alarmed and waited for advice, for they saw that at any moment we might be called upon to deal with a situation that neither they nor we had ever been trained to meet. Unexpectedly help came. A parcel was delivered for each company labelled, 'Gas Masks, Type 1'. Unpacked, the parcel revealed bundles of small squares of blue flannel, just large enough to cover the mouth, with a tape on each side to tie round behind the head. Whatever benign personage contrived these amiable death-traps I do not know. But anything more futile could never have been devised by the simplicity of man. On the whole we preferred to resort to the face-towels dipped in our own urine, which an earlier order had suggested would be a temporary palliative. Nor was our confidence restored a day later by the arrival of 'Gas Masks, Type II', which was to replace the first. On unpacking my particular bundle I found that the new masks consisted of large pieces of hairy Harris tweed about three feet long and one in width, again with tapes nattily fixed to the sides. With much laughter the men tried to don their new masks. But at the bottom of the parcel I found a small printed label briefly entitled 'BODY BELTS'. So without further enquiries I ordered my men to put them to whatever use seemed best to them. To a man they placed them round their long-suffering stomachs.

I have often wondered what inspired genius was at work away back in England to give us these gifts. I have been told since that Gas Mask Type I was invented by the fertile brain of a Cabinet Minister. I feel tempted to attribute Type II to the Archbishop of Canterbury.

Stanley Casson

289.

In the German trenches, August 1915.

ONE of the next starlit summer nights, a decent Landwehr chap came up suddenly and said to 2/Lt Reinhardt, 'Sir, it's that Frenchie over there singing again so wonderful.' We stepped out of the dug-out into the trench, and quite incredibly, there was a marvellous tenor voice ringing out through the night with an aria from *Rigoletto*. The whole company were standing in the trench listening to the 'enemy', and when he had finished, applauding so loud that the good Frenchman must certainly have heard it and is sure to have been moved by it in some way or other as much as we were by his wonderful singing.

Herbert Sulzbach

290.

An infantry officer daydreams about his fellow students at the Fourth Army tactical school in France, most of whom were shortly doomed to wounds or death on the Somme.

MY woolgatherings were cut short when the lecturer cleared his throat; the human significance of the audience was obliterated then, and its outlook on life became restricted to destruction and defence. A gas expert from G.H.Q. would inform us that 'gas was still in its infancy'. (Most of us were either dead or disabled before gas had had time to grow up.) An urbane Artillery General assured us that high explosive would be our best friend in future battles, and his ingratiating voice made us unmindful, for the moment, that explosives often arrived from the wrong direction. But the star turn in the schoolroom was a massive sandy-haired Highland Major whose subject was 'The Spirit of the Bayonet'. Though at that time undecorated, he was afterwards awarded the D.S.O. for lecturing. He took as his text a few leading points from the *Manual of Bayonet Training.*

He spoke with homicidal eloquence, keeping the game alive with genial and well-judged jokes. He had a Sergeant to assist him. The Sergeant, a tall sinewy machine, had been trained to such a pitch of frightfulness that at a moment's warning he could divest himself of all semblance of humanity. With rifle and bayonet he illustrated the Major's ferocious aphorisms, including facial expression. When told to 'put on the killing face', he did so, combining it with an ultra-vindictive attitude. 'To instil fear into the opponent' was one of the Major's main maxims. Man, it seemed, had been created to jab the life out of Germans. To hear the Major talk, one might have thought that he did it himself every day before breakfast. His final words were: 'Remember that every Boche you fellows kill is a point scored to our side; every Boche you kill brings victory one minute nearer and shortens the war by one minute. Kill them! Kill them! There's only one good Boche, and that's a dead one!'

Afterwards I went up the hill to my favourite sanctuary, a wood of hazels and beeches. The evening air smelt of wet mould and wet leaves; the trees were misty-green; the church bell was tolling in the town, and smoke rose from the roofs. Peace was there in the twilight of that prophetic foreign spring. But the lecturer's voice still battered on my brain. 'The bullet and the bayonet are brother and sister.' 'If you don't kill him, he'll kill you.' 'Stick him between the eyes, in the throat, in the chest.' 'Don't waste good steel. Six inches are enough. What's the use of a foot of steel sticking out at the back of a man's neck? Three inches will do for him; when he coughs, go and look for another.'

Siegfried Sassoon

291.

A new commanding officer takes over 6th Royal Scots Fusiliers, December 1915.

THE first intimation we had was when Charlie Broon, our Company runner, came into our billet and announced: 'We're gettin' a new C.O.—some fella ca'd Churchill.' I asked him if it was the ex-First Lord of the Admiralty, the ex-Home Secretary, the M.P. for my home town of Dundee. 'Aw Ah ken is that he's ca'd Churchill.'

At the battalion parade on the morning following Churchill's arrival we soon sensed that a new force had come among us. In his initial address to us he said: 'You men have had a hard time. Now you're going to have it easy for some time, I hope.' On the previous evening, to the assembled officers he spoke these now-historic words: 'Gentlemen, we are now going to make war—on the lice!' Cleaning, scrubbing and de-lousing were now the order of the day. Huge stocks of clothing arrived at the quartermaster's stores. We all needed new rig-outs. We got them. Steel helmets were by then being issued to the British Army. We were among the first to get them. We found, too, a vast improvement in our rations. Bully beef and biscuits were only memories.

We took over the sector to the right of 'Plugstreet' Wood in early February. It had always been regarded as one of the 'cushy' sectors of the front. But with the coming of Churchill it was soon evident that the live-and-let-live atmosphere that had always prevailed here was coming to an end.

He visited the front line daily and nightly. He went on lone reconnaissance missions into 'no-man's-land'. We often got the order: 'Pass it along—no firing. The C.O.'s out in front.' In the fire bays, he scrutinized every man and sometimes questioned them. I remember one night in the front line when Sergeant McGee, an old Regular, was rousing men in the dugouts to form a fatigue party. He was doing this by his usual method—pulling up the sacking flap, kicking the soles of protruding feet, then addressing the inhabitants in a mixture of profanity and Hindustani. He was unaware of Churchill's presence until a narrow beam of light from the C.O.'s torch pinpointed his three stripes.

'Ah, a sergeant.'

'Sir.' McGee's heels clicked.

'Are you an old soldier, sergeant?'

'Yes, sir. Eight years' service.'

'Well, sergeant, if you live to see the end of this war—which I hope you do—you are going to be a *very* old soldier.'

Robert Fox

292.

The excesses of the campaign to drive young civilians into uniform became one of the most distasteful features of the Home Front.

SOME of the crudest psychological pressure on women was applied by women. Baroness Orczy, creator of the 'Scarlet Pimpernel', founded the Active Service League, which urged women to sign the following pledge:

> At this hour of England's grave peril and desperate need I do hereby pledge myself most solemnly in the name of my King and Country to persuade every man I know to offer his services to the country, and I also pledge myself never to be seen in public with any man who, being in every way fit and free for service, has refused to respond to his country's call.

Today, the harping on England's peril might seem no way to win recruits from Scotland, Wales or Ireland; but England was unabashedly used for Britain in those days, not least by poets (even in World War Two the song went, *There'll Always Be An England*). In any event, the Baroness had the excuse that she was born in Hungary. It was now an enemy nation, but her readers obviously trusted her, for they signed her pledge in hundreds and some may even have honoured it. In her autobiography she omits to mention this episode in her life.

The Mothers' Union urged its members to say: 'My boy, I don't want you to go, but if I were you I should go.' On his return, hearts would beat high with thankfulness and pride. If, however, God had 'another plan for him' . . .

' . . . you will have a yet deeper cause for thankfulness that he is among the long roll of English heroes, ever to be held in highest honour while the English name lasts, and better—far better even than that—the welcome of the King of Kings will greet him—"Well done, good and faithful servant, enter thou into the joy of thy Lord." '

The notion of distributing white feathers to young men (a symbol of cowardice made familiar by A. E. W. Mason's *The Four Feathers*, 1902) is supposed to have come from an admiral at a recruiting rally in Folkestone. One of the earliest distributions, less than a month from the outbreak of war, was at Deal, where the Town Cryer was induced to shout: 'Oyez! Oyez! The White Feather Brigade. Ladies wanted to present to young men of Deal and Walmer who have no one dependent on them the Order of the White Feather for shirking their duty in not offering their services to uphold the Union Jack of Old England. God Save The King!' Before the announcement was cried, a number

of young men had been befeathered without realizing the significance
of the decoration. Handing out these insults was a healthy open-air
game in which hoydens and old ladies could for once unite. The former
delighted to embarrass young men of a higher social class and the latter
gave them out indiscriminately to teach the lesson that it is the duty of
youth to die for age. Compton Mackenzie had a theory that 'idiotic
young women' were using white feathers to get rid of boyfriends of
whom they were tired. In autobiographies one may read of receiving
feathers but never of giving them. Lord Brockway claims to have had a
collection which he spread out like a fan; others tell of receiving them
when they were schoolboys. According to Daphne Fielding, the
capricious Rosa Lewis, who ran the Cavendish Hotel, 'distributed
white feathers indiscriminately, sometimes making terrible gaffes, and
Kippy, her Aberdeen terrier, was trained to fly at the heels of any man
not in uniform'. In Parliament, Cathcart Wason asked the Home Secretary if he was aware that State employees were subject to 'insolence
and provocation at the hands of some advertising young women presenting them with white feathers', and whether he would authorize the
arrest of such persons for conduct likely to disrupt the peace. Reginald
McKenna agreed that the practice was unlikely to aid recruiting, but
felt the danger of disorder was slight. However, it emerged that thousands of dock workers at Chatham were being issued with protective
badges testifying that they were serving King and Country.

The author of *The Unspeakable Scot*, T. W. H. Crosland, wrote a
song called *The White Feather Legion*:

> Yes, somehow and somewhere and always,
>   We're first when the shoutings begin,
> We put up a howl for Old England
>   The Kaiser can hear in Berlin,
>   Dear boys!
> He hears it and quakes in Berlin.
> Yes, a health to ourselves as we scatter
>   In taxis to get the last train,
> Cheer oh, for the White Feather Legion
>   Goes back to its females again,
>   Regards!
> Goes back to its slippers again,
>   Hurrah!
> The Bass and the lager again,
>   Here's how!

And so on.

For the man not in uniform, the hazards of the streets included women in mourning, with reproachful looks and sometimes accusing words. He might run foul of noisy recruiting parties, with military bands, tots bearing placards saying 'My Dad's At the Front' and strong-armed recruiting sergeants doing their best to hustle him off to the enlisting office. Refuge could be hard to find. In Hyde Park, London, cantered Winifred and Ivy Mulroney, two Irish sisters in semi-military uniform, their saddle-cloths proclaiming 'Do Not Hesitate: To Arms: King And Country', who bore down on young men and urged them to join up. Nancy Astor had her own way of applying pressure. Driving with Sylvia Pankhurst to Cliveden from the local station she espied a young horseman, put her head through the window and shrieked, 'Charlie McCartney, pride of the knuts! Why aren't you in uniform?'

Feminine blackmail could find an outlet in the Personal Columns of newspapers. In *The Times* of July 8, 1915, appeared this warning: 'Jack F. G. If you are not in khaki by the 20th I shall cut you dead. Ethel M.' The Berlin correspondent of the *Cologne Gazette* telegraphed a translation of this item to his journal and made the threat read, 'I shall hack you to death'—'hacke ich dich zu Tode'.

E. S. Turner

293.

I SPENT the rest of my watch in acquainting myself with the geography of the trench-section, finding how easy it was to get lost among culs-de-sac and disused alleys. Twice I overshot the company frontage and wandered among the Munsters on the left. Once I tripped and fell with a splash into deep mud. At last my watch was ended with the first signs of dawn. I passed the word along the line for the company to stand-to-arms. The N.C.O.s whispered hoarsely into the dug-outs: 'Stand-to, stand-to', and out the men tumbled with their rifles in their hands. As I went towards company head-quarters to wake the officers I saw a man lying on his face in a machine-gun shelter. I stopped and said: 'Stand-to, there.' I flashed my torch on him and saw that his foot was bare. The machine-gunner beside him said: 'No good talking to him, sir.' I asked: 'What's wrong? What's he taken his boot and sock off for?' I was ready for anything odd in the trenches. 'Look for yourself, sir', he said. I shook the man by the arm and noticed suddenly that the back of his head was blown out. The first corpse that I saw in France was this suicide. He had taken off his boot and sock to pull the trigger of his rifle with his toe; the muzzle was in his mouth. 'Why did he do it?' I said. 'He was in the last push, sir and that sent him a bit queer, and on top of that, he got bad news from Limerick about his girl and another chap.' He was not a Welshman, but belonged to the Munsters; their machine-guns were at the extreme left of our company. The suicide had already been reported and two Irish officers came up. 'We've had two or three of these lately', one of them told me. Then he said to the other: 'While I remember, Callaghan, don't forget to write to his next-of-kin. Usual sort of letter, cheer them up, tell them he died a soldier's death, anything you like. I'm not going to report it as suicide.'

Robert Graves

294.

When Robert Graves was transferred from the Second Welsh Regiment to the Royal Welch Fusiliers, he found himself subjected to all the withering petty humiliations to which some regular officers' messes traditionally subjected newly joined subalterns fresh from Sandhurst. A fellow-sufferer briefed him on what he might expect.

'THEY treat us like dirt; in a way it will be worse for you than for me because you're a full lieutenant. They'll resent that with your short service. There's one lieutenant here of six years' service and second-lieutenants who have been out here since the autumn. They have already had two Special Reserve captains foisted on them; they're planning to get rid of them somehow. In the mess, if you open your mouth or make the slightest noise the senior officers jump down your throat. Only officers of the rank of captain are allowed to drink whisky or turn on the gramophone. We've got to jolly well keep still and look like furniture. It's just like peace time. Mess bills are very high; the mess was in debt at Quetta last year and we are economizing now to pay that back. We get practically nothing for our money but ordinary rations and the whisky we aren't allowed to drink.

'We've even got a polo-ground here. There was a polo match between the First and Second Battalions the other day. The First Battalion had had all their decent ponies pinched that time when they were sent up at Ypres and the cooks and transport men had to come up into the line to prevent a break through. So this battalion won easily.

Can you ride? No? Well, subalterns who can't ride have to attend riding-school every afternoon while we're in billets. They give us hell, too. Two of us have been at it for four months and haven't passed off yet. They keep us trotting round the field, with crossed stirrups most of the time, and they give us pack-saddles instead of riding-saddles. Yesterday they called us up suddenly without giving us time to change into breeches. That reminds me, you notice everybody's wearing shorts? It's a regimental order. The battalion thinks it's still in India. They treat the French civilians just like "niggers", kick them about, talk army Hindustani at them. It makes me laugh sometimes. Well, what with a greasy pack-saddle, bare knees, crossed stirrups, and a wild new transport pony that the transport men had pinched from the French, I had a pretty thin time. The colonel, the adjutant, the senior major and the transport officer stood at the four corners of the ring and slogged at the ponies as they came round. I came off twice and got wild with anger, and nearly decided to ride the senior major down. The funny thing is that they don't realize that they are treating us badly— it's such an honour to be serving with the regiment. So the best thing is to pretend you don't care what they do or say.'

I protested: 'But all this is childish. Is there a war on here or isn't there?'

'The battalion doesn't recognize it socially', he answered. 'Still, in trenches I'd rather be with this battalion than in any other that I have met. The senior officers do know their job, whatever else one says about them, and the N.C.O.'s are absolutely trustworthy.'

The Second Battalion was peculiar in having a battalion mess instead of company messes. The Surrey-man said grimly: 'It's supposed to be more sociable.' This was another peace-time survival. We went together into the big château near the church. About fifteen officers of various ranks were sitting in chairs reading the week's illustrated papers or (the seniors at least) talking quietly. At the door I said: 'Good morning, gentlemen', the new officer's customary greeting to the mess. There was no answer. Everybody looked at me curiously. The silence that my entry had caused was soon broken by the gramophone, which began singing happily:

> We've been married just one year,
> And Oh, we've got the sweetest,
> And Oh, we've got the neatest,
> And Oh, we've got the cutest
> Little oil stove.

I found a chair in the background and picked up *The Field*. The door burst open suddenly and a senior officer with a red face and angry eye burst in. 'Who the blazes put that record on?' he shouted to the room. 'One of the bloody warts I expect. Take it off somebody. It makes me sick. Let's have some real music. Put on the *Angelus*.' Two subalterns (in the Royal Welch a subaltern had to answer to the name of 'wart') sprang up, stopped the gramophone, and put on *When the Angelus is ringing*. The young captain who had put on *We've been married* shrugged his shoulders and went on reading, the other faces in the room were blank.

'Who was that?' I whispered to the Surrey-man.

He frowned. 'That's Buzz Off ', he said.

Before the record was finished the door opened and in came the colonel; Buzz Off reappeared with him. Everybody jumped up and said in unison: 'Good morning, sir.' It was his first appearance that day. Before giving the customary greeting and asking us to sit down he turned spitefully to the gramophone: 'Who on earth puts this wretched *Angelus* on every time I come into the mess? For heaven's sake play something cheery for a change.' And with his own hands he took off the *Angelus*, wound up the gramophone and put on *We've been married just one year*. At that moment a gong rang for lunch and he abandoned it. We filed into the next room, a ball-room with mirrors and a decorated ceiling. We sat down at a long, polished table. The seniors sat at the top, the juniors competed for seats as far away from them as possible. I was unlucky enough to get a seat at the foot of the table facing the commanding officer, the adjutant and Buzz Off. There was not a word spoken down that end except for an occasional whisper for the salt or for the beer—very thin French stuff. Robertson, who had not been warned, asked the mess waiter for whisky. 'Sorry, sir,' said the mess waiter, 'it's against orders for the young officers.' Robertson was a man of forty-two, a solicitor with a large practice, and had stood for Parliament in the Yarmouth division at the previous election.

I saw Buzz Off glaring at us and busied myself with my meat and potatoes.

He nudged the adjutant. 'Who are those two funny ones down there, Charley?' he asked.

'New this morning from the militia. Answer to the names of Robertson and Graves.'

'Which is which?' asked the colonel.

'I'm Robertson, sir.'

'I wasn't asking you.'

Robertson winced, but said nothing. Then Buzz Off noticed something.

'T'other wart's wearing a wind-up tunic.' Then he bent forward and asked me loudly. 'You there, wart. Why the hell are you wearing your stars on your shoulder instead of your sleeve?'

My mouth was full and I was embarrassed. Everybody was looking at me. I swallowed the lump of meat whole and said: 'It was a regimental order in the Welsh Regiment. I understood that it was the same everywhere in France.'

The colonel turned puzzled to the adjutant: 'What on earth's the man talking about the Welsh Regiment for?' And then to me: 'As soon as you have finished your lunch you will visit the master-tailor. Report at the orderly room when you're properly dressed.'

There was a severe struggle in me between resentment and regimental loyalty. Resentment for the moment had the better of it. I said under my breath: 'You damned snobs. I'll survive you all. There'll come a time when there won't be one of you left serving in the battalion to remember battalion mess at Laventie.' This time came, exactly a year later.

Robert Graves

295.

TOWARDS the end of May [1916], a dozen recruits joined the company, young reinforcements, boyish and slight. Early one morning the enemy began to shell the trench with whizz-bangs; it was a sudden angry storm, too fierce and too localized to last long. I had just passed the fire-bay in which Delivett was frying a rasher of bacon, with five of these lads watching him and waiting their turn to cook. I stopped in the next bay to reassure the others. Suddenly a pale and frightened youth came round the corner, halting indecisively when he saw me, turning again, but finally going back reluctantly to his fire-bay in despair of finding any escape from his trap. Between the crashes of the bursting shells a high-pitched sing-song soared up.

'You'll 'ev 'em all over,' . . . Crash . . . 'All the milky ones.' . . . Crash . . . 'All the milky coco-nuts . . . ' ' . . . You'll 'ev 'em all over . . . All the milky ones.' . . . Crash . . . 'Therree shies a penny . . . All the milky coco-nuts . . . You'll 'ev 'em all over' . . .

Crash—and then silence, for the morning had ended as suddenly as it began.

I walked to find Delivett still frying bacon, and the five youths smiling nervously, crouched below the firestep. I sent them away on some improvised errand and faced Delivett.

'That's a fine thing you did then, Delivett', I said. He looked up, mess-tin lid in his hand, saying nothing, but the lines round his mouth moved a little.

'You saved those lads from panic—they were frightened out of their wits', I added.

'Yes, sir, they was real scared', he replied.

'Delivett, you've spent a lot of time on Hampstead Heath.'

'Yes sir . . . I ran a coco-nut shy there once . . . '

With these words a man and an environment fused into a unity, satisfying and complete in itself; here at last was a credible occupation for this quiet stranger.

'I'm going to tell the Colonel all about this', I said. Delivett thought hard for several seconds, and put his bacon back on the fire.

'Well, sir,' he said diffidently, 'if it's all the same to you, I'd much rather you made me Sanitary man.'

'Do you mean that you'd really like to go round with a bucket of chloride of lime, picking up tins and . . . '

'Yes, sir, I'd like that job.'

'You shall have it here and now. You are made Sanitary man for valour in the field, this very moment.'

In half an hour Delivett was walking round with a bucket, his head a little higher in the air, spitting a little more deliberately than before, as his new dignity demanded. He had found a vocation.

Wyn Griffith

296.

THIS is what happened the other day. Two young miners, in another company, disliked their sergeant, who had a down on them and gave them all the most dirty and dangerous jobs. When they were in billets he crimed them for things they hadn't done. So they decided to kill him. Later they reported at Battalion Orderly Room and asked to see

the adjutant. This was irregular, because a private is not allowed to
speak to an officer without an N.C.O. of his own company to act as go-
between. The adjutant happened to see them and said: 'Well, what is it
you want?' Smartly slapping the small-of-the-butt of their sloped rifles
they said: 'We've come to report, sir, that we are very sorry but we've
shot our company sergeant-major.' The adjutant said: 'Good heavens,
how did that happen?' They answered: 'It was an accident, sir.' 'What
do you mean? Did you mistake him for a German?' 'No, sir, we mistook
him for our platoon sergeant.' So they were both shot by a firing squad
of their own company against the wall of a convent at Béthune. Their
last words were the battalion rallying-cry: 'Stick it, the Welsh!' (They
say that a certain Captain Haggard first used it in the battle of Ypres
when he was mortally wounded.) The French military governor was
present at the execution and made a little speech saying how gloriously
British soldiers can die.

Robert Graves

297.

*The epitome of tragic contrast between the spirit and reality of the Battle of the Somme
lay in the footballers of zero hour on 1 July 1916. The practice has been attributed to
several units at different times, but the best documented episode was inspired by
Captain W. P. Nevill of the 8th East Surreys.*

NEVILL was a young officer who liked to stand on the fire-step each
evening and shout insults at the Germans. His men were to be in the
first wave of the assault near Montauban and he was concerned as to
how they would behave, for they had never taken part in an attack
before. While he was on leave, Nevill bought four footballs, one for
each of his platoons. Back in the trenches, he offered a prize to the first
platoon to kick its football up to the German trenches on the day of the
attack. One platoon painted the following inscription on its ball:

The Great European Cup
The Final
East Surreys v. Bavarians
Kick-off at Zero

Nevill himself kicked off. 'As the gunfire died away [wrote a survi-
vor], I saw an infantryman climb onto the parapet into No Man's Land,

beckoning others to follow. As he did so he kicked off a football; a good kick, the ball rose and travelled towards the German line. That seemed to be the signal to advance.'

. . . The winning footballers of the 8th East Surreys were unable to collect the prize money from their commander. Captain Nevill was dead.

Martin Middlebrook

298.

A moment on the Somme: 9th Royal Sussex Regiment, 7 July 1916.

As I was travelling light and the men were loaded with all sorts of junk, I got to the enemy line all alone. It was blown all to hell, but the dugouts were obvious. There was not a soul in the trench and I realized I had got there before the Germans had come out of their burrows. I sat down facing the dug-out doors and got all the Germans as they came up. They had no idea I was there even, the ground was so blown up and I was in a hole; they never knew what hit them. Broughall, a plucky little Canadian, was about the next of our people to arrive; he was very excited at my bag, but disgusted at their 'hats' as they all had steel helmets or flat caps and he had promised himself the best spiked helmet (*pickelhaube*) in France.

This craving for a trophy was the cause of his getting to the fourth line . . . While we were cleaning up the front line we put up a big German wearing a very smart spiked helmet. Broughall, unaware that there were dozens of other helmets in the dug-outs, at once gave chase to the wearer. His platoon rallied to the cry of 'Get that bloody hat' and followed him. The quarry ran up a communication trench and was finally pulled down in the German fourth line, where Broughall and his platoon settled him and held their own against repeated counter-attacks.

While we were rounding up the prisoners I came upon one of the Fusiliers being embraced round the knees by a trembling Hun who had a very nice wrist-watch. After hearing the man's plea for mercy the Fusilier said, 'That's all right, mate, I accept your apology, but let's have that ticker.'

Captain H. Sadler

299.

WHEN Rumania declared war in August 1916, it is said that one of the first army orders, after mobilization, was that only officers above the rank of major were allowed to use make-up.

Ronald Lewin

300.

A British artillery officer discovers unexpected virtue in one of his gunners.

BRIGGS brought off one feat which endeared him to the battery. He couldn't read or write, but he was no fool, and he was about the best and most intelligent scrounger we had—an extremely useful accomplishment in those hard times. The late winter of 1916–17 was extremely bitter, and the ground that we were holding then had been frozen iron hard. The issue of fuel was down to a minimum, and conditions in the lines were arctic. Men shivered in the shallow dugouts round the guns and were too cold to sleep. One morning I had the Maltese cart sent up to the Battery, called for Briggs, and told him to go off with it into the blue anywhere and do his damnedest to come back with any sort of fuel. There wasn't much hope, for all the ruined frostbound villages round about had been stripped to the bone. Every window-frame and every rafter had long since been extracted for firewood. However, Briggs set off. Some distance in the rear he came to the shelltorn village of Colincamps. There was a tall post in the pitted market square of the village with a placard on it DANGER, DON'T LOITER! Briggs naturally tied his horse and cart up to this post and started to reconnoitre. Most of the little houses were rubble, but the walls of the church still stood. Briggs clambered over broken stones and entered. The roof was gone and so were the rafters, the pews, and the benches, and apparently everything else in the slightest degree combustible. Dangling the battery axe thoughtfully in one hand, Briggs wandered round the building. He saw that at man-height from the ground there was a series of niches, each occupied by one highly coloured member of the select company of the Saints. Their primitive colours of scarlet and blue and gold were still untarnished amid this desolation. Were they marble? Stone? Plaster? Concrete? Briggs approached the nearest, and tapped Saint Peter firmly on the shin. He tapped again hard. A light as of pious awe illuminated his Yorkshire face.

Some hours later the Maltese cart arrived at the Battery position.

Piled high with chopped and painted timber, it was seized upon by the shivering but happy gunners, and soon a dozen varieties of fug were making things homely and comfortable in the dugout. Before morning dawned the good news went down the wagon lines, the sergeant-major collected the rest of the heavenly choir in a G.S. wagon, and for many days after the troops cooked their morning bacon and stoked their midnight fires with the chopped anatomies of Saints, Virgins, and Apostles. And it gave us all an added zest to know that half the British Army must have seen these images and passed them by, and that it had been left to our Briggs with his little battery axe to discover that the Saints were made of wood.

Lewis Hastings

301.

THE iron deck of a barge under a single awning in the fantastic temperature of a Mesopotamian summer is about as near hell as one can get this side of the Styx—and our 'P' boat was as firmly embedded in the palms as ever. No relief was to be expected from there. I searched our bank. It seemed competely deserted until I caught a glimpse of tents among the trees about half a mile downstream towards Basra. This looked more hopeful. I decided to explore.

I found a couple of large E.P. tents inside a barbed-wire enclosure that was stacked with crates, boxes, sacks and supplies of all kinds. I passed an Indian sentry at the gate and made for one of the tents. Inside, seated at a packing-case fitted roughly as a desk, was a lieutenant-colonel of the Supply and Transport Corps. He was a tall, cadaverous, yellow-faced man with a bristling moustache. He looked very fierce and military— officers who dealt with bully-beef and biscuit in the back areas so often did—and he gave short shrift to my timid suggestion that his dump might possibly provide something in the way of additional awnings or tents for us. No, his Supply Depot contained nothing but supplies. Then, perhaps, a little something extra in the way of rations . . . ? I was informed that his supplies were not for issue to any casual subaltern who cared to ask for them, and, if my detachment had not got everything that was necessary for its comfort, it was because either:

(a) I was incompetent,
(b) The staff at the Reinforcement Camp was incompetent, or
(c) A combination of (a) and (b).

I gathered he rather favoured the first alternative. He ended with the final warning: 'And don't let your fellows come hanging round here. The British soldier is the biggest thief in Asia and his officers encourage him.'

It is not a very profitable pastime for subalterns to quarrel with lieutenant-colonels, so I swallowed all this as best I could...

We did not sail in the morning; in fact we spent two more infernal nights on those moored barges. We had, however, one pleasant surprise. On the evening of the second day our rations, which up to then had been limited strictly to the regulation bully, biscuit, dried vegetables—horrible things—tea and sugar, were suddenly supplemented by a liberal issue of tinned fruit. As I squatted on my valise, making a leisurely choice between pineapple and peaches, I thought of the kind heart that S. and T. colonel must hide beneath his fierce exterior. Next morning when we all breakfasted off first-class bacon, followed by admirable Australian quince jam, while tinned milk flowed in streams, and every man seemed to have a handful of cigarettes, I meditated on how one could be misled by first impressions.

I will not deny that certain suspicions did flit across my mind. There was a tinge of apprehension on the mahogany face of my acting quartermaster-sergeant when I suggested it would be a graceful act of courtesy if he would accompany me to thank the good colonel for his generosity. Well, well; perhaps the colonel was one of those splendid fellows who rejoiced in doing good by stealth and thanks might be embarrassing—most embarrassing.

On the last afternoon of our stay another subaltern and I were standing in the stern of a barge, clad only in our topis, heaving buckets of tepid water over one another, when an agitated quartermaster-sergeant interrupted our desperate attempt to avert heat-stroke.

'They've caught 'im, sir!' he panted, as if announcing the fall of a second Kut.

'Caught who?'

'Chuck, sir!'

I groped for a pair of shorts.

'Who's caught him and why?' I demanded.

'The colonel at the dump, sir. Says Chuck's been pinchin' 'is comforts, sir. There's a warrant officer and a gang of natives come to search the barges, sir.'

'Search the barges?'

'Yes, sir, to see if any of the stuff's 'idden.'

One look at my sergeant's face told me what to expect if the search took place.

'How long do you want?' I asked.

''Arf an hour, sir,' he answered hopefully.

With as much dignity as I could muster I walked to the gangway and confronted the warrant officer, who informed me with the strained politeness of a hot and angry man that his colonel had sent him to search the barges. With the utmost indignation I spurned the idea that any unauthorized supplies could be concealed on my barges. Did he think my men were thieves? He made it quite clear that he did. I shifted my ground. What authority had he? No written authority! I could not think of permitting a search without written authority until I had seen the colonel. We would go back to the colonel.

I dressed, and we went to the supply depot. It was in an uproar. Indian *babus* and British N.C.O.s were feverishly checking stores in all directions, while from the office tent came roars of rage as each fresh discrepancy was reported. I entered in some trepidation to be greeted by a bellow.

'Do you know how much those Birmingham burglars of yours have looted from my hospital comforts? Look at this!'

He thrust a list under my nose, item after item: condensed milk, tinned fruit, cigarettes, jam.

'But—but how do you know *my* men have taken all this, sir?' I gasped.

'Caught 'em! Caught 'em in the act! Bring that hulking great lout who said he was in charge!'

Chuck, seemingly quite unmoved, and if anything slightly amused by the uproar, was marched in between two British sergeants.

'That's the feller!' exploded the colonel, stabbing a denunciatory pencil at Chuck. 'Caught him myself, marching out as bold as brass with a fatigue party of your robbers and a case of lump sugar—the only lump sugar in Mesopotamia! Lifting it under my very nose! Said he'd picked it up by mistake with the other rations, blast his impudence!'

Chuck stood there stolidly, his jaws moving slowly as he chewed gum—more hospital comforts, I feared. His eyes roamed over the tent, but as they passed mine they threw me a glance of bored resignation.

'He'll be court-martialled,' continued the colonel, 'and'—he glared at me—'you'll be lucky if he's the only one that's court-martialled! Now I'm going to search those barges of yours.'

Chuck grinned ruefully as I passed and I caught a whisper of, 'It's a fair cop, all right.' I was afraid it was. We left him chewing philosophically while he and his escort awaited the arrival of the provost-marshal's police.

The colonel, to give him his due, searched those barges thoroughly. He even had the hatches off and delved among the sacks of *atta* that formed the cargo. He and his men grew hotter, dustier, and more furious, but not an empty condensed milk tin, not the label of a preserved pineapple could they find. He turned out the men's kits, he rummaged in the cooks' galley; he even searched the sick-bay we had rigged up in the bows for the sick awaiting removal by bullock *tonga*.

It was empty, except for one may, who lay stretched out flat on his blankets, under a mosquito-net. The colonel glared through the net at the wretched man who with closed eyes was breathing heavily.

'Suspected cholera!' the quartermaster-sergeant whispered hoarsely.

The sick man groaned and clasped his stomach. I thought his complexion was rather good for a cholera case, but then I am no clinical expert. Nor was the colonel. He called off his men, and, breathing threats, left us.

That evening we sailed. After much chuffing and chugging, to the accompaniment of a great deal of yelling in good Glasgow Scots and bad British Hindustani, a squat little tug had hauled our steamer out of the palm grove. We were lashed, a barge on each side, and staggered off up-river. But we left Chuck behind us, and I was thinking, rather sadly and not without some prickings of conscience, that we should miss him, especially at mealtimes, when the quartermaster-sergeant interrupted my gentle melancholy.

'Will you 'ave peaches or pineapple for dinner, sir?'

'Good lord, Quartermaster-Sergeant, I thought you'd chucked it all overboard?' I gasped.

'So we did, sir,' he grinned. 'But we tied a rope to it with a bit of wood for a float, and when the colonel 'ad gone we pulled it up again. Some of the labels 've come off the tins, but that's all.'

'What about the cigarettes; they weren't in tins?'

'Oh, that chap in the sick-bay, 'e lay on 'em!'

Viscount Slim

302.

The leader of an Arab guerrilla army in Palestine, a man of classical education, is moved by their marching songs to recall the ballads of the legions.

THERE came a warning patter from the drums and the poet of the right wing burst in strident song, a single invented couplet, of Feisal and the pleasure he would afford us at Wejh. The right wing listened to the verse intently, took it up and sang it together once, twice and three times, with pride and self-satisfaction and derision. However, before they could brandish it a fourth time the poet of the left wing broke out in extempore reply, in the same metre, in answering rhyme, and capping the sentiment. The left wing cheered it in a roar of triumph, the drums tapped again, the standard-bearers threw out their great crimson banners, and the whole guard, right, left and centre, broke together into the rousing regimental chorus,

> I've lost Britain, and I've lost Gaul,
> I've lost Rome, and, worst of all,
> I've lost Lalage—

only it was Nejd they had lost, and the women of the Maabda, and their future lay from Jidda towards Suez. Yet it was a good song, with a rhythmical beat which the camels loved, so that they put down their heads, stretched their necks out far and with lengthened pace shuffled forward musingly while it lasted.

                                                    T. E. Lawrence

303.

OUR first impressions, formed in Serbia in 1915, were that the Bulgar was little better than an uncivilized savage, who lived for a lust of blood, and would delight in torturing his enemy for the pure joy of seeing him writhe. We heard terrible stories of the tortures inflicted on French soldiers who fell into their hands, and I have with my own eyes seen a Bulgar thrust his bayonet through an unarmed British soldier, who, cut off from his comrades, was offering to surrender.

The more we have seen of the Bulgar soldier, however, the more we have come into the way of thinking that he is not such a bad sort of fellow after all, and that he will play the game as long as his opponent plays the game too. Of the British he has no instinctive dislike. I am perfectly sure that, given the choice, individually, he would much prefer to fight with us than against us, especially after sampling the doubtful pleasures of German comradeship, during these many months of war. The Germans have done their best to instil a feeling of hatred for us in his mind, but apparently, with not quite so much success as they desire.

It is quite the Teutonic way to tell the less 'kultured' Bulgar that horrible treatment awaits him at the hands of the British should he fall into our hands, either voluntarily or involuntarily. One deserter, who came in, assured us that he had been told he would be eaten alive.

'That is why you came across?' questioned our Intelligence officer, cynically.

'I didn't believe it', replied the deserter.

In the struma fighting throughout the Bulgar has, up to the present, revealed a sporting quality with which few people, who do not know him, would credit him. The most striking instance of this was given at the Battle of Yenikoj after a fiercely delivered counter-attack had temporarily given the enemy a slight footing at the far end of the village. Both sides were engaged in the invigorating pastime of pouring 'rapid' into each other at a distance of 100 yards or so, when three of our men, observing that three wounded comrades were lying in the open between the Bulgars and ourselves, dashed over the top in order to bring them in. The Bulgar fire on the particular part of the line where this very gallant deed was being performed, immediately ceased, though it continued in every other part, with the result that the three wounded men were safely brought in to our line, and their rescuers were untouched. It was an incident that revealed the Bulgar in a different light to that which many had previously considered him in. But this is by no means an isolated instance of the Bulgar's sporting qualities. I remember being on outpost duty at Topalova, in front of which a troop of Yeomanry were pursuing their task of keeping the Bulgar patrols in check. Several hundred yards in front lay Prosenik, a once flourishing town on the railway, which was then still in the enemy's possession. The troop of cavalry had dismounted when an unexpected Bulgar H.E. fell among the horses, and one frightened animal dashed away in a dead line for Prosenik. A trooper promptly jumped on to his horse and galloped after the runaway. So exciting went the chase that in a few seconds our infantry were following it from their parapets standing up in full view of any wily Bulgar sniper who might be waiting for the opportunity of an exposed head. On dashed the runaway, the trooper still following it up, and then we realized that the Bulgar garrison of Prosenik had followed our example and was breathlessly following the race. It was a strange spectacle—Bulgar and British standing up in full view of each other, watching a runaway horse. At length the trooper headed the animal back towards our own lines, and returned with his captive without a single shot having been fired at him.

'The Bulgar is a humorous devil', is a remark one often hears passed, and it is certain that he possesses a deal greater sense of humour than his friend, the Bosche. There was rather a rage for some weeks on the part of ourselves, as well as the Bulgars, to post up (during expeditions into opposing territory) little messages for the edification of enterprising patrols on either side. I forget what the particular message was that I have in mind (they were legion) but on the day following its posting, pinned to the identical tree on which our message had been fixed, was the reply, and a P.S. which read, 'For goodness' sake, Englishmen, write in English next time. Your French is awful.' Needless to say, we rarely racked our mental French vocabulary after this in composing our letters to the enemy.

When told in one message from us that any Bulgar who would like to look us up would be welcomed and given plenty of bread (a subtle invitation in view of the enemy's reported shortage of bread), a reply was sent to the effect that any Britisher who thought of doing likewise would be warmly welcomed and that they had enough bread to feed all who came across, including the Commandant of— (the officer who signed our original message). The Bulgars invariably commenced their message with the prefix 'Noble Englishmen', and often reproached us for having invaded their 'peaceful Macedonian soil'. A subtle but amusing reference to Ireland was frequently included. But one day came a blood-curdling message to the effect that every loyal and true Bulgar's sole ambition was to plunge his bayonet deep in the breast of the hated British, and was so unlike our hitherto cordial exchange of letters that we unanimously ascribed it to a Teutonic hand. And I fancy we were not erring.

One day, a scratch football match was in progress behind our line, and well within view and range of the enemy guns, and it certainly was somewhat surprising that not a single shell came over to interrupt our game. It was in consequence of this forbearance on the part of our friends over the way that a conscientious O.C. Company, seeking an opportunity to fill up a sleepy hour by improving the bearing of his company by an hour's drill, paraded his company in as unexposed a spot as he could find and commenced arm drill. A shrapnel shell quickly dissipated the idea that this could be indulged in with impunity (to the delight of the whole company), and the following day a patrol discovered a message worded, as near as I can recollect—'We like to see you playing football, and we shall not shell you while you are playing football, and we are if we are going to watch you doing company drill.'

A. Donovan Young

304.

A visit to GHQ in France, August 1917.

I WENT to lunch with an old friend, Colonel Tandy of the Operations Branch of the General Staff. I was naturally plied with questions and I expressed my views with considerable candour and vigorous language . . . I wound up by definitely stating that, in my opinion, the battle was 'as dead as mutton', and had been so since the second day. . . .

I went with Tandy to his office. . . . While I sat there, an orderly came in and told me that Brigadier-General Davidson (at that time, Director of Operations, afterwards Major-General Sir John Davidson, K.C.B., D.S.O.) would like to see me before I left.

On entering Davidson's office, I found him seated at his table, his head in his hands.

'Sit down,' he said. 'I want to talk to you.' I sat down and waited.

'I am very much upset by what you said at lunch, Baker', he began. 'If it had been some junior officer, it wouldn't have mattered so much, but a man of your knowledge and experience has no right to speak like you did.'

'You asked me how things really were, and I told you frankly.'

'But what you say is impossible.'

'It isn't. Nobody has any idea of the conditions.'

'But they can't be as bad as you make out.'

'Have you been there yourself?'

'No.'

'Has anybody in O.A. been there?'

'No.'

'Well then, if you don't believe me, it would be as well to send somebody up to find out. I'm sorry I've upset you, but you asked me what I thought, and I've told you.'

Brigadier C. D. B. S. Baker-Carr

305.

Unexpected duties of a Guards officer in London, early 1918.

LATE one morning, I was sent for to the Regimental Orderly Room. Hastening as quickly as I could to the temple, I was commanded to proceed at once, with the regulation escort of a lieutenant and ensign, to St Pancras Station, and there arrest, as he stepped out of the train on to the platform, a 'young officer'. The charge against him was unspecified, but, I was given to understand, of a serious nature. In fact, I must use force, if necessary, to nab him: for he might prove a battling captive. And in this connection, let me remind the reader that the term 'young officer' was technical, youth consisting in short regimental service rather than in lack of years, and that, during the 1914–18 war, when many were already middle-aged before they took commissions, the accused might be old enough to be my father. And so, indeed, he proved. The poor old chap seemed very surprised when, placing his hat on his grey hair, he stepped out of the carriage and found two other officers and myself waiting for him, with, if I remember correctly military procedure, our swords drawn. He enquired, with an engaging air of puzzlement and timidity, what we could have against him. I replied that he would shortly learn, in the Regimental Orderly Room. According to orders, we marched there in fine style, and were received with considerable disciplinary pomp.

'Mr Crouchend,' the Lieutenant-Colonel observed, looking over the top of a pair of beautifully made spectacles with a terrifying mildness, 'there is a serious charge against you!'

'Sir!' Mr Crouchend replied dutifully, in the sacrificial monosyllable that is the correct reply to a superior officer in the Brigade of Guards.

'You gave a false address when on leave last week,' the Lieutenant-Colonel continued in the voice of an oracle. 'You wrote in the book 42 Clarges Street: we have evidence that you were staying at 12 Half Moon Street.'

With the cry of a wild animal that has been snared, poor Mr Crouchend broke away from tradition and wailed,

'But it's the same building, sir! It's Fleming's Hotel!'

Silence of a rather portentous kind followed this disclosure, and the junior officers of the escort, I observed, stared in front of them with peculiarly unseeing eyes. Already the mind's ear could detect the thunder of reprimand and rebuke that would, when we had departed, roll through the room: for the idol would speak, of that there could be no doubt. At last he roused himself from the coma into which he seemed to be descending, and called,

'March that officer out at once! I will go into the matter later.'

Osbert Sitwell

306.

March Retreat, 1918, viewed by a sniper of the Black Watch.

THE first two or three days, the bloodiest and most feverishly distraught of that magnificent rearguard action, were finished before myself was added to it; and though I was involved in some disagreeable episodes, my roundest recollections are of consuming, with great relish, a bottle of looted champagne and a jar of the best plum jam I have ever tasted; of sleeping very comfortably between two convenient graves in a shattered churchyard; and of listening, during a whole day of battle, to an Irishman discussing his next war.

Fragments and wandering details of many regiments were fighting together, and by chance I found myself in company with two men of the South Irish Horse. A plump and rather surly young trooper, and an elderly leather-skinned band-sergeant, a talkative fellow with a single mind. His opinion of the war, in which we were then so closely engaged, was simple and instructive: it was useful training for the approaching conflict with England. Even without their presence it would have been an interesting day, for we were retreating across open country, and behaving exactly as we had been taught: two platoons going back while others gave covering fire, and the latter retiring under the shelter of the rifles and Lewis guns of those who had preceded them. It was an admirable picture of the benefits of education; but to the Irish sergeant it was still a schoolroom exercise.

'Now stop shoving about', he would cry to the trooper, as we settled into a fold of the ground. 'Haven't I been telling you all morning to run like hell when you mean to run, and lie like a bloody rock when you're down? It's open country we'll be in when we're fighting the English, and now's your time to learn how to behave, and not make a target of yourself by thrusting your great round bottom in the air like a porpoise under the Old Head of Kinsale. What are your sights at?'

'Four hundred', shouted the plump young trooper, puffing and blowing.

'God Almighty! Give me patience! They were four hundred, weren't they, when you were down in the ditch beyond? And now you're a hundred yards nearer the sea, God help you, and by the same extent farther from Jerry, you fool, so put them up, you devil, and remember the wind that's blowing.'

I lay on his other side, and turning his head he spoke earnestly to me. 'If there's one thing I hate to see more than another,' he said, 'it's wasting good ammunition, and the waste that goes on here would frighten a millionaire. It breaks my heart to see the boys throwing off a bandolier because it's too heavy to carry, and to think what we could do with it in Ireland.'

'So you're going to fight the English?'

'We are that.'

'When?'

'As soon as we get finished with this blasted pigsty of a war, though I shouldn't be speaking against it, for it's good practice for boys the like of that lad there, who didn't know the touch of a trigger from the toe of my boot when he came out. But he's learning. He's learning every day, and he'll be a good boy yet.'

We retired again when a couple of light field-guns, motor-drawn, opened fire on us; and the Irish sergeant and I lay side by side in a stony gully.

'You ought to come in with us yourself', he said. 'Scotland and Ireland together: we'd knock the bloody English to hell.'

'I haven't any quarrel with England', I said.

'Ach, everybody has a quarrel with England, if they'd only the bloody sense to see it! It's England that has spoiled the whole world with its scheming and money-making and the righteousness, God save us, that says England knows the way of it, and all the rest are niggers or talking nonsense like children. Let the Scotch and Irish join together, and give England what Cromwell gave Drogheda, the bastard.—And what in hell are *you* thinking of, Michael James? Can you not see that bloody machine-gun there? And for the love of God put your sights up. Now all together: three rounds rapid—fire!'

Eric Linklater

307.

With the American Expeditionary Force in France.

As we march, houses appear more numerous. Soon they line the road. Still no sign of life in any of them. It seems as though a pestilence had swept over this part of the country. We do not see any signs of fighting, not even a solitary shell-hole.

Soon we are in cobble-paved streets. We see shops.

No shopkeepers. We look at the signs over the entrances of the stores.

We are in the city of Arras.

It is a large city for northern France. There are hotels, churches, stores, wine-shops. It is broad daylight now, but there is not a single soul in sight other than the marching troops. Our heavy footsteps echo down the empty streets.

There is an old-world quaintness about the buildings. We pass a soft brown Gothic cathedral, and in a few minutes are marching past the enormous rococo Hotel de Ville. We look at the signs at the street corners. We read: Grande Place. The square is flanked by Flemish houses which are built with their upper stories projecting over the footways and supported by columns so as to form an arcade. Not a civilian soul can be seen.

We halt. We are in one of the main streets. On both sides of the street are stores—grocery stores, tobacco shops, clothing stores, wineshops. In the windows we see displays of food and cigarettes temptingly displayed—tins of lobster, glass jars of caviare, tinselcapped magnums of champagne. I look through a glass window and read: *Veuve Cliquot*—the bottle looks important and inviting. In another window I read: 'Smoke De Reszke cigarettes.'

We ask our captain—a fidgety, middle-aged man by the name of Penny—why the town is deserted. He explains that the Germans dropped a few long-range shells into the city a few days ago, and the inhabitants, thinking that Heinie was about to enter, fled leaving the city as we now see it.

We rest on the kerb of the street, looking hungrily at the food and cigarettes behind the thin glass partitions. Little knots of soldiers gather and talk among themselves.

As I stand talking to Broadbent a man in the company ahead of us idly kicks a cobble-stone loose from its bed. He picks it up and crashes it through a wide, gleaming shop window. The crash and the sound of the splintering, falling glass stills the hum of conversation. The soldier steps through the window and comes out with a basketful of cigarettes. He tosses packages to his comrades.

Another crash!

More men stream through the gaping windows.

Officers run here and there trying to pacify the men.

As far as I can see, men are hurling stones through windows and clambering in for supplies.

The street is a mass of scurrying soldiers.

Discipline has disappeared.

I step through an open, splintered window and soon come out laden with tins of peas, lobster, caviare, bottles of wine. Broadbent and I visit many shops. In each are crowds of soldiers ransacking shelves, cupboards, cellars. Some of them are chewing food as they pillage.

When we have filled our bags with food, drink and cigarettes, we make off to look for a place to rest.

We climb through a window of a pretentious-looking dwelling. It is deserted. We prowl through the house. In the dining-room the table is set for the next meal. There is no sign of disorder—the inhabitants must have fled without preparation of any sort.

We dump our sacks down in the centre of the room and begin to prepare the food. In a little while we are tackling lobster salad, small French peas, bread and butter, and washing it down with great gulps of Sauterne. We do not speak, but simply devour the food with wolfish greed.

At last we are sated. We search in the sacks and find tins of choice Turkish cigarettes. We light up, putting our dirty feet on the table and smoke in luxury.

We hunt through the house and find the owner's room. Water is boiled and soon we are shaved and powdered with the late owner's razor and talcum. We throw ourselves on the valanced beds and fall asleep.

We are wakened by the sound of crashing noises downstairs. We descend. A party is going on in the drawing-room. Some of our men have found the house. They are drunk. Some sprawl on the old-fashioned brocaded gilt furniture. Some dance with each other.

More men arrive.

One of the recruits, a machine-gunner, draws his revolver from his holster and takes pot-shots at a row of china plates which line a shelf over the mantelpiece.

His companions upbraid him:

'Hey, cut out that bloody shooting; you're filling the damned room with smoke.'

The conversation is boastful and rowdy.

'Some of the men bust into the church and took all the gold and silver ornaments. . . . '

' . . . There's wine-cellars in this town as big as a house. They'll never get the outfit out of here. . . . '

'They'll send for the M.P's . . . '

'We'll give 'em what-for when they come, don't worry. . . . '

Broadbent and I go out into the street. It is nearly dark. Men stagger about burdened with bags of loot. They are tipsy. The officers are nowhere to be seen. Up towards the line the sky is beginning to be lit with the early evening's gun flashes.

Over to the south side of the town a red glow colours the sky. Some of our men must have set fire to some houses. As we look we see flames and a shower of sparks leap into the air.

We look at each other in amazement.

'Do you know that this is looting a town?' Broadbent says.

'Of course it is.'

'There will be merry hell to pay for this.'

We turn into the Grande Place. Men lie drunk in the gutters. Others run down the street howling, blind drunk.

There is nothing to do, so we walk into a wineshop. We find a bottle of cognac and drink it between us. We go out again.

The streets are bedlams.

From the houses come sounds of pianos as though they were being played by madmen. Men laugh, sing, brawl.

We find an officer and ask where we are to report. He is a little drunk, too. He does not know and staggers on.

The flames of the fire to the south leap higher and higher.

Overhead we hear the whirr of motors. Planes are reporting that the city is occupied. Shells begin to scream into the city. The detonations sound louder in the echoing streets.

Falling masonry and bricks make it dangerous to stay out of doors.

The shells come faster and faster.

Bodies begin to litter the streets.

The explosions swell into the steady roar of bombardment.

The streets are lit with the flashes of the shell-bursts.

Buildings take fire.

Men run to shelter. The revelry turns into nightmare.

Broadbent and I find a deep cellar. Over our heads the rafters shiver with the force of the shell-bursts.

Other men come streaming down the stairs. The bombardment has sobered them.

Sacks of food and drink are piled into the corners of the cellar.

After a while we fall asleep. . . .

In the morning we awake with champagne hang-overs. We feel groggy and thirsty. We go out into the streets. Soldiers are scurrying about carrying sacks of looted provisions.

By noon most of the men are drunk again. Men stagger through the streets waving empty wine bottles. Some of them have found a French quartermaster storehouse where some French officer uniforms were stored. They cut ludicrous figures in the ill-fitting blue tunics.

News of the looting has spread to Army Head-quarters.

A detachment of mounted English Military Police approach the town.

The police are our traditional enemies.

We organize a volunteer defence corps.

We post ourselves on the roofs of houses which overlook the road which leads into the city. We are armed with rifles, machine-guns, hand-grenades.

As the police canter close to the town they are met with a burst of rifle-fire.

Two horses are hit and rear madly into the air. The M.P.'s draw rein and about face.

This is our first victory over the police. The retreat is greeted with cheers.

We celebrate the event by going back into the main streets and drinking more wine.

Comrades meet and relate incidents of the day.

' . . . the officers are as drunk as we are. . . . '

' . . . two guys got into a cellar that had one of those big vats . . . they turned on the faucet and started to drink out of their mess-tins . . . got so drunk that they forgot to turn it off after a while . . . when we looked through the trap-door this morning they were floating in about five feet of wine . . . '

' . . . God, who would've thought that plain gravel-crushers like us would ever get rich pickin's like this . . . '

' . . . the soldier's dream come true, all right, all right . . . '

' . . . hey, the frogs is supposed to be our allies . . . '

'What, with *vin rouge* at five francs a bottle?'

'Well, why the hell didn't they bring the grub up . . . '

Charles Yale Harrison

308.

TEN days before the end, the battery was in action before Le Ques-noy. Merredew had left to command a battery in the north. The guns were in a little field, sloping down to a stream on the other side of which was a large mill. The only road to the front ran over the bridge past the mill. All day long the columns of men, guns, and transport passed over this bridge, and all day long the enemy shelled it with a high-velocity gun. In the afternoon when the gunners had ceased firing they lay back on the grass and speculated which of the endless teams of horses and mules, limbers and guns would get safely across the bridge. The sappers were working hard at repairs under this steady shell-fire. A gallant party of military police and others were clearing away the dead horses and men that littered the road both sides of the stream. A gun team would come trotting down the hill towards the bridge and a hundred yards from it, break into a gallop. 'Hooray! they are safely across. Here come the next lot! Bang! That's got them. No, it hasn't—!' as horses and men, less one driver, emerge from the smoke, and gallop up the road into safety the other side. At dusk the enemy ceased fire, and the mill being the only available billet, the men moved into its vast, underground store-room, whilst Shadbolt and the officers occupied an upstairs room, where there were some beds. Soon after midnight that accursed gun began again. Whee-oo! Whoosh! Bang! The shells sailed over the mill-house and crashed on to the road beyond. An argument began between Queenie and the Cherub as to whether a retirement to the cellar would not be sound policy. CRASH! and Shadbolt woke up, soaked to the skin, his bedclothes in ribbons— unhurt! The shell had come through the roof and burst in the attic above, upsetting a bucket of water and ripping a great hole in the ceil-ing. At this critical moment Mr Prout appeared, dignified and urbane even at that hour. 'Excuse me, sir, but before retiring to rest I deemed it advisable to put the officers' kit in the cellar. I have laid out your valise and placed your flannel trousers and a clean shirt under the pillow.'

The next day they moved forward again and supported the New Zealanders in the assault on Le Quesnoy. The brigade car was the first to enter the town, where the Colonel, to his intense embarrassment, was soundly kissed by a grateful old woman. He was so unnerved that on his return to head-quarters he poured himself out a tumblerful of neat gin and started to drink, thinking it was water. His staff watched him with amusement. Expressions of astonishment, anger, defiance, and gratification chased each other in succession across his face as without a word, he emptied the tumbler.

Alone 2XX went forward into the Forest of Mormal. It was here, on the 8th of November, that news was received that Merredew had been killed four days earlier at Moen on the Scheldt.

Very early on the last morning Shadbolt was watching the men dragging the heavy howitzers into a little clearing in the wood. The day was grey and overcast and the raindrops from a recent shower were dripping sadly off the trees. Above them a few pigeons, disturbed by the movements and cries of the men, circled and wheeled. A despatch rider rode up and handed him a message form. 'Hostilities will cease at 11 a.m. to-day. A.A.A. No firing will take place after this hour.' He sat down on the stump of a tree. In any case, the order did not affect them. The enemy was already out of range, and they could move no further.

This then, was the end. Visions of the early days, their hopes and ambitions, swam before his eyes. He saw again his pre-historic howitzer in the orchard at Festubert, and Alington's long legs moved towards him through the trees. He was back with the Australians in their dug-out below Pozieres. He saw the long slope of the hill at Heninel, covered with guns, ammunition dumps, tents and dug-outs. Ypres, the Salient, Trois Tours, St Julien—the names made unforgettable pictures in his mind. Happy days at Beugny and Beaussart, they were gone and the bad ones with them. Hugh was gone, and Tyler and little Rawson; Sergeant Powell, that brave old man; Elliot and James and Johnson—the names of his dead gunners strung themselves before him. This was the very end. What good had it all been? To serve what purpose had they all died? For the moment he could find no answer. His brain was too numb with memories.

'Mr Straker.'

'Sir.'

'You can fall the men out for breakfast. The war is over.'

'Very good, sir.'

Overhead the pigeons circled and wheeled.

Lt.-Col. F. Lushington

309.

11 November 1918.

. . . the grim business of war itself went on as usual, right up to 11 a.m., and, at one or two points along the line, even beyond. Thus a captain commanding an English cavalry squadron which took the Belgian village of Erquelinnes wrote that morning:

At 11.15 it was found necessary to end the days of a Hun machine-gunner on our front who would keep on shooting. The armistice was already in force, but thee was no alternative. Perhaps his watch was wrong but he was probably the last German killed in the war—a most unlucky individual!

Elsewhere on the British front an officer commanding a battery of six-inch howitzers was killed at one minute past eleven—at which his second-in-command ordered the entire battery to go on firing for another hour against the silent German lines.

But generally, any firing still going on ended on the last second of the tenth hour, sometimes with droll little ceremonies—as on the British front near Mons, where another and more fortunate German machine-gunner blazed off his last belt of ammunition during the last minute of the war and then, as the hour struck, stood up on his parapet, removed his steel helmet, bowed politely to what was now the ex-enemy opposite, and disappeared.

The British division on whose front that little incident took place had lost, during that one final week of the war, two officers killed and twenty-six wounded, and among the other ranks one hundred and seventeen killed, six hundred and ninety-three wounded and sixty-one missing. Small wonder that its historian recorded 'no cheering and very little outward excitement' as peace came.

Gordon Brook-Shepherd

310.

A British officer returns to an old battlefield.

THE village was flooded when last I was here; the Germans had gone the night previously, and no guns were firing, for the enemy had walked out of range.

I remember the Bengal Lancers filing through the ruins: bearded, turban'd, dark-skinned soldiers, with the pennons on their upheld lances scarcely fluttering in the windless air. A battalion of the Yorkshire Regiment was 'on fatigue', laying balks of timber over the liquid mud of the broken road. As I passed on my horse I saw a pallid hand sticking out between two balks, and a sodden grey uniform cuff; a young soldier laughingly put the handle of a broken spade between the stiff fingers, saying, 'Now then, Jerry, get on wi' it; no bluudy skrimshankin' 'ere.'

I entered an *estaminet* near the station and asked for bread and cheese and wine. It was an untidy place like the village, a place of shapeless shacks and sheds made of rusty sheets of wartime corrugated sheet-iron among buildings partly rebuilt. There were several young men in the room watching two men playing a game of billiards. An idiot child was running about the room, and seeing me, but without human recognition, it came up and took my stick out of my hand. Its father, a man of about thirty-five years of age, in slovenly clothes, shouted something as he raised himself from a leaning position over the billiard table, and then resumed his preparation for a stroke. A female voice replied shrilly and rapidly from the unseen kitchen, and a moment later a woman ran out, seized the child by its wrist, wrenched the stick out of its fingers, returned it to me without a glance, and dragged the child through a door into the kitchen.

I waited five minutes, ten minutes, but no one took any notice of me; the game continued with much jabbering of voices, which is another way of saying that I understood only one word in fifty of the language of the country in which I was a foreigner.

At the end of a quarter of an hour madame cam back, less untidy and less worried, and agreed to cook me an omelette.

I ate in silence when it arrived; and I had just finished it when the game ended and the patron (I am ignorant of the right word; my authority for this term is a hazy boyish memory of the international works of the late Mr William Le Queux) came to speak with me. I told him in my weak French that I was a returned soldier; I gave him a laboured account of the village as it had appeared in the winter of 1916–17. He said that his wife had been there until November, 1916, when the English advanced up the valley from Beaumont Hamel; le pauvre petit—he indicated the idiot child—had been a baby of two years then, and had been struck in the head by a piece of English shell—c'est la guerre. . . . The other men stopped talking, and listened; I explained that I was meditating a novel, or novels, of the War, the story of an insignificant and obscure family which had helped, in its small way, to prepare and make the Great War. I would of course, have to draw on some of my own experiences, as Henri Barbusse had in *Le Feu*.

Their eyes lit up; they exclaimed with enthusiasm at that name. That was reality, la verité! Only the week before a German soldier, looking for the grave of his brother, had come to the village, and it so chanced that he had read Barbusse, and had declared that it was true for the German soldier as well as for the French! He was a comrade, that Boche . . . no, Boche was a bad word, part of the old world: pas vrai! He was a man like themselves, but in the War his uniform happened to be a different colour. He was a brother!

It was amazing, the animation on the faces of those men. Their eyes were lit by inner fire; they smiled eagerly, their gestures and attitudes were vital and happy. What had brought this miracle—to use a term of the old world? A stranger had come, a German; a stranger had come, an Englishman; after the mention of a name there was no reserve, no suspicion, no distrust; all shared a common humanity. Something not supernatural, but supernational.

'Bonne chance, camarade! Bonne chance!'

I settled the very small bill, adding a few francs extra, and left gaily in the rain, and turned to see them watching me from the doorway. All of us waved together.

Henry Williamson

311.

An act of misguided chivalry by Colonel George S. Patton, entirely in character with the legend revealed in the Second World War.

ON a summer night in 1922, while driving his roadster from the [horse] show to his hotel in Garden City, he spotted three rough-looking characters with a damsel in apparent distress. They seemed to be pushing the girl into the back of a truck. Patton stopped his car, jumped out and forced the men at gun point to release the young woman. Then it developed that the girl was the fiancée of one of the men, who merely were helping her to climb into the truck.

The incident was reminiscent of Don Quixote's encounter with the six merchants of Toledo on the road to Murcia and his spirited defence of Dulcinea's unquestioned virtue. When later Patton laughingly related the story of his gratuitous intervention to a spell-bound lady of Long Island society, he was asked, 'How come, Georgie, that you go armed to a civilian horse show?'

'I believe in being prepared', he told her. 'I always carry a pistol, even when I'm dressed in white tie and tails.'

Ladislas Farago

312.

THE parade sergeant-major was addressing the King's Squad of the Royal Marines:

'On the 26th June, 1926, you will be marching into the arena at Olympia. Seated in the Royal box will be 'er Majesty, Queen Mary. 'Er 'usband, King George V, our Colonel-in-Chief, will not be present as 'e is sick-a-bed at Buckingham Palace . . .

'You will go through your stuff, and when you 'ave done, 'er Majesty will get into 'er carriage and drive back to Buckingham Palace . . . She will say: "I've bin to Olympia, George", and 'e will say: "Oh, 'ave you, Mary, and 'ow was those young Marines of mine?" and she will say: "Well, excuse me, George, but they was bloody awful"—AND SO YOU ARE.'

Sir Robert Bruce Lockhart

313.

A timeless sample of military bureaucracy, as recorded by a Military Assistant to the Chief of the Imperial General Staff in the 1920s.

I HOPE I shall not fall foul of the Official Secrets Act if I quote verbatim the following branch memorandum. On March 10, 1926, the C.I.G.S. asked me for a pair of dividers, costing, I suppose, eighteen pence. How did I obtain them? Here is the answer:

1

'Q.M.G.9.
'Would you be good enough to obtain a pair of dividers for the use of C.I.G.S.?

J. F. C. Fuller,
Colonel G.S., M.A. to C.I.G.S.'

10th March, 1926.

2

'X Compass, drawing, shifting leg, double jointed, II. Q.M.G.F. (b).
'We propose to convey approval to the permanent issue of a Compass as at X above. Have you any remarks from a financial point of view?
Q.M.G.9 (a).
11th March, 1926.

J. Gardner,
For D.A.D.E.O.S.'

3

'Q.M.G.9 (a).
'No financial objection. Will you let us have this B.M. again when the Compass has been issued?
Q.M.G.F. (b).
15th March, 1926.

G. Lillywhite.'

4

'A.D.O.S.P.
'Will you please arrange issue of a Compass, drawing, shifting leg, double-jointed II. to— M.A. to C.I.G.S. Room 217, War Office? Issue will be permanent.
Q.M.G.9 (a).
16th March, 1926.

J. Gardner,
For D.A.D.E.O.S.'

5

'Q.M.G.9 (a).
'Issue has been arranged.
'I.O.P.4.D/4186 dt. 18.3.26.
18th March, 1926.

H. E.,
For A.D.O.S. Provision.'

6

'M.A. to C.I.G.S.
'Please let me know when the compass is received.
Q.M.G.9. (a).
19th March, 1926.

J. Gardner,
For D.A.D.E.O.S.'

7

'Q.M.G.9 (a).

'Compass received, thank you.

J. F. C. Fuller,

24th March, 1926.   Colonel G.S., M.A. to C.I.G.S.'

J. F. C. Fuller

314.

A young officer leaves Sandhurst in 1929.

WHEN I sat for the final exams I discovered with pleasure mixed with surprise that they came quite easily to me and as I had also accumulated a very nice bonus of marks for being an Under-Officer, my entry into the Argylls seemed purely a formality. Everything in the garden was beautiful—a fatal situation for me.

Just before the end of term, all cadets who were graduating were given a War Office form to fill in:

'Name in order of preference three regiments into which you desire to be commissioned.'

I wrote as follows:

1. The Argyll and Sutherland Highlanders
2. The Black Watch

and then for some reason which I never fully understood, possibly because it was the only one of the six Highland Regiments that wore trews instead of the kilt, I wrote

3. Anything but the Highland Light Infantry.

Somebody at the War Office was funnier than I was and I was promptly commissioned into the Highland Light Infantry.

David Niven

315.

Late in life, the British Army's official historian of the First World War, General Sir James Edmonds, compiled a fascinating list depicting the fate of his fellow students on the Staff College course of 1896. After detailing the obvious generals and casualties on the battlefield, the count becomes somewhat more exotic.

PLACED on the retired list for quelling a riot by

machine-gun fire in India (Dyer)   1

Joined the Sudan Civil Service	1
Retired on coming into money	2
Shot his mother-in-law and her lawyer and committed suicide	1
Last heard of keeping a brothel in Smyrna—his father married a Levantine during the Crimean War	1

Sir James Edmonds

316.

A fellow officer of the author in the Highland Light Infantry, one John Royal, reaches the abrupt termination of his military career after being posted to India.

SOON after his arrival, the officers of the Second Battalion were invited to a ball given by the local maharajah and John became sleepy, so after dinner he lay down behind some potted palms and stole forty winks. He was awakened by a captain of a cavalry regiment who stirred him, none too gently, with his foot.

'Stand up', said the Captain. John stood.

'You are drunk', said the Captain.

'You are right', said John and flattened him with a left hook.

He then composed himself once more behind the potted palms. Pretty soon he was awakened again, this time by a full colonel of Artillery.

'Stand up', said the Colonel. John stood.

'You are drunk', said the Colonel and collected a right cross.

John was court-martialled and insisted on conducting his own defence. He had been dropped on his head as a baby, he said, and this had the unfortunate effect of making him lash out at the first person he saw when he was woken from a deep sleep.

The prosecuting officer smiled faintly. 'Perhaps you would tell the court what happens to your batman when he wakes you up in the morning?'

'Nothing,' said John, unmoved. 'I have issued him with a fencing mask.'

David Niven

317.

The perils of frontier life with the Bengal Lancers.

I DO not know how far discipline of the sex life is a good thing. But I know that a normal sex life is more necessary in a hot than a cold country. The hysteria which seems to hang in the air of India is aggravated by severe continence of any kind; at the end of Ramzan, for instance, my fasting squadron used to become as lively as a basket of rattlesnakes. Many good brains in India have been bound like the feet of a mandarin's wife, so that they can only hobble ever after; and such cramping of the imagination may lose us the Empire.

Many times have I said that I would write these things. But now that I have done so, in this grey London weather, I cannot believe that I am not exaggerating. I cannot believe that it was too hot to bear a sheet on my skin, that I ingested six glasses of milk and soda for breakfast, had a malaria temperature twice a week for months on end, that my brain grew addled, and my liver enlarged, and my temper liable to rise like the fires of Stromboli. Yet so it was. Men's brains and bodies, like other machines, work differently at different temperatures; and India would be a happier country if we could always remember that, especially in Whitehall.

One night, when the temperature had risen apoplectically (for a ceiling of thunderclouds had closed in on us) and I lay gasping on the roof of my quarters, a revolver shot rang out from a neighbouring bungalow. A moment before I had been drinking tepid soda water, and thinking of England, and cursing this stifling night through which the angel of sleep would not come. But now Providence had sent something better—raiders?

Voices cries 'Halaka ghula di!' (' 'Ware thief!'). Khushal arrived with the first weapon to his hand, a lance.

I went out in my pyjamas to explore. Crossing the road in the direction of the shot, I found myself with a group of officers in the elderly Major's bungalow, where a curious story was related to me.

The elderly Major had been celebrating his approaching departure with more than enough champagne. On reaching his bed he had lain down quietly; in a stupor, no doubt. Then his shattered nerves began to conjure up visions, and by the glimmer of the night-light which he always kept burning beside him, he saw a skinny outline at the foot of the bed. When he moved, it moved. Seizing a revolver in his trembling hand, he fired; then he roared with pain, for he had shot not a face, but his own foot.

Next morning, he was hurried down to Kohat, with an orderly to put ice on his mangled toes and on his poor, deluded head.

F. Yeats-Brown

318.

A newly joined subaltern with the Duke of Cornwall's Light Infantry in India in 1934.

I CAN live with the memory of my first day in the awe-inspiring and gloomy splendour of an officers' mess. It was in Bareilly, and I was still nineteen. I sat down to tea at the polished table and cautiously admired a large fruit cake in front of me. After licking my lips for five minutes, I screwed up my courage and asked the captain next to me whether I might be allowed to have some cake. He turned, looked at me with an indescribable expression of scorn and astonishment, and said coldly, 'Yes. That's a mess cake. You're not at your prep school now.'

Christmas came. I had ceased to be nineteen, and on Christmas Day it was my turn to be orderly officer. On this day my duties included following the colonel, the second-in-command, and the adjutant round every mess hall in the battalion—seven of them—and, in each mess, drinking toasts from half-tumblers of whisky thinly diluted with fizzy lemonade. The British soldiers, far from home and families, tried to forget their exile in a riot of snowballing, singing, and drinking. The sergeants waited on them at table.

After a couple of hours our bedraggled and hardly conscious convoy reached the officers' mess and sat down, without hunger, before an enormous Christmas dinner. The lieutenant at the head of the table suddenly remembered that this day was traditionally a topsy-turvy one for rank and discipline. He picked a leg of turkey off his plate and flung it accurately at the officer sitting at the other end, who happened to be a senior major. The colonel smiled, but after all he was no longer in his twenties. He collected the majors with his eye and left us. As the field officer crept silently out the air grew thick with flying potatoes, pudding, turkey, gravy, and oranges.

I watched in amazement. If we had behaved like this at the Royal Military College we would have been rusticated on the spot and told we were quite unfit to be officers. Apparently when one actually became an officer the rules were different. Amazement gave place to loneliness and a despair born of all those toasts, for I was not at all used to drinking. I have tried so hard to be an officer, I thought tearfully. I want so much to be treated as one of the family. But no one is throwing anything at *me*. They haven't forgiven me about the cake yet.

Then—oh, ecstasy!—hard fingers were rubbing brandy butter into my hair and stuffing Christmas pudding into my ears. I was forgiven, accepted! I flung myself with abandon into the riot, and the steaming rum punch flew faster round the table and the snow flew thicker outside the windows.

When all our fiendish energy had at last been spent, and we were preparing to go and clean ourselves, someone heard a faint muttering from the floor. We knelt and looked under the wide table. We saw two doctors, both medical majors, lying comfortably on their sides, their heads pillowed on cushions. A bottle of brandy stood between them and they were arguing in an involved way about horsebreeding for they were, of course, like most army doctors, Irishmen. They must have been there for hours and no one knew how or when they had arrived. We sent another bottle of brandy down to them, with the compliments of the regiment, and trooped out into the snow.

John Masters

319.

One of the most celebrated incidents in the Spanish Civil War took place in the summer of 1936, during the defence of Toledo by a 1,300-strong Nationalist garrison under Colonel José Moscardó.

FROM Madrid, the minister of education, the minister of war, and General Riquelme had been furiously telephoning the 58-year-old infantry colonel, Moscardó, commander of the nationalist garrison still holding out in the Alcázar, in an attempt to persuade him to surrender. Finally, on 23 July, Cándido Cabello, a republican barrister in Toledo, telephoned Moscardó to say that if Moscardó did not surrender the Alcázar within ten minutes, he would shoot Luis Moscardó, the Colonel's 24-year-old son, whom he had captured that morning. 'So that you can see that's true, he will speak to you', added Cabello. 'What is happening, my boy?' asked the Colonel. 'Nothing,' answered the son, 'they say they will shoot me if the Alcázar does not surrender.' 'If it be true,' replied Moscardó, 'commend your soul to God, shout *Viva España*, and die like a hero. Good-bye my son, a last kiss.' 'Good-bye father,' answered Luis, 'a very big kiss.' Cabello came back on to the telephone, and Moscardó announced that the period of grace was unnecessary. 'The Alcázar will never surrender', he remarked, replacing the receiver. Luis Moscardó was not, however, shot there and then, but was executed with other prisoners in front of the Tránsito synagogue on 23 August, in reprisal for an air raid.

Hugh Thomas

320.

A British volunteer with the Republican army reflects upon the tragi-comic incompetence which characterized the conduct of the Spanish war.

THE difficult passwords which the army was using at this time were a minor source of danger. They were those tiresome double passwords in which one word has to be answered by another. Usually they were of an elevating and revolutionary nature, such as *Cultura—progreso*, or *Seremos—invencibles*, and it was often impossible to get illiterate sentries to remember these highfalutin' words. One night, I remember, the password was *Cataluña—eroica*, and a moon-faced peasant lad named Jaime Domenech approached me, greatly puzzled, and asked me to explain.

'*Eroica*—what does *eroica* mean?'

I told him that it meant the same as *valiente*. A little while later he was stumbling up the trench in the darkness, and the sentry challenged him:

'*Alto! Cataluña!*'

'*Valiente!*' yelled Jaime, certain that he was saying the right thing.

Bang!

However, the sentry missed him. In this war everyone always did miss everyone else, when it was humanly possible.

George Orwell

321.

Manœuvres with the Oxford University Cavalry Squadron.

THE Baron—we never caught his real name; it sounded like the Vicomte de Broncoute—was of Belgian extraction. A stout, bespectacled individual of Teutonic mien, he was immediately dubbed 'Baron Von Braunshnaut'. The nobleman, who had few friends, was anathema to Sergeant Rhimes and a goldmine to the grooms. He had an arrogant conceit. That he was well equipped was reluctantly accepted; that his horse was a superior type of Hanoverian with impeccable manners and certain dressage ability, could not be denied; but in camp such niceties were considered superfluous. . . .

It was an episode in the Long Valley which proved the Baron's undoing. This is what happened, as described by an eye-witness:

The Oxford University Cavalry Squadron was about to mount, but the call 'Boots and Saddles' found Von Braunshnaut unprepared. Tubbs, waiting with his horse, enquired anxiously for 'the foreign gentleman', for names were quite beyond him.

Just at the off, the gallant horseman, who had been in London overnight, appeared and mounted in hot haste, but failed to notice that his girths needed final adjustment. Officer cadets in theory saddled their own chargers, but the rich and lazy chaps often paid the grooms to do it for them. Gathering up the reins he cantered off, despite shouts of warning from the stableman.

Once formed up, the Oxford Cavalry proceeded at a trot to join the big parade in the Long Valley, where General Blakiston Houston was to review the troops. The regiments rode past: at a trot, canter and finally at gallop. In this last manœuvre the Oxford Cavalry followed the Life Guards; behind them thundered two lancer regiments. It was a brave show and the horses enjoyed it as much as the men who rode them. At middle pace the band played us by to 'The Irish Washer Woman', then disaster struck!

The Baron was not far in front of me and I saw his saddle begin to turn. He made a gallant effort to stay on board and Oliver Woods and Bailey, a powerful New Zealander from Magdalen, edged forward to catch him, but to no avail. His saddle slipped and the Baron bit the dust! Two rocking, galloping regiments rode over him. Above the thunder of the charge came the cool voice of Percy Rhimes, our peerless instructor: 'Keep your head under your saddle, Sir. The Seventh Hussars are close behind.'

At the end of the parade the Reverend Tubbs approached me in the horse-lines; he looked worried, for the Baron was a good customer. 'Where has he got to, sir?' he asked hoarsely. 'What's left of him is down in the Long Valley,' came the callous reply. 'You'd better take a cab and pick up the bits.'

The unfortunate Continental finally limped in bruised and minus his hat, and immediately had his name taken for being improperly dressed. 'Where's your Service Dress cap?' enquired Neville. The Baron was incensed. 'Up your arse!' came the swift riposte! Braunshnaut was learning fast; even so Crump got the better of him.

Charged next morning at Adjutant's Orders, with loss of army equipment, the Baron's parting shot told against him. Now he faced two offences under various Army Acts:

1. Returning improperly dressed from the Major-General's Inspection.

2. Failing to report the loss of Government Property—one Service Dress cap.

Neville supplied the details: 'On being questioned where he had put this article of clothing, the officer cadet replied "Up your arse, schweinhund" or words to that effect. I immediately took his name for making a statement that I knew to be false, and placed him on the Charge Sheet, Sir.' The Baron was ordered to make good the deficiency.

Lord Lovat

322.

A Yeomanry subaltern learns the business of war on exercises in 1937.

THE squadron huddled together on horseback under cover of a wood. Tense with the excitement of the chase, Victor Bone sat erect on his horse, his heavy cavalry moustache stirred gently by the morning breeze. He sniffed the air as if to sense from it the whereabouts of the missing enemy. Then, with a few curt orders, he sent a patrol forward to reconnoitre. I wondered whether the time would ever come when I would attain to a comparable grasp of these complex matters.

The patrol assembled itself without seeming haste; and without seeming haste trotted off ahead. Obviously we had some time to wait before fighting could recommence. I took out a packet of cigarettes and offered one to my idol.

'Have a smoke, sir?'

His prominent, rather red-rimmed blue eyes stared at me in outraged astonishment.

'We never smoke during battle,' he said angrily.

John Verney

323.

An ambitious young regular captain of the British Army recalls 3 September 1939.

I CAN still clearly remember the exact text of one message: 'War has broken out with Germany only.' The first person I told was an RASC Captain who leapt for joy, saying: 'Marvellous! Marvellous! I was terrified that old Chamberbottom would settle up once again.'

However, most other people heard the news rather solemnly. My foremost thought was that it might mean promotion.

John Frost

324.

'Officer under instruction' in 1939.

I ARRIVED at the racecourse grandstand, which was then serving the Infantry Training Centre as its officers' mess, at about eight o'clock in the evening.

The Adjutant, summoned from his dinner by the mess corporal, was young, a regular soldier, and properly proud of his regiment and its traditions.

'Those trousers', he muttered, averting his eyes.

I apologized, explaining the circumstances.

'You can't', he kept on repeating, 'come into the mess in those God-awful trousers.'

I had been travelling all day. I was tired, hungry and rather frightened. Visions of a drink, followed by dinner, began to fade.

Taking me out into the decent obscurity of the platform at the top of a long flight of concrete steps, the Adjutant asked if I had brought a civilian suit. I told him I had.

'In that case,' he said with evident relief, 'you must go and change into it at once. *At once.*'

He organized transport to take me to my billet, an opulent villa, full of pink lampshades, situated about a mile and a half from the mess. The driver waited while I changed out of the faulty uniform which I had put on so proudly. I was driven back to the mess, where a late supper had been laid on. The Adjutant darted in and out like a flustered mother-bird. He did his best to dispel an unfortunate first impression, but I was painfully aware that whenever he set eyes on me during my sojourn at the ITC the recollection of those khaki slacks came between him and a proper appreciation of my military potentialities.

He had, poor chap, plenty of other troubles in connection with the newly joined wartime officers, of whom I was only one among many.

Three days after we had reported for duty he announced that a special parade had been laid on for us in the dining-room. When we assembled we observed that one place, and one place only, had been laid on the long mahogany dining-table which had been transported to the grandstand from the regimental mess. There was a lavish display of knives, forks, spoons and wine-glasses. Had we, the Adjutant inquired, brought our notebooks? Some of us had; others, imagining perhaps that we were to receive encouragement in the shape of a buckshee and supplementary meal, had not. While the ill-equipped retired to make good their deficiencies, the rest of us regarded the dining-room table with puzzled concern. When we were all in a state of readiness the object of the exercise was explained.

The Colonel, the Adjutant told us, had been concerned and shocked on the previous evening—a guest night—to observe that some of the newly joined officers had been in doubt about the correct implements and glasses to employ for the successive courses. If we would be kind enough to pay attention and take notes, he would give us a practical demonstration. Without batting an eyelid this impeccable young man then sat down at the table and an equally solemn mess waiter served him first with token soup, then with token fish, then with token meat, then with a token pudding and finally with a token savoury. The wine waiter went through the motions of pouring out sherry, burgundy, port and brandy. Somewhere I still possess the valuable notes I made.

Ralph Arnold

325.

Lord Yarborough reported for duty with his Yeomanry regiment with two hunters as his chargers, his personal valet as his servant, his stud groom as his second servant. To the peer's dismay, in France early in 1940 one of the horses developed colic.

THE horse chose to go sick in the middle of France, miles from civilization. The train clanked to a halt at a small country station. The horse was let down on to the platform. Corporal Harrison, former stud groom at Welbeck, tossed out numerous bales of straw, then jumped down to keep the horse company. The train puffed on, leaving the pair behind.

Harrison led the horse into the waiting room, surrounded it with straw, locked the door, and walked off briskly to the shops, whence he returned armed with several bottles of brandy.

The brandy cure had to be persisted with, and took some time. Outside, the frost could have chilled enough brass monkeys to provide fifty million Frenchmen with doorknockers. The travelling population, red-nosed and blue-cheeked, stormed the waiting room demanding admission. Harrison and his horse held the fort. The door was still locked.

After a time, both the brandy and the horse were exhausted. Harrison racked his brain, and remembered that there was a Liaison Officer between the British and French Commands, and that Officer was none other than the Duke of Gloucester. He commandeered the stationmaster's telephone, and by sheer effort of will bludgeoned a chain of operators into connecting him with His Royal Highness.

Harrison's explanation was brief and to the point. 'You remember when you visited Welbeck there was one horse with a wart on its nose?'

His Royal Highness had not forgotten.

'Well—I've got this horse here in the waiting room, and it's got the colic.'

Within the hour, a special carriage was hooked on to the next train. In the carriage were three veterinary officers from the Indian Army, equipped for any contingency.

By the time the Regiment reached Marseilles, Harrison and the horse (now thoroughly alive and kicking) proudly caught up with them.

T. M. Lindsay

326.

On 1 June 1940, Colonel A. D. Wintle determined that only personal, direct action by himself, making use of his old friends of the French air force, might enable some proportion of its strength to be flown to Britain and saved. What followed was one of the great eccentric sagas of the Second World War.

I . . . REALIZED that I hadn't a hope in hell of getting official sanction for a fast move. *Immediate* action was called for. I knew that if I failed to pull off the stunt I had in mind I would either be shot by the enemy or court-martialled by our side. But I considered it a worthwhile risk as long as there was the slightest chance of success.

I rang the Commandant at Heston Airfield, giving every password and code sign I knew, and claiming to be a senior Staff Officer at the Air Ministry. 'Please prepare an aircraft with all speed to take a Colonel A. D. Wintle to Bordeaux immediately. He will arrive shortly in a French Mission car. Absolute secrecy must be observed.'

It appeared to go down quite well. I was satisfied and drove out to the airport in the Mission car I had commandeered through my influential French friend. Unfortunately the preparation of the plane had taken less time than I had anticipated. As I reached Heston the Commandant was on the 'phone to the Air Ministry, crowing that the plane was ready. The response, of course, was: 'What bloody plane . . . ?' The flight was cancelled.

I thought quickly and attacked. I called the Commandant a blithering idiot for not maintaining secrecy and stormed out. I then drove straight to the Air Ministry and stormed into the office of Air Commodore Boyle, the Director of Intelligence, whose name and manner I had assumed when making the 'phone call ordering the plane.

I pleaded with him to allow me to fly to France that night. I begged him, as a patriot, to take this chance of salvaging France's air strength. He answered sharply that I would be court-martialled and that I could meanwhile, if I wished, make my suggestion in writing. It would have to proceed through the normal channels. I could not take the law into my own hands, as I would see.

I saw all right. I saw red and cursed him fluently. 'While you sit there,' I concluded, 'blood is flowing in France, not ink. And I am deadly serious.' I then drew my revolver and waved the muzzle under his nose like a warning finger. 'You and your kind ought to be shot', I snorted. And I named a few top people who deserved it as much as he did. I then broke my revolver, spilled out the bullets to show I had not been bluffing and left him shaking with fright.

I returned to my unit in the North that night. Next morning I was arrested. This seemed a trivial happening while the fate of Europe was in the balance. But I was given an escort and a warrant, to be placed under close arrest in the Tower of London while charges were prepared.

The rest of this story is more like a comedy play than an episode in a major war. You can always trust the Army (or, rather, the non-combatant part of it) to provide the laughs where they are least expected.

My escort, a timid little re-employed officer of the Lancashire Fusiliers, spent the whole journey from the camp to Liverpool fumbling through his pockets to see that the documents were safe. A dozen times he opened and shut my revolver holster, which he was carrying, to make sure the gun was still there. Yet, for all this worrying, when we got to the station the travel warrant was missing. He went through his pockets again and again, getting more flustered each time. We had about ten minutes left to catch the train. The next would land us in

London in the middle of the night—a prospect I did not relish. So I said to him: 'For heaven's sake stop fumbling. Wait here by the baggage while I go and get another warrant.'

He obeyed meekly and stood watching with an unhappy expression as his prisoner disappeared. But I had no desire to escape. I found the RTO's office and asked for a warrant. As no other officer was present, I signed it myself. This must surely make me the first—and only—prisoner who has ever signed his own travel warrant to the Tower of London.

Nothing else happened on the journey to disturb my escort's peace of mind. At the end of it he saw me lodged in a room in the forbidding stone tower with heavily barred windows. A Scots Guardsman, with fixed bayonet, took up a post at the door.

My life in the Tower had begun. How different it was from what I had expected. Officers at first cut me dead, thinking I was some kind of traitor; but when the news of my doings leaked out they could not do enough for me. My cell became the most popular meeting place in the garrison and I was as well cared for as if I had been at the Ritz. I would have a stroll in the moat after breakfast for exercise. Then sharp at eleven each morning, Guardsman McKie, detailed as my servant, would arrive from the officers' mess with a large whisky and ginger ale. He would find me already spick and span, for, though I have a great regard for the Guards, they have not the gift to look after a cavalry officer's equipment. The morning would pass pleasantly. By noon visitors would begin to arrive. One or two always stayed to lunch. They usually brought something with them. I remember a particularly succulent duck in aspic—it gave me indigestion—and a fine box of cigars brought by my family doctor. Tea-time was elastic and informal. Visitors dropped in at intervals, usually bringing along bottles which were uncorked on the spot. I don't recall that any of them contained tea. Dinner, on the other hand, was strictly formal. I dined sharp at eight and entertained only such guests as had been invited beforehand. After a few days of settling in, I was surprised to find that—as a way of life— being a prisoner in the Tower of London had its points. If there hadn't been a war on I might well have tried to get a life sentence.

Of course, I had to forgo the joys of freedom: pleasures like queuing up for rations, doing a useful job of work . . . or fighting the enemy; but I made up for that somehow and plenty of friends came to wish me well and cheer me up.

Only one visitor was unwelcome. He was an officer of the Judge-Advocate's department, the people who were bringing the case against me. I didn't in the least mind his questions, but he took the liberty of calling me 'old boy'—a slovenly form of address which I don't like from friends and can't bear from strangers. This gentleman told me he wanted to be 'perfectly frank'—a figure of speech which always puts me on my guard. It usually means exactly the opposite. After a lot of beating about the bush, it turned out that the War Office wanted to kiss and make up. Some of the brasshats were getting cold feet. 'After all, old boy,' said my 'frank' visitor, in honeyed tones, 'we don't want a Court Martial, do we?'

'You may not,' I answered tartly, 'but I do. I came here through the "usual channels" and that is the way I propose to leave. Now, sir, I will not detain you if you have pressing business elsewhere. Good day.' Looking like a little boy who has just been ticked off at school, he departed. He even forgot to say 'old boy' as he said goodbye. . . .

The day of my Court Martial came. I was escorted to the Duke of York's Headquarters, Chelsea, and led into the court. I felt a tension in the air and wondered what was in store for me. Then I read the charges and had great difficulty in stopping myself from laughing aloud. This, I could see, was going to be great fun. Most of the original charges (some dozens of them) had been dropped. Only three remained, and these were:

'Stating that certain of His Majesty's Ministers ought to be shot—thereby committing common assault.'

'Endeavouring to evade active service by feigning blindness in one eye.'

'Threatening a superior officer with a revolver.'

I was delighted to see that whoever was responsible for bungling the trial had made a first-class job of it. I did not deny the first charge. I carefully explained that in the Army there is a slogan 'no names, no packdrill'.

'It is a corporal's slogan,' I went on, 'and as I have never been a corporal I do not uphold it. I propose to name names. And if I forget anybody it will only be because of my inadequate memory and the fact that my list is so long.'

I then carefully and loudly named all those of His Majesty's Ministers whom I *still* thought should be shot, but I was not allowed to finish. When I got to Kingsley Wood, about seventh on my mental list, the prosecuting advocate interrupted. In an embarrassed tone of voice he rose to say that he did not propose to proceed with this charge. I was almost disappointed.

On to the second charge. Here, I proved conclusively that I had in fact volunteered for active service several times. I had not faked blindness or anything else. Instead, to try to get into action I had pretended *not* to be blind in an eye which was blind. I called Sir Edmund Ironside, CIGS, as a witness and he gave me an excellent reference as an eccentric and a fighter for England. If anything, this charge was dropped rather more quickly than the first.

Then came the third and last. It was argued at length. Great stacks of books were brought out. Learned counsel nodded and whispered together. I felt like a criminal specimen under a legal microscope. Then my 'friend in court', J. D. Casswell, QC, revealed that the man I was alleged to have threatened was not my superior officer at all, nor was he anyone else's. He was a perfectly ordinary Civil Servant, who had merely been given permission to wear the King's uniform while the war was on. The prosecution looked as though they'd had something for lunch that had disagreed with them badly. But, of course, they had to have a face-saver. This they achieved by the swift reduction of the third charge to one of ordinary civil assault. Now, if you threaten a person with your fist when within striking distance of him, even though you have no intention of striking, it is technically an assault. So, on these minor grounds, I was found guilty and sentenced to a severe reprimand.

The brasshats' faces were saved. I had a sense of victory. Technically, I was a naughty boy. Actually, I felt grand. Back at the Tower the Scots Guards greeted me like a conquering hero. Their CO, Gavin Maxwell, almost ran across the square to hand back my sword-belt and revolver and insisted on making me his guest for the evening. I was invited to continue using the room which had been my cell, the difference being that I now had the key of the door. Now these kindnesses, I am sure, were not demonstrations of affection for myself. They were an expression of the frustration that all true soldiers feel at seeing their country's flag dragged in the mire by a bunch of dithering incompetents.

A. D. Wintle

327.

On the beaches of Dunkirk in the dying days of May 1940.

THE picture will always remain sharp-etched in my memory—the lines of men wearily and sleepily staggering across the beach from the dunes to the shallows, falling into little boats; great columns of men thrust out into the water among bomb and shell splashes. The foremost ranks were shoulder deep, moving forward under the command of young subalterns, themselves with their heads just above the little waves that rode in to the sand. As the front ranks were dragged aboard the boats, the rear ranks moved up, from ankle deep to knee deep, from knee deep to waist deep, until they, too, came to shoulder depth and their turn.

Some of the big boats pushed in until they were almost aground, taking appalling risks with the falling tide. The men thankfully scrambled up the sides on rope nets, or climbed the hundreds of ladders, made God knows where out of new, raw wood and hurried aboard the ships in England.

The little boats that ferried from the beach to the big ships in deep water listed drunkenly with the weight of men. The big ships slowly took on lists of their own with the enormous numbers crowded aboard. And always down the dunes and across the beach came new hordes of men, new columns, new lines.

On the beach was the skeleton of a destroyer, bombed and burnt. At the water's edge were ambulances, abandoned when their last load had been discharged.

There was always the red background, the red of Dunkirk burning. There was no water to check the fires and there were no men to be spared to fight them. Red, too, were the shell bursts, the flash of guns, the fountains of tracer bullets.

The din was infernal. The batteries shelled ceaselessly and brilliantly. To the whistle of shells overhead was added the scream of falling bombs. Even the sky was full of noise—anti-aircraft shells, machine-gun fire, the snarl of falling planes, the angry hornet noise of dive bombers. One could not speak normally at any time against the roar of it and the noise of our own engines. We all developed 'Dunkirk throat', a sore hoarseness that was the hallmark of those who had been there.

Yet through all the noise I will always remember the voices of the young subalterns as they sent their men aboard, and I will remember, too, the astonishing discipline of the men. They had fought through three weeks of retreat, always falling back, often without orders, often without support. Transport had failed. They had gone sleepless. They had been without food and water. Yet they kept ranks as they came down the beaches, and they obeyed commands.

While they were still filing back to the beach and the dawn was breaking with uncomfortable brilliance, we found one of our stragglers—a navy whaler. We told her people to come aboard, but they said that there was a motor-boat aground and they would have to fetch off her crew. They went in, and we waited. It was my longest wait, ever. For various reasons they were terribly slow. When they found the captain of the motor-boat, they stood and argued with him and he wouldn't come off anyway. Damned plucky chap. He and his men lay quiet until the tide floated them later in the day. Then they made a dash for it, and got away.

We waited for them until the sun was up before we got clear of the mole. By then, the fighting was heavy in-shore, on the outskirts of the town, and actually in some of the streets.

Going home, the dive bombers came over us five times, but somehow left us alone though three times they took up an attacking position. A little down the coast, towards Gravelines, we picked up a boatload of Frenchmen rowing off. We took them aboard. They were very much bothered as to where our 'ship' was, and said quite flatly that it was impossible to go to England in a thing like ours. Too, too horribly dangerous!

One of the rare touches of comedy at Dunkirk was the fear of the sea among French *poilus* from inland towns. They were desperately afraid to forfeit solid land for the unknown perils of a little boat. When, on the last nights of the evacuation, the little boats got to the mole many refused to jump in, despite the hell of exploding shells and bombs behind them.

David Divine

328.

The British Expeditionary Force in France in 1940 was commanded during the last stages of its evacuation from Dunkirk by its senior Corps commander, General Sir Harold Alexander. As the great drama of Dunkirk drew to a close, it was Alexander himself, accompanied by his driver Corporal Wells and a handful of staff officers, who sought to ensure that every possible Englishman had been taken off the beaches and quays.

As soon as it was dark on June 2nd, the remnants of the BEF began to embark on destroyers at the mole. The arrangements worked without a hitch. All the men were aboard by 11.40 p.m. When the destroyers sailed for Dover, Alexander with Brigadier Parminter (the military embarkation officer) and half a dozen others including Corporal Wells, boarded a motor boat in the harbour, ordering a single destroyer to await them at the mole. There was no shelter on the boat from the incessant gunfire. They zig-zagged out of the harbour, and then turned east parallel to the beaches for about two miles, as close inshore as the draught of the boat would allow. Twice they grounded on sand-bars. The sea, Wells remembers, was covered with a film of oil, in which were floating the corpses of many soldiers. Alexander took a megaphone and shouted over and over again, in English and French, 'Is anyone there? Is anyone there?' There was no reply. They returned to the harbour, shouted the same question round the quays, and then boarded the waiting destroyer. Unharmed, they reached Dover as dawn was breaking.

When Alexander landed in England he went immediately to see Anthony Eden at the War Office. 'After he had given me an account of what had passed,' Eden wrote in his Memoirs, 'I congratulated him, and he replied, with engaging modesty, "We were not pressed, you know." '

Nigel Nicolson

329.

The Dunkirk spirit, exemplified by a captain of engineers in the Orkneys.

IT was, I think, a few days after the beaching of the *Iron Duke* that I was summoned, with other local commanders, to a conference at Head-quarters, Orkney and Shetland Defences, in Stromness. Our general, sometime a Horse Gunner in India, was vigorous, swiftly moving, with a thin, bony, claret-coloured face, lively blue eyes, a meagre sward of ginger hair, and a patch of ginger bristles on a long upper lip. His temper could flare fierce as a blow-lamp—there was much occasion for it—and it consumed in its fire many of the obstructions that our ignorance created; but in his private habit—when in friendly company he unbuttoned—Ginger Kemp was a man of immense geniality who gathered affection, not fear.

We had been summoned to discuss what could best be done to meet an attempted landing on our shores. We had been subject to sea-borne attack and attack from the air, and the Fleet had been driven from an anchorage we could not defend: it was not unreasonable to suppose that the Germans would follow up success by trying to put small parties of soldiers ashore to destroy such military installations as we had. We listened to explanation of the general plan for defence, and then, each in turn, we were asked what local and particular instructions we had given to the soldiers in our own commands. I, responsible for a stony segment of the island of Flotta in which it was impossible to dig trenches, replied meekly, 'Don't shoot till you see the whites of their eyes.'

'Don't be a damned fool!' exclaimed our fiery general. 'This is no time for joking, this is a serious occasion.'

'I have, sir, two Lewis guns, each with two drums of ammunition, and only ten rounds to a rifle. I thought it would be advisable to conserve ammunition.'

Eric Linklater

330.

FRANCE had fallen. Great Britain stood alone. She was awaiting the next assault. The Brigade of Guards had already suffered lamentable losses. In consequence my battalion could only spare the minimum time for training raw officers. Like Lord Lloyd who in 1931 assumed that I was going to prove a good secretary, my battalion in this desperate summer of 1940 assumed that I would prove a good officer. I regret that this assumption was not justified.

At once I felt at a great disadvantage with my co-ensigns who unlike me had reached the rank after many months of arduous training at Caterham. They knew the ropes. I did not. Their extreme youth was as disconcerting as their prowess. The extreme youth of my seniors in rank did not matter so much because these full lieutenants and captains were of course expected to be versed in the intricacies of regimental practice. I rather enjoyed being coached in social etiquette by a wonderfully self-confident lieutenant of 19. 'When you go to London,' he cautioned, 'don't say "I'm off to town." Whatever you do, never, never be seen carrying a parcel, not even a tube of toothpaste.' 'What then should we do if we find ourselves obliged to buy some toothpaste?' we asked in bewilderment. 'You must have it sent', said this young man who had just returned from a week's participation in the carnage of Calais, 'round to the Ritz, or wherever you may be staying. And one more thing,' he went on. 'When someone greets you with "How d'you do?" you must not reply, "I'm doing nicely, thanks." ' 'Thank you', we said, 'for the hint. We won't.'

The Medical Officer's advice was likewise useful. 'You *must* wash under the arms, you know,' he said fiercely. 'And after every evacuation you must have a bath.' 'A bath every time?' one of us asked. 'Even if I have what is euphemistically termed diarrhoea?' 'I repeat, after *every* evacuation, a bath.' The Medical Officer was emphatic. Only the Battalion Chaplain made allowances for the human flesh. 'Don't think I don't know that boys will be boys. Of course they will be. Don't think Our Blessed Lord wouldn't also have been, if indeed he had been one, which of course he never was. At least not in the sense you mean, I mean. Anyway, boys, don't be boys too often, if you know what I mean. Got it?' He was a good man, brimful of the milk of human understanding.

*

I had spent barely a month at the training barracks at Lingfield, when I was posted to Dover. The Battle of Britain was in full swing. Hitler's invasion of England was expected at any moment. We lived on the alert. Day and night an officer was kept on duty awaiting from some higher intelligence the warning code signal, 'Oliver Cromwell'. When this ominous name came down the telephone the officer knew that the invasion was on the way. He must instantly without wasting a second ring through to the Colonel and arouse the whole battalion. At 3 o'clock one morning it was my turn to be on duty. Rather drowsily I was reading *Barchester Towers*. The telephone rang. I picked up the receiver. 'This is Higher Command QE2X speaking', came from a rather sissy voice a long way off. 'I say, old boy, sorry to tell you— Oliver Cromwell.' 'What?' I screamed, my heart in my boots. 'Are you sure? Are you absolutely sure?' I had no reason for questioning the man's words beyond the utter horror of the announcement. 'Well, I may have got it wrong,' the voice said affectedly. 'Then for dear Christ's sake,' I pleaded, 'do get it right.' There was a pause, during which I had my finger on the special telephone to the Colonel's bedroom, as it were on the pulse of England. 'Sorry, old chap,' the voice came back again. 'It's only Wat Tyler. I get so confused with these historical blokes.'

James Lees Milne

331.
Evelyn Waugh writes to his wife Laura, 31 May 1942.

No. 3 Commando was very anxious to be chums with Lord Glasgow, so they offered to blow up an old tree stump for him and he was very grateful and he said don't spoil the plantation of young trees near it because that is the apple of my eye and they said no of course not we can blow a tree down so that it falls on a sixpence and Lord Glasgow said goodness you are clever and he asked them all to luncheon for the great explosion. So Col. Durnford-Slater DSO said to his subaltern, have you put enough explosive in the tree. Yes, sir, 75 lb. Is that enough? Yes sir I worked it out by mathematics it is exactly right. Well better put a bit more. Very good sir.

And when Col. D Slater DSO had had his port he sent for the subaltern and said subaltern better put a bit more explosive in that tree. I don't want to disappoint Lord Glasgow. Very good sir.

Then they all went out to see the explosion and Col. DS DSO said you will see that tree fall flat at just that angle where it will hurt no young trees and Lord Glasgow said goodness you are clever.

So soon they lit the fuse and waited for the explosion and presently the tree, instead of falling quietly sideways, rose 50 feet into the air taking with it $\frac{1}{2}$ acre of soil and the whole of the young plantation.

And the subaltern said Sir, I made a mistake, it should have been $7\frac{1}{2}$ lb not 75. Lord Glasgow was so upset he walked in dead silence back to his castle and when they came to the turn of the drive in sight of his castle what should they find but that every pane of glass in the building was broken.

So Lord Glasgow gave a little cry and ran to hide his emotion in the lavatory and there when he pulled the plug the entire ceiling, loosened by the explosion, fell on his head.

This is quite true.

Evelyn Waugh

332.

Philip Pinkney was an early recruit to the commandos.

WHEN his troop went raiding in the Channel Islands Philip is said to have visited the Dame of Sark, entering her bedroom through the french windows. Recognizing the blackened face of an Allied intruder, the good lady sat up in bed with the cry, 'Thank God to see a decent-sized man at last!'

*

The stars who emerged from commando soldiering were not confined to the officer class or to the famous regiments. Take Lance-Sergeant Peter King of the Royal Dental Corps. A tall, fine-looking man, drafted on mobilization into the wrong branch of the service, he quickly became bored with the inactivity of his professional duties. Stationed near Dover, he decided to raise a private army of his own, consisting of two other men. They 'borrowed' a boat in the harbour and set out on a raid across the Channel. Wind and weather were against them, the engine broke down and they drifted for two days before being ignominiously towed home by a naval patrol. King was court-martialled and reduced to the ranks. He immediately applied to join No. 4 Commando.

Lord Lovat

333.

Evelyn Waugh's biographer recalls the novelist's return from the débâcle in Crete of 1941, in which he had served with the commandos.

THE battle of Crete was Evelyn's first experience of military action. Bob Laycock was impressed by the cool courage which he showed throughout the action. In one place Waugh describes the dive-bombing which more than anything else succeeded in shattering the morale of the troops as 'monotonous', and in another he says that 'it was overdone, like everything German'. While they were crossing back to Alexandria in a crammed vessel, Bob asked him what his impressions were of his first battle. 'Like German opera,' replied Evelyn, 'too long and too loud.'

Christopher Sykes

334.

Admiral Sir Walter Cowan, KCB, DSO, commanded a Nile gunboat during the Sudan campaigns of the 1890s, commanded the Devonport destroyer flotilla in 1902, and in 1941 at the age of 74 was attached at his own request to the Eighth Army in the Western Desert, where he was captured. Cowan was bitterly affronted to find himself released by the Italians as 'of no further use' to the British war effort, and had himself attached to No. 8 Commando along with Waugh.

A VERY old, minute hero who came out as a kind of mascot to Pedder's Commando and was left behind with gross discourtesy when they went to Cyprus . . . Most of his experience had been with the Army and he showed great intolerance of signalmen, who he could not bear anywhere near him. He neither smoked nor drank wine, and ate all his food on the same plate, porridge, fruit, meat, eggs in a single mess. He was exquisitely polite, almost spinster-like in conversation; churchgoing with a belief in British-Israel. He sat behind me in the boat at Bardia bearing the weight of fifteen men. I could feel him fluttering like a bird in the hand. Later he said 'Young Waugh is uncommon heavy.' He read nothing but Surtees. He was popularly believed to spend his leisure in sniping at Italian prisoners with a catapult. He certainly loathed them almost as violently as he loathed signallers. I was once talking to him when a group marched past us with distinguishing patches in the seats of the trousers. He had been asking solicitously, like an aunt, after my health. He suddenly broke off and said with extravagant venom; 'That's the place to mark the sods.' He went with the *Aphis* party on their abortive raids and greatly enjoyed the bombing. 'They ought to have got us', he said very regretfully.

Evelyn Waugh

335.

The difficulties facing the professional service chiefs compelled to conduct the war amid the Prime Minister's extravagant enthusiasms are vividly described by Sir James Marshall-Cornwall, a corps commander in July 1940, in a memoir he entitled 'Mad Hatter's Dinner Party'.

On Friday 26 July, I was rung up by General Sir John Dill, the CIGS, to say that I was commanded to spend Saturday night with the Prime Minister at Chequers. Thunder-struck, I asked Jack Dill what it was all about. He replied that he hadn't the faintest notion, but that he had been invited also. I was to come up to London by train the following morning and a War Office car would take me to Chequers in the afternoon. I reached Chequers about six o'clock and was told that the PM was resting. Two hours later we sat down to dinner. It was indeed a memorable meal. I was placed on the PM's right, and on my right was Professor Frederick Lindemann, Churchill's scientific adviser. The others around the oval table were Mrs Churchill, Duncan Sandys and his wife, 'Pug' Ismay (Military Secretary to the War Cabinet), Jack Dill, Lord Beaverbrook, and one of the PM's private secretaries.

Churchill was bubbling over with enthusiasm and infectious gaiety. I marvelled how he could appear so carefree with the enormous load of anxieties on his shoulders, and I wish that I could remember some of the splendid sentences that rolled off his tongue. As soon as the champagne was served he started to interrogate me about the condition of my Corps. I told him that when I had taken it over I had found all ranks obsessed with defensive tactical ideas, the main object of everyone being to get behind an anti-tank obstacle. I had issued orders that only offensive training exercises were to be practised, and that the III Corps motto was 'Hitting, not Sitting', which prefaced every operation order. This went down tremendously well with the PM, who chuckled and chortled: 'Splendid! That's the spirit I want to see.' He continued, 'I assume then that your Corps is now ready to take the field?' 'Very far from it, Sir,' I replied. 'Our re-equipment is not nearly complete, and when it is we shall require another month or two of intensive training.' Churchill looked at me incredulously and drew a sheaf of papers from the pocket of his dinner-jacket. 'Which are your two Divisions?' he demanded. 'The 53rd (Welsh) and the 2nd (London)', I replied. He pushed a podgy finger on the graph tables in front of him and said, 'There you are; 100 per cent complete in personnel, rifles and mortars;

50 per cent in field artillery, anti-tank rifles and machine-guns.' 'I beg your pardon, Sir,' I replied. 'That state may refer to the weapons which the ordnance depots are preparing to issue to my units, but they have not yet reached the troops in anything like those quantities.' The PM's brow contracted; almost speechless with rage, he hurled the graphs across the dinner-table to Dill, saying, 'CIGS, have those papers checked and returned to me tomorrow.'

An awkward silence followed; a diversion seemed called for. The PM leant across me and addressed my neighbour on the other side: 'Prof! What have *you* got to tell me today?' The other civilians present were wearing dinner-jackets, but Professor Lindemann was attired in a morning-coat and striped trousers. He now slowly pushed his right hand into his tail-pocket and, like a conjuror, drew forth a Mills hand-grenade. An uneasy look appeared on the faces of his fellow-guests and the PM shouted: 'What's that you've got, Prof, what's that?' 'This, Prime Minister, is the inefficient Mills bomb, issued to the British infantry. It is made of twelve different components which have to be machined in separate processes. Now *I* have designed an improved grenade, which has fewer machined parts and contains a 50 per cent greater bursting charge.' 'Splendid! Splendid! That's what I like to hear. CIGS! Have the Mills bomb scrapped at once and replaced by the Lindemann grenade.' The unfortunate Dill was completely taken aback; he tried to explain that contracts had been placed in England and America for millions of Mills bombs, and that it would be impracticable to alter the design now, but the PM would not listen. To change the subject he pointed a finger at Beaverbrook across the table. 'Max! What have *you* been up to?' Beaverbrook replied, 'Prime Minister! Give me five minutes and you will have the latest figures.' He rose and went to a telephone box at the far end of the room; after a very few minutes he returned with a Puckish grin on his face. 'Prime Minister,' he said, 'in the last 48 hours we have increased our production of Hurricanes by 50 per cent.' When I repeated this story later to a distinguished Air Marshal, I was told that the Minister's claim was quite illusory; a temporary spurt in production had been made by cannibalizing machines awaiting other components and by delaying the output of bombers, but no real improvement had been achieved. In fact, during the month of July our production of fighter aircraft had risen from 446 to 496, but during August it fell to 476.

The brandy and coffee had now circulated and the PM lit his cigar.

'I want the Generals to come with me', he said, and stumped off to an adjoining room, followed by Dill, Ismay and myself. On a large table was a rolled-up map, which the PM proceeded to spread out. It was a large-scale map of the Red Sea. The PM placed his finger on the Italian port of Massawa. 'Now, Marshall-Cornwall,' he said, 'we have command of the sea and the air; it is essential for us to capture that port; how would you do it?' I was in no way prepared to answer a snap conundrum of this kind, and indeed had no qualifications for doing so. I saw Dill and Ismay watching me anxiously and felt that I was being drawn into some trap. I looked hard at the map for a minute and then answered, 'Well, Sir, I have never been to Massawa: I have only passed out of sight of it, going down the Red Sea. It is a defended port, protected by coast defence and anti-aircraft batteries. It must be a good 500 miles from Aden, and therefore beyond cover of our fighters. The harbour has a very narrow entrance channel, protected by coral reefs, and is certain to be mined, making an opposed landing impracticable. I should prefer to wait until General Wavell's offensive against Eritrea develops; he will capture it more easily from the land side.' The PM gave me a withering look, rolled up the map and muttered peevishly, 'You soldiers are all alike; you have no imagination.'

We went to bed. I left the Wonderland of Chequers on the following afternoon, after a walk in the woods with Duncan Sandys, whom I have never found very communicative. On our way back to London Jack Dill said to me, 'I'm thankful, Jimmy, that you took the line you did last night. If you had shown the least enthusiasm for the project, I should have been given orders to embark your Corps for the Red Sea next week.'

Sir James Marshall-Cornwall

336.

More of the same, from the pen of the Director of Military Operations.

THE Prime Minister made a practice of telephoning, from time to time, to junior officers in the War Office. One night, during the Syrian campaign, he asked to be put through to M.O.5, the section of my staff which dealt with the Middle East. Presently he was told that M.O.5 was on the line. The following conversation ensued:

Prime Minister: Is that M.O.5?
Voice: Yes.

Prime Minister: How do you think the operations are going in Syria?
Voice: Oh, I think everything is going all right.
Prime Minister: What about that turning movement the French are trying to make?
Voice: Oh, that seems to be all right.
Prime Minister: Who are you?
Voice: Corporal Jones, Duty Clerk, M.O.5
   End of conversation

                                                      Sir John Kennedy

337.

General Ismay, the Prime Minister's Chief of Staff, used to lunch each day at the United Services Club until he found it intolerable to be importuned with constant advice and requests from retired officers.

IN the end I was compelled to go elsewhere for my midday meal. White's proved ideal. All the young, and many of the not-so-young members were away fighting, and those who were too old to be accepted had no bright ideas for winning the war, and were careful not to embarrass me by asking questions which it would have been difficult to answer. One or two of them did not follow the war very closely. General Alexander, fresh from his triumphs in Italy, came into the Club one day in a flannel suit, and was greeted by a contemporary who lived in Ireland: 'Hullo Alex, I haven't seen or heard of you since the war started. What have you been doing with yourself?' To which Alexander replied: 'I'm still soldiering.'

                                                              Lord Ismay

338.

A novelist's vision of the Chief of the Imperial General Staff, Sir Alan Brooke, on the steps of the War Office.

MY companion's attention, my own too, was at that moment unequivocally demanded by the hurricane-like imminence of a thickset general, obviously of high rank, wearing enormous horn-rimmed spectacles. He had just burst from a flagged staff-car almost before it had drawn up by the kerb. Now he tore up the steps of the building at the charge, exploding through the inner door into the hall. An extraordinary current of physical energy, almost of electricity, suddenly pervaded the place. I could feel it stabbing through me. This was the CIGS. His quite remarkable and palpable extension of personality, in its effect on others, I had noticed not long before, out in the open. Coming down Sackville Street, I had all at once been made aware of something that required attention on the far pavement and saw him pounding along. I saluted at admittedly longish range. The salute was returned. Turning my head to watch his progress, I then had proof of being not alone in acting as a kind of receiving-station for such rays—which had, morally speaking, been observable, on his appointment to the top post, down as low as platoon commander. On this Sackville Street occasion, an officer a hundred yards or more ahead, had his nose glued to the window of a bookshop. As the CIGS passed (whom he might well have missed in his concentration on the contents of the window), this officer suddenly swivelled a complete about-turn, saluting too. No doubt he had seen the reflection in the plate glass. All the same, in its own particular genre, the incident gave the outward appearance of exceptional magnetic impact. That some such impact existed, was confirmed by this closer conjunction in the great hall. Vavassor, momentarily over-awed—there could be no doubt of it—came to attention and saluted with much more empressement than usual. Having no cap, I merely came to attention. The CIGS glanced for a split second, as if summarizing all the facts of one's life.

'Good morning.'

It was a terrific volume of sound, an absolute bellow, at the same time quite effortless. A moment later, he was on the landing halfway up the stairs. . . . Then he disappeared from sight.

Anthony Powell

339.

Orde Wingate made his reputation operating behind the Italian lines in Abyssinia in 1941. But on his return to Cairo, suffering from acute exhaustion and delusions brought on by excessive prescriptions of drugs, he was driven to desperation.

A T three o'clock in the afternoon of July 4th he took his temperature and read that it was standing at 104 degrees. He had no more atabrin left. He got out of bed, made his way downstairs and out into the street, and tried to walk to the doctor's house. He could not find it although he had been there more than once. He became terrified. He now believed that his loss of memory was the beginning of madness. In his weakness he had to hold on to the walls as he made his way back to the hotel. In his confusion and despair he had now made up his mind.

In the bedroom corridor he found the floor-waiter who used to bring him meals. He said something to him, thanking him for his services. The waiter noticed something odd in his behaviour, followed him to the door and waited outside it. Wingate wanted to lock the door, but feared to increase the waiter's suspicions, so he half-locked it and waited till the man had gone. Then he took out his pistol and saw that it had not been cleaned for a long time and was still choked with Ethiopian sand. It was empty and he could not find the ammunition. (In fact Akavia had forgotten to pack it when Wingate left Addis Ababa.) He put the pistol away and took out a hunting-knife which a friend had given him. He went to the mirror above the wash-basin. He held the knife in his right hand and thrust into the left side of his neck. He found the effort of cutting through greater than he had guessed. He saw he must try again and suddenly remembered that the door was not locked. With the knife still in his neck, and drenching blood from the wound he went to the door and locked it, went back to the mirror, plucked out the knife, and taking it in his left hand, thrust with all his force at the jugular vein on the right, then fell unconscious on the floor.

He would have died within the hour, but rescue came quickly. In the next room Colonel Thornhill was enjoying a siesta. He heard unusual sounds through the wall. They gave him an idea (though there was no shout or cry) that something untoward was happening. He decided he had better look into it. He gave his reasons afterwards. He said: 'When I hear a feller lock a door, I don't think anything about it, and if I hear a feller fall down, that's his affair, but when I hear a feller lock his door and then fall down—it's time for action.' He pulled on his clothes quickly, went out into the corridor and knocked on the door. There was no sound that he could hear. He shook the handle and pushed. He ran to the lift, went down, rushed to the manager's office for the master key. He and the manager and others ran back, swept up the corridor, and forced the door because the key was in. As they burst in, Wingate came back to partial consciousness. He remembered after that it seemed to him that he was dead and in hell.

Christopher Sykes

340.

John Masters encountered the Yeomanry in the Iraq campaign of 1941, and describes a staff conference he attended, which encapsulates all the British Army's fantasies about the Yeomanry view of war.

The General: 'Well, I think we should sent a patrol up the Euphrates for fifty miles or so, to make sure no one's lying up in the desert out there.'

One of his Yeomanry colonels: 'Good idea, George.'

The General: 'From your regiment, I thought, Harry. About a troop, with a couple of guns, eh?'

The Colonel: 'Oh yes, George . . . I think I'll send Charles.'

The General (horror in his face): 'Charles? *Charles?* Do you think he'll go?'

We learned later that though 2nd Lieutenant Charles was distinctly vexed at being sent on such a piddling mission, he did finally agree to go, since George and Harry seemed to set so much store on it.

They were delightful people. My own favourite story about them concerns an early inspection, by the general, of one of the regiments. The Yeomanry colonel, going down the line introducing his officers, stopped before one captain, and said, 'This is Captain . . . Captain . . . ' He shook his head, snapped his fingers and cried genially, 'Memory like a sieve! I'll be forgetting the names of me hounds next.'

John Masters

341.

MONTGOMERY'S allegedly austere personal habits gave rise to a number of disobliging comments and anecdotes. His appalled reaction to the clouds of cigar smoke with which Churchill had filled his tent in the desert was the subject of much amusement, as was Churchill's reply to a questioner in the House of Commons who complained that Montgomery had invited von Thoma, the defeated German general, to dinner in his desert caravan. 'Poor von Thoma,' said Churchill gravely. 'I, too, have dined with Montgomery.'

Lord Chalfont

342.

A portrait of Eighth Army's commander by his ADC.

MONTY'S habits in the desert and thereafter were simple and regular. He would be called by his soldier servant, Corporal English, at 6.30 every morning with a cup of tea and would not come out of his caravan till 8 to walk across to the mess tent for breakfast. You could set your watch by his regular visit to the W.C. He would retire to bed at 9.30 in the evening no matter who was visiting the headquarters. Even when George VI came he would say: 'If you will excuse me, Sir, we have the battle to win and I must go to bed. These lads will sit up all night drinking and I trust they will look after you.' He went to bed as usual at 9.30 on the eve of the Normandy landing, saying 'Come and tell me the news at 6 a.m.' He was awake when I went in and just said quietly, 'What's the news?'

Living conditions were sometimes quite spartan. In southern Italy we were once in a very primitive house. As I walked down the passage I noticed Monty trying to have a bath where there was no running water. He was calling out to Corporal English to bring him some cold water. Noticing a jerry can in the passage which I presumed to be full of water, I opened the door to come to the rescue. He was standing up in the bath lifting his feet in and out of the very hot water. He took the can and poured what turned out to be Marsala wine over a vulnerable area above the knees. He was not at that moment as amused as I was, but afterwards frequently enjoyed telling the story of how I was unable to tell the difference between wine and water.

Dinner in the evening was the only period of relaxation. In the desert there were often not more than three or four of us, though there would be a greater number in Europe. Nearly every night he would provoke a conversation, often of a trivial, bantering nature, which would often run something like this:

Monty: 'Johnny, have you read my latest pamphlet on military training?'

Reply: 'No, matter of fact I haven't.'

Monty: 'Well, you will never make a soldier if you don't get down to that.'

Reply: 'But I don't want to be a soldier.'

Monty: 'Alright, what do you want to do?'

Reply: 'I don't really know, but perhaps I might go into the City.'

Monty: 'Oh, you want to make money, do you? That won't do you any good. Anyway, it's no good saying "You don't know"—you had better make up your mind.'

One evening in Belgium he sat down and asked us for our definition of a gentleman. He clearly thought we weren't doing very well, as indeed we weren't so he said: 'Well, we'll ask Winston when he comes out next week.' On Winston's first night we had not been sitting down long before Monty duly remarked: 'I have been asking these fellows for a definition of a gentleman and they aren't very good at it—what's yours?' Winston thought for a moment and said: 'I know one when I see one,' and then added; 'I suppose one might say—someone who is only rude intentionally.'

Monty had a good sense of humour and could tell a story really well, often against himself. He enjoyed recounting a story which dated from pre-war days when he was commanding a battalion of the Royal Warwickshire Regiment in Egypt. One of his young officers was, in Monty's view, doing himself no good by being out too often with the girls. 'So I gave him an order not to have another woman without my permission, though if I thought it necessary I would give it.' Some weeks later he was dining in Cairo with the Ambassador, Lord Killearn. During dinner the butler announced that there was a telephone call for Colonel Montgomery. The Ambassador said 'Ask who it is and what he wants.' The butler returned and gravely announced: 'It is Lieutenant X and he wants to ask the Colonel if he can have a woman.' Permission was granted.

J. R. Henderson

343.

A tale of the North African Desert.

BREAKFAST was not a success. The fire smouldered dejectedly until the Professor teased it with a gill of petrol, and then it sprang up in a fury and singed his moustache; when he assaulted the sausages the tin counter-attacked and cut his finger; the water refused to boil, and while he was not looking tipped itself over into the fire. 'Oh, the malice—the cursed, diabolical malice of inanimate objects!' muttered the Professor ferociously between clenched teeth. 'Here, let me help', I said. 'You keep away', he snarled. 'If they want to be bloody-minded, I'll show them, by God I will', booting the empty sausage-tin into a cactus bush. I knew from past experience that it was no good interfering. I had given 'Pinafore' her fuel and water and tested the tyres, so I picked the tin of cigarettes out of the ration box, sat down on the tailboard and watched him begin to rekindle the fire.

It was half-past six on a June morning in 1943. 'Pinafore', a thirty-cwt truck, was parked in a disused railway cutting about sixty miles east of Algiers. The Professor really had occupied a distinguished chair of learning until the outbreak of war, when he had enlisted as an infantryman. Now he was my senior officer, and if he was a singular and in some ways unorthodox Lieutenant-Colonel, he certainly looked more like a soldier than an absent-minded scholar. He was still in his early thirties, stockily built, with a pale face and brown hair *en brosse*. His eyes were greenish, very penetrating and rather sinister; they indicated something of their owner's intellectual brilliance and something of his force of character. . . .

The Professor's life had been crammed with scholarly achievement; but in the days of his youth he had never been a Boy Scout, and during the war he had been too busy for sixteen hours a day creating confusion in the ranks of the enemy to have time to learn how to look after himself in the open. It is true that before the war he had on a number of occasions, for several days on end, trudged the English and Welsh roads on foot at an average rate of five and a half miles per hour (about half a mile an hour slower than his normal rate of progression for short distances). But on these expeditions he had never cooked his own food; and he had slept on railway station platforms, in barns, or in even more civilized places. Another consideration of some importance was that he could not drive. He was quite candid about this. He possessed a certificate, carefully tucked away in his pocket-book, stating that he was authorized to drive any Government road vehicle; but I gathered that this had been presented to him when he had been a cadet by an over-optimistic Sergeant Instructor before his first and only driving lesson. Since then he had displayed characteristic courage and determination, and quite remarkable ineptitude, in endeavouring to master an Army motor-bicycle.

The Professor recounted all these shortcomings to me in detail, and it may well be wondered why I consented to make the journey with him at all, let alone agree to teach him to drive on the way. My motives were various; apart from my personal desire to travel to Cairo by road, I felt sure that the Professor was minimizing his abilities. Moreover, although I did not really profess to be a hardened campaigner or knowledgeable mechanic, I rather enjoyed the prospect of looking after the two of us and 'Pinafore'. It would be a distinctly agreeable experience, I thought, for me to give instructions to the Professor for a change.

The Professor insisted on preparing breakfast unaided on that first morning, and it made a bad start to the day. The sausages were cold and flabby, tea-leaves floated on top of a grey, tepid liquid which I tactfully consumed with feigned relish. But the Professor was not deceived and went about shaking his head muttering 'Bloody inefficient! bloody inefficient!' too angry to eat. If he had a failing it was an overbearing intolerance of stupidity and inefficiency. People less acute and less energetic than himself, that is practically every other human being with whom he came in contact, were very liable to incite his wrath. I myself had of course already been the cause of many outbursts, and I had witnessed more than one explosive scene when the offenders had been very senior officers indeed and had not taken kindly to his blunt exposure of their brainlessness. But this was something new. I had never before seen the Professor really angry with himself, because I had never before seen him make a fool of himself. While I had been working with him I had often almost exasperated him, but he had been very patient with me and had taught me a great deal. I wondered just how far our roles were now to be reversed.

By half-past seven we were ready to start, and the Professor decided to take his first spell at the wheel. He already knew the lay-out of the controls and became piqued when I insisted on pointing out which was the accelerator and which was the brake. In fact, as I was about to learn, his difficulties were much more complex than being unable to distinguish one pedal from another: they involved problems which would not even have occurred to a normal beginner. I did not realize this at the time, and do not remember feeling particularly apprehensive as we jerked and jolted off towards the main road. I had taught other people to drive and was quite confident in my ability to teach him.

The main difficulty, according to the Professor, lay in the steering. His diagnosis was at least partly correct, as I discovered when we had to turn back on to the main road. Instead of slowing down he suddenly accelerated, at the same time swaying about in his seat as though wrestling for possession of the wheel. We turned neither to right nor left, but shot straight on towards a stone wall on the far side. We stopped with a lurch a few inches short of the wall and I found that I had subconsciously pulled the handbrake hard on.

'You see what I mean?' asked the Professor, quite unperturbed.

'Yes, I see,' I replied, wiping the sweat off my hands, determined to be equally composed. 'Now, to turn her it's no good just shifting your weight about in the seat; you must take a grip of the steering-wheel and turn it like this.'

'Of course, of course, I quite understand. I must remember I am not on that motor-bicycle,' he said.

'Take it easy, don't be in a hurry, reverse her and try again.' He reversed without much difficulty, but in two seconds we had shot back across the road and were again facing the wall.

'Never mind,' I said, wiping my hands again, 'just take it steady—try again.'

'I'll manage it,' muttered the Professor with the most ferocious look of resolution. Next time he certainly did manage it. We turned a good deal more than the necessary right angle and narrowly missed the ditch on the wrong side of the road. 'Done it!' beamed the Professor as we swerved back into the centre of the road. I was too unnerved to make any comment.

The road to Bougie forks short of Tizi Ouzou, and at the fork was a large notice stating that the coast road was 'closed to W.D. transport'. The Professor chose it accordingly. We soon realized the reason for the notice. The road was narrow and began to mount and wind in tortuous convolutions through the hills. 'Good practice for steering', he said, crashing his gears as he negotiated a steep hairpin from which we looked down into the plain, hundreds of feet below. As a matter of fact his steering improved remarkably rapidly, and I had just told him how pleased I was with his progress when quite suddenly and unexpectedly 'Pinafore' slewed hard to port and was only prevented from slipping over the edge of a precipice by hitting the end of a stone bridge. 'How did that happen?' asked the Professor innocently as we inspected the damage. We were relieved to find that we had only stove in an iron bracket and crumpled the oil and water cans held in place by it. They were now oozing their contents into the dust. The Professor seemed to take the accident very much as a matter of course, but for fear that he should lose confidence I screwed up my courage and suggested that he should continue to the top of the pass. . . .

It often happened that we would not speak to another soul for two or three days at a time, and in this sense the journey was lonely. We soon found our flow of random conversation running dry, and might sit for two or three hours in dead silence. This was boring and could be dangerous; in the heat of the driving-cab, lulled by the desolate monotony of the road and the steady note of the engine, it was all too easy for the driver to fall asleep.

Some weeks previously I had implied in the course of conversation with the Professor that Xerxes had been the opponent of Alexander. The Professor had started as though jabbed deeply with a needle and had glared at me as if I had caused him some personal injury. I now proposed that the long hours of driving should be employed in his remedying my ignorance. The Professor consented on condition that when I was not driving I in turn should improve his knowledge. This was an awkward proviso. In the first place, I found that I simply could not relax while the Professor was driving. Indeed it was considerably more tiring to have to watch him than to drive myself, and I did not feel that I should be able to divert much of my attention to this parallel course of instruction. My second and even greater difficulty was to choose a subject on which I was better informed than he was. The Professor's range of knowledge was mortifyingly wide, as I discovered when I made a blundering attempt with French painting. But with his usual obstinacy he made it quite plain that unless I talked he would not. I cast about desperately for a subject, until the narrow scope of my own experience, and the discovery that the Professor had never ridden horseback, resulted in agreement to my talking discursively on horses and hunting.

I was treated to a course of brilliant impromptu lectures on Greek and Roman history, art and literature. We anticipated the chronological sequence of events so that the Punic Wars could be described as we passed through the territory of Carthage. Cato died as we traversed the battlefield of Utica, and as we bowled along the Via Balbia I received a truly peripatetic introduction to the philosophy of Aristotle. It seemed ludicrous at first to intersperse the story of the Odyssey with episodes from 'Mr Sponge's Sporting Tour', or to follow the Professor's discourse on Roman military strategy with a description of what I knew about the art of working a pack of foxhounds. But my diffidence at trying to deliver a 'sporting lector' was soon dispelled by the Professor's unexpectedly eager interest. We each became so engrossed in the other's subject that in the evenings after supper the Professor would illustrate verse forms and teach me the Greek alphabet, while I would draw for him bits of harness, the points of a horse, and other intricacies which would have necessitated his taking his eyes off the road if I had tried to explain them while he was driving. Of the various characters I introduced into my talks Squire Mytton was one of his favourites. I

wondered why this should be so, and it occurred to me that perhaps
the Professor recognized in Mytton's mentality a kindred streak of
what the euphemists call eccentricity. I knew Nimrod's biography of
the man almost as well as I knew 'Handley Cross' and 'Market Har-
borough' and was able to repeat most of the stories with fair accuracy.
An anecdote which particularly amused him was that of Mytton driving
an acquaintance home in a gig. The acquaintance nervously suggested
that they should slacken speed lest they should overturn, an unpleasant
experience which he had so far been spared. 'What!' cried Mytton,
'never upset in a gig?' and drove straight into the ditch. Hitherto my
story-telling had been mainly confined to children, and with them you
can rely on ringing the changes with two or three well-tried favourites.
But if the Professor was more exacting because he never wanted to
hear the same tale twice, I could not possibly have desired a more
attentive or enthusiastic listener. 'By Jove!' he exclaimed one day when
I had finished the more or less true account of an eventful day's hunting, 'what I've been missing!—"the image of war without its guilt and
only five-and-twenty per cent of its danger!" I believe that fellow
Jorrocks knew what he was talking about.' Then quite solemnly he
said, 'I've made up my mind. I shall hunt.' I never took him seriously,
of course. The idea of the Professor hunting was diverting—but quite
preposterous.

We took a brief look at the appalling destruction and desolation of
Bizerta and Ferryville and set off on the road to Tunis with the Professor at the wheel. It was a good road, and the Professor was taking
advantage of it. I remarked rather acidly that the speedometer needle
was wavering at over forty m.p.h. 'Just repeat the ingredients of the
bran mash again—I must get all this quite clear', replied the Professor
with his foot hard down on the accelerator. At that moment I saw two
hundred yards ahead a barrier across the road and a military policeman
waving us down a diversion to the right. Forty yards from the barrier
the Professor had still not slackened speed. I yelled. The policeman
began to run. The Professor suddenly wrenched the wheel over and
we careered down the side road straight into a three-foot ditch. There
was a moment's silence while we sprawled at an angle of forty-five
degrees and collected our wits. Then the Professor began to roar with
laughter; 'Ha-ha-ha!' he gasped, 'never been upset in a gig?'

*

I did not see the Professor again until the other day. It was a

December evening and I boarded a London-bound train on the out-skirts. I could not have missed that pale face and those arresting eyes; I would in any case have taken a second look at him because of his clothes. He was wearing a bowler hat with a mud-smeared dent in it, a black cutaway coat with a muddied shoulder, a stock with a fox-head pin, and mud-spattered breeches and boots.

'Ever been upset in a gig?' he grinned, digging me in the ribs with his hunting-crop.

'It looks as though you have,' I replied, 'quite recently.'

'Yes, I took four tosses today—but the last two were at jumps.'

'You don't mean to say you've been hunting?'

'Of course I've been hunting. I told you I was going to hunt, and hunt I do. It's all your fault, you know; ever since I last saw you I've been taking riding lessons when I could, and now I hunt regularly every Saturday. Judging by the number of bowlers I've smashed I'm inclined to think that "five-and-twenty per cent of the danger" is an underestimate, but my luck holds and "all time is lost wot is not spent in 'unting." '

'Well done!' I cried, 'but what are you doing in the train?'

'Well, I live in London and have to get to and from the meets some-how—train, bus, horse-box, or pony-trap. The other day I walked the last six miles in my boots in just under the hour and got there before they moved off.'

'This petrol rationing is the devil,' I sympathized.

'Oh, I wouldn't *drive*,' he replied, 'even if I could get all the petrol I needed—I haven't got the nerve.'[1]

'M.L.S.'

344.

A portrait of General Patton by a British officer—who pseudonymizes himself as Meego—who spent some months attached to his staff in 1942, before and during the TORCH landings in North Africa. Here he calls at the general's house for the first time.

IN the hall he met Mrs Patton, a gracious and minute lady of wonderful charm and spirit. She was carrying in both hands a lump of primitive carving in lava rock. Somewhat battered, it seemed to be a

---

[1] 'The Professor' was Lt.-Col. J. Enoch Powell.

carved head with the hair curled up in a peak. 'Meet Charlie!' she said to Meego. 'He's very, very old, and very, very distinguished. They gave him to the General in Hawaii. He's a warrior. You can tell he's a warrior from his peak.'

'Do they have warriors in Hawaii?' Meego asked.

'They used to have, one time', Mrs Patton said. 'This is a warrior idol. If you're a warrior yourself, he brings you good luck. But if you're not a warrior, it's quite the reverse. Would you care to have him, Larry?'

'Doesn't the General want him?'

'I don't know what you've done to the General today', Mrs Patton said. 'He's in a terrible wax.'

Although Mrs Patton must have been twenty or thirty years younger than Meego's grandmother Micholls she seemed to belong to that same generation and to have been brought up on similar traditions which had allowed them to borrow from their brothers at Oxford or in the Army such rather daring slang as 'wax', or as 'swell' used as a noun but not as an adjective, and as 'don't' and 'ain't' used in the third person singular. Our grandmother would have said, for instance: 'He's no end of a swell these days. He don't have the time . . . He ain't asking . . . ' All, of course, as a kind of joke borrowed from her kin in the mounted regiments who had got it from the cockney cabby.

'The General', Mrs Patton continued, 'came right home and threw Charlie right in the pond. I just fished him out.' She thrust the idolized lump into Meego's hands. It was quite a weight. 'I warned you about being a warrior', she said. They were walking towards the drawing-room. 'One other thing, Larry . . . If you take him, you must take him with you.'

'Take him where?' Meego asked.

'Take him in the little boats,' she said. 'I must be promised that. He has to go to Casablanca with the General to bring him luck.' Meego was shocked at the indiscretion and must have shown it. 'Doesn't *your* wife know where you're going when you go off?' Mrs Patton asked. 'The General didn't exactly tell me,' Mrs Patton added, 'I must have just kind of guessed. I'm kind of psychic like that.'

*

A few weeks later, on 6 November 1942, Patton landed in North Africa.

As Patton stepped ashore, Meego met him with Charlie in his hands. Patton said: 'Goddamit, Larry, didn't I tell you to stay in your goddam ship?'

Meego said: 'Mrs Patton made me promise to bring Charlie ashore with the assault.'

Patton said: 'So she did!' Then he asked what had happened and was happening. Meego told him and explained also that the chaos, which Patton was reviewing at the time, was due mainly to the dereliction of the 'Shore parties'.

Patton stood there, with his two pearl-headed pistols, surveying the long beach. The scene was silent, sunlit and tranquil. An Arab was leading a donkey laden with sacks along the stranded craft. He was filling the sacks with such oddments and trifles of American equipment as he thought were of worth. Nobody else was doing any work. They had even stopped digging, for they had no longer any pretext of danger to dig against. This picture of total idleness and untroubled chaos provoked Patton to say—and he said it then, and he said it to Meego and to nobody else—he said:

'Jesus, I wish I were a corporal!'

At this moment Meego took the General's photograph. Shortly afterwards he took another photograph to record the historic occasion when Patton actually consulted with the Navy.

. . . while Patton was talking to the naval officer, he saw the itinerant Arab with his donkey come upon a rifle which some American soldier had let fall rather than carry. As the Arab was stowing it away in his sack, Patton sent a shot across his bows from one of his pearl-handled pistols. The result was satisfactory . . . the rifle let go, and the donkey sent scurrying in panic, with the Arab after him.

Robert Henriques

345.

Henriques, shortly after stepping ashore with the TORCH forces, found himself involved in a gruesome incident.

MEEGO, advancing warily, skirted the top of the cliff until he came to a ruined cowshed which, it was clear, had recently been hit by a shell.

From inside it there came an appalling odour and a terrible sound: a sound at the very top of, and almost beyond, the sonic scale; a sound that was a prolonged shrieking but with no voice to it. Forcing himself to look inside, Meego saw the debris of a milking-stook, a milk pail, a cow and a deep black Senegalese soldier in French uniform. Meego was instantly sick. Then, forcing himself to advance through the slime of blood and milk with which the floor was awash, he had to observe that neither the cow nor the man were dead but only horribly broken. Both their bellies had been blasted open, and their innards were intermingled. This was the cause of the stench. The sound that Meego had heard was issuing from the man's tattered mouth, but the man was quite unconscious.

With his pistol Meego shot the cow at once. What could he do about the man? Nothing in his 'field dressing' was of any use for a wound such as this. There was no other person in sight from the vicinity of the cowshed. He already knew that there was no American doctor—though there were several medical orderlies—on his side of the bridge or even as yet ashore. He had not realized how near the fort he had got—that the cowshed was almost an annexe to the fort—for the ground rose so steeply at this point in a convex slope that the closer he got to the fort, the less he could see of it. From the cowshed it was invisible. Again and again he stumbled out of the cowshed, pursued by that thin, voiceless scream, and again and again he returned to the scream's source. The man by now was nothing in Meego's mind but the scream's source; and Meego was engulfed in a frenzy of rage, horror and helplessness, an utter panic such as he had never before experienced. He shot the man through the head.

That night, eager to unburden himself of guilt, he told the horrid story to a senior Army doctor, a southerner, from the very deep South. 'The man couldn't have lived?' Meego asked.

'He probably could', the doctor said, 'with these sulphur drugs. These days we'd have stuffed his guts back with sulphanamide and stitched 'em up, and he'd have been all right. . .' Observing Meego's distress, he patted Meego's shoulder, adding, 'Don't worry, son! What's one nigger the less?'

Robert Henriques

346.

Chance encounter on a troopship to India.

I FOUND myself sharing a cabin with Peter Smith-Dorrien, whom I had never met before: he was going out to fill the slot on Heywood's staff which I had inadvertently left vacant. Far more *piquant*, his father had been my father's Corps Commander from August of 1914, throughout Mons, Le Cateau and the Aisne, until he had suddenly sacked him one day in November. Then in February of 1915, French decided to sack Smith-Dorrien, and deputed the future C.I.G.S., 'Wullie' Robertson, who rose from Trooper to Field-Marshal, to break the news gently. This Robertson did, so legend still maintains, with the words: ''Orace, you're for 'Ome.' It was my father who came out to relieve Smith-Dorrien in the command of the Corps, and there was never any rancour between them thereafter.

Bernard Fergusson

347.

Field Marshal Lord Wavell, in 1942 Viceroy of India, must be among the few military commanders in history to have edited an anthology of poetry—'Other Men's Flowers'—and indeed, his literary passions formed an important part of his legend. His Military Assistant records the following example.

WHEN the Japanese menace to India was at its height, an order had gone forth from GHQ in Delhi that all officers should have revolver practice; so everyone, myself included, suddenly became very revolver-minded, and I remember Wavell's ADC in India, Sandy Reid-Scott, who was adept, coaching me in small-arms practice, in the garden of the C-in-C's house, and pretty bad I was at it.

One evening Wavell sent for me to his office. His desk was littered with books, and all the drawers were open as if he had been looking for something. 'Peter,' he said, 'I can't find my Browning. You did not borrow it, I suppose?'

I spent the next hour frantically searching for a Browning revolver, though it was the Collected Works the C-in-C had meant.

Peter Coats

348.

General Sir William Slim was perhaps the outstanding British commander of the Second World War, displaying a greatness of spirit in human relations that eluded Montgomery. Here, he was commanding Burcorps at the low point of the retreat in April 1942.

MORE Japanese were coming in from the east and were reported on the river. The situation was grave. At half-past four in the afternoon, Scott reported on the radio that his men were exhausted from want of water and continuous marching and fighting. He could hold that night, he thought, but if he waited until morning his men, still without water, would be so weakened they would have little or no offensive power to renew the attack. He asked permission to destroy his guns and transport and fight his way out that night. Scott was the last man to paint an unduly dark picture. I knew his men were almost at the end of their strength and in a desperate position. I could not help wishing that he had not been so close a friend. I thought of his wife and of his boys. There were lots of other wives, too, in England, India, and Burma whose hearts would be under that black cloud a couple of miles away. Stupid to remember that now! Better get it out of my head.

I thought for a moment, sitting there with the headphones on, in the van with the operator crouching beside me, his eyes anxiously on my face. Then I told Scott he must hang on. I had ordered a Chinese attack again with all available tanks and artillery for the next morning. If Burma Division attacked then we ought to break through, and save our precious guns and transport. I was afraid, too, that if our men came out in driblets as they would in the dark, mixed up with Japanese, the Chinese and indeed our own soldiers, would fail to recognize them and their losses would be heavy. Scott took it as I knew he would. He said, 'All right, we'll hang on and we'll do our best in the morning, but, for God's sake, Bill, make those Chinese attack.'

I stepped out of the van feeling about as depressed as a man could. There, standing in a little half-circle waiting for me, were a couple of my own staff, an officer or two from the Tank Brigade, Sun, and the Chinese liaison officers. They stood there silent and looked at me. All commanders know that look. They see it in the eyes of their staffs and their men when things are really bad, when even the most confident staff officer and the toughest soldier want holding up, and they turn where they *should* turn for support—to their commander. And sometimes he does not know what to say. He feels very much alone.

'Well, gentlemen,' I said, putting on what I hoped was a confident, cheerful expression, 'it might be worse!'

One of the group, in a sepulchral voice, replied with a single word: 'How?'

I could cheerfully have murdered him, but instead I had to keep my temper.

'Oh,' I said, grinning, 'it might be raining!'

Two hours later, it was—hard. As I crept under a truck for shelter I thought of that fellow and wished I *had* murdered him.

Viscount Slim

349.

The Japanese treatment of their prisoners in the Second World War will remain an eternal blot upon their nation's history. Here one of the victims, an Australian, describes an indescribable moment in his own experience.

OUTSIDE Kanu, in the small stream that trickled down from the mountain above, lay a naked man. When asked why he lay there, he pointed to his legs. Tiny fish nibbled at the rotten flesh round the edges of his ulcers. Then he pointed inside the camp. Other ulcer-sufferers, reluctant to submit to this nibbling process, wore the only dressings available—a strip of canvas torn from a tent soaked in Eusol. Their ulcers ran the whole length of their shin bones in channels of putrescence. Looking back at the man in the stream it was impossible to decide, even though he was insane, which treatment was the best.

We reached the next camp, and found it practically deserted—almost all the original inhabitants were dead. There were proud signs of the struggle for survival those men had put up. Carefully constructed latrines, spotless surrounds, an overhead pipeline made from bamboos which brought cholera-free water from its source two or three miles away and hundreds of feet up at the top of the mountain. This pipeline led to a shower-centre with a bamboo floor and separate cubicles (pathetic symbol of man's desire for even a little privacy) and to a cookhouse that was all clean wood and carefully-swept packed earth. All of these were refinements installed after gruelling sixteen-hour shifts of work at the expense of sleep and the re-charging of their energies so vital to the next day's shift. But none of this had been enough—flies carried the cholera germs and mosquitoes the malarial parasites. Starvation and slavery did the rest. Now, as we set out back to our own camp, there were only a few skeleton-like travesties of humanity left and the big fire where they burnt their dead.

These fires flared at every camp where cholera struck. They lighted the way out to work in the dark before dawn: they guided the men back through the dark wetness of the jungle long after dusk. And, always, lying round them in stick-like-bundles, were the bodies that awaited cremation—bodies at which the returning men peered closely as they came in to see if any of their mates lay among them. And every now and then, as they filed past, came that muttered: 'Half his luck.'

About these fires a strange story was told. At one camp the task of attending to the pyre and of consigning the bodies to the flames was given to an Australian who, being without brains or emotions or finer susceptibilities of any kind, was more than happy in his work.

He stripped the dead of their gold tooth caps; he stole fearlessly from the guards who dared not touch him lest he contaminate them: he cooked what he stole—for one only stole food, or something that could be bartered for food or tobacco, in those days—on the fire where he burnt the bodies. He was a complete moron.

It was his practice before dealing with the fresh batch of bodies that arrived each morning to boil himself a 'cuppa cha' and watch the working party fall-in to be marched away to the cuttings. He liked watching the working parties fall-in to march away because *he* stayed at home by his fire where, even in the monsoonal rains, he could keep warm and do his cooking. Upon one particular morning he sipped his tea out of the jam tin that served as a mug and watched the parade. As he watched he rolled some tobacco in a strip of the tissue that clings to the inside of a bamboo: then, his fag completed, he picked up a body and tossed it easily from yards off (for it was only light) on to the fire. He enjoyed the revulsion this caused. He did it every morning just before the workers marched out. Grinning at them as they glowered angrily, he then shambled to the fringe of the fire to light his cigarette.

As he leant forward to pick up a faggot the body he had just tossed into the flames, its sinews contracted, suddenly sat bolt upright and grunted, and in its hand thrust out a flaming brand on to the cigarette in the moron's mouth.

With a scream of terror the man who had burnt hundreds of bodies with callous indifference fell backwards, his hands over his eyes. When the workers reached him he was jabbering and mad.

They took him to the hut that housed the sick, an attap roof draped over a patch of mud in which—all over one another—lay hundreds of men. For days he lay there silent, knowing nothing. Then one night he suddenly remembered and screamed, screamed piercingly and long so that, even though it was forbidden, the medical orderly lit a resin flare and rushed down to where he lay to see why he screamed.

Russell Braddon

350.

It is easier for those who were not commanded by Orde Wingate to be funny about him (though it is also characteristic of military men to show astonishing tolerance to those who have led them to disaster). Travelling to Quebec with the British party for the Quadrant conference in 1943, he suddenly accosted one of the secretaries among his fellow passengers.

WINGATE turned his penetrating gaze on her and said portentously: 'We have met before.' She denied this politely. 'Ah,' said Wingate, *'not in this world.'* As he turned to leave, he added, 'without religion man is nothing'.

Faced with a crisis he was apt to react hysterically. There is a well attested account of an occasion in 1943 when, on receiving bad news, he publicly flung himself on the ground in an access of frustration. There was also an incident of a similar sort in 1944 at the very moment when the fly-in of the Chindits was about to begin.

Shelford Bidwell

351.

Disgraceful incidence of unchivalrous conduct to animals in the field reported by David Smiley, serving as a British liaison officer with the Albanian partisans, 1943.

I BOUGHT a riding mule for myself costing five sovereigns, and I christened her Fanny (we always referred to our mentor in Cairo as Fanny Hasluck). Fanny had a very sweet nature and I became devoted to her; she carried me everywhere for the next six months of my stay in Albania. On leaving the country I handed her over to Alan Hare of the Life Guards. While on leave in England I sent a signal asking news of Fanny. It was a very severe winter, and our mission at the time was not only on the run from the Germans, but was very short of food. Even so,

Hare could not have been a true cavalryman, as his reply was short and to the point: 'Have eaten Fanny.'

David Smiley

352.

In Sicily in the late summer of 1943, having established a remarkable reputation as an energetic and effective commander, General George Patton committed a series of acts which resulted in his dismissal from field command, and would have terminated his military career but for the support of Eisenhower, who secured his reinstatement in time to lead an Army in North-West Europe.

CASUALTIES had left gaping holes in the line, and Patton saw a tangible connection between them and his difficulties. Moreover, he was told that an increasing number of the men had gone to the hospital with nothing but combat fatigue, a form of neurosis for which he had neither understanding nor sympathy. The departure of these men from the tough battle for Troina was felt seriously by the hard-pressed regiments, which were becoming substantially reduced anyway by *bona fide* casualties. Since no replacements could be obtained, every man was indispensable.

It was with the fresh memories of his visit to the 1st Division boiling in him, on this 3rd August, that Patton spied signs on the road to Mistretta showing directions to the 15th Evacuation Hospital. He told Sergeant George Mims, his driver, 'Take me to that Evac', not so much to seek solace this time but to see for himself how crowded it was with those combat-neurosis cases. . . .

The grand round inside the tent cheered Patton, because the men appeared to be legitimate casualties so far as he could judge from the abundance of bandages. . . . He was about to leave the tent when his eyes fell on a boy in his mid-twenties who was squatting on a box near the dressing station with no bandage on him to indicate that he had been wounded. He was Private Charles Herman Kuhl, ASN 35536908, of Mishawaka, Indiana, a bright-faced, good-looking young soldier eyeing the General with what Patton thought was a truculent look.

'I just get sick inside myself,' Patton later told his friend, Henry J. Taylor, a millionaire businessman who doubled as a war correspondent in Sicily, 'when I see a fellow torn apart, and some of the wounded were in terrible, ghastly shape. Then I came to this man and asked him what was the matter.

'The soldier replied: "I guess I can't take it."'

'Looking at the others in the tent, so many of them badly beaten up, I simply flew off the handle.'

What happened next was described the day after by Kuhl himself in a letter to his father. 'General Patton slapped my face yesterday,' he wrote, 'and kicked me in the pants and cussed me. This probably won't get through, but I don't know. Just forget about it in your letter.'

When Patton was through, he turned to Colonel Wasden.

'Don't admit this sonuvabitch,' he yelled. 'I don't want yellow-bellied bastards like him hiding their lousy cowardice around here, stinking up this place of honour.' Then turning to Colonel Leaver and still shouting at the top of his high-pitched voice, he ordered:

'Check up on this man, Colonel. And I don't give a damn whether he can take it or not! You send him back to his unit at once—you hear me, you gutless bastard,' he was now shrieking at Kuhl again, 'you're going back to the front, *at once!*'

Kuhl was picked up by a group of corpsmen attracted to the scene by the noise. They took him to a ward, where he was found to have a temperature of 102.2°. It also developed that he had been suffering from chronic diarrhoea ever since he joined the 1st Division at the front. A blood test then showed that he had malaria.

Neither the medical staff, nor Kuhl nor his folks in Mishawaka followed up the incident, and that seemed to close the case. Patton himself dismissed it from his mind.

*

On 10th August, Truscott's 3rd Division moved closer to Brolo, where it was to rendezvous with Colonel Bernard's sea-borne force. But the advance was not fast enough, and Bradley called Patton again, pleading with him to postpone the landing a day. Patton remained hard. . . . He was not immune from once in a while suspecting his commanders of sabotaging his decisions which they disliked, and now he feared that Bradley and Truscott might pull something to delay the landing after all. He dropped everything, sent for Mims and drove to II Corps command post for a showdown with Bradley.

Patton was highly agitated on the drive and eager to get to Bradley as quickly as possible. But when he saw signs of the 93rd Evacuation Hospital in the valley near Sant' Agata di Militello, he ordered Sergeant Mims to take him there. He walked unannounced to the admission tent, where Colonel Donald E. Currier, commanding officer of the hospital, hastily advised of the General's arrival, caught up with him. Patton greeted Currier amicably. The surgeon was from Boston and was a friend of his family. The visit thus started out auspiciously.

Waiting at the entrance to the admission tent was Major Charles Barton Etter, the Receiving Officer. . . . What followed was described most graphically by Major Etter in the report he prepared for 'Surgeon, II Corps, A.P.O. 302, U.S. Army (Att'n: Colonel Richard T. Arnest).' It read in full:

1. On Monday afternoon August 10, 1943, at approximately 1330, General Patton entered the Receiving Ward of the 93rd Evacuation Hospital and started interviewing and visiting the patients who were there. There were some ten or fifteen casualties in the tent at the time. The first five or six that he talked to were battle casualties. He asked each what his trouble was, commended them for their excellent fighting; told them they were doing a good job, and wished them a speedy recovery.

He came to one patient who, upon inquiry, stated that he was sick with high fever. The general dismissed him without comment. The next patient was sitting huddled up and shivering. When asked what his trouble was, the man replied, 'It's my nerves', and began to sob. The General then screamed at him, 'What did you say?' He replied, 'It's my nerves. I can't stand the shelling any more.' He was still sobbing.

The General then yelled at him, 'Your nerves Hell, you are just a Goddamn coward, you yellow son of a bitch.' He then slapped the man and said, 'Shut up that Goddamned crying. I won't have these brave men here who have been shot seeing a yellow bastard sitting here crying.' He then struck at the man again, knocking his helmet liner off and into the next tent. He then turned to the Receiving Offier and yelled, 'Don't you admit this yellow bastard, there's nothing the matter with him. I won't have the hospitals cluttered up with these sons of bitches who haven't the guts to fight.'

He turned to the man again, who was managing to 'sit at attention' though shaking all over, and said, 'You're going back to the front lines and you may get shot and killed, but you're going to fight. If you don't, I'll stand you up against a wall and have a firing squad kill you on purpose. In fact,' he said, reaching for his pistol, 'I ought to shoot you myself, you Goddamned whimpering coward.' As he went out of the ward he was still yelling back at the Receiving Officer to send that yellow son of a bitch to the front lines. . . .

Colonel Currier was beside himself. He rushed back to his office and put a call to Colonel Arnest, Surgeon of II Corps.

'Dick,' he told Arnest, 'this is Currier, 93rd Evac. You better come over here as fast as you can make it.'

353.

High on an Italian hillside in 1943, travelling with the correspondent Wynford Vaughan Thomas, the novelist Eric Linklater—who was serving as an official chronicler of the campaign—encountered a miraculous oasis of culture overrun by the war.

IT was a union of little castle and large villa, an ancient tower rising among cypresses on a small hillside above the plain high walls of a sixteenth-century building. It was, we discovered, the Castello di Montegufoni, the property of Sir Osbert Sitwell. In recent years incongruities have been as common as violent death, but, unless the mind has been numbed by too much exposure, the latter still dismays and the former continue to excite a curious pleasure. If it was engaging to find the Mahratta Light Infantry in residence in a Tuscan castle, it was delightful to learn that it belonged to Sir Osbert: the Indian soldiers looked like new images, domiciled as urbanely as their many divers predecessors, in the Sitwells' eclectic hospitality; and we may have been fractionally prepared for the greater, the superb, the enchanting surprise that awaited us within the walls. . . .

Idly we looked into a courtyard, and within a minor entrance to the house discovered to our surprise three or four pictures propped against a wall. Elderly dark paint on wooden panels, and some tarnished gold: a Virgin, the Child and the Virgin, a painted Crucifix. The yellow faces were drawn with the severe and melancholy stare of the earliest Florentine painting.

We sat on our heels to examine them more closely. One of us said with astonishment, 'But they're very good!'

'They must be copies', said another.

I answered like an auctioneer, with the conviction of faith rather than of knowledge: 'Genuine Italian primitives!'

We went into a room where many more pictures were stacked against the walls, some in wooden cases, some in brown paper, and others naked in their frames. Two or three of those that were exposed to view aroused in us the dishonest pretence of recognition so common in visitors to an art gallery. 'Why,' we said, 'surely that's by So-and-so. Not Lippo Lippi, of course, but—oh, what's his name?'

We were not the only occupants of the room, however. Half a dozen soldiers were rummaging in a large desk which seemed to have been roughly opened. It would be altogether too harsh to accuse them of looting, they were only looking for small souvenirs. But they may have been careless, for there was broken glass on the floor and books which

had been tidily stacked were scattered about in some confusion. I
looked at some neatly tied bundles of yellowish paper, and saw that
they were legal documents of Sir George Sitwell's time. I found a copy
of *Before the Bombardment* inscribed by Osbert to his mother, and some
invitation cards which announced that Lady Ida Sitwell would be At
Home on such-and-such a date, when there would be Dancing.

Presuming on the slightest sort of acquaintanceship—I had met
Osbert once or twice—I said to the soldiers, very mildly, 'I don't think
you should take anything from here. I know the owner of the house.'

A genial well-fed sergeant at once replied, 'Oh well, sir, that makes
all the difference, doesn't it? If we'd known that, we wouldn't have
touched a thing. Not a thing,' he repeated, as though shocked by the
very idea.

Nayar and Quereshi and Vaughan Thomas had gone to explore the
farther rooms, and now Vaughan Thomas, his rosy face tense with
excitement, reappeared. 'The whole house is full of pictures,' he
exclaimed, 'and some of the cases are labelled. They've come from the
Uffizi and the Pitti Palace!'

Hastily I followed him into the next room, where a score of wooden
cases stood against the walls, and then to the room beyond. There a
very large picture lay upon trestles. It was spattered with little squares
of semi-transparent paper, stuck for protection over imperilled areas
where the paint was cracking or threatening to flake. On the near side
there were cherubs, or angel-young, with delicate full lips, firm chins
and candid eyes wide open over well-defined cheek-bones. Against a
pale blue sky the Virgin floated in splendour. Two reverent, benign
and bearded figures held a crown above her head.

We failed to recognize it. We knew now that we were in the presence
of greatness, and a bewildered excitement was rising in our minds.
Recognition could not yet speak plainly, but baffled by the vast
improbability merely stammered. Stupidly we exclaimed, 'But that
must be . . .'

'Of course, and yet . . .'

'Do you think it is?'

By this time we had gathered a few spectators. Some refugees had
been sleeping in the castello—their dark bedding lay on the floor—and
now, cheerfully perceiving our excitement, they were making sounds of
lively approval, and a couple of men began noisily to open the shutters
that darkened the last of the suite of rooms. This was a great chamber
that might have served for a banquet or a ball, and as we went in the

light swept superbly over a scene of battle: over the magnificent rotundities of heroic war-horses, knight tumbling knight with point of lance—and beside it, immensely tall, an austere and tragic Madonna in dark raiment upon gold.

Vaughan Thomas shouted, 'Uccello!'

I, in the same instant, cried, 'Giotto!'

For a moment we stood there, quite still, held in the double grip of amazement and delight. Giotto's Madonna and Uccello's Battle of San Romano, leaning negligently against the wall, were now like exiled royalty on the common level. They had been reduced by the circumstance of war from their own place and proper height; and they were a little dusty. We went nearer, and the refugees came round us and proudly exclaimed, 'E vero, è vero! Uccello! Giotto! Molto bello, molto antico!'

Now Vaughan Thomas is a Welshman, more volatile than I, quicker off the mark, swifter in movement, and while I remained in a pleasant stupefaction before the gaunt Virgin and the broad-bottomed cavalry, he was off in search of other treasures. A stack of pictures in the middle of the room divided it in two, and he, with Nayar and Quereshi, was on the other side when a helpful Italian took down the shutters from the far end, and let in more light. Then I heard a sudden clamour of voices, a yell of shrill delight from Nayar, and Vaughan Thomas shouting 'Botticelli!' as if he were a fox-hunter view-halloing on a hill. I ran to see what they had found, and came to a halt before the Primavera.

I do not believe that stout Cortez, when he first saw the Pacific, stood silent on a peak in Darien. I believe he shouted in wordless joy, and his men with waving arms made about him a chorus of babbling congratulation. We, before the Primavera, were certainly not mute, and the refugees—some had been sleeping side by side with Botticelli—were as loudly vocal as ourselves. They had a fine sense of occasion, and our own feeling that this was a moment in history was vigorously supported by the applause they gave to our exclamation and delight . . .

Commanding officers who have lately been engaged in battle and are roused from their entitled sleep are sometimes difficult; but fortunately for us Colonel Leeming of the Mahrattas was a good-humoured man. He listened politely, then with growing attention to what I told him. He knew there were some pictures in the house, but he had had no time to look at them, he said, and he had supposed they belonged to the family. The castello was the property of the Sitwells, who were artistic people, weren't they?

To describe the wealth of treasure that lay below him, I used all the superlatives I could put my tongue to—and still the Colonel listened, unprotesting. To the north we could hear the noise of war, and so much concern for a few yards of paint may have seemed excessive to him, whose care was men; but he was very patient. He admitted that he knew little about art, and wistfully added that if his wife were there she would be more impressed. She took a great interest in pictures, he said.

He put on his shoes and came down to look at the Primavera. He stood silent for some time, and still without comment walked slowly past the other pictures, into the adjoining rooms and back again, as though he were making his rounds of a Sunday morning after church parade. He was evidently pleased with what he saw, and now permitted himself—with a decent restraint—to be infected by our enthusiasm. He would do everything in his power to keep the pictures safe, he promised.

Several other officers had appeared, and to one of them he said: 'Have all these rooms put out of bounds, and get a guard mounted. You'll have to find somewhere else for the refugees to sleep; there's plenty of room in the place.'

We explained to the Professor [guardian of the castello] that his pictures were now under official protection—Mahratta bayonets would guard them night and day, we told him—and at once he grew boisterously happy, and danced about thanking everyone in turn. . . .

In the morning we returned to Montegufoni, and found dark sentries, grave of feature and dignified in their bearing, outside the doors. Then the Professor appeared with one of the Mahrattas' English officers, and we went inside. The Colonel's orders had been strictly obeyed, and the rooms had now the untenanted peace of a museum on a fine morning. We opened the shutters, and with more leisure made further discoveries. Many pictures that we had scarcely noticed in our first excitement now appeared like distinguished guests at a party, obscured by numbers to begin with, who, when at last you meet them, are so dignified or decorative that it seems impossible they could have remained unrecognized even though their backs were turned and a multitude surrounded them. Lippo Lippis came forward smiling, a Bronzino was heartily acknowledged, Andrea del Sartos met our eyes and were more coolly received.

Beside the Giotto Madonna stood a huge equestrian portrait of Philip IV of Spain—by Rubens or Velasquez? I do not know which—and peering round Philip's shoulder, absurdly coy, was the stern and antique countenance of another great Virgin. With some difficulty we moved the King and revealed a Madonna of Cimabue. In a room on the other side of the courtyard, that we had not visited before, we found Duccio's Sienese Madonna, the Rucellai Madonna. Here also were many altar-pieces, triptychs in lavish gold, and painted crucifixes of great rarity in long-darkened colours with mouths down-drawn in Byzantine pain.

Then, privily, I returned to the great room and Botticelli's Primavera. I was alone with his enchanting ladies, and standing tiptoe I was tall enough, I kissed the pregnant Venus, the Flowery Girl, and the loveliest of the Graces: her on the right. I was tempted to salute them all, but feared to be caught in vulgar promiscuity. Some day, I said, I shall see you again, aloft and remote on your proper wall in the Uffizi, and while with a decently hidden condescension I listen to the remarks of my fellow-tourists, I shall regard you with a certain intimacey: with a lonely, proud and wistful memory. The officials, I thought sadly, will certainly not allow me to take a ladder into the gallery.

Eric Linklater

354.

An officer of the Special Air Service captured in Sardinia escapes through Italy until he comes at last within reach of the British lines.

I REACHED the hill-top as dawn broke, but the morning mist was too thick to see anything. I longed to be challenged by a British sentry, but there were none about.

Descending the hill on the far side, I met three Italians on donkeys.

'Are there any Germans round here?' I asked them in Italian.

Suspiciously, they asked if I was German. Hearing I was English, their manner changed immediately. They embraced me and told me to keep going for half a mile when I would reach their village, Montenero, and find English soldiers everywhere.

'Niente tedeschi, niente tedeschi!' they laughed.

The sun broke through the morning mist as I came in sight of the village. Approaching it, I deliberately dawdled and finished the last mouthful of Italian bully.

'Well, here you are,' I said aloud. 'I suppose you'll remember the next minutes all your life.'

And I was quite right.

From a hundred yards away the much-battered buildings appeared deserted. Then I noticed a Bren-carrier behind a wall, a few trucks under camouflage netting in a yard. As I limped slowly into the main street, a solitary shell whistled overhead, exploding somewhere at the farther end. A group of British soldiers, the first I had seen, in long leather waistcoats and khaki cap-comforters, chatted unconcernedly in a doorway across the cobbles from me. I glanced shyly at them, but they took no notice. Just another bedraggled peasant haunting the ruins of his home. . . .

The conventional inhibited Englishman is ill-equipped by temperament for such occasions. I would have liked to dance, to shout, to make some kind of demonstration. A Frenchman, an Australian, would have done it naturally, but somehow I could not. So I walked slowly on, holding off the pleasure of the long-awaited moment, the exclamation of surprise, the greeting from a compatriot.

English voices and laughter came from a house. I crossed the threshold and found, in what had been the peasants' kitchen but was now the usual military desolation of a billet, two half-dressed Privates cooking breakfast. One of them saw me, standing there grinning at them.

'Christ, Nobby, look what the cat's brought in,' he said.

I tried to be hearty but failed. 'I've just come through. I'm soaked. Can I warm up by your fire?' I heard my bored voice say politely.

Neither of the soldiers was much surprised by this sudden entry of what was, to all appearances, a dank and bearded Italian, who spoke fluent English with a B.B.C. accent. Sensibly enough, they were more interested in breakfast.

'What are you? Escaped P.O.W. or something?'

'Yes.'

It didn't cause much of a sensation and they asked no more questions. They treated me, as they might have a stray dog, with a sort of cheery kindness and without fuss. In a few minutes I was sitting naked before their fire, drinking a cup of char and feeling the warmth return to my numbed body.

A Corporal and others of the section came in for their breakfast. My back view may have mildly surprised them.

'Bloke's an escaped P.O.W.,' Nobby explained.

'Lucky sod. They'll send you home,' the Corporal said, offering me a Players.

Savouring every puff of the tobacco, every sip of the tea, I wondered whether Amos was doing the same somewhere nearby. We had so often pictured just this situation in the past three months. Superstitiously, I put off asking them if they had heard of him. If they had, they would surely say so. And I didn't want to hear them say they hadn't.

Long-anticipated pleasures seldom come up to expectation. Neither the tea, the tobacco nor even the warmth were now quite as delicious as I had imagined they would be. The scene was unreal, unbelievable. Though the soldiers' gossip around me was vivid enough.

'Ginger, go and swipe some clothes for him off the C.Q.M.S.'s truck,' the Corporal said to one of the men.

'Do you think the C.Q.M.S. can spare me something?'

'The C.Q.M.S. won't know,' Ginger winked as he left the room.

Certainly I was back with the British Army all right.

Later, in the miscellaneous garments swiped by Ginger (the C.Q.M.S. would, I am sure, have supplied them voluntarily—but that, of course, would have been more trouble) I visited R.H.Q. in another part of the village. Nothing had been heard there of Amos and the C.O. refused at first to credit my story that I had walked through his outposts unobserved, until I traced my route for him on the map. Evidently I had indeed walked slap through C Company's position.

'Can't think why they didn't shoot you,' the Colonel said irritably. 'Remind me to have a word with the Company Commander about that,' he added to his Adjutant.

He seemed to treat my personal survival as a discredit to his blasted Battalion. He was about my age, had a pink face and a toothbrush moustache and the manners of a bilious Scoutmaster. We disliked one another on sight.

I ventured a facetious joke. I hadn't made one for years.

'It was only eight o'clock. Perhaps they were all still asleep.'

'That is not very probable.'

We had little in common and I was glad when he told the Adjutant to take me over. The latter rang through to Brigade and then to Division, but they, too, had heard nothing of Amos. The Divisional I.O.

wanted to see me as soon as possible so the Adjutant arranged for me
to travel back there on a truck.

'Be a good chap,' he whispered as we parted, 'and don't mention
that you walked through our lines unopposed.'

'Of course I won't,' I smiled. Nor have I, till this day.

John Verney

355·

*Having fought in Russia for two years with the Gross Deutschland division and mira-
culously survived the murderous retreat across the Dneiper of October 1943, Private
Guy Sajer looked forward yearningly to a long-promised leave. He was disappointed.*

THERE were two noncoms and a lieutenant in our group. We went
into the building, which had its own generator and was brightly lit. Our
state of extreme filth suddenly made us feel awkward. Military men of
all ranks and military police were sitting facing us behind a row of long
tables. An *obergefreite* came up to us, yelling as in the old days at training camp. He told us to get over to the tables to be screened. We
should be ready to produce on demand the papers and equipment
entrusted to us by the army. This reception only increased our sense of
astonished unease.

'First, your documents,' an M.P. shouted across the table.

The lieutenant, who was directly ahead of me in the line, was being
interrogated.

'Where is your unit, lieutenant?'

'Annihilated, Herr Gendarme. Missing or dead. We had a hard
time.'

The M.P. said nothing to this, but went on leafing through the
lieutenant's papers.

'Did you leave your men, or were they killed?'

The lieutenant hesitated for a moment. We were all watching in
frozen silence.

'Is this a court-martial?' The lieutenant's voice was exasperated.

'You must answer my questions, Herr Leutnant. Where is your
unit?'

The lieutenant clearly felt caught in a trap, as did we all. Very few of
us could have answered that question with any precision. He tried to
explain. But there is never any point in explaining to an M.P.: their

powers of comprehension are always limited to the form they wish to fill.

Further, it appeared that the lieutenant was missing a great many things. This fact obsessed his interrogator. It didn't matter that the man in front of him was effecting a miracle simply by staying on his feet, and had lost at least thirty pounds since entering the army. The M.P. only noted that the Zeiss fieldglasses, which are part of an officer's equipment, were missing. Also missing were a map case, and the section telephone, for which the lieutenant was responsible. In fact, the lieutenant, who had managed to save only his life, was missing far too many things. The army did not distribute its papers and equipment only to have them scattered and lost. A German soldier is expected to die rather than indulge in carelessness with army property.

The careless lieutenant was assigned to a penal battalion, and three grades were stripped from his rank. At that, he could think himself lucky.

The lieutenant's eyes were wild, and he seemed to be fighting for breath. He was a pitiful and terrifying sight. Two soldiers dragged him off to the right, toward a group of broken men, who'd been dealt with in the same way.

Then it was my turn. I felt stiff with fright. I pulled my rumpled documents from an inside pocket. The M.P. rifled through them, throwing me a reproving look. His bad temper seemed to soften somewhat at the sight of my apprehensive, mortified face, and he continued his inventory in silence.

Fortunately, I had been able to reintegrate with my unit and had saved the scrap of white cardboard which stated that I had left the infirmary to take part in an attack. My head was swimming, and I thought I was going to faint. Then the M.P. read off a list of articles which ordinary soldiers like myself were supposed to carry at all times. The words rolled off his tongue, but I didn't catch them quickly enough, and didn't immediately produce the items still in my possession. The M.P. then treated me to a certain German word, which I was hearing for the first time. It appeared I was missing four items, including that fucking gas mask I had deliberately abandoned.

My pay book was passed from hand to hand to be inspected and stamped. In my panic, I made an idiotic move. Hoping to gain favour, I produced nine unused cartridges from my cartridge belt. The M.P.'s eyes lit on these like the eyes of an alpinist who spots a good foothold.

'You were retreating?'

'Ja, Herr Unteroffizier.'

'Why didn't you try to defend yourself? Why didn't you fight?' he shouted.

'Ja, Herr Unteroffizier.'

'What do you mean – ja?'

'We were ordered to retreat, Herr Unteroffizier.'

'God damn it to hell!' he roared. 'What kind of an army runs without shooting?'

I held back my tears with difficulty. Finally the M.P.'s right fingers handed back my liberty. I had not been assigned to a penal battalion, but my emotion overwhelmed me anyway. As I picked up my pack, I sobbed convulsively, unable to stop. A fellow beside me was doing the same.

The crowd of men still waiting stared at me in astonishment. Like a miserable tramp, I ran past the line of tables and left by a door opposite the one we'd entered by. I felt that I had disgraced myself.

I rejoined my comrades, who were standing in the rain in the other part of the camp. They weren't resting on the soft beds we'd dreamed of before coming to this place, and the rain streaming down their shoulders and backs was another hope disappointed.

Guy Sajer

356.

At war, the Yeomanry regiments of the British Army preserved the social standards of the country society from which they were drawn with splendid determination. This narrative picks up the experience of a Scottish unit training in England in 1943.

THE final fling in Yorkshire was exercise 'Eagle', probably the most realistic ever to be held in the country. One Yeoman remarked that the sooner the invasion began the better, as these exercises were killing him. The realism was due to the dreadful weather, which would have been enough to wash most exercises out; to the deliberately short rations, the absence of Canadian umpires and the issue of only one blanket per head—all ranks. It was just before leaving for such an exercise . . . dressed in full marching order, steel helmets but no greatcoats, which were forbidden, they were finishing a glum, silent breakfast at 4.55 a.m. Outside it was raw and lashing with rain; inside tempers were rough and morale at rock bottom. Just as all were gloomily savouring the last warmth they would enjoy for the next fortnight, Gnr H. E. Barnicoat entered. He was batman to Major The Lord Montgomerie. Standing solemnly to attention he announced: 'Excuse me, my Lord. Your Lordship's tank is at the door.'

Gnr Barnicoat was later severely wounded in Holland, but completely recovered and rejoined Major Montgomerie who was by then G.S.O.2 (R.A.) at the School of Infantry. Looking exactly like a stage butler, Barnicoat had been hall porter at the Cambridge Hotel, Farnborough. On one occasion he was handing a glass of sherry to the Divisional Commander who was visiting the Yeomanry for lunch, when the General remarked that his face was familiar and asked where he had seen him before, to which the bold Barnicoat replied, 'At the Cambridge Hotel, sir, where I helped to put you to bed after the Staff College dinner.'

Not much had changed on the battlefield in Normandy a year later.

R.H.Q. at this time was in a pig-sty. On one occasion Lieut. Gray and Sergeant Burton were sitting in it, heavily engaged at the wireless sets and somewhat concerned at the prospect of being cut off by the infiltrating Germans. Just then L/Bdr Symington entered with two cups of cocoa on a tray. He was always known as 'Robert', and never failed to display all the professional dexterity of a butler. He placed the cocoa carefully before the two hard-pressed men, and leaned over in the confidential way he had, murmuring, 'Excuse me, sir, it is reported that a German patrol is coming up through the wood behind. Thank you, sir.' He then withdrew as quietly and as gracefully as he had entered.

W. S. Brownlie

357·

At the river Sangro on Christmas Day 1943, Montgomery's chief of intelligence, the brilliant Balliol don Colonel Bill Williams, heard on the BBC that Montgomery had been nominated to command the Allied landing force in North-West Europe for D-Day. Passionately keen both to serve on his staff and to have an opportunity to see England again after three years in North Africa and Italy, he set off to see 'Master' with his driver, Private Currell.

I F the Army Commander takes me back with him,' I told him en route, 'I'll see to it that you get home too.'

The enemy were spending a quietish Christmas on their side of the river and the only information I had of interest for my Commander for that morning's breakfast was not about them but that I had gathered that General Freyberg was proposing to swim the river that night and that it might perhaps be a good idea to stop him. 'I've got good news for you, Bill', said the Army Commander. My heart jumped. 'Here it comes', I thought. 'Yes,' he went on, 'I remembered that you and Mr Harwood (his clerk) both smoke pipes; so I have been saving this tin of tobacco for you for Christmas.' I thanked him slightly less than warmly, saluted after my fashion and went down the steps of the caravan to Currell's expectant face. We drove back in a loud sheepish silence to my truck at Main HQ, where Corporal Young, the clerk, was waiting impatiently. 'ADC on the line, sir', he said. 'What is it, Johnny?' I asked Johnny Henderson. 'I've only just left the little so-and-so.' 'Well, he wants to talk to you.' 'Gee One Eye[1] here, sir', I reported. 'Is that you, Bill?' came that familiar high-pitched voice: 'Army Commander speakin'. I forgot to tell you that I'm taking you back to England with me. D'you want to come?' (Currell arrived in England a few days later.)

E. T. Williams

358.

In 1944, the British resident minister in the Mediterranean was the quintessential Old Etonian, Harold Macmillan. He recorded the following in his diary after the Allied entry into Rome.

I GO this evening to a Fourth of June dinner. I sent General Alexander a telegram running as follows:

Many congratulations on the successful development of your battle and all good wishes for its exploitation. It was most thoughtful of you as an old Harrovian to capture Rome on the Fourth of June.

General Alexander replied, 'Thank you. What is the Fourth of June?'

Harold Macmillan

[1] The abbreviation for General Staff Officer, Grade One, Intelligence—a Lieutenant-Colonel's appointment.

359.

Special operations in the Second World War gave birth to innumerable acts of derring-do. Few caught the public imagination so vividly as the kidnapping of Major-General Karl Kreipe, German officer commanding in Crete, by Major Patrick Leigh Fermor and Captain Stanley Moss of Special Operations Executive on 26 April 1944. Here Moss takes up the story as the two officers, disguised as German soldiers, reach the road by which they expected the general's car to pass.

It was eight o'clock when we reached the T-junction. We had met a few pedestrians on the way, none of whom seemed perturbed at seeing our German uniforms, and we had exchanged greetings with them with appropriately Teutonic gruffness. When we reached the road we went straight to our respective posts and took cover. It was now just a question of lying low until we saw the warning torch-flash from Mitso, the buzzer-man. We were distressed to notice that the incline in the road was much steeper than we had been led to believe, for this meant that if the chauffeur used the foot-brake instead of the hand-brake when we stopped him there would be a chance of the car's running over the edge of the embankment as soon as he had been disposed of. However, it was too late at this stage to make any changes in our plan, so we just waited and hoped for the best.

There were five false alarms during the first hour of our watch. Two *Volkswagen*, two lorries, and one motor-cycle combination trundled past at various times, and in each of them, seated primly upright like tailors' dummies, the steel-helmeted figures of German soldiers were silhouetted against the night sky. It was a strange feeling to be crouching so close to them—almost within arm's reach of them—while they drove past with no idea that nine pairs of eyes were so fixedly watching them. It felt rather like going on patrol in action, when you find yourself very close to the enemy trenches, and can hear the sentries talking or quietly whistling, and can see them lighting cigarettes in their cupped hands.

It was already one hour past the General's routine time for making his return journey when we began to wonder if he could possibly have gone home in one of the vehicles which had already passed by. It was cold, and the canvas of our German garb did not serve to keep out the wind.

I remember Paddy's asking me the time. I looked at my watch and saw that the hands were pointing close to half-past nine. And at that moment Mitso's torch blinked.

'Here we go.'

We scrambled out of the ditch on to the road. Paddy switched on his red lamp and I held up a traffic signal, and together we stood in the centre of the junction.

In a moment—far sooner than we had expected—the powerful headlamps of the General's car swept round the bend and we found ourselves floodlit. The chauffeur, on approaching the corner, slowed down.

Paddy shouted, 'Halt!'

The car stopped. We walked forward rather slowly, and as we passed the beams of the headlamps we drew our ready-cocked pistols from behind our backs and let fall the life-preservers from our wrists.

As we came level with the doors of the car Paddy asked, 'Ist das das General's Wagen?'

There came a muffled 'Ja, ja' from inside.

Then everything happened very quickly. There was a rush from all sides. We tore open our respective doors, and our torches illuminated the interior of the car—the bewildered face of the General, the chauffeur's terrified eyes, the rear seats empty. With his right hand the chauffeur was reaching for his automatic, so I hit him across the head with my cosh. He fell forward, and George, who had come up behind me, heaved him out of the driving-seat and dumped him on the road. I jumped in behind the steering-wheel, and at the same moment saw Paddy and Manoli dragging the General out of the opposite door. The old man was struggling with fury, lashing out with his arms and legs. He obviously thought that he was going to be killed, and started shouting every curse under the sun at the top of his voice.

The engine of the car was still ticking over, the hand-brake was on, everything was perfect. To one side, in a pool of torchlight in the centre of the road, Paddy and Manoli were trying to quieten the General, who was still cursing and struggling. On the other side George and Andoni were trying to pull the chauffeur to his feet, but the man's head was pouring with blood, and I think he must have been unconscious, because every time they lifted him up he simply collapsed to the ground again.

This was the critical moment, for if any other traffic had come along the road we should have been caught sadly unawares. But now Paddy, Manoli, Nikko, and Stratis were carrying the General towards the car and bundling him into the back seat. After him clambered George,

Manoli, and Stratis—one of the three holding a knife to the General's throat to stop him shouting, the other two with their Marlin guns poking out of either window. It must have been quite a squash.

Paddy jumped into the front seat beside me.

The General kept imploring, 'Where is my hat? Where is my hat?'

The hat, of course, was on Paddy's head.

We were now ready to move. Suddenly everyone started kissing and congratulating everybody else; and Micky, having first embraced Paddy and me, started screaming at the General with all the pent-up hatred he held for the Germans. We had to push him away and tell him to shut up. Andoni, Grigori, Nikko, and Wallace Beery were standing at the roadside, propping up the chauffeur between them, and now they waved us good-bye and turned away and started off on their long trek to the rendezvous on Mount Ida.

We started.

The car was a beauty, a brand-new Opel, and we were delighted to see that the petrol-gauge showed the tanks to be full.

We had been travelling for less than a minute when we saw a succession of lights coming along the road towards us; and a moment later we found ourselves driving past a motor convoy, and thanked our stars that it had not come this way a couple of minutes sooner. Most of the lorries were troop transports, all filled with soldiery, and this sight had the immediate effect of quietening George, Manoli, and Stratis, who had hitherto been shouting at one another and taking no notice of our attempts to keep them quiet.

When the convoy had passed Paddy told the General that the two of us were British officers and that we would treat him as an honourable prisoner of war. He seemed mightily relieved to hear this and immediately started to ask a series of questions, often not even waiting for a reply. But for some reason his chief concern still appeared to be the whereabouts of his hat—first it was the hat, then his medal. Paddy told him that he would soon be given it back, and to this the General said, 'Danke, danke.'

It was not long before we saw a red lamp flashing in the road before us, and we realized that we were approaching the first of the traffic-control posts through which we should have to pass. We were, of course, prepared for this eventuality, and our plan had contained alternative actions which we had hoped would suit any situation, because we knew that our route led us through the centre of Heraklion, and that in the course of our journey we should probably have to pass through about twenty control posts.

Until now everything had happened so quickly that we had felt no emotion other than elation at the primary success of our venture; but as we drew nearer and nearer to the swinging red lamp we experienced our first tense moment.

A German sentry was standing in the middle of the road. As we approached him, slowing down the while, he moved to one side, presumably thinking that we were going to stop. However, as soon as we drew level with him—still going very slowly, so as to give him an opportunity of seeing the General's pennants on the wings of the car—I began to accelerate again, and on we went. For several seconds after we had passed the sentry we were all apprehension, fully expecting to hear a rifle-shot in our wake; but a moment later we had rounded a bend in the road and knew that the danger was temporarily past. Our chief concern now was whether or not the guard at the post behind us would telephone ahead to the next one, and it was with our fingers crossed that we approached the red lamp of the second control post a few minutes later. But we need not have had any fears, for the sentry behaved in exactly the same manner as the first had done, and we drove on feeling rather pleased with ourselves.

In point of fact, during the course of our evening's drive we passed twenty-two control posts. In most cases the above-mentioned formula sufficed to get us through, but on five occasions we came to roadblocks—raisable one-bar barriers—which brought us to a standstill. Each time, however, the General's pennants did the trick like magic, and the sentries would either give a smart salute or present arms as the gate was lifted and we passed through. Only once did we find ourselves in what might have developed into a nasty situation. . . .

Paddy, sitting on my right and smoking a cigarette, looked quite imposing in the General's hat. The General asked him how long he would have to remain in his present undignified position, and in reply Paddy told him that if he were willing to give his parole that he would neither shout nor try to escape we should treat him, not as a prisoner, but, until we left the island, as one of ourselves. The General gave his parole immediately. We were rather surprised at this, because it seemed to us that anyone in his position might still entertain reasonable hopes of escape—a shout for help at any of the control posts might have saved him.

According to our plan, I should soon be having to spend twenty-four hours alone with Manoli and the General, so I thought it best to find out if we had any languages in common (for hitherto we had been speaking a sort of anglicized German). Paddy asked him if he spoke any English.

'Nein,' said the General.

'Russian?' I asked. 'Or Greek?'

'Nein.'

In unison: 'Parlez-vous francais?'

'Un petit peu.'

To which we could not resist the Cowardesque reply, 'I never think that's quite enough.'

W. Stanley Moss

360.

As the war progressed, the difficulties of finding employment for Captain Evelyn Waugh became almost insuperable, as his diary records.

March 2nd 1944

Luncheon with General Thomas, who accepted me as ADC in spite of my warnings against it. I thought him a simple soldier but heard later that he is a man of insatiable ambition and unscrupulous in his means of self-advancement. On Tuesday I went to his headquarters for a week's trial—today returned unaccepted. This is a great relief. The primary lack of sympathy seemed to come from my being slightly drunk in his mess on the first evening. I told him I could not change the habits of a lifetime for a whim of his.

May 11th 1944

Interview in the afternoon. I found the room at Hobart House full of the scouring of the Army, pathetic old men longing for a job, obvious young blackguards. We were seen in turn by a weary but quite civil lieutenant-colonel and a major. The colonel said 'We've two jobs for you. I don't know which will appeal to you the more. You can be a welfare officer in a transit camp in India.' I said that was not one I should choose. 'Or you can be assistant registrar at a hospital.' I said if I had to have one or the other I would have the latter. Then he said, 'By the way are you educated? Were you at a university?'

'Yes, Oxford.'

'Well, they are very much in need of an educated officer at the War
Office, G3 Chemical Warfare.'

'My education was classical and historical.'

'Oh, that doesn't matter. All they want is *education*.'

Evelyn Waugh

361.

Montgomery's Military Assistant recalls an incident in the spring of 1944.

ABOUT a month before the invasion Monty, whose personal vanity
was markedly not diminished by his new status as the nation's conquering hero, decided that he must have his portrait painted. Since I
knew Augustus John slightly I suggested him as the most appropriate
artist. John agreed to do the portrait for a very modest fee. After the
first sitting my bell rang loudly and I found myself confronted with an
outraged Monty—'Kit, who is this terrible man you have sent me to?
His clothes are dirty, I think he was rather tight and there are dozens
of women in the background. I shan't go again unless you come with
me.' So I found myself attending all future sittings, where I was usually
made to sit in the corner with my face to the wall. This far from cordial
atmosphere was considerably lightened during a visit made to the stu-
dio one day by Bernard Shaw with whom Monty struck up an immediate rapport. What transcribed is described in letters written by Shaw
on successive days, later shown to me by the recipient and quoted in
Monty's *Memoirs*:

4, Whitehall Court,
London S.W.1
26th February 1944

Dear Augustus John,

This afternoon I had to talk all over the shop to amuse your sitter
and keep his mind off the worries of the present actual fighting. And as
I could see him with one eye and you with the other—two great men at
a glance—I noted the extreme unlikeness between you. You, large, tall,
blonde, were almost massive in contrast with that intensely compacted
hank of steel wire, who looked as if you might have taken him out of
your pocket.

A great portrait painter always puts himself as well as his sitter into
his work; and since he cannot see himself as he paints (as I saw you)

there is some danger that he may substitute himself for his subject in the finished work. Sure enough, your portrait of B.L.M. immediately reminded me of your portrait of yourself in the Leicester Gallery. It fills the canvas, suggesting a large tall man. It does not look at you, and Monty always does this with intense effect. *He* concentrates all space into a small spot like a burning glass; *it* has practically no space at all, you haven't left room for any.

Now for it. Take that old petrol rag that wiped out so many portraits of me (all masterpieces), and rub out this one until the canvas is blank. Then paint a small figure looking at you straight from above, as he looked at me from the dais. Paint him at full length (some foreground in front of him) leaning forward with his knees bent back gripping the edge of his campstool, and his expression one of piercing scrutiny, the eyes unforgettable. The background; the vast totality of desert Africa. Result; a picture worth £100,000. The present sketch isn't honestly worth more than the price of your keep while you were painting it. You really weren't interested in the man.

Don't bother to reply. Just take it or leave it as it strikes you.

What a nose! And what eyes!

Call the picture INFINITE HORIZONS AND ONE MAN.

Fancy a soldier being intelligent enough to want to be painted by you and to talk to me!

Always yours,
(Sgd) GBS
C. P. Dawnay

362.

Eisenhower has been found wanting by some historians as a battlefield commander. Yet in the hours before D-Day, 6 June 1944, he demonstrated his greatness as Allied Supreme Commander by the manner in which he carried the intolerable burden of decision to launch the invasion.

THE evening of June 3, Eisenhower met in the mess room at South-wick House with his commanders and RAF Group Captain J. M. Stagg, his chief weatherman. Staff had bad news. A high-pressure system was moving out, and a low was coming in. The weather on June 5 would be overcast and stormy, with a cloud base of five hundred feet to zero and Force 5 winds. Worse, the situation was deteriorating so rapidly that forecasting more than twenty-four hours in advance was highly undependable. It was too early to make a final decision, but word had to go out to the American Navy carrying Bradley's troops to Omaha and Utah beaches, since they had the farthest to travel. Eisenhower decided to let them start the voyage, subject to a possible last-minute cancellation. He would make the final decision at the regular weather conference the next morning.

At 4.30 a.m. on Sunday, June 4, Eisenhower met with his subordinates at Southwick House. Stagg said sea conditions would be slightly better than anticipated, but the overcast would not permit the use of the air forces. Montgomery said he wanted to go ahead anyway. Tedder and Leigh-Mallory wanted a postponement. Ramsay said the Navy could do its part but remained neutral when asked whether or not the whole operation should go. Eisenhower remarked that Overlord was being launched with ground forces that were not overwhelmingly powerful. The operation was feasible only because of Allied air superiority. If he could not have that advantage, the landings were too risky. He asked if anyone present disagreed, and when no one did he declared for a twenty-four hour postponement. The word went out to the American fleet by prearranged signal. Displaying superb seamanship, the fleet drove through the incoming storm, regained its ports, refueled, and prepared to sail again the next day.

That evening, June 4, Eisenhower ate at Southwick House. After dinner he moved into the mess room. Montgomery, Tedder, Smith, Ramsay, Leigh-Mallory, Strong, and various high-ranking staff officers were already there. The wind and the rain rattled the window frames in the French doors in staccato sounds. The mess room was large, with a heavy table at one end and easy chairs at the other. Two sides of the room were lined with bookcases, most of which were empty and forlorn. A third side consisted of the French doors: the fourth wall was covered with a huge map of southern England and Normandy, filled with pins, arrows, and other symbols of Allied and German units. The officers lounged in easy chairs. Coffee was served and there was desultory conversation. Stagg came in about nine-thirty with the latest weather report. Eisenhower called his associates to order and they all sat up to listen intently.

Stagg reported a break. Kenneth Strong recalled that at Stagg's prediction 'a cheer went up. You never heard middle-aged men cheer like that!' The rain that was then pouring down, Stagg continued, would stop in two or three hours, to be followed by thirty-six hours of more or less clear weather. Winds would moderate. The bombers and fighters ought to be able to operate on Monday night, June 5–6, although they would be hampered by clouds. Leigh-Mallory remarked that it seemed to be only a moderately good night for air power. Tedder, his pipe clenched between his teeth and forcibly blowing out smoke, agreed that the operations of heavies and mediums were going to be 'chancy'. Eisenhower countered by pointing out that the Allies could call on their large force of fighter-bombers.

The temptation to postpone again and meet the following morning for another conference was strong and growing, but Ramsay put a stop to that idea by pointing out that Admiral Alan G. Kirk, commanding the American task force, 'must be told in the next half hour if Overlord is to take place on Tuesday [June 6]. If he is told it is on, and his forces sail and are then recalled, they will not be ready again for Wednesday morning. Therefore, a further postponement would be forty-eight hours.' A two-day delay would put everything back to June 8, and by that time the tidal conditions would not be right, so in fact postponement now meant postponement until June 19.

Whatever Eisenhower decided would be risky. He began pacing the room, head down, chin on his chest, hands clasped behind his back. Suddenly he shot his chin out at Smith. 'It's a helluva gamble but it's the best possible gamble', Smith said. Eisenhower nodded, tucked his chin away, paced some more, then shot it out at Montgomery, huddled in his greatcoat, his face almost hidden. 'Do you see any reason for not going Tuesday?' Montgomery straightened up, looked Eisenhower in the eye, and replied, 'I would say—Go!' Eisenhower nodded, tucked away his chin, paced, looked abruptly at Tedder. Tedder again indicated he thought it chancy. Finally Eisenhower halted, looked around at his commanders, and said, 'The question is just how long can you hang this operation on the end of a limb and let it hang there?'

If there was going to be an invasion before June 19, Eisenhower had to decide now. Smith was struck by the 'loneliness and isolation of a commander at a time when such a momentous decision was to be taken by him, with full knowledge that failure or success rests on his individual decision'. Looking out at the wind-driven rain, it hardly seemed possible that the operation could go ahead. Eisenhower calmly weighed the alternatives, and at 9.45 p.m. said, 'I am quite positive that the order must be given.'

Ramsay rushed out and gave the order to the fleets.More than five thousand ships began moving toward France. Eisenhower drove back to his trailer and slept fitfully. He awoke at 3.30 a.m. A wind of almost hurricane proportions was shaking his trailer. The rain seemed to be travelling in horizontal streaks. He dressed and gloomily drove through a mile of mud to Southwick House for the last meeting. It was still not too late to call off the operation. In the now familiar mess room, steaming hot coffee helped shake the gray mood and unsteady feeling. Stagg said that the break he had been looking for was on its way and that the weather would be clear within a matter of hours. The long-range prediction was not good, to be sure, but even as he talked the rain began to stop and the sky started to clear.

A short discussion followed, Eisenhower again pacing, shooting out his chin, asking opinions. Montgomery still wanted to go, as did Smith and Ramsay. Smith was concerned about proper spotting for naval gunfire but thought the risk worth taking. Tedder was ready. Leigh-Mallory still thought air conditions were below the acceptable minimum.

Everyone stated his opinion. Stagg withdrew to let the generals and admirals make the decision. No new weather reports would be available for hours. The ships were sailing into the Channel. If they were to be called back, it had to be done now. The Supreme Commander was the only man who could do it. Eisenhower thought for a moment, then said quietly but clearly, 'O.K., let's go.' And again, cheers rang through Southwick House.

Then the commanders rushed from their chairs and dashed outside to get to their command posts. Within thirty seconds the mess room was empty, except for Eisenhower. The outflow of the others and his sudden isolation were symbolic. A minute earlier he had been the most powerful man in the world. Upon his word the fate of millions depended. The moment he uttered the word, however, he was powerless. For the next two or three days there was almost nothing he could do that would in any way change anything. The invasion could not be stopped, not by him, not by anyone. A captain leading his company onto Omaha, or a platoon sergeant at Utah, would for the immediate future play a greater role than Eisenhower. He could now only sit and wait.

Eisenhower was improving at killing time. He visited South Parade Pier in Portsmouth to see some British soldiers climb aboard their landing craft, then returned to his trailer. He played a game of checkers on a cracker box with Butcher, who was winning, two kings to one, when Eisenhower jumped one of his kings and got a draw. At lunch they exchanged political yarns. After eating, Eisenhower went into a tent with representatives of the press and announced that the invasion was on. Smith called with more news about de Gaulle. After hanging up, Eisenhower looked out the tent flap, saw a quick flash of sunshine, and grinned.

When the reporters left, Eisenhower sat at his portable table and scrawled a press release on a pad of paper, to be used if necessary. 'Our landings . . . have failed . . . and I have withdrawn the troops,' he began. 'My decision to attack at this time and place was based upon the best information available. The troops, the air and the Navy did all that bravery and devotion to duty could do. If any blame or fault attaches to the attempt it is mine alone.' Putting the note in his wallet, Eisenhower went to dinner.

Stephen Ambrose

363.

Montgomery established his headquarters at Creully in Normandy in the aftermath of D-Day, 6 June 1944.

MONTGOMERY started up a private zoo almost as soon as he landed. In Bayeux he caught sight of Major Sobilov—a Russian—whose scrounging exploits were notorious throughout the Allied forces. Montgomery called Sobilov over and told him to get him a budgerigar by 4 p.m. or he would be sacked. The Russian seemed confused at first; but as he strolled off down the street he saw a birdcage in a window, rushed into the house and claimed it. The inhabitants were too astonished to resist. So the menagerie was under way. There was potential excitement, too, when a German soldier was discovered hiding in the bushes less than thirty yards from Montgomery's caravan; but he was too frightened to do anything. There were elements of almost pure farce. One was the army biscuit problem. Montgomery broke his false teeth on one of these rock-like objects, soon after landing. The teeth were sent back to London, where they were rapidly mended. The next week, another army biscuit shattered this repaired set. After that a softer diet was strictly applied. On another occasion Madame de Druval, who had remained in residence in her château at Creully, was asked to provide Montgomery with a chamber-pot for his caravan. The ADC entrusted with the mission decided to use tact, and instead of demanding the object bluntly, he asked for a vase. After she had brought him all the flower vases in the château, and he had rejected them all, 'Madame, having great intuition and no small sense of humour, immediately sensed what was wanted.' So the general's caravan was fully furnished.

Lord Chalfont

364.

Normandy, 15 June 1944: a British NCO makes his report.

'WE were told to clear the church steeple, but we couldn't get at it, so I took my piat into the upstairs bedroom of the house opposite, stuck it up on the window-sill, and let fly at the tower. The bursts knocked half the top off. And later we found twelve dead Jerries up there; some had been killed by our stens, and the piat got the rest.'

'Was the church badly damaged?' asked the colonel. 'Not inside it wasn't, sir,' . . . 'We just knocked the top off; we wouldn't have touched it if the snipers hadn't been there. And when I went in, sir, I did take my hat off.'

Corporal Tom Galeen

365.

Scavenging for fresh food in Normandy.

IN the no-man's-land between the two sides, in the deserted farmsteads, there were plenty of fowls if you could catch them. I couldn't. These chickens, as soon as they saw anybody in battledress, however much he whistled disinterest, scrambled up the nearest rampart, and you could not get after them without revealing yourself in a field of machinegun fire. But I discovered a flock of geese, and I broke my penknife trying to slaughter the first. When I had at last killed them all and loaded them into my jeep for my hungry colleagues, I was covered from top to tail with feathers. A soldier looking like one out of a Giles wartime cartoon, climbed out of a slit trench and said to me balefully, 'Them was laying eggs.'

Macdonald Hastings

366.

There seem grounds for holding some reservations about the heroic place in history of the German army's conspirators against Hitler, most of whom summoned the nerve to act not out of moral conviction, that the Nazi cause was wrong, but out of belated despair that Germany's battle was lost. An assassin might have killed Hitler at any time had he been willing to sacrifice his own life in the process. But Count von Stauffenberg left the conference room before his bomb exploded on 20 July 1944, and thus the conspirators made their move in ignorance that Hitler still lived. The grotesque débâcle in Berlin that evening sounded the death knell of the old German army.

ABOUT nine o'clock Field-Marshal Witzleben, muttering, 'This is a fine mess', climbed into his car and drove back to the Lynar estate at Seesen, and almost at the same time it became known that the commander of *Wehrkreis III* (von Thüngen) and the military Commandant of Berlin (von Hase) had accepted the order of General Reinecke, a notorious Nazi who had also been on the telephone to Hitler, to withdraw their troops, surrender their authority and consider themselves under arrest.

Olbricht thereupon assembled in his room those officers who were privy to the conspiracy and begged them to resist the assault which was now inevitably imminent and to fight it out to the end. This they agreed to do and orders were given to put the building into some state of defence. With Beck and Hoepner, von Quirnheim, von Stauffenberg and Werner von Haeften, Olbricht then retired to Fromm's old room (now Hoepner's) on the floor above to hold a last council of war.

Scarcely had they assembled than shots were heard on the stairs and in the corridors outside, and a group of officers, headed by Colonel Bodo von der Heyde, all armed with tommy guns and grenades, forced their way into the room and at pistol point demanded that Fromm should be released and handed over to them. It was the counter-*Putsch* and the nemesis of misplaced mercy. It was an error of judgment—equal almost in catastrophic consequences to Fellgiebel's failure and the omission to provide an alternative method of radio transmission—to have allowed Fromm and von Kortzfleisch and their fellow-prisoners to have remained in open custody in the same building with the conspirators. If they had not been shot out of hand—a fate which most of them richly deserved and which they did not hesitate to mete out when their turn came—they should at least have been closely confined. Instead, they had been accorded the honours of war and food and wine had been provided for them; in the confusion they had eluded their guards and found arms.

Olbricht showed fight and was overpowered. Von Stauffenberg was shot in the back as he was retreating into his own room next door. The others remained rooted where they stood. Then Fromm appeared.

This wretched man had been all things to all men for many years. An ardent Nazi when the fortunes of the *Führer* and the Nazi régime were in the ascendant, he had been privy to and compliant with the conspiracy which was being hatched in his own office, and, had the attempt upon Hitler's life succeeded, would have been among the first to hail the new régime in Germany. There were many who were aware of how much he knew and his conduct in the early afternoon had been anything but unequivocal. Now at the last moment he sought to rehabilitate himself in the eyes of the winning side by eliminating the chief conspirators, ostensibly as a proof of his undying loyalty to the *Führer* but actually to destroy the incriminating evidence against himself. It is of some satisfaction to know that, though he succeeded in carrying out this weasel plan, it profited him nothing.

Urged on by the knowledge that retribution was hard on his track if he did not act at once, Fromm proceeded with ruthless and indecent haste. He ordered the prisoners to be disarmed and constituted himself and his recently released fellow-prisoners a drum-head court-martial of summary procedure. Beck, who had sat as if stunned throughout this last swift passage of events, asked to keep his pistol as he wished to use it for 'private purposes'. 'You would not deprive an old comrade of this privilege,' he said to Fromm with quiet dignity.

So this was the end. He, Ludwig Beck, had seen it coming for a long time. In his deepest heart he had never believed in success for the *Putsch* but he had been convinced that it must be attempted as an act and gesture of expiation. 'There is no use. There is no deliverance,' he had said to a friend only a few weeks before. 'We must now drain little by little the bitter cup to the bitterest end.' And why? Because men of high character such as himself had once allowed themselves to be beguiled by the enticements and seductions of National Socialism. Beck had not scrupled to defend his subalterns, Scheringer and Ludin, when charged with the propagation of what was then (1931) the subversive doctrine of the Nazi Party. He had not been shaken in his belief that there was something good for Germany in all that Hitler promised until the first exhibition of bestial gangsterism in the Blood Bath of June 30, 1934. Yet a few weeks later he had taken the Oath of

Allegiance, albeit with grave and heart-searching reservations, to the man who had ordered this massacre. Not till the defiling hand of the Party was laid upon the sacrosanct privileges of the Army itself, four years later, was Beck roused to open opposition, but it must be stated that once he had been thus aroused he never looked back. From 1938 until now, on the sultry night of July 20, 1944, when he stood at the end of the road, he had fought and struggled to free Germany and the German Army from the fetters of National Socialism which he and many of his comrades had helped to rivet upon their wrists. He symbolized the best in German military resistance, the man who saw the error of his ways and did what he could, however futile and ineffective, to undo the harm which he had done. Beck was no band-wagon jumper, as had been Fromm and von Kluge and Rommel; he had watched inactive the Nazi circus go past him when all his world was following admiring in its train, but the years since 1938 had been a hell upon earth for him.

Something of all this must have been in his mind as he stood now, pistol in hand, confronting Fromm, with his fellow-conspirators, now his fellow-prisoners, about him. 'I recall the old days . . .' he began, but Fromm interrupted him with crude brutality, increased by his own guilty anxiety for speed, and ordered him to get on with the business in hand. Beck gave him one contemptuous glance, and looked once in farewell to his friends. Then he put the pistol to his grey head and pulled the trigger.

His intention was better than his aim. The bullet grazed his temple, giving him a slight flesh wound, and buried itself in the ceiling. Beck staggered to a chair and collapsed into it, his head in his hands. 'You'd better give the old man a hand,' said Fromm callously, and left the room.

It was at this moment, shortly after ten o'clock, that Lieutenant Schlee and his detachment of the *Wachbataillon* made their unmolested entrance into the War Ministry. As they made their way up the deserted stairs and along the empty corridors, proceeding with caution lest a trap awaited them, they heard a single shot. There was silence for a moment, then a burst of voices and a general officer, whom Schlee recognized as Fromm, came into the passage. Schlee reported himself and placed his detachment under the General's orders. Fromm then went back to his office.

The scene was macabre. In a chair, supported by two officers, sat Beck, his face ashen and blood from his flesh wound running unchecked down his cheek. Half lying in another chair, attended by his brother and Werner von Haeften, was Claus von Stauffenberg, wounded from Bodo von der Heyde's bullet in the back. At the central table Olbricht and Hoepner were writing farewell letters to their families. Fromm looked evilly portentous: 'In the name of the *Führer*, a summary court-martial called by myself, has reached the following verdict: Colonel of the General Staff Mertz von Quirnheim, General Olbricht, the Colonel—I cannot bring myself to name him [von Stauffenberg]—and Lieutenant von Haeften are condemned to death.'

They were taken immediately to the courtyard below, von Haeften supporting the staggering von Stauffenberg. The headlights of the military trucks shone in their eyes, all but blinding them. The men of Schlee's detachment formed the firing-party. There was only one volley.

Left alone with Beck and Hoepner, Fromm offered the latter a pistol but Hoepner was not prepared for this. He refused the way of suicide and allowed himself to be arrested. 'I am not a swine', he said, 'that I should have to condemn myself.' It was a decision which he was doubtless later to repent.

'Now how about you?' Fromm asked Beck roughly, shaking him by the shoulder. Beck asked in a weak and weary voice for another pistol and it was given him. This time he was successful.

The remaining prisoners who had been arrested in Olbricht's room, including Peter Yorck, Fritz von der Schulenburg, Eugen Gerstenmaier, Ulrich von Schwerin-Schwanenfeld, von Stauffenberg's brother Berthold and von Haeften's brother Bernd, were now herded down into the courtyard where, under Fromm's orders, a second firing-party had been ordered. But here Fate again intervened.

Before the second batch of executions could be carried out, thereby removing virtually the last traces of Fromm's complicity, there arrived at the Bendlerstrasse a group of Gestapo officials, escorting Kaltenbrunner and Skorzeny, with explicit orders that no further summary justice should take place. It was the first indication of the policy which *Reichsführer*-SS Heinrich Himmler, Minister of Interior and now Commander-in-Chief of the Home Army, was to pursue. The mere slaughter of the *Führer*'s enemies was of no importance to him. They should die, certainly, but not before torture, indignity and interrogation had drained from them the last shred and scintilla of evidence which should lead to the arrest of others. Then, and only then, should the blessed release of death be granted them.

And thus the day, which was to have heralded the downfall of the Nazi tyranny, closed with the opening of a new era of hideous and sadistic persecution.

Sir John Wheeler-Bennett

367.

The most wretched fate of all was reserved for Field Marshal Irwin Rommel, hero of the North African campaign, almost certainly not an active member of the conspiracy against Hitler, but doomed because the plotters had regarded him as a suitable figure-head to lead negotiations with the Western Allies. His son describes his last hours as follows.

WHEN my parents arrived back at Herrlingen again after the long car journey, they found a telephone message awaiting them to the effect that two Generals were coming next day to talk to my father about his 'future employment'.

My battery, to which I had returned several weeks before, had given me leave for the 14th October [1944]. I left the gun position very early in the morning and arrived at Herrlingen at 7.00 a.m. My father was already at breakfast. A cup was quickly brought for me and we break-fasted together, afterwards taking a stroll in the garden.

'At twelve o'clock today two Generals are coming to see me to dis-cuss my future employment,' my father started the conversation. 'So today will decide what is planned for me; whether a People's Court or a new command in the East.'

'Would you accept such a command,' I asked.

He took me by the arm, and replied: 'My dear boy, our enemy in the East is so terrible that every other consideration has to give way before it. If he succeeds in overrunning Europe, even only temporarily, it will be the end of everything which has made life appear worth living. Of course I would go.'

Shortly before twelve o'clock, my father went to his room on the first floor and changed from the brown civilian jacket which he usually wore over riding-breeches, to his Africa tunic, which was his favourite uniform on account of its open collar.

At about twelve o'clock a dark-green car with a Berlin number stopped in front of our garden gate. The only men in the house apart from my father, were Captain Aldinger, a badly wounded war-veteran corporal and myself. Two generals—Burgdorf, a powerful florid man, and Maisel, small and slender—alighted from the car and entered the house. They were respectful and courteous and asked my father's permission to speak to him alone. Aldinger and I left the room. 'So they are not going to arrest him,' I thought with relief, as I went upstairs to find myself a book.

A few minutes later I heard my father come upstairs and go into my mother's room. Anxious to know what was afoot, I got up and followed him. He was standing in the middle of the room, his face pale. 'Come outside with me', he said in a tight voice. We went into my room. 'I have just had to tell your mother', he began slowly, 'that I shall be dead in a quarter of an hour.' He was calm as he continued: 'To die by the hand of one's own people is hard. But the house is surrounded and Hitler is charging me with high treason. "In view of my services in Africa," he quoted sarcastically, 'I am to have the chance of dying by poison. The two generals have brought it with them. It's fatal in three seconds. If I accept, none of the usual steps will be taken against my family, that is against you. They will also leave my staff alone.'

'Do you believe it?' I interrupted.

'Yes,' he replied. 'I believe it. It is very much in their interest to see that the affair does not come out into the open. By the way, I have been charged to put you under a promise of the strictest silence. If a single word of this comes out, they will no longer feel themselves bound by the agreement.'

I tried again. 'Can't we defend ourselves . . . ' He cut me off short.

'There's no point,' he said. 'It's better for one to die than for all of us to be killed in a shooting affray. Anyway, we've practically no ammunition.' We briefly took leave of each other. 'Call Aldinger, please,' he said.

Aldinger had meanwhile been engaged in conversation by the General's escort to keep him away from my father. At my call, he came running upstairs. He, too, was struck cold when he heard what was happening. My father now spoke more quickly. He again said how useless it was to attempt to defend ourselves. 'It's all been prepared to the last detail. I'm to be given a state funeral. I have asked that it should take place in Ulm. In a quarter of an hour, you, Aldinger, will receive a telephone call from the Wagnerschule reserve hospital in Ulm to say that I've had a brain seizure on the way to a conference.' He looked at his watch. 'I must go, they've only given me ten minutes.'He quickly took leave of us again. Then we went downstairs together.

We helped my father into his leather coat. Suddenly he pulled out his wallet. 'There's still 150 marks in there,' he said. 'Shall I take the money with me?'

'That doesn't matter now, Herr Field Marshal,' said Aldinger.

My father put his wallet carefully back in his pocket. As he went into the hall, his little dachshund which he had been given as a puppy a few months before in France, jumped up at him with a whine of joy. 'Shut the dog in the study, Manfred,' he said, and waited in the hall with Aldinger while I removed the excited dog and pushed it through the study door. Then we walked out of the house together. The two generals were standing at the garden gate. We walked slowly down the path, the crunch of the gravel sounding unusually loud.

As we approached the generals they raised their right hands in salute. 'Herr Field Marshal', Burgdorf said shortly and stood aside for my father to pass through the gate. A knot of villagers stood outside the drive. Maisel turned to me, and asked: 'What battery are you with?'

'36/7, Herr General', I answered.

The car stood ready. The S.S. driver swung the door open and stood to attention. My father pushed his marshal's baton under his left arm and with his face calm, gave Aldinger and me his hand once more before getting in the car.

The two generals climbed quickly into their seats and the doors were slammed. My father did not turn again as the car drove quickly off up the hill and disappeared round a bend in the road. When it had gone Aldinger and I turned and walked silently back into the house. 'I'd better go up and see your mother,' Aldinger said. I went upstairs again to await the promised telephone call. An agonizing depression excluded all thought.

I lit a cigarette and tried to read again, but the words no longer made sense. Twenty minutes later the telephone rang. Aldinger lifted the received and my father's death was duly reported. That evening we drove into Ulm to the hospital where he lay. The doctors who received us were obviously ill at ease, no doubt suspecting the true cause of my father's death. One of them opened the door of a small room. My father lay on a camp-bed in his brown Africa uniform, a look of contempt on his face.

It was not then entirely clear what had happened to him after he left us. Later we learned that the car had halted a few hundred yards up the hill from our house in an open space at the edge of the wood. Gestapo men, who had appeared in force from Berlin that morning, were watching the area with instructions to shoot my father down and storm the house if he offered resistance. Maisel and the driver got out of the car, leaving my father and Burgdorf inside. When the driver was permitted to return ten minutes or so later, he saw my father sunk forward with his cap off and the marshal's baton fallen from his hand. Then they drove off at top speed to Ulm, where the body was unloaded at the hospital; afterwards General Burgdorf drove on to Ulm Wehrmacht Headquarters where he first telephoned to Hitler to report my father's death and then on to the family of one of his escort officers to compose the menu for that night's dinner. General Burgdorf, who was hated for his brutality by 99 per cent of the Officer Corps, ended his own life in Berlin in April 1945, after staggering round drunk with Bormann for several days in the Fuehrer's bunker.

Perhaps the most despicable part of the whole story was the expressions of sympathy we received from members of the German Government, men who could not fail to have known the true cause of my father's death and in some cases had no doubt themselves contributed to it, both by word and deed. I quote a few examples:

In the Field
16 October 1944

Accept my sincerest sympathy for the heavy loss you have suffered with the death of your husband. The name of Field Marshal Rommel will be for ever linked with the heroic battles in North Africa.

ADOLPH HITLER

Fuehrer's Headquarters
26 October 1944

The fact that your husband, Field Marshal Rommel, has died a hero's death as the result of his wounds, after we had all hoped that he would remain to the German people, has deeply touched me. I send you, my dear Frau Rommel, the heartfelt sympathy of myself and the German Luftwaffe.

In silent compassion, Yours,

GOERING, Reichsmarschall des
Grossdeutschen Reiches

Manfred Rommel

368.

An incident during the German winter offensive in the Ardennes, December 1944.

IT is not surprising that the enemy detected in the westerly battles a scarcity of American infantry grievous enough to warrant a surrender demand. About noon on December 22, four Germans under a flag of truce entered the lines of Company F of the 327th. A major, a captain, and two enlisted men, they described themselves as 'parlementaires'. The commander of the 327th could not immediately be found, so it was the regimental operations officer who received from the Germans a written note from 'The German Commander', which he delivered to division headquarters. The note referred to the progress of German spearheads farther west toward the Meuse as evidence of the futility of holding out at Bastogne, which adds perspective to the importance of the battles concurrently being fought by the 2nd and 3rd Armored and 84th Infantry Divisions in front of the Meuse crossings. Thus suggesting that the German tide was irresistible anyway, the note demanded the surrender of the encircled town within two hours, on pain of annihilation of 'the U.S.A. troops in and near Bastogne'.

[Brigadier-General Anthony C.] McAuliffe received this demand just as he was about to leave headquarters to congratulate the defenders of a roadblock who had given an especially good account of themselves. He dropped the message on the floor, said 'Nuts', and left.

When he returned his staff reminded him of the message, and for the first time he gave it serious enough thought to ask what he should say in reply. His G-3 suggested, 'That first remark of yours would be hard to beat.'

'What did I say?' asked McAuliffe, and he was told. So the formal reply, typed on bond paper and delivered to the officer parlementaires at the F Company command post by Colonel Joseph H. Harper of the 327th, read:

To the German Commander:
  Nuts!
                 The American Commander

Harper naturally found the parlementaires uncertain about the translation. He also found them apparently assuming their surrender demand would be met. Settling at first for advising them that the reply was decidedly not affirmative, by the time he had escorted the German officers back to the Company F outpost line, where they picked up the two enlisted men, Harper had pondered long enough on what he took to be their arrogance to send them off with: 'If you don't understand what "Nuts" means, in plain English it is the same as "Go to hell". I will tell you something else—if you continue to attack, we will kill every goddamn German that tries to break into this city.'

Russell F. Weigley

369.

THAT particular night [in Germany, early in 1945], as the dusk was gathering prematurely under the high canopy of trees, I was just about to signal the infantry through when there was the most alarming spurt of flame, followed by a very loud bang indeed. For a moment I thought Joe's tank, which was leading, had been hit by a bazooka shell, but seconds later I heard him come up on the intercom to his driver with such volume that I did not need earphones. There was a crashing of gears, a roaring of engines and Joe charged into the trees. This remarkable escapade was to earn him a doubly-deserved Military Medal.

Where was I, the reader may well ask, while all this banging and crashing was going on? Actually I was in the rear tank with only Wally between me and the action. In fact a second bazooka took a pot-shot at me before Joe blew him up. I can only say that the bazooka operator must have been in a fairly jittery state because at about twenty yards he almost missed completely, the shell passing harmlessly through the back flange of my almost stationary tank.

We were very lucky. An armour-piercing shell amidships is not a pleasant experience. The shell is apt to rattle round the inside of the turret like an angry wasp, causing considerable damage to life and limb before, as likely as not, setting fire to the whole contraption for good measure.

With this excitement over, only the clash of gears could be heard as Joe, Wally and I backed hard into the trees and heaved a sigh of relief as the forward platoon of the Argylls materialized unscathed out of the darkness. A tot or two of the blessed rum and so to bed.

The following morning, as Brigsy reversed the tank back into business, there rose from literally under the left-hand track, with hands held well above his head, as dishevelled, grimy and altogether miserable a figure as anyone could imagine. His grey German uniform was scarcely recognizable under its coating of mud and oil.

As we stared in amazement at this apparition, he grimaced and pointed to a narrow slit trench in which he had evidently been trapped under the tank track all night. There was something about that gesture which rang the very faintest of bells. I signalled to him to climb on to the turret. Sitting on top of the tank, we just stared at each other in total disbelief.

In those long-ago sunlit days of the 1930s, when God was in his heaven and all was well with the world, my father had decreed that my brother and I should have a German tutor. His name had been Willie Schiller. Now the same Willie Schiller was facing me.

There was nothing much either of us could do about it. He may have said 'Gott in Himmel', but I can't really remember. We just had a rum or two and smoked a cigarette. Then I gave Bolton the job of escorting him back to rear HQ.

'See he gets there safely,' I ordered. It was the least I could do. There had been cases, particularly of captured snipers, not making it all the way back.

After the war I was telling my mother about this extraordinary affair.

'Nonsense,' she said firmly. 'It could not have been Willie. You must have been drunk.'

'I was not drunk,' I responded indignantly. 'Why do you say it could not have been Willie?'

'Because,' she said firmly, 'Willie was always so perfectly turned out.'

Douglas Sutherland

370.

At the court of Adolf Hitler in the apocalyptic days of April 1945.

GOEBBELS told Schewerin von Krosigk how he had recently been reading aloud to the Fuehrer, to solace him in his universal discomfiture. He was reading from his favourite book, Carlyle's *History of Frederick the Great*; and the chapter he was reading described 'how the great king himself no longer saw any way out of his difficulties, no longer had any plan; how all his generals and ministers were convinced that his downfall was at hand; how the enemy was already counting Prussia as destroyed; how the future hung dark before him, and in his last letter to his minister, Count Finckenstein, he gave himself one last respite: if there was no change by February 15th, he would give it up and take poison. "Brave king!" says Carlyle, "wait yet a little while, and the days of your suffering will be over. Already the sun of your good fortune stands behind the clouds, and soon will rise upon you." On February 12th the Czarina died; the Miracle of the House of Brandenburg had come to pass.' At this touching tale, said Goebbels, 'tears stood in the Fuehrer's eyes'. They discussed the matter to and fro, and in the course of the discussion sent for two horoscopes that were carefully kept in one of Himmler's research departments: the horoscope of the Fuehrer, drawn up on 30th January 1933, and the horoscope of the Republic, dated 9th September 1918. These sacred documents were fetched and examined, and 'an astonishing fact' was discovered, which might well have repaid an earlier scrutiny. 'Both horoscopes had unanimously predicted the outbreak of war in 1939, the victories till 1941, and then the series of defeats culminating in the worst disasters in the early months of 1945, especially the first half of April. Then there was to be an overwhelming victory for us in the second half of April, stagnation till August, and in August peace. After the peace there would be a difficult time for Germany for three years; but from 1948 she would rise to greatness again. Next day Goebbels sent me the horoscopes. I could not fathom everything in them; but in the subjoined interpretation, newly drawn up, I found it all; and now I am eagerly awaiting the second half of April.'

Hugh Trevor-Roper

371.

A British officer drives through Germany in the first days after the German surrender.

I PASSED a farm wagon headed for the village. I glanced casually at the two men sitting up behind the horse. Both wore typical farmer headgear and sacks were thrown over their shoulders protecting them from a light drizzle. We were just past them when something made me slam on the brakes and back up. I was right, the man who was not driving was wearing field boots. I slipped out from behind the wheel, pulled my revolver from its holster and told the corporal to cover me with his Tommy gun.

I gestured to the men to put their hands over their heads and told them in fumbling German to produce their papers.

'I speak English,' said the one with the field boots, 'this man has papers—I have none.'

'Who are you?' I asked.

He told me his name and rank—'General'.

'We are not armed,' he added, as I hesitated.

Sandhurst did it—I saluted, then motioned to them to lower their hands.

'Where are you coming from, sir?'

He looked down at me. I had never seen such utter weariness, such blank despair on a human face before. He passed a hand over the stubble of his chin.

'Berlin', he said quietly.

'Where are you going, sir?'

He looked ahead down the road towards the village and closed his eyes.

'Home,' he said almost to himself, 'it's not far now . . . only . . . one more kilometre.'

I didn't say anything. He opened his eyes again and we stared at each other. We were quite still for a long time. Then I said, 'Go ahead, sir,' and added ridiculously . . . 'please cover up your bloody boots.'

Almost as though in pain, he closed his eyes and raised his head, then with sobbing intake of breath, covered his face with both hands and they drove on.

David Niven

372.

ARMY Health specialists [of whom the author was one] credit Moses with an enlightened attitude to hygiene and sanitation in camp and on the march; and it is not only doctors who admire his ability as a military leader, as the following anecdote illustrates.

Field Marshal Montgomery visited the Headquarters of 15 (Scottish) Division shortly before he was to address the undergraduates of St Andrews University. During lunch, after being told that I am a native of St Andrews, he first asked me how to find Butts Wynd, where Montrose shot with the bow and arrow, and then asked if I would like to hear what he proposed to say to the students. 'I shall take three great soldiers in History—I shall describe their methods—and with them I shall compare my own—my own. I shall take Cromwell, Napoleon—and Moses.' I said that the choice of Moses might surprise them, and he went on, 'Have you ever considered Moses' task—to conquer Canaan with a crowd of fellahin–DPs? Do you suppose that the children

of Israel were *lost* in the Sinai Desert for 40 years? Not a bit of it. They
were training—training.'

Of course I lacked the courage to say that *he* had not been our
Moses but had had the luck to be Joshua. One might wish that the
Field Marshal could have given more credit to those who played
Moses to his Joshua—Auchinleck and Wavell, whose *History of the
Palestine Campaign* shows how generously 'Joshua' Allenby acknowl-
edged his debt to 'Moses' Murray—Sir Archibald Murray, his prede-
cessor in command.

                                                          F. M. Richardson

373.

Return of a prisoner of war.

IN the early summer of 1945 I climbed into a Dakota on an airfield in
East Germany with all my worldly posessions—a pistol and ten rounds,
and a few cigarettes. There were a dozen other men on the plane, all
very dirty and most of them asleep. Nobody talked much, and at three
in the afternoon we came down on a runway in a field full of buttercups
in Oxfordshire. I had been away four years. It was England all right:
there was that special kind of early summer light calming down the
romantic distances and making the hedgerows into dark blue mists.
Sweet reason was the prevailing atmosphere on the air-strip. Soothing
girls gave us tea, rock cakes and cigarettes and asked soothing, ridiculous questions. They took down our names and units and addresses,
doctors plied their stethoscopes, beat on our knees with little rubber
hammers, and took blood samples. Quartermasters of a new kind to
me, young and deploying a winsome charm, issued new underclothes
and shoes. Orderlies showed us into bedrooms with beautiful white
sheets and bathrooms attached. The first bath for three years was such
a revelation for me that I made it last nearly two hours. Then I hacked
off my beard and shaved.

They're softening you up, I said to myself from time to time. It's a
trap. My neighbour in the next room, a bald major, put his head round
the door with another version of events. 'I can only suppose', he said,
'that the man who runs this place wants to get into Parliament.'

'I'm not stopping here,' I told him, 'no matter what they say or do. If
I have to bust out I'm taking off tonight.'

'Oh, I don't know,' the major murmured, 'might give the bed a trial.'
At this innocent speech such a fury rose in me that I had to move away
at a run in case I fell upon him tooth and claw. So I went into the
assembly hall where there was to be an announcement.

'Won't waste your time with speeches,' the commandant was saying,
'The sergeants sitting at tables down both sides of this room are
experts in cutting red tape. They're here to see you get your advances
on pay, temporary identity card, ration books, coupons, and all the
bumf you need nowadays in the quickest possible time. Only one snag.
Nobody leaves here until he is past the psychiatrist. The examination
will take some time. There are 25 of you and three psychiatrists, so
some of you will be staying the night. Any volunteers?' To my amazement and contempt he got 12.

The psychiatrist was Viennese and cat-like. 'I am not at all sure that
you're fit to take your place in the civilian world. I ask you to stay. Will
you stay?'

'No,' I said. 'I'll break out.'

'That would be very foolish, but also of some inconvenience to me,'
the psych said. 'Have you a permanent address, a telephone number,
somebody to look after you during your first three or four weeks?'

'My wife has taken a flat in South London,' I said, 'and she is
expecting me.'

Quite suddenly I had to put on an absolutely blank face over one of
those appalling rages which had been invading me every since I got
free from the prisoner-of-war camp. Deceit was the only thing. Bluff
your way out. 'Oh, I think I'll be all right,' I said easily.

'Very well, you get three months' leave,' and he filled in a card. I
hadn't taken him in, though: I saw the card later: 'Manic depressive
type. Educated. High IQ. Possibly disturbed. Marked aggression.'
Then two red asterisks.

'Have a drink', said this abominable man, and I drank a large whisky
very slowly to deceive him.

Twelve of us left for London by the 9.30 train, and if I was madder
than most of them there wasn't much to choose between us. By midnight seven wives had a drama on their hands once more for better or
for worse, and for the first time in history their dramas were being produced by the War Office. When I first heard this I was so furious I
thought I would going to have a stroke. 'Do you mean to say', I yelled,
'that the bloody army gave you lessons in how to be married to me?'

'Well, they told us what we might expect.'

'To hell with that', I roared, and went off to the pub and stayed away for three days.

When I got back I said: 'I took off because I will not have my life interfered with.' 'Oh yes,' my wife said, 'they told us about that, too.'

René Cutforth

374.

[As CIGS] Monty took me [Under-Secretary of State at the War Office] down to the Staff College at Camberley on one memorable occasion. There were in my recollection, possibly inflated, several hundred officers in uniform. I, the only civilian present, perched uneasily on the platform while Monty delivered a spellbinding address. He ended this way: 'And remember, gentlemen. Never forget, gentlemen, the politicians.' All eyes turned in my direction. 'They are our masters (considerable laughter). It's up to us—to lead them—up the garden path—(the laughter now was happy and prolonged) gentlemen dismiss.'

Lord Longford

375.

Colonel Richard Meinzerhagen, a retired officer and passionate Zionist sympathizer, found himself aboard a liner which docked briefly at Haifa in the midst of Israel's war of independence. The author was already a man of almost 70.

23. IV. 1948.
WE arrived at Haifa, on my way back from Arabia, at dawn and tied up. There is a company of Coldstream Guards on board; some of the officers knew Dan [the author's son] and we spoke about him; that pleased me beyond measure; this company disembarked here to the tune of a full-scale battle along the sea-front between the Arabs and the Jews. By 4 p.m. the Arabs were on the run and the Jews in control of the port except for the small depot still occupied by the British Army. The Coldstreams walked right into the fight, their job being to protect Government stores. Both rifle fire and the ping of bullets continued throughout our stay in Haifa with an occasional mortar shell or bomb.

Now I must relate my grossly irregular behaviour in Haifa. I realized that the Jews were going to be strained to the utmost with seven Arab States invading them from all sides and with an unsympathetic Great Britain. I was quite determined to help if even in a small way. A private soldier in the Coldstream detachment knew Dan and he was sick and unable to land with the detachment. I went to his cabin and asked him if he would lend me his complete equipment, rifle, uniform and ammunition to which he agreed with a typical 'Take the whole bloody lot, as far as I'm concerned.' So I took the 'whole bloody lot' and marched ashore behind the Coldstream detachment, unnoticed by the officers and falling-in in the rear. I had no difficulty in getting ashore and on leaving the breakwater I broke away from the detachment of Coldstreams and walked to where I could hear firing. I soon found the front line—about twenty Haganah well entrenched in sand. So I ran up, scraped a hole and lay low for a bit. I had my field glasses and sighted my rifle on an empty barrel, some 200 yards away. Some Arabs, about 600 yards away, had fired at me as I ran up to take position beside the Haganah, so I crawled forward by degrees taking every advantage of folds in the ground and eventually got a fine little scrape in the sand no more than 250 yards from some Arab snipers. Three Haganah did likewise and we four opened fire. I saw an Israeli looking at me and he said something which I did not hear; he then shouted to his friends and yelled at me in Hebrew. I paid no attention. My first shot was a bull's-eye and there was a cheer from the Haganah as the man rolled over and writhed about on the sand. I crept forward to a better position and found I could take the Arabs in the flank; which I proceeded to do. Two more paid the penalty. The Haganah kept up with me and between us we got five more and one got up and ran towards us with his arms above his head so we captured him. There were now some twenty Arabs firing at us, at ranges between 300 and 600 yards; so we crept on and bagged four more: I had a narrow squeak when a bullet hit my little parapet and spluttered me with sand. We were doing well when one of the Haganah shouted at me, but not understanding I paid no attention. He then got up and ran back. About an hour later, after we had disposed of all the Arabs in front of us, a Coldstream officer came along, asked who the hell I was and on recognizing me, he ordered me back to the ship, which I had to obey; but it mattered little as by then I had fired all my 200 rounds. So off I went, rather sheepishly, and without further incident got aboard, returned my uniform to my friend, cleaned his rifle and then ordered a large

bottle of champagne which we shared in his cabin. Altogether I had
had a glorious day. May Israel flourish!

Richard Meinzerhagen

376.

*General Douglas MacArthur was relieved of his command in Korea by President
Truman on 11 April 1951, after publicly threatening an extension of the war to
mainland China.*

ALMOST at the very moment yesterday that the news of General
MacArthur's relief was coming over the radio at the divisional command post on the western front where I have been spending a few
days, a terrific wind blew across the camp site, leveling a couple of
tents. A few minutes later, a hailstorm lashed the countryside. A few
hours after that, there was a driving snowstorm. Since the weather had
been fairly springlike for the previous couple of weeks, the odd climatic
goings on prompted one soldier to exclaim, 'Gee, do you suppose he
really is God, after all?'

E. J. Kahn

377.

*The French GCMA—Groupement de Commandos Mixtes Aeroportes—teams which
fought behind Vietminh lines in Indo-China were founded on Second World War
maquis experience. Each was composed of native tribesman fighting under the leadership of French officers and NCOs, supplied by air. One of the most extraordinary and
tragic stories of that war was the fate of surviving GCMA groups which could never be
evacuated after the French withdrawal.*

THE cease-fire of July 1954 also brought an end to G.C.M.A. operations. Frantic efforts were made by the French to broadcast messages
to all the groups operating behind Communist lines to fall back to
Laos, the 17th parallel, or to the shrinking Haiphong perimeter before
the Bamboo Curtain rang down on them for good. But for many, the
broadcasts came too late, or the T'ai or Meo could not reconcile themselves to leave their families exposed to the Communist reprisals which
now were sure to come. And the Frenchmen who were with them and
who could not possibly make their way back across hundreds of miles

of enemy territory, stayed with them, to fight with the tribesmen to the end.

This was a fight to the finish, and no quarter was given on either side. One by one, as the last commandos ran out of ammunition, as the last still operating radio sets fell silent, the remnants of the G.C.M.A. died in the hills of North Viet-Nam. There was no 'U-2' affair, no fuss: France did not claim the men, and the Communists were content to settle the matter by themselves. French officers recalled with a shudder the last radio message picked up from somewhere in North Viet-Nam nearly two years after the fighting had officially stopped. The voice was a French voice and the message was addressed to the French. It said:

You sons-of-bitches, help us! Help us! Parachute us at least some ammunition, so that we can die fighting instead of being slaughtered like animals!

But the cease-fire was in effect and the last French troops left Indo-China in April 1956, in compliance with the demands of the Vietnamese nationalists. Yet the few remaining G.C.M.A.'s kept on fighting. No less an authoritative source than the Communists' own weekly *Quan-Doi Nhan-Dan* ('People's Army') of September 3, 1957 reported that from July 1954 to April 1956 their forces in the mountain areas east of the Red River had, 'in spite of great difficulties and hardships', killed 183 and captured 300 'enemy soldiers', while inducing the surrender of 4,336 tribesmen and capturing 3,796 weapons. Some of the luckier tribesmen, such as the Muong and Nung who were closer to the French lines, made their way to South Viet-Nam and are now resettled in the southern hills near Dalat, in a setting and climate very close to that of their beloved T'ai country. Others continue to trickle into neighboring Laos, whose own mountain tribes are their close relatives.

By 1959, the struggle was over. The mountaineers were thoroughly purged of all 'reactionary' elements and whatever Frenchmen there had been left among them were now dead or captured. Only one Frenchmen, Captain C—, who was thoroughly familiar with several mountain dialects, is known to have made his way out of the Communist-occupied zone after a harrowing 500-mile trek through the mountains from tribe to tribe. And thus ended the French experiment of anti-Communist guerilla warfare in Indo-China.

Bernard Fall

378.

The 1956 Suez operation was marked by military confusion quite as great as the political misjudgement. In the weeks following mobilization, the British expeditionary force assembled for war with painful sluggishness.

WHEN the units started to collect their vehicles and stores from depots which were spread around the country and manned mostly by civilians who took the week-end off, it was found that mobilization scales were out-of-date, that numerous items were out-of-stock and that many of the vehicles were, to say the least, decrepit. To move the tanks from Tidworth to Portland and Southampton, where they were to be loaded into L.S.T.s, help had to be sought from Pickfords to supplement the few tank-transporters still left to the Army. Pickford's men were subject to trade-union rules and civilian regulations, and their massive transporters took a week for a journey which an army convoy could complete in three days; behind each bunch of their vehicles trailed a number of empty spares, as was required by the Regulations of British Road Services. It was hardly surprising that it took four weeks to move and load ninety-three tanks.

*

When ships which had been loaded for so many weeks eventually off-loaded their cargoes at Port Said there were some unexpected surprises. At the fishing harbour a senior staff officer one day noticed a 3-ton lorry, so overladen that its rear springs were all but concave and stuck fast on the ramp. 'Who the bloody hell are you', he enquired kindly, 'and what are you doing?' 'I, sir,' responded a voice of much dignity, 'am the mess-sergeant of Her Majesty's Life Guards, and I have with me the officers' mess silver and champagne.'

Roy Fullick and Geoffrey Powell

379.

Harold Macmillan described to an interviewer his final encounter with Field Marshal Alexander.

'THE last time I saw him before he died, we were going into the theatre together. I said one of those old man's things to him: "Alex, wouldn't it be lovely to have it all to do over again?"

'Alex turned to me and said, "Oh, *no*. We might not do *nearly* so well." '

Max Hastings

380.

A young officer of the American Marines describes his introduction to war, posted to Da Nang in March 1965.

IT was a peculiar period in Vietnam, with something of the romantic flavour of Kipling's colonial wars. It was not so splendid for the Vietnamese, of course, and in early April we got a hint of the nature of the contest that was being waged in the bush. Two Australian commandos, advisers to an ARVN Ranger Group, walked into Charley Company's area. They were tough-looking characters, with hatchet-hard faces, and were accompanied by an even tougher-looking ranger, whose eyes had the burned-out look of a man no longer troubled by the things he had seen and done. The Aussies looked up Sergeant Loker, Tester's platoon sergeant, who had once served as adviser with them. There was a noisy reunion. A few of us, curious about these strangers, gathered nearby to listen. The Australians were describing a fire-fight they had been in that morning. The details of this clash have vanished from my memory, but I recall the shorter of the two saying that their patrol had taken a 'souvenir' off the body of a dead VC, and pulled something from his pocket and, grinning, held it up in the way a fisherman posing for a photograph holds up a prize trout. Nothing could have been better calculated to give an idea of the kind of war Vietnam was and the kind of things men are capable of in war if they stay in it long enough. I will not disguise my emotions. I was shocked by what I saw, partly because I had not expected to see such a thing and partly because the man holding it was a mirror image of myself—a member of the English-speaking world. Actually, I should refer to 'it' in the plural, because there were two of them, strung on a wire; two brown and bloodstained human ears.

Philip Caputo

381.

Perhaps the outstanding war correspondent's dispatch from Vietnam.

AFTER a light lunch last Wednesday [1 June 1966], General James F. Hollingsworth, of Big Red One, took off in his personal helicopter and killed more Vietnamese than all the troops he commanded.

The story of the General's feat begins in the divisional office, at Ki-Na, twenty miles north of Saigon, where a Medical Corps colonel is telling me that when they collect enemy casualties they find themselves with more than four injured civilians for every wounded Viet Cong—unavoidable in this kind of war.

The General strides in, pins two medals for outstanding gallantry to the chest of one of the colonel's combat doctors. Then he strides off again to his helicopter, and spreads out a polythene-covered map to explain our afternoon's trip.

The General has a big, real American face, reminiscent of every movie general you have seen. He comes from Texas, and is forty-eight. His present rank is Brigadier General, Assistant Division Commander, 1st Infantry Division, United States Army which is what the big red figure one on his shoulder flash means.

'Our mission today', says the General, 'is to push those goddam VCs right off Routes 13 and 16. Now you see Routes 13 and 16 running north from Saigon toward the town of Phuoc Vinh, where we keep our artillery. When we got here first we prettied up those roads, and cleared Charlie Cong right out so we could run supplies up.

'I guess we've been hither and thither with all our operations since, an' the ol' VC he's reckoned he could creep back. He's been puttin' out propaganda he's goin' to interdict our right of passage along those routes. So this day we aim to zapp him, and zapp him, and zapp him again till we've zapped him right back where he came from. Yes, sir. Let's go.'

The General's UH18 helicopter carries two pilots, two 50-calibre machine-gunners, and his aide, Dennis Gillman, an apple-cheeked subaltern from California. It also carries the General's own M16 carbine (hanging on a strut), two dozen smoke bombs, and a couple of CS anti-personnel gas-bombs, each as big as a small dustbin. Just beside the General is a radio console where he can tune in on orders issued by battalion commanders flying helicopters just beneath him, and company commanders in helicopters just below them. Under this interlacing of helicopters lies the apparently peaceful landscape beside Routes 13 and 16, filled with farmhouses and peasants hoeing rice and paddy fields.

So far today, things haven't gone too well. Companies Alpha, Bravo and Charlie have assaulted a suspected Viet Cong HQ, found a few tunnels but no enemy. The General sits at the helicopter's open door, knees apart, his shiny black toecaps jutting out into space, rolls a filter-tip cigarette to-and-fro in his teeth, and thinks.

'Put me down at Battalion HQ,' he calls to the pilot.

'There's sniper fire reported on choppers in that area, General.'

'Goddam the snipers, just put me down.'

Battalion HQ at the moment is a defoliated area of four acres packed with tents, personnel carriers, helicopters and milling GIs. We settle into the smell of crushed grass. The General leaps out and strides through his troops.

'Why General, excuse us, we didn't expect you here,' says a sweating major.

'You killed any 'Cong yet?'

'Well no General, I guess he's just too scared of us today. Down the road a piece we've hit trouble, a bulldozer's fallen through a bridge, and trucks coming through a village knocked the canopy off a Buddhist pagoda. Saigon radioed us to repair that temple before proceeding—in the way of civic action, General. That put us back an hour. . . . '

'Yeah. Well Major, you spread out your perimeter here a bit, then get to killin' VCs will you?'

Back through the crushed grass to the helicopter.

'I don't know how you think about war. The way I see it, I'm just like any other company boss, gingering up the boys all that time, except I don't make money. I just kill people, and save lives.'

In the air the General chews two more filtertips and looks increasingly forlorn. No action on Route 16, and another Big Red One general has got his helicopter in to inspect the collapsed bridge before ours.

'Swing us back along again,' says the General.

'Reports of fire on choppers ahead, sir. Smoke flare near spot. Strike coming in.'

'Go find that smoke.'

A plume of white rises in the midst of dense tropical forest, with a Bird Dog spotter plane in attendance. Route 16 is to the right; beyond it a large settlement of red-tiled houses.

Two F105 jets appear over the horizon in formation, split, then one passes over the smoke, dropping the trail of silver, fish-shaped canisters. After four seconds' silence, light orange fire explodes in patches along an area fifty yards wide by three-quarters of a mile long. Napalm.

The trees and bushes burn, pouring dark oily smoke into the sky. The second plane dives and fire covers the entire strip of dense forest.

'Aaaaah,' cries the General. 'Nice. Nice. Very neat. Come in low, let's see who's left down there.'

'How do you know for sure the Viet Cong snipers were in that strip you burned?'

We don't. The smoke position was a guess. That's why we zapp the whole forest.'

'But what if there was someone, a civilian, walking through there?'

'Aw come son, you think there's folks just sniffing flowers in tropical vegetation like that? With a big operation on hereabouts? Anyone left down there, he's Charlie Cong all right.'

I point at a paddy field full of peasants less than half a mile away.

'That's different son. We know they're genuine.'

The pilot shouts: 'General, half-right, two running for that bush.'

'I see them. Down, down, goddam you.'

In one movement he yanks his M16 off the hanger, slams in a clip of cartridges and leans right out of the door, hanging on his seatbelt to fire one long burst in the general direction of the bush.

'General, there's a hole, maybe a bunker, down there.'

'Smokebomb, circle, shift it.'

'But General, how do you know those aren't just frightened peasants?'

'Running? Like that? Don't give me a pain. The clips, the clips, where in hell are the cartridges in this ship?'

The aide drops a smoke canister, the General finds his ammunition and the starboard machine-gunner fires rapid bursts into the bush, his tracers bouncing up off the ground round it.

We turn clockwise in ever tighter, lower circles, everyone firing. A shower of spent cartridge cases leaps from the General's carbine to drop, lukewarm, on my arm.

'I . . . WANT . . . YOU . . . TO . . . SHOOT . . . RIGHT . . . UP . . . THE . . . ASS . . . OF . . . THAT . . . HOLE . . . GUNNER.'

Fourth time round the tracers flow right inside the tiny sand-bagged opening, tearing the bags, filling it with sand and smoke.

The General falls back off his seatbelt into his chair, suddenly relaxed, and lets out an oddly feminine, gentle laugh. 'That's it,' he says, and turns to me, squeezing his thumb and finger into the sign of a French chef's ecstasy.

We circle now above a single-storey building made of dried reeds. The first burst of fire tears the roof open, shatters one wall into fragments of scattered straw, and blasts the farmyard full of chickens into dismembered feathers.

'Zapp, zapp, zapp', cries the General. He is now using semi-automatic fire, the carbine bucking in his hands.

Pow, pow, pow, sounds the gun. All the noises of this war have an unaccountably Texan ring. . . .

'There's nothing alive in there', says the General. 'Or they'd be ske-daddling. Yes there is, by golly.'

For the first time I see the running figure, bobbing and sprinting across the farmyard towards a clump of trees dressed in black pyjamas. No hat. No shoes.

'Now hit the tree.'

We circle five times. Branches drop off the tree, leaves fly, its trunk is enveloped with dust and tracer flares. Gillman and the General are now firing carbines side by side in the doorway. Gillman offers me his gun: No thanks.

Then a man runs from the tree, in each hand a bright red flag which he waves desperately above his head.

'Stop, stop, he's quit', shouts the General, knocking the machine-gun so tracers erupt into the sky.

'I'm going down to take him. Now watch it everyone, keep firing round-about, this may be an ambush.'

We sink swiftly into the field beside the tree, each gunner firing cau-tionary bursts into the bushes. The figure walks towards us.

'That's a Cong for sure,' cries the General in triumph and with one deft movement grabs the man's short black hair and yanks him off his feet, inboard. The prisoner falls across Lieutenant Gillman and into the seat beside me.

The red flags I spotted from the air are his hands, bathed solidly in blood. Further blood is pouring from under his shirt, over his trousers.

Now we are safely in the air again. Our captive cannot be more than sixteen years old, his head comes just about up to the white name patch—Hollingsworth—on the General's chest. He is dazed, in shock. His eyes calmly look first at the General, then at the Lieutenant, then at me. He resembles a tiny, fine-boned wild animal. I have to keep my hand firmly pressed against his shoulder to hold him upright. He is quivering. Sometimes his left foot, from some nervous impulse, bangs hard against the helicopter wall. The Lieutenant applies a tourniquet to his right arm.

'Radio base for an ambulance. Get the information officer with a camera. I want this Commie bastard alive till we get back . . . just stay with us till we talk to you, baby.'

The General pokes with his carbine first at the prisoner's cheek to keep his head upright, then at the base of his shirt.

'Look at that now,' he says, turning to me. 'You still thinking about innocent peasants? Look at the weaponry.'

Around the prisoner's waist is a webbing belt, with four clips of ammunition, a water bottle (without stopper), a tiny roll of bandages, and a propaganda leaflet which later turns out to be a set of Viet Cong songs, with a twenty piastre note (about 1s 6d) folded in it.

Lieutenant Gillman looks concerned. 'It's OK, you're OK', he mouths at the prisoner, who at that moment turns to me and with a surprisingly vigorous gesture waves his arm at my seat. He wants to lie down.

By the time I have fastened myself into yet another seat we are back at the landing pad. Ambulance orderlies come aboard, administer morphine, and rip open his shirt. Obviously a burst of fire has shattered his right arm up at the shoulder. The cut shirt now allows a large bulge of blue-red tissue to fall forward, its surface streaked with white nerve fibres and chips of bone (how did he ever manage to wave that arm in surrender?).

When the ambulance has driven off the General gets us all posed round the nose of the chopper for a group photographer like a gang of successful fishermen, then clambers up into the cabin again, at my request, for a picture to show just how he zapped those VCs. He is euphoric.

'Jeez I'm so glad you was along, that worked out just dandy. I've been written up time and time again back in the States for shootin' up VCs, but no one's been along with me like you before.'

'I'll say perhaps your English generals wouldn't think my way is all that conventional, would they? Well, this is a new kind of war, flexible, quickmoving. Us generals must be on the spot to direct our troops. The helicopter adds a new dimension to battle.

'There's no better way to fight than goin' out to shoot VCs. An' there's nothing I love better than killin' Cong. No sir.'

                                                                Nicholas Tomalin

382.

On 6 October 1973, the Syrian and Egyptian attack on the Israeli army achieved devastating surprise, and in its first hours came close to achieving a decisive break-through. But the Israeli genius for improvisation on the battlefield proved sufficient—just sufficient—to stem the assault. The defence of the Golan Heights against overwhelming odds will always stand as an epic of military endeavour. By the after-noon of 9 October, the position of the Israeli 7th Brigade had become critical. Lt.-Col. Yossi had become world famous in June 1967, when his photograph appeared on the cover of Life magazine swimming in the Suez Canal after the triumphal climax of the Sinai campaign. Now, he found himself in battle once again under very different circumstances.

THEY had been fighting for four days and three nights, without a moment's rest or respite, under constant fire. On average each tank was left with three or four shells. At the height of battle Avigdor turned and spoke to his operations officer. The officer began to reply but suddenly in the middle of his sentence slid to the floor of the armoured carrier, fast asleep. Avigdor spoke to Raful and told him that he did not know if he could hold on. Already in a daze, he described the condition of his brigade. Raful, as ever quiet, calm and encouraging, pleaded with him, 'For God's sake, Avigdor, hold on! Give me another half an hour. You will soon be receiving reinforcements. Try, please, hold on!'

At this critical moment, Lieut.-Col. Yossi, leading remnants of the Barak Brigade with a force of eleven tanks, entered the divisional area and was directed by Raful to Avigdor. Yossi had handed over command of his battalion in the Barak Brigade on 4 September and decided that his honeymoon would be a non-conventional one. So with his newly wed wife, Naty, he flew to the Himalayas. On Yom Kippur eve they rode by motorbike to the Chinese frontier. Back in Katmandu for Yom Kippur, the receptionist in the hotel said to him, 'You're from Israel, aren't you? Something is happening in your area. You ought to listen to the news.' Racing against time Yossi and Naty, using every form of subterfuge, managed to fly back to Israel via Teheran and Athens. From Athens Yossi phoned his family to bring his uniform and equipment to the airport. As he rushed northwards, little did he realize that he would receive command of the remnants of his former brigade. He hurried to Hofi's advanced headquarters and heard what had happened to the Barak Brigade. It was Tuesday morning.

When Dov had reached the Barak Brigade centre, remnants of the brigade began to arrive in dribs and drabs. Oded had in the meantime evacuated from the area of Tel Faris, taking with him some 140 infantry men who arrived on foot down the Gamla Rise. Dov and the other officers organized technical teams and began to recover abandoned tanks in the field, while ordnance units began to repair them. At noon on Tuesday a psychiatrist arrived from the medical centre of Tel Hashomer to take care of the soldiers of the Barak Brigade. He stood and looked at the dishevelled, unshaven, gaunt-eyed soldiers, some of them burnt and most of them blackened by the smoke and flames, working silently on the damaged tanks and putting them in shape. It was a moving and sobering sight. He asked them what they were doing and they explained that they were preparing the tanks to take them back into battle again. 'If they are going into battle again, I had better forget everything I ever learnt,' he remarked.

Dov notified command headquarters that he already had thirteen tanks ready for battle. He organized crews, brought in ammunition, begged some mortars and then he heard from command headquarters that Yossi was arriving to take command. The news of Yossi's arrival spread and Shmulick, who had been Yossi's second-in-command and who had been wounded in the first day of battle, escaped from the hospital in Safed and came to rejoin him and go back into battle. Conscious of the fact that they were to avenge the comrades of their brigade, Dov led Yossi's force to the front in a jeep. As they appproached and received orders to join the 7th Brigade, Yossi heard on the radio that Tiger on the southern sector of the brigade front was out of ammunition and unable to hold out on the slopes of the 'Booster' against the Syrian advance.

Tiger's force was by now left with two shells per tank. 'Sir,' he radioed in a tone of desperation to the brigade commander, 'I can't hold on.' 'For heaven's sake hold on for only ten minutes,' implored Avigdor. 'Help is on the way.' When Tiger ran out of shells completely, he began to fill his pockets with hand grenades and withdraw. At this moment Yossi moved up to the 'Booster', opened fire and in the initial clash destroyed some thirty Syrian tanks. He had arrived just as the 7th Brigade, left with 7 running tanks out of an original total of approximately 100, was on the verge of collapse. Both sides had fought to a standstill. Avigdor had told Raful that he could not hold the Syrian attack, but suddenly a report came in from the A3 fortification (surrounded by Syrians and well behind the Syrian advance forces), that the Syrian supply trains were turning round and withdrawing. The Syrian attack had been broken; their forces broke and began to withdraw in panic.

The remnants of the 7th Brigade, including Yossi's reinforcements, totalled some twenty tanks. Exhausted, depleted to a minimum, many wounded, with their tanks bearing the scars of war, they now began to pursue the Syrians, knocking out tanks and armoured personnel carriers as they fled. On the edge of the anti-tank ditch, they stopped: the brigade had reached the limits of human exhaustion.

Avigdor stood in a daze looking down on the Valley of the Tears. Some 260 Syrian tanks and hundreds of armoured personnel carriers and vehicles lay scattered and abandoned across this narrow battlefield between the Hermonit and the 'Booster'. In the distance he could see the Syrians withdrawing in a haze of smoke and dust, the Israeli artillery following them. Raful's quiet voice came through on the earphones as he addressed them on the network of the 7th Brigade. 'You have saved the people of Israel.'

Chaim Hertzog

383.

Lt. Hiroo Onoda of the Imperial Japanese Army provided one of the strangest postscripts to the Second World War. Along with many other Japanese soldiers, he merely retired into the wilderness when his position in the Philippines was overrun by the Americans in 1945. In the years that followed, first the Americans, then the Philippines army and police, and finally Japanese well-wishers conducted a series of attempts to hunt down the fugitives. Almost all were killed or induced to surrender. But when a young Japanese traveller finally made contact with Onoda in his fastness early in 1974, the soldier declined to surrender, or even to concede the reality of Japan's defeat until he had received orders to this effect from his former commander, Major Taniguchi. At last, the profoundly wary Onoda approached a rendezvous.

I HID in the bushes, waiting for the time to pass. It was a little before noon on March 9, 1974, and I was on a slope about two hours away from Wakayama Point. My plan was to wait until the time of the evening when it is still just possible to tell one face from another and then approach Wakayama Point rapidly, in a single manoeuvre. Too much light would mean danger, but if it were too dark, I would not be able to make sure that the person I was meeting was really Major Taniguchi. Also, late twilight would be a good time for making a getaway, if I should have to.

Just after two in the afternoon, I crept cautiously out of my hiding place and crossed the river above the point. Making my way through a grove of palms that ran along the river, I soon came to an area where the islanders cut trees for building.

At the edge of a clearing, I stopped and looked the place over. I could see nobody around. I supposed that the workers must be taking the day off, but to be on the safe side, I camouflaged myself with sticks and dried leaves before dashing across the shelterless area.

I crossed the Agcawayan River and reached a position about three hundred yards from the appointed spot. It was only about four o'clock, so I still had plenty of time. I changed to a camouflage of fresh leaves. There used to be paddy fields at the point, but now it is a grassy plain with a palm tree here and there. Along the river grow bamboo and shrubs.

I started up a little hill from which I would be able not only to look down on the point but to keep an eye on the surroundings. This was the place where I had met and talked with Norio Suzuki two weeks before. Just two days earlier a message from Suzuki asking me to meet him here again had been left in the message box we had agreed on, and I had come. I was still afraid it might be a trap. If it was, the enemy might be waiting for me on the hill.

I proceeded with the utmost caution but saw no signs of life. At the top of the hill, I peered out from among the trees and bushes, and on the edge of the point, where Suzuki had put up his mosquito net, I saw a yellow tent. I could make out a Japanese flag waving above it, but I could not see anybody. Were they resting in the tent? Or were they hiding somewhere else waiting for me to show up?

After thirty tense minutes, during which there was no change, I came down the slope and approached a spot only about one hundred yards from the tent. I shifted my position a little to get a different view, but still I saw no one. I decided they must be in the tent and settled down to wait for sunset.

The sun began to sink. I inspected my rifle and retied my boots. I was confident: I could have walked to the tent with my eyes shut, and I felt strong because I had rested while keeping watch. I jumped over a barbed-wire fence and made for the shade of a nearby *bosa* tree, where I paused, took a deep breath, and looked at the tent again. All was still quiet.

The time came. I gripped my rifle, thrust out my chest, and walked forward into the open.

Suzuki was standing with his back to me, between the tent and a fireplace they had rigged up by the riverbank. Slowly he turned around, and when he saw me, he came toward me with arms outstretched.

'It's Onoda!' he shouted. 'Major Taniguchi, it's Onoda!'

In the tent, a shadow moved, but I went forward anyway.

Suzuki, eyes bursting with excitement, ran up to me and with both hands clasped my left hand. I stopped about ten yards from the tent, from which there came a voice.

'Is it really you, Onoda? I'll be with you in a minute.'

I could tell from the voice that it was Major Taniguchi. Motionless, I waited for him to appear. Suzuki stuck his head in the tent and brought out a camera. From inside, the major, who was shirtless, looked out and said, 'I'm changing my clothes. Wait just a minute.'

The head disappeared, but in a few moments Major Taniguchi emerged from the tent fully clothed and with an army cap on his head. Taut down to my fingertips, I barked out, 'Lieutenant Onoda, Sir, reporting for orders.'

'Good for you!' he said, walking up to me and patting me lightly on the left shoulder. 'I've brought you these from the Ministry of Health and Welfare.'

He handed me a pack of cigarettes with the chrysanthemum crest of the emperor on them. I accepted it and, holding it up before me in proper respect for the emperor, fell back two or three paces. At a little distance, Suzuki was standing ready with his camera.

Major Taniguchi said, 'I shall read your orders.'

I held my breath as he began to read from a document that he held up formally with both hands. In rather low tones, he read, 'Command from Headquarters, Fourteenth Area Army' and then continued more firmly and in a louder voice: 'Orders from the Special Squadron, Chief of Staff's Headquarters, Bekebak, September 19, 1900 hours.

'1. In accordance with the Imperial Command, the Fourteenth Area Army has ceased all combat activity.

'2. In accordance with Military Headquarters Command No. A–2003, the Special Squadron in the Chief of Staff's Headquarters is relieved of all military duties.

'3. Units and individuals under the command of the Special Squadron are to cease military activities and operations immediately and place themselves under the command of the nearest superior officer. When no officer can be found, they are to communicate with the American or Philippine forces and follow their directives.

'Special Squadron, Chief of Staff's Headquarters, Fourteenth Area Army, Major Yoshimi Taniguchi.'

After reading this, Major Taniguchi paused slightly, then added, 'That is all.'

I stood quite still, waiting for what was to follow. I felt sure Major Taniguchi would come up to me and whisper, 'That was so much talk. I will tell you your real orders later.' After all, Suzuki was present, and the major could not talk to me confidentially in front of him.

I watched the major closely. He merely looked back rather stiffly. Seconds passed, but still he said no more. The pack on my back suddenly seemed very heavy.

Major Taniguchi slowly folded up the order, and for the first time I realized that no subterfuge was involved. This was no trick—everything I had heard was real. There was no secret message.

The pack became still heavier.

We really lost the war! How could they have been so sloppy?

Suddenly everything went black. A storm raged inside me. I felt like a fool for having been so tense and cautious on the way here. Worse than that, what had I been doing for all these years?

Gradually the storm subsided, and for the first time I really understood: my thirty years as a guerrilla fighter for the Japanese army were abruptly finished. This was the end.

I pulled back the bolt on my rifle and unloaded the bullets.

Hiroo Onoda

384.
A war correspondent's view of the last day of the Falklands War, June 14 1982.

I AWOKE from a chilly doze on Monday morning to find a thin crust of frozen snow covering my sleeping-bag and equipment in the dawn. Around me in the ruined sheep pen in which we lay, a cluster of snow-covered ponchos and rucksacks marked the limits of battalion headquarters. The inexhaustible voice of Major Chris Keeble, second in command of 2 Para, was holding forth into a radio handset as decisively as it had been two hours earlier when I lost consciousness. All firing in front of us, where the battalion's rifle companies had stormed a succession of enemy positions in the darkness, was ended. Desultory Argentinian shells were falling on untenanted ground some 600 yards to the right. We could hear heavy firing of all calibres further south, where the Guards and the Gurkhas were still fighting for their objectives.

Might I go forward, I asked? By all means, said the energetic Major. He pointed across the hill to the new positions of the rifle companies, and detailed a soldier from the defence platoon who had crossed the ground during the night to show me the way. We left the headquarters group huddled around their radios and bivouacs dusted with snow, and began to stride across the frozen tussock grass, my guide chattering busily about men he knew who had been hit during the night, and the amazing helicopter pilot John Greenhalgh who flew in his Gazelle without benefit of night vision aids to bring up ammunition and recover the wounded in the midst of the battle.

We began to pass the abandoned enemy positions, strewn with weapons and ammunition, clothing and food. 'Not short of much, was they?' said the Para. 'So much for the navy's blockade.' We reached 'A' Company, a few hundred yards frontage of unshaven scarecrows surrounded by arms and equipment, their positions dotted with flickering flames from the little hexamine cookers on which they were brewing hot chocolate and porridge from their arctic ration packs. Nearby stood the Scorpion and Scimitar light tanks which had supported the battalion in the attack. The delightful Lord Robin Innes-Ker, who had seemed at times less keen than some of his more homicidal comrades about passing the summer soldiering in the South Atlantic, had at last entered into the spirit of the thing. 'Did you see us?' he enthused. 'It was tremendous. We fired a hundred and fifty rounds. Once we saw somebody light a cigarette in front of us and that was it . . . ' Everybody agreed that the night had been a huge success, not least because those doing the talking had come through it alive. I sat down in an untenanted bivouac—a poncho flapping uneasily above a peat hag—to write a dispatch. The obliging Blues and Royals had carried my typewriter in the back of a Scorpion from San Carlos Bay to Wireless Ridge, complaining somewhat that it was taking up precious ammunition space. At last it came into its own.

A forward gunnery observation officer came and sat beside me. He asked in vain (as every soldier asked every correspondent throughout the campaign) if I had the faintest idea what was going on. I said I only knew that I was due to join 3 Para late in the afternoon, in time to see tham launch the next—and everybody hoped final—attack of the war that night. A cheeky eighteen-year-old private soldier put his head under the poncho and demanded a cigar, which I was not cheeky enough to refuse him. 'We did pretty good, didn't we? You get paid extra for doing this? Why does BBC always tell everybody where we're going to attack? How many more days do you reckon?'

Suddenly we heard men calling to each other in the snow shower outside: 'They're running away! It's on the radio! The Argies are running everywhere!' The Company Commander, Major Dair Farrar-Hockley, shouted to his platoon commanders to be ready to move in five minutes. I pulled my dispatch from the typewriter, ran over the ridge to where I had heard a helicopter engine idling, and thrust it, addressed optimistically to Brigade Headquarters, into the pilot's hand. Then I began to gather up my own equipment.

'Do you want a lift?' called Roger Field of the Blues and Royals. One of the most pleasant parts of this war was that, after so many weeks together, so many people knew each other. I climbed clumsily on to his Scimitar, and clung fervently to the smoke projector as we bucketed across the hillside. We halted for a few moments by one of the enemy positions captured during the night. The men picked a path through the possible souvenirs. We speculated about the identity of a sad corpse covered with a poncho, its feet encased in British-issue rubber boots.

*

We clattered down the ridge to meet the long files of 2 Para who had arrived before us. As we approached the skyline, we saw soldiers lying, standing, crouching along it, fascinated by the vision below. Jumping down from the tank, I walked forward to join them. They were looking upon the wreckage of a cluster of large buildings at the head of the estuary, perhaps three hundred yards beneath us. It was the former Royal Marine base at Moody Brook. Two or three miles down a concrete road east of it, white and innocent in the sudden winter sunshine, stood the little houses and churches of Port Stanley. Suddenly in a few minutes of the morning, the climax of all our ambitions, apparently as distant as the far side of the moon at breakfast, lay open for the taking. The soldiers, three nights without sleep, began to chatter like schoolboys. The Battalion Commander, David Chaundler, was giving his orders: ' . . . I'm not having anybody going down that road unless that high ground is covered, so I'm getting "B" Company up there. The tanks will stay here and provide a firebase . . . '

The first men of 'B' Company were already threading their way through Moody Brook and up the opposite hillside. The Blues and

Royals took up position down among the rocks from which they could cover the entire road into Port Stanley. 'A' Company was to march straight up the road. I trotted after Dair Farrar-Hockley. We crossed Moody Brook amidst orders shouted down the line to stay rigidly in file on the track because of the danger of mines. With disgracefully selfish professional ambitions in my mind, I started to reflect aloud on the risk that 45 Commando might already be approaching Stanley from the other flank, that if negotiations started our advance would be stopped in its tracks. The word was called forward to quicken the pace. Dair Farrar-Hockley, signaller and correspondent trailing in his wake, began to hasten past the files of the leading platoon to take position among the point section, each man praying silently for the radio to remain mute.

We passed a building burning opposite the seaplane jetty, abandoned vehicles, loose ammunition littering the road like sweet papers in Hyde Park. Then we were among the first demure little bungalows of the Stanley seafront. 'We've got to stop, sir, and wait for the CO!' shouted a signaller. There was a groan, then reluctant acquiescence. The men dropped into a crouch by the roadside, peering ahead towards the town centre. Then an NCO at the point of the Company called: 'I think I can see a Panhard moving in front.' The soldiers hastily adopted tactical positions on either roadside, searching the distance for the threatened armoured car. A man with a rocket launcher doubled forward, just in case. Nothing happened except that a trawler began to move out across the harbour, showing a white flag. Through binoculars, I began to study scores of men, evidently enemy, standing idly watching our progress from the hillside perhaps a mile across the bay.

Then there was more excited chatter around the signallers: 'The Argies have surrendered! No one to fire except in self-defence.' Men called forward. Up the road behind us strode a knot of officers led by the colonel. 'Get in behind the Colonel's party, "A" Company', ordered Dair Farrar-Hockley urgently. 'Nobody but "A" is to get in behind the Colonel.' Every man who had not lost his red beret was wearing it now, passionately conscious that a unique opportunity for regimental glory was within their grasp.

*

The Battalion's officers had advanced perhaps two hundred yards beyond our initial halting place when a new signal was brought to the

Colonel's attention. No British soldier was to advance beyond the racecourse, pending negotiations. There was a bitter mutter of disappointment. Where was the racecourse? Beside us now. There was a brief chorus about Nelsonian blind eyes, rapidly stifled. The Colonel ordered 'A' Company to turn aside on to the racecourse. Suddenly, the tiredness of the men seeped through. They clattered on to the little wooden grandstand and sat down, still draped in weapons and machine-gun belts, to cheer one of their number as he clambered out on to the roof and, after some technical difficulties, tore down the Argentinian flag on the little flagpole, and raised that of 2 Para. At their urging, I took a group photograph of this memorable gathering of desperadoes on the stepped benches. Then, inevitably, men began to brew up and to distribute a few cases of Argentinian cigarettes they found in the starter's hut, first booty of the battle.

I wandered down to the road. It stretched empty ahead, the cathedral clearly visible perhaps half a mile away. It was simply too good a chance to miss. Pulling off my web equipment and camouflaged jacket, I handed them up to Roger Field in his Scimitar, now parked in the middle of the road and adorned with a large Union Jack. Then with a civilian anorak and a walking stick that I had been clutching since we landed at San Carlos Bay, I set off towards the town, looking as harmless as I could contrive. 'And where do you think you are going?' demanded a Parachute NCO in the traditional voice of NCOs confronted with prospective criminals. 'I am a civilian', I said firmly, and walked on unhindered.

Just round the bend in the road stood a large building fronted with a conservatory that I suddenly realized from memories of photographs was Government House. Its approaches were studded with bunkers, whether occupied or otherwise I could not see. Feeling fairly foolish, I stopped, grinned towards them, raised my hands in the air, and waited to see what happened. Nothing moved. Still grinning and nodding at any possible spectres within, I turned back on to the road and strode towards the Cathedral, hands in the air. A group of Argentinian soldiers appeared by the roadside. I walked past them with what I hoped was a careless 'Good morning'. They stared curiously, but did nothing.

Then, ahead of me, I saw a group of obviously civilian figures emerging from a large, official-looking building. I shouted to them: 'Are you British?' and they shouted back 'Yes'. Fear ebbed away, and I walked to meet them. After a few moments conversation, they pointed me towards the Argentinian colonel on the steps of the administration block. I introduced myself to him quite untruthfully, as the correspondent of *The Times* newspaper, on the basis that it was the only British organ of which he might have heard. We talked civilly enough for a few minutes. He kept saying that most of my questions could be answered only after four o'clock, when the British General was due to meet General Menendez. Could I meanwhile go and talk to the British civilians, I asked? Of course, he said. I walked away towards that well-known Stanley hostelry 'The Upland Goose' down a road filled with file upon file of Argentinian soldiers, obviously assembling ready to surrender. They looked utterly cowed, totally drained of hostility. Yet I did not dare to photograph their wounded, straggling between comrades. It was only when I saw officers peering curiously at me from their vehicles that I realized that my efforts to look civilian were defeated by my face, still blackened with camouflage cream.

Walking into the hotel was the fulfilment of a dream, a fantasy that had filled all our thoughts for almost three months. 'We never doubted for a moment that the British would come,' said the proprietor, Desmond King. 'We have just been waiting for the moment.' It was like liberating an English suburban golf club.

Max Hastings

SOURCES AND ACKNOWLEDGEMENTS

The editor and publishers gratefully acknowledge permission to reproduce copyright material in this book:

Stephen Ambrose: from *Eisenhower the Soldier*. Copyright © 1983 by Stephen E. Ambrose. Reprinted by permission of George Allen & Unwin (Publishers) Ltd., and Simon & Schuster, Inc.

Sergeant Ancell: quoted from *The Blessed Trade* by Marjorie Ward (1971). Reprinted by permission of Michael Joseph Ltd.

Lord Anglesey: from *One Leg: The Life and Letters of Henry William Paget, 1st Marquess of Anglesey, K.G.* (1961). Reprinted by permission of Jonathan Cape Ltd.

The Anglo-Saxon Chronicle, translated and edited by Whitelock, Douglas, and Tucker (Eyre & Spottiswoode, 1962).

Ralph Arnold: from *A Very Quiet War* (Hart-Davis, 1962).

Arrian: from *The Life of Alexander the Great*, translated by Aubrey de Sélincourt (Penguin Classics, 1958), pp. 134–6, 252–3. Copyright © the Estate of Aubrey de Sélincourt 1958. Reprinted by permission of Penguin Books Ltd.

John Aubrey: from *Brief Lives* (Boydell Press, 1982).

Lt. Aubusey: quoted in *The Fire of Liberty*, by Esmond Wright, published by The Folio Society for its Members in 1984.

Brigadier C. D. B. S. Baker-Carr: from *From Chauffeur to Brigadier* (Ernest Benn, 1930). Reprinted by permission.

The Baronage of England (London, 1737).

Henry Belcher: from *The First American Civil War* (Macmillan, 1911).

Douglas Bell: from *Wellington's Officers* (Collins Publishers, 1938).

Mark Bence-Jones: from *The Cavaliers* (1976). Reprinted by permission of Constable Publishers.

The Bible: Authorized Version. All rights in respect of the Authorized King James Version of the Holy Bible are vested in the Crown in the United Kingdom and controlled by Royal Letters Patent.

Shelford Bidwell: from *The Practitioner*, vol. 223 (November 1979). Reproduced by kind permission of the Editor.

Matthew Bishop: *Life and Adventures* (London, 1744).

Robert Blakeney: from *A Boy in the Peninsular War* (John Murray, 1899).

John Blakiston: from *Twelve Years' Military Adventures in Three Quarters of the Globe*, vol. i (Henry Colburn, 1829).

Lesley Blanch: from *The Game of Hearts: Harriette Wilson and her Memoirs* (Gryphon, 1957).

Russell Braddon: from *The Naked Island* (Michael Joseph: London). By permission of the author.

Gordon Brook-Shepherd: from *November 1918* (1981). Reprinted by permission of Collins Publishers.

Richard Brooke: from *Visits to Fields of Battle in England of the Fifteenth Century* (London, 1857).

Captain T. W. Brotherton: quoted in *The British Cavalry* by P. Warner (J. M. Dent, 1984).

Dee Brown: from *Bury my Heart at Wounded Knee: An Indian History of the American West* (Barrie & Jenkins, 1970: Holt, Rinehart & Winston, 1971). Reprinted by permission of A. D. Peters & Co Ltd.

W. S. Brownlie: from *The Proud Trooper* (Collins Publishers, 1964).

Sir Robert Bruce Lockhart: from *The Marines Were There* (Putnam, 1950). Copyright © Robin Bruce Lockhart 1950. By permission.

The Diaries of Private Horace Bruckshaw, edited by Martin Middlebrook (1979). Reprinted by permission of Scolar Press Ltd.

John Buchan: from *Oliver Cromwell* (Hodder, 1934). Reprinted by permission of A. P. Watt Ltd., on behalf of The Right Hon. Lord Tweedsmuir.

Dr John Butter: from *Autobiography* (London, 1847).

Caesar: from *Gallic Wars*, Book IV, translated by John Warrington (Everyman, 1965). Reprinted by permission of J. M. Dent & Sons Ltd.

Philip Caputo: from *A Rumour of War* (New York: Holt Rinehart, 1977).

Maurice Carpenter: from *The Indifferent Horseman—The Divine Comedy of Samuel Taylor Coleridge* (Elek, 1954).

Samuel Carter III: from *Blaze of Glory* (St Martin's Press, 1971).

Stanley Casson: from *Steady Drummer* (1935). Reprinted by permission of Bell & Hyman Ltd.

Bruce Catton: from *Grant Takes Command* (1969). Reprinted by permission of Little, Brown & Company. From *This Hallowed Ground: the story of the Union Side of the American Civil War*. Copyright © 1955, 1956 by Bruce Catton. Reprinted by permission of Doubleday & Company, Inc.

Lord Chalfont: from *Montgomery of Alamein* (1976). Reprinted by permission of Weidenfeld & Nicolson Ltd.

David Chandler: from *Waterloo and the Hundred Days* (Osprey, 1980). Courtesy of the author, D. G. Chandler.

John Chaney: quoted in *The Fire of Liberty*, by Esmond Wright published by The Folio Society for its Members in 1984.

Winston S. Churchill: from *My Early Life* (1941). Reprinted by permission of Newnes Books, a division of the Hamlyn Publishing Group Limited.

Peter Coats: from *Of Generals and Gardens* (1976). Reprinted by permission of Weidenfeld & Nicolson Ltd.

Hubert Cole: from *Beau Brummell* (Hart-Davis, 1977).

Arthur Conan Doyle: from *The Great Boer War* (Smith Elder, 1902).

E. A. Cook: from *Letters* (London, 1855).

Sir Edward Creasey: from *Fifteen Decisive Battles of the Western World* (Everyman, 1908). Reprinted by permission of J. M. Dent & Sons Ltd.

René Cutforth: from the *Listener*, 19 December 1968.

David Dalrymple, Lord Hailes: from *Annals of Scotland*, vol. i (Edinburgh, 1819).

C. P. Dawnay: from *Montgomery at Close Quarters*, edited by T. E. B. Howarth (Leo Cooper, 1985). Reprinted by permission of A. D. Peters & Co. Ltd.

Daniel Defoe: from *The Life and Adventures of Mrs Christian Davies, Commonly Called Mother Ross*.

David Divine: from *Dunkirk* (Faber, 1945). Reprinted by permission of David Higham Associates Ltd.

Christopher Duffy: from *The Army of Maria Theresa* (1974). Reprinted by permission of David & Charles.

Sir James Edmonds: quoted from *Montgomery of Alamein* by Lord Chalfont (1976). Reprinted by permission of Weidenfeld & Nicolson Ltd.

Bernard Fall: from *Street Without Joy* (1961). Reprinted by permission of Stackpole Books.

Ladislas Farago: from *Patton: Ordeal and Triumph* (1966). Copyright © 1963, 1966 by Faracorn Ltd. First published in Great Britain by Arthur Barker Ltd. Reprinted by permission of Weidenfeld & Nicolson Ltd., and Tessa Sayle.

James Farrar: from *Military Manners and Customs* (London, 1885).

Byron Farwell: from *Queen Victoria's Little Wars* (Allen Lane, 1973: Harper & Row, 1973). Copyright © Byron Farwell, 1973. By permission.

Bernard Fergusson: from *The Trumpet in the Hall* (Collins Publishers, 1970). Copyright Bernard Fergusson 1970. Reproduced by permission of Curtis Brown Ltd.

Ronald Finucane: from *Soldiers of the Faith* (1983). Copyright © 1983 by Ronald Finucane. Reprinted by permission of J. M. Dent & Sons Ltd., and St Martin's Press, Inc.

Gordon Fleming: from *The Young Whistler* (1978). Reprinted by permission of George Allen & Unwin (Publishers) Ltd.

Florus: from *Epitome of Roman History*, Book II, translated by Edward Forster (1927). Reprinted by permission of William Heinemann Ltd., and Harvard University Press.

Robert Fox: from the *Listener*, 17 September 1964.

Joseph Frank: from *Dostoevsky: The Seeds of Revolt, 1821–1849*. Copyright © 1976 by Princeton University Press. Reprinted by permission of Robson Books and Princeton University Press.

Sir John Froissart: from *Chronicles of England, France, Spain and the Adjoining Countries*, books i and ii, translated by Thomas Johnes (Willim Smith, 1839).

Major-General John Frost: from *A Drop Too Many* (Cassell, 1980). Copyright J. D. Frost 1980. By permission of the author.

J. F. C. Fuller: from *Memoirs of an Unconventional Soldier* (Nicolson, 1936).

Roy Fullick and Geoffrey Powell: from *Suez: The Double War* (Hamish Hamilton, 1979). Reprinted by permission of A. M. Heath & Co. Ltd.

Corporal Tom Galeen: quoted by Chester Wilmot in *BBC War Report* (OUP, 1946). By permission.

Geoffrey of Monmouth: from *The History of the Kings of Britain*, translated by Lewis Thorpe (Penguin Classics 1966). Copyright © Lewis Thorpe, 1966. Reprinted by permission of Penguin Books Ltd.

Edward Gibbon: from *Autobiography* (London, 1796). From *The Decline and Fall of the Roman Empire*, vols. i and ii (Everyman, edn., 1938).

G. N. Godwin: from *Memorials of Old Hampshire* (London, 1906).

General John B. Gordon: from *Reminiscences of the Civil War* (Constable, 1904).

U. S. Grant: from *Personal Memoirs*, vol. i (Low, 1885).

William Grattan: from *Adventures with the Connaught Rangers, 1808–1814*, edited by Charles Oman (Edward Arnold, 1902).

Robert Graves: from *Goodbye to All That* (Cape, 1929). Reprinted by permission of A. P. Watt Ltd., for the author.

Fulke Greville: from *The Life of the Renowned Sir Philip Sidney* (London, 1652).

Wyn Griffith: from *Up to Mametz*.

Captain Gronow: from *Last Recollections* (Selwyn & Blount, 1934). From *Reminiscences and Recollections*, abridged by John Raymond (Bodley Head, 1964).

Major H. R. Hadow: quoted in *Sandhurst*, by Sir John Smyth (1961). Reprinted by permission of Weidenfeld & Nicolson Ltd.

Alan Hankinson: from *Man of Wars: William Howard Russell and 'The Times', 1820–1907* (Heinemann Educational, 1982, distributed by Gower Publishing Company). Used by permission.

Dr Hare: from *Journal*. Quoted from *Marlborough: His Life and Times*, vol ii (Harrap, 1934).

Charles Yale Harrison: from *Generals Die in Bed* (Noel Douglas, 1930).

Lewis Hastings: from *Dragons are Extra* (Penguin Books 1947). Copyright 1947 by Lewis Hastings. Reprinted by permission of Penguin Books Ltd.

Macdonald Hastings: from *Gamebook* (Michael Joseph, 1979). By permission.

Max Hastings: from *Montrose: The King's Champion.* (Gollancz, 1977). Reprinted by permission of the author and Curtis Brown Ltd. From the *Spectator*, 26 June 1982. © Max Hastings 1982. From the *Standard*, 6 October 1983. © Max Hastings 1983. By permission of the author.

Lt.-Col. G. F. R. Henderson: from *Stonewall Jackson and the American Civil War*, vol. i (Longmans Green & Co., 1898).

J. R. Henderson: from *Montgomery at Close Quarters*, edited by T. E. B. Howarth (Leo Cooper, 1985). Reprinted by permission of A. D. Peters & Co. Ltd.

Henrici Quinti Angliae Regis Gesta, edited by B. W. Williams. Quoted from

English Historical Documents, 1327–1485, vol. iv, edited by A. R. Myers (Eyre & Spottiswoode, 1969).

Robert Henriques: from *A Biography of Myself: A Posthumous Selection of the Autobiographical Writings* (Secker & Warburg, 1969). Reprinted by permission of John Farquharson Ltd., on behalf of the Estate of Robert Henriques.

Aubrey Herbert: from *Mons, Anzac and Kut* (Edward Arnold, 1919).

Herodotus: from *The Histories*, Books III, IV, and VII, translated by Aubrey de Sélincourt (Penguin Classics, 1954). Copyright © the Estate of Aubrey de Sélincourt 1954. Reprinted by permission of Penguin Books Ltd.

Chaim Hertzog: from *The War of Atonement* (1975). Reprinted by permission of Weidenfeld & Nicolson Ltd.

Christopher Hibbert: from *Agincourt* (1964, n. e. 1978). Reprinted by permission of B. T. Batsford Limited.

Raymond Horricks: from *Marshal Ney: The Romance and the Real* (Midas Books, 1982). Reprinted by permission of the author and Sheila Rossini, Author's Agent.

Michael Howard: from *The Franco-Prussian War* (Hart-Davis, 1961). Reprinted by permission of David Higham Associates Ltd.

David Howarth: from *A Near Run Thing* (1971). Reprinted by permission of Collins Publishers.

Captain Sir Edward Hulse: from *Letters from the English Front in France*.

William Hulton: from *The Battle of Bosworth Field* (Nichols, Son & Bentley, 1813).

Lord Ismay: from *Memoirs* (Heinemann, 1960).

Josephus: from *The Jewish War*, translated by G. A. Williamson (Penguin Classics, Revised edition 1970). Copyright © G. A. Williamson, 1959, 1969. Reprinted by permission of Penguin Books Ltd.

E. J. Kahn: from the *New Yorker*, 24 April 1951.

Sir John Kennedy: from *The Business of War* (1957). Reprinted by permission of Hutchinson Publishing Group Ltd.

Sir John Kincaid: from *Adventures in the Rifle Brigade* (T. W. Boone, 1838). From *Random Shots from a Rifleman* (T. W. Boone, 1835).

Captain John Knox: from *Historical Journal*. Quoted from *The Englishman at War*, by J. Freeman (George Allen & Unwin, 1941).

F. S. Larpent: from *Private Journal of F. S. Larpent During the Peninsular War*, edited by G. Larpent (Bentley, 1854).

Blaise de Lasseran-Massencenere, Seigneur de Monlue: from *Commentaries*.

T. E. Lawrence: from *Seven Pillars of Wisdom*. Copyright 1926, 1935 by Doubleday & Company, Inc. Reprinted by permission of Jonathan Cape Ltd., Doubleday and The Seven Pillars Trust.

James Lees Milne: from *Another Self* (Hamish Hamilton, 1970). Reprinted by permission of David Higham Associates Ltd.

Letters and Papers Illustrative of the Wars of the English in France During the Reign of Henry VI, edited by Joseph Stevenson. Rolls series, vol. xxi (Longman, Green & Roberts, 1861–4).

Ronald Lewin: from his own *Commonplace Book*.

Earl Ligonier: quoted from *Field Marshal Lord Ligonier*, by Rex Whitworth (1958). Reprinted by permission of Oxford University Press.

T. M. Lindsay: from *The Sherwood Rangers* (Burwyn Mathieson, 1952).

Eric Linklater: from *Fanfare for a Tin Hat* (Macmillan, 1970). Reprinted by permission of A. D. Peters & Co. Ltd. From *The Man on My Back* (1941). Copyright Eric Linklater 1941. Reprinted by permission of Macmillan, London & Basingstoke, and Curtis Brown Ltd.

Paul Lintier: from *My Seventy-Five: Journal of a French Gunner* (Peter Davies, 1929).

Lives of the Two Illustrious Generals, John, Duke of Marlborough, and Francis Eugene, Prince of Savoy, vol. i, anon. (A. Bell, 1713).

Livy: from *History of Rome*, Books, II, V, VIII, XXI, XXII, and XXV, translated by Church and Broadrill (Macmillan, 1890).

Elizabeth Longford: from *Wellington: The Years of the Sword* (1969). Reprinted by permission of Weidenfeld & Nicolson Ltd.

Lord Longford: quoted in *Montgomery at Close Quarters*, edited by T. E. B. Howarth (Leo Cooper, 1985). Reprinted by permission of A. D. Peters & Co. Ltd.

Lord Lovat: from *March Past* (1973). Reprinted by permission of Weidenfeld & Nicolson Ltd.

Lt.-Col. Franklin Lushington: from *The Gambardier* (Ernest Benn, 1930). Reprinted by permission.

A. G. Macdonell: from *Napoleon and His Marshals* (1936). Reprinted by permission of Macmillan, London & Basingstoke.

Harold Macmillan: from *War Diaries: Politics and War in the Mediterranean 1943–1945* (1983). Copyright © 1983 by Harold Macmillan. Reprinted by permission of Macmillan, London & Basingstoke and St Martin's Press, Inc.

Sir Patrick Macrory: from *The Siege of Derry* (Hodder & Stoughton, 1980).

Philip Magnus: from *Kitchener* (1964). Reprinted by permission of John Murray.

Baron Marcellin de Marbot: in *Memoirs*, translated by A. J. Butler (Longmans Green & Co., 1893).

Sir James Marshall-Cornwall: from *Wars and Rumours of Wars* (1984). Reprinted by permission of Secker & Warburg Ltd.

Philip Mason: from *A Matter of Honour* (Cape, 1974).

Robert K. Massie: from *Peter the Great: His Life and World*. Copyright © 1980 by Robert K. Massie. Reprinted by permission of Alfred A. Knopf Inc., and the author.

John Masters: from *Bugles and a Tiger* (1956). From *The Road Past Mandalay* (1961). Reprinted by permission of Michael Joseph Ltd.

Thomas James Mathias: from *The Pursuits of Literature* (London, 1796).

Richard Meinzerhagen: from *Middle East Diary* (Cresset Press, 1959).

Cavalier Mercer: from *Journal of the Waterloo Campaign* (London, 1877).

Martin Middlebrook: from *The First Day on the Somme* (Allen Lane, 1971). Copyright © Martin Middlebrook, 1971. Reprinted by permission of Penguin Books Ltd., and A. P. Watt Ltd.

Robert Middlekauft: from *The Glorious Cause: The American Revolution 1763–1789*. Copyright © 1982 by Oxford University Press, Inc. Reprinted by permission.

Nancy Mitford: from *Voltaire in Love* (Hamish Hamilton, 1957). Reprinted by permission of A. D. Peters & Co. Ltd.

'M.L.S.', *Blackwood's*, May 1949.

Field Marshal Viscount Montgomery of Alamein: from *Memoirs* (Collins Publishers, 1956). Reprinted by permission of A. P. Watt Ltd., on behalf of the Executors of the Estate of Viscount Montgomery.

James Carrick Moore: from *The Life of Lieutenant-General Sir John Moore*, vol. ii (London, 1834).

Edmund Morris: from *The Rise of Theodore Roosevelt* (1979). Reprinted by permission of Collins Publishers.

Leonard Mosley: from *Castlerosse* (Arthur Barker, 1956). Reprinted by permission of John Farquharson Ltd.

W. Stanley Moss: from *Ill Met by Moonlight* (1950). Reprinted by permission of Harrap Ltd.

William Napier: from *Life of General Sir William Napier*, vol. i, edited by H. A. Bruce (Murray, 1864).

A Book of Naval and Military Anecdotes, anon. (London, 1824).

Cornelius Nepos: from *Lives*, Book XVIII, translated by John C. Rolfe (1929). Reprinted by permission of William Heinemann Ltd.

Nigel Nicolson: from *Alex* (1973). Reprinted by permission of Weidenfeld & Nicolson Ltd.

David Niven: from *The Moon's a Balloon* (Hamish Hamilton, 1971). Reprinted by permission of John Farquharson Ltd., on behalf of the Estate of the late David Niven.

Notker the Stammerer: from 'Charlemagne' from *Two Lives of Charlemagne*, translated by Lewis Thorpe (Penguin Classics, 1969). Copyright © Lewis Thorpe, 1969. Reprinted by permission of Penguin Books Ltd.

MacCarthy O'Moore: from *The Romance of the Boer War: Humour and Chivalry of the Campaign* (Elliot Stock, 1901).

Hiroo Onoda: from *No Surrender: My Thirty Year War* translated from the Japanese by Charles S. Terry (London: Deutsch/New York: Kodansha, 1975). By permission.

The Order Book of the Staffordshire County Committee of the Parliamentary Army, edited by D. H. Pennington and I. A. Roots (Manchester University Press, 1957).

George Orwell: from *Homage to Catalonia*. Copyright 1952, 1980 by Sonia Brownell Orwell. Reprinted by permission of A. M. Heath & Co. Ltd., on behalf of the Estate of the late Sonia Brownell Orwell & Secker & Warburg Ltd., and of Harcourt Brace Jovanovich Inc.

Lt.-Col. Arthur Osburn: from *Unwilling Passenger* (Faber & Faber, 1932).

J. Outram: quoted from *A Season in Hell*, by Michael Edwardes (Hamish Hamilton, 1973). By permission of Campbell Thomson & McLaughlin Ltd.

Robert Parker and the Comte de Merode-Westerloo: from *Military Memoirs*, edited by D. G. Chandler (Londman, 1968).

Roger Parkinson: from *The Fox of the North* (Peter Davies, 1980). © Roger Parkinson 1976. Reprinted by permission of Mrs Betty Parkinson.

Francis Parkman: from *Montcalm and Wolfe*, vol. ii (Macmillan, 1906).

Miss Payne: quoted from *Memoirs of Sir Harry Smith*, vol. ii, by G. C. M. Smith (Murray, 1901).

Hesketh Pearson: from *The Hero of Delhi* (Penguin Books, 1948). Copyright 1948 by Hesketh Pearson. Reprinted by permission of Penguin Books Ltd.

The Percy Anecdotes, edited by S. and R. Percy (London, 1823).

Plutarch: from *Lives*, translated by B. Perrin (Loeb Classical Library, 1917).

The Poem of the Cid, translated by Hamilton and Perry, edited by I. D. Michael (Manchester University Press, 1975), pp. 73–7. Reprinted by permission of the publisher.

Anthony Powell: from *Marcel Proust, 1871–1922: A Centenary Volume*, edited by Peter Quennell. Reprinted by permission of Weidenfeld & Nicolson Ltd. From *The Military Philosophers* (1968). Reprinted by permission of William Heinemann Ltd., and David Higham Associates Ltd.

Sydnam Poyntz: from *The Relation of Sydnam Poyntz, 1624–1636* (Camden Third Series, vol. xiv, 1908). By permission of the Royal Historical Society.

John Prebble: from *Glencoe: The Story of the Massacre* (1966). From *Mutiny: Highland Regiments in Revolt, 1743–1804* (1975). Reprinted by permission of Secker & Warburg Ltd., and Curtis Brown Ltd.

William H. Prescott: from *History of the Conquest of Mexico*, vol. i (Bentley, 1843).

Procopius: from *History of the Wars*, Book I, translated by H. B. Downing (Loeb Classical Library, 1914: Harvard University Press: William Heinemann). By permission.

Christopher Pulling: from *They Were Singing* (1952). Reprinted by permission of Harrap Limited.

Ludwig Reiners: from *Frederick the Great*, translated by Lawrence Wilson (1960). Reprinted by permission of Oswald Wolff (Publishers) Ltd.

Frank Richards: from *Old Soldier Sahib* (Anthony Mott edn., 1983).

F. M. Richardson: from *Fighting Spirit* (Leo Cooper, 1975). Reprinted by permission of the publisher.

Lord Roberts: from *Forty-One Years in India* (Bentley, 1898).

William Robson: from *The Great Sieges of History* (London, 1855).

H. B. C. Rogers: from *Wellington's Army* (Ian Allan, 1979).

Manfred Rommel: from *The Rommel Papers*, edited by Basil Liddell Hart, translated by Paul Findlay. Reprinted by permission of Collins Publishers.

Gabriel Ronay: from *The Tartar Khan's Englishman* (Cassell, 1978). © 1978 by Gabriel Ronay. Reprinted by permission of the author.

Lord de Ros: from *The Young Officer's Companion* (Murray, 1868).

Steven Runciman: from *A History of the Crusades*, vol. ii. (1952). Reprinted by permission of Cambridge University Press.

Captain H. Sadler: from *The History of the Seventh (Service) Battalion, The Royal Sussex Regiment 1914–1919*, ed. Owen Rutter (London, 1934).

Guy Sajer: from *Forgotten Soldier* (London: Weidenfeld & Nicolson Ltd., 1971/New York: Harper & Row, 1971). Reprinted by permission of Weidenfeld & Nicolson Ltd., and Editions Robert Laffont.

Siegfried Sassoon from *Memoirs of an Infantry Officer* (1931). By permission of Faber & Faber Ltd., and the K. S. Giniger Company Inc., and Stackpole Books.

Maurice de Saxe: from *Reveries, or Memoires Upon the Art of War* (London, 1786).

James Settle: from *Anecdotes of Soldiers in War and Peace* (Methuen, 1905).

'S. H.': quoted from *History of the British Army*, vol. vi, by Sir John Fortescue (Macmillan, 1899–1930).

William T. Sherman: from *From Atlanta to the Sea*, vol ii (New York: Charles Webster, 1891).

William Siborne: from *History of the War in France and Belgium*, vol. ii (Boone, 1844). From *Waterloo Letters: Hitherto Unpublished, Bearing on 16–18 June 1815* vol. ii, edited by H. T. Siborne (Cassell, 1891).

Edith Simon: from *The Piebald Standard* (Cassell, 1959). Reprinted by permission of David Higham Associates Ltd.

Osbert Sitwell: from *Great Morning* (Macmillan 1951). Reprinted by permission of David Higham Associates Ltd.

Field Marshal Viscount Slim: from *Defeat Into Victory* (Cassell, 1956). From *Unofficial History* (Cassell, 1959). Reprinted by permission of David Higham Associates Ltd.

David Smiley: from *Albanian Assignment* (1984). Reprinted by permission of the author and Chatto & Windus/The Hogarth Press.

Sir Harry Smith: from *Memoirs of Sir Harry Smith*, vol. i, edited by G. C. M. Smith (Murray, 1901).

The Soldier's Companion, anon.

Sir Edward Spears: from *Liaison 1914* (Heinemann, 1930).

Philip Henry Stanhope, 5th Earl: from *Conversations with the Duke of Wellington, 1831–1851* (Oxford, 1947).

Richard Steele: from *Tatler*, no. 164, 27 April 1710.

William B. Stevens: quoted in *Storm Over Savannah: The Story of Count d'Estaing and the Siege of the Town in 1779*, by Alexander A. Lawrence (University of Georgia Press, 1951).

Suetonius: from *The Twelve Caesars*, translated by Robert Graves (Allen Lane, 1979), pp. 27–8, 29–30, 38, 56–7, 154–5, 247. Translation © Robert Graves 1979. Reprinted by permission of A. P. Watt Ltd.

Herbert Sulzbach: from *With the German Guns*, translated by Richard Thonger (Leo Cooper, 1973). Reprinted by permission of the publisher.

Douglas Sutherland: from *Sutherland's War* (1984). Reprinted by permission of Secker & Warburg Ltd.

Christopher Sykes: from *Evelyn Waugh* (1975). Reprinted by permission of Collins Publishers. From *Orde Wingate* (Collins, 1959). Reprinted by permission of A. D. Peters & Co. Ltd.

Julian Symons: from *England's Pride*. Copyright © Julian Symons 1964. Reprinted by permission of Hamish Hamilton Ltd. and Curtis Brown Ltd.

Le General Baron Paul François Charles Thiébault: from *Memoirs*, vol. i, translated by A. J. Butler (Smith Elder, 1896).

Hugh Thomas: from *The Spanish Civil War* (1961). Reprinted by permission of Hamish Hamilton Ltd., and Harper & Row Publishers Inc.

Nicholas Tomalin: 'Zapping Charlie Kong' from the *Sunday Times*, 5 June 1966. Reprinted by permission of Times Newspapers Limited.

Geoffrey Trease: from *The Condottieri* (1970). Reprinted by permission of Thames & Hudson Ltd.

Hugh Trevor-Roper: from *The Last Days of Hitler* (1978). Reprinted by permission of Macmillan, London & Basingstoke, and A. D. Peters & Co. Ltd.

Barbara Tuchman: from *A Distant Mirror* (1978). Reprinted by permission of Macmillan, London & Basingstoke. From *August 1914* (Constable), published in America by Macmillan as *The Guns of August*. © Barbara W. Tuchman 1962. Reprinted by permission of Constable Publishers and Macmillan Publishing Company, New York.

E. S. Turner: from *Dear Old Blighty* (1980). Reprinted by permission of Michael Joseph Ltd. From *Gallant Gentlemen* (1956). Reprinted by permission of Michael Joseph Ltd.

Sun Tzu: from *The Art of War*, edited and translated by James Clavell (1981). Reprinted by permission of Hodder & Stoughton Ltd., and the author.

Unnamed British medical officer: quoted from *Incidents in the China War* (London, 1862).

John Verney: from *Going to the Wars* (1955). Reprinted by permission of Collins Publishers.

Voltaire: from *Ancient and Modern History*, vol. xiv, translated by William Fleming (Dingwall-Rock, New York, 1927). From *Siècle de Louis XIV*, translated by Max Hastings. By permission.

Arthur Waley: *The Secret History of the Mongols* (1963). Reprinted by permission of George Allen & Unwin (Publishers) Ltd.

Sir William Waller: quoted from *Cornwall in the Great Civil War and Interregnum, 1642–1660* (Barton, 1977).

Warkworth's Chronicle: quoted from *English Historical Documents, 1372–1485*, vol. iv, edited by A. R. Myers (Eyre & Spottiswoode, 1969).

Philip Warner: from *The British Cavalry* (1984). Reprinted by permission of J. M. Dent & Sons Ltd.

Evelyn Waugh: from *The Diaries of Evelyn Waugh*, edited by M. Davie (1976). From *The Letters of Evelyn Waugh*, edited by Mark Amory (1980). Reprinted by permission of Weidenfeld & Nicolson Ltd.

C. V. Wedgwood: from *The King's War*. Copyright © C. V. Wedgwood 1958. Reprinted by permission of Deborah Owen Ltd.

Russell F. Weigley: from *Eisenhower's Lieutenants: The Campaigns of France and Germany, 1944–1945*. © 1981 by Russell F. Weigley. Reprinted by permission of Sidgwick & Jackson Ltd., and of Indiana University Press.

James Wellard: from *The French Foreign Legion* (1981). Reprinted by permission of André Deutsch and Rainbird Publishing.

Nehemiah Wharton: quoted from *The Blessed Trade*, by Marjorie Ward (1971). Reprinted by permission of Michael Joseph Ltd.

William Wheeler: from *The Letters of Private Wheeler*, edited by Basil Liddell Hart (1951). Reprinted by permission of Michael Joseph Ltd.

Sir John Wheeler-Bennett: from *The Nemesis of Power* (1954). Copyright © 1954 by John Wheeler-Bennett. Reprinted by permission of Macmillan, London & Basingstoke, and St Martin's Press, Inc.

John Manchip White: from *Marshal of France* (Hamish Hamilton, 1962). © John Manchip White 1962. Reprinted by permission of Curtis Brown Ltd., and the author.

Adrian Carton de Wiart: from *Happy Odyssey* (Cape, 1950). Reprinted by permission of Lady Carton de Wiart.

Charles Wickins: from *The Indian Mutiny Journal of Charles Wickins*, in *Journal of the Society for Army Historical Research*, vol. xxxv (1957).

Frank Wilkeson: from *The Soldier in Battle* (Redway, 1896).

Brigadier E. T. Williams: from *Montgomery at Close Quarters*, edited by T. E. B. Howarth (Leo Cooper, 1985). Reprinted by permission of A. D. Peters & Co. Ltd.

Henry Williamson: from *The Wet Flanders Plain* (Faber, 1929). Reprinted by permission of the Estate of Henry Williamson and A. M. Heath & Company Ltd.

Beckles Willson: from *Life and Letters of James Wolfe* (Heinemann, 1909).

A. D. Wintle: from *The Last Englishman* (1962). Reprinted by permission of Michael Joseph Ltd.

Cecil Woodham-Smith: from *Florence Nightingale* (1950). From *The Reason Why* (1953). Reprinted by permission of Constable Publishers.

Alexis Wrangel: from *The End of Chivalry: Last Great Cavalry Battles*,

1914–1918 (New York: Hippocrene Books, 1982; London: Secker & Warburg, 1984). By permission.

Esmond Wright: from *The Fire of Liberty*, published by The Folio Society for its Members in 1984.

Xenophon: from *Anabasis*, Book IV, translated by J. S. Watson (London, 1907).

F. Yeats-Brown: from *The Bengal Lancer* (Gollancz, 1930). Reprinted by permission of David Higham Associates Ltd., on behalf of the Estate of Francis Yeats-Brown.

A. Donovan Young: from *A Subaltern in Serbia, and Some Letters from the Struma Valley* (1922).

While every effort has been made to secure permission, we may have failed in a few cases to trace the copyright holder. We apologize for any apparent negligence.

INDEX OF PRINCIPAL NAMES AND PLACES

References are to pages